Private Law and Practical Reason

OXFORD PRIVATE LAW THEORY

Oxford Private Law Theory publishes leading work in private law theory. It commissions and solicits monographs and edited collections in general private law theory as well as specific fields, including the theoretical analysis of tort law, property law, contract law, fiduciary law, trust law, remedies and restitution, and the law of equity. The series is open to diverse theoretical approaches, including those informed by philosophy, economics, history, and political theory. Oxford Private Law Theory sets the standard for rigorous and original work in private law theory.

Series Editors
Paul B. Miller, University of Notre Dame
John Oberdiek, Rutgers University

Advisory Board
Marietta Auer, Max Planck Institute for Legal History and Legal Theory
Molly Brady, Harvard University
Hanoch Dagan, Tel Aviv University
John Goldberg, Harvard University
Matthew Harding, University of Melbourne
Irit Samet-Porat, King's College, London
Seana Shiffrin, University of California, Los Angeles

ALSO PUBLISHED IN THIS SERIES
Rights, Wrongs, and Injustices
The Structure of Remedial Law
Stephen A. Smith

Civil Wrongs and Justice in Private Law
Edited by Paul B. Miller and John Oberdiek

Private Law and Practical Reason

Essays on John Gardner's Private Law Theory

Edited by
HARIS PSARRAS
SANDY STEEL

OXFORD
UNIVERSITY PRESS

Great Clarendon Street, Oxford, OX2 6DP,
United Kingdom

Oxford University Press is a department of the University of Oxford.
It furthers the University's objective of excellence in research, scholarship,
and education by publishing worldwide. Oxford is a registered trade mark of
Oxford University Press in the UK and in certain other countries

© The several contributors 2023

The moral rights of the authors have been asserted

First Edition published in 2023

All rights reserved. No part of this publication may be reproduced, stored in
a retrieval system, or transmitted, in any form or by any means, without the
prior permission in writing of Oxford University Press, or as expressly permitted
by law, by licence or under terms agreed with the appropriate reprographics
rights organization. Enquiries concerning reproduction outside the scope of the
above should be sent to the Rights Department, Oxford University Press, at the
address above

You must not circulate this work in any other form
and you must impose this same condition on any acquirer

Public sector information reproduced under Open Government Licence v3.0
(http://www.nationalarchives.gov.uk/doc/open-government-licence/open-government-licence.htm)

Published in the United States of America by Oxford University Press
198 Madison Avenue, New York, NY 10016, United States of America

British Library Cataloguing in Publication Data

Data available

Library of Congress Control Number: 2022940914

ISBN 978-0-19-285733-0

DOI: 10.1093/oso/9780192857330.001.0001

Printed and bound by
CPI Group (UK) Ltd, Croydon, CR0 4YY

Links to third party websites are provided by Oxford in good faith and
for information only. Oxford disclaims any responsibility for the materials
contained in any third party website referenced in this work.

Contents

List of Abbreviations	ix
List of Contributors	xi

1. Introduction: John Gardner's Philosophy of Private Law   1
   Haris Psarras and Sandy Steel
   1. Justifying Private Law: General Issues   1
   2. Responding to Wrongs   7
   3. Specific Areas   12

PART I GENERAL PRIVATE LAW THEORY

2. Gardner on Duties in Tort   19
   Leo Boonzaier
   1. Definitions   19
   2. Wrongs and Fault   22
   3. Reasons Continuity   28
   4. The Argument   29
   5. The Assessment   31
   6. Core and Penumbra   39
   7. Conclusion   41

3. Are There Any Moral Duties?   43
   Nicholas J McBride
   1. Law as the Mirror of Morality   43
   2. What Is a Mirror of What?   44
   3. In the Realm of Morality   46
   4. A Place for Moral Duties?   48
   5. E versus M   52
   6. Why Did M Win?   56
   7. The Mirror Crack'd   58

4. Reasons to Try   59
   Ori J Herstein
   1. Introduction   59
   2. Preliminary Clarifications   59
   3. Reasons to Try and the Law   60
   4. Trying as a Means to an End   63
   5. Trying as an End: The Intrinsic Value of Trying   67
   6. Conclusion   74

vi CONTENTS

5. Legality and Capacity 76
Frederick Wilmot-Smith

   1. Introduction 76
   2. The Two Maxims 76
   3. Gardner's Accounts 82
   4. Resolution 84
   5. Diagnosis 90

6. Gardner on Justice 92
Tatiana Cutts

   1. Introduction 92
   2. Allocation 93
   3. Scope 95
   4. Competition 97
   5. Method 100
   6. Correction 102
   7. Conclusion 104

7. Distributing Corrective Justice 106
Rebecca Stone

   1. Kantian Corrective Justice 107
   2. Gardner's Scheme 109
   3. Comparing the Gardnerian and Kantian Conceptions 112
   4. An Intermediate Conception 113
   5. Substantive versus Procedural Dimensions of Justice 116
   6. The Relationship Between Corrective and Distributive Justice 119

8. Deterrence in Private Law 123
Sandy Steel

   1. The Necessity of Deterrence 125
   2. The Sufficiency of Deterrence 127
   3. Deterrence Considerations as Reasons which Make a Difference 128
   4. Overdeterrence 134
   5. General Objections to Deterrence 136
   6. Conclusion 141

PART II RESPONDING TO WRONGS

9. Finishing the Reparative Job: Victims' Duties to Wrongdoers 145
Cécile Fabre

   1. Introduction 145
   2. Reparative Justice: A Primer 146
   3. Acceptance 148
   4. Use 152
   5. Complications 156
   6. Conclusion 159

CONTENTS vii

10. Wrongs, Remedies, and the Persistence of Reasons: Re-Examining the Continuity Thesis 161
John Oberdiek
   1. Introduction 161
   2. The Continuity Thesis and Its Presuppositions 162
   3. The Criticism 164
   4. Reasons, Relationality, and Claims 168

11. The Next Best Thing to a Promise 177
Dori Kimel
   1. Has the Promise Been Broken? 180
   2. Is the Promised Action Otherwise Required? 183
   3. Bilaterality 186
   4. Variations in Fault 189
   5. Relationship Norms 196
   6. Conclusions 198

12. The Place of Regret in the Law of Torts 203
Zoë Sinel
   1. Reparation for Wrongs: Puzzles and Gardner's Solutions 204
   2. The Place of Regret 209
   3. No Regrets (in the Law of Torts) 219
   4. Conclusion 221

13. Primary Duty = Secondary Duty? 223
Claudio Michelon
   1. Primary Duties, Secondary Duties, and Their Identity 224
   2. Grounds, and the Identity of Primary and Remedial Duty 229
   3. Duties, Reasons, and Continuity 232

14. The Role of Plaintiffs in Private Law Institutions 239
Larissa Katz and Matthew A Shapiro
   1. The Power to Sue—Three Models 239
   2. Three Queries 244
   3. Power-Sharing Revised 253
   4. Conclusion 257

15. Private Law Rights and Powers of Waiver 259
Haris Psarras
   1. Introduction 259
   2. Waivability and Types of Private Law Rights 260
   3. The Waivability of Primary Rights 265
   4. Limitations on the Waivability of Rights to Remedies 271
   5. Conclusion 277

viii CONTENTS

PART III THEORIZING PARTICULAR AREAS OF PRIVATE LAW

16. How is Tort Law Political? — 281
Jenny Steele
    1. Introduction — 281
    2. Three "Political" Connections: Choice, Distribution, and Power — 285
    3. Reflecting on Security and Private Law — 290
    4. Tort, Politics, and Security Rights — 293
    5. Conclusion — 295

17. The Value of the Neighbour Relation — 297
Christopher Essert
    1. Introduction — 297
    2. Gardner on Relational Duties — 297
    3. The Duty of Care as a Liability-Limiting Principle — 301
    4. The Value of Line-Drawing — 304
    5. Relating as Equals, Relating as Neighbours — 307
    6. Doing Things as Equals — 309

18. The Liberal Promise of Contract — 311
Hanoch Dagan
    1. Introduction — 311
    2. Gardner on Contract — 312
    3. Gardner as a Transfer Theorist — 316
    4. From Transfer to a Joint Plan — 319
    5. Liberal Contract Meets Gardner — 324
    6. Private Law and Liberalism — 329

19. The Reasonably Loyal Person — 330
Andrew S Gold
    1. Buck Passing and the "Reasonably Loyal" Trustee — 330
    2. Assessing Arguments Against a "Reasonably Loyal" Trustee Standard — 333
    3. Fiduciary Loyalty as a Different Kind of Loyalty — 335
    4. The Existence of a Law-Independent Counterpart — 340
    5. The Buck Passing Account Revisited — 343
    6. Conclusion — 347

20. Corrective Justice and the Right to Hold on to What One Has — 348
John CP Goldberg and Benjamin C Zipursky
    1. Agents and Patients; Duties and Rights — 348
    2. Value Theory and the Continuity Thesis Reconceived — 351
    3. Qualified Liberalism in Torts — 355
    4. Why We Don't Sign On — 356
    5. Conclusion — 360

Name Index — 361
Subject Index — 367

List of Abbreviations

BMA	British Medical Association
CUP	Cambridge University Press
FPLPL	*From Personal Life to Private Law*
IOC	International Olympic Committee
kph	kilometers per hour
OC	ought-implies-can
OUP	Oxford University Press
TAOW	*Torts and Other Wrongs*
UPR	Universal Principle of Right

List of Contributors

Leo Boonzaier, Lecturer in Law, University of Cape Town

Tatiana Cutts, Associate Professor of Law, University of Melbourne

Hanoch Dagan, Stewart and Judy Colton Professor of Legal Theory and Innovation, Tel Aviv University

Christopher Essert, Associate Professor of Law, University of Toronto

Cécile Fabre, Senior Research Fellow, All Souls College, University of Oxford

Andrew S Gold, Professor of Law, Brooklyn Law School

John CP Goldberg, Carter Professor of General Jurisprudence, Harvard University

Ori J Herstein, Professor of Law, Hebrew University of Jerusalem & King's College, London

Larissa Katz, Professor and Canada Research Chair in Private Law Theory, University of Toronto

Dori Kimel, Reader in Legal Philosophy, University of Oxford

Nicholas J McBride, Fellow in Law, Pembroke College, University of Cambridge

Claudio Michelon, Professor of Philosophy of Law, University of Edinburgh

John Oberdiek, Distinguished Professor of Law, Rutgers University

Haris Psarras, Associate Professor of Law, University of Southampton

Matthew A Shapiro, Associate Professor of Law, Rutgers University

Zoë Sinel, Associate Professor of Law, University of Western Ontario

Sandy Steel, Professor of Law and Philosophy of Law, University of Oxford

Jenny Steele, Professor of Law, University of York

Rebecca Stone, Professor of Law, University of California Los Angeles

Frederick Wilmot-Smith, Fellow, All Souls College, University of Oxford

Benjamin C Zipursky, James H. Quinn '49 Chair in Legal Ethics, Professor of Law, Fordham University

1
Introduction
John Gardner's Philosophy of Private Law

Haris Psarras and Sandy Steel

During his lifetime, John Gardner was best known for his work on the philosophy of criminal law and the philosophy of law in general.[1] For the last ten years of his career he became increasingly interested in the philosophy of private law.[2] The contributors to this volume engage with his influential work in this area, in some cases by detailed engagement with particular arguments, in others by using Gardner's philosophically rich ideas as a basis for development of novel lines of thought. In this introduction, we provide an overview of the essays in the volume, setting them in the context of Gardner's thinking. The introduction mirrors the structure of the book, with a division between general, overarching issues in the philosophy of private law, issues specifically connected to responding to wrongs, and those connected to particular areas of private law.

1. Justifying Private Law: General Issues

1.1 Duties

For Gardner, tort and contract law, as areas of law, are partly constituted by their providing remedies for breaches of certain kinds of legal duty, and these legal areas are, in turn, justified in so far as their existence contributes to the fulfilment of the moral duties which the legal duties constitute or reflect, and to the promotion of or respect for other valuable goods.[3] Tort law's concretizing of individuals' abstract moral duties of corrective justice, for instance, is a "necessary" part of its justification.[4] The idea—a general theme of Gardner's work—is that legal institutions are *pro tanto* justified to the extent that they promote conformity to the reasons, including duties, that people

---

[1] For overviews of John's scholarship, see J Edwards, "John Gardner" in M Sellers and S Kirste (eds), *Encyclopedia of the Philosophy of Law and Social Philosophy* (Springer 2021); H Collins and A Duff, "John Gardner" in *Biographical Memoirs of Fellows of the British Academy, XX*, 1–24 <https://www.thebritishacad emy.ac.uk/publishing/memoirs/20/gardner-john-1965-2019/>.

[2] In J Gardner, *From Personal Life to Private Law* (OUP 2018) ("*FPLPL*") 4 he dates his beginning "more serious" work on private law from 2008. See, earlier, J Gardner, "The Purity and Priority of Private Law" (1996) 46 University of Toronto Law Journal 459, and chs 4, 5, and 8 of *Torts and Other Wrongs* (OUP 2019) ("*TAOW*").

[3] See *FPLPL* (n 2) 8: "ultimately the only considerations that are relevant to defending the law are considerations that are also relevant to defending what people do quite apart from the law."

[4] *TAOW* (n 2) 32.

Haris Psarras and Sandy Steel, *Introduction* In: *Private Law and Practical Reason*. Edited by: Haris Psarras and Sandy Steel, Oxford University Press. © Haris Psarras and Sandy Steel 2023. DOI: 10.1093/oso/9780192857330.003.0001

have independently of the law. Private law is no different—to the extent it differs from other fields of law, its difference resides in the nature of the duties conformity to which it supports, or in the mode by which it seeks to promote conformity.

Nicholas McBride and Leo Boonzaier each challenge, in very different ways, the central place occupied by duties in Gardner's account of private law. McBride's chapter raises doubts about the very existence of moral duties. If there are no moral duties, then private law cannot be justified, as Gardner would have it, in so far as it secures conformity to them. McBride's argument proceeds by sketching an account of morality which, he contends, dispenses with the notion of "moral duty," and defending the superiority of this account to a moral-duty-based view "M." In this eudaimonic (ie flourishing-cantered) account, "E," morality is concerned with "(i) evaluation; (ii) transitions; (iii) temptations; (iv) concern for others; and (v) transcendence."[5] Morality's evaluation is of when a state of being constitutes flourishing for a human being (rather than whether an action is in breach of a duty). Transition and temptations are a matter of providing guidance for moving from a non-flourishing to a flourishing state, and of avoiding human inclinations to subvert one's own flourishing, respectively. Concern for others is partly constitutive of what it is to flourish. Finally, transcendence is the part of morality concerned with goods that go beyond flourishing. McBride's case for E over M focuses on cases in which M appears not to register an intuitively justifiable feature of our moral reactions to particular moral problems. Sometimes, the wrongness of a particular action is only captured by its falling under the description of a "thick" ethical concept, such as "bestial" or "cowardly," concepts which McBride holds to fall more naturally within E rather than M.

Boonzaier's chapter is not skeptical of the very idea of moral duties but rather of Gardner's contention that the breach of a primary moral duty is a necessary condition of justified tort liability to compensate. Gardner followed Raz in understanding duties as special kinds of reason. A reason to φ is a duty only if the reason is categorical (the reason's existence is independent of the aims of the person for whom it is a reason) and mandatory (there is a reason not to act upon at least some of the reasons against φ-ing). Boonzaier examines the case for Gardner's view that there must be non-conformity to a *mandatory* reason to justify tort liability. One argument considered is that, given the negative consequences inflicted upon a liable person in tort, the imposition of these consequences can only be justified when the person has behaved *objectionably*. As Boonzaier points out, this idea does not lend support to Gardner's view. On Gardner's view, a person can act contrary to a mandatory reason and yet be justified. Justified breaches of duty are possible. If so, the link between "breach of a duty" and "objectionable conduct" is broken: breaching a duty might in the circumstances even be *required* and so not be straightforwardly objectionable. Nor, Boonzaier argues, does Gardner's justification of compensatory action itself support a mandatoriness condition. According to the continuity thesis justification of compensation, the reasons which grounded a person's primary duty at time point t continue to demand conformity after breach. In so far as conformity can still (imperfectly) be achieved by compensation, there is a reason to compensate. Why believe, however, that only *mandatory*

---

[5] McBride, Chapter 3, this volume, 46.

reasons can hang around demanding conformity after non-conformity? In principle, non-conformity to a non-mandatory, weighty reason could require compensatory action. Boonzaier argues there is a robust, *contingent* connection between the breach of a primary duty and justified tort liability, but that, ultimately, the case for a necessary connection is not established.

1.2 Practical reasons in general

Private law attributes normative significance to the outcomes of one's conduct. A person's legal liability to pay compensation normally depends (absent an enforceable agreement to pay compensation) upon whether the person's conduct was a cause of the outcome in respect of which compensation is sought. The result is that private law accepts a significant degree of luck in assigning entitlements to compensation. Although two drivers may have imposed equal, unreasonable, risks of harm, only the driver whose risk imposition materializes in harm may be faced with a substantial compensatory liability. Some regard this as a puzzling instance of "moral outcome luck."[6]

Gardner argued for the pervasive bearing of outcome luck upon certain kinds of moral assessment. He did so, in part, by drawing attention to the existence of certain kinds of reason: reasons to succeed.[7] The argument is that a basic form of reason we have are reasons to *succeed*. We have reasons to keep our promises, not merely to try to keep our promises; reasons not to harm each other, not merely reasons to try not to harm each other. If our non-mandatory reasons include reasons to produce or not to produce certain outcomes, then a burden of proof is cast upon those who would claim that our mandatory reasons cannot have this form.[8] If the outcomes one has caused or failed to prevent can impact upon the reasons one has failed to conform to, then it becomes less puzzling that the harm-causer is subject to a liability to which the mere harm-risker is not. The two agents fail to conform to different reasons: the harm-causer fails to conform not only to the reason not to impose unreasonable risk but also to the more fundamental reason not to harm itself.

Ori Herstein's chapter takes up the "reasons to try" side of Gardner's fruitful distinction and elucidates the connections between reasons to try and the law, various ways in which there can be a value in trying, and the reasons to which these values give rise. Herstein first articulates a particular moral problem with legal duties to try: since trying-to-φ involves forming an intention-to-φ, legal requirements to try mandate specific mental states, an interference with liberty which is normally considered especially difficult to justify. His discussion then moves to the various values of trying, dividing between cases in which trying is valuable as a means to some valuable end, and cases in which trying has intrinsic value. In the first category, beyond the relatively

---

[6] See J Waldron, "Moments of Carelessness and Massive Loss" in D Owen (ed), *Philosophical Foundations of Tort Law* (Clarendon 1997).

[7] For another argument, a Nagel-inspired *reductio* based on the consequences of denying the role of luck in moral life, see *TAOW* (n 2) ch 5.

[8] *TAOW* (n 2) 171–72.

straightforward instance in which trying to φ is a means to φ-ing, Herstein examines three others: reasons to try to φ that arise as a means of aspiring to φ, even when φ-ing is unattainable (a pianist's reason to try to become a consummate pianist); reasons to try to φ as a means to the achievement of a valuable end other than φ-ing (a child's reason to try to win school sports competitions arising at least in part in virtue of the health or developmental benefits to the child); and reasons to fail-to-φ-by-trying-to-φ (the reason to fail at first attempt, because success later will be all the sweeter). Herstein also seeks to demonstrate the existence of reasons to try based on the intrinsic value of trying. An important class of cases here, Herstein claims, are those in which there is an expressive value to trying to φ, even when it is futile (and so the reason to try cannot be derivative of the prospect of success at φ-ing). Moving beyond the much-discussed Gardner example of a person who, atop a hillside, is manifestly unable to assist a drowning person below—Gardner claimed such a person has a reason to succeed in rescuing, but not a reason to try—Herstein elaborates other examples that make expressively justified trying plausible: "think how, upon hearing of a friend's advanced terminal illness, is there really no point to one's silent prayer for a miraculous recovery, even if one is a non-believer?"[9]

Accepting the idea of reasons to succeed does not itself settle the issue of when one has such a reason. Gardner held a rather expansive view: one could have a reason-to-φ even when one is unable to φ. He rejected at least some versions of "ought-implies-can" (OC). Frederick Wilmot-Smith draws attention to a tension between Gardner's rejection of OC and his defenses of the rule of law. He identifies common theoretical motivations for both the OC maxim and the rule of law ideal: guidance and fairness. A prominent motivation for OC is that it is in the nature of normative reasons that they *guide* action. Similarly, the rule of law is an ideal conformity to which is intended to render the law capable of guidance. The idea that it would be *unfair* for a person to be subject to moral requirements to which she is unable to conform is also adduced in support of OC and against legal requirements that demand the impossible. How, then, can one reject OIC and accept the moral demands of the rule of law? Ultimately, Wilmot-Smith argues that the tension can be dissolved. First, the guidance requirements that the rule of law imposes on legal norms have a different content to the guidance requirements on purely moral norms. This is because legal norms are directed to both law-appliers and legal subjects. This creates special problems because what constitutes good guidance for law-appliers may be rather different from what constitutes good guidance for legal subjects. No parallel problem exists in the purely moral domain. Second, Wilmot-Smith argues, the ideal that norms should provide guidance applies to all persons in relation to every action in morality, but "the value of legality will be met so long as a sufficient number of individuals who are to be guided by the norm—be they citizens or officials—can be guided by it."[10] One reason is that the value of legality will itself be subverted if laws are tailored to the particular abilities of each individual: the result would be a legal system that is incapable of providing satisfactory guidance.

[9] Herstein, Chapter 4, this volume, 74.
[10] Wilmot-Smith, Chapter 5, this volume, 86.

1.3 Justice

A prominent theme in contemporary philosophizing about private law is the exploration of connections between private law and justice. On one view, associated with Ernest Weinrib's work, private law's sole justified task is the provision of corrective justice, while public law is properly concerned with distributive justice.[11] Gardner disagreed. Private law is partly constituted by norms of corrective justice, but only partly—many of the primary duties imposed by tort law, for instance, are not themselves norms of justice, and some justified norms of private law are norms of distributive justice.[12]

Gardner's view rests upon a concept of justice as concerned with *allocations*. Norms of justice are allocative norms. Corrective justice norms regulate a particular kind of allocation: they are norms that allocate "back" after a transaction, including a wrong. The wrongness of torture is not a wrong of justice since it is not wrong in virtue of allocating something incorrectly. Tatiana Cutts' chapter challenges Gardner's conception of justice and questions the theoretical need to establish the "subject matter" or domain of justice in philosophizing about private law. According to Cutts, allocation of (scarce) goods is neither necessary nor sufficient for an activity to be a matter of justice. It is not necessary because issues of justice are intuitively raised by the proportionality of punishment to crimes, even though freedom from punishment is not a scarce good. It is not sufficient because, for instance, decisions about distributing one's attention among potential dating partners do not raise issues of justice. Cutts suggests that the thread relating these examples—including one within justice and excluding the other—is whether an action bears upon rights. However, her chapter's more fundamental point is that the theoretical value of first characterizing a problem as a problem of "justice" in allocation is non-obvious, and potentially detrimental: "Framing problems of justice as 'allocative' tends to focus our attention on the relative strength of two parties' competitive claims to some specific set of goods at a particular moment in time, on the basis of known facts."[13] Such a framing directs attention away from the question of justifying a *rule* that regulates particular situations, and the reasons there may be for valuing the existence of such a rule.

As noted above, Gardner's position is that private law raises issues of corrective *and* distributive justice and is justifiably concerned with both. One way in which he argued for this was to point to decisions about the legal institutionalization of moral rights and duties of corrective justice. Moral duties of corrective justice arise as a manifestation of reasons which grounded primary moral rights and duties, but which moral duties of corrective justice should be legally regulated, and upon whom should legal rights of corrective justice be conferred? These, Gardner held, are inevitably allocative questions, the domain of distributive justice. Private law is, in this way, in the business of resolving questions of distributive justice about the distribution of legal rights to corrective justice. Rebecca Stone's chapter agrees with Gardner that private law is

---

[11] E Weinrib, *The Idea of Private Law* (reprint, OUP 2012).
[12] See *TAOW* (n 2) 31–44.
[13] Cutts, Chapter 6, this volume, 103.

justifiably concerned with distributive and corrective justice, but argues that the interrelationship between the two is more complicated than in Gardner's account.[14] In Stone's account, moral rights and duties are resolutions of conflicts between different normative standpoints that reflect the governing moral reasons bearing upon a choice. Moral rights and duties are, in this sense, inherently allocative since they give normative priority to some normative standpoint over another in relation to a particular choice. In this sense, moral rights and duties are all inherently a matter of distributive justice. Stone agrees with Gardner that corrective duties arise as a means of imperfect conformity to the moral reasons that generated the primary moral rights and duties. So it might seem that, for Stone, justified legally regulated corrective justice is wholly dependent upon legal rights reflecting the underlying, distributively just, moral rights. Stone's view allows for a partial independence between substantive distributive justice and justified corrective justice, however. The idea is that the law can justifiably and authoritatively resolve normative uncertainty about substantive distributive justice, even when it wrongly assesses the moral reasons bearing upon a particular situation. Here the parties, relative to the moral facts, do not have the substantive moral rights which the law claims they have. Nonetheless, given the reasonableness of the resolution of the normative uncertainty in question, the parties could be morally bound by the legal determination of their rights and duties. Consequently, there could be a moral duty of corrective justice independent of the primary rights and duties being substantively justified as a matter of distributive justice.

1.4 Instrumentalism

Gardner urged against false oppositions in the philosophy of law, considering the tendency to package together sets of theses as rival schools a "blight" on the subject.[15] Vague labels can obscure underlying agreement (or mislocate disagreement). For instance, if "instrumentalism" is the thesis that "private law [is] a means of forwarding the community's aggregate welfare through a strategy of maximisation often expressed in economic terms,"[16] then both Gardner and Weinrib are anti-instrumentalists. If instrumentalism is the thesis that "private law [is] a means to something else,"[17] it is also not entirely clear that Gardner and Weinrib are in disagreement on this point. If "is a means to" is understood to include both relationships of facilitation and part-constitution, then Weinrib and Gardner are probably both instrumentalists. If Weinrib accepts that the content of private law is partly determined by social facts about judicial and legislative conduct (as his writing a casebook on torts would imply), then it seems likely that these social facts are only valuable to the extent that they part-constitute people as moral equals. The law is still justified only in so far as it contributes to the realization of an ideal that is partly independent of the law.

---

[14] Stone, Chapter 7, this volume.
[15] J Gardner, *Law as a Leap of Faith* (OUP 2013), vi.
[16] Weinrib *The Idea of Private Law* (n 11) 48.
[17] ibid 49. See *TAOW* at 328ff for discussion.

Agreement on the fact that private law is valuable (at least partly) as an instrument to morally valuable states or outcomes does not settle, of course, what those are or how exactly the instrument should operate. Sandy Steel's chapter addresses the role of deterrence—a particular mode, he notes, of influencing the conduct of others—within non-consequentialist accounts of private law. It seeks to vindicate Gardner's view that considerations about the beneficial or negative deterrent impact of private law are relevant to its justification within a non-consequentialist outlook. His chapter argues that while the beneficial deterrent impact of a private law norm is neither necessary nor sufficient for its justification, it can decisively determine which private law norms ought to be adopted among those which have a non-consequentialist justification and enter into the design of private law institutions whose duties are incurred by choice.

2. Responding to Wrongs

2.1 Victims' duties to wrongdoers

As Cécile Fabre observes in her chapter, the far greater part of philosophical attention in the domain of reparative justice has been focused on wrongdoers' reparative duties to victims.[18] A neglected question, posed by Gardner in *From Personal to Life to Private Law*, is whether victims have duties to wrongdoers to accept their offers of amends, and in so far as that amounts to financial compensation, to use the compensation to effect repair of the wrong. Gardner sketched a view according to which victims were so duty-bound.[19] Fabre's chapter uses Gardner's remarks as a springboard to examine the issue more fully. It argues against victim duties to accept financial compensation and against a duty to use financial compensation, if accepted, to repair the wrong. Consider first duties to accept compensation. Fabre gives a case for moral duties not to thwart others' performance of their moral duties: such a duty is supported by others' well-being (in so far as living a life in accordance with moral duties contributes to one's well-being) and respect for their moral agency. However, she argues that the interests of the victim which ground reparative duties to compensate also ground victim powers to waive such duties, and a permission for the victim vis-à-vis the wrongdoer to do so. Part of the argument draws on a comparison with duties to rescue: the victim's interest grounds this duty but it also grounds a permission to release a person from their duty to rescue. If this is true in relation to duties of rescue, it is unclear why the same should not be true in relation to duties to improve another's position through compensation. Consider next duties to use compensation to repair the wrong. Here Fabre's negative case focuses on the fact that, if the victim uses money compensation for a purpose other than repair of, say, wrongfully damaged property, this merely involves the victim doing something that they had an option to achieve through their property prior to the wrong. For instance, if the victim uses the payment for a replacement car to fund her daughter's holiday, she does something which she could have achieved by selling the car prior to the wrong. Fabre points out

[18] Fabre, Chapter 9, this volume.
[19] ibid 145.

2.2 Wrongdoers' duties to victims

Why are there duties to compensate for harm caused by one's wrongdoing? Gardner's answer was his well-known "continuity thesis."[20] Although the breach of a duty may mean that the duty no longer exists, the reasons which grounded that duty continue, after breach, to exist and demand conformity. Perfect conformity after breach is impossible, according to Gardner, because the reason constituted by the breached duty is itself no longer available for conformity.[21] However, in so far as the reasons that grounded one's duty *can* still be conformed to, and in so far as compensation will constitute conformity to those reasons, one has a reason to compensate. Typically if those reasons amounted to a duty prior to breach, Gardner claims, they will also have duty-bearing force after breach. This is an elegant explanation of why duties to compensate arise, an explanation that avoids appeal to an independently justified principle of corrective justice: the justification of compensatory duties just is the continued force of the reasons for one's original duties.

The continuity thesis follows from a general principle about reasons to which Gardner subscribed: the "conformity principle," which holds that one ought to conform to reason completely and if one cannot do so, one ought to come as close as possible.[22] The fact that the continuity thesis is a special application of a general thesis about *reasons*, regardless of whether they are *mandatory* and *categorical* reasons, and regardless of why a person failed to conform to a reason, has given rise to an important critique of the thesis as an explanation of compensatory duties. The critique, as John Oberdiek explains in his chapter, is that the thesis accords no distinctive significance to *wrongs*. Non-conformity to any reason, not just reasons whose non-conformity amounts to a wrong, entails a reason to do the next best thing to conformity. Further, the fact of non-conformity itself is only a causal condition for the duty to compensate; the wrong itself is not a normative reason for the duty to compensate. The fact that one committed a wrong is not, after all, among the reasons which justified one's original duty so, the objection runs, the continuity thesis cannot capture the sense in which one's wronging another is part of the positive justification of why one is under a duty to compensate them.

Oberdiek aims to defend the continuity thesis against this criticism by showing that it accommodates a distinctive significance to wrongs. His central point is that non-conformity to a relational duty—a duty owed to another—*is* distinctive from other forms of non-conformity to reason in that it amounts to the frustration of a *claim*.

---

[20] See *TAOW* (n 2) 61.

[21] *TAOW* (n 2) 62.

[22] A principle stated by Raz: J Raz, "Personal Practical Conflicts" in P Baumann and M Betzler (eds), *Practical Conflicts: New Philosophical Essays* (CUP 2004) 189–93.

This can be registered by the continuity thesis because a person's claim amounts to a reason for the original, primary, duty, and the secondary duty that arises upon breach. Further, the continuity thesis is also, Oberdiek suggests, compatible with the idea, distinctive to relational duties and so to wrongs, that there is a value in accountability. Part of what justifies primary relational duties is the value of accountability and this value also partly justifies secondary relational duties.

Although Gardner developed the continuity thesis in detail in a paper about the role of corrective justice in tort law, one of the examples with which he illustrated the idea was a promissory one.[23] A father promises his children to take them to the beach at the weekend, but an emergency precludes him from doing so. Intuitively, Gardner thinks, the father cannot simply move on without further ado in the face of the broken promise. Rather, the reasons that grounded the primary duty to perform continue to demand conformity—these reasons now require some next best action for the benefit of the children promisees, such as a substitute beach trip another day. Generalizing, Gardner holds that the breach of a promise generates a duty to do the next best thing, even if the breach was justified.

Dori Kimel's chapter critically scrutinizes the idea that breach of a promise always gives rise to a duty of next-best conformity. He agrees with Gardner that the breach of a promise *always* generates a duty, but disagrees that it always triggers a duty of *next-best conformity*. For Kimel, the justified breach of an altruistic promise gives rise to a duty to give an *account* to the promisee of, at least, the fact that there was a justification for the breach, but it may not require more. Whether a duty to do the next-best thing arises depends upon a host of factors, Kimel argues, including the non-promissory background norms which govern the parties' relationship. For instance, a parent might owe next best conformity of a justifiably breached promise to their child in virtue of their special relationship but not to a stranger. Kimel challenges the idea that the reasons which contributed to a promised action being obligatory—the fact that a promise has been made and whatever the reasons are why promises are binding— are not "satisfied" in cases of justified breach. In such cases, the promisor adequately weighs in deliberation the rational force of the promise. Only in cases of disregard or undue weight being given to the promise does the promisor have a duty of next best conformity.

Wrongdoers' duties to victims—as all duties—are reasons. Do reason-based accounts of reparation in private law leave room for emotions to play any normatively significant role? Answering this question in the affirmative is more straightforward when it comes to a victim's emotions. You suffered an accident—probably due to another person's negligence. You are disappointed and angry at the injustice you feel was done to you, so you sue the suspected wrongdoer. You may have reasons to sue them, but your emotions also motivate you.

When it comes to the wrongdoers' emotions, any possible link between them and private law and civil litigation is less evident. In her chapter, Sinel inquires into how wrongdoers' emotions may matter to private law, argues that Gardner treated regret as the most relevant emotion to the remedial obligations that a wrongdoer owes to

---

[23] Borrowed from N MacCormick, "The Obligation of Reparation" in N MacCormick, *Legal Right and Social Democracy* (OUP 1982) 212.

the person she wronged.[24] Sinel endorses Gardner's insight into the normative potential of regret, but only when it comes to moral obligations to remedy your wrong.[25] According to Sinel, regret is irrelevant to remedial obligations in law. The largest part of her argument is dedicated to the defense of the idea that the irrelevance of regret to the wrongdoer's reparative duties is due to the fact that the normative power of reasons that remained non-conformed to at the time the wrong was committed, does not revive to support reparative duties. What Sinel takes as a fact here is what she describes as "the normative inertness" of past wrongs.[26] Her approach directly opposes Gardner's continuity thesis. But in addition to her argument against the continuity thesis, Sinel also argues that reasons in favor of the irrelevance of regret to law underlie even the continuity thesis itself; that is because, the argument continues, the continuity thesis endorses an automatic revival of violated duties in the form of reparative duties that leaves no room for emotional responses with any normative weight.[27] This paves the way to the second point that Sinel raises in her chapter: regret can develop its normative appeal in the moral sphere, precisely because reparation under the law leaves no room for grounding responsibility and reparation on emotions, such as regret.[28]

In the concluding chapter of the section on wrongdoers' duties to victims, Michelon offers a fresh and moderate defense of the continuity thesis. He does so through constructively comparing it with the identity thesis which he associates with some of the theoretical models in private law against which Gardner often leveled his criticism, such as those devised by Weinrib and Ripstein.[29] Interestingly, Michelon's argument begins not with taking sides in the debate between the two theses, but with clearing the ground for the strengths of each thesis to shine as each deserves, safe from the conceptual confusion that he finds to have bedeviled part of their critical reception to date. As the argument develops, Michelon engages with what he proposes as a fair charge against even a fine-grained version of the identity thesis, namely its unpersuasive attempt to individuate duties on the basis of act-individuation. A contrast of act-individuation with an alternative manner of individuating duties that Michelon considers as "ground-based individuation" provides the identity thesis with a better chance to move on in its account of primary and remedial duties in private law; a chance which, according to Michelon's argument, explains why ground-based individuation is also favored by Weinrib.[30] However, Michelon's close scrutiny of the justificatory potential of ground-based individuation brings to light the close ties between this form of individuation of duties and a higher-level duty. Michelon argues that this undermines the credibility of the identity thesis not least because the monistic normative foundation that the high-level duty provides—or rather imposes—to the ground-based individuation leaves no room for acknowledging the relevance of other normative reasons.[31] The final stage of the argument unfolds through carefully

---

[24] Sinel, Chapter 12, this volume, 208.
[25] ibid 225.
[26] ibid 217.
[27] ibid 214.
[28] ibid 225–26.
[29] See eg *TAOW* (n 2) ch 2. See also Michelon, Chapter 13, this volume, 227.
[30] Michelon, Chapter 13, this volume, 232, 233.
[31] ibid 236.

demonstrating why the continuity thesis is safe from the charge that the identity thesis is found to be exposed to when it comes to the normative grounding of primary and reparatory duties.[32] In fact, the chapter's moderate defense of the continuity thesis owes much to Michelon's strategy of highlighting the continuity thesis's comparative advantages over its adversary. But this strategy can also be seen as paving the way to a promising restatement of the continuity thesis that would bring it closer to the views of its rivals, while retaining its distinctiveness, and would therefore arguably increase its appeal to theorists who are still undecided as to which side they are on.

2.3 Victims' powers

Gardner's consideration of genuine reasons in law as moral reasons that, thanks to the institutionalization that they normally undergo in the course of power-conferring practices, concretize either their mandatory or their permissive properties, enabled him to furnish normative accounts not only of duties, but also of other normative relations in private law.[33] Gardner's theory covers not only "initial entitlements,"[34]—that is, rights correlative to duties not to wrong another through a tortious act or breach of contract—but also remedial entitlements as well as powers to have such entitlements crystallized in the form of enforceable court orders.

Though Gardner theorized on all three aforementioned types of entitlements and on multiple intersections among them, his philosophical exploration of this area of private law intensified at a later stage of his career; due to his untimely death, it now reaches us more in the form of fragments of a work in progress[35] than in a definitive manner, as is typical of his work on the place of corrective justice in private law or on strict liability. Yet it is precisely this excitingly open-ended dimension of Gardner's innovative treatment of private law entitlements in terms of moral reasons, legal rights, and procedural powers that appears to have inspired some contributors to this volume.

Katz and Shapiro, in their jointly written chapter, embark on a constructive critique of Gardner's theory on the reasons that underlie the plaintiff's power to sue; a critique that inevitably extends to Gardner's intentionally provocative consideration of plaintiffs as "acting officials" in civil litigation.[36] The brevity of Gardner's remarks on the institutional role of litigants does not make it easy to speculate as to whether his acknowledgment of an open scope of possible justifications for civil proceedings in light of a plurality of values[37] is open enough to accommodate Katz and Shapiro's justification of the power to sue on the basis of those moral reasons that survive the violation of the plaintiff's primary rights.[38] But even that justification, though it opposes Gardner's

---

[32] ibid 239–41.

[33] *FPLPL* (n 2) 191–92.

[34] G Calabresi and D Melamed, "Property Rules, Liability Rules, and Inalienability: One View of the Cathedral" (1972) 85 Harvard Law Review 1089, 1097; cited ibid 192.

[35] See eg his debate with Stephen Smith on the normative reasons for damages awards in J Gardner, "Damages Without Duty" (2019) 69 University of Toronto Law Journal 412.

[36] *TAOW* (n 2) 106.

[37] *FPLPL* (n 2) 208–09

[38] Katz and Shapiro, Chapter 14, this volume, 254–55.

dissociation of the normative grounding of enforcement rights from considerations of corrective justice,[39] builds on his idea that the reasons underlying primary rights also provide the foundation for remedial rights. Taking this idea further, Katz and Shapiro claim that the normative appeal of corrective justice and of Gardner's continuity thesis reaches beyond remedial rights and is equally relevant to the plaintiff's enforcement rights.[40] At the start of their argument, they devise three different conceptualizations of the plaintiff's power to sue that are detectable in Gardner's writings: the public authority conscription model, the power-sharing model, and the model of plaintiffs as quasi-officials. After endorsing the public authority model as the one that most closely reflects Gardner's approach to the institutional role of the plaintiff, they discuss three puzzles that a solely institution-based approach to civil litigation cannot address satisfactorily. This leads Katz and Shapiro to a formulation that encompasses the strengths of Gardner's portrayal of plaintiffs as institutional actors but also overcomes the limitations of a solely institution-based approach to the power to sue. This is achieved through calling attention to the fact that plaintiffs may act in a personal capacity in order to vindicate rights in light of moral reasons that are also personal, in the sense that there is a personal value in standing up for their rights when there would be a challenge to their dignity in not so doing.

Gardner's classification of entitlements in private law into primary, secondary, and tertiary rights—with secondary rights being rights to remedy, and the class of tertiary rights roughly corresponding to powers often described as enforcement rights—has also provided a springboard for another chapter. In his chapter on private law rights and powers of waiver, Psarras uses Gardner's tripartite classification as the starting point for an approach to waiving rights that intends to challenge and qualify the view that a right-holder in private law can give up any of her rights. Psarras associates this view with another which takes all private law rights to correlate to duties over which a right-holder has full control. After rejecting both views, the argument advances an alternative take on the waivability of private law rights which considers the three different types of rights highlighted by Gardner as indicative of three different types of waivability. In this framework, primary rights are seen as clusters of claim-rights, powers to waive claim-rights and powers to revoke such waivers, while secondary rights are taken to be non-waivable in light of the service they render not only to the right-holder but also to the promotion of corrective justice under the law. Finally, tertiary rights are analyzed in terms of waivable powers toward wrongdoers, but also in terms of non-waivable powers inextricably linked to courts' authority to vindicate substantive rights and remedy their breaches.

3. Specific Areas

Among all different areas of private law, the one that attracted Gardner's interest far more than any other is tort. His work on other areas was often a working out of the ways in which tort is distinctive from other areas of private law, such as equity or contract.[41]

---

[39] ibid 248.
[40] ibid 253.
[41] See eg *TAOW* (n 2) Ch 1.

It is this well-known side of Gardner's interests that the third and last part of this edited collection celebrates by paying tribute to Gardner's theoretical contributions to specific areas of private law. It includes two chapters on tort, one chapter on contract, one on equity, and a final chapter that is not as much a chapter on tort as it is on the intertwinement of tort with questions of personal responsibility and interpersonal moral duties in our life under the law and beyond.[42] Thus, the volume concludes with a reminder that even Gardner's theoretical writings on specific areas of private law take us back to his general philosophy of private law and personal life.

In her chapter, Steele explores in what respect Gardner's tort theory can be taken to have emancipatory political potential, while she also constructively discusses what she sees as the limitations of his theory in the domain of institutionalized forms of social power that could rival wealth. The element of Gardner's account of tort that Steele highlights as most relevant to a project of political change is his original view that tort, as a whole, and, more specifically, the negligence standard protect security rights—a claim that can be juxtaposed to the classical liberal conception of tort as primarily serving individual autonomy.[43] Though Gardner's claim is that security rights are, in essence, rights to corrective justice,[44] his vision, as appositely encapsulated in Steele's argument, is that tort not only safeguards, but also—and most importantly—distributes security rights.[45] Considering that the distribution of security rights also involves a distribution of powers—both in substantive law and in civil litigation—whose institutional dimension (possibly, with a little help from the judiciary) could challenge the non-institutional expansionist power of accumulated wealth, tort law can be seen as political; provided, of course, that we see the distributive considerations, which tort could enhance and concretize, as inherently political. Yet Steele's argument also emphasizes that tort's service to security is a double-edged sword: claims to security also tend to sustain a long-standing social order that has generated or favored unequal allocation of resources in the first place.[46]

While McBride and Boonzaier, as noted above, argue that Gardner is, in different ways, over-reliant on duties, Chris Essert's chapter argues that Gardner underplays the role of strictly *relational* duties in tort law, specifically the tort of negligence in England and Canada. Essert and Gardner agree that private law is partly constituted by relational legal duties: duties owed by particular persons to other particular persons. In *From Personal Life to Private Law*, Gardner distinguished between "strictly" and "loosely" relational duties.[47] A duty is strictly relational if at least part of the duty's justification is the value of the relationship that it partly constitutes. The duties of a parent to a child are strictly relational according to Gardner: the value of the relation of parent–child is part of the justification of the duties that constitute the relationship. Loosely relational duties, by contrast, are ones which are owed to another person, but not in virtue of an independently comprehensible relation, to use Essert's term, between the duty-bearer and the counterparty. Gardner argued that the duty of care

---

[42] Goldberg and Zipursky, Chapter 20, this volume, 348.
[43] Steele, Chapter 16, this volume, 288, 293.
[44] ibid 291.
[45] ibid 293–94.
[46] ibid 295–96.
[47] *FPLPL* (n 2) 23–26.

in the tort of negligence between Atkin neighbors is a loosely relational duty: what justifies the duty is not the value of the relation in which the parties stand.[48] The trigger for the duty is one party being situated such that it is reasonably foreseeable as more than a far-fetched possibility that one's careless act will physically damage the other—but what *value* is there in such a relation? Essert argues, to the contrary, that the duty of care between Atkin neighbors *is* strictly relational and owes its existence to the value of the relation it constitutes. The Atkin neighbor principle draws lines between persons to whom a special kind of concern is owed and those to whom it is not: it determines who will be wronged when a person fails to take reasonable care. If there were no such line-drawing, Essert argues, then each of us would forever be wronging the other: for instance, the materialization of any unforeseeable risk of bodily harm, or the creation of even far-fetched risks, would constitute a wrong: "Duties like that would, given the inevitability of risk-creation, effectively make it impossible for us to live our lives, to do anything at all."[49] So there is, he concludes, a value in the Atkinian neighbor relation—the value resides in its excluding certain people from the remit of a kind of special concern, which, in turn, allows people enough elbow room to live their lives freely.

In his critically alert exploration of Gardner's tentative approach to modern contract law, Dagan starts by acknowledging Gardner's highly skeptical position toward a number of unqualified endorsements of freedom of contract[50] that idolize contract law and lose sight of the service that private law, more broadly conceived, is intended to render to an array of moral values, some of which incorporate considerations not directly relevant to the value of freedom, such as perfectionist or distributive considerations. Dagan, who has, over the years, developed his own philosophical project on contract, endorses Gardner's criticism of a narrow liberal rhetoric that echoes a dated model of contractual relations (the "this for that" model, as Dagan labels it). Yet Dagan also argues in favor of the inherence of some liberal values in private law.[51] In this spirit, he places particular emphasis on the value of autonomy.[52] Overall, Dagan's chapter joins Gardner in his rejection of theories that slavishly serve the principle of formal equality among contract parties and fail to prevent phenomena of alienation, exploitation, or subordination that the inequality of parties' bargaining power tends to lead to. However, the approach to contract that Dagan proposes as an alternative is different to approaches we know from Gardner's work. More specifically, it is premised on Dagan's consideration of contract as a primarily power-conferring institution[53] that can counterbalance the tendency of some contractual arrangements to generate long-term substantive inequality. Such a counterbalancing potential is, according to Dagan, a matter of ensuring secure interpersonal arrangements between a better-off and a less well-off party with a contract thus amounting to a joint plan co-authored by both parties.[54]

---

[48] *FPLPL* (n 2) 46–52.
[49] Essert, Chapter 17, this volume, 303.
[50] *FPLPL* (n 2) 198.
[51] Dagan, Chapter 18, this volume, 329.
[52] ibid.
[53] ibid 322.
[54] ibid 324.

Gold takes a different path to explore Gardner's more peripheral yet equally note-worthy engagement with another area of private law: fiduciary law. Rather than fo-cusing on Gardner's investigation into normatively significant differences between tort and equity—like those reflected in Gardner's comparison between reparative damages for tortious wrongdoing and remedies for equitable wrongs[55]—Gold calls attention to a question that Gardner insightfully raised without yet attempting to answer it, but only in passing: why is there no legal counterpart of what in ordinary language is a "reasonably loyal" person?[56] More specifically, why does fiduciary law not include the concept of a reasonably loyal trustee? Gold relates this question to a broader puzzle that Gardner also concerned himself with, the puzzle over the desir-ability of the use of non-legal concepts and criteria to further concretize legal duties that have been articulated in inevitably indeterminate terms or may have been left intentionally open-ended.[57] This strategy is familiar to courts. It can be seen as a form of legal interpretation that judges or other law-appliers resort to when the law offers no answer as to how an abstract concept they find embedded in a legal rule applies to a case or an area of practice—and that is a regular occurrence. Gold acknowledges that the issue has broader implications for law, and then concentrates on additional complications or opportunities that feeding non-legal elements into law (or, in other words, *buck passing*, as this technique has been termed by Gardner) brings with it, specifically when it comes to fiduciary loyalty obligations.[58] The argument develops through an examination of three reasons in favor of the use of buck passing in fidu-ciary law; reasons that highlight positive outcomes that buck passing may have for eq-uitable reasoning (eg offering guidance for assessing fiduciary loyalty)[59] and for legal reasoning, more broadly, as opening law to non-legal collective experience enables law to evolve in tune with other normative realms.[60]

Goldberg and Zipursky, whose influential civil recourse theory of tort[61] was praised by Gardner as a reinvigoration of the classical interpretation of the common law of torts (an interpretation which part of his own work also aimed to vindicate),[62] pay tribute to the philosophical outlook of Gardner's tort law theory and explore points of convergence and divergence between his theoretical model and theirs. Their argu-ment begins by calling attention to the moral foundations of Gardner's conceptuali-zation of remedying civil wrongs as a matter of restoring the wronged party's life to the shape it had before she suffered the wrong. Goldberg and Zipursky identify the roots of Gardner's commitment to the idea of restoration as a basis for civil remedies in his theory's affinity to Bernard Williams's commitment-based account of value.[63] If what makes a value or a set of values more significant for one person than it may be for others is that person's commitment to it, then securing one's life against others'

---

[55] *TAOW* (n 2) 6–11.
[56] Gold, Chapter 19, this volume, 330.
[57] ibid 346.
[58] ibid 340–41.
[59] ibid 344.
[60] ibid 345–46.
[61] See its recent upshot in JCP Goldberg and BC Zipursky, *Recognizing Wrongs* (Harvard University Press 2020) chs 1–5.
[62] *TAOW* (n 2) 1.
[63] Goldberg and Zipursky, Chapter 20, this volume, 349.

wrongful or even harmful interference safeguards not only legitimate personal choices but also states of affairs that are as valuable as also are the personal attachments created and sustained through them over time. Goldberg and Zipursky credit this philosophical background of Gardner's thought with a transformative potential that can trigger a move from corrective-justice-based theories, like Weinrib's or Ripstein's, to rights-based theories of tort, like theirs. Though Goldberg and Zipursky note Gardner's reluctance to undertake such a move openly,[64] they endorse his treatment of security as a value that private law institutions should promote also in light of considerations of distributive justice. Of course, Gardner considered the institutionalization of security demands in private law in terms of security rights, though Goldberg and Zipursky favor security safeguards in the form of the conferral of key powers in civil litigation to individuals.[65] Yet Goldberg and Zipursky welcome Gardner's insistence in making a place for distributive justice in the foundations of private law as an acknowledgment that such foundations also rest on political morality.[66]

[64] ibid 354–55.
[65] ibid 358.
[66] ibid 355.

PART I
GENERAL PRIVATE LAW THEORY

2
Gardner on Duties in Tort

Leo Boonzaier

Being taught by John Gardner as a master's student, and then supervised by him for my doctorate, was one of the great privileges of my life. Like many of my peers, I was drawn tightly into John's orbit, which was a wonderful place to be. He was brilliant and captivating. The ideas that poured from him were bold and distinctive. But they were also closely argued, deeply rooted in philosophical learning, and, in my view, thoroughly convincing. This chapter is about a rare respect in which John's work left me unpersuaded, and in part puzzled. It is about his endorsement of the claim that tort liability is grounded upon a wrong (or, equivalently, a breach of duty) by the defendant. Why did John endorse this claim? And was he right to? My first task in this chapter will be to explain why these questions are worth asking. In the process I will try to bring out some features of John's tort scholarship which make the answers non-obvious. My second task will be to assess John's argument for the claim that torts are wrongs and offer some criticisms of it. I will conclude that the argument is unsound but nevertheless illuminating.

1. Definitions

My interest, then, lies in Gardner's claim that a breach of duty is necessary (and defeasibly sufficient) to justify the imposition of tort liability.[1] Indeed he thought that, unless one identifies a breach of duty, one has not identified a tort.[2] This claim can be boiled down, for most purposes, to one I call "TW":

(TW) Torts are, necessarily, wrongs.

My willingness to query this claim may seem surprising, perhaps sacrilegious. Isn't the claim *obviously* true? Doesn't virtually *every* tort theorist believe it? At any rate, doesn't every "non-instrumental"[3] or (as Gardner put it) "moralistic"[4] tort theorist believe it? Skepticism about private law's primary duties is usually thought to be the preserve of

---

[1] J Gardner, "Backward and Forward with Tort Law" in JK Campbell, M O'Rourke, and D Shier (eds), *Law and Social Justice* (MIT Press 2005) 275–77.

[2] ibid 256. See also his "Torts and Other Wrongs" (2011) 39 Florida State University Law Review 43, 45–46.

[3] This terminology is usually associated with Ernest Weinrib: see eg *The Idea of Private Law* (Harvard University Press 1995) 48–55.

[4] J Gardner, "Tort Law and Its Theory" in J Tasioulas (ed), *The Cambridge Companion to the Philosophy of Law* (CUP 2020).

Leo Boonzaier, *Gardner on Duties in Tort* In: *Private Law and Practical Reason.* Edited by: Haris Psarras and Sandy Steel, Oxford University Press. © Leo Boonzaier 2023. DOI: 10.1093/oso/9780192857330.003.0002

20   LEO BOONZAIER

the legal economists, and of Oliver Wendell Holmes, who inspired them.[5] The centrality of duties has since been reasserted by virtually all leading writers in the field.[6] So it is only natural, one might think, that Gardner stood among them, denouncing the "Holmesian heresy."[7]

Well, I don't find any of this reassuring. And that is only partly because, as Gardner wrote in an adjacent context:

> Many philosophers ... regard the fact that a proposition is widely accepted, or plausible, as counting in favor of its being true, or at least being treated as true in philosophical argument. I tend to count it the other way. Our main job as philosophers is to expose the difficulties with what most people, even other philosophers, take to be obvious. The more obvious it seems, the more work still needs to be done.[8]

In fact the near-universal agreement on the truth of TW "immediately puts me on my guard."[9] For it seems likely that the agreement, or the appearance of it, is made possible by the "vagueness or equivocation" inherent in the claim.[10] Only because of its many ambiguities has it been endorsed by writers who otherwise disagree about so much.

As is well known, Gardner followed Raz in analyzing duties in terms of categorical and mandatory reasons.[11] More precisely, to have a duty to φ entails that one has a reason to φ that (i) is not conditional upon the aims of the person who has it ("categorical"); and (ii) is protected by an exclusionary reason, in other words one has a reason not to act on (at least some of) the reasons to not-φ ("mandatory"). Exclusionary reasons are one kind of second-order reason. Whereas first-order reasons are reasons for or against an action, and compete with one another by weight, second-order reasons are reasons to act for (or, in the case of exclusionary reasons, *not* to act for) one or more first-order reasons. Exclusionary reasons prevail outright over the first-order reasons they exclude; they defeat them just in virtue of being reasons of a higher order, and regardless of any question of weight. Hence, when a reason to φ is coupled with an exclusionary reason, the reason to φ is "protected," in the sense that it is not liable to be outweighed by (some of) the reasons against φ-ing. Rather, those latter reasons are defeated outright, in virtue of their being excluded. To have a duty, for Raz and for Gardner, entails that one is subject to a combination of just this kind: that is, a reason to φ that is protected by exclusionary force. The further feature, as mentioned, is that

---

[5] See eg JCP Goldberg and BC Zipursky's historical sketch in *Recognizing Wrongs* (Harvard University Press 2020) 44ff.

[6] To give only a small sample: A Ripstein, *Private Wrongs* (Harvard University Press 2016); S Hershovitz, "Treating Wrongs as Wrongs: An Expressive Argument for Tort Law" (2018) 10 Journal of Tort Law 405; Goldberg and Zipursky, *Recognizing Wrongs* (n 5).

[7] "Torts and Other Wrongs" (n 2) 46.

[8] J Gardner, "As Inconclusive as Ever" (2019) 19 Jerusalem Review of Legal Studies 204, 209.

[9] ibid.

[10] ibid.

[11] For example, J Gardner, "The Wrongdoing That Gets Results" (2004) 18 Philosophical Perspectives 53, 58; J Gardner, "What Is Tort Law For? Part 1. The Place of Corrective Justice" (2011) 30 Law and Philosophy 1, 31. The analysis is from J Raz, "Promises and Obligations" in PMS Hacker and J Raz (eds), *Law, Morality and Society* (OUP 1977); J Raz, *Practical Reason and Norms* (2nd edn, OUP 1999).

the reason to φ is categorical: it does not depend upon the aims or goals of the person who has it.

Raz's account of duties is much discussed, but when introduced into tort-theoretical debates is perhaps surprisingly distinctive. To begin with a point that is obvious: Raz's account distinguishes "A has a duty to φ" from "A has reason to φ."[12] The former entails the latter, but the reverse is not true; to say that A has a duty means that one has a reason *with special further features*.[13] And Raz's account of the specialness of duties is precise. "A has a duty to φ" does not mean "A has a reason to φ, and that reason is very weighty." Nor does it mean "A has a reason to φ, and φ is not supererogatory." And so we can already see that to endorse the Razian analysis is to distance oneself from the many writers who, within tort-theoretical debates and without, understand "A has a duty to φ" in one of the senses just mentioned, or who do not adopt any precise or stable usage at all. It also shows that, for Gardner, endorsing TW means something more specific than that tort law is about "interpersonal morality" (and not only about "policy") or about "corrective justice" (and not only about "distributive justice"). Duties are, on his understanding, only *one component* of interpersonal morality, and wrongdoing only *one kind* of transaction that ought justly to be corrected.[14]

Here is another thing to notice: Raz analyzes duties exclusively in terms of their bearing on the agent's practical reasoning at the moment when they fall to be conformed to. It cashes out TW in terms of the kinds of reasons that apply to the defendant at the time the tort is committed (call this "t_1"). Whether a defendant had a duty, and whether he breached it, turn on the following questions: did the defendant have a reason to φ at t_1? Was that reason categorical? Was it mandatory? Did the defendant φ at t_1? And, if he did not φ, was he, in doing so, acting for a reason that was excluded? All pertain to the reasons that applied to the defendant at t_1 and his conformity, or non-conformity, to them.

This point may seem innocuous, but is not. The kicker is that, on Raz's account, duties are understood independently of the normative consequences of their breach. Contrast, for example, the view that duties have a conceptual connection with the corresponding right-holder's standing to hold the wrongdoer accountable.[15] Or take the still more venerable tradition that understands a duty as that which, once breached, exposes the wrongdoer to the legitimate use of coercion.[16] Neither view understands duties independently of the normative consequences of their breach. Rather, a certain normative consequence is built into the concept. It follows that, when we apply these views to tort law, we are a short step away from the truth of TW. Provided only that one thinks, very plausibly, that the imposition of tort liability is a form of accountability, or that it involves a form of coercion, the truth of TW is assured. Of course, these

---

[12] Compare Raz, "Promises and Obligations" (n 11) 210–11.

[13] The more far-reaching point about Raz's account is that "A has a duty to φ" does not entail that "A ought (all things considered) to φ." I return to this at length in section 2.

[14] See for discussion of some related points J Gardner, "Corrective Justice, Corrected" (2012) 12 Diritto e Questioni Pubbliche 9, 34ff.

[15] Compare S Darwall and J Darwall, "Civil Recourse as Mutual Accountability" (2011) 39 Florida State University Law Review 17, 18.

[16] This can be traced, with many subtleties I gloss over here, to Immanuel Kant, *The Metaphysics of Morals* (1797), especially his introduction to the Doctrine of Right.

traditions (which I am greatly simplifying) may nevertheless cast much illumination. But TW, of itself, is studiously unexciting. Its truth is guaranteed as soon as we understand what duties are.

For Gardner, by contrast, the connection between the breach of a duty at t_1 and the justified imposition of liability at t_2 is far from analytic. It has to be earned, through argument. It has to be shown that, of all the kinds of defendant conduct upon which tort liability might, in principle, be grounded, the only eligible conduct is the breach of a duty.

2. Wrongs and Fault

In explaining this connection between wrongdoing and liability, one enduring line of thought goes something like this: tort liability subjects the defendant to a very serious burden in response to something that he or she has done; the infliction of serious negative consequences upon a person can be justified only when that person's conduct was objectionable; and the notion of wrongdoing (or the breach of a duty) serves to capture the sense in which it was indeed objectionable. TW is thus borne of the idea that tort liability is a response to conduct by the defendant that is, or is thought by the law to be, seriously deficient. "What justifies the imposition of tort liability upon a defendant?" "Answer: his bad behavior when he committed the tort." "And what makes his behavior bad?" "Answer: the fact that it was a breach of duty."

But how exactly should we understand the badness of breaching a duty? Some early writers, like John Austin, suggested that wrongdoing entailed culpability.[17] But, when applied to tort law, this suggestion quickly faced criticism—notably from Holmes[18]— and I doubt anyone would defend it now. The counterexamples are notorious.[19] These led Holmes, rather too quickly, to give up on the idea of torts as wrongs altogether. The better response, however, is to drop the "unduly moralistic"[20] association between wrongdoing and culpability and opt for something more ecumenical. A natural way to go is to understand duties as requirements or prohibitions: statements of the form, "Do not do x."[21] For McBride, for example, "[t]o say that someone has a legal duty to do x is a shorthand way of saying that the law tells, or requires, him or her to do x."[22] For Smith, "[t]he straightforward and indeed unavoidable meaning of a statement to the effect that 'everyone has a duty to φ' is simply that everyone ought to φ."[23]

---

[17] J Austin, *Lectures on Jurisprudence, or, The Philosophy of Positive Law* (R Campbell ed, J Murray 1869) Lecture XXIV.

[18] For example, OW Holmes, "Book Notices" (1872) 6 American Law Review 723; OW Holmes, *The Common Law* (Little, Brown 1881) 81–82.

[19] Namely the torts of strict liability, like trespass, and, even within negligence, cases like *Vaughan v Menlove* (1837) 132 ER 490.

[20] Goldberg and Zipursky, *Recognizing Wrongs* (n 5) 206.

[21] ibid 89.

[22] NJ McBride, "Duties of Care—Do They Really Exist?" (2004) 24 Oxford Journal of Legal Studies 417, 417 fn 1.

[23] SA Smith, "Duties to Try and Duties to Succeed" in A Dyson, J Goudkamp, and F Wilmot-Smith (eds), *Defences in Tort* (Hart Publishing 2015) 67–68.

These views are not unusual. Their importance here is that they yield the thought that "A has a duty to φ" entails "A ought (all things considered) to φ." In other words, breaching a duty to φ entails that one had a conclusive reason to φ (and not merely that one had a *pro tanto* reason, or indeed a sufficient one).[24] McBride, at any rate, is explicit on the point. As he puts it in his recent book, the law's imposition of a duty to x

> is meant to do more than just give me a reason to do x, in the sense of counting in favour of doing x—it is meant to provide me with a conclusive reason to do x: it is meant to decide the issue for me of whether or not I will do x.[25]

In general moral philosophy, the understanding of duties as "absolute" is usually associated with Kant.[26] But it seems to have a different source of attraction to modern-day legal theorists, who believe it is a function of law, including tort law, to guide its subjects, and that in order to serve this function its primary duties must settle what those subjects ought to do.[27] Either way, the upshot is clear. One cannot, on this view, breach a (legal) duty while behaving as one ought (in the law's view) to behave. To breach a duty is, necessarily, to behave unreasonably. It is also (therefore) to behave without justification.[28] True, breaching a duty does not entail that one lacked an excuse.[29] Hence wrongdoing can be blameless—which suffices to distance this model from the outmoded Austinian one. But the important point, to repeat, is that wrongdoing entails doing what one ought not to. We can call this view, then, the "ought-inclusive" account of duties.

With the ought-inclusive account of duties plugged in, TW copes well with the tort of negligence. For it is built into that tort's headline element that liability will not be imposed unless the defendant behaved unreasonably. And it seems plausible that the intentional torts, or most of them, can be reconciled with the same thought. For isn't it obvious that defaming, assaulting, and so on are things one ought not to do? But, as is also well known, cases like *Rylands v Fletcher*[30] and *Vincent v Lake Erie Transportation Co*[31] become troubling. In *Rylands*, liability was imposed, famously, on a defendant whose reservoir had burst and flooded his neighbor's property, and without regard to whether his conduct was unreasonable. In *Vincent*, liability was imposed even though the court was adamant the defendant's conduct was *not* unreasonable. The defendant ship's captain moored without consent to the plaintiff's dock, and, having done so, caused damage to it, but his conduct was reasonable, being necessary to keep the ship

[24] See Raz, *Practical Reason and Norms* (n 11) 27ff.

[25] NJ McBride, *The Humanity of Private Law: Part I: Explanation* (Hart Publishing 2019) 36.

[26] See eg L Alexander and M Moore, "Deontological Ethics" in EN Zalta (ed), *The Stanford Encyclopedia of Philosophy* (Stanford University Press 2021). In Raz's terms, it may be wise to distinguish "conclusive" from "absolute," but nothing turns on the point here.

[27] This is how I understand views such as P Jaffey, "Duties and Liabilities in Private Law" (2006) 12 Legal Theory 137, 138–39. McBride's and Smith's views seem to be based on similar thoughts: compare McBride, *The Humanity of Private Law* (n 25) 37–39; SA Smith, *Rights, Wrongs, and Injustices: The Structure of Remedial Law* (OUP 2019) 199, 259.

[28] Acting with a justification is a more complex notion than acting reasonably. But acting with a justification entails acting reasonably, which suffices for the point.

[29] Compare JCP Goldberg, "Inexcusable Wrongs" (2015) 103 California Law Review 467.

[30] *Rylands v Fletcher* (1868) LR 3 HL 330.

[31] *Vincent v Lake Erie Transportation Co* 124 NW 221 (Minn 1910).

24   LEO BOONZAIER

safe from an impending storm. Hence these cases are powerful counterexamples to TW—or so they seem. Many strategies have been employed to discount them; perhaps the best-known is Weinrib's attempt to re-explain *Vincent* on the basis of unjust enrichment.[32] Fortunately, there is no need to rehearse the debate about whether these strategies succeed. The pertinent point here is only that they are thought to be needed. Because the orthodox view accepts the truth of TW, and because it takes wrongdoing to entail unreasonable conduct, it is imperative that cases like *Rylands* and *Vincent*, in which liability is not conditional upon unreasonable conduct, are marginalized in some way.[33] They are not consistent with TW, and so they create a problem that needs solving.

Gardner, by contrast, did not think these cases create any problem at all. He thought the attempts to reinterpret *Vincent* as an enrichment case are not so much wrong as "unnecessary."[34] For in truth, he said, *Vincent* can be read "unproblematically" as a case of tortious wrongdoing.[35] He thought that it and *Rylands* are "not counterexamples [to TW] at all."[36] Why not? The reason is not far to seek. It lies in Gardner's analysis of duties. For the ought-inclusive view of duties was one he did not share. Much of his work in criminal law theory had been aimed at resisting it.[37] He sought to show that wrongdoing can be justified, and (therefore) reasonable. It may even be praiseworthy. But, for all that, it is still wrongdoing.

How can that be? Gardner's analysis is famously complex.[38] But its bare bones will suffice. The central point is that on Raz's schema the exclusionary force of a duty need not be total. The duty need not, in other words, exclude *all* the countervailing reasons. It may exclude only some of them. True, when the duty *does* exclude all countervailing reasons, its breach can never be justified—which means Raz's schema can accommodate absolute duties, in so far as they exist. But whether the duty does indeed exclude all of them, or, if not, which reasons the duty excludes, depend on the case for having it—in other words, on the duty's "rationale." Duties thus contain, on Gardner's approach, an air of paradox. They work by excluding first-order reasons: that accounts for their special trumping power, their capacity to defeat first-order reasons outright, "in advance."[39] And yet at the same time duties are subordinate to reasons, for they exist only in so far as there is reason for having them.

Be that as it may, the key point is that the reasons that are not excluded by the duty continue to exert their usual force in determining what the duty-bearer ought to do. And it may be that the force of those unexcluded countervailing reasons is sufficient

---

[32] Weinrib, *The Idea of Private Law* (n 3) 196ff.

[33] McBride's and Smith's recent books are admirably clear about this: McBride, *The Humanity of Private Law* (n 27) 60–61, 68–69; Smith, *Rights, Wrongs, and Injustices* (n 27) 259–61, 268. And see, for eg, Weinrib, *The Idea of Private Law* (n 3) 197; Jaffey, "Duties and Liabilities" (n 27) 139–43.

[34] J Gardner, "Wrongs and Faults" in A Simester (ed), *Appraising Strict Liability* (OUP 2005) 56.

[35] ibid.

[36] Gardner, "Torts and Other Wrongs" (n 2) 46 fn 9. Indeed *Rylands* reveals, he says, tort law's "moral essence": J Gardner, "Obligations and Outcomes in the Law of Torts" in J Gardner and P Cane (eds), *Relating to Responsibility: Essays in Honour of Tony Honoré on his 80th Birthday* (Hart Publishing 2001) 125.

[37] See especially chs 4, 5, and 7 of his *Offences and Defences* (OUP 2007).

[38] J Gardner, "Justifications and Reasons" in AP Simester and ATH Smith (eds), *Harm and Culpability* (OUP 1996), republished as *Offences and Defences* (n 37) ch 5.

[39] *Offences and Defences* (n 37) 105.

to defeat the reasons to conform to the duty (which include, prominently, the first-order reason given by the duty itself). Or, at any rate, the force of those countervailing reasons may be sufficient to ensure that they are not themselves defeated. In the second case, the duty-bearer may permissibly breach the duty. In the first, more dramatic, case, the duty-bearer *ought* to breach it. *Vincent* was a case of this kind. True, the defendant had a duty not to trespass on the defendant's dock. Perhaps that duty was at one stage absolute.[40] But, as *Vincent* shows, it did not remain so. The court decided that the exclusionary force of the duty did not extend to the reasons upon which the defendant acted in that case. It thus granted to the defendant what Gardner, following Raz, calls a "cancelling permission."[41] The court, by the exercise of a normative power, canceled the (thitherto absolute) exclusionary force of the duty in the circumstances of *Vincent*. And hence the countervailing reasons—the reasons that stood *in favor* of the defendant's mooring to the dock—are allowed back into the equation. And these were, in the exigent circumstances of *Vincent*, compelling: with the storm approaching, trespassing on the dock was the only means available to save the ship. That is why the court was adamant that the defendant acted rightly. And yet it does not follow that he had no duty to act otherwise. *Au contraire*. Only because he had a duty were the exigencies of the storm necessary to overcome it.

The Razian analysis of duties has well-known attractions in general moral philosophy. For tort lawyers, it allows cases like *Vincent* to be explained perhaps more satisfyingly than on the orthodox view. Both the defendant's duty not to trespass and his compelling reasons to do so can be given their due, and the conflict between them resolved into its elements. And one can imagine the ship's captain, wavering at the dockside, afflicted by Raz's "peculiar feeling of unease" in the face of "two incompatible assessments of what ought to be done":[42] his action is both reasonable (since compelled by the need to save the ship) and wrongful (since contrary to the mandatory reason borne of the plaintiff's right to exclude). For Gardner, then, *Vincent* "isolates a general proposition of central importance to the common law: the mere fact that one was justified (=not wrong) in acting wrongfully does not mean that one did not act wrongfully."[43]

So much for *Vincent*. What about *Rylands*? Here there is a vital step still missing. It must be the case that one can have a duty to secure a result, and not (only) a duty to try to secure it. In other words, it must be possible to have a duty to make it the case that *p*, and not (only) a duty to take certain steps with a view to ensuring that *p*. Otherwise, cases like *Rylands* would not be reconcilable with TW. Any (supposed) duty not to flood the plaintiff's property would inevitably fall to be reinterpreted as a duty *to take reasonable steps* not to flood the plaintiff's property. This interpretation would accord with a certain Kantian thought that a person who has done all that he could to conform to his duty must, *eo ipso*, have conformed to it. And it would accord, also, with the thought that the law is in the business of providing guidance, and that any guidance that strict duties are alleged to provide would be either misleading or

---

[40] ibid 106 (though here he had in mind the criminal law).
[41] J Raz, *The Authority of Law* (OUP 1979) 18; Gardner, *Offences and Defences* (n 37) 106.
[42] Raz, *Practical Reason and Norms* (n 11) 41.
[43] "Wrongs and Faults" (n 34) 56.

unattainable. But it would mean that the liability in *Rylands*—since it was *not* conditioned upon any failure by the defendant to take reasonable steps—cannot be based upon the breach of a duty.

These objections to strict liability, or rather to the strict duties upon which liability is purportedly based, persist among theorists of private law.[44] Gardner spent much time rebutting their arguments.[45] In fact he turned the tables. Not only are "duties to succeed," as he called them,[46] fully rationally intelligible, they are the basic case. And wrongdoing without fault, far from being exceptional, "is the ordinary or basic kind of wrongdoing."[47] This is because reasons to succeed enjoy logical priority over reasons to try. The intelligibility of reasons to try to φ depends, in other words, on the intelligibility of reasons to φ. The case for trying not to flood my neighbor's property, for example, is that doing so will (usually) contribute to my succeeding in not flooding it; unless there can be a reason for the latter, there can be no reason for the former.[48] To be sure, that does not quite show there are *duties* to succeed. But there is no good case to doubt that reasons to succeed may be mandatory and categorical, Gardner argued,[49] and indeed a good case to be made that some of them are.[50]

All this is part of a wider story about the way in which Gardner sought to separate the incurrence of adverse normative consequences (including legal liabilities) from fault and other kinds of rational failure on the part of those who incur them. He sought to rehabilitate what he called "the Aristotelian story" against the rival, and now more orthodox, Kantian one.[51] The Razian account of duties that I have been sketching was one important part of that story:[52] a wrongdoer may have done all he could not to commit the wrong, and may have been amply justified in committing it, but for all that he is still a wrongdoer. Hence *Vincent* is not a counterexample to TW merely because

---

[44] For example, SA Smith, "Strict Duties and the Rule of Law" in LM Austin and D Klimchuk (eds), *Private Law and the Rule of Law* (OUP 2014); Smith, "Duties to Try and Duties to Succeed" (n 23). See further n 27 above.

[45] "The Purity and Priority of Private Law" (1996) 46 University of Toronto Law Journal 459, 483–93; "Obligations and Outcomes" (n 36); "The Wrongdoing That Gets Results" (n 11); "Reasons and Abilities: Some Preliminaries" (2013) 58 American Journal of Jurisprudence 63; "Some Rule-of-Law Anxieties about Strict Liability in Private Law" in LM Austin and D Klimchuk (eds), *Private Law and the Rule of Law* (OUP 2014). Gardner's disagreement with Smith spilled over into the question whether there is a (legal) duty to pay damages (in advance of the court's ordering one to do so). Gardner's response was published, shortly before his death, as "Damages without Duty" (2019) 69 University of Toronto Law Journal 412.

[46] "The Purity and Priority of Private Law" (n 45) 486; "Obligations and Outcomes" (n 36) 117–18. See for discussion Ori Herstein, Chapter 4 in this volume.

[47] *Offences and Defences* (n 37) 150.

[48] It does not follow that one has a reason to try to φ only when trying to φ will contribute to one's φ-ing. Gardner explains why not in "Obligations and Outcomes" (n 36) 138.

[49] ibid 134–35.

[50] Gardner's most celebrated example was the clifftop hiker's duty to rescue the drowning stranger in the sea below. But the specific example drew perhaps more attention than he would have liked: compare "As Inconclusive as Ever" (n 8) 215–17. The clearer cases are (some) promissory duties, and perhaps (some) duties within special relationships.

[51] "The Purity and Priority of Private Law" (n 45) 493; "The Mark of Responsibility" (2003) 23 Oxford Journal of Legal Studies 157, 158–59. See too "Wrongs and Faults" (n 34); *Offences and Defences* (n 37) 81–82.

[52] Its equally important counterpart is Gardner's spare account of "basic responsibility": see "The Mark of Responsibility" (n 51); "The Negligence Standard: Political Not Metaphysical" (2017) 80 Modern Law Review 1; *From Personal Life to Private Law* (OUP 2018) 75, ("*FPLPL*").

the defendant behaved reasonably. Still less is *Rylands* a counterexample merely because the defendant was not found to have behaved *unreasonably*.

In that respect, then, Gardner's account might seem congenial to TW. Yet in another, more important respect, it makes his endorsement of the claim surprising—which is really the key point I wished to make in this section. To motivate TW, it is not enough to deal with examples that purport to show the claim is false. One must provide some positive reason for believing the claim is true. And the point of this section has been to show that one familiar reason for believing the claim is true—the reason that is implicit in the folk understanding of tort law with which I began this section—does not carry over to Gardner's account at all. That is because the folk understanding has whatever appeal it does *because* it ties wrongdoing to objectionable conduct. The positive reason that it provides for believing in TW's truth lies in the fact that wrongdoers are guilty (in the law's eyes, at any rate) of a significant rational failure. They have done what they should not have done: hence they may be justly held liable for it. But Gardner's account, by contrast, distances itself from precisely that source of appeal. Not only does he reject the connection between wrongdoing and culpability (as had almost every tort theorist since Holmes), he rejects the connection between wrongdoing and doing that which one should not. Indeed for Gardner it is possible to have "wrongful actions that were performed without the slightest rational error."[53] It may even be praiseworthy to breach one's duty, as it was for the defendant in *Vincent*.

True, such cases are likely to be rare. Even on Gardner's view, wrongful conduct will usually be unreasonable. The special (and perhaps sometimes absolute) force of the duty ensures as much. But it is also integral to Gardner's account that, in those cases where the breach of a duty does *not* entail rational failure, the usual argument in favor of imposing tort liability still goes through. That is why *Vincent* and *Rylands* are, in his view, unproblematic cases of tort liability. So the striking thing about Gardner's view is that, *even absent* the premise that the defendant's conduct was objectionable, the (defeasibly) sufficient conditions for the imposition of tort liability remain. But if the sufficient conditions for liability do not include that premise, then the case for the wrongs-based picture cannot have anything to do with the fact that the presence of wrongdoing makes the premise true.

This marks a significant fork in the road. Whereas many other moralists have tried to hang on to the basic model underlying the folk understanding (albeit while making suitable refinements), Gardner's account gives up on it altogether. And that is one reason why I share Liam Murphy's sense that, although Gardner sometimes proclaimed his agreement with other defenders of TW, he did so "rather breezily."[54] He did not share the deeper commitments on which their endorsement of TW rests. Indeed he had sought to refute them. My point is that, having done so, he needs to seek his reason for believing in the truth of TW elsewhere. The next two sections discuss where he found it.

---

[53] *Offences and Defences* (n 37) 81.
[54] L Murphy, "Purely Formal Wrongs" in PB Miller and J Oberdiek (eds), *Civil Wrongs and Justice in Private Law* (OUP 2020) 22.

3. Reasons Continuity

Gardner developed his own account of how tort liability is justified. The central pillar of it is his justly famous "continuity thesis," to which he gave most detailed expression in 2011's "What Is Tort Law For? Part 1."[55] According to it, the reason (call it "r") in virtue of which the defendant in a tort case has a duty to compensate the plaintiff at t_2 is the same reason that grounded the defendant's duty not to commit the tort at t_1. He ought to compensate the plaintiff at t_2 simply because that constitutes conformity to the same reason that existed, and to which he failed to conform, at t_1. The continuity thesis thus locates the incurrence of a duty to compensate when one commits a tort in general truths about reasons: a reason calls for conformity; it continues to do so after one has failed to conform to it initially, and that is true even if one failed to conform to it in order to conform to other reasons.[56] And hence the explanation for tort liability partakes of the same explanation as other aspects, including humdrum aspects, of rational life. It is, at base, the same as the explanation of why, if I miss the 12:00 train, I should catch the one at 12:30; and of why, if I breach a promise to φ on Monday, I should φ on Tuesday (or, failing that, on Wednesday), and so on.

The challenge is, of course, to show that, even when the first action is "committing the tort" and the second action is the strikingly dissimilar one of "paying damages to the plaintiff," this really can be explained continuously with these other cases. Gardner's attempts to do that faced much resistance.[57] But I do not intend to repeat the debate here. Suffice to say that the continuity thesis provides the crucial underpinning to Gardner's views that I sketched in section 2. It explains how it might be that, even when the defendant's harm-causing conduct was reasonable at t_1, he ought to be liable for it at t_2. He ought to be liable for it because he can conform to r now by paying compensation. Whether r was a conclusive reason not to commit the tort at t_1, with the implication that he ought not to have committed the tort all things considered, is irrelevant. It matters only that r was a reason to which he failed to conform, and to which he ought to conform now. There is no need to appeal to the thought that the defendant behaved culpably, unjustifiably, or contrary to what he ought to have done.

But all this raises an obvious question. The continuity thesis is spare, but can it not be made even sparer? Though Gardner stated it in terms of duties (or obligations)— the breach of a *duty* at t_1, he always said, gives rise to the duty to compensate at t_2—it is not immediately obvious what work the primary duty is doing. After all, it is not as though the duty itself continues. Indeed Gardner was adamant that it doesn't.[58] Duties, he points out, are individuated by the action they require.[59] And plainly there are two

---

[55] "What Is Tort Law For? Part 1" (n 11).

[56] Compare J Raz, "Personal Practical Conflicts" in P Baumann and M Betzler (eds), *Practical Conflicts: New Philosophical Essays* (CUP 2004) 189–90.

[57] For example, McBride, *The Humanity of Private Law* (n 27) 29–30, fn 134; Smith, *Rights, Wrongs, and Injustices* (n 27) 184–87; Goldberg and Zipursky (n 5) 157–58.

[58] "What Is Tort Law For? Part 1" (n 11) 29–30; see also "The Negligence Standard" (n 52) 4. This marks a change from his earlier view, which was that the duty of repair "is the same primary duty that one violated when one breached the contract or committed the tort": "Wrongs and Faults" (n 34) 59. This accords with Weinrib's view (see eg Weinrib (n 3) 135) which Gardner later rejected.

[59] But cf S Steel, "Compensation and Continuity" (2020) 26 Legal Theory 250, 263.

distinct actions, and therefore two distinct duties, at t_1 and t_2. What continues, then, is not the primary duty, but the reasons that grounded it. For "[r]easons are individuated differently from obligations. Every reason for action is potentially a reason for multiple actions."[60] So it is the reason, not the duty, that continues from t_1 to t_2, becoming a reason for a new and different action. And it is this continuity of reasons—which is entailed, as I said, by reasons' basic nature—that explains why the defendant ought to compensate.

All this raises the following simple-minded question: if one has a reason to compensate at t_2 just in virtue of the failure to conform to that reason at the earlier time, then why might not mere non-conformity to a reason be sufficient to support the imposition of liability? Given that continuity is a property of reasons, and not of duties, can we not restate our explanation of tort liability thus:

> The defendant in a tort case has a reason, r, to compensate the plaintiff at t_2 just in virtue of the fact that the defendant failed to conform to r when he committed the tort at t_1.

It seems clear that Gardner would agree this proposition is true.[61] And, that being so, his own continuity thesis deepens the puzzle, at least initially, about why he subscribed to TW. Having resolved the duty into its more basic elements—reasons—the question arises why we need to insist on the superstructure.

4. The Argument

The answer begins with a truism. To justify the imposition of liability, it is not sufficient that the defendant has a (*pro tanto*) reason to compensate. The reason must be conclusive. It must be the case that the defendant ought, all things considered, to compensate, not only that he had a *pro tanto* reason to do it.[62] But the reason, r, that the continuity thesis picks out is not necessarily conclusive. As Gardner puts it, the continuing reason "only counts for as much as it counts for."[63] What the continuity thesis establishes is only "that, still being available for conformity, [that reason] counts for something."[64] Being a *pro tanto* reason, it justifies one in repairing one's initial nonconformity only if, in light of all the other reasons that apply to one at t_2, one ought to perform the act for which it is a reason. Plainly it will not always do so, for, "[n]aturally, other reasons may countervail."[65] That is simply what it means to be a *pro tanto* reason, which must compete in the struggle with the countless other reasons that feature in determining what ought to be done.

---

[60] "What Is Tort Law For? Part 1" (n 11) 31.
[61] This is clear, *inter alia*, from the quotation provided at n 66.
[62] No doubt there are other conditions for liability to be justified. In the text I focus on the pertinent one.
[63] "What Is Tort Law For? Part 1" (n 11) 32–33.
[64] ibid 33. See also Raz, "Personal Practical Conflicts" (n 56) 191.
[65] "What Is Tort Law For? Part 1" (n 11) 32. Hence "a reparative step that is called for by the continuity thesis is not necessarily called for, all things considered": *FPLPL* (n 52) 104.

30   LEO BOONZAIER

Hence the continuity thesis itself leaves much to be said about what kinds of reasons will be conclusive, and when. And it is here that Gardner's argument for the truth of TW is located. He did not develop this argument in "What Is Tort Law For? Part 1." We find it in his proto-statements of the continuity thesis some years earlier. As he put it in "Wrongs and Faults," for example, in 2005:

> When we do not fully conform to a non-categorical and/or non-mandatory reason, the reason that remains to haunt us still is non-categorical and/or non-mandatory. Such a reason is therefore permanently vulnerable to the abandonment of old goals and/or to defeat by the new reasons that militate powerfully in favour of getting on with our lives. When things are not so easy is when we are left with old unconformed-to reasons that are both categorical and mandatory, i.e. when we had duties that we failed to perform, and hence acted wrongfully. In such cases the reason left over and still awaiting conformity does not surrender to a change in our personal goals. And it continues to exert mandatory force such that at least some conflicting reasons (some of the otherwise powerful reasons that we have to get on with our lives) are excluded from consideration and cannot suffice to defeat it.[66]

The argument is not difficult to understand. It invites us to imagine a case in which r is non-mandatory. It is true, Gardner grants, that non-conformity to that reason at t_1 will mean it continues to call for conformity at t_2. That is a truth about all reasons. But it would not follow that the reason is conclusive. In fact—and this is the key move—it will necessarily *not* be conclusive because it is bound to be defeated by the powerful reasons that militate against conforming to it. Its rational hold will be feeble and insignificant against the countervailing reasons that exist for "getting on with our lives" rather than "crying over spilt milk."[67] So any reason of this kind cannot be a sufficient basis for a duty to compensate. It can provide a sufficient basis only if, instead, it is categorical and mandatory, for in that case the countervailing reasons may be defeated by exclusion. Absent that trumping force, however, r is bound to be defeated. Unless r is mandatory and categorical—unless there is a duty—it will inevitably fail to be conclusive at t_2.

The only remaining step is to connect this to the justified imposition of tort liability, which is not hard to do. In Gardner's view, the justification for holding a defendant (legally) liable to compensate the plaintiff is that (morally) he ought to do so.[68] And since, by the argument just given, the defendant ought (morally) to do so only when r was mandatory and categorical, it follows that tort liability can be justified only for the breach of a duty. Hence we have a proof of TW.

---

[66] "Wrongs and Faults" (n 34) 58–59. This is a compressed form of what he had written a year earlier with T Macklem in "Reasons" in JL Coleman and others (eds), *The Oxford Handbook of Jurisprudence and Philosophy of Law* (OUP 2004) 467–68. The argument appears, substantially unchanged, in *FPLPL* (n 52) 126.

[67] "Reasons" (n 66) 467–68.

[68] Compare "Wrongs and Faults" (n 34) 59.

5. The Assessment

But does the move from a *pro tanto* reason to a conclusive one really need duties, in the way that Gardner says? It would be excellent if it did. For if it did, it would mean that Gardner had offered an analysis of, and an argument for, the connection that others have perceived between wrongdoing and compensation. Some writers, as I mentioned in section 1, have tended to treat that connection as something close to analytic. Others, though convinced of the connection, have frankly admitted they cannot explain it.[69] Gardner improves upon both. Duties are understood by their features at t_1. Via the continuity thesis, however, and thence by the argument I set out in the previous section, he ties these mandatory and categorical features of duties to the special claim to repair that wrongdoing has at t_2. Thus he unites the two commonly perceived faces of duties: the special force they have in the first place, and the "residue"[70] or "remainder"[71] they leave behind upon breach. That, at any rate, is what his argument promises to do. But I am not sure it succeeds.

5.1 Reasons, outweighing, and excluding

The first worry is that the argument, even at best, does not establish quite what it needs to. Recall that TW, as both Gardner and I stated it, claims there is a necessary connection between tort liability and wrongdoing. And we now see that, in the argument set out in section 4, this depends on a necessary connection between r's having mandatory force and its being a secure basis for the imposition of legal liability. But all that Gardner's argument seems to establish is a *probabilistic* connection. It is hard to deny, in other words, that when r is mandatory, and thus protected by exclusionary force, r is much more likely to be a conclusive reason to compensate. By definition, the exclusionary force defeats (some of) the reasons that countervail. That cannot but make r more likely to be an undefeated reason than it would otherwise have been. But is it *essential* that r has that protection? Will it *necessarily* be defeated in the absence of exclusionary force?

It is hard to see why one should think so. After all, being excluded by a reason of a higher order is just one way in which a reason can be defeated. Another is, of course, to be outweighed by reasons of the same order. Obversely stated: where r is a very weighty reason, it is hard to see why it might not be capable of prevailing in the battle of reasons that Gardner describes. So his line of thought does not establish that the exclusionary force of the reasons against committing the tort is essential in order to ground the liability to compensate. That is indeed one way of creating a conclusive reason to compensate, and hence of justifying liability. But the same line of thought suggests it is not the only way: reasons against committing the tort that do not have exclusionary force, but do have very great weight, also tend to be conclusive. Hence

---

[69] JJ Thomson, "Rights and Compensation" (1980) 14 Noûs 3, 14.
[70] JJ Thomson, *The Realm of Rights* (Harvard University Press 1990) 85.
[71] "What Is Tort Law For? Part 1" (n 11) 34–35.

they, too, may plausibly justify a liability to compensate in the event that they are not conformed to. Gardner's argument succeeds in establishing a contingent connection, then, between r's being mandatory and its capacity to justify liability. But we were looking for a necessary one.

To be sure, the contingent connection is strengthened when we remind ourselves that the law regulates generally, across a range of cases, and with limited flexibility in response to changing circumstances. For the imposition of tort liability to be justified, it needs to be justified for *all* defendants who perform the act-types picked out by that precedent, not only one or other of them, and the liability will remain in place regardless of the defendant's changing circumstances (including, pertinently here, a change in the defendant's goals). That last point virtually guarantees that r must be categorical to justify the imposition of liability. The more difficult question is whether the same is true of mandatoriness. It seems fair to suppose, again, that a reason with mandatory force stands up better against a wide set of diverse countervailing considerations. It rules out those considerations and does not have to compete with them in weight. But even a strongly contingent connection is not a necessary one.

In a way, then, Gardner's argument for TW has returned us to the general debate about whether practical reasoning can be adequately explained in terms of the balancing or weighing-up of reasons of the same order, or whether (and to what extent) the trumping force of duties occupies an important space. One could, in principle, deny that the trumping force of duties is necessary to explain how r might be a (stably and generally) conclusive reason for repair at t_2, and yet accept all other aspects of Gardner's account.[72] One could go almost all the way with him, in other words accepting the logic of the continuity thesis, and that it provides the justification for the imposition of tort liability, but get off the bus just before the final stop. One could part ways with him only when the time comes to ask whether r might be a secure basis for tort liability just in virtue of its great weight.

And there are some respects, I think, in which Gardner's argument sidelines that possibility too quickly. It contrives a seemingly necessary role for mandatoriness illegitimately. Gardner invites us to imagine that there is a systematic first-order case *against* conforming to r at t_2, and hence, the thought continues, r must have mandatory force if it is to have any hope of prevailing. For how else can a reason be (stably and generally) conclusive, in the face of powerful reasons that militate against it, unless the latter are knocked out by exclusion? The supposed first-order case against conforming to r, on which this line of thought rests, consists of the reasons that one has "for getting on with one's life," rather than "crying over spilt milk."[73] And Gardner shores it up with the reasons we have not to become consumed by regret for all the reasons we have failed to conform to.[74] "Clearly a person should move on with their

---

[72] Compare Stephen Smith's argument that utilitarians can, in principle, accept the continuity thesis as the explanation of tort liability: "Duties, Liabilities, and Damages" (2012) 125 Harvard Law Review 1727, 1736–38.

[73] Gardner and Macklem (n 66) 467.

[74] See especially the way Gardner introduces the argument in "Wrongs and Faults" (n 34) 58–59. Perhaps the most obvious line of attack here is to deny that each and every failure to conform to even a *pro tanto* reason is cause for regret. I do not pursue that point. But see for related discussion Sinel, Chapter 12, this volume.

life," Gardner invites us to think, "rather than dwelling upon past failures to conform to each and every reason. Hence there can be a conclusive case for repairing one's past non-conformity—one should dwell upon them—only if those countervailing reasons are excluded." But aren't these countervailing reasons being over-inflated? Whereas Gardner suggests there is a powerful, across-the-board case to move on from our feelings of regret, and not to attend to our past failings, the better reading of these ideas is surely more attenuated. True, in other words, we may have reason to forget about *unproductive* feelings of regret, regret for things we can do nothing to amend. Equally, there will always be a strong case against *futile* attempts to make amends, against taking steps that do not in fact contribute to one's amending. But these more moderate proposals no longer support Gardner's argument. For their obverse is that, when taking reparative steps *is* productive—when we *can* still do something to conform to r—then the countervailing reasons do not apply. The case for conforming to r is unaffected, and no longer subject to the inevitable defeat that Gardner supposed.[75] But that is often the situation in which we find ourselves. The animating thought behind the continuity thesis, after all, is that often we *can* conform to r at t_2 (albeit imperfectly), even after we failed to conform to it at t_1. Differently put, Gardner contrasts "moving on with one's life" with repairing one's mistakes. But why can't one move on with one's life *by* repairing one's past mistakes? The lesson of the continuity thesis is precisely that one can.

To be sure, there are also certain features of Gardner's wider philosophical commitments that led him to ascribe a central role to the mandatory force of duties. All of them relate to what McBride aptly calls "the multiplicity of reasons" to which Gardner believed we are subject.[76]

(1) First, Gardner took an almost uniquely expansive view of what reasons apply to us, relative to our ability to conform to them. In his view, "A has a reason to φ only if at least one conceivable human being has the capacity to φ and A is a human being."[77] He rejects a range of other possible views, including, for example, the view that A has a reason to φ only if A *himself* had the capacity to φ.[78] Thus even a wheelchair-bound person, he says, "could have reasons to run a four-minute mile or to climb Mount Everest."[79] And on Gardner's view, I take it, I have reason to rescue a person who is drowning in a lake in Outer Mongolia, even if I do not know it is happening and would have no hope of preventing it if I did.[80]

---

[75] None of that is to deny that there usually are countervailing reasons against conforming to r. Doing so is burdensome, expensive, and so on. But those reasons stand or fall within the ordinary first-order calculus. What Gardner needs is a *general and systematic* first-order case against conforming to r, for only then is there a general and systematic role for duties.

[76] NJ McBride, "Book Review" (2019) 78 Cambridge Law Journal 217, 217.

[77] "Reasons and Abilities" (n 45) 72.

[78] A more plausible view might limit the kinds of capacities that count here; A's lack of *some* capacities (such as his being so evil that he could never bring himself to φ) would not plausibly preclude A's having a reason to φ. But Gardner rejects any view of this kind.

[79] "Reasons and Abilities" (n 45) 72–73.

[80] Compare "Obligations and Outcomes" (n 36) 137.

(2) Second, Gardner's view was that "all reasons, by their nature, are impersonal in respect of attention."[81] He did not think there are any reasons that apply to P and yet are "none of Q's business"[82]—that do not, in other words, call for conformity by Q. To the contrary, "any reason for P to φ is equally a reason for any action by anyone, familiar or stranger, that contributes to P's φing."[83] "So while I am sitting here typing," as McBride explains it, "I also have reason to help you and everyone else in the world to do whatever it is that you and they have reason to do."[84] True, those reasons may turn out to be "none of Q's business" in the relatively superficial sense that he (unlike P) ought not to (try to) conform to them, all things considered. But they are still reasons for Q. It is only that they are defeated by other considerations.[85]

(3) Third, when are we (basically) responsible for failing to conform to a reason? Again, Gardner has a very wide view: one is responsible provided only that one had "the ability and the propensity to have and to give self-explanations in the currency of reasons."[86] He rejects other prominent views that limit responsibility to, say, intentional actions and those one is ordinarily able to perform successfully.[87]

These claims, taken together, yield a very wide set of reasons that apply to persons. That includes a very wide set of reasons that may be reasons for reparative actions at t_2. And that leaves Gardner in a precarious position among theorists of tort law. That is because he needs to reconcile his account with our intuitions and moral practices, which consider reparative actions, and the imposition of liability to perform them, to be justified relatively rarely. Or perhaps one should say Gardner *would* be in a precarious position, but for the intervention of duties. Wrongdoing provides the kind of "in principle" limitation on the justified imposition of liability that his account needs. Other theorists would screen out many more reasons at the outset, as it were, in the move from value to reasons, and from reasons to responsibility. For Gardner, however, they all apply at t_1, and indeed continue to t_2, provided only that they were not fully conformed to. What causes them to fall away, at the final hurdle, is the fact they are not supported by a duty. And so, whereas I made the preliminary suggestion in section 3 that Gardner's continuity thesis-cantered account does not really need duties, the truth is, in a sense, the opposite: Gardner needs duties perhaps more than anyone else, in order to reign in his very wide views about reasons.

Merely making these observations does not show that wrongdoing *is* an "in principle" limitation on liability, of course. It only shows that it would be nice for Gardner's

---

[81] *FPLPL* (n 52) 108. See also *Offences and Defences* (n 37) 62–65; "Corrective Justice, Corrected" (n 14) 22–23, fn 18; T Macklem and J Gardner, "Human Disability" (2014) 25 King's Law Journal 60, 76–78.

[82] Compare "The Negligence Standard" (n 52) 11.

[83] *FPLPL* (n 52) 109.

[84] McBride, "Book Review" (n 76) 217.

[85] Gardner notes a few such considerations in *FPLPL* (n 52) 109–10.

[86] See n 52 above.

[87] This is a rough sketch of Raz's view, which Gardner rejects as "untenabl[e]": see J Raz, "Responsibility and the Negligence Standard" (2010) 30 Oxford Journal of Legal Studies 1; Gardner, "The Negligence Standard" (n 52) 13.

account if it were. But one can get closer to an argument for a necessary role for wrong-doing by adding a fourth feature of his wider philosophy:

(4) Gardner believes in the incommensurability of reasons, and indeed that in-commensurability is "pervasive."[88] Hence, supposing that r calls for conformity through some action, φ, and even supposing further that r is undefeated, it still does not follow that φ ought, on balance, to be performed. For it may be the case that there is *also* an undefeated reason in favour of not-φ-ing. That is just what it means for r to be incommensurable with the reasons that countervail. There is a rational case for both φ-ing and not-φ-ing, since there are reasons in favour of both, and, these reasons being incommensurable, neither outweighs the other. As Gardner says, "very often there is no defeat. There are undefeated reasons on both sides and one is left with a choice of justifiable actions."[89] Hence "the principle of rationality ... does not adjudicate as between the two alternatives."[90]

This greatly aggravates the difficulties entailed by (1) to (3). It is not as though we can simply tot up the many pros and cons of φ-ing, in light of the mass of first-order reasons that we are left with, and hence extract from them a conclusive case for φ-ing. Often that is simply not possible.

The net effect is to leave us in a serious rational predicament. We are in danger of being so overwhelmed by the multiplicity of reasons that we cannot hope to extract from them conclusive reasons for action, unless by some further means we are able to limit the set that has rational salience. Before reasonable engagement is even possible, there is a need "to bring order to the chaos of value that we confront."[91] And what does that? What makes it possible even to engage with this multiplicity of reasons, and on occasion to extract from it a conclusive case for φ-ing? The answer, above all, is second-order reasons. We need them if we are to have a hope of navigating the turbulent sea of reasons on which we are adrift. And this does much to explain why Gardner was drawn to write about goals,[92] schemes,[93] roles,[94] relationships,[95] responsibilities,[96] rules and norms,[97] promises and undertakings,[98] and of course duties. The second-order reasons that they create are vital in settling rational conflict at the first-order level.

These views about the nature of rationality in general apply, of course, to tort law in particular, and more pertinently still to the tort defendant in respect of whom the

---

[88] Gardner and Macklem (n 66) 470–74.

[89] J Gardner, "Why Blame?" in I Solanke (ed), *On Crime, Society, and Responsibility in the Work of Nicola Lacey* (OUP 2021) 84.

[90] Gardner and Macklem (n 66) 471.

[91] *FPLPL* (n 52) 12.

[92] Gardner and Macklem (n 66) 458–60; *FPLPL* (n 52) 172–74.

[93] Macklem and Gardner (n 81) 75–76.

[94] J Gardner, "Criminals in Uniform" in RA Duff and others (eds), *The Constitution of the Criminal Law* (OUP 2013).

[95] *FPLPL* (n 52) ch 1.

[96] "The Negligence Standard" (n 52).

[97] *Offences and Defences* (n 37) 105–6, 146–52.

[98] J Gardner, *Law as a Leap of Faith: Essays on Law in General* (OUP 2012) 189–90.

imposition of tort liability is to be justified. And here we should not forget that *other* persons may also have reasons to repair the harm in question. This might be because they, too, failed to conform to a reason when the harm was caused, and so have a continuity thesis-derived reason to repair it. Or their reasons may be "original"[99]—that is, not based on any prior non-conformity—such as where an insurer has reason to compensate for a loss it did not cause, where the state ought to socialize it, or where the victim's wealthy aunt should take pity on him. These considerations mean that the rational case for any *particular* person's taking the reparative steps is often inconclusive. Or again, more accurately, it is inconclusive *but for the mediating influence of second-order reasons*. Responsibility to repair the harm must be assigned to one of the available candidates—and often is assigned by the law.[100] The law does so by imposing a duty to repair on one or other person, in virtue of which that duty-bearer's case for repairing it becomes conclusive. There may be a better or worse case for selecting one candidate to bear this duty, rather than another. But the core of the case for imposing the duty to repair the harm is simply that, unless it is imposed, no-one has a conclusive case to repair it. By solving the coordination problem, the duty makes it possible for us to conform to the reasons that existed apart from it.

One can see, from these positions staked out by Gardner, why the prospect is minimal of the defendant's having a conclusive case to repair absent a duty to do so. My objection in this section has traded on the gap between "reasons that are stably and generally conclusive" (read: the justified imposition of liability) and "reasons that are mandatory and categorical" (read: the existence of a duty). But for Gardner that gap is paper-thin. The all-important reason, r, will never emerge from the roiling multiplicity of first-order reasons and provide a stably and generally conclusive reason for a given defendant to make repair *unless* it is mandatory and categorical.

How plausible are these Gardnerian views, with which his defense of TW is bound up? That is, inevitably, too large a question to answer here. But some will find his argument disappointing. It depends on too many controversial upstream commitments. The truth of TW becomes a function of the "extravagance with which Gardner spreads wrongdoing" through all aspects of our rational lives[101]—which includes tort law, to be sure, but only *en passant*. And Gardner's notion of wrongdoing, as we saw, does not carry the usual condemnatory sting. It does not mark out tort law as a domain of particularly serious moral failings by defendants. To be sure, wrongdoing remains a "particularly serious" moral failing in the sense that it creates sticky and inescapable reasons to make amends. What it does not do, however, is bear out the thought that those reasons to make amends derive from a particularly grave shortcoming by the person who incurs them. "So much the better," Gardner would of course say; it was his aim to carve out a role for duties shorn of their overheated moralism, as he saw it. But that may not be the role for TW for which its proponents were hoping.

---

[99] The helpful terminology is from E Voyiakis, *Private Law and the Value of Choice* (Bloomsbury 2017) 12–13.

[100] "The Negligence Standard" (n 52).

[101] RA Duff, "Cliff-Top Predicaments and Morally Blemished Lives" (2019) 19 Jerusalem Review of Legal Studies 125, 129.

5.2 The relative independence of primary and reparative duties

In my view, however, the critical shortcoming in Gardner's argument is a quite different one. Thus far, I was commenting on the connection between r's being mandatory at t_2 and its being (stably and generally) conclusive at t_2. I was exploring Gardner's reasons for thinking the connection is a necessary one. What I took for granted was a silent but crucial premise in his argument: that if r is mandatory at t_2, it must have been mandatory at t_1 also. It is this which connects the justified imposition of tort liability not (only) to a duty to pay compensation but to the breach, at an earlier time, of a *primary* duty. It is this premise, in other words, that gets us where we need to be for TW to be true. But unfortunately the premise is false. There is no reason to think r's mandatoriness is, as it were, a constant property. Or, at any rate, not necessarily.

For Gardner, tort liability is justified only if there is at t_2 a reason, r, to which the defendant failed to conform at t_1.[102] That is the implication of the continuity thesis itself. But by the argument I considered in section 4 he *also* supposes that tort liability is justified only if r was mandatory at t_1. That is his route to endorsing TW. There was a duty at t_1 (grounded upon r) which upon breach generates a duty (also grounded upon r) to repair the breach at t_2. The duty's presence at t_2 is necessary to explain why r is not merely *pro tanto*. And, since the duty at t_2, not unlike r itself, descends from t_1, we have our necessary role for primary duties. One way to read Gardner here is, as Sinel puts it, that "the exclusionary force of the [primary duty] sticks around"; what persists is not only the reason but "the deontic structure, or form, of the obligation," in virtue of which that reason is (contrary to the usual run of things) a conclusive one to pay compensation.[103] But the more ecumenical reading, perhaps, which sidesteps the puzzling metaphysics, is simply that the judgment that the defendant had a duty to conform to r at t_1 entails that, all else being equal, he had a duty to conform to it also at t_2.

Yet notice that, even as we formulate the point, it has an obvious shortcoming. It is not adequate for Gardner's conclusion. True, *if* there was a duty to conform to r at t_1, *then* there is (all else being equal) a duty to conform to r at t_2. But what Gardner's argument needs is the inverse. He needs it to be the case that, *if* there is a duty to conform to r at t_2, *then* there was a duty to conform to r at t_1. (Even the parenthetical "all else being equal" causes trouble for him.) Only if having the duty to compensate at t_2 necessarily implies there was a duty to conform to r at t_1 can the truth of TW be established. We may grant, in other words, everything that Gardner says in defense of what he sometimes called the "obligation-in, obligation-out" principle: once we have a primary duty, its rationale is sufficient, all else being equal, to justify a secondary duty to do whatever counts as next-best conformity to it.[104] But Gardner's argument needs a stronger principle. He needs, as it were, an "obligation-out, obligation-in" principle: a principle that one cannot get an obligation out *unless* one put an obligation in. It seems highly plausible, or so we may grant, that if the defendant had a duty not to commit the

---

[102] Of course, there can also be what I earlier called "original" reasons to repair. I take it these are not plausibly considered *tort* duties, except perhaps in an extended or peripheral sense.

[103] Sinel, Chapter 12, this volume, 216.

[104] "What Is Tort Law For? Part 1" (n 11) 33.

38   LEO BOONZAIER

tort at t_1 then, in the absence of some compelling argument, some relevant difference between the situations at t_1 and t_2, the duty's mandatory force extends also to t_2, when it comes time to pay compensation. But, if we suppose that the defendant did *not* have a duty to conform to r at t_1, does that make it impossible for there to be a duty to conform to it at t_2? It seems odd to rule that out, in the way that Gardner seems to. Surely, one wants to say, it all depends on the duty's rationale?

The obvious case where one wants to say this is *Rylands*. On Gardner's account, the liability of the defendant in *Rylands* is to be explained by his breach of a strict duty not to harm the plaintiff's property. But the problem, as Raz says, is that "we lack an explanation for the duty."[105] It is not that strict duties are not possible, nor that their breach is not a possible basis for liability. We can agree with Gardner that they are. The problem is that we lack a discernible rationale for *this* strict duty—the strict duty, that is, not to harm one's neighbor's property by flooding. That is not to deny that the defendant has a (*pro tanto*) reason not to flood his neighbor's property. Plainly he does. Nor is it to claim that the law, or anyone else, is "indifferent" about the flooding; "[t]he hoped-for result," as Raz says, "is that the harm does not occur."[106] (That is why there is a reason, perhaps a weighty one, not to cause it.) The critical question, however, is whether there is a case for that reason to be strengthened, and allowed to punch above its weight in rational conflict, by the existence of a duty. And here one is left puzzled. There is no explanation that I can see, and I'm not sure Gardner has offered one either.

To be clear, what we do *not* lack is a rationale for the strict *liability*. We may draw that rationale from all the familiar ways in which *Rylands* has conventionally been justified. It lies in the social value of providing a means of compensation for those affected by extraordinary risks, and especially in the fact that, of the two parties, it is better that the person who exercised some choice in creating that risk, who takes the corresponding benefits, and who is more likely to be able to bear the resulting loss, is the one who will indeed bear it.[107] But what does that justify? Surely what that justifies (or purports to justify) is the imposition, by law or social practice, of a duty to compensate. But our question, again, is whether that duty rests, in turn, upon the breach of a prior duty not to cause the harm that is being compensated. And the rationale just mentioned does not seem to count in favor of one. It points to the value of compensation's being paid and of assigning responsibility for doing so to the person who caused the loss. It does not suggest that the defendant had a duty at t_1 in the precise sense that Gardner means it, namely that his admitted reasons not to flood his neighbor's property were protected by mandatory force, and excluded the reasons that countervail.[108]

---

[105] Raz, "Responsibility and the Negligence Standard" (n 87) 8.

[106] ibid 7–8.

[107] All this is compatible with, and reinforced by, Gardner's own explanation of the considerations that bear on the choice between strict and fault-based liability. See "Some Rule-of-Law Anxieties" (n 45).

[108] We might, as ever, drift into looser usages. We might say, for example, that *Rylands* establishes that flooding one's neighbor's property is "non-optional"—and thus "the breach of a duty"—in the sense that, if one does it, the law will intervene to impose liability. But that does not show that the liability is grounded upon an anterior breach of duty (which is the point on which Gardner's analysis is rightly focused). It simply substitutes that claim for another one.

6. Core and Penumbra

In sum, Gardner's argument of section 4 amply explains why, when there is a primary duty that the defendant has breached, that bears powerfully and often decisively on the case for tort liability. The further step he takes, which outstrips his argument, is to say that the breach of a primary duty is necessary. Here, then, is an alternative to TW that seems to me more plausible:

A breach of duty is (defeasibly) sufficient to justify the imposition of tort liability.

That ascribes a very important role to primary duties in tort law. But it does not, of course, establish the claim with which we started.

What this "reading down" of TW does imply is what we may call, with apologies to HLA Hart,[109] a "core" of cases in which tort liability is grounded upon a breach of duty and a "penumbra" in which it is not. There are some instances of tort liability which are justified by the fact that the defendant breached a (primary) duty. In fact the breach of duty provides a (defeasibly) sufficient justification: in the absence of special countervailing considerations, liability ought to be imposed. That is a consequence of the exclusionary force of the primary duty which carries over, all else equal, to t_2. However, there are also instances of tort liability which may be justified even in the absence of a breach of duty. This is possible, however, only in special cases—that is to say, only where a rationale can be given for the imposition of a duty to compensate that does not apply equally to the imposition of a duty not to cause the harm being compensated. It is already apparent, from this, that the former group is likely to be larger than the latter. Where there is a breach of duty, liability is (all else equal) justified. Whereas in the absence of a breach of duty, liability is (all else equal) *un*justified. Where there is the breach of a primary duty, we get a secondary duty without more. But absent a primary duty, the duty to compensate has to be earned. And usually it will not come cheaply.

This schema—a "core" of tort cases in which TW is true and a "penumbra" of exceptions in which it is not—may seem banal. Hasn't that always been the orthodox way of dealing with apparent counterexamples, like *Rylands* and *Vincent*? In a way, yes. But the resemblance is only superficial. The distinctive features of the Gardnerian account I have been sketching are significant. First, it draws the line between the core and penumbra in a quite different place. This we saw most clearly with *Vincent*, which is a case firmly within the core, and not marginal at all. Torts like this one (and many other intentional torts, I suspect) are strong cases for the truth of TW. This is because the case for the primary duty—perhaps even for the strict duty—can be explained, and its exclusionary force is palpable when we think about the scenario in which the tort might be committed.[110] Second, and more importantly, the core and penumbra share a common explanation. In both sets of cases, the justification for the liability is supplied by the same, "ordinary vanilla case for repair,"[111] namely the continuity

---

[109] HLA Hart, "Positivism and the Separation of Law and Morals" (1958) 71 Harvard Law Review 593, 607.

[110] See text at n 42 above.

[111] *FPLPL* (n 52) 155.

thesis. The difference between the core and penumbra is a relatively superficial one: it is a function of the two different ways the continuity thesis may play out. It may be that the continuing reason, r, that grounds the defendant's duty to compensate at t_2 gets its force from the fact that it was mandatory at t_1. Or it may be that the force of r is to be explained differently: by the distinctive case for the defendant's paying compensation.

Third, and following from this, it is a mistake to think that when the liability to compensate does not rest upon the breach of a duty, it falls "outside tort law," as it were, requiring explanation on some entirely different basis. Take *Rylands*. I argued that, even on Gardner's account, it is a mistake to regard the liability there as grounded upon a breach of duty. Hence one should accede to the mainstream view of the case (albeit for reasons other than those usually given), and regard the liability in *Rylands* as "free-standing."[112] What one should *not* do is take the further step of thinking that *Rylands* liability must therefore be explained in unjust enrichment,[113] as an "isolated victory" for the economists,[114] or by analogy to the liability of an insurer.[115] Such responses are both unnecessary and too extreme. What each of these alternative explanations abandons or obscures is the fact, which we surely want to hang on to, that the defendant in *Rylands* is being held liable at t_2 in virtue of what he has done at t_1. He is liable to repair a harm that he has caused, and the fact that he has caused it is a central part of the justification for his being so liable. By contrast, this forms no part of the justification for liability in unjust enrichment or the liability of an insurer; the defendant in these contexts usually has not caused, and certainly need not have caused, the loss for which he is being held liable. That contrast is preserved by remembering that *Rylands*, in common with all other instances of tort liability, is to be explained by the defendant's failure to conform to the reason that he had not to cause harm to the plaintiff. The case's special feature is only that the rationale for that reason's being conclusive at t_2 lies not in the mandatory protection it received at t_1, but in the distinctive case for the defendant's conforming to it by paying compensation.

Which other cases are in the penumbra? I began with *Rylands* because it is the thin end of the wedge. But plausibly the number of cases in the penumbra is much larger. One can see already that it might include strict products liability, where the familiar rationale for the liability is similar to *Rylands*, and the case for a strict primary duty not to harm similarly mysterious. But might the penumbra extend even to the tort of negligence, or parts of it? That suggestion, which inverts the familiar picture with which I began section 2, may sound alarming. But perhaps it should not. For one thing, the balancing of the risk of harm against the costs of avoiding it, which is so integral to the negligence standard, seems naturally explicable as a weighing-up of first-order reasons for and against the defendant's actions. It is not easy to see the exclusionary force of a primary duty at work. And Liam Murphy may

---

[112] Compare McBride, *The Humanity of Private Law* (n 27) 60–62.
[113] See again n 32 above.
[114] *Transco plc v Stockport MBC* [2004] 2 AC 1 [29] (Lord Hoffmann).
[115] Raz, "Responsibility and the Negligence Standard" (n 87) 7–8. See also "Some Rule-of-Law Anxieties" (n 45) 221, where Gardner suggests this same contrast.

be right that we lack a plausible explanation for "an outcome-inclusive moral duty not to injure negligently," and that the case for negligence liability is, rather, the social value of having it, in so far as it "promote[s] the twin goals of compensation and deterrence."[116]

The difference between the core and penumbra, after all, redirects us to, rather than settles, the perennial question: What is the most plausible justification for a given instance of tort liability? My argument does not attempt to settle the answers to this question. But what it does say is that the breach of a duty will not feature in all of them.

7. Conclusion

Is it a bad thing if Gardner's argument fails to establish the truth of TW? Not to my eye. Certainly we must account for the role of primary duties in tort law: it does seem that tort liability is often imposed for the breach of a primary duty *stricto sensu*, and that one cannot understand why it is imposed—and why many duties of repair are so "sticky"—without the exclusionary force the primary duty entails. And Gardner's account shows why that is. But it also leaves open the possibility of justified tort liability even when there is no exclusionary force at t_1 for the duty of repair to inherit. Then the duty to repair must be made to stand on its own two feet, by means of the independent value of the defendant's paying compensation. Or so I have argued.

True, this means that not all torts are wrongs in the sense set out in section 1. And, for some, that is too high a price to pay. After all, many moralists treat TW as an axiom—indeed as constitutive of moralism. They imply that unless TW is true, the whole edifice of moralism collapses, and they will have to succumb to the economists. But that does not follow. At least, not on Gardner's account.[117] That is because, even in those cases where TW does *not* hold, the continuity thesis provides a unified explanation of tort liability that exposes the mistake made by the economists. The continuity thesis, in other words, of itself secures the success of moralism. It shows how defendants have reasons of repair at t_2 just in virtue of their reason non-conformity at t_1. And that, in turn, constitutes the complete case for imposing tort liability, in so far as there is one. Invoking the further consequences to which the imposition of liability is an instrument—deterrence, the optimization of insurance arrangements—in order to justify it, as the economists do, is therefore unnecessary and indeed misconceived. A complete, moralistic explanation for the imposition of tort liability exists regardless of them.

With that explanation in place, then, the truth or falsity of TW lies downstream. Whether an instance of tort liability is grounded upon the breach of a duty, or merely upon the non-conformity to a weighty reason, is a question about how the general

---

[116] Murphy, "Purely Formal Wrongs" (n 54) 35.

[117] For Gardner's own remarks about the malign tendency to overdraw the distinction between the economists and the moralists, see his "Tort Law and Its Theory" (n 4) 352–53; also "Backward and Forward with Tort Law" (n 1). The points in the text are my own.

explanation plays out in particular cases. It is a question that arises only once the debate between the economists and the moralists has been settled. And since that debate has been settled, I have suggested, by John's continuity thesis, and since I have been relying throughout upon features of his wider account, my argument in this chapter—though it has taken issue with some of John's conclusions—is still very much in his spirit.

3
Are There Any Moral Duties?

Nicholas J McBride

1. Law as the Mirror of Morality

One of the habits that John Gardner picked up from his mentor, Joseph Raz, was that of adding to our understanding of law and life by advancing, naming, and considering various theses about the same. In a modest attempt to follow Gardner and Raz's example, I advance (for the purpose of attacking) the following "mirror thesis":

Mirror thesis. Our legal duties reflect, in some way, our moral duties.

Many different legal theorists—including Gardner—endorse the mirror thesis but disagree on the way in which law operates as a mirror of our moral duties. A popular version of the mirror thesis goes as follows:

(α) In a properly functioning legal system, our legal duties will replicate some, but not all, of our moral duties.

Ronald Dworkin's last work on jurisprudence[1] might be taken as endorsing an identity relation between our legal duties and a subset of our moral duties:

(β) The legal duties that we have *are* the moral duties that we have by virtue of the institutional history of our law-making institutions.

Gardner would have rejected (α)[2] and (β),[3] but he might have agreed that:

(γ) When our law-making institutions impose a legal duty to φ on us, they claim that we have a moral duty to φ.[4]

---

[1] R Dworkin, *Justice for Hedgehogs* (Harvard University Press 2011) ch 19.

[2] Gardner would have rejected (α) because (α) overlooks how our legal duties do not just replicate moral duties but can also constitute them by shaping and rendering more concrete moral duties that are relatively amorphous "in the wild": see J Gardner, *From Personal Life to Private Law* (OUP 2018) ("*FPLPL*") 7–8, 13, and J Gardner, *Torts and Other Wrongs* (OUP 2019) 45.

[3] J Gardner, "Law's Aims in *Law's Empire*" in S Hershovitz (ed), *Exploring Law's Empire: The Jurisprudence of Ronald Dworkin* (OUP 2009).

[4] "Might have agreed" because (γ) seems inconsistent with Gardner's rejection of Robert Alexy's view that the law claims to be morally *correct* when it imposes legal duties on us: J Gardner, "How Law Claims, What Law Claims" in his *Law as a Leap of Faith* (OUP 2012) 139–44. But Gardner seems to be saying something very like (γ) in J Gardner, "Ethics and Law" in J Skorupski (ed), *The Routledge Companion to Ethics* (Routledge 2010) 420–21.

Nicholas J McBride, *Are There Any Moral Duties?* In: *Private Law and Practical Reason*. Edited by: Haris Psarras and Sandy Steel, Oxford University Press. © Nicholas J McBride 2023. DOI: 10.1093/oso/9780192857330.003.0003

And he certainly would have agreed with the more cautious claim that:

(δ) When our law-making institutions impose a legal duty to φ on us, they claim to be an authoritative guide as to what moral duties we are subject to.

Gardner's explanation of private law was inspired by his endorsement of (δ) and (possibly) (γ). Gardner's book *From Personal Life to Private Law* vindicates the moral claim that he thinks private law is making in imposing legal duties on us by showing a strong continuity between the private law duties that we owe each other and the moral duties that he sees us as owing each other in ordinary private life, with the result that "what private law would have us do is best understood by reflecting on what we should be doing quite apart from private law."[5]

By contrast, HLA Hart was skeptical as to whether the mirror thesis was true, in any of its forms.[6] Hart's skepticism focused on the law end of the mirror thesis: he did not question whether there were such things as moral duties but was skeptical as to whether they were reflected—in one way or another—in what legal duties we have. I want to question the mirror thesis from the other end, and consider whether there are such things as moral duties. If there are not, then the mirror thesis is untrue, in at least some of its forms.

2. What Is a Mirror of What?

I can anticipate the typical reader's incredulity at the enterprise on which I am embarked. How could anyone think that there are no such things as moral duties? However, as Gardner observed, "Uncontroversial ideas need not less but more critical scrutiny, since they generally get such an easy ride."[7] And ideas don't come more uncontroversial than the idea that there are such things as moral duties.

In order to open up the reader's mind to the possibility that there may be something problematic about the very idea of a moral duty, I point out that anyone who reads the seminal secular writings on the nature of moral duties could easily be excused for concluding that *moral duties are modeled on legal duties.*[8] This is the flat opposite of what the mirror thesis tells us is the case. According to the mirror thesis, legal duties in some way reflect our moral duties. But these writings give us every reason to believe that legal duties came *first*, and that moral duties were conceived as being law-like.

The above point hardly needs to be made out when it comes to Kant. Kant could not write five lines on the nature of moral duties without bringing in the concept of law.

---

[5] *FPLPL* (n 2) 8.

[6] Hart, "Legal Duty and Obligation" in his *Essays on Bentham* (OUP 1982). Hart would, however, have endorsed a variation on (α), that in a properly functioning legal system a subset of our legal duties will replicate a subset of our moral duties.

[7] *FPLPL* (n 2) 189–90.

[8] This point applies even more strongly to *non-secular* writings on moral duties, which see such duties as arising out of the command of the ultimate law-giver, God. In her "Modern Moral Philosophy" (1958) 33 Philosophy 1, Elizabeth Anscombe argues (at 6) that the notion of a moral obligation *only* make sense against that background, and should therefore be given up by those who do not believe in such a thing as divine law. As I am writing for a secular audience, I will not pursue this point further in this chapter.

As Schopenhauer observed, Kant simply assumed that morality took the form of laws. Schopenhauer could see no reason why Kant would make that assumption other than that he had been influenced by the model of the Ten Commandments.[9]

The notion that moral duties are modeled on legal duties becomes even more pronounced in the writings of the utilitarians, not least because it is in those writings that the idea first gains traction that morality "could be a *force*," in Bernard Williams' phrase.[10] An explicit link between moral duties and their being enforceable in some sense was made by John Stuart Mill in his essays on *Utilitarianism*:

> It is a part of the notion of Duty *in every one of its forms*, that a person may rightfully be *compelled* to fulfil it. Duty is a thing which may be *exacted* from a person, *as one exacts a debt*. Unless we think it might be exacted from him, we do not call it his duty.[11]

Given this, the possibility must be considered that the notion of a moral duty has depended from its very inception on a kind of optical illusion—a projection onto the moral plane of something that has actually only ever existed in the legal arena. Unsurprisingly, this illusion (if illusion it be) is not confined to the progenitors of the concept of a moral duty. Modern-day writers on morality can also be seen as falling foul of the tendency to construct morality in the image of law.

For example, R Jay Wallace's account of interpersonal morality in *The Moral Nexus*[12] seems to involve a straight transposition to the moral realm of ideas and concepts that any first-year law student would be familiar with, starting with the idea of a relational obligation. In Wallace's view, the paradigmatic example of a relational moral obligation is a "transactional duty," which concept covers duties "created by promises and other forms of agreement or exchange." Such duties "represent what is often thought to be the original notion of obligation: an obliging of one agent by another, which brings into existence a normative debt that must be repaid."[13] But transactional duties do not exhaust the range of relational moral obligations that we owe to others. Other relational obligations:

> specify what we owe to people just in virtue of the fact that they occupy a world in common with us, and are therefore liable to be affected in one way or another by the things that we might decide to do.[14]

The comparisons with contract law and tort law are too obvious to belabor. However, the parallels with our private law obligations do not stop there. Wallace's scheme of relational obligations even includes "secondary obligations" that apply "when people

---

[9] Schopenhauer, *On the Basis of Morality* (1839) §4 ("On the imperative form of the Kantian ethics").

[10] B Williams, *Ethics and the Limits of Philosophy* (Routledge 2006) 23 (emphasis in original).

[11] JS Mill, *Utilitarianism* (Longmans 1871), Chapter V ("On the Connection between Justice and Utility") 72–73 (emphasis added, except for the italicized "exacted," which is italicized in the original).

[12] RJ Wallace, *The Moral Nexus* (Princeton University Press 2019).

[13] ibid 50.

[14] ibid 53.

have flouted a primary moral obligation" and require the person in breach to "acknowledge their moral failing and apologize for what they have done."[15]

Adherents to the mirror thesis may feel some vindication in Wallace's establishing such an amazingly close correlation between our moral duties and our legal duties. However, all but the most purblind must acknowledge that there is a possibility that our legal duties appear to him and them to mirror our moral duties because the existence of our legal duties has persuaded us to imagine that there also exist (or even that there *must* also exist) moral duties that parallel those legal duties.

3. In the Realm of Morality

Of course, none of this establishes that what we think of as our moral duties are actually illusory. But if they are, the question naturally arises: If there are no such things as moral duties, then what is morality "about"? Five things: (i) evaluation; (ii) transitions; (iii) temptations; (iv) concern for others; and (v) transcendence.

First, morality is concerned with evaluating certain states of (human) being as flourishing, and other states as non-flourishing. We engage with this part of morality when we form "second-order" desires: desires about our desires.[16] These second-order desires either reflect our happiness at having certain desires that strike us as compatible with, or contributing to, our enjoying a flourishing existence; or they involve our disowning certain desires we have, whose mere existence seems to us incompatible with our being able to think of ourselves as flourishing, or that threaten—if acted on— to get in the way of our enjoying a flourishing existence.

Second, morality is concerned with how someone can transition from a non-flourishing existence to a flourishing existence. As Alasdair MacIntyre observes, this was the central concern of the "moral scheme ... [which] came for long periods to dominate the European Middle Ages from the twelfth century onwards":

> Within [this] scheme there is a fundamental contrast between man-as-he-happens-to-be and man-as-he-could-be-if-he-realized-his-essential-nature. Ethics is the science which is to enable men to understand how they make the transition from the former state to the latter.[17]

It is this aspect of morality that MacIntyre has sought to rehabilitate, in the face of a modern sensibility that sees morality as addressed not to what we could *be* as human beings, but to what we should *do*.

Third, Simone Weil has observed that when it comes to their flourishing, human beings are conflicted. Some part of their soul wishes to attain a flourishing existence, while another—mediocre—part wishes for anything else:

---

[15] ibid 89.

[16] H Frankfurt, "Freedom of the Will and the Concept of a Person" (1971) 67 Journal of Philosophy 5; C Taylor, "What is Human Agency?" in his *Human Agency and Language: Philosophical Papers 1* (CUP 1985).

[17] A MacIntyre, *After Virtue* (3rd edn, Bloomsbury 2013) 62.

When the soul flies from anything it is always trying to get away, either from the horror of ugliness, or contact with what is truly pure. This is because all mediocrity flies from the light; and in all souls, except those which are near perfection, there is a great part which is mediocre.[18]

It follows that human beings will always be faced with temptations to turn their backs on their own flourishing. The third part of morality is concerned with how such temptations can be avoided, and if not, managed.

Fourth, it has long been acknowledged that any decent conception of human flourishing will include within it a proper concern for the flourishing of others.[19] Anyone who feels no such concern cannot be counted as flourishing, not least because—by definition—they will feel no love for anyone else, as it is in the nature of love that one cannot count oneself as flourishing if the object of one's love is not. More broadly, I have argued that: (i) no-one can count themselves as flourishing if their "flourishing" has been purchased at the expense of another's flourishing; and (ii) it is unlikely that anyone can flourish without living in a community that is concerned to foster the flourishing of all its members.[20] The fourth part of morality deals with the level of concern for the flourishing of others that someone needs to feel if they are to count as flourishing themselves.

Fifth, in Wayne Sumner's phrase, human flourishing is "something in between" a life that is going badly and a life that could go as well as it could possibly go.[21] While someone who is leading a flourishing life is entitled to be perfectly content with how their life is going, there is a good for human beings that transcends their flourishing, the achievement of which would make their life even more complete than it is. The fifth part of morality is concerned with what that good might be, in what circumstances it might be appropriate to seek to achieve that good, and what is required to achieve that good.

This account of morality—call it "E" for short—is *eudaimonic* in nature in that "the reasonableness of different course of action and of the cultivation of different traits of character is to be assessed by reference to one's own happiness, not by reference to some point of view external to the interests of the agent."[22] MacIntyre calls our modern day, duty-saturated, conception of morality, " 'Morality' ... with a capital M."[23] I will follow his example by calling this conception of morality "M" for short.

There are two obvious differences between E and M. First, unlike M, E makes no obvious reference to the existence of moral duties. Second, E is concerned to *assist* an agent to live a good life, and is not—as M is—concerned to place *limits* on an agent's pursuit of a good life. The second difference is the reason for the first: an account of morality that is not interested in placing limits on my pursuing a good life will tend not to have much use for the concept of duty.

---

[18] S Weil, "Forms of the Implicit Love of God" in S Weil, *Waiting for God* (Harper Perennial 2009) 64.

[19] Aristotle, *Nicomachean Ethics*, IX.8.

[20] NJ McBride, *The Humanity of Private Law, Part I: Explanation* (Hart Publishing 2019) 99–107.

[21] W Sumner, "Something in Between" in R Crisp and B Hooker (eds), *Well-Being and Morality: Essays in Honour of James Griffin* (OUP 2000).

[22] T Irwin, "Prudence and Morality in Greek Ethics" (1995) 105 Ethics 284, 284–85.

[23] A MacIntyre, *Ethics in the Conflicts of Modernity* (CUP 2016) 65, 151.

4. A Place for Moral Duties?

However, it may be that E does in fact have a place for the concept of a moral duty. There are five ways in which the concept of a moral duty might figure within E: (i) via the idea of a duty to oneself; (ii) via the fact that under E certain actions, practices, thoughts, and dispositions are designated as being evil or vicious; (iii) via the importance of someone's being just if they are to count as flourishing as a human being; (iv) via the importance of someone's being reliable to people's flourishing generally; (v) via the importance of law to people's flourishing generally.

4.1 Duties to oneself

It might be argued, first, that the account of morality presented by E is underpinned by a basic moral duty—a duty, owed to oneself, to flourish as a human being. If such a duty exists, then—by extension—everything else touched by E becomes a matter of moral obligation. However, it seems unlikely that there is such a thing as a moral duty, owed to oneself, to flourish as a human being.

Bernard Williams described the notion of a duty owed to oneself as "fraudulent,"[24] explaining that the concept of a duty owed to oneself had been invented to solve problems created by M in accounting for why it is permissible under M for people to spend time on improving themselves, or engaging in morally indifferent activities.[25] And even under M, it seems implausible that people who waste their talents do anything *wrong* in not making more of what they are given. Test it this way: we don't normally give people praise or credit for doing their duty. But someone who achieves their potential tends to receive praise and credit for doing so. So even under M, there is no duty to flourish as a human being; and if there is no such duty under M, it would be implausible to think there would be one under E.

4.2 Evil and vice

A more promising entry point for the concept of a moral duty into E is the fact that under E certain actions will be designated as being evil or vicious because of their being, or having the tendency to be, extremely damaging to the flourishing of the agent, or the flourishing of someone who will be impacted by those actions. Surely, it might be argued, we can say that under E an agent has a moral duty not to perform those actions?

Consider, for example, Vaclav Havel's example of the greengrocer who, operating behind the Iron Curtain and seeking to ingratiate himself with the authorities and enjoy a quiet life, puts a notice in his shop window saying "Workers of the World, Unite!"[26] There is no doubt that E would take a very dim view of this action—it would

---

[24] Williams, *Ethics and the Limits of Philosophy* (n 10) 182.
[25] ibid 50, 182.
[26] V Havel, *The Power of the Powerless* (Sharpe 1985) 27.

ARE THERE ANY MORAL DUTIES? 49

be regarded by E as cowardly and as a result incompatible with the greengrocer's flourishing as a person. The question is whether E would have any use for the proposition that the greengrocer had a *moral duty* not to put up the sign. It is hard to see why it would. Characterizing the greengrocer's putting the sign in the window as cowardly tells us (if we are interested in flourishing as human beings) everything we need to know as to whether such an action is to be done or not to be done. To say *as well* that the greengrocer had a moral duty not to put the sign in the window seems to be superfluous.[27]

This point can be put another, more technical, way. Raz explains that your being subject to a duty to φ usually supplies you with a first-order reason to φ, while giving you a second-order reason—in deliberating whether or not to do φ—to disregard as irrelevant various reasons that you might otherwise have had not to do φ.[28] But it is not just duties that operate in this way.[29] What Bernard Williams called "thick ethical concepts" also have this effect.

Such concepts, Williams explains, are "action-guiding" in that "they often provide ... someone with a reason for action, though that reason may not be a decisive one."[30] But at the same time, thick ethical concepts are "world guided": they "may be rightly or wrongly applied" with the result that "their use *is* controlled by the facts."[31] An example of a thick ethical concept is "cowardly" and when rightly applied to a greengrocer's putting a sign in a shop window saying "Workers of the World, Unite!" it supplies the greengrocer with a first-order reason not to post the sign in the window, and renders irrelevant—for the purpose of his deliberating as to what to do—the reasons he might otherwise have to put the sign in the window; principally, that doing so will secure him a quiet life.

It follows that saying that the greengrocer has a duty not to put the sign in the window is redundant. Designating such an act as cowardly does all the work that the existence of a duty not to put the sign in the window would have done in terms of affecting the architecture of the reasons that apply to the greengrocer. Generalizing, the same will be true of any action or practice that is designated by E as evil or vicious. Such an action or practice will already fall under a (negative) thick ethical concept, marking it out as involving danger of one kind or another for the agent's or another's flourishing and, as such, something we have compelling reason not to do. As a result, *also* saying that there is a moral duty not to perform that action or engage in that practice would be pointless.

4.3 Justice

Being just, and wishing to see justice done, is generally regarded as an important component of someone's flourishing as a human being.

---

[27] Anscombe, "Modern Moral Philosophy" (n 8) 8–9.
[28] J Raz, *Practical Reason and Norms* (Princeton University Press 1990) 58–59, 73–76.
[29] Raz gives a decision to φ as an example of something that is not (in his terminology) a mandatory norm but creates an exclusionary reason to φ: ibid 65–71.
[30] Williams, *Ethics and the Limits of Philosophy* (n 10) 140.
[31] ibid 141 (emphasis in original).

The reasoning in the previous section indicates that it would be superfluous for E to say of someone that they had a moral duty not to act in an unjust way. The fact that φ-ing would be unjust gives us all the reason we need not to φ. But the importance of justice to E might mean that E has to acknowledge that people owe others moral duties. This is because, according to what we can call the *classical* understanding of justice, justice is to be identified as giving people what is *due* to them.[32] What could that word "due" connote, other than a moral duty?

To see what "due" might mean under E, consider the story told by Peter Geach, about someone who was casting doubt "on the very existence of any fixed standard of justice" because "one cannot measure justice." Geach's daughter, Mary Gormally, responded sharply, "Without justice there is no measurement." Geach reflected that:

> A little thought shows how deep this retort penetrates. For measurement there must be *true* weights and measures; the results of measurement must be *truly* reported and recorded; and we must trust our fellows that there are such *true* reports. Otherwise the practice of measurement is futile. So there can be no measurement without a species of justice.[33]

He concluded that when it came to justice, "Ethics and epistemology are ... closely intertwined."

It is therefore possible to define what is *due* to someone not as whatever someone else has a moral duty to give them but what they would receive *if they were dealt with honestly*. So someone who is given an unfair mark in their exams is treated unjustly because a claim is made when they are given that mark—"This is the mark your exam performance merited"—and that claim is not true. Someone who is unfairly passed over for promotion at work is treated unjustly because a claim is made when they are told the outcome of the promotion exercise—"We gave the promotion to the best qualified person"—and that claim is not true. The same could be said of legal injustice, where what a claimant or defendant receives at the hands of the law is inconsistent with the claim that is made when what they receive is doled out to them: "This is what the law requires you be given."[34]

If this is right, then the importance that E places on doing justice and avoiding injustice does not require it to accept that there are such thing as moral duties in relation to how one allocates goods and bads to other people. Moreover, the above account of what justice and injustice involves allows us to understand better *why* E would place such importance on being just. If, as I have contended elsewhere,[35] there is a deep link between human flourishing and truth and truthfulness, it is inevitable that E will be urgently concerned with promoting justice and discouraging injustice: the first involves truthful dealing with another; the second, untruthful dealing.

---

[32] J Finnis, *Natural Law and Natural Rights* (2nd edn, OUP 2011) 162.

[33] Geach, "Truth, Truthfulness and Trust" in his *Truth and Hope* (University of Notre Dame Press 2001) 47 (emphasis added).

[34] Of course, Gardner took a very different view of justice, confessing that the idea that there was some hypocrisy—a form of dishonesty—involved in legal injustice "leaves me cold": J Gardner, "The Virtue of Justice and the Character of Law" in *Law as a Leap of Faith* (n 4) 239.

[35] NJ McBride, *The Humanity of Private Law, Part II: Evaluation* (Hart Publishing 2020).

4.4 Reliability

It may be that there are extremes of unreliability that endanger one's (or others') flourishing and that E would consequently designate as evil or vicious. However, there is a lower-level form of unreliability that does not directly endanger an agent's flourishing, or that of anyone else's. Instead, if it is repeated on a sufficiently large enough scale, it exerts a kind of "moral drag" on the community, creating so much irritation and aggravation that it becomes unnecessarily harder for the members of that community to enjoy a flourishing existence. It follows that E would be concerned to discourage this lower-level form of unreliability.

One way of doing this would be through law. Another way—involving a lighter touch—would be to recognize people as having moral duties not to behave in an unreliable fashion. This is the role that Bernard Williams saw moral obligations as playing, arguing that "[o]bligation works to secure reliability, a state of affairs in which people can reasonably expect others to behave in some ways and not in others."[36] The social importance of securing reliability might also mean that E has use for the concept of moral duty in a Bradley-esque "My station and its duties" sense of moral duty.[37] Certainly, social life would become very difficult in the absence of a felt sense of duty among people occupying different positions in society to fulfil the expectations attached to those positions.

However, there should be some discomfort attached to using the term *moral duty* to describe what we might call, generically, a *reliability-assuring norm*. First, the term is being used instrumentally—we are *saying* that A is subject to a moral duty *in order to* make A more reliable in performing certain functions. Only utilitarians tend to think of moral duties in such instrumental terms. Second, the moral duty that A is subject to is only as strong as our interest in A's being reliable in performing a particular function. While we do have such an interest, it is not hugely strong and does not warrant subjecting A to a duty that is as strong as we would normally expect a moral duty to be.

Given this, instead of calling reliability-assuring norms moral duties, a much more appropriate name would be *social responsibilities*. There is therefore no necessary reason why our general interest in people's being reliable would result in E's acknowledging that people are subject to moral duties. It would instead acknowledge that people have certain social responsibilities that are cantered around the general social importance of people's being reliable in performing certain functions and roles.

4.5 Law

Within the account of morality presented by E, the role of law is twofold. The first is to proscribe certain of the actions and practices designated by E as being evil or vicious, on the grounds of either their damaging effect on the agent's, or another's, flourishing

---

[36] ibid 187.

[37] FH Bradley, *Ethical Studies* (2nd edn, OUP 1970) essay V. "Bradley-esque" because Bradley meant a lot more by that phrase than just the responsibilities attached to one's position in social life.

or their tendency to have such an effect. The second is coordinative: distributing legal rights, duties, powers, liabilities, and so on among the law's subjects in order to provide those subjects with a fair chance of leading a flourishing existence.

For law to be able to perform these roles—and in particular, the second—it has long been acknowledged that it is important that the vast majority of the law's subjects think that they *ought* to be obey the law. It is likely that that "ought" will need to have a much stronger weight in people's deliberations as to what they should do than a mere social responsibility would have. Given this, it is entirely possible that E would acknowledge people's as having (in the right circumstances, where law plays the role assigned to it under E) a moral duty to obey the law. That moral duty would then mean that if an agent A had a legal duty to φ then A would have a corresponding moral duty to φ.

However, even if this is so, it should be noted that it would no longer be possible to say, as the mirror thesis does, that our legal duties reflect, in some way, our moral duties. The reverse would be the case: our moral duties would reflect our legal duties. So even if E did acknowledge the existence of moral duties arising out of our legal duties, such an acknowledgment would do nothing to establish that moral duties exist in a way that might support the mirror thesis.

It follows that if E is true then there exist no *relevant* moral duties that might support the mirror thesis, in at least some of its forms. But is the account of morality that E offers us actually true?

5. E versus M

In addressing this question, it is not possible to consider the merits of E in isolation. Instead, we should proceed by comparing E to M and ask ourselves—if we make the transition from E to M, what happens? From the perspective that M provides us, do we take the view that our understanding of the nature of morality has become more perspicuous than it was when we adopted the perspective that E provided us? Or has, by contrast, our understanding become more cloudy?

If the first, then we should prefer M to E and regard M, and not E, as true until some third rival account of the nature of morality (T) comes along and demonstrates that the move from M to T represents an epistemic gain in the same way that the move from E to M enhanced our understanding of the nature of morality. If, on the other hand, we can acknowledge from the perspective that M provides us that our understanding of the nature of morality is diminished as compared with the understanding that E provided us, then we should prefer E to M and regard E as true, again until the transition from E to a third rival account of the nature of morality is shown to represent an epistemic gain.[38]

I have suggested elsewhere that the transition from E to M involves an epistemic loss, rather than epistemic gain.[39] I don't intend to rehearse the arguments for thinking

---

[38] In support of this way of proceeding, see C Taylor, "Explanation and Practical Reason" in M Nussbaum and A Sen (eds), *The Quality of Life* (OUP 1993).

[39] McBride, *The Humanity of Private Law, Part I* (n 20) 21–26. Key texts supporting that conclusion are MacIntyre, *After Virtue* (n 17); Williams, *Ethics and the Limits of Philosophy* (n 10) ch 10; C Taylor, "Perils of Moralism" in his *Dilemmas and Connections* (Harvard University Press 2011).

that here,[40] but instead want to reinforce those arguments by considering how Gardner—as a fully paid-up supporter of M—dealt with a couple of moral issues in his writings. Gardner's treatment of those issues shows that M does not provide us with the resources to deal with those issues adequately, while E does.

5.1 The wrongness of rape

In a paper on "The Wrongness of Rape," John Gardner and his co-author Stephen Shute undertook to identify "*what* is wrong with rape."[41] Although the word "duty" is never used in their paper, to a supporter of M such as Gardner, the question "what is wrong with rape?" is identical to the question "why is there a duty not to rape someone else?"[42] And it is clear that Gardner and Shute were concerned in their paper with explaining the existence of a *moral* duty not to rape, and only derivatively (as one would expect, given the mirror thesis) with the legal duty not to rape.

If we dispense (as we should) with the idea of a duty owed to oneself, the answer to the question of why A has a moral duty not to rape B tends to focus on B, and what it is about B that generates A's having a moral duty not to rape B. In trying to answer this question, Gardner and Shute focused on what they called the case of "pure" rape, where A has sex with an unconscious B, and B suffers no ill-effects from A's actions and B never finds out what A did to her (and nor does anyone else). Given that B is unaffected by A's actions in any material way, it is unsurprising that in explaining what is wrong about A's actions, Gardner and Shute have to have recourse to the Kantian argument that it is wrong to use another as a mere means: "Rape, in the pure case, is the sheer use of a person... the sheer use of a person, and in that sense the objectification of a person, is a denial of their personhood. It is literally dehumanizing."[43]

However, this argument makes rape, as a wrong, a near neighbor of C and D's engaging in consensual sex, where each is making sheer use of the other's person; for example, where C is a prostitute and D is a client. Gardner and Shute acknowledged the point, and argued that while rape should be criminalized, a "dehumanizing" consensual sexual encounter involving the sheer use of another should not be because "allowing people ... to pursue" the option of having dehumanizing sexual encounters with others "is, up to a point, rehumanizing, because it credits them with moral agency, without which credit their dehumanization is only compounded. This rehumanizing

---

[40] But briefly: (i) our moral exemplars tend not to act out of a sense of duty, and someone who refrains from φ-ing only because they think they have a duty not to do so usually counts less well in our estimations than someone who would never dream of φ-ing in the first place; (ii) likewise, someone who comes to morally regret their actions tends not to do so because they think that they breached a duty in acting in the way they did, but because the *facts* of what they did are now clearer to them; (iii) M does not cope well with the idea that certain actions or practices are morally commendable, but not morally compulsory; (iv) likewise, M has a tough time explaining why, when someone is normally subject to a duty not to φ, they might on occasion be permitted to φ; (v) M cannot explain at all why we might make an adverse moral judgment on someone based on their *thoughts*.

[41] J Gardner and S Shute, "The Wrongness of Rape" in J Gardner (ed), *Offences and Defences* (OUP 2007) 1 (emphasis in original).

[42] In a follow-up article on the wrongness of rape—J Gardner, "The Opposite of Rape" (2018) 38 Oxford Journal of Legal Studies 48—the language of "duty" is used throughout.

[43] Gardner and Shute, "The Wrongness of Rape" (n 41) 16.

value combines with the general value of personal autonomy to yield a right to sexual autonomy."[44] It follows that when C genuinely consents to being used as a sex object by D, D's use of C "is not a violation of [C's] right to sexual autonomy, and so not a wrong *against* [C]."[45]

Gardner subsequently confessed that while he thought his and Shute's answer to the question of what is wrong with rape was "in the right neighbourhood … I am not as confident about the details as I once was."[46] It is not hard to see the reason for Gardner's unhappiness. If you make rape, as a wrong, a near neighbor of using prostitutes or pornography for sexual satisfaction, the unspeakable and horrific nature of rape becomes much harder to explain. No-one regards having sex with a prostitute or watching pornography as unspeakable or horrific, even though those activities involve the "sheer use" of another. Moreover, the lack of horror attached to these activities as compared with rape cannot sensibly be explained on the basis that the former do not involve a violation of a right to sexual autonomy while the latter does.

What went wrong with Gardner and Shute's analysis is that M did not provide them with the resources they needed to understand what was wrong with rape. In the "pure" case of rape that they focused on, M left them with nowhere to go in understanding what is wrong with A's having sex with B except to locate A's breach of duty in the "sheer use" A made of B.

Only E provides Gardner and Shute with the resources they needed to understand what is wrong about A's actions in the "pure" case they considered. As it happens, Gardner and Shute came tantalizingly close to accessing those resources when they observed that the defendants in *DPP* v *Morgan*[47] "were animals *par excellence*."[48] Indeed, the thick ethical concept "bestial" is the one that most appropriately describes what rape involves, at least so far as the perpetrator is concerned. It is a concept that warns A—in the case where he is in a position to have sex with an unconscious B—that doing so will strip him of his capacity for human flourishing because he will no longer even be able to count himself as human (at least until he recovers his humanity by repenting of what he did to B).[49] As such, it is not even a question for E that A's having sex with B will be forbidden.

It may be argued that by shifting our attention from B to A—when accounting for the wrongness of A's having sex with B—we are making a mistake. The wrongness of rape, the argument would go, must always be located in facts about B, not A. But Gardner and Shute's "pure" rape scenario makes that implausible, given that it has been constructed so that A's having sex with B will make no difference to how B's life goes. When it comes to the *central* case of rape—where *both* A *and* B know that A is

---

[44] ibid 20.

[45] ibid (emphasis in original).

[46] R Marshall, *Ethics at 3:AM: Questions and Answers on How to Live Well* (OUP 2017) 174.

[47] [1976] AC 182 (HL). The defendants in *Morgan* gangraped a woman and then tried to claim that her husband had encouraged them to think that she would welcome having sex with all of them.

[48] Gardner and Shute, "The Wrongness of Rape" (n 41) 26 (italics in original).

[49] This point has the important legal implication that not only is the victim of a rape allowed to use lethal force to bring the rape to an end, they should be allowed to do so without any inquiry being made as to the reasonableness of their doing so.

having sex with B without B's consent—E will find more than enough reason to forbid A's action on both A *and* B's side of the ledger.

On A's side because of the bestiality of his act. On B's side because of the impact that their treatment at A's hands is likely have on their capacity to flourish. That impact will radiate out from the terror felt by B, in realizing that they are in the power of someone who has deprived themselves of their humanity and from whom no humanity can therefore be expected. The predictable sequelae of that terror will be such flourishing-impairing harms as: a constant dwelling by B on their treatment by A and what they could have done to avoid it; traumatic memories of their treatment by A; an inability to form intimate relationships with others; and even an inability to believe that good exists in the world.

It follows that far from neighboring the wrong of rape, the wrong involved in using prostitutes or consuming pornography (if it is wrong) does not even live in the same district. *None* of the specific reasons that E has for forbidding rape apply to the use of prostitutes or pornography. The wrongs that neighbor the wrong of rape are wrongs such as torture or bestiality. Most people would agree with this; but only E tells us why this is. As Gardner and Shute's example shows, M leads us in completely the wrong direction in understanding the wrongness of rape.

5.2 *Sophie's Choice*

At the climax of William Styron's novel, *Sophie's Choice*,[50] Sophie tells the narrator, Stingo, that when she and her two children, Jan and Eva, were transported to Auschwitz, they were required to line up for inspection by a doctor who would select who would be sent to the gas chambers and who would be allowed to live.

In an attempt to save her and her children's lives, Sophie told the doctor that she was not Jewish and was a believing Christian (which was true). The doctor told her that in light of that fact, he would permit her and one of her children to live; he told her to choose which of Jan and Eva would die and which live. If she did not choose, then both would be selected to die. Sophie initially refused to choose, but faced with both of her children being taken away from her, she picked Eva to be sent to the gas chambers.

After spending the night with Stingo, Sophie leaves him while he is still asleep and goes back to her long-term boyfriend Nathan. At the end of the novel, Sophie and Nathan have killed themselves. We can suppose that Sophie's suicide is linked with the guilt she feels over Eva's death: in a note Sophie left for Stingo after their night together she confessed that "[I] now feel this Hate of Life and God. FUCK God and all his Hände Werk, And Life too. And even what remain of Love."[51]

Gardner discusses Sophie's choice in his book *From Personal Life to Private Law*.[52] He argues that the "terrible secret behind Sophie's suicidal depression" was that by choosing to save Jan over Eva, she "failed in her duty to be impartial" between the two children, but that her failure was justified or excused because she had to choose

---

[50] W Styron, *Sophie's Choice* (Jonathan Cape 1979).
[51] ibid 500.
[52] *FPLPL* (n 2) 39, 51, 138, 181 n 28.

between her children "in order to perform (in the case of one of the children) another duty, namely the duty to protect her children from danger." As a result, Sophie "had to fail as a parent in order to do what a parent must do."[53]

This M-based account of the significance of Sophie's choice and its effect on Sophie hardly seems adequate. How could a breach of a duty to be impartial between one's children result in one's feeling a hatred of life, God, and even love itself?

For a more perspicuous analysis of Sophie's choice, we again have to turn to E and look first at the doctor who made Sophie make her choice. Dismissed by Gardner as a "thug,"[54] he is in fact presented in Styron's novel in far more complex terms.[55] He was, like Sophie, a believing Christian who originally intended to be a priest until he was forced by his father to become a doctor. Life in Auschwitz broke his belief in God, and the doctor wanted "to restore his belief in God ... by committing the most intolerable sin that he was able to conceive"—for if there is such a thing as sin then there must be such a thing as God. And the worst sin he is able to think of is making a mother choose to send one of her children for execution.

There is no thick ethical concept available to describe the doctor's actions. While a negative thick ethical concept normally operates as a harbinger of evil, a warning that proceeding further will take you or someone else into a dark place ethically, the evil involved in the doctor's actions speaks for itself—it is evil in its most brazen and unadorned form because it is aimed straight at the complete destruction of another individual's capacity for flourishing as a human being.

That destruction is worked in Sophie's case by freezing her in time so that she is condemned to live forever in her worst moment, when she helped bring about her daughter's death. Sophie tries to break out of that moment through frenzied sexual encounters, such as with Stingo on her last night with him. However, she cannot escape—she is destined always to return to that moment in her memories and ponder what she could have done differently. Trapped in time, she cannot but end up hating life, her love for Eva that makes it impossible for her to move on from what she did, and the God who allows her to be tortured over and over again by her memories of her last moments with Eva.

There is therefore no need to account for Sophie's suicidal depression by reference to her having breached a moral duty in making the choice she did. Instead, E is perfectly able to account for why Sophie's ultimate fate was sealed the moment she was made to choose which of Jan and Eva would be killed.

6. Why Did M Win?

At this point, the challenge might be made: if the transition from E to M involved an epistemic loss, rather than an epistemic gain, why did it happen? What non-epistemic features of M account for why M, rather than E, defines the way we conventionally think about morality today? The challenge can easily be answered. There are two

[53] ibid 39.
[54] ibid 181, n 28.
[55] Styron, *Sophie's Choice* (n 50) 484–87.

features of our modern condition that M caters for in a way that E never could, and account for why we moderns are much happier thinking about morality in the way that M invites us to, rather than the way E would have us do.

The first feature of modernity is our desire for *certainty*. In his brilliant account of the genesis of modernity, *Cosmopolis*,[56] Stephen Toulmin traces the origins of modernity to the convulsions that seized Europe during the course of the Thirty Years' War (1618–1648) that was triggered by the assassination of King Henry IV of France in 1610. In response to this chaos, the sort of humanistic toleration of differences of opinion represented by Montaigne (who died in 1592) fell out of fashion, and a deep desire for "some *rational method* for demonstrating the essential correctness or incorrectness of philosophical, scientific, or theological doctrines"[57] took its place. As a result, "[a]ll the protagonists of modern philosophy promoted theory, devalued practice, and insisted equally on the need to find foundations for knowledge that were clear, distinct, and certain."[58] Kant and the utilitarians can be seen as heirs to this project, in seeking clear, distinct, and certain bases for our knowledge of morality. But only a morality of *duty* is capable of being provided with such a clear, distinct, and certain basis. It is certainly possible to suggest any number of tests for determining whether or not one has a moral duty to φ,[59] but it is impossible to imagine doing the same for the much more complex and multi-faceted account of morality provided by E—what would one be testing *for*?

The second feature of modernity that M caters to is our desire for *moral purity*. E scores very badly on this front. On its account of morality, morality is always further on up the road, beckoning us on, pointing out the moral progress we will make if we make the move from where we are at the moment to the position from where morality is speaking to us. So under E, there is always more room for moral progress. Even if we attain a flourishing existence—an existence that anyone would be content to enjoy—there is a good beyond flourishing for us that invites us to transcend our current circumstances and reach higher. It follows that if we adopt E's view of morality, morality comes across as exhausting and demeaning. M, on the other hand, absolves us of the feelings of inadequacy that E inculcates in us. M tells us that so long as we do our duty we are entitled to think well of ourselves, and entitled to demand that others think well of us. In other words, M provides us with an account of morality that respectable people can feel comfortable with.

If this is right, then the transition from E to M that has undoubtedly occurred since the seventeenth century did not occur because making that transition provided a more perspicuous understanding of the nature of morality, but because our conception of morality was remodeled to accommodate new needs and desires that began to be felt from the seventeenth century onwards. However, those needs and desires have led us astray: they have led us to adopt a picture of morality that is inferior to the picture that it superseded.

---

[56] S Toulmin, *Cosmopolis: The Hidden Agenda of Modernity* (University of Chicago Press 1990).

[57] ibid 55 (emphasis in original).

[58] ibid 70.

[59] For recent attempts, see TM Scanlon, *What We Owe To Each Other* (Harvard University Press 1999) and D Parfit, *On What Matters*, Vol One (OUP 2011).

7. The Mirror Crack'd

I hope I have said enough by now to allow my incredulous reader to think that, at the very least, a case can be made for thinking that the answer to the question posed by the title of my paper is "No." But if the answer to that question is "No," where does that leave the mirror thesis? The first two forms of the mirror thesis would have to be rejected out of hand—if there are no moral duties then we cannot say that our legal duties ought to replicate, or are identical to, a subset of our moral duties.

However, the last two forms of the mirror thesis may survive its being established that there are no moral duties. That fact (if fact it is) does not prevent the law from operating under the spell of M—which tells the law that there are plenty of moral duties—and *claiming* when it imposes a duty to φ on us, that we have a moral duty to φ; or *claiming* when it imposes a duty to φ on us that we will do better in terms of complying with our moral duties if we comply with all of our legal duties, including our duty to φ. The law would be mistaken in making those claims, but it could still make them.

It seems, then, that the forms of the mirror thesis that I have labeled (γ) and (δ) can be maintained even if we accept that there are no moral duties. However, (γ) and (δ) are undermined in another way by its being established that there are no moral duties. The principal argument made for thinking that the law makes the claims that (γ) and (δ) say it makes is that law *necessarily* makes those claims.[60] But suppose that everyone were convinced by the sort of arguments made in this chapter, and elsewhere, that there are no such things as moral duties. In such a case, the sort of claims that (γ) and (δ) see the law as making would and could no longer be made. Would law then disappear? Of course not. It follows that what we might call the *necessity thesis*—that law *necessarily* makes claims (γ) or (δ)—must be given up, and with it the principal argument for thinking that the law makes claims (γ) or (δ) *at the moment* falls away.

Even if the necessity thesis is untrue—and, by extension, (γ) and (δ)—those like Gardner who see the law as making moral claims for itself could fall back to a weaker form of the necessity thesis, according to which law necessarily claims to pursue morally beneficent ends.[61] Happily, that is a thesis that is consistent with E's being true. It is also one that Gardner would have accepted. But it remains to be seen whether the explanations of private law advanced by Gardner in *From Personal Life and Private Law* and *Torts and Other Wrongs* are compatible with our seeing law as simply making a claim to pursue morally beneficent ends, as opposed to the stronger claims that (γ) or (δ) see law as making.

---

[60] See eg Gardner, "Ethics and Law" (n 4) 420–21.

[61] For a recent defense of this thesis, see D McIlroy, *The End of Law: How Law's Claims Relate to Law's Aims* (Elgar 2019).

4
Reasons to Try

Ori J Herstein[*]

1. Introduction

The value of trying is various and complex, yielding reasons to try to do numerous different things in diverse contexts. Demonstrating this richness, I draw on cultural insights and on examples from everyday life, with a special focus on the law and on morality. The chapter builds on the work of John Gardner, who has done more than anyone to further our understanding of reasons to try.

The chapter opens with some conceptual and terminological clarifications (section 2). The next section is devoted to discussing some connections between reasons to try and the law (section 3). Next, following the distinction between value as a means and intrinsic value, the bulk of the chapter explores different types of values of trying, and the reasons that those values give rise to (sections 4 and 5).

2. Preliminary Clarifications

The terms "to φ" and "φ-ing" refer both to actions and to states of affairs that are the outcomes of actions. Notice also that when referring to actions, "φ-ing" may refer to actions and omissions alike. In discussing reasons to try we may, therefore, find straightforward reasons to try-to-φ as well as reasons to try-*not*-to-φ. For our purposes, to "try to φ" is to act with the intent or with the aim of φ-ing. More specifically, to try to φ is to engage in an "appropriately oriented endeavor or effort."[1] As such, there appear at least two conditions for an action to qualify as an instance of trying: to try to φ one must ψ with the intent or aim of thereby φ-ing; and, loosely, one's trying to φ must satisfy some agent-independent standard for qualifying as an intelligible attempt toward φ-ing (eg one cannot reasonably try to slice a tomato by washing one's car, even if in some sense one genuinely believes that is what one is trying to do).

Following Gardner, I use the colloquially appealing terminology of "trying" and "succeeding." Yet, to avoid the pitfalls of colloquial usage, notice that while *trying*-to-φ invariably involves some measure of intention to φ, the same is not necessarily true of all instances of *succeeding* at φ-ing—as there are instances where one can φ without intending to do so. That said, in natural language "to succeed" may appear to incorporate

---

[*] For their helpful comments on previous drafts of this chapter I am grateful to Andrew Gold, Sandy Steel, and to the participants of the workshop devoted to this volume. For editorial assistance I am grateful to Rotem Ortas.

[1] K Brownlee, "Reasons and Ideals" (2010) 151 Philosophical Studies 235, 437.

Ori J Herstein, *Reasons to Try* In: *Private Law and Practical Reason*. Edited by: Haris Psarras and Sandy Steel, Oxford University Press. © Ori J Herstein 2023. DOI: 10.1093/oso/9780192857330.003.0004

60   ORI J HERSTEIN

an assumption about one having tried to succeed. Yet, here I aim to explore reasons to try-to-φ and their relation to reasons to successfully-φ also in those cases where successful φ-ing does *not* require trying or intending to φ.[2] Accordingly, to avoid confusion I will not always use "success" talk when discussing (successfully) φ-ing, and will take "reason to succeed-at-φ-ing" to simply mean "reason to φ."

One should resist viewing all reasons to try-to-φ in terms of reasons to (successfully) φ. While it is obviously possible to describe any instance of trying-to-φ as an instance of succeeding—namely as cases of successfully trying-to-φ—this is a *non sequitur*. In order to truly reduce all trying to succeeding, what is required is that all instances of trying-to-φ be reducible to instances of success at φ-ing, which is clearly a non-starter. Success at trying-to-φ is not necessarily an instance of successful φ-ing, given that it is possible to (successfully) try-to-φ and still fail to φ. The same is true, *mutatis mutandis*, of *reasons* to φ and of *reasons* to try-to-φ. While all reasons to try-to-φ just are reasons to succeed-at-*trying*-to-φ, not all reasons to try-to-φ are instances of reasons to succeed-at-φ-ing. In fact, as is explained later in this chapter, reasons to try-to-φ are often grounded in values other than the value of φ-ing, even allowing for cases in which there is reason to try-to-φ without a reason to succeed-at-φ-ing.

Finally, that there is reason to φ does not necessarily entail that one *ought* to φ. It does not even entail that one has strong reason to φ. This is important to emphasize given that this chapter is devoted to pointing out the wide scope of reasons to try and their grounding values, which might invite the mistake of assuming that I endorse trying in all cases in which I identify a reason to do so. I do not. This chapter is devoted to expanding our appreciation of the reasons bearing on whether or not we ought to try to do certain things, not on the bottom line of whether or not—given all the relevant considerations—we indeed ought (or may, or ought not, etc) to try to do any one of those things in any particular case.

3. Reasons to Try and the Law

It is illuminating to reflect upon reasons to try not only in the abstract but also through their manifestation in specific and across normative realms. Of particular interest to me are the realms of morality and law, examples from which appear throughout the chapter.

Looking to law, one should appreciate that laws providing *legal* reason to try-to-φ come with a cost. Given that trying assumes intending, such laws amount to mandating not only the conduct involved in an act of trying-to-φ but also mandate coupling that conduct with certain specific mental states, namely intending to act with the purpose of achieving some outcome. Such laws, therefore, constitute legal directives—typically stigmatizing as well as enforceable through censure, liability, or sanction—to hold a specific mental state.

To appreciate the concern with laws mandating specific mental states, consider first laws that forbid them. Legal prohibitions on specific mental states are widely

---

[2] For more on this, see RA Duff, "Cliff-top Predicaments and Morally Blemished Lives" (2019) 19 Jerusalem Review of Legal Studies 125, 126.

considered anathema to liberal values, mostly falling well outside the purview of legitimate state power. Imposing obligations and sanctioning people purely for having certain thoughts or intentions can significantly interfere with personal privacy, autonomy, and agency, as well as with the freedoms of thought and conscience.

Still, as problematic as laws *prohibiting* specific mental states are, laws *mandating* specific mental states are potentially worse. Laws prohibiting a specific mental state still provide liberty to embrace any and all other mental states that are not forbidden. Of course, the broader these prohibitions become and the more of them you have, the less liberty remains. Yet, at least when taken in isolation, laws exhibiting the logic of specific prohibitions assume a normative backdrop or default of liberty. In contrast, laws exhibiting the logic of specific mandates are bans on all other relevant options— they are the type of laws fitting the appetites of totalitarianism.

Moreover, the type of mental state required by mandates to try impacts personal agency in a fairly robust way. Intending to try involves acting with what the law calls a "specific intent," which involves volitionally ψ-ing with the intention of thereby φ-ing. Accordingly, a mandate to try directs not only what one must do but also how one ought to guide one's own actions in doing so. This seems particularly offensive to the inviolability of personal agency.

Notice that the concern with laws mandating specific mental states is not mitigated by the law's frequent *prohibitions* on the coupling of certain specific actions with certain specific mental states, as is the case in much of criminal law. Such laws *do not mandate* coupling specific actions with specific mental states. Rather, they merely *prohibit* certain specific couplings, allowing all others. Hence, their proliferation and apparent legitimacy in law does not directly bear on the matter of legal reasons to try.

I do not mean to sound overly alarmist. A legal system can remain legitimate even recognizing or imposing the occasional legal duty to try, as do all legal systems, to some degree. For instance, courts allow as well as enforce contractual clauses mandating trying, such as "best efforts" clauses. Another example of arguably justifiable legal duties to try are norms directing legal officials to try to carry out their duties with certain aspirations. Mine, therefore, is an argument from degree, prescribing an economical use of such norms in law.

And still, laws mandating coupling actions with specific mental states are not the ideal building blocks of a liberal legal system. Thus, while it is perhaps understandable for morality or religion to mandate, for example, that thou "*love* thy God" or "*honor* thy parents," this is something that civil law should probably mostly shy away from. As a rule of thumb, while morality may merit and even demand of us specific mental states, people's specific thoughts, attitudes, sentiments, values, and intentions are mostly best left outside the purview of legal obligation. When it comes to legal norms, it is, therefore, mostly advisable to adhere to the creed of "render[ing] unto Caesar the things that are Caesar's, and unto God the things that are God's."[3]

Legal mandates to φ can trigger non-legal reasons, including reasons to try-to-φ.[4] Actually, this is fairly common. Perhaps most obviously, a legal norm to φ can trigger

---

[3] The Bible, *Matthew* 22:20–22, King James Version (Chrtitian Art Publishers 2016).

[4] On how facts (including the fact of a legal norm) can trigger moral norms see D Enoch, "Reason-Giving and the Law" (2011) 1 Oxford Studies in the Philosophy of Law 1.

a *prudential* reason to try-to-φ as a means of avoiding negative legal consequences for having failed to φ. Similarly, a legal norm can trigger *moral* reasons. For instance, in those cases where we have moral reason to obey the law's directives, we often also have a derivative moral reason to try to do so as a means of doing so. This is perhaps most salient in the case of legal norms that are *mala prohibita*, so that had the law not directed us to φ we would have had no moral reason to do so. It is the legality of such norms (or some closely related implication of a norm's legality) that triggers the moral reason to comply with them—reasons from which may derive moral reasons to *try*-to-comply.

Gardner's discussion of strict liability in private law offers a helpful example for fleshing out the complex relations between law and non-legal reasons to try.[5] Strict liability for φ-ing does not involve a legal reason to try-to-avoid- φ-ing. Indeed, strict liability for φ-ing attaches regardless of whether and to what extent one tried to avoid φ-ing. In contrast, as with all obligations, legal obligations imposing strict liability for φ-ing obviously do involve legal reasons to avoid φ-ing. In this respect, as Gardner points out, strict liability law involves legal reasons to succeed, not to try. That said, strict liability laws can trigger *non*-legal reasons to try-to-φ in those cases where trying to avoid φ-ing is an effective means for not φ-ing.

Yet, while perhaps common, it is noteworthy that this is not always the case. In fact, under certain circumstances trying to avoid φ-ing is actually counterproductive. This is nicely demonstrated by Gardner's example of the overcautious driver, whose excessive efforts at driving with care only make him more of a menace.[6] Thus, while given the law the driver has non-legal reasons to avoid causing an accident, he does not, at least from a certain point, thereby also have a non-legal reason to *try* to avoid an accident.[7] Accordingly, rules imposing strict liability for φ-ing can trigger prudential and moral reasons to try-to-avoid-φ-ing. Yet, at the point from which more trying becomes self-defeating, the law ceases triggering such non-legal reasons to try. Indeed, at that point the law begins triggering a non-legal reason to *not*-to-try-to-avoid-φ-ing (which is not a reason to try but rather a reason to succeed at not trying).

Am I being overly formalistic? If in order to conform to the law's obligations one is left with little choice—morally or prudentially—but for trying to φ, thereby embracing a certain specific attitude, intent, or other mental state, then, does not my call to keep law relatively light on express requirements for such mental states rest, at the end of the day, on a distinction without a practical difference? Worse still, does such formal purity not risk concealing the reality of law's trespasses against the same liberal values that I set out to protect?

All I can say here is that, holding all else equal, laws triggering *non*-legal reasons to try-to-φ do not seem to raise some of the same type or extent of difficulties briefly discussed earlier with positive and expressive *legal* reasons to try. It seems important that the law, where possible, mostly stay out of our agency and provide space for

---

[5] J Gardner, *Torts and Other Wrongs* (OUP 2019) 133–51 ("*TAOW*").

[6] ibid 138.

[7] This example assumes a legal regime of strict liability for injuries caused in car accidents, more typical of civil law systems.

avoiding breaching legal duties not only through acting with the specific intention of acting as the law mandates (*de re*) but also through luck, instinct, subconscious drive, habit, and for the grace of others. Moreover, it is exactly in the face of tyranny that conformity without conviction allows for preserving something of an inner citadel for the self, free of compulsion. Finally, I expect that there is a slippery slope concern lurking somewhere here. Because once law is allowed robustly, expressly, and directly to partake in the business of mandating, nudging, incentivizing, and enforcing specific mental states, and once legal status turns more and more on what we are legally required to intend, wish, believe, think, and value, things are liable to get very bleak very fast.

Next, I turn to my primary end of exploring different types of values of trying and the reasons that they give rise to.

4. Trying as a Means to an End

Success is counted sweetest
By those who ne'er succeed.
To comprehend a nectar
Requires sorest need.

Emily Dickinson, Success is Counted Sweetest (1859)

One primary type of ground for reasons to try-to-φ is the value of trying as a means toward some valuable end. Here are four such cases.

4.1 Trying-to-φ as a means of φ-ing

Obviously, reasons to try follow from reasons to succeed when trying is advantageous toward succeeding. The end, if you will, wills the means. Examples of reasons to try deriving from reasons to succeed are numerous. For instance, given that a student has reason to do well on her exams, and given that typically the best (legitimate) way to do well on exams is to try (within reason) to do well on one's exams, the student's reason to succeed on her exams gives rise to a reason to try to do so, as a means toward such success. Or, given that I have reason to be a good father and given that capable parenthood typically requires some effort, presumably I thereby also have a moral reason to try to become a good father as a means toward successfully attaining the end of good fatherhood. More generally, many moral reasons to *try* to act for the benefit of others in need—such as the moral duty to try to rescue a person in peril—are often partially derivatives of one's moral reasons to succeed in benefiting those others.

64   ORI J HERSTEIN

What about the law? Notwithstanding my worries about legal reasons to try, as already granted some such legal norms seem perfectly fine. For example, consider the oath of office for the Presidency of the United States:

> I do solemnly swear (or affirm) that I will faithfully execute the Office of President of the United States, and will to the best of my ability, preserve, protect and defend the Constitution of the United States.[8]

The oath involves a self-imposed quasi-legal obligation to do one's best, that is to *try* to one's utmost ability to preserve, protect, and defend the Constitution, and, presumably part of the justification for this legal duty to try is the value of the president actually *succeeding* in doing so. The same is likely true of the grounds of many other norms giving legal reasons to try.

4.2 Trying-to-φ as aspiration toward φ-ing

Both Gardner and Ulrike Heuer appear to subscribe to what Kimberley Brownlee has labeled the "sufficiency condition" for having reasons to try,[9] which is that reasons to try-to-φ can only derive from reasons to φ if trying will (ultimately) or, at the very least, in some sense *can* yield success at φ-ing.[10] Challenging this view, Brownlee points out that the sufficiency condition rules out reasons to try to pursue what I will label "aspirational values" which, by definition, are never fully attainable. The example that Brownlee focuses on are ideals, which she understands as models of excellence one can orient one's conduct and thinking toward, but never fully attain. And still, she plausibly claims, we can have reasons to try to realize ideals, even if not fully realizable. For example, a pianist can have reason to try to become the consummate pianist, even if that is an unattainable goal. Now, the value of trying to achieve an ideal as a form of aspiration is likely rich and complex. Yet, likely often part of the value of trying is its role in improving conformity with the ideal, even if never fully attaining it.

In law, aspirational norms are perhaps rare, yet they do exist. Such norms can give legal reasons to aspire to realize certain ends, even when the law itself presents those ends as not fully realizable. Accordingly, aspirational legal norms can give legal reasons to *try* to pursue a certain ideal, as well as trigger non-legal reasons to do so. Here's an example. Law can exhibit what we may label background or meta-legal reasons to try. Without stepping into the thicket of general jurisprudence and the debate over the nature of law, legal systems—in their prouder moments—typically aspire toward the loftiest of values, such as truth and justice. Of course, no legal system is ever perfect in this regard. Yet, at least ideally, legal systems in a sense expect and even implicitly direct legal officials (judges, prosecutors, governmental legal counsel, as well as rank and file lawyers) to aspire—that is, to try—toward such perfection.

---

[8] US Const. art II, § 1, cl. 8.

[9] J Gardner, "The Wrongdoing that Gets Results" (2004) 18 Philosophical Perspectives 53, 55; U Heuer, "Reasons and Impossibility" (2008) 147 Philosophical Studies 235, 244.

[10] Brownlee, "Reasons and Ideals" (n 1) 437.

4.3 Trying-to-φ as a means toward ends other than φ-ing

Trying can also serve as a means toward attaining ends other than the end that one is trying to achieve. After all, frequently "life is what happens to you while you're busy making other plans."[11] For instance, the primary value of young children trying to win at team sports is less the end of winning any particular game or tournament, but is rather found more in the health and developmental benefits, as well as the social skills and character traits that engaging in team sports can foster. Thus, while in order to wholeheartedly engage in team sports one must play with a genuine aim of winning, the value of *trying* to win is only partially explained by the value of winning.[12] In qualifying trying as "genuine" I aim to emphasize that trying means just that. So that a reason to try-to-φ in a sense means reason to try-to-φ-with-the-aim-of-φ-ing. For example, accepting that wholehearted engagement in team sports requires trying to win, and given the value that playing team sports has for one, it follows that in playing team sports one has a reason to *really* try to win. Accordingly, given the key role that trying has in realizing the aforementioned ends of playing team sports, although one's reason to try-to-φ (ie to try to win) derives from one's reason to ψ (eg to learn how to cope with losing), it is not reducible to it—one must really and genuinely try to do one thing (φ) in order to succeed at something else (ψ); thus, the derivative reason of one's reason to ψ is not a reason to try-to-ψ but rather a reason to try-to-φ.

Moving to another example, is there reason to try to rescue others even when there is no chance of success? Unsurprisingly, this question has drawn the attention of the literature on reasons to try,[13] as the context of rescue brings into focus a more general moral question pertaining to reasons to try: are there *moral* reasons to try to act for the benefit of others, independent of the likelihood of thereby succeeding in benefiting them? Illustrative is Jennifer Hornsby's example of having a reason to try to rescue a drowning man, even when one knows that success is in fact impossible—a reason arising, according to Hornsby, not from the value of a successful attempt at rescuing but from the value of being perceived to have tried.[14] In other words, for Hornsby it is the communicative value of trying to come to the aid of others which can give reason to do so.

Following on the example from Hornsby, does law communicate valuably by providing *legal* reasons to try? One such instance arises from the aforementioned notion that, at least ideally, legal systems ideally and even typically provide legal officials with legal reasons to pursue values such as truth and justice in carrying out their official roles. In adopting such aspirational values, a legal system communicates a most valuable message to the general public: that even if imperfect, the officials populating the

---

[11] J Lennon, "Beautiful Boy (Darling Boy)" (*Double Fantasy*, 17 November 1980). Originally attributed to A Saunders, see "Life Is What Happens to You While You're Busy Making Other Plans" (*Quote Investigator*, May 6, 2012) <https://quoteinvestigator.com/2012/05/06/other-plans/> accessed July 12, 2021.

[12] For a similar analysis in the context of the presumed value of teamwork, see LD Katz, "The Intrinsic Value of Teamwork: Reinterpreting Gardner" (2019) 19 Jerusalem Review of Legal Studies 187, 193.

[13] More on this type of scenario at section 5.4 of this chapter.

[14] J Hornsby, "On What's Intentionally Done" in S Shute, J Gardner, and J Horder (eds), *Action and Value in Criminal Law* (OUP 1993).

legal system mean well and are expected to try their best. This message is important for assuring public trust in the legal system. In addition, and what is perhaps less obvious, is the importance of this message for the victims of the law's many imperfections. Even the best of legal systems let some people down, distorting their story or failing to avert, ameliorate, or even directly perpetrating an injustice against them. Believing that one's case was an aberration, and that the system is basically oriented toward truth and justice, may, for some, provide a measure of solace, renewed trust, and mitigation in the understandable sense of betrayal, isolation, and alienation from the law, the state, and from the public which they represent.

4.4 Reason to fail-to-φ-by-trying-to-φ

At times, the value of trying is wrapped up in the instrumental value of failing, such as when trying-and-failing serves as a means for enhancing one's appreciation for having succeeded, if and when such success is later achieved. And even if this reason to try-and-fail does not always override one's related reasons to succeed, it is a reason nonetheless; a reason detected in the meaningfulness and unique joy that comes with success that follows failure; boons enhanced and perhaps even made possible only if one's past failures were not for want of trying to succeed. I am reminded of a statement by Michael Jordan, given upon winning his first of six NBA championships and following years of falling short of that mark: "This has been a seven-year struggle for me ... I don't know if I'll ever have this same feeling again."[15] Relatedly, this possible instrumental value of failing-by-trying entails cases in which there is reason to try-to-φ even when one has no real chance of success, so long as failing-by-trying *now* serves as a means for enhancing the value of succeeding later.

4.5 Reasons to try-not-to-try

Not all reasons incorporating "trying" in their description are reasons to try. For instance, reasons to not-try-to-φ are not reasons to try but rather reasons to succeed; namely, to succeed at not trying. Moreover, such reasons do not necessarily even trigger or give rise to reasons to try. Because, depending on the context, one may avoid trying-to-φ without trying. In fact, there are many things that we ought not to try to do, which we succeed in not trying to do without ever trying not to try to do them(!)

In the law, for instance, crimes of attempt give legal reason to not-to-try-to-commit certain crimes. Yet, not only are these legal reasons to *succeed* (at not trying) and not reasons to try (not-to-try), they usually do not even trigger moral or prudential reasons to try (not-to-try). We are constantly blissfully unaware of our daily effortless success at not committing a slew of crimes of attempts. Thus, for most people, most of the time, not committing most crimes requires neither effort nor awareness.

---

[15] C Brown, "Jordan Transformed" *New York Times* (New York, June 16, 1991).

That said, reasons to not-to-try-to-φ give rise to or trigger reasons to *try*-not-to-try-to-φ in those cases where trying is a means toward not-trying-to-φ. Returning to the example of criminal law, for people inclined or driven to try to commit a crime, crimes of attempts often do trigger prudential as well as moral reasons to try-not-to-try.

Other types of reasons to-try-not-to-try become apparent when noticing that some ends become unrealizable through their own pursuit and are, therefore, only achievable as side effects of pursuing some other ends. In fact, as already demonstrated above in the example of the driver, pursuing certain ends is even counterproductive to obtaining them. Indeed, under such conditions not only does a reason to φ not give rise to a derivative reason to try-to-φ, but it can actually yield a derivative reason to not-to-try-to-φ and perhaps even a reason to try-not-to-try-to-φ. Other examples are trying to impress people, or trying to be funny, or trying to make oneself popular, all of which might yield the opposite effect.[16]

Happiness is another such example. The road to happiness involves less pursuing it by trying to be happy and more through engaging—genuinely and for their own sake—in happiness-fostering projects, relationships, and activities. Thus, while one may pursue happiness as an overarching end, in order to succeed one must genuinely engage in activities that foster happiness but do not, in and of themselves, incorporate the active pursuit of happiness as part of the activity. To achieve happiness one must, therefore, bracket one's overarching end of happiness when pursuing it through pursuing other ends. Now, for citizens of Western capitalist societies, believing in the pursuit of personal happiness is almost dogma. Indeed, the US Declaration of Independence actually enshrines the "pursuit of happiness" as an unalienable and Godly-endowed right of all.[17] For those of us who are the products of this culture it is sometimes difficult not to engage in the futile endeavor of actively and directly pursuing our own happiness. Accordingly, assuming that we have an interest in our own happiness, we have reason to actively try-to-not-to-pursue (ie try to)-happiness.

5. Trying as an End: The Intrinsic Value of Trying

> If in life's great, onward battle
> You have done your best and lost,
> If amid the din and rattle
> You regarded not the cost,
> If you met your foeman bravely,
> If you dared to do or die,
> God will credit you, most surely,
> For your fearless, honest try.
>
> William Henry Dawson, *God will Count Your Honest Try* (1910)

Ours is an efficiency obsessed age. And unsurprisingly, the appreciation and evaluation of acts of trying is regularly reduced solely to their contribution as means toward

---

[16] J Gardner, "Reason and Impossibility" (2002) 8 Legal Theory 495, 495.
[17] The Declaration of Independence (US 1776).

some valuable end. As has been attributed to WC Fields: "[i]f at first you don't succeed, try, try again. Then quit. There's no point in being a damn fool about it." Accordingly, Gardner's use of the term "success" is apt exactly because of its somewhat obnoxious "go-getting" undertones, capturing something of this devaluation.

Yet, trying is valuable not only as a means of production. And the same is likely to be true of related actions, such as striving, aspiring, devoting, toiling, and persevering. In this respect, like much of analytic philosophy devoted to clarifying aspects of the normative landscape, the analysis of reasons to try and their relation to reasons to succeed is not only theoretically explanatory but also aspires to serve as an exercise in self-knowledge, aiming toward a fuller appreciation of the value of our actions. Moreover, gaining a richer appreciation for trying is a form of inoculation against the prevailing purely utilitarian and overly pragmatic notions of its value.

5.1 Trying to φ as a form of φ-ing

Sometimes trying to φ just *is* to succeed at φ-ing. What I have in mind are cases where trying to φ is—in and of itself—a manifestation of φ-ing. And when that is the case, if there is reason to φ there is also *ipso facto* reason to try-to-φ; a reason that is satisfied by one's trying (even if one fails to succeed). For instance, striving toward good fatherhood is not only typically an effective means toward attaining that end, it is also—in and of itself—a partial realization of that end. Such striving exhibits the attitude, care, and regard of a good father. So that striving to improve as a parent is to manifest the virtue of good parenthood. Deploying the language of "reasons"—reasons in favor of good fatherhood just are reasons for striving (ie trying) toward good fatherhood.

5.2 Succeeding-by-trying

Trying to φ can be a *constituent* of φ-ing. Here, unlike in the section above, to try is not in and of itself to succeed, but rather *part* of what constitutes success. Put differently, while in the previous section trying was sufficient (although not necessary) for succeeding, here trying is necessary (although not sufficient). Thus, in such cases if there is reason to φ there is also reason to try to φ as part and parcel of the reason to φ.

For instance, Gardner explores what he calls "reasons for succeeding-by-trying,"[18] which are found in many contexts. For an example, Gardner points out that reasons for winning at most games are reasons to win-by-trying-to-win. Indeed, certainly when approaching playing a game from the game's internal point of view, the idea of winning without trying involves a distortion of the concept of winning; winning by its very nature involves having tried to win. In such cases, when fleshed out, reasons to win just are reasons to succeed-in-one's-attempt-at-winning. Given this, if one has reason to win one thereby has reason to try to win. Accordingly, trying is a constituent of winning so that if winning is of value, so is trying.

---

[18] Gardner "The Wrongdoing that Gets Results" (n 9) 53.

What about legal rules providing *legal* reasons to succeed-by-trying? Keeping with my skepticism of legal reasons to try, my sense is that such laws are scarce, and that we are likely to be better off for it. Gardner, however, can be understood to have thought otherwise, having argued that the duty of care found in the tort of negligence has the form of a duty to try; relatedly, for Gardner the tort of negligence more generally (including its duty of care) has the form of a duty to succeed-by-trying. I'll explain why.

Let's begin with the duty of care. Four elements comprise the tort of negligence: duty of care; breach of that duty; harm to the person to whom that duty is owed; and a causal connection between the breach and the harm. Gardner's view is that the "duty of care" element in negligence is a duty to try.[19] Accordingly, here to "take care" is to: (i) act (reasonably) with (ii) the view, aim, or intent of thereby averting causing harm. For Gardner the duty of care is, therefore, a duty not only to act in a way that generates only reasonable risk (to those one owes the duty) but also to thereby positively "engage in a certain kind of mental activity."[20]

From Gardner's conception of the duty of care it follows that the tort of negligence involves a legal duty to succeed-by-trying. At its core, the tort of negligence as a whole involves a duty not to harm carelessly. And, therefore, liability in negligence only attaches to those who carelessly cause harm to someone to whom they owed a duty to take care not to do so. As we saw, according to Gardner "acting with care" means *trying* to avoid harming, which involves a conjunction of acting reasonably while intending to do so. Thus, if we accept Gardner's account of the duty of care as a duty to try, it would seem that the tort of negligence as a whole involves a duty to not-φ-by-not-(reasonably)trying-not-to-φ (where "φ-ing" stands for harming), which is a duty to succeed-by-trying.

If right, this picture raises a challenge for the law of negligence. As discussed above, laws mandating trying-to-φ are worrisome given that they involve a legal mandate to have a specific mental state. And in the case of the tort of negligence, this worry is amplified given that if the duty of care is indeed a duty to try, it comes close to a legal mandate to hold certain moral attitudes and even sentiments. After all, Gardner's duty of care is a duty to act with the aim and intention of (reasonably) caring for the interests of others. This seems in tension with liberal limits on legal obligations, especially considering the extraordinarily wide reach of the tort of negligence into numerous facets of people's lives.

Gardner's conception of the duty of care entails a revisionary conception of the tort of negligence. Or so it seems to me. Because in a way, Gardner effectively reverses foundational assumptions about the tort of negligence as reflected, for example, in Lord Atkin's seminal construction of the duty of care in *Donoghue v Stevenson*.[21] As you may recall, Atkin's maneuver is to construct a general legal principle of negligence from the various specific pockets of negligence liability found in the common law of the period. That general legal principle, according to Atkin, is an articulation of a general *moral* principle into legal form, fashioned to fit the contours and limitations of

---

[19] See eg *TAOW* (n 5) 139.
[20] J Gardner, "The Purity and Priority of Private Law" (1996) 46 University of Toronto Law Journal 459, 486.
[21] *Donoghue v Stevenson* [1932] UKHL 100, [1932] AC 562 (HL).

70 ORI J HERSTEIN

a legal system. The general moral principle Atkin has in mind is the Judeo-Christian edict that "you are to love your neighbour" which, in law, takes the form of negligence's duty of care. As Atkin puts it:

> The rule that you are to love your neighbour becomes in law, you must not injure your neighbour; and the lawyer's question, "Who is my neighbour?" receives a restricted reply. You must take reasonable care to avoid acts or omissions which you can reasonably foresee would be likely to injure ....[22]

Atkin's account of negligence law as a "translation" of a moral duty of love into a legal duty to take reasonable precautions to avoid causing reasonably foreseeable harm is, if you will, the epitome of rendering "unto Caesar only the things which are Caesar's." It constructs legal liability so that it turns not on the defendant's actual mental state— that is what one actually did or did not "foresee"—but rather on what one could have *reasonably* foreseen. Moreover, Atkin's formulation of negligence is oriented toward the reasonableness of one's actions or omissions, not of one's mental states.

Gardner, however, can be interpreted as reading Atkin's "take reasonable care to avoid acts or omissions" to incorporate not only conduct but also its accompanying mental states. In articulating negligence as a legal mandate for acting with a type of moral regard for others (or at least with a regard for their interests), Gardner effectively turns some of the moral duty of love into legal obligation, thereby "rendering unto Caesar" a good measure of what liberalism favors keeping outside the jurisdiction of the state.

Thankfully, these worries only arise if Gardner's description of the duty of care is accurate, of which I have doubts.[23] In a nutshell, imagine a defendant who not only did not intend to act carefully, but actually wholeheartedly intended to act carelessly and with the hope of harming others; yet, his efforts notwithstanding, unbeknownst to him he failed and ended up acting reasonably safely. Let's further assume that had he lived up to Gardner's duty to try, his conduct would have been more than reasonably safe, to the extent of assuring that his conduct could in no way harm the person to whom he had owed the duty of care. Under Gardner's account of the duty of care, were the reasonably safe actions of this defendant to harm the person to whom he owed care, he would be liable in negligence. This is because the defendant's breach of her duty of care—failing to try—would have caused harm to the person to whom he owed the duty. Nevertheless, contrary to the implications of Gardner account, the fact is that such a defendant is likely not liable in negligence as a matter of law, even if his reasonable conduct did happen to cause harm to the person to whom he had owed a duty of care. Accordingly, as a matter of law it seems that such a defendant acted reasonably, not breaching his duty of care; demonstrating that the duty of care in the tort

---

[22] ibid 580.

[23] OJ Herstein, "Responsibility in Negligence: Why the Duty of Care is not a Duty to Try" (2010) 23 Canadian Journal of Law and Jurisprudence 403. At one point it seemed that Gardner had taken on my critique. See J Gardner, "The Negligence Standard: Political Not Metaphysical" (2017) 80 The Modern Law Review 1, 31 (Gardner "The Negligence Standard: Political Not Metaphysical"). Yet later, Gardner may have reverted back to his original view. See *TAOW* (n 5) 215.

of negligence is not a duty to try but rather a duty to succeed. From which it follows that as a whole, the tort of negligence does not involve a duty to succeed-by-trying.

Yet, what if it turned out that there are other central norms of private law exhibiting the form of a duty to try and, more generally, directing people to have specific mental states? Would this not erode my argument against Gardner's view of the duty of care? Perhaps in some way it would. Moreover, it would certainly cut against my general objection to over-proliferation of such legal norms, as it would disprove my semi-dystopic projection. Some obvious candidates for legal obligations to try and, more generally, for having specific mental states, seem to include the legal duties of guardians and the duty of good faith such as in the performance or negotiation toward contract.

In fact, while the question of whether or not the duty of care in negligence involves a duty to try has received little scholarly attention, there is a similar yet more robust debate regarding the legal duties of fiduciaries. Framed in Gardner's terms, some view the duties of fiduciaries as essentially legal duties to try (ie intend) to act for the benefit of the beneficiary.[24] While others present a contrary view of fiduciary duties that is, at least to an extent, more along the lines of a duty to succeed.[25]

Whether these legal norms constitute mostly duties to try or objective duties to succeed (which is what I expect), exploring this matter is well beyond the scope of this essay. That said, it is worth gesturing toward this matter as it suggests that Gardner's distinction between reasons to try and reasons to succeed may track a fundamental tension or issue cutting across private law.

5.3 Trying as a constituent of value

Trying to φ is at times a constituent of something else which has value, so that failure to try to φ entails the dilution or even the complete dissolution (or non-constitution) of the value it is a constituent of. Hence, unlike in the section above, here trying to φ is not a constituent of φ-ing but of some other value.

Here is an example of the constitutive relation I have in mind. Arguably, friendship is valuable as such, while fidelity is not. In the case of fidelity, we would likely want to hear more about to what and to whom one is showing fidelity before we are ready to label it valuable. Fidelity to your spouse—good; fidelity to a members only

---

[24] For instance, focusing on the duty of loyalty, Stephen Galoob and Ethan Leib argue that a "fiduciary obligation characteristically shapes the fiduciary's deliberation vis-à-vis her beneficiary in a particular way. A fiduciary whose deliberation is not shaped in this way does not live up to her fiduciary obligation, no matter what else she does.' S Galoob and E Leib, "Intentions, Compliance, and Fiduciary Obligations" (2014) 20 Legal Theory 106. Along similar lines, Lionel Smith has argued that "the heart of the fiduciary obligation is the surveillance and the justiciability of motive. Whatever powers a fiduciary has, he must exercise them … with a particular motive. He must act … in what he perceives to be the best interests of the beneficiary." L Smith, "The Motive, Not the Deed" in J Getzler (ed), *Rationalizing Property, Equity, and Trusts: Essays in Honour of Edward Burn* (OUP 2003) 53.

[25] Paul Miller, for instances, claims that "[t]he no conflict rule, for example, requires only that fiduciaries avoid situations of conflict of interest or duty. The rule does not require that the fiduciary adopt a particular state of mind (i.e., hold certain beliefs, have certain feelings, weigh certain reasons in a particular way, and so on)." PB Miller, "Dimensions of Fiduciary Loyalty" in DG Smith and AS Gold (eds), *Research Handbook on Fiduciary Law* (Elgar 2018) 180.

72 ORI J HERSTEIN

racist organization—not so much. That said, fidelity is a constituent of friendship—forsaking or betraying a friend *ipso facto* dwindles and even undercuts the friendship. Fidelity to one's friends is, therefore, intrinsically valuable as a constituent of friendship.

Trying to φ can have this sort of constitutive value. Here to, the value of trying is most easily isolated in those cases where trying is futile or is at least likely to fail. For example, there is a certain nobility to sticking by one's mates or to toiling together toward a common goal, even when futile or facing overwhelming odds. This value of trying partly derives from its role as a constituent of one's valuable group affiliation or of one's comradery and friendship. The assumption being that even if futile, if you do not "go down with the ship," or "fight till the last bullet," or "show up when it counts most," etc, you are not a full member of the group, not a true friend, etc.

As is assumed throughout this chapter, value can beget reasons. And here to, the constitutive value of one's trying gives rise to a reason in favor of doing so. Which is a reason grounded in the (constitutive) value of trying itself, and not at all in the value of succeeding.

5.4 The expressive value of trying

According to Michelle Dempsey trying can exhibit expressive value, giving rise to reasons to try, and this is true whether or not trying to φ is futile as a means of φ-ing, and whether or not one is aware of that futility.[26] Gardner's view is less clear on this point.[27] I agree with Dempsey. The following few paragraphs aim to convince through examples.

But first, what is expressive value? A working conception sufficient for our purposes is to look at expressive actions that have value *vis-à-vis* or as a manifestation of the value that they express. And as for the specific matter of reasons to try, I would say that we have reason to express a value through an act of trying (ie we have an expressive reason to try) when said trying is valuable *vis-à-vis* or as a manifestation of the value that it expresses.

Imagine walking along a deserted cliff-top by the ocean, spotting a drowning swimmer in the stormy waters below. You realize that there is absolutely nothing that you can realistically do to save him.[28] Let's further assume that neither the swimmer nor anyone else is aware of your presence. Do you have reason to try to save the swimmer? As mentioned, Gardner seems to claim that you do not, because you are

---

[26] MM Dempsey, "What We Have Reason to Do: Another View from the Cliff-Top" (2019) 19 Jerusalem Review of Legal Studies 141, 145.

[27] On the one hand, he did seem to recognize expressive reasons to try. See Gardner "The Wrongdoing that Gets Results" (n 9) 57. Yet, on the other hand, Gardner was clear that at least when one is aware of the futility of trying to rescue others, one does not have a reason to try to do so. *See* J Gardner, *From Personal Life to Private Law* (OUP 2018) 145 ("*FPLPL*").

[28] The example is one that Gardner returned to several times. See eg J Gardner, "Justifications and Reasons" in J Gardner (ed), *Offences and Defenses* (OUP 2007) 93; J Gardner, "Obligations and Outcomes in the Law of Torts" in P Cane and J Gardner (eds), *Relating to Responsibility*)2001) 137; Gardner, "The Wrongdoing that Gets Results" (n 9) 55; *FPLPL* (n 27) at 145.

aware that trying would be futile. This notwithstanding, Dempsey convincingly fleshes out how trying to rescue the swimmer, even under such dire and hopeless conditions, can have expressive value, giving rise to a reason to do so:

> Any observer would have success-independent, expressive reasons to try to save the drowning man, simply because he is suffering, a human life is being lost, and the observer is well-positioned to serve as a witness to this tragedy and express the horror of such facts. The expression of horror, through a futile attempt to save him ... pays respect to the tragedy unfolding below and thus respects the value of the man's life, the disvalue of his suffering, etc.[29]

Now, the cliff-top scenario is both helpful and limiting for exploring the expressive value of trying. It is helpful because it clears out some obvious (and therefore less theoretically interesting) possible grounds for reasons to try to come to the aid of another, such as providing an example for others or giving the drowning swimmer a sense that he is not forsaken. In clearing out such reasons, the scenario brings into focus the question of whether there is any intrinsic value to a (knowingly) futile attempt to aid others in peril. Nevertheless, the example is also limiting, because it narrows the scope of the question to the very specific and rather rare scenario. If trying to help others in dire need can indeed have expressive value, that value surely is at play in numerous other more common (be they less "clean") types of cases, where the value of trying is varied and where the grounds of one's reasons to try are many, including expressive value.

But before turning to a few such examples, a word about the modality they assume. The way the debate on reasons to try is set up is to ask whether trying is valuable even if success is in some sense impossible. Yet, modal terms (such as "possible," "impossible," and "necessary") are notoriously beguiling. Derek Parfit labels cases that are impossible on account of the laws of nature "deeply impossible."[30] There are, however, impossibilities that are, as Heuer puts it, "shallow,"[31] in the sense that they can be overcome in later situations (eg while I can't play the piano, it is not impossible for me to come to learn how to play in the future). And Parfit also discusses impossibilities that are as he puts it "technical," that is more a matter of factual contingency than of physics (or, for that matter, metaphysics or human nature).[32] Now, the notion that one can have reason to try to do that which is "deeply impossible" might, to some, seem especially puzzling, even more so perhaps where one is aware of the impossibility. Accordingly, the examples below purposely aim at a range of modalities, ranging from the shallow to the very deep.

Imagine that you have a close friend who divorced her spouse months after they had a baby. A custody battle ensued. While the spouse proves abusive to the child, your friend is continuingly unable to convince the courts to grant her sole custody of the child. Moreover, there is simply no chance that she will ever succeed in extracting

---

[29] Dempsey, "What We Have Reason to Do" (n 26) 146.
[30] D Parfit, *Reasons and Persons* (OUP 1984) 119.
[31] Heuer, "Reasons and Impossibility" (n 9) 237.
[32] Parfit, *Reasons and Persons* (n 30) 119.

the child from the clutches of that abusive environment. The spouse is just too clever and too gifted a liar, the abuse too obscure and unfathomable, the court too aloof, and the child welfare authorities too overworked. No matter, your friend felt obliged to engage in a decade-long court battle that she was sure to lose, spending all her money, handicapping her career, neglecting her own health and social circle, and immersing herself and those closest to her in a never-ending circle of emotional mire. Yet, all this notwithstanding, your friend feels that she cannot but stay the course and keep trying. Or think how, upon hearing of a friend's advanced terminal illness, is there really no point to one's silent prayer for a miraculous recovery, even if one is a non-believer?[33] Or, imagine that the good name of a gifted film-maker who is a childhood hero of yours is being publicly besmirched, his career destroyed, and his artistic contribution and legacy erased, all on the grounds of what you confidently believe are false allegations. What if, in a moment of frustration, you were to take to Twitter and, in an attempt at changing global public opinion, tweet "#he'sInnocent" to all your 83 followers, fully aware that your efforts will have less of an impact than a cricket holding its breath has on a hurricane. Similar expressive arguments are presumably also available in support of reasons we have to try to bring about social change through political activism or voting.

These knowingly futile attempts at rescuing, or promoting the good, or assisting others in peril all strike me as reasonable. That is, they are not only intelligible but also seem fitting and appropriate. They are, in other words, responsive to reasons. Namely, they are responsive to reasons to try, where trying is expressive of those values that ground these reasons to try, such as: expressing (the value of) nonwavering love and devotion for one's child; expressing (the value of) friendship; and, expressing respect for (the values of) justice and artistic genius.

6. Conclusion

As the partial overview offered here demonstrates, the value of trying is wide in scope, various, and rich, providing for reasons to try traversing all normative realms and found in all walks of life. Alas, this is a multiplicity frequently obscured by a prevailing shallow version of a purely production-driven approach to practical reasoning, which assumes that the only reason to try to do *anything* is as a means for succeeding at doing that very same thing. Building and elaborating on the work of John Gardner, this chapter tried to widen and enrich the appreciation of the value of trying and of the reasons it favors. Whether or not I succeeded in doing so, I do not know. But even if not, I feel that it was still worth the try.

By way of concluding, working on this chapter I was reminded of an evening spent lounging in front of the television with my wife, watching a movie. The characters on the screen were also married, and they were discussing what a "successful marriage they had had." Now, at this point it is key to pause in order to point out that my wife

---

[33] Dempsey briefly raises the expressive value of prayer. Dempsey, "What We Have Reason to Do" (n 26) 25.

grew up in Soviet Russia, by which I mean that along with many progressive values, she also holds dear some non-Western "old-world" ethical commitments. Returning to the story, I recall looking at my wife and, half-jokingly, asking her whether she thought that we too had a "successful marriage." While wielding a pillow toward the backside of my head, she turned toward me and said: "Don't be an idiot!"

5

Legality and Capacity

Frederick Wilmot-Smith[*]

1. Introduction

John Gardner denied any allegiance to grand themes. "I don't have a theory of law," he said. "I have quite a lot of thoughts about law in general and I can only hope that they turn out to be consistent with one another."[1] So let me, instead, suggest a minor theme and an apparent inconsistency.

First, the theme. Gardner was far more comfortable with strict legal duties (whether primary or secondary) than many scholars of private law. One of his most illuminating essays was concerned to vindicate strict primary duties against various assaults;[2] his last paper on private law defended the notion of a duty to pay damages against Steve Smith's formidable attack.[3]

Next, the apparent inconsistency. Gardner rejected the notion that "ought implies can" (OC) but was a fierce defender of the rule of law. Maybe it is not obvious that these twin commitments *are* in tension with one another. However, as I will seek to demonstrate, OC and legality are closely related maxims, both in their motivation and their demands. It is therefore—at least at first blush—puzzling for someone to be committed to one but not the other.

I aim to cast some light on the theme by showing that there is no inconsistency. Although I take issue with Gardner's own account of OC, his commitment to the rule of law gave him good reason to reject OC as a constraint on good laws.

2. The Two Maxims

2.1 OC and Legality

A number of philosophers claim that "ought implies can" (OC), that is, that an agent ought to ϕ only if they are able to do so. OC is a deeply ambiguous maxim. Thus

---

[*] All Souls College, Oxford. I am grateful to the editors and attendees of the conference for their comments on an earlier draft. Tom Adams and Chris Essert spared me particularly embarrassing errors, so special thanks to them.

[1] J Gardner, "Preface" in *Law as a Leap of Faith* (OUP 2012) v.

[2] J Gardner, "Obligations and Outcomes in the Law of Torts" in P Cane and J Gardner (eds), *Relating to Responsibility: Essays for Tony Honoré* (Hart 2001). See, too, J Gardner, "The Wrongdoing that Gets Results" (2004) 18 Philosophical Perspectives 53.

[3] J Gardner, "Damages Without Duty" (2019) 69 University of Toronto Law Journal 412. See generally S Smith, "Duties, Liabilities and Damages" (2012) 125 Harvard Law Review 1727 and S Smith, "Wrongs" in *Rights, Wrongs and Injustices* (OUP 2019) 197–200.

Frederick Wilmot-Smith, *Legality and Capacity* In: *Private Law and Practical Reason*. Edited by: Haris Psarras and Sandy Steel, Oxford University Press. © Frederick Wilmot-Smith 2023. DOI: 10.1093/oso/9780192857330.003.0005

scholars debate the meaning of "ought," "implies," "can," and even 'ϕ'. I will return to these debates below, when I consider Gardner's interpretation in more detail. For now, I will assume a candidate maxim: stipulate "ought" means a moral obligation (rather than, say, a *pro tanto* reason); "implies" is a material conditional (rather than, say, a conversational implicature); "can" concerns the ability of a particular agent at a particular point in time (rather than, say, metaphysical possibility for a conceivable human); and ϕ denotes action tokens, not action types.

The canonical launchpad for modern discussions of legality is Lon Fuller's parable of an inept law-maker, Rex. Rex attempts to make law eight times and fails on every occasion. From this parable Fuller derives "eight routes to disaster" or "principles of legality."[4] Thus laws must be general, public, prospective, intelligible, constant, fairly administered, and (crucially, for our purposes) such that the affected party can conform with them.

There are numerous disagreements about legality which I want to set to one side. One question is whether Fuller was right to think of these standards as embodying a "morality."[5] Another is whether other legal standards are properly seen as falling under the banner of legality.[6] The important point is that this list (or something like it) is widely endorsed.[7] For the purposes of this essay, two distinctions are crucial: between criteria and desiderata, and between laws and legal systems.

Consider first the distinction between criteria and desiderata. These things, as Gardner explained, are conceptual chasms apart.[8] There is no necessary normative defect in failure to satisfy a criterion; it simply prevents the thing (for which there are criteria) from instantiation. Desiderata play no such constitutive role. In the legal context, for example, we cannot begin to assess some norm *qua* legal norm unless it is a *valid* legal norm. It makes no sense to say of a token law that it is both not a law *and* that it is a bad law.

People sometimes use "legality" as an umbrella for a set of criteria with which to determine whether a token law or (more often) legal system exists. Failure to meet these standards means the token "law" is not a law, or system is not a system of law. What counts as compliance with these criteria is not an easy thing to pin down—nor is it rewarding to try to do so. Although these criteria do have limits—a wholly retrospective system of "laws," for example, is not a system of laws—perfect compliance is unnecessary for the system to exist.[9]

---

[4] LL Fuller, *The Morality of Law* (Rev., Yale University Press 1969) 39.

[5] R Dworkin, "Philosophy, Morality and Law—Observations Prompted by Professor Fuller's Novel Claim" (1965) 113 University of Pennsylvania Law Review 672, 668–78; Fuller, *The Morality of Law* (n 4) 162; HLA Hart, "Lon Fuller: *The Morality of Freedom*" in *Essays in Jurisprudence and Political Philosophy* (OUP 1983) 347–53.

[6] For example, T Bingham, *The Rule of Law* (Penguin 2011); J Waldron, "The Rule of Law and the Importance of Procedure" (2011) 50 Nomos 3; J Gardner, "How to Be a Good Judge" (*London Review of Books*, July 8, 2010) ⟨https://www.lrb.co.uk/the-paper/v32/n13/john-gardner/how-to-be-a-good-judge⟩ accessed 30 December 2020.

[7] For example, J Raz, "The Rule of Law and its Virtue" in *The Authority of Law: Essays on Law and Morality* (OUP 1979) 214–18; HLA Hart, "Problems of the Philosophy of Law" in *Essays in Jurisprudence and Political Philosophy* (OUP 1983) 114; J Finnis, *Natural Law and Natural Rights* (2nd edn, OUP 2011) 270–71.

[8] J Gardner, "On the Supposed Formality of the Rule-of-Law" in *Law as a Leap of Faith* (OUP 2012) 196, fn 5.

[9] For example, MH Kramer, *Objectivity and the Rule of Law* (CUP 2007) 105.

At other times, people use these phrases to denote desiderata which individual laws or legal systems ought to meet. John Rawls, for example, writes that the precepts of legality are "those that would be followed by any system of rules which perfectly embodied the idea of a legal system."[10] He adds, however, that "existing laws" do not "necessarily satisfy these precepts in all cases." Instead, laws should "approximate" to the ideal.[11] John Finnis, similarly, says that "the Rule of Law" is "[t]he name commonly given to the state of affairs in which a legal system is legally in good shape."[12] These claims suggest that there is a virtue in compliance with the rule of law: the ideal of legality, on this understanding, connotes desiderata.

Let us turn now to the two things to which these operators—criteria and desiderata—are applied. The first is token laws. Someone might say, in other words, that Fuller's list gives criteria of or desiderata for a token law. The criterial claim would hold that laws are valid only if they have, in the customary lexicon, the requisite form.[13] It is rare to see someone make that kind of claim. Few, for example, would think that a retrospective law is not a law; indeed, an important part of the objection *to* retrospective laws is precisely that they *are* laws (and, for example, bring with them further consequences such as legal sanctions).[14] More often the list—or some components of the list—is held up as a desiderat(um/a) of token laws. A retrospective law is a bad law; a law to which it is impossible for its subject to conform is a bad law; and so on. For example, John Gardner writes that

> a legal norm that is retroactive, radically uncertain, and devoid of all generality, and hence dramatically deficient relative to the ideal of the rule of law, is no less valid *qua* legal, than one that is prospective, admirably certain, and perfectly general.[15]

These operators, of criteria and desiderata, can also be applied to legal systems.[16] Fuller's list is most often understood in this way, as criterial standards for legal systems.[17] Any system must comply with them (to some sufficient extent), on this view, if it is to count *as* a legal system. As Fuller puts this point,

> A total failure in any one of these eight directions does not simply result in a bad system of law; it results in something that is not properly called a legal system at all.[18]

---

[10] J Rawls, *A Theory of Justice* (Belknap Press 1999) 207.

[11] ibid 207; HLA Hart, "Positivism and the Separation of Law and Morals" (1957) 71 Harvard Law Review 593, 595. Compare Hart, "Positivism and the Separation of Law and Morals" (n 11) 623.

[12] Finnis, *Natural Law and Natural Rights* (n 7) 270.

[13] The language of "form" is often unhelpful: Gardner, "On the Supposed Formality of the Rule-of-Law" (n 8). But it would delay things too much to question it here.

[14] Compare T Hobbes, *Leviathan: The English and Latin Texts* (i) (N Malcolm (2012) ed, *The Clarendon Edition of the Works of Thomas Hobbes*, vol 4, OUP 1651) 458. Note that Hobbes does not suggest prospectivity as a condition of the directive being a *law*; the condition is on *obligation*.

[15] J Gardner, "Legal Positivism: 51 Myths" in *Law as a Leap of Faith* (OUP 2012) 31.

[16] Perhaps the better view is, though, that sufficient compliance with legality is a precondition of a legal system's efficacy, and efficacy is a criterion of a legal system: see T Adams, "The Efficacy Condition" (2019) 25 Legal Theory 225.

[17] For example, Kramer, *Objectivity and the Rule of Law* (n 9) 105.

[18] Fuller, *The Morality of Law* (n 4) 39.

Fuller does, though, sometimes conflate laws and systems. For example, he says that

> where one would have been most tempted to say, "This is so evil it cannot be a law," one could usually have said instead, "This thing is the product of a system so oblivious to the morality of law that it is not entitled to be called a law."[19]

Here he mixes the evil of a token law—which, in the first statement, is said to vitiate the validity of the law—with the evil of the legal system (the apparent object of assessment in the second statement). These notions can come apart. If the system is so flawed that it is not a legal system, no token utterance within it can instantiate a law—even if that token act is not *itself* defective on any of the Fullerian grounds. Similarly, if the legal system exists, many people will say that the validity of a token law is a function of the legal system's own rules; a retrospective law is then a law just so long as it has satisfied the legal system's criteria of validity.

Legality can, therefore, be understood to propose (1) criteria or (2) desiderata of (A) laws or (B) legal systems. All four possible formulations, from (1)(A) to (2)(B), are visible in the literature; the most prominent are (1)(B) and (2)(A). Since, in this chapter, I seek to explore the relation between legality and OC, the candidate thesis to isolate is the one which will make that discussion most illuminating. For that reason, we should consider legality as it applies to laws: there is no analogue to OC as a criterion of moral systems (rather than individual norms). However, we should also consider a plausible thesis of legality, and very few scholars hold that compliance with legality is a *criterion* of a particular law. Thus the best formulation of legality for our purposes will be (2)(A): legality as an ideal of individual laws.

2.2 Common foundations?

Fuller's sixth requirement of legality was that laws should not require the impossible. Yet, as he recognized, one might wonder whether

> most of the other desiderata that make up the internal morality of law are not also ultimately concerned with the possibility of obedience. Just as it is impossible to obey a law that requires one to become ten feet tall, so it is also impossible to obey a law that cannot be known, that is unintelligible, that has not yet been enacted, etc.[20]

So Fuller seems to think that an OC-like idea lies at the very heart of his principles of legality. He does not pursue the thought because

> my concern is not to engage in an exercise in logical entailment, but to develop principles for the guidance of purposive human effort.

---

[19] LL Fuller, "Positivism and Fidelity to Law: A Reply to Professor Hart" (1958) 71(4) Harvard Law Review 630, 661.

[20] Fuller, *The Morality of Law* (n 4) 70, fn29.

80 FREDERICK WILMOT-SMITH

This distracts him from any thorough investigation of these links.

Fuller is not alone in suggesting that OC and legality relate. Numerous other scholars have drawn, explicitly or implicitly, connections between OC and legality.[21] For example, John Rawls wrote that

> Given that the legal order is a system of public rules addressed to rational persons, we can account for the precepts of justice associated with the rule of law. These precepts are those that would be followed by any system of rules which perfectly embodied the idea of a legal system.[22]

One such precept "associated with the rule of law" was OC.[23] Rawls proceeds to derive numerous requirements which an ideal legal system should seek to achieve, such as a requirement that impossible duties be avoided and that impossibility of performance be recognized as a defense (or "mitigating circumstance").[24]

It is especially intriguing to notice that there appears to be a yet deeper connection between OC and legality: the theoretical motivations of both the maxim and the ideal appear to be precisely the same.

2.2.1 Guidance

The most prominent theoretical motivation of OC is the idea that it is in the nature of normative reasons that they can guide action.[25] David Copp, for example, writes that "the point of moral requirements is to affect our decisions, and to lead us to do what is right, by being taken into account in our deliberation."[26] From the notion that morality should act as a guide, therefore, Copp derives OC.[27]

---

[21] Another important example is J Waldron, "The Rule of Law in Contemporary Liberal Theory" (1989) 2 Ratio Juris 79, 86–87.

[22] Rawls, *A Theory of Justice* (n 10) 207.

[23] ibid 208. Rawls describes these precepts as "implied" by the rule of law, which suggests a logical relation between the two. Surely, though, Rawls did not mean that OC was derived from legality. Hence his earlier statement that the precepts are "associated" with the rule of law is a more charitable reading of his view.

[24] ibid.

[25] There is a related strand of literature on normative reasons' capacity to *explain* actions: eg B Williams, "Internal and External Reasons" in *Moral Luck: Philosophical Papers 1973–1980* (CUP 1981) 102, 106; SL Darwall, *The British Moralists and the Internal "Ought," 1640–1740* (CUP 1995) 10–12; J Raz, "Reasons: Explanatory and Normative" in *From Normativity to Responsibility* (OUP 2011) 27.

[26] D Copp, "'Ought' Implies 'Can,' Blameworthiness, and the Principle of Alternative Possibilities" in M McKenna and D Widerker (eds), *Moral Responsibility and Alternative Possibilities: Essays on the Importance of Alternative Possibilities* (Ashgate 2003) 273.

[27] Copp's argument can be made more formally, which uncovers its shakiest premiss. We can use the following three-place relations: Reason(x,y,ϕ): x is a reason for y to ϕ; Explains(x,y,ϕ): x explains y's ϕing; and the following two-place relation: Ability(y,ϕ): y is able to ϕ. Copp's argument is:

A $\forall x\,((\neg°\text{Explains}(x,y,\phi)) \rightarrow \neg\text{Reason}(x,y,\phi))$

This is the conceptual claim about reasons. From this we can infer:

B $\neg\exists x\,(°\text{Explains}(x,y,\phi)) \rightarrow \neg\exists x\,(\text{Reason}(x,y,\phi))$.

We now need an additional premiss:

C $\neg\text{Ability}(y,\phi) \rightarrow \neg\exists x\,(°\text{Explains}(x,y,\phi))$.

The rationale for this premiss is as follows. If someone is unable to ϕ, it follows that they cannot ϕ; if they cannot ϕ, no fact can explain their ϕing (for there is no ϕing to explain). The principal concern I have with this is that "can" and "able" may have different modal domains; it is, therefore, arguable that a fact can explain *A*'s ϕing even if *A* cannot ϕ in the actual world. Nevertheless, the premiss is intuitive enough and it may be what proponents of this argument, like Copp, have in mind. With that additional premiss we can, from B and C, therefore conclude:

D $\neg\text{Ability}(y,\phi) \rightarrow \neg\exists x\,(\text{Reason}(x,y,\phi))$.

The most prominent strand of writing on the rule of law *qua* ideal claims, similarly, that it is an ideal for laws that they be capable of guiding action. Thus Joseph Raz writes that legality has two features: "(1) that people should be ruled by the law and obey it, and (2) that the law should be such that people will be able to be guided by it."[28] When Raz comes to develop his list of principles his principal justification of each precept is the guidance requirement. Laws should be prospective, open, and clear, he claims, because "[o]ne cannot be guided by a retroactive law";[29] "[s]tability is essential if people are to be guided by law in their long-term decisions";[30] and the judiciary must be independent because "it is futile to guide one's action on the basis of the law if when the matter comes to adjudication the courts will not apply the law and will act for some other reasons."[31]

This feature—that the law should be capable of guiding individuals—has featured prominently in many contemporary discussions of the rule of law.[32]

2.2.2 Fairness

A second ground for OC sometimes proposed is that morality should be fair.[33] David Copp writes that the "most basic motivation for [OC] begins with the thought that it would be unfair to expect a person to do something, or demand or require that she do it, if she lacked the ability to do it."[34] He adds that "agent-requirements are morally unfair if the person required to act in a certain way is unable to act in that way ... Hence an adequate moral theory ... must imply [OC]."[35]

This concern for fairness is also apparent in writing on legality. This thought is most popular in accounts of legality proposed by lawyers (rather than legal philosophers).[36] For example, Arthur Chaskalson, former Chief Justice of South Africa, wrote that

What was missing [from South Africa's apartheid government] was the substantive component of the rule of law. The process by which the laws were made was not fair (only whites, a minority of the population, had the vote). And the laws themselves were not fair.[37]

---

[28] Raz, "The Rule of Law and its Virtue" (n 7) 213.

[29] ibid 214.

[30] ibid 215.

[31] ibid 217.

[32] T Endicott, "The Impossibility of the Rule of Law" (1999) 19 Oxford Journal of Legal Studies 1, 17–8; J Coleman, *The Practice of Principle: In Defence of a Pragmatist Approach to Legal Theory* (OUP 2003) 206; A Marmor, "The Rule of Law and its Limits" (2004) 23 Law and Philosophy 1, 2; J Gardner, "Introduction" in J Gardner (ed), *H.L.A. Hart's Punishment and Responsibility: Essays in the Philosophy of Law* (OUP 2008) xxxvi, xlvii; S Smith, "Strict Duties and the Rule of Law" in LM Austin and D Klimchuk (eds), *Private Law and the Rule of Law* (OUP 2014) 198.

[33] MS Moore, *Educating Oneself in Public: Critical Essays in Jurisprudence* (OUP 2000) 169.

[34] Copp, "'Ought' Implies 'Can', Blameworthiness" (n 26) 271.

[35] ibid 272.

[36] However, see further Finnis, *Natural Law and Natural Rights* (n 7) 273–74. Consider, too, that the "negative virtue" of the rule of law is to protect individuals from arbitrary (ie unfair) burdens created by law itself: Raz, "The Rule of Law and its Virtue" (n 7) 224.

[37] A Chaskalson, Remarks at the World Justice Forum I, July 2008.

3. Gardner's Accounts

3.1 On OC

Gardner considered OC on a number of occasions.[38] His account held that "*A* has a reason to ϕ only if at least one conceivable human being has the capacity to ϕ and *A* is a human being."[39] This ability constraint on reasons is incredibly austere. This enabled Gardner to reject any OC-based critique of laws which concern others, such as the objective standard of care in tort law.

The attraction of Gardner's account is that it is robust in the face of personal vices. Moral faults, shortfalls of skill, and weakness of will do not remove the agent's reasons; they are "incapacities to do what one has reason to do."[40] This theme—a stringency about the demands of rationality—is quintessentially Gardnerian. Yet there are two puzzling features of his account.

First, Gardner's maxim bears no obvious relation to the theoretical motivations for OC. It is odd to think that the guidance concern is satisfied by some fact being capable of guiding "at least one conceivable human being." Reasons, surely, are to guide their actual subjects (not some merely possible human). Likewise, the stringency of Gardner's maxim means any concerns of fairness will not be met: it is slim comfort, when faced with sheer impossibility, to be told that there is no unfairness in the moral demand made because a *conceivable* human could have performed the action in question.

Consider, second, Gardner's famous clifftop case:

> I am on a clifftop miles from anywhere looking down helplessly on a man drowning in the stormy sea below. Because no amount of trying would bring me closer to success, my reasons to save the man do not yield any reasons to try to save him. Yet I still have the same reasons to save him that I would have if doing so were perfectly straightforward. That is why the situation is so horrifying.[41]

Gardner is on a clifftop (in some iterations, incapable of swimming) to emphasize that the impossibility of saving the drowning man is quite deep; it is not as if the man could be saved if only Gardner had a rubber ring. But this suggests that his maxim

---

[38] See J Gardner, "Justifications and Reasons" in *Offences and Defences: Selected Essays in the Philosophy of Criminal Law* (OUP 2007) 92–93; "Obligations and Outcomes" (n 2) fn 8, 42; "The Wrongdoing that Gets Results" (n 2) 54; "Damages Without Duty" (n 3) 416–17. The most complete treatment is J Gardner, "Reasons and Abilities: Some Preliminaries" (2013) 58 American Journal of Jurisprudence 63.

[39] Gardner, "Reasons and Abilities" (n 38) 72. The clarification on the nature of "ought" is important, since not every ought is understood, even by defenders of OC, to entail "can": cf PBM Vranas, "'Ought' Implies 'Can' but Does Not Imply 'Must': An Asymmetry Between Becoming Infeasible and Becoming Overridden" (2018) 127(4) Philosophical Review 487.

[40] Gardner, "Reasons and Abilities" (n 38) 70.

[41] Gardner, "Obligations and Outcomes" (n 2) 137. See, for the same case, "Justifications and Reasons" (n 38) 93; "The Wrongdoing that Gets Results" (n 2) 55.

is inconsistent with the suggested lesson of his hypothetical. No conceivable human can save the drowning man; there can, on Gardner's view, be no reason to save the drowning man.[42]

For these reasons, I think it better to say simply that Gardner rejected OC.[43]

3.2 Legality

Gardner was firmly committed to the value of legality. He was committed, in particular, to a guidance interpretation of the ideal. Thus he writes that legality "requires that the law's conduct rules should be capable of guiding those who are subject to them."[44] Given the austerity of Gardner's account of OC, it is interesting to note that his account of legality sometimes appears to be *incredibly* demanding. He writes that "the definitions of criminal offences ... should be such that *everyone* can be guided by them."[45] One of his last pieces claims that "we should *all* be able to be guided by the law."[46] Thus Gardner appears to claim that there is a rule of law concern if an individual of below-average ability cannot be guided by a norm because of the norm's complexity.[47]

3.3 A puzzle

Gardner was very concerned that the law should be able to guide its subjects, all subjects, and endorsed a demanding ideal of legality in consequence. By contrast, although he accepted that it is in the nature of reasons that they guide actions,[48] he did not cash that concern out in anything similar to his account of legality. Why not?

There is here a puzzle about Gardner's thought—how the claims fit together—but it is broader than that. There is, I have suggested, a general question about how OC and legality relate to one another, a question which has not received sufficient investigation. I pursue that investigation in more detail in the next section. In so doing, I aim to vindicate the core of Gardner's thought—and, more specifically, to argue that Gardner's commitment to legality helped to justify his rejection of OC.

---

[42] I agree with Gardner on the phenomenology of the case, but this only goes to show that a situation can be horrifying even when we have no reason to change it. Given the horrors of history—which we surely have no reason to *change*—this is no great surprise.

[43] So Gardner seemed to recognize: "Damages Without Duty" (n 3) 416, fn 26.

[44] Gardner, "Justifications and Reasons" (n 38) 115.

[45] J Gardner, "The Gist of Excuses" in *Offences and Defences: Selected Essays in the Philosophy of Criminal Law* (OUP 2007) 138 (emphasis added).

[46] J Gardner, "Damages Without Duty" (2019) 43 Australasian Journal of Legal Philosophy 1, 14 (my emphasis; Gardner emphasized *able*).

[47] For other suggestive passages, see J Gardner, "Reply to Critics" in *Offences and Defences: Selected Essays in the Philosophy of Criminal Law* (OUP 2007) 239; Gardner, "On the Supposed Formality of the Rule-of-Law" (n 8) 211–13.

[48] Gardner, "Reasons and Abilities" (n 38) 69, fn 8.

4. Resolution

4.1 Guidance: Asymmetries

In respect of the guidance ideal, there are a number of asymmetries between the demands made of law and of morality. In consequence, one cannot endorse OC on guidance grounds *and* legality: they make inconsistent demands. This shows that there was no tension in Gardner's thought on this account.

4.1.1 The agents to guide
To say that law and morality should guide leaves silent the agents it is supposed to guide. Morality is, in that respect, relatively simple: it applies to its subjects, and those are the ones norms seek to guide. Many laws are similar. They are intended to guide citizens: don't steal; perform your contracts; and so on. Those parts of law can, therefore, be seen as direct analogies with moral norms. However, laws are more complicated than this. Beyond citizens, laws are also supposed—indirectly and directly—to guide norm-appliers, in other words judges.[49]

Consider the law of contract. The central principle of the law of contract is—at least, as customarily understood—*pacta sunt servanda*.[50] Since contractual obligations are, at least in theory, voluntarily imposed, this principle provides citizens with two kinds of instruction. First, and most obviously, it tells them that they must perform the contracts they agree. Second, perhaps less obviously, it cajoles them only to agree to the contracts they believe they can keep. So far, so consistent with an extra-legal analogue, promissory morality. However, the very same principle, *pacta sunt servanda*, also provides judges with guidance. Most obviously, they should order citizens to perform their contracts when morality permits it; when specific performance is not morally permissible, they should order that damages be paid.[51] Judges should develop the common law principles of damages to better ensure that the principle is satisfied.[52]

This institutional feature—that legal norms, like Janus, face in "two directions"[53]—illustrates a key difference between law and morality. The distinction would, perhaps, be relatively trivial if it were possible cleanly to divide the legal landscape into "law for citizens" and "law for judges." If that division were possible, each norm would have to

---

[49] One interesting and understudied of Gardner's claims is that defenses need not answer to the rule of law since they are not supposed to guide citizens: "Justifications and Reasons" (n 38) 117; "Introduction" (n 32) xlvii. Even defenses, though, should guide law-appliers.

[50] This point is contentious among legal scholars. Some point to the absence of specific performance as (in common law countries) proof that the law does not regard performance as mandatory. That view is not compatible with various basic doctrinal facts: it is a common law tort to induce a breach of contract (*Lumley v Gye* (1854) 3 El & Bl 114, 118 ER 1083 (QB)); specific performance is granted where it is morally defensible (*Cooperative Insurance Society Ltd v Argyll Stores (Holdings) Ltd* [1998] AC 1 (HL)).

[51] *Robinson v Harman* (1848) 1 Ex 850, 855; 154 ER 363, 365 (Parke B).

[52] I have tried, in this expression, to be ecumenical: the same basic point should be acceptable, regardless of whether you regard the law as presently conforming with the underlying normative principles. Compare SV Shiffrin, "The Divergence of Contract and Promise" (2007) 120(3) Harvard Law Review 708 (arguing that contract law fails, in this respect, to live up to moral demands).

[53] J Waldron, "The Rule of Law" in EN Zalta (ed), *The Stanford Encyclopedia of Philosophy* (Fall 2016, Metaphysics Research Lab, Stanford University 2016).

be assessed for its guidance potential for the relevant group; law would simply require a bit more attention than morality, since we would have to tailor norms to the appropriate group. As any (thoughtful) legislator would tell you, though, it is rarely possible to carve so cleanly in practice. Consider the law of contract again. The rules on performance, you might think, are supposed to guide citizens; rules for the orders to make on breach of those duties, the thought continues, are to guide judges. However, it is not possible—even if it were desirable—to draw a "cone of silence" between the primary and secondary norms.[54] Judges, most obviously, sculpt judicial remedies for breach in light of the primary norm; citizens, too, approach their duties of performance with half an eye to the consequences of breach. It follows that individual norms will provide guidance both for citizens and for judges—even a norm addressed squarely to one will guide, even indirectly, the other.

How, then, does this distinction matter? It shows that the guidance ideal not only means something quite different in law as opposed to morality, but also that the ideal creates different, specifically legal, problems. The inextricability of these guidance requirements creates burdens of design for legal norms, ones not found in morality. For example, a norm which constrains an official (= provides clear guidance) will sometimes provide less useful guidance than a standard (ie one which generates more useful guidance). Many laws, therefore, contain necessary imperfections; it is not possible to realize both ideals perfectly. Consider, for example, that some norms are incapable of providing individuals with precise guidance and yet *because of those features which mean they cannot guide individuals* are good guides for judges (and sound norms in general). Most legal systems, for example, have drink-driving laws specifying very precise standards. Individuals are rarely guided by those standards: they tend to rely on rules-of-thumb about the amount of drinks ingested rather than the precise alcohol content in the blood. The guidance the norm gives to agents is, therefore, at best indirect. The rule can, however, be applied without much discretion on the part of the law-applier: the police, the judge, and so on. The rule is, therefore, fairer to individuals than a vague standard.[55]

The same point can be made in reverse. A norm which provides good guidance for individuals may provide judges with unhealthy discretion. Legal norms embedding evaluative standards—"be reasonable," "don't drive dangerously"—may provide as helpful guidance as is possible to give to individuals. Yet when a case comes before a judge, who is called upon to decide whether an individual violated these standards, such standards will allow for a range of possible interpretations; the judge, ultimately, will have to pick.

All this shows two ways in which the ideal, that the norms in question guide, differs when applied to law and to morality. First, all legal norms must address both citizens and norm-appliers; this makes the legal ideal necessarily more complex than

---

[54] This metaphor comes from M Dan-Cohen, "Decision Rules and Conduct Rules: On Acoustic Separation in Criminal Law" in *Harmful Thoughts* (Princeton University Press 2002).

[55] I take this example from T Endicott, "The Value of Vagueness" in A Marmor and S Soames (eds), *Philosophical Foundations of Language in the Law* (OUP 2011) 19. A similar point is made, for example, by J Gardner, "Rationality and the Rule of Law in Offences Against the Person" in *Offences and Defences: Selected Essays in the Philosophy of Criminal Law* (OUP 2007) 44–45.

86 FREDERICK WILMOT-SMITH

morality's. Second, this complexity is such that laws will often be deficient along one dimension or another.

4.1.2 Who is in the group?

We now know the type of agents morality and law are supposed to guide. But the precise group to guide can still be specified with greater precision. For example, Bernard Williams held that "If it is true that A has a reason to ϕ, then it must be possible that he should ϕ for that reason."[56] Similarly, Joseph Raz's explanatory-normative nexus, an import from Williams's work, "is interpreted to apply to each individual agent and reason."[57] As these formulations suggest, the most natural reading of OC is that its restriction on oughts applies to specific individuals: for some fact to be a duty *for me*, it must be possible *for me* to act on it; for some fact to be a duty *for you*, it must be possible *for you* to act on it.

What does legality require? Does it require, in other words, that laws be capable of guiding each individual of whom the norm makes demands? Or is its value met when laws are capable of guiding some group of individuals? Some scholars have approached the question through the lens of OC; unsurprisingly, they have objected to token norms on agent-specific grounds, protesting that a particular individual lacks an ability.[58] As I pointed out above, Gardner's claims were similar. By contrast, Joseph Raz claims that "the law should be such that *people* will be able to be guided by it."[59] He does not say that *each person* must be capable of being guided by *each norm* at *every possible moment*.

Raz is right. The value of legality will be met so long as a sufficient number of individuals who are to be guided by the norm—be they citizens or officials—can be guided by it. That is for two reasons.

First, it would be indirectly self-defeating to try to calibrate each norm to each individual: the law would be so fragmentary and disjointed that no-one would be able to figure out which norms applied to them, much less be guided by the norms that do. The consequence of this point is that objections to so-called strict duties—duties which are not leveled to each individuals' ability, such that they can be breached in individual instances by those who were unable to comply—have this puzzling feature: any call to erase strict duties from the law is *eo ipso* a call to reduce the quality of the legal system by the lights of the rule of law. This suggests that Gardner's commitment to the value of legality, properly understood, was a ground for him to reject orthodox understandings of OC.

Second, adjusting the content of norms to make them intelligible to each individual would require, on occasion, that the content of the norm (rather than its expression)

---

[56] B Williams, "Internal Reasons and the Obscurity of Blame" in *Making Sense of Humanity* (CUP 1995) 39. See, further, B Williams, "Replies" in JEJ Altham and R Harrison (eds), *World, Mind, and Ethics* (CUP 1995) 192 (those who lack the capacity "have no reason to try to be like a *phronimos*, to the extent that such a life lies beyond their competence.").

[57] Raz, "Reasons: Explanatory and Normative" (n 25) 34.

[58] For examples, B Chapman, "Ethical Issues in the Law of Tort" in ME Bayles and B Chapman (eds), *Justice, Rights, and Tort Law* (D Reidel Pub Co 1983) 35–36.

[59] Raz, "The Rule of Law and its Virtue" (n 7) 213 (emphasis added). See too Kramer, *Objectivity and the Rule of Law* (n 9) 169.

be adjusted. Some people might, in other words, not be able to understand the complicated rules governing the licensing of pharmaceuticals; they could only be guided by those rules if the rules themselves were changed. Doing this would violate deeply held convictions of equality before the law: Friedrich Hayek talked of an ideal of "general and equal laws" where the rules "are the same for all";[60] John Rawls, similarly, said that "formal justice requires that in their administration laws and institutions should apply equally (that is, in the same way) to those belonging to the classes defined by them."[61] This ideal could not be met if legality required individual norms to be tailored to each individual—and, even if the ideal of legality is distinct from that of the rule of law, it is implausible to suggest that the latter requires violation of the former.

Here, then, is another way in which the ideal of guidance differs between morality and law: moral norms should be capable of guiding each individual; legality is not so demanding of law. A distributive question thus arises in law which does not in morality. When considering whether the ideal of legality is met in a particular case there may be difficult questions of whether some norm (or set of norms) provide sufficient guidance when the norm (or set) can guide only the very able (or very rich) few. Some norms are, for example, intelligible only to those who have the benefit of expensive legal advice. For these, if the ideal of legality is not met, lawyers must then consider whether the compensating benefits of having those norms is such that any defect in legality is justified.

4.2 Fairness: Asymmetries

4.2.1 The orthodox account

Consider Thomas Nagel's statement, that "strict liability may have its legal uses but seems irrational as a moral position."[62] This passage suggests that it might be possible for the law to be (justifiably) unfair, but that morality should not (or cannot) be so. That, I suggest, is the orthodox account of the place of fairness in law and in morality.

Many scholars of private law have objected, in response, that there is no such disconnect between law and morality. This means either that Nagel's account of morality or of law is wrong. Many think Nagel wrong about the law; they say that strict liability in law is just as immoral as it is irrational in morality.[63] Gardner agreed with the premise—that there is no disjunct between morality and law—but thought Nagel wrong about morality.[64]

---

[60] FA Hayek, *The Constitution of Liberty* (R Hamowy ed, first published 1960, University of Chicago Press 2011) 222.

[61] Rawls, *A Theory of Justice* (n 10) 51.

[62] T Nagel, "Moral Luck" in *Mortal Questions* (CUP 1979) 31. There is a similar claim in O Wendell Holmes Jr, *The Common Law* (Little, Brown and Company 1881) 86.

[63] See generally J Steiner, "Putting Fault Back into Products Liability: A Modest Reconstruction of Tort Theory" (1982) 1 Law and Philosophy 419, 437; Chapman, "Ethical Issues in the Law of Tort" (n 58) 35–6; A Beever, *Rediscovering the Law of Negligence* (Hart Publishing 2007) 77–8; Kramer, *Objectivity and the Rule of Law* (n 9) 165; A Slavny, "Should Tort Law Demand the Impossible?" in PB Miller and J Oberdiek (eds), *Civil Wrongs and Justice in Private Law* (OUP 2020) 374.

[64] For the general claim, about the relationship between legal and moral norms, see Gardner, "Obligations and Outcomes" (n 2) 121.

88 FREDERICK WILMOT-SMITH

No one has it quite right. Facial similarities between the demands made of both law and morality are, on analysis, distinct. Nagel's thought is, in that respect, congenial—and the reformist thoughts are not. Even so, the orthodox account does not have things quite right. There is *a* sense in which morality can seem unfair—the cosmic unfairness of the tragedian, perhaps. But that is only a manner of speaking. Fairness is simply not an appropriate norm with which to assess moral standards. The law, by contrast, can be unfair—of course it can!—but (less obviously) the law *cannot* be justifiably unfair.

4.2.2 Morality and unfairness

Certain theorists of OC claim that morality must be fair (and propose OC as a tool to ensure this fairness). The claim is puzzling. Most obviously, morality *seems* unfairly demanding in a number of ways. Here are three ways related to impossible standards.

First, moral appraisals of our actions can depend upon "resultant luck."[65] To take a common example, the only difference between driving dangerously and causing death by dangerous driving might be the presence of an individual in the road, something the driver has no control over. The driver who kills is unlucky: she had no control over the facts which made her action worse. True enough, a number of scholars have proposed amendments to moral requirements to try to insulate the normative realm from luck.[66] But these attempts fail to do justice to our basic moral intuitions: the dangerous driver's life bears no moral stain as deep or indelible as one who *killed* by dangerous driving.

Second, morality sometimes places us in situations of dilemma. An individual faces a moral dilemma if they will do something wrong no matter what they do.[67] A typical example is Sophie's choice. On arrival at Auschwitz, Sophie is told that one of her children will be murdered—and she has to decide which it is to be. The tragedy of Sophie's life is that she cannot but commit a grave wrong. This seems unfair, so unfair that many attempt to amend morality to spare Sophie her fate.

Third, morality can demand us to act on facts which we are not in a position to know.[68] It is plausibly wrong, for example, to purchase goods which are produced or distributed in an immoral manner: think of blood diamonds, cocaine, or ivory. For goods which cannot be produced in a moral manner, morality's demands are transparent; for example, it tells us (with no silent "ifs") not to buy ivory. For the other goods, morality's demands are conditional: diamonds and cocaine *can* be produced ethically. So I might purchase a diamond, acting upon the best evidence available (which suggests that the diamond is clean), and end up purchasing a blood diamond.

---

[65] I take this terminology from Nagel, "Moral Luck" (n 62) 28.

[66] This reading of the literature is proposed by, variously, R Sorensen, "Unknowable Obligations" (1995) 7(2) Utilitas 247, 249 and A Srinivasan, "Normativity without Cartesian Privilege" (2015) 25 Philosophical Issues 273.

[67] Some claim that moral dilemmas refute OC: eg EJ Lemmon, "Moral Dilemmas" (1962) 71(2) Philosophical Review 139. See, however, B Williams, "Ethical Consistency" in *Problems of the Self: Philosophical Papers 1956–1972* (CUP 1973) 180; and compare J Jarvis Thomson, *Normativity* (Open Court Press 2008) 145, fn 4.

[68] See Srinivasan, "Normativity without Cartesian Privilege" (n 66).

I commit a moral wrong; yet (stipulate) I was not in a position to know that I would commit a wrong.

The right response to these cases is not to say that morality can be unfair. Fairness, being a part of morality, cannot itself be used to criticize claims about morality. Thus the orthodox account is correct: morality cannot be unfair. Yet the orthodox account is correct because fairness is not an apt standard to apply to morality, not because morality is necessarily fair.[69]

4.2.3 Law and fairness

The law, likewise, sometimes makes demands which can seem unfair. It instructs us to meet objective standards of care, even if we simply do not measure up in our daily lives;[70] to suffer legal sanctions for actions we took while legally insane;[71] to pay damages even when we are not in a position to know the quantum;[72] and so on.

There are two points to make about these unfair legal rules, neither of which apply to morality. First, it is always a criticism of law that it is unfair. By contrast, it makes scant sense to criticize morality as being unfair; morality either makes its demands, or it does not.

Second, more important, the orthodox view is that a law which makes unfair demands can be justified by some advance in value in some other domain.[73] It is, for example, unfair on its face that citizens are legally proscribed from escaping prison even when wrongfully convicted of crimes, or for people to have to pay court orders where the obligation recorded is not consistent with the facts. Such duties might be justifiable if any alternative system of rules, such as one which permitted the truly innocent to except themselves from the court's orders, would be worse. But, on this view, the *pro tanto* unfairness of the obligation is outweighed by some wider benefit.

The orthodox account is wrong to think that such laws are unfair but justified: when a law is justified, its claims are not unfair.[74] A fairness-based objection to a law claims that the law places either undue or unequal burdens on the burden-bearer. The objection is that the burden-bearer's interests have not been properly taken into account. But a law could only be justified if the legislator *had* taken such a person's interests properly into account—if they had, for example, concluded that the risk of wrongful imprisonment was a price worth paying to avoid the ills of a system where there is no duty to obey court orders. Once such a determination has been reached, there is no logical space for a fairness-based objection to the impact of a rule.

---

[69] Compare Geoffrey Sayre-McCord's argument, that any moral theory which demands the impossible has a "fairer counterpart" which is less demanding: G Sayre-McCord, "A Moral Argument Against Moral Dilemmas" (May 24, 2013) 11. Notice that Sayre-McCord's claim is not that morality cannot be unfair; his claim is ordinal, on the ranking of theories.

[70] *Vaughan v Menlove* (1837) 3 Bing NC 468, 132 ER 490.

[71] *Kahler v Kansas*, 589 US (2020).

[72] *Photo Production Ltd v Securicor Transport Ltd* [1980] AC 827 (HL).

[73] cf Hart, "Positivism and the Separation of Law and Morals" (n 11) 619.

[74] There is some analogy here with Tony Honoré's justification of the objective standard of care: T Honoré, "Responsibility and Luck" in *Responsibility and Fault* (Hart Publishing 1999).

5. Diagnosis

John Gardner was right to reject OC as a tool for criticism of the law: one cannot both endorse the ideal of legality and hold that OC should directly constrain legal standards. I have argued, further, that despite the apparent symmetry of the ideal and the maxim, scholars are wrong to invoke fairness as a basis of OC. Why, if I am right, are these thinkers going wrong?

One possible diagnosis is that those who endorse fairness requirements for morality are too given to thinking like—and thinking of morality in the terms of—lawyers.[75] Consider, for example, that the principal proponent of OC, as his work is customarily understood, is Immanuel Kant.[76] Kant's system of moral thought is lawyerly.[77] Most obviously, his *Foundations* and *Metaphysics* are replete with references to the Formula of Universal Law: "act only according to that maxim through which you can at the same time will that it become a universal law."[78] By the time of the *Metaphysics*, that formula is explicitly invoked in the context of (and confined to) the principle of right.[79] At its most general, the signature Kantian move is to think of morality as a set of rules to be followed—and law *just is* that system of rules. Small wonder common concepts creep across both domains.[80]

The lawyerly nature of certain theorists' approaches is more widespread than this. It also seems present in the sensibilities of some moral theorists to approach morality as a tool to solve hard cases. I have in mind certain of those theorists who approach moral problems through a series of increasingly intricate thought experiments (sometimes called "cases"). I do not mean to rehearse the pros and cons of this method of doing philosophy, nor, absurdly, to say that all those who engage in thought experiments are proto lawyers. My point is that certain practitioners of this method sometimes seem to think of morality, as we lawyers often think of law, as having an answer to all problems.

So why was Gardner different? Why did he endorse legality while rejecting OC? I argued that his commitment to legality gave him good reason to reject OC as directly applicable to legal standards. A more obvious answer is also important: John was no Kantian and nor did he think of morality as a social institution. His conception of morality had space for tragedy and conflict, taking more from Aristotle, Nussbaum, and

---

[75] Having formed this rather vague diagnosis, I discovered that James Penner beat me to the punch: J Penner, *Property Rights: A Re-Examination* (OUP 2020) 191. See, too, Nick McBride's chapter in this volume, Chapter 3.

[76] Compare R Stern, "Does 'Ought' Imply 'Can'? And Did Kant Think It Does?" (2004) 16(1) Utilitas 42.

[77] This is a familiar claim: cf B Williams, *Ethics and the Limits of Philosophy* (Routledge 2015) 223, fn 17.

[78] I Kant, *Foundations of the Metaphysics of Morals* (J Timmermann ed, MP Gregor and J Timmermann trs, first published 1797, Library of Liberal Arts 2013) 4:421; I Kant, *The Metaphysics of Morals* (L Denis ed, M Gregor tr, 2nd edn, first published 1797, CUP 2017) 6:376.

[79] Kant, *The Metaphysics of Morals* (n 78) 6:230. See, too, Kant, *The Metaphysics of Morals* (n 78) 6:246 (conduct is right if it can "coexist with the freedom of everyone in accordance with a universal law.").

[80] See eg Sayre-McCord, "A Moral Argument Against Moral Dilemmas" (n 69) 9, where Sayre-McCord explicitly invokes a legislator and a legal system to discuss fairness in moral claims.

Williams than it ever took from Kant. So the basic urge which leads some to endorse OC—that morality must be fair—inevitably had no effect on him.

John's account—and mine—leaves a lot of questions. I wish that he was here to help answer them. But we must do what we can even if, at times, it does not seem enough.

6

Gardner on Justice

Tatiana Cutts

1. Introduction

"Driving" describes a certain kind of activity. It sets some baseline conditions for qualification: I must have control over a moving vehicle. But it tells us nothing about whether I am doing it well. "Justice," by contrast, wears two hats: it designates a sphere of activity (a "matter of justice"), and a standard for success against which actions within that sphere may be measured ("a just decision").[1] John Gardner gave us a compelling theory of the first hat, which has had a profound influence on the evolution of private law theory.

For Gardner, questions of justice were "distinctive in being allocative questions,"[2] or questions about "who is to get how much of what and why".[3] Who should be treated for or vaccinated against COVID-19 as a matter of priority? Who should have access to the courts' remedial arsenal, and who (if anyone) should suffer criminal incarceration? In Gardner's terms, these were allocative questions in that "there must be losers as well as winners";[4] the task of the justice-seeker is to decide who wins and who loses, and in what degree.[5]

According to Gardner's theory of justice as allocation, these questions arise in private law at a particular stage. For Gardner, the rationale for private law duties, like other legal duties, was to help each of us to conform to reasons that apply to us:[6] to distil the "chaos" of value that we confront in our daily lives;[7] to help us choose among rationally defensible options;[8] and to provide the security that we need to continue on the track that, for better or worse, we have chosen.[9] Yet, for Gardner, most of that work did not raise the sort of questions of "interpersonal allocation" that belong within the

---

[1] And it sometimes wears a third hat when it refers to the role of decision-maker within that sphere ("justice," "justicier").

[2] J Gardner, "Legal Justice and Iudic Fairness" (2020) 11 Jurisprudence 468. They are questions about "who stands to gain what, and who stands to lose what, and whether those are the people who should be gaining or losing whatever it is they stand to gain or lose." See also J Gardner, "The Virtue of Justice and the Character of Law" in *Law as a Leap of Faith: Essays on Law in General* (OUP 2012) 238.

[3] ibid.

[4] Gardner, "Legal Justice" (n 2) 468.

[5] ibid.

[6] "The law exists to improve how people (including its own officials) will act. Indeed, the reason should be stated even more capaciously than that. The law exists to improve people's conformity with reasons that already apply to them, including but not limited to reasons to act." J Gardner, *From Personal Life to Private Law* (OUP 2018) ("*FPLPL*") 77.

[7] ibid 12–13.

[8] ibid 13.

[9] ibid 183.

Tatiana Cutts, *Gardner on Justice* In: *Private Law and Practical Reason.* Edited by: Haris Psarras and Sandy Steel, Oxford University Press. © Tatiana Cutts 2023. DOI: 10.1093/oso/9780192857330.003.0006

realm of justice.[10] By contrast, once a wrongful transaction had occurred, courts were required to confront questions such as "who is to bear the costs of the alleged breach, and in what proportions, and on what grounds, etc."[11] Those questions, for Gardner, were questions of justice.

In what follows, I argue that Gardner was correct to emphasize that there is a "normative distance" to be traveled from the fact of failure to perform some original duty to the imposition of a remedial burden,[12] but that we need not travel this distance via a distinct frame of theoretical reference. We justify private law rules and responsibilities of all forms in the same way, by identifying the reasons that people have to want legal protection, and the costs to other interests of providing it.[13] The remedial exercise is not, and should not be treated as, a distinct project of interpersonal (re)allocation.

The first argument is one of scope, which engages with the definitional project on its own terms. I argue that there are central problems of justice that do not involve the allocation of benefits and burdens among individuals, and the fact that a problem does involve allocation does not make it a problem of justice.

The second argument addresses the methodological goal directly. I argue that we do not need to define the "subject matter of justice" to answer important questions, such as: are our social institutions justifiable, and what follows from the conclusion that they are? When and how does equality matter, and what departures from it are admissible? Does a given norm impose too great a burden on any individual?

The third argument is a product of the first two: we will do a better job of figuring out what we ought to do in concrete cases if we ask these questions directly. I argue that framing private law remedies as exercises in "allocating back" transactional outputs can obscure facts that are relevant to figuring out whether legal intervention is justifiable, and what form that intervention should take.[14]

2. Allocation

For Gardner, norms of justice were norms for "tackling allocative moral questions," or questions "about who is to get how much of what,"[15] and the "distinctive preoccupation of the justice-seeker" was with making sure that "the right goods and ills are

---

[10] Or other defective transactions: see eg J Gardner, "What is Tort Law For? Part 1. The Place of Corrective Justice" (2011) 30 Law and Philosophy 1, 22.

[11] Gardner, "The Virtue of Justice" (n 2) 256.

[12] I borrow this language from Voyiakis: "there is a normative distance to travel between the failure to discharge an original burden and the justification for imposing the burden of repair." E Voyiakis, *Private Law and the Value of Choice* (Hart Publishing 2017) 37.

[13] Here, I use the language of Tim Scanlon: TM Scanlon, "Rights, Balancing and Proportionality" in L Kioussopoulou and Others (eds), *Human Rights in Times of Illiberal Democracies, Liber Amicorum in Memoriam of Stavros Tsakyrakis* (Nomiki Bibliothiki 2020) 35. NB though the context in which he uses that language is with respect to certain rights (eg freedom of expression, rights of due process) claimed against the state.

[14] Specifically, whether some interest is best protected through legal intervention, and how, and whether that protection can be provided at acceptable cost to other interests See eg Scanlon, "Rights, Balancing and Proportionality" (n 13) 35; TM Scanlon, "Rights, Goals, and Fairness" (1975) 11 Erkenntnis 81; and Scanlon, "Contractualism and Justification" (n 13).

[15] Gardner, "Part 1. The Place of Corrective Justice" (n 10) 6.

assigned to the right people and on the right grounds."[16] This is not a political theory of justice or a theory of the justice of social institutions more broadly conceived.[17] It is an account of justice across social institutions and individual interactions—from "low-stakes" games to life-changing rules about criminal punishment.[18]

I have called this a "formal" theory of justice, though that label may invite confusion. Gardner's theory of justice as allocation tells us what counts as a matter of justice and what does not. This is a matter of "demarcating the subject-matter of justice"[19]—identifying what is "distinctive"[20] about questions of justice, among a range of other questions that we might ask about the law. It does not tell us whether we have done justice, or how we would know. For Gardner, a particular norm or action belongs within the realm of justice if it involves allocation, whether or not it allocates "the right things to the right people on the right grounds."[21]

For Gardner, as for Hume, the central cases of justice involved competition for goods that were in short supply.[22] "As a rule" he said, "allocative questions are forced upon us only when people make competing claims to assignable goods";[23] in these cases, when there is not enough to satisfy everyone's wants, needs, or claims, the justice-seeker must confront a decision about who will receive some of whatever is up for allocation (and how much) and who will not.

Yet, Gardner came to be persuaded that there were other "non-competitive" problems of justice.[24] He argued that one cannot make sense of the idea of punishment without some sort of discrimination between those who deserve to be punished (on the basis of whatever it is that they have done wrong) and those who do not.[25] And this, he concluded, made punishment an "essentially allocative action," such that "one cannot separate the question of whether to indulge in it at all from the question of how to distribute it."[26] Gardner argued that punishment "is by its nature exacted *for* something (viz. for some wrong or supposed wrong)."[27] And, he said, "as soon as one

---

[16] Gardner, "The Virtue of Justice" (n 2) 242.

[17] See eg Scanlon "Individual Morality and the Morality of Institutions" (2016) 27 Filozofija I Društvo 3, 4.

[18] For games, Gardner used the language of "fairness": "I tend to think that an unfairness is something that would be an injustice if only it were more important, while an injustice is something that would be a mere unfairness if only it were less important." Gardner, "Legal Justice" (n 2) 471.

[19] ibid 468.

[20] ibid.

[21] Gardner, "The Virtue of Justice" (n 2) 242.

[22] Hume wrote that justice would be "totally useless" in a world of "extreme abundance," in which "every individual finds himself fully provided with whatever his most voracious appetites can want." "For what purpose," he asked, "make a Partition of Goods, where every one has already more than enough?" Thus, the "jealous virtue of justice" was needed only on account of competition for goods that were in short supply (D Hume, *An Enquiry Concerning the Principles of Morals* (reprinted edn, Public Domain Books 1912) 9–10. For Rawls, too, justice concerned "the proper distribution of the benefits and burdens of social cooperation," and the need to address these questions arose from conditions of "moderate scarcity" in which "natural and other resources are not so abundant that schemes of cooperation become superfluous, nor are conditions so harsh that fruitful ventures must inevitably break down": J Rawls, *A Theory of Justice* (Belknap Press of Harvard University Press 1971) 128.

[23] Gardner emphasized that "Many morally significant goods, including many relevant to politics and law, are either not competed for or not assignable." Gardner, "Part 1. The Place of Corrective Justice" (n 10) 6.

[24] ibid 7.

[25] J Gardner, "Finnis on Justice" in J Keown and R George (eds), *Reason, Morality, and the Law: The Jurisprudence of John Finnis* (OUP 2012) 151.

[26] Gardner, "Part 1. The Place of Corrective Justice" (n 10) 7.

[27] ibid.

asks 'For what?' one implicitly asks "To whom?" '[28] Thus for Gardner, punishment, like competition for scarce resources, was the sort of task that entails "losers as well as winners," such that we have to make an allocative decision about "who will fall into which category."[29]

By contrast, in Gardner's scheme, torture was a problem of inhumanity, not "objectionable under the heading of justice."[30] There was, he said, "an infinite amount" of non-torture to go around,[31] and the idea of torture did not demand an equivalent discrimination between the deserving and undeserving.

3. Scope

Gardner found support for his formal theory of justice as allocation in Rawls' *A Theory of Justice*. According to Gardner, the "Rawlsian project" had a central "preoccupation with allocation."[32] "For Rawls" he said, "the whole problem of social organization fell to be constructed, first and foremost, as a problem of who gets how much of what and why,"[33] and "all moral conflicts are to be interpreted primarily as allocative conflicts calling for adjudication."[34] There are, however, important differences between the way in which Rawls conceptualized principles of allocation, and their role in Gardner's theory of justice.

The subject matter of *A Theory of Justice* is "the way in which the major social institutions distribute fundamental rights and duties and determine the division of advantages from social cooperation."[35] For Rawls, this meant structuring and restructuring society according to principles that reflect the individual interests of each person, no one person's interests being overridden by the broader "welfare of society."[36] These principles demanded: equal liberty (a fair "system of public rules defining rights and duties" and the constraints that they entail);[37] a level playing field of opportunity;[38] an inclusive political system;[39] and a distribution of economic and social advantages (wealth, income, authority and responsibility) that benefits everyone.[40]

Rawls distinguished this theory of social justice from a model of fairness as the allocation of some independently existing set of benefits and burdens.[41] For Rawls, "allocative justice applies when a given collection of goods is to be divided among definite individuals with known desires and needs."[42] In Rawls' words, his scheme of social

---

[28] Gardner, "The Virtue of Justice" (n 2) 267.
[29] Gardner, "Legal Justice" (n 2) 468.
[30] ibid 470.
[31] Gardner, "The Virtue of Justice" (n 2) 264.
[32] ibid 260.
[33] ibid.
[34] ibid 259.
[35] John Rawls, *A Theory of Justice* (Revised ed, Harvard University Press 1975) 6.
[36] ibid 11. Thus, for Rawls "justice is the first virtue of social institutions"—that mechanism for reflecting the individual interests and "rational ends" of each person within a society 3, 513.
[37] ibid 177.
[38] ibid 72ff
[39] ibid 65ff.
[40] ibid 57.
[41] See further TM Scanlon, *Why Does Inequality Matter?* (OUP 2018) 140.
[42] Rawls, *A Theory of Justice* (n 35) 76.

justice "does not interpret the primary problem of distributive justice as one of allocative justice."[43] "The problem of social justice" is not, he said "that of allocating *ad libitum* various amounts of some thing, whether it be money, or property, or whatever, among given individuals."[44]

The basic structure at the heart of *A Theory of Justice* is a system for specifying certain public rules that make possible various forms of interaction through which benefits are produced, and the resulting distribution (equal or otherwise) is justifiable by reference to features needed to do this.[45] Thus, there can be "no answer" to the question of whether "one distribution of a given stock of things to definite individuals" at any moment in time is better than another—only to the question of whether that structure, and the modes of interaction that it facilitates, is fair.[46] Unequal outcomes can be entailed by a proper balancing of the interests of participants in an animate ecosystem, part constituted by social norms.

Gardner did not advocate any bigger role for allocation in understanding and justifying the "system of public rules defining rights and duties";[47] rather, he advocated a smaller role for justice. Many of the values, goals, and concerns that Rawls considered under the rubric of social justice crop up in Gardner's scheme, but almost all of them do so *outside* of the realm of justice. For Gardner, the rationale of law is to shape our actions toward a specific end—to "improve people's conformity with reasons that already apply to them."[48] Like Rawls, Gardner was concerned here to ensure that individual reasons for action are reflected properly in specific rights and duties. According to Gardner, those specific duties—of "honesty, considerateness, trustworthiness, loyalty, humanity and so on"—help to concentrate our efforts properly[49] and carry through to the justification for certain remedial responses.[50]

But for Gardner, these duties were not, by and large, duties of justice. In Gardner's words "laws, like other rules, are forced into the forms of justice only at the point at which their benefits and burdens fall to be rationed, and not before."[51] He continued:

> For the most part the benefits and burdens of legal rules do not have to be rationed at all. I don't have a quota of contracts to make and break this week, so the legal rules to the effect that I am empowered to make contracts but forbidden from breaking them have no built-in allocative dimension. They are basic rules of trustworthiness. But they do come to have a secondary allocative dimension, or secondary allocative implications, whenever a case for breach of contract comes before the courts. For at this point the court cannot but face up to the question of who is to bear the costs of the alleged breach, and in what proportions, and on what grounds, etc. It is now a situation in which there are no winners without losers, no gains without losses, and

---

[43] ibid.

[44] ibid 136.

[45] ibid 76.

[46] ibid.

[47] To use Rawls' terminology 177.

[48] *FPLPL* (n 6) 77.

[49] Gardner, "Part 1. The Place of Corrective Justice" (n 10) 23.

[50] The "continuity thesis" insists that facts that are reasons to act in particular ways can be reasons for "next best" or steps when the moment for perfect conformity has passed: ibid 30.

[51] Gardner, "The Virtue of Justice" (n 2) 256.

questions of how to allocate these gains and losses cannot but arise. Some of these questions may be corrective questions about whether and how to restore the parties to some status quo ante or status quo alter; some may be distributive questions about how to divide up the costs, or how to scale the penalties, in the event of multiple wrongdoers or multiple contributions to wrongdoing.[52]

Gardner argued that we confront two primary kinds of allocative question in private law, each of which is concerned with concrete questions about how to use the courts' resources to rectify (or prevent) wrongs. First, we confront questions about whether and how to reverse defective transfers from one person to another.[53] For Gardner, these are questions of "corrective justice," which is "a specialized juridical scheme for allowing some people, often at the expense of others, to hold on more tightly, with the support of the law, to what they already have, or recently had, in their lives."[54] That scheme directs the reversal of transactions between two potential holders (the "'arithmetic' model of addition and subtraction").[55] Second, we confront questions about who gets access to this scheme,[56] which are questions of "distributive justice," about how to divide up goods among multiple possible holders (the "'geometric' model of division'").[57] We may also confront local distributive questions between the two parties to a corrective claim, about the extent of the recoverable loss (via doctrines such as mitigation, remoteness and contributory negligence).[58]

So, Rawlsian social justice is about ensuring that the processes, systems, and norms for social cooperation create conditions in which everyone is able to pursue their individual plans. Whether justice has been done is a question that we ask about a social structure according to which allocations are made. Gardner's allocative justice is a different and smaller domain, concerned with dividing up a defined set of goods among two or more parties. It aims at outcome fairness across distributions, and it sometimes aims specifically at "arithmetic proportionality"—ensuring an alignment between what has been taken from the wronged party and what is restored to them via remedial action. Whether justice has been done is a question that we can only ask after the allocation has been made.

4. Competition

The allocative account fits many cases of justice quite well. In 2020, the British Medical Association (BMA) issued guidance to doctors faced with dwindling resources with

---

[52] ibid 256–57.

[53] See generally Gardner, "Part 1. The Place of Corrective Justice" (n 10).

[54] *FPLPL* (n 6) 192.

[55] Gardner, "Part 1. The Place of Corrective Justice" (n 10) 9.

[56] "[T]he law of obligations cannot be assigned to the role of doing 'corrective justice" as opposed to "distributive justice"; for what the law of obligations must do above all is justice in the distribution of the very corrective justice that it dispenses'. *FPLPL* (n 6) 192–93.

[57] Gardner, "Part 1. The Place of Corrective Justice" (n 10) 9.

[58] J Gardner, "What is Tort Law For? Part 2. The Place of Distributive Justice" in J Oberdiek (ed), *Philosophical Foundations of Tort Law* (OUP 2014) 349.

which to treat acute cases of COVID-19.[59] Doctors were advised to set a "threshold for admission to intensive care or use of scarce intensive treatments such as mechanical ventilation" by reference to factors associated with treatment survival, including severity of acute illness, co-morbidity and age.[60] The BMA envisaged both winners and losers of the treatment process, and a decision-making process that would determine who should fall into which category.

We can conceptualize many other competitions for scarce benefits in this way—sports matches and races, games, and sortition. There can only be one winner and one runner-up of each of the Wimbledon singles events; it is up to the Chair Umpire to determine, according to the rules of lawn tennis, who gets to claim those titles.[61] Even if there can be more than one successful candidate, lottery winnings are a limited pot to be distributed among those who were lucky enough to select the winning number.

But many problems of justice are harder to reconcile with an allocative paradigm. The UK driving test has four components: multiple choice theory and hazard perception tests, eyesight test, and practical assessment. Assessment criteria and thresholds are standardized: a candidate must score ≥ 43 out of 50 on the theory test, ≥ 44 out of 75 on the hazard perception test, ≥ 0.8 and 0.1 on the Snellen scale on the vision test, and ≤ 15 minor faults (and no major faults) in the practical. A candidate who meets those thresholds passes their test and receives a license to drive. The Driver and Vehicle Licensing Agency is not in the business of dividing up, or "allocating," passes and fails among candidates. Rather, the decision-making process is a matter of assessing candidates against a common and pre-determined standard.

This is typical of aptitude-based assessment, unless we are allocating grades over a normal distribution (grading to a bell-curve).[62] It is also typical of punishment. Gardner noted that "a court sometimes has to determine how much to punish whom for what,"[63] or "to whom is this punishment due?"[64] But that's an odd way of expressing the fact that it may be up to a court to determine how to act on the conclusion that a particular defendant has committed a wrong. Unlike the Wimbledon Chair Umpire, BMA, and International Olympic Committee, the court is not deciding who, among possible candidates, should win or lose (and how much by). Like decisions about who should pass their driving test, sentencing is a matter of assessing individuals against common criteria.

---

[59] Dominic Norcliffe-Brown and Others, "COVID-19: Ethical Issues When Demand for Life-Saving Treatment is at Capacity" (2021) Journal of Medical Ethics <http://dx.doi.org/10.1136/medethics-2021-107507>.

[60] ibid 6.

[61] Possibly, Gardner did not mean that there must actually be only one winner of any given competition. In the 2021 Summer Olympics high jump final, Qatar's Mutaz Essa Barshim and Italy's Gianmarco Tamberi each cleared 2.37 meters (m) and failed at 2.39 m. Refusing to perform a "jump off," the two athletes chose instead to share a gold medal finish. There were no *necessary* losers, or burdens to bear, but Gardner, I think, would still call this a matter of justice as between the two competitors. What matters is that this is the sort of decision in which there may be winners and losers. If everyone can always have what they want to have, we not in the realm of allocation.

[62] And if we *are* grading to a bell curve, there is a good case for saying that what we are doing is not fair: candidates' performances may be adjusted by reference to facts that have nothing to do with their performance on the relevant assessment, or broader intellectual ability.

[63] Gardner, "Legal Justice" (n 2) 468.

[64] Gardner, "Finnis on Justice" (n 25) 157.

Gardner noted that his thinking about punishment and justice had been influenced by Green—specifically, by a paper (as yet unpublished) called "The Germ of Justice."[65] In it, Green borrows an example from Waldron's "The Primacy of Justice,"[66] which I will call *Crime Ring*:

> We hear on television that a judge has sentenced five members of an organised crime ring to a total of two hundred years in prison.

For Green as for Waldron, we don't yet know whether those sentences are just, because "we are still missing the most important thing, justice-wise, which is how those penalties are distributed amongst the offenders."[67] For instance, asks Waldron, "does this mean that each of them was sentenced to forty years? Or does it mean that four of them got five years each and the other was sentenced to 180 years?"[68] For each writer, justice is about "who is punished, how severely, and on what grounds, and that matters even when there are enough lawyers to go round and plenty of space in jails."[69]

There are two things to note here. First, Waldron, Green, and Gardner each conclude that punishment is not a matter of competition, because there is no scarcity of available punishment.[70] But the hypothetical is designed to focus our attention on a small group and a set number (200). The effect is to make freedom appear as if it *is* a scarce good: if none of the gang members can have all the freedom they want, we need to know how to divide up the 200 years of non-freedom among them. That, in turn, makes us think about the relative treatment of gang members: if four of them got five years each and the other was sentenced to 180 years, that seems *prima facie* unjust as a matter of treatment *inter se*.

But that isn't how a judge goes about the sentencing exercise, nor is it how we should assess the exercise. Freedom from incarceration is not a scarce good, and criminal punishment *is* a comparative matter, but it is not a matter of comparing persons against one another.[71] Rather, it is a matter of comparing facts about persons against predetermined criteria, which (ought to) reflect the reasons for punishment.[72] Thus, the most important thing, justice-wise, is not how the penalties are distributed among the offenders. It is whether each penalty can be justified by the reasons for criminal

---

[65] L Green, "The Germ of Justice," Oxford Legal Studies Research Paper No. 60/2010 (revised version, 2021).

[66] J Waldron, "The Primacy of Justice" (2003) 9 Legal Theory 269, 275.

[67] Green, "The Germ of Justice" (n 65) 10.

[68] Waldron, "The Primacy of Justice" (n 66) 275.

[69] Green, "The Germ of Justice" (n 65) 10.

[70] Gardner, "Part 1. The Place of Corrective Justice" (n 10) 4. Thus, he concluded, "Questions of justice are forced upon us whenever an allocable good or ill is *either* in short supply *or* essentially allocative." Gardner, "The Virtue of Justice" (n 2) 267.

[71] Gardner acknowledged this in "Finnis on Justice" (n 25) 161: "there are also plentiful non-comparative questions of justice, such as whether a particular punishment (or criticism or reward or compliment or electoral defeat, etc.) is deserved, or whether a particular procedure (e.g. for determining guilt or awarding a license) is fair, irrespective of parity with any other instances or recipients." See also J Gardner, "Hart on Legality, Justice, and Morality" in *Law as a Leap of Faith: Essays on Law in General* (OUP 2012) 238, 230 ("There are also principles of justice with no competitive, and hence no inevitably interpersonal, dimension").

[72] See generally J Feinberg, "Noncomparative Justice" (1974) 83 The Philosophical Review 297.

100 TATIANA CUTTS

punishment, which are specified in concrete terms by sentencing criteria (the gravity of the crime, mitigating factors, and so on).

Yet, this description—the idea that punishment is a matter of deciding how to treat someone by reference to rules or reasons—will not help us to distinguish justice from other moral matters that Gardner excluded from his scheme (eg charity and the alleviation of suffering, torture, honesty, and betrayal).[73] Moreover, the fact that something *is* about dividing up benefits and burdens doesn't tell us that it will qualify as a matter of justice, or even a moral matter at all. Take the following example:

> *Hot Date*: Sam signs up to a dating website. Several people have viewed his profile and would like to spend time with him—many more than he has time or inclination to date.

Hot Date raises an allocative problem as between would-be dating partners: some people are going to miss out on Sam's excellent dinner conversation; who should bear that burden? But it does not raise a problem of justice, or (unless Sam has made any specific representations about how he will spend his time) any problem of morality broadly conceived.

So, we still need to determine what sets matters of justice apart from other moral matters. "Allocation" won't do that work for us: there are central problems of justice that do not involve the allocation of benefits and burdens among individuals, and the fact that a problem does involve the allocation of benefits and burdens among individuals does not make it a problem of justice. If *Crime Ring* is a matter of justice but *Hot Date* is not, and if Gardner is correct that the boundary between cases such as these is something worth drawing, we still need to know why.

5. Method

One possible basis for distinguishing *Hot Date* from *Crime Ring* is that the latter implicates rights (among others, the right not to be incarcerated), while the former does not. For Gardner, however, rights theories of justice did not hold water. It was, he said, "common to all plausible accounts of rights ... that a right is to something that the rightholder either does or should welcome,"[74] while the outcome of the justice exercise might be a bad grade, demerit points, a speeding fine, or (a case in point) criminal incarceration. Gardner acknowledged that having others recognize that one is a "morally responsible agent" can be valuable; indeed, he advocated that claim strongly.[75] But, he said, even if criminal punishment can have a "silver lining," it "needs on the whole to be a cloud"; that is its "defining purpose."[76]

Few people want to be punished, even fewer to be labeled a criminal and stripped of many of their rights, liberties, and privileges. But I can have rights to things that I have

---

[73] See generally Gardner, "Legal Justice" (n 2) and Gardner, "The Virtue of Justice" (n 2).
[74] Gardner, "Finnis on Justice" (n 25) 156.
[75] See generally J Gardner, "The Mark of Responsibility" (2003) 23 Oxford Journal of Legal Studies 157.
[76] ibid.

reason to welcome, regardless of whether I do welcome those things. I can have reason to welcome punishment, if it sets me on the right track, or perhaps (in Gardner's words) if it "takes the heat out of the situation" by managing the "retaliatory impulses" of victims.[77] Moreover, I can have rights to things that I do not have reason to want, such as onerous property rights, if property rights are the sort of things that people generally have reason to want. And I can have rights to things that I do not have reason to want overall, if they are the sort of thing that people with certain characteristics or capacities (eg citizen, promise, competitor) have reason to want.[78]

But let us grant Gardner's basic claim: it *does* seem awkward to talk of a "right to be punished," even if punishment is something we can have reason to want. Does that mean that rights talk is inapt in matters of punishment, and thus (if punishment is a matter of justice) in matters of justice more generally? I do not think so. Many rights are conditional: if I buy a ticket, arrive on time, and (as of writing) wear my face mask, I have a right to travel on the 10.45 a.m. train from Marshall station to Melbourne Southern Cross Station. And these are the sort of rights that we often talk about in relation to justice: a candidate who meets the conditions specified by each element of the UK driving test is entitled to receive a pass mark and their license; a driver who exceeds the speed limit may receive one or more demerit points; an individual who unlawfully kills another person may be sentenced to a term of imprisonment. In each case, the relevant individual has the right to some privilege (to travel by train, to start or continue driving, to remain free from incarceration) that depends upon their satisfying other conditions.

But all of this begs the question: why should we worry about whether the subject matter of justice corresponds to that of rights?[79] Indeed, why should we worry about what counts as a matter of justice at all (in law, or in morality more generally); why is "demarcating the subject matter of justice" a worthy goal?[80]

One answer might be that we are and ought to be particularly concerned with understanding whether our social institutions can be justified, and with the consequences of finding that they are. We might want to know whether a particular rule, decision, or action places too great a burden on any one individual—for instance, whether torture is ever acceptable, and if so under what circumstances. We might want to work out when and why equality matters (in the context of social institutions or elsewhere), and how it matters. All of these questions are important, but we don't need a formal theory of justice—a theory of what counts as a matter of justice—to ask and answer them. And in what follows, I argue that such a theory can make it harder to justify and formulate concrete norms.

---

[77] See further J Gardner, "Crime: In Proportion and in Perspective" in *Offences and Defences: Selected Essays in the Philosophy of Criminal Law* (OUP 2007). Gardner, "Finnis on Justice" (n 25) 156.

[78] Their rights "serve their interests as individuals with those characteristics, but they may be against their interests overall": J Raz "On The Nature of Rights" (1984) 93 Mind 194, 208.

[79] See generally Scanlon's "Reply to Leif Wenar" (2013) 10 Journal of Moral Philosophy 400, 403: "I believe that a contractualist theory can explain all the phenomena that Wenar would count as rights, along with other facts about moral right and wrong. What such a theory does not do is answer the question that Wenar poses: "Which of these moral phenomena involves a right?" I did not address this question in *What We Owe to Each Other* because it did not occur to me, and it still does not seem to me a question that it is important to answer."

[80] Gardner, "Legal Justice" (n 2) 468.

6. Correction

We have already seen that Gardner adopted Aristotle's distinction between two types of allocative norm: norms of distributive justice regulate the division of goods or ills between several potential holders (the "'geometric' model of division");[81] norms of corrective justice direct the reversal of transfers of goods or ills between two potential holders (the "'arithmetic' model of addition and subtraction").[82] Gardner argued that certain responses to tortious and contractual wrongs belonged to this latter model: they were cases involving "wrongful transactions," which the law reverses by requiring the defendant to make good losses "wrongfully occasioned" through breach.[83]

For Gardner the corrective artillery of private law encompassed cases, generally understood to belong to the law of unjust enrichment, in which "the only relevant wrong is that of failing to correct the transaction."[84] In *Kelly v Solari*,[85] Mr Solari had died before paying the final premium of a policy insuring his life, and the insurers had marked the policy as "lapsed." Unaware of this fact, Mr Solari's widow and executrix (Mrs Solari) claimed, and the insurers paid, the sum that would have been owing if the policy had not lapsed. Subject to retrial on a question of fact, the insurers were held to be entitled to recover the funds, even though Mrs Solari did not and could not have known about the insurers' mistake

Yet, for who endorse the view that private law is concerned (here and elsewhere) with reversing transfers and "allocating back" gains, *Kelly v Solari* appears to be something of a puzzle. The corrective justice account compares the position of Mrs Solari and her insurer against their position prior to payment: Mrs Solari is required to "allocate back" gains made in departure from that baseline, thus restoring the parties' pre-transaction positions. But to justify restoring the parties to that baseline, we need to identify some reason why the insurer, having made a mistake, now has a good claim to co-opt Mrs Solari's choices about what to do with her assets. And it is very difficult to do that.[86]

Some have argued that the mistaken payee should have to effect restitution because doing so causes her no harm; it is a remedy for the claimant with no downside for the defendant.[87] But this is only true relative to the pre-transaction baseline—and restoring the parties to that baseline is precisely what we have to justify.[88] Gardner

---

[81] Gardner, "Part 1. The Place of Corrective Justice" (n 10) 9.

[82] ibid.

[83] ibid 16: "the norm of tort law according to which (legally recognized) wrongdoers are required to pay reparative damages in respect of those (legally recognized) losses that they wrongfully occasion on the ground that they wrongfully occasioned those losses, is one such [norm of corrective justice]."

[84] Gardner, "Part 1. The Place of Corrective Justice" (n 10) 22.

[85] (1841) 152 ER 24.

[86] See eg F Wilmot-Smith, "Should the Payee Pay?" (2017) 37 Oxford Journal of Legal Studies 844.

[87] See eg P Birks, Unjust Enrichment (2nd edn, OUP 2005) 7; J Beatson and W Bishop, "Mistaken Payments in the Law of Restitution" (1986) 36 University of Toronto Law Journal 149, 150; M McInnes, "Enrichment Revisited" in J Neyers and Others (eds), *Understanding Unjust Enrichment* (Hart Publishing 2004) 169; R Chambers, "Two Kinds of Enrichment" in R Chambers and Others (eds), *Philosophical Foundations of the Law of Unjust Enrichment* (OUP 2009) 267; S Smith, "A Duty to Make Restitution" (2013) 26 Canadian Journal of Law & Jurisprudence 157, 172.

[88] Wilmot-Smith, "Should the Payee Pay?" (n 86).

made this point in a different context. In *From Personal Life to Private Law*, he asks us to consider a bedroom tax, designed with the goal of ensuring maximum occupancy of social housing. Gardner argues that there is a good case for excepting the currently housed from the scope of that tax, or for phasing in changes for that group slowly, because "[p]eople should be given an opportunity to hold on, to continue on the same track, to keep the lives they already have. They should not be treated as if they did not already have those lives, as if their home were just an empty space up for distribution from scratch."[89]

The question, then, is what can justify disrupting the life that the payee is currently living. There is no sense in which she "wrongfully occasions" the loss that she is being asked to make good, and it is no answer to say that she has some causal or transactional connection to it if we cannot also explain why this should matter. When corrective justice describes a sort of formal equality relative to rights, those rights are justified by reference to a specific set of reasons pertaining to the parties' interests (individual freedom, or some broader set of interests). Restitutionary responses to unjust enrichment do not protect primary rights, so that we must appeal to those considerations directly. But if individual freedom or some other interest justifies doing anything other than letting the mistaken payee carry on with her life undisturbed, we still need to explain why.

Perhaps there is no great mystery here. Framing problems of justice as "allocative" tends to focus our attention on the relative strength of two parties' competitive claims to some specific set of goods at a particular moment in time, on the basis of known facts.[90] But what we need to justify is not an administrative direction requiring a specific payee to effect restitution, but rather a *rule* in the form "unless there is a valid reason for reducing or defeating their liability, payees must restore funds mistakenly paid to them."[91]

So, the relevant question is not who has the better claim to the sum mistakenly paid, or who should bear some set burden. Rather, it is whether there are good reasons for intervening through law—at all, or via a rule to the effect that claimants can trigger court-enforced restitution. Answering that question requires us to think not only about the immediate impact of restitution but also about the prospective (behavior guiding) impact of a restitutionary rule upon the full range of persons whom those rules will affect.

Without beginning from the position that we are trying to achieve some sort of allocative equality between the parties, it is much easier to see that payors and payees are not distinct individuals: all users of the payments system regularly transact in each capacity, so that protecting the interests of would-be payors appropriately is precisely the same task as protecting the interests of all users of the payments system appropriately. Thus, our question becomes: what reasons do (current and would-be) users of the payments system have to want protection against the consequences of their mistakes;

---

[89] *FPLPL* (n 6) 167.

[90] In Rawls' words, "allocative justice applies when a given collection of goods is to be divided among definite individuals with known desires and needs." Rawls, *A Theory of Justice* (n 35) 76.

[91] See further T Cutts, "Unjust Enrichment: What We Owe to Each Other" (2021) 41 Oxford Journal of Legal Studies 114.

which mechanism will provide that protection; and can it be provided at acceptable cost to other interests?

We all have reasons to value the ability to make and receive payments. I have argued elsewhere that a restitutionary rule prevents users from suffering mightily from a small mistake (eg failing to cancel a direct debit, or entering the incorrect recipient or amount in an online transfer), thus allowing us to transact with greater confidence. We all have reasons to want this protection—what McBride calls a "reassurance" argument.[92] And we all have reasons to want the payee to be the person to mitigate that risk: giving up an unplanned-for ("windfall") gain is far less burdensome than losing money upon which one has founded plans and expectations.[93] Thus, we all have reasons to want a rule that allocates to payees the burden of risk for mistake and allows them to claim the upside of that protection for any transaction in which they are situated as payor.[94]

Gardner demonstrated clearly that those facts which justify original duties, which include the right-holder's interest in performance, can point in the direction of substitute performance. Their normative force is not spent by breach.[95] And he also demonstrated clearly that we nevertheless have normative distance to travel from the failure to perform some original duty to the justification for subjecting someone to a remedial duty.[96] But we do not need to travel that normative distance via a separate frame of theoretical reference—a project of legal justice as allocation, as distinct from the justification for law in general. And I have argued that we should not—that approaching remedial questions as questions of corrective justice can make it harder to work out what which principles of law are justifiable.

7. Conclusion

Gardner gave us two stories of private law: a story about the justification for original burdens, which requires us to think about how to help people conform to the reasons that apply to them; and a story about interpersonal (re)allocation, which begins at the moment of wrongdoing and requires us to think about "who is to bear the costs of the

---

[92] As McBride puts it, "by assuring the debtor that should he make a mistake in paying his debts he will be able (other things being equal) to get the value of his money back, the law encourages him to pay his debts." He expressed it thus in a paper presented at the Obligations XIII Conference (2016) in Cambridge ("Restitution and Unjust Enrichment: The Coming Counter-Revolution") and expands on this idea of "confidence" or "reassurance" in *The Humanity of Private Law I* (Hart Publishing 2018) 191. In his unpublished article, McBride argues that the confidence theory applies and justifies restitution where "(1) C was engaged in some valuable activity A, (2) as a result of which, D acquired from C something of value V, (3) but the circumstances in which D acquired V are such that if C were not able to recover the value of V from D, people would be discouraged from engaging in activity A."

[93] If there is a glimmer of truth to the "no harm" thesis, it is this. See further T Cutts, "Unjust Enrichment: What We Owe to Each Other" (2021) 41 Oxford Journal of Legal Studies 114, 135.

[94] I have argued elsewhere that a restitutionary principle makes a good deal more sense than a principle that "socializes loss" by requiring us to pay into a sort of public insurance scheme: Oxford Journal of Legal Studies 114, 136–37.

[95] Voyiakis, *Private Law and the Value of Choice* (n 12) 19: "the normative force of the considerations that justify the imposition of an original burden on a person is not exhausted or extinguished when that person has failed to discharge that burden."

[96] ibid 37.

alleged breach, and in what proportions, and on what grounds, etc."[97] For Gardner, the second is a story of justice, in that the court must decide who wins and who loses, and in what degree.

Yet, as Voyiakis' asks, "if we have a story that justifies the imposition of original burdens, why can't we use the same story to justify the imposition of the burden of repair too?"[98] I have argued that the theory of justice as allocation makes it difficult to capture all considerations that are relevant to the questions of whether legal intervention is justifiable, and what form it should take. Instead, we should pursue the logic of Gardner's "continuity thesis" through to its methodological conclusion— "continuing" our reflections on the moral implications' of the original duty in precisely the same way.

---

[97] Gardner, "The Virtue of Justice" (n 2) 256.
[98] Voyiakis, *Private Law and the Value of Choice* (n 12) 37.

7
Distributing Corrective Justice

Rebecca Stone[*]

When we create a system of tort law that gives wronged persons a legal right to corrective justice, John Gardner argues, we inevitably confront an important question of distributive justice: does "the system justly distribute access to the corrective justice it dispenses[?]"[1] It would be distributivity unjust were the system to give one person the legal right to corrective justice of some wrong without giving the same to similarly situated others. At the same time, Gardner contends, the good that tort law is distributing here is "irreducibly corrective ... [which] lends a certain explanatory priority to corrective over distributive justice."[2]

Gardner might simply be observing that because the creation of private legal relations that have a distinctively corrective flavor affect the distribution of benefits and burdens among members of the polity, tort law inevitably raises distributive questions. But for Gardner, a sound legal norm of corrective justice must be grounded in a sound moral norm of corrective justice.[3] And so he may be suggesting something more interesting—namely, that access to legal support of morally required corrective justice is directly regulated by norms of distributive justice in much the same way as access to ordinary goods such as food and water is so regulated.

There is something at least *prima facie* puzzling about the idea that corrective justice is regulated by distributive justice as ordinary goods are. The fact that the system has distributed access to water unjustly doesn't call into question the value of water to those who have access to it. It is unjust that some have more access than others, but the value of the water to a given person seems independent of that fact. But if the system has distributed access to corrective justice unjustly, such that only a subset of persons who have been morally wronged are able to seek it, it is less clear that it makes sense to say that the system is doing justice of any kind. Saying that the system doles out justice unjustly has an oxymoronic quality that saying the system doles out a valuable good like water unjustly does not.

Is it in fact puzzling to understand corrective justice in the way Gardner suggests? Do Gardner's observations support the idea that corrective justice enjoys some kind of "explanatory priority" over distributive justice? Can corrective justice be conceptualized prior to and independent of questions of distributive justice? I don't think we can get a full answer to these questions without delving more deeply into the nature of private legal rights. I therefore explore them by examining the conception of private legal

---

[*] Thanks very much to Jonathan Quong for helpful comments.
[1] J Gardner, *Torts and Other Wrongs* (OUP 2019) 87 ("*TAOW*").
[2] ibid 91.
[3] ibid 51–53.

Rebecca Stone, *Distributing Corrective Justice* In: *Private Law and Practical Reason*. Edited by: Haris Psarras and Sandy Steel, Oxford University Press. © Rebecca Stone 2023. DOI: 10.1093/oso/9780192857330.003.0007

rights that Gardner adheres to alongside the Kantian conception that Gardner rejects. I then propose and defend an intermediate conception. On my conception, there is a singular question of justice at the fundamental moral level that entails corrective and distributive principles whose prescriptions depend on the circumstances. There is no fundamental norm of corrective justice that is distinct from some other fundamental norm of distributive justice. On the contrary, the moral soundness of any corrective legal norm depends inescapably on distributive considerations.

1. Kantian Corrective Justice

On the Kantian conception of corrective justice as it has been developed by Ernest Weinrib and Arthur Ripstein, considerations of corrective justice and distributive justice operate independently of one another and cannot be combined in a single relationship. Corrective justice in the Kantian sense can be conceptualized without reference to distributive considerations and vice versa.[4] At the same time, it seems that Kantian corrective justice is not something that can be the object of distributive justice in a straightforward way. This is because Kantian principles imply that there cannot be corrective justice unless it is available to all.

To see why, we need to look to the principles that underpin the Kantian scheme. The master principle is the universal principle of right, a principle of reciprocity that requires each to respect the like freedom of all. It implies the principle of independence: each must be free to set her own purposes independently of the will of particular others.[5] The principle of independence in turn implies that persons' rights against one another must be defined and coercively enforced by an appropriately constituted state that represents the will of all. Unless private rights are omnilaterally defined, particular persons may impose their conceptions of private rights on everyone else. Unless they are omnilaterally enforced, each will lack assurance that their rights are secure from interference by particular others.[6] In short, publicly-minded construction and enforcement mechanisms are constitutive of a system of private rights that

---

[4] On Weinrib's view, the two forms of justice "connote categorically different structures of justification. Neither of them can integrate the other within it." Weinrib, *Corrective Justice* (OUP 2012) 270. "For purposes of justifying a determination of liability, corrective justice is independent of distributive justice." ibid 19. Thus, "considerations of poverty have no effect on the definition and application of property rights." ibid 297. On Ripstein's view, the moral idea that no-one is in charge of any other entails that "I cannot take or use your property without authorization" or "act in ways that are inconsistent with your being in charge," but "is silent on the further question of what citizens, acting as a collective body through their governments, should do about the distribution of property." A Ripstein, *Private Wrongs* (Harvard University Press 2016) 44.

[5] A Ripstein, *Force and Freedom* (Harvard University Press 2009) 13–15.

[6] The principle of right requires "a state that will render the demands of right determinate, through legislation and adjudication, and will render the enforceability of those demands reciprocal through an enforcement mechanism." A Ripstein, "Authority and Coercion" [2004] 32 Philosophy & Public Affairs 27. See also E Weinrib, *The Idea of Private Law* (Harvard University Press 1995) 107 ("Since the vindication of right includes the prevention or reversal of violations of right, the freedom of all is immediately joined with a reciprocal universal coercion."); Weinrib, *Corrective Justice* (n 4) 111 ("a claim of right implies a judicial role in interpreting and enforcing the claim").

secures everyone's independence—a system of private rights that ensures that "no person is in charge of another."[7]

The contours of private rights, moreover, cannot depend on anyone's purposes. In the terminology of the common law, private rights are rights against misfeasance, not rights against nonfeasance.[8] There can't be privately enforceable relational duties that require private persons to serve other private persons' needs and purposes.

The equal freedom that is instantiated by the Kantian scheme is therefore a thin, formal kind. Each has a right to do as they wish with their rightful means unencumbered by duties to serve the purposes of others, even when they could do so with minimal impact on the pursuit of their own ends. It doesn't matter, from the standpoint of Kantian corrective justice, that some have a greater ability to pursue their ends than others so long as each person's rights to his means are exercisable without reference to anyone else's purposes.

In this way, the Kantian scheme erects a firewall between corrective justice and justice in the distribution of the means. A system of corrective justice honors each person's ability to use the means that she has free from interference by particular others. Ensuring that those means are fairly distributed such that each has the ability to pursue her ends successfully is another matter entirely. This is not to say that distributive considerations are irrelevant, only that they are irrelevant from the standpoint of corrective justice. Distributive justice is a matter of what the community as a whole owes to each, not what particular private persons owe to particular others. It is a matter of public, not private, right.

It should now be clear why on the Kantian conception it doesn't make sense to say that corrective justice is a good that can be distributed in the same way that we might distribute the ordinary means that persons use to pursue their ends. Everyone's private rights must be omnilaterally defined and coercively enforced for those rights to instantiate the equal freedom of all. Imperfect access to tort law institutions of corrective justice, even if that imperfect access is equally distributed, violates this condition, leaving persons' independence in peril. Therefore, unless everyone has full access to corrective justice for all infringements of their private rights, there can be no corrective justice at all. In other words, an absolute distributive imperative is part and parcel of the system of corrective justice itself: everyone's rights must be omnilaterally defined and enforced for there to be justice of the corrective kind at all. At the same time, the distributive imperative requiring that each has full access to corrective justice doesn't have implications for run-of-the-mill questions about the distribution of means. The way in which the polity decides to resolve distributive questions of the latter kind has no impact on the justice of the corrective scheme.

In so far as we agree with the Kantians that independence is an important value, their conception is an appealing one when both public and private institutions are doing what they are supposed to be doing—discharging distributive and corrective justice respectively. It becomes less appealing when one or other is not. Suppose that

---

[7] Ripstein, *Private Wrongs* (n 4) 12.

[8] ibid 53–55. See also Weinrib, *Corrective Justice* (n 4) 11 ("as participants in a regime of liability, the parties are viewed as purposive beings who are not under duties to act for any purposes in particular, no matter how meritorious").

public institutions fail to implement a plausible principle of distributive justice such that the means of some to pursue their ends unjustly exceed the means of others to do likewise. Why think that a system that protects the means of each against interference by particular others is doing any kind of justice at all? The system may be securing each person's independence to use their legally rightful means as they wish. But it is doing so by entrenching injustice in the distribution of means. Why give priority to the former over the latter?

A response might be to say that navigating trade-offs between corrective and distributive justice is just a question that the theory doesn't speak to. But if it is possible to navigate such trade-offs in a principled fashion, then there must exist a more fundamental principle of justice that tells us how to do so. Otherwise, all we have is either an ideal theory that has little bearing on our actual, non-ideal world or two conceptions of different types of justice—corrective and distributive—that don't generate all-things-considered prescriptions.[9]

2. Gardner's Scheme

Let's now drop the Kantian idea that private rights are constituted by their omnilateral definition and enforcement and suppose with Gardner that rights can exist at the moral level independently of such state action. It remains true that the state will be involved in the definition and enforcement of private rights in so far as it creates legal rights that institutionalize moral rights. But the underlying moral rights exist—they are the source of binding moral obligations—prior to their legal institutionalization. The process of institutionalization may modify the rights to some extent by resolving indeterminacy about their content and transforming them into meaningful legal rights. But the state's actions in creating those legal rights are justified in so far as they reflect and protect underlying moral rights that exist in a robust sense prior to being elaborated and enforced by legal institutions.

Gardner will say that the underlying moral rights and associated moral obligations exist because of the set of moral reasons that gives rise to them.[10] Once a right has been infringed, the associated primary obligation can no longer be performed, but the reasons that gave rise to it persist generating a moral duty to do the next best thing, such as paying the right-holder compensation. This is the moral duty of corrective justice that follows from Gardner's continuity thesis.[11] And it points to a way of justifying a system of tort law that creates a system of primary and secondary legal duties that track underlying primary moral rights and associated corrective moral duties.

The substantive claim that private legal rights derive their normative force from pre-existing moral rights that they instantiate and enforce is a plausible and familiar one. But Gardner conceptualizes the relationship between private rights and justice in a way that may obscure some of what the Kantian conception illuminates. On both

---

[9] We have a theory that calls out for a "resolution principle" but hasn't supplied it. D Priel, "The Impossibility of Independent Corrective Justice" (unpublished manuscript 2018), on file with author.
[10] *TAOW* (n 1) 57–58.
[11] ibid.

110 REBECCA STONE

conceptions, duties of repair owed by the wrongdoer to the right-holder arise when primary private rights are infringed. But whereas the Kantians view the infringements themselves—the prior wrongs that give rise to the duty to correct—as violations of norms of (corrective) justice, Gardner contends that "[m]ost torts are not injustices at all, let alone corrective injustices. They are violations of norms of honesty, considerateness, trustworthiness, loyalty, humanity, and so on."[12]

This picture of the relationship between rights and justice emerges from particular features of the conceptual scheme that Gardner endorses. On Gardner's picture, moral rights are rights that arise from moral norms that are grounded in the interests of the right-holder and impose upon the duty-bearer a duty to take or refrain from particular actions.[13] Norms of justice, in turn, are moral norms for "tackling *allocative* moral questions," narrowly defined as questions about who is to get how much of morally significant assignable goods.[14] Moral rights therefore count as rights of justice only if they arise from moral norms that tackle allocative questions of this kind. In this way, a duty of justice in the form of a duty of repair can arise from the breach of a moral right that is not a right of justice. This is because the reasons underpinning the moral right persist after it is violated giving rise to a duty on the part of the wrongdoer to do the next best thing for the right-holder, and the resulting obligation to do the next best thing responds to an allocative moral question. The right-holder has not received the performance she was owed. The duty-bearer cannot go back in time and render that performance. Thus, the duty-bearer must give her something as close as possible to the original performance to make up for her loss. Thus, a duty of justice can arise from the infringement of a primary duty that was not itself an answer to an allocative problem of justice—and thus not a norm of justice within Gardner's scheme.

Gardner's concept of justice is thus a deflationary one. Justice is not part of the normative landscape at the fundamental moral level. The fundamental building blocks are moral reasons that are themselves not understood as entailments of justice. Rights of justice are simply those that arise from moral norms that handle certain allocative moral question. Moral rights and duties of all kinds, whether they are norms of justice or not, exist in virtue of the reasons that justify them and so their existence isn't a matter of justice. They "come and go with the reasons for and against their existence, and irrespective of their use, observance, recognition, or adoption," and so are "incapable of being distributed."[15]

This way of carving up the moral universe leads to the jarring conclusion that the moral right not to be tortured is not a right of justice.[16] It qualifies as a right because "the interests of the person who is not to be tortured suffice to justify the obligation not to torture."[17] But it doesn't qualify as a right of justice because it is an obligation of humanity not an allocative right. It gives rise to a right of corrective justice when it is infringed because the claim of a tortured person for reparation from her torturer is

[12] ibid 50.
[13] ibid 74.
[14] ibid 31–32.
[15] ibid 84.
[16] ibid 31–32, 74.
[17] ibid 74.

a claim that the losses she has suffered at the hands of the torturer be reallocated between them.[18] But this is a feature of the secondary right not the primary right.

On this picture of justice, it is clear why the institutionalization of norms of corrective justice raises questions of distributive justice. In determining which moral norms will count as torts, the system determines which wronged persons will have their claims for corrective justice legally recognized and publicly supported, which is an allocative problem of the right kind.[19] But the Gardnerian scheme doesn't tell us much about the nature of the allocative problem and how it should be solved beyond the observation that it concerns the allocation of something that alters the overall distribution of benefits and burdens.

Perhaps it is enough to categorize the problem as an allocative one. Some prescriptions straightforwardly follow. It would be obviously problematic, for example, if the system arbitrarily defined torts with reference to characteristics of the right-holder and/or duty-bearer such as their race or gender.

Yet much remains underdetermined. We could eliminate problems of arbitrariness by getting rid of the tort entirely instead of eliminating the discriminatory limitations. When we set aside such problems and the question we ask instead is "should we recognize a type of wrong against all relevant right-holders by all relevant duty-holders?" the answer will, on Gardner's conception, be driven in significant part by the reasons that underpin the moral norms themselves. Observing that the problem is an allocative one doesn't offer much in the way of guidance. The institutionalization of moral norms raises an additional set of difficulties that aren't reducible to questions about the significance of the norms being institutionalized. Some norms may be costlier to define and adjudicate than others. But holding such considerations constant, decisions to recognize one set of moral norms legally at the expense of another will be regulated by the reasons that lie behind the two sets of moral norms. If a choice must be made, norms that are supported by weightier reasons should be recognized at the expense of others.

It is also not clear in what sense this picture vindicates the notion that "corrective justice in tort law enjoys some kind of explanatory priority."[20] Suppose that the system distributes access to corrective justice unjustly by recognizing some torts instead of others that were more worthy of recognition. Suppose, for example, tort law recognizes a set of wrongs that are disproportionately suffered by the rich while failing to recognize another set that are disproportionately suffered by the poor. The system's failure and the injustice that ensues from lack of recognition and enforcement of the latter, it is plausible to suppose, will alter the set of reasons that lie behind the underlying moral norms. Perhaps certain minimal infringements of the legal property rights of the rich by the poor no longer count as morally wrongful when the poor may not rely on tort law to vindicate their own more significant claims. But if that is so, then when the system gives the rich a remedy in the face of such infringements of their legal rights, it cannot be doing corrective justice of any kind.

[18] ibid.
[19] ibid 85–87.
[20] ibid 82.

Gardner might respond that this misses the point. Precisely because the legal right isn't supported by moral reasons that would give rise to a duty of repair pursuant to the continuity thesis, any corrective legal norm that would provide the rich person with a remedy in these circumstances must be unsound. Conceding this is compatible with maintaining that moral duties of repair continue to arise from infringements of primary moral norms that reflect the full set of reasons that arise under these distributively unjust conditions. In this sense, corrective justice has a kind of explanatory priority.

But if this is the explanatory priority corrective justice retains, it is a thin, formal kind of priority. For it is compatible with injustice in the distribution of access to corrective justice altering the content of the very norms that any institution of corrective justice should support. In short, access to corrective justice doesn't look like an ordinary good that can straightforwardly be distributed, because the substantive content of sound corrective norms will be affected by the way in which access to corrective justice is distributed.

3. Comparing the Gardnerian and Kantian Conceptions

While both offer rights-based justifications of private law, there are at least two significant respects in which the Kantian and Gardnerian conceptions diverge. The first concerns the relationship between substance and procedure. The second concerns the extent to which rights necessarily confer freedom of choice on the right-holder or simply serve the interests of the right-holder.

Consider the relationship between substance and procedure first. On the Kantian conception, private rights must instantiate the independence of all, a requirement that entails only procedural constraints on the particular content of those rights. The cardinal sin is unilateralism—the unilateral imposition of particular persons' wills on particular others. Thus, private rights are necessarily constituted by omnilateral state action that resolves indeterminacy about their content and coercively enforces the omnilaterally defined rights—rights that must be defined without reference to particular persons' needs and purposes. On the Gardnerian conception, by contrast, private rights are a function of the underlying substantive moral reasons and can exist whether or not they are legally institutionalized.

As we have seen, it is the proceduralism of the Kantian account that creates the firewall between corrective and distributive justice. The substantive concerns that may require a more egalitarian distribution of means are simply not relevant to the question whether each is free to use his means independently of the purposes of others. And since independence is the master principle as far as corrective justice is concerned, corrective justice doesn't depend on such substantive concerns. Gardner's conception erects no such firewall, but at the expense of diminishing the significance of corrective duties, as the content of primary and secondary duties are entirely determined by the full set of underlying moral reasons including those that arise from the prevailing distribution of means.

As for the role of freedom in the two accounts, Kantian private rights establish domains in which persons are free to do as they wish with their rightful means, whereas the hallmark of a right on the Gardnerian conception is whether it has as part of its rationale the interests of the right-holder. Thus, on the Gardnerian conception, moral rights necessarily serve the interests of the right-holder, but they don't necessarily confer on her any protected domain of freedom of choice. In other words, whereas the Kantians offer a will-based theory of the function of rights, Gardner's is an interest-based account.

Despite these differences, sound private legal rights are closely connected to their moral counterparts on both conceptions. On the Kantian conception, the two come into existence together: full-fledged private rights must be legally institutionalized to count as genuine rights. On the Gardnerian conception, moral rights provide a justification for their legal counterparts, which must therefore closely mirror those moral rights.

In the remainder of this chapter, I'll sketch an alternative conception of private rights that is in various respects intermediate between the Kantian and Gardnerian conceptions on both dimensions while retaining what I consider to be the most normatively plausible features of each. The account also departs from both accounts in detaching justified legal rights from their moral counterparts while retaining a significant role for the latter in the justification of the former.

4. An Intermediate Conception

Like Gardner, I begin with the idea that reasons are morally fundamental and underpin our rights against one another. Persons ought to make choices that reflect the balance of moral and prudential reasons that apply to them. A plausible conception of rights should reflect that fact.

This cannot be the entire story, however, if, as it is plausible to suppose, rationality requires each of us to give special weight to our own interests and those with whom we stand in particular relationships—family, friends, and members of the larger communities of which we are part. For then some of the reasons each of us should rationally weigh are partial reasons that can make it the case that what it is rational for me to do when faced with a particular choice won't correspond with what another would rationally want me to do. Partial reasons, in other words, entail that rationality will be indexed to a particular person's standpoint. And if persons' standpoints conflict, we will need a way of rationally navigating those conflicts. Appealing only to the reasons that define persons' standpoints will result in an impasse whenever standpoints conflict. This suggests that there exists a further set of rational considerations orthogonal to those reasons that tell persons whose standpoint governs a choice in the event of a conflict.

This last point may not seem immediately obvious. Why aren't the choices that a particular person faces necessarily governed by her standpoint? She is the one who must choose. Surely rationality requires that she should choose the option that is prescribed by her standpoint.

Though superficially plausible, such an allocation of standpoints to choices doesn't withstand scrutiny. Without more, the non-normative fact that I am the one doing the choosing can't entail the normative conclusion that the partial reasons that define my standpoint prevail over those that define others' standpoints. This point is most obvious when it comes to choices made by those who stand in certain relationships of trust with others. The teacher's choice of learning material for her students, for example, should clearly be informed by her students' standpoint, not her own. But the point applies more generally. The significance of the set of choices the rich get to make is much greater than that of the poor. It can't be that their standpoint controls those choices just because they happen to be the ones making them. We are, of course, morally responsible for our choices, which might make it seem that we must always do what we rationally think is best. But the set of choices we face is in significant part a function of circumstances that are out of our control. It surely isn't fair for the standpoint of one whose life by good luck presents him with many significant choices—significant not just for himself but also for many others—to govern all those choices when many other persons have lives that because of misfortune present them with fewer such significant choices. Fairness seems to dictate a more equitable allocation of standpoints to choices.

Is a more equitable allocation best understood as a requirement of justice? I think it is, though within Gardner's scheme it wouldn't be. In Gardner's scheme, recall, justice solves problems about the allocation of assignable goods. The fairness considerations that I have just identified help to solve an allocative problem. But the allocative problem is deeper than the type of problem that Gardner identifies as a problem of justice, because while it may have implications for problems of allocating assignable goods, it isn't fundamentally a problem about allocating goods. Rather, it is an allocative problem that is built into the fabric of moral reality at the fundamental level. Just as there are reasons that define persons' rational standpoints, there are considerations of justice that tell us how rational standpoints should be allocated among choices and thus how conflicts among standpoints should be resolved.

If we view justice in this way—as allocating standpoints among choices—we are naturally led to a conceptualization of persons' rights according to which there is an intimate connection between rights and justice. To have a right over a particular choice means that the all-things-considered balance of considerations of justice require that that one's standpoint be allocated to that choice. A right to have one's standpoint determine how that choice is to be made is thus a right of justice. On my conception, therefore, unlike on Gardner's, it isn't a mistake to view a question of rights as necessarily involving a question of justice. If justice would assign a torturer's victim's standpoint to the torturer's choice whether to torture him, then the torturer's victim's right not to be tortured is a right of justice.

My conception is compatible with an interest-based conception of rights in so far as reasons and considerations of justice—rather than the right-holder's will—control what agents are duty-bound to do. The right-holder's standpoint controls the choices that are governed by it, whether these be her own choices or the choices of others, and considerations of justice determine which choices the standpoint governs. The prescriptive content of the standpoint and the just allocation of standpoints to choices are in turn determined by reasons and considerations of justice, not by anyone's will.

If, however, there is metaphysical or epistemic uncertainty about the content of persons' standpoints or the just allocation of standpoints to choices, persons will need mechanisms for settling that normative uncertainty—mechanisms that necessarily aren't reducible to the underlying reasons and considerations of justice given that the latter don't yield certain prescriptions. This means that we must answer a further question: how is moral authority to settle normative uncertainty allocated among persons? Given the allocative nature of the question, it makes sense to view it as a question of justice.

What is the just solution to this second-order problem of justice—that of allocating moral authority to settle normative uncertainty about first-order justice (the allocation of standpoints to choices) and the content of persons' rational standpoints? Liberal-egalitarian principles suggest that considerations of autonomy and equal respect for persons will figure in the just solution, such that the just allocation of authority will ensure that persons whose rights are or may be affected by the resolution of the uncertainty must (presumptively at least) have an equal say in how it is to be resolved. Each person's autonomy is furthered by an allocation that gives her authority to settle uncertainty about her own standpoint and a say in resolving uncertainty about how her standpoint is to be justly allocated among possible choices. The value of equal respect for persons is advanced by an allocation of authority that ensures that each person has an equal say in the selection among plausibly just allocations that may affect her rights.

As I argue in detail elsewhere, this is where normative powers of decision-making, consent, promise, and agreement enter into the picture.[21] Such acts are normatively significant precisely because they settle normative uncertainty about the content of persons' rational standpoints and the just allocation thereof by the persons or groups of persons who are authorized by justice to resolve it. When an agent makes a decision about what she should do or consents to an action by another where her own standpoint is allocated to her own or the other's choices, she settles normative uncertainty about the content of her standpoint as it pertains to her own or another's choices respectively. When agents make promises or agreements, they resolve normative uncertainty about justice by together settling uncertainty about how their rational standpoints should be justly allocated among possible choices they may face. As an example of the former, suppose that an agent's standpoint controls whether another person may perform a surgery on her. According to my conception, her morally valid consent to the surgery involves her settling normative uncertainty about her standpoint in favor of her undergoing the procedure. As an example of the latter, suppose that two persons enter into a morally valid agreement to exchange widgets for money. According to my conception, the parties thereby settle normative uncertainty about what justice between them demands in favor of the buyer's standpoint controlling who gets the widgets and the seller's standpoint who gets the money.

When the rights of many agents would be implicated by the resolution of normative uncertainty, mechanisms of promise and agreement may not work because a requirement of unanimity may not be achievable or desirable. Thus, agents may have to resort to legal institutions to settle uncertainty about background rights. But those legal institutions should answer to a similar set of considerations of justice. They should be designed to allocate settling authority among persons in a way that is compatible with liberal egalitarian principles.

---

[21] R Stone, "Normative Uncertainty, Normative Powers, and Limits on Freedom of Contract" (unpublished manuscript 2020), on file with author.

5. Substantive versus Procedural Dimensions of Justice

Much more needs to be done to fill in and defend the picture sketched here, some of which I attempt to do elsewhere.[22] The important point for present purposes is that agents simultaneously face (i) substantive problems of reason and justice, and (ii) procedural questions about who is authorized to settle normative uncertainty about agents' standpoints and the just allocation of those standpoints to choices. Thus, the framework admits of injustice on two dimensions: there is substantive injustice when someone acts contrary to the just assignment of standpoints to choices; and there is procedural injustice when someone acts contrary to a valid settlement of normative uncertainty about (substantive) injustice—that is, when someone fails to respect the settlement that reflects the just assignment of authority to settle normative uncertainty, even if the result imposed by ignoring those determinations might accord with substantive justice. To illustrate, return to the simple doctor–patient example. The doctor engages in substantive injustice if he operates on the patient when undergoing such a procedure is proscribed by the patient's standpoint. The doctor engages in procedural injustice when he operates on the patient in the face of normative uncertainty about what the patient's standpoint prescribes where the patient has validly exercised her settling authority to determine that she not undergo the procedure. Some amount of substantive injustice is inevitable in a world of imperfectly rational beings for whom the demands of justice are epistemically opaque. Procedural injustice, by contrast, is eliminable even for such beings, at least in principle.

Injustice of the procedural sort is analogous to the injustice that the Kantians associate with the infringement of private rights, if, as I suggest, authority to settle normative uncertainty is justly assigned to those who are most implicated by it: the possessor of the standpoint when it comes to normative uncertainty about a standpoint; and those whose first-order rights may be implicated by the settlement when it comes to normative uncertainty about justice. Contra the Kantian conception, however, procedural rights ultimately serve a substantive conception of justice and so are substantively constrained. The assignment of authority is an assignment of authority to settle normative uncertainty and valid resolutions of the uncertainty must plausibly do exactly that. Agents must consider in good faith the substantive problem at hand and their settlement must be substantively plausible. Valid exercises of settling authority are therefore not pure acts of will. They are valid only in so far as they respect and are consistent with the underlying reasons and considerations of justice, uncertainty about which they purport to settle.

Both types of injustice arise from a departure from a just allocation—an allocation of standpoints and an allocation of authority respectively. In this sense, we can view them as different forms of distributive injustice (though what I'm referring to as substantive justice most likely tracks more closely what people usually have in mind when they speak of distributive justice). We might then define two notions of corrective justice corresponding to any secondary duties of repair that arise from injustices of each

---

[22] ibid; R Stone, "Putting Freedom of Contract in Its Place" (unpublished manuscript 2021), on file with author.

type. Such corrective duties are clearly derivative of allocative considerations, and so we may be tempted to conclude that corrective justice is wholly dependent on distributive justice.

This conclusion is too quick, however, because a substantive injustice doesn't always generate a duty of repair that could be knowable and so action-guiding given normative uncertainty about justice. If an action is transparently an injustice—because it would count as such under any plausible settlement of the uncertainty about justice—then a duty to repair capable of guiding action clearly arises. It doesn't matter how applicable normative uncertainty about justice has been resolved, because any attempt to resolve it in a way that yields the conclusion that the conduct is not unjust is invalid regardless of the validity of the procedure. But in other cases—where, given the prevailing normative uncertainty, it isn't clear whether an action is unjust—it matters how the applicable normative uncertainty has been resolved as agents can't be sure whether the action was unjust. And so procedural considerations come to the fore. An action that runs contrary to the procedurally valid resolution of the uncertainty about justice would count as a procedural injustice, even if we cannot say that it is also a substantive injustice, giving rise to a duty of repair on that dimension. Table 7.1 sets out the possibilities.

In contending that all that matters from the standpoint of private right is the omnilateral definition and enforcement of private rights, the Kantian conception focuses our attention exclusively on the middle two rows of Table 7.1. It ignores the substantive dimension of justice entirely, using the term corrective justice to denote both the primary legal duties that emerge alongside secondary duties to correct infringements of them. Mapping their framework onto this one, the Kantians contend in effect that the substantive considerations of justice that regulate the allocation of standpoints to choices are irrelevant as far as the content of persons' private rights and duties are concerned. Hence, corrective justice is independent of questions of distributive justice.

This picture is normatively plausible if normative uncertainty is pervasive and purely metaphysical—that is, if it is always present and all-encompassing and there aren't better or worse ways of resolving it. Under these assumptions the rows at the top

Table 7.1 When do corrective duties capable of guiding action arise?

	No Procedural Injustice (no infringement of valid legal right)	Procedural Injustice (infringement of valid legal right)
Transparent Substantive Justice	Clear absence of a corrective duty of any kind	Clear absence of a corrective duty of any kind
Contestable Substantive Justice	Unknowable absence of a corrective duty	Clear duty to correct infringement of legal rights
Contestable Substantive Injustice	Unknowable duty to correct substantive injustice	Clear duty to correct infringement of legal rights
Transparent Substantive Injustice	Clear duty to correct substantive injustice	Clear duty to correct substantive injustice

118 REBECCA STONE

and bottom of Table 7.1 can be ignored, and all private duties have content that is entirely procedurally defined.

The Kantian picture is less plausible if normative uncertainty has an epistemic component, such that there are substantively better or worse ways of assigning standpoints to choices. Under such conditions, a procedurally impeccable process may be transparently substantively flawed. It is unclear why procedure must always trump substance, given that the point of the procedure is to resolve a substantive epistemic problem. Yet insisting that substance should always take precedence over procedure also seems to go too far in the face of significant epistemic normative uncertainty about justice and associated reasonable disagreement about its content.

Thus, we need to strike a balance between these two extremes. The requirement that epistemic uncertainty about justice be resolved reasonably rather than perfectly justly looks like a promising way to do this. Procedurally valid legal rights would then be the end of the story only when reasonable people would disagree about what substantive justice has to say about its content. In the absence of such reasonable disagreement, substantive considerations would determine the content of persons' private rights directly. If we follow the Kantians in associating corrective justice with what I am calling procedural justice, and distributive justice with what I am calling substantive justice, the zone of the reasonable would then limit the extent to which corrective justice could operate independently of distributive considerations.

A sceptic might object at this point that introducing a reasonableness requirement is simply serving as a placeholder—identifying a trade-off without giving us tools to resolve it. Thus, the conception leaves us no better off than the Kantian conception does in navigating tensions between corrective and distributive justice.

A full response to this objection is beyond the scope of this chapter. But it is clear that any such response will have to build more content into the idea of the reasonable. An extremely thin conception of the reasonable—for instance, one requiring nothing more than internal consistency—will leave corrective justice effectively unconstrained by considerations of substantive justice. A more robust conception will render it more constrained.

How should we choose among the possibilities? We aren't seriously settling normative uncertainty about justice if the only desiderata of such a settlement is internal consistency. Such a thin constraint could leave persons vulnerable to legal action by another based on conduct that is transparently not an infringement of the former's rights. To settle normative uncertainty about justice we must seriously engage with a substantive normative problem and arrive at a resolution that is normatively plausible given the nature of the problem sufficient to justify enforcement of a plaintiff's legal rights against the defendant. At the same time, it is important that our conception of the reasonable not require persons to arrive at the truth or something too close to it, given the epistemic complexity of the substantive problem of justice. Such a demanding conception would make a conscientious plaintiff reluctant to stand on her rights in situations where it is likely that her rights have been infringed. An intermediate solution is therefore required. Exactly what this entails is difficult to specify with precision, but it must tolerate disagreement among those who reasonably engage with the problem of resolving normative uncertainty about justice—that is among those who are committed to a solution that instantiates substantive principles of fairness and flourishing.[23]

A response of this form concedes that there is uncertainty about the criterion that we use to distinguish acceptable and unacceptable resolutions of the uncertainty—that the reasonable can't be specified with precision. But this isn't a fatal problem. Many of our moral concepts require us to exercise judgment in the face of vagueness about their range of application, but that doesn't render those concepts practically inert. The idea of the reasonable is such a concept. There will be a range of settlements of normative uncertainty about justice that are close to the line and so difficult to classify as reasonable or unreasonable. But there will also be a range of possible settlements that are easy for us to classify because they clearly fall above or below it.

6. The Relationship Between Corrective and Distributive Justice

Instead of starting by conceptualizing a corrective form of justice distinct from a distributive form, I began with a unitary conception of justice within which we can locate distributive and corrective concerns. In a world of normative certainty and determinacy, justice entails an allocation of standpoints to choices that is responsive to distributive considerations. This entails a system of private rights pursuant to which each has the duty to act in accordance with another's standpoint whenever justice has assigned the latter's standpoint to his choice. Private persons will have primary duties to so act alongside secondary corrective duties to do the next best thing should they infringe another's rights. But both types of duties are ultimately derivative of the assignment of standpoints to choices that is given by substantive justice.

If we were to follow Gardner here, we would say that duties of corrective justice are just the secondary duties of repair that arise when these primary duties are infringed. Alternatively, if we were to follow the Kantians by viewing corrective justice as demarcating the set of rights and duties that define private parties' relationships with one another including but not confined to associated duties of repair, we might label the entire domain as one of corrective justice, albeit one whose content is, contra the Kantian conception, distributively determined.

Normative uncertainty adds an additional layer of complexity by forcing us to reckon with the procedural dimension of injustice with which the Kantian corrective justice theorists are exclusively concerned. Agents must continue to honor the substantive constraints imposed by the reasons that define controlling standpoints and by considerations of justice in so far as they are certain. But in so far as there is uncertainty about their content, agents must now also honor the just assignment of

---

[23] This suggestion has a Rawlsian flavor though Rawls suggests that private law may not be subject to the exacting demands of justice to which the basic structure are subject to, or at least that the principles that do apply are distinct from and independent of the principles that regulate the basic structure. See J Rawls, *Justice as Fairness: A Restatement* (EI Kelly ed, 2nd edn, Harvard University Press 2021) 11. For further argument that something more than internal consistency but considerably less than the truth is the correct constraint, see R Stone, "Private Liability without Wrongdoing," University of Toronto Law Journal (forthcoming).

authority to reasonably settle that normative uncertainty. Thus, a duty-bearer can infringe a presumptive right-holder's rights by acting as if his own standpoint controls the choice even if such an allocation of standpoints is compatible with some plausible resolution of extant normative uncertainty about justice, when those authorized to resolve normative uncertainty about the just assignment of standpoints to choices have plausibly settled the uncertainty differently by assigning the presumptive right-holder's standpoint to the choice instead.

Does corrective justice enjoy any kind of "explanatory priority" once normative uncertainty is in the picture? I've argued that corrective duties depend on the basic assignment of standpoints to choices being reasonably just. If normative uncertainty about the just assignment has been settled unreasonably, then the primary and secondary duties that are entailed by the settlement are not morally binding. In other words, the outer limit of persons' moral authority to settle normative uncertainty about justice is distributively determined.

On the other hand, if reasonableness captures the correct trade-off between procedural and substantive considerations, corrective justice also achieves a modicum of independence from substantive justice. This is because agents will be required to respect substantively unjust settlements of normative uncertainty about justice in their interactions with other private parties when those settlements are reasonable. In these cases, distributive considerations governing how standpoints and authority to resolve normative uncertainty about justice should be allocated are important determinants of corrective duties, but so are the determinations of those thereby authorized to settle the applicable normative uncertainty about justice—determinations that are content-independent within substantively constrained bounds.

The framework can vindicate Gardner's claim that the occasion of a tort dispute can confront us with "questions of distributive justice that are already pre-localized, that already assume the context of a bilateral zero-sum conflict."[24] If the polity's assignment of standpoints to choices is reasonable but not perfectly just, then the occasion of a tort dispute could provide the parties to the dispute with an opportunity for refining that assignment as between them in the light of what has transpired. In other words, the tort dispute would provide them with an opportunity to refine the allocation of standpoints to choices to better approximate what justice between them requires. In my framework, though, in contrast to Gardner's, corrective justice is not thereby enjoying "explanatory priority."[25] The refinement is justified by the relationship-specific questions of substantive justice that come to the fore—questions that the parties are morally authorized to settle when the answers are normatively uncertain. Indeed, the parties could use the tort dispute to reshape their vision of their primary rights and duties against one another in which case any resulting refinements of their corrective duties would be derivative of their reconfiguration of their primary rights.[26]

Does it make sense to think of corrective justice as a good to be distributed in accordance with considerations of justice—something we can characterize prior to and

[24] Rawls, *Justice as Fairness* (n 23) 97.
[25] ibid.
[26] For further development of this idea see R Stone, "Who Has the Power to Enforce Private Rights" in P Miller and J Oberdiek (eds), *Oxford Studies in Private Law Theory*, Vol. II (OUP forthcoming).

independently of how it is in fact distributed by the polity? As Gardner's observations make clear, there is more to assigning standpoints to choices than defining private parties' rights against one another. This is because the polity must also confront the question what resources are to be devoted to the enforcement of such rights and duties. This, of course, is a question of non-ideal theory, for it wouldn't arise if everyone always did what justice required of them—if every private actor discharged his primary duties of corrective justice. But once people are imperfectly motivated to conform to justice, we face a question of non-ideal justice: how should the polity organize itself in order to respond to such non-compliance?

Given that resources are scarce, it won't be possible for the polity to confront this second question without it having an impact on the first question—the question how to allocate standpoints to choices in the first place. Indeed, the decision to allocate some resources to enforcement is an allocative decision of this kind. The state is deciding, in effect, to allocate a public standpoint to control of those resources. But for precisely this reason, I don't see how corrective justice can be characterized as a simple good or resource to be distributed, as Gardner seems to suggest that it can. Corrective duties arise from infringements of the primary rights, which are themselves given by the basic assignment of standpoints to choices, which must be responsive to the problem of ensuring that rights are respected when some are imperfectly motivated to conform to justice.

To be more concrete, consider the reasonable person standard in torts. With a few exceptions, the law evaluates the reasonableness of a defendant's conduct by comparing it to the reasonable behavior of a person of "ordinary prudence"—a standard that is thus invariant to many of the actual capabilities of the defendant.[27] Such a standard is more burdensome for those who are less capable of meeting the standard than others (say because they are naturally slower, clumsier, or less perceptive than the ordinary person).[28] Ideal justice, it is plausible to suppose, would require that the standard be perfectly tailored to the actual capabilities of the defendant at least where the defendant can't be held responsible for failing to develop capabilities comparable to those of the ordinary person. But greater tailoring would, of course, increase litigation and administration costs and burdens on potential victims trying to protect themselves from the carelessness of others in the face of imperfect compliance and enforcement. And so, it may make sense from the standpoint of non-ideal justice to compromise. But notice that in doing so, the legal system doesn't simply make a decision to allocate resources to enforcement in a particular way. It alters the substantive content of the primary duties that the tort system imposes on private parties. They are duty-bound to adhere to this capability-invariant standard even though ideal justice would seemingly require something more fine-grained. In short, the system reduces enforcement costs and increases the general level of conformity with the primary assignment to the

---

[27] Restatement (Second) of Torts (1965) § 283 cmt. c.

[28] As Oliver Wendell Holmes explained: "If ... a man is born hasty and awkward, is always having accidents and hurting himself or his neighbors, no doubt his congenital defects will be allowed for in the courts of Heaven, but his slips are no less troublesome to his neighbors than if they sprang from guilty neglect. His neighbors accordingly require him, at his proper peril, to come up to their standard, and the courts which they establish decline to take his personal equation into account." OW Holmes, Jr. *The Common Law* (The Lawbook Exch., Ltd. 2009) 108.

benefit of all, especially potential victims. But this is achieved by creating inequities in the distribution of the burdens of conforming to the standard and by recognizing the moral rights of some but not others. It might seem that in doing so, the legal system has simply chosen to recognize some wrongs as such instead of others, such that the *moral* corrective duties remain unchanged despite the legal system's decision not to recognize them. But an objective standard may also create legal duties where none exists at the moral level. More importantly, if in formulating the non-ideal standard the polity is doing so in a way that honors underlying considerations of non-ideal justice, the resulting legal duties, though they inevitably depart from the ideal, might reflect what the parties (non-ideally) owe to each other.[29]

Thus, in confronting what looks like a simple distributive problem—the problem of distributing access to corrective justice—the system may end up changing the contours of the primary rights at the (non-ideal) moral level. But this means that it is the ultimate assignment of standpoints to choices in the non-ideal circumstances in which the polity finds itself that has explanatory priority. The fact that the assignment needs only to be reasonable will give the polity some scope to make decisions about enforcement without altering the contours of the primary and secondary rights entailed by the basic assignment. But that only allows for a qualified kind of independence between the rights themselves and the decision to enforce. And, of course, what counts as reasonable—the content of the constraint that allows for such a modicum of independence—will depend on the underlying considerations of substantive justice.

---

[29] For further elaboration of this argument, see J Quong and R Stone, "Rules and Rights" in D Sobel, P Vallentyne, and S Wall (eds), *Oxford Studies in Political Philosophy*, Vol. 1 (OUP 2015).

8
Deterrence in Private Law

Sandy Steel[*]

Non-consequentialist justifications of private law liability foreground the role of the law in setting out, part-constituting, and providing enforcement of interpersonal moral rights and duties at the suit of right-holders.[1] The justificatory role of deterrence is either explicitly rejected or not given much attention.[2] The impression given is that deterrence is somehow necessarily inconsistent with the justificatory role of interpersonal moral rights and duties. My aim in this chapter is to show that this is not the case. I try to outline a general account of the normative role of deterrence in the justification of private law norms and enforcement. In making this argument, I will ultimately be affirming John Gardner's view that deterrence matters, non-trivially, to private law, while not being the whole story, or even the most important story.[3] In a nutshell, the thesis is that deterrence is neither necessary nor sufficient for a private law norm to be justified, but deterrence can play an important, difference-making, justificatory role when individuals do not have a reasonable individual objection to the deterrence-justified norm.

A number of preliminaries are in order. First, my concern is with the justification of private law norms, not their claimed justification by legal officials. It is not controversial that legal officials claim that some private law norms are or can be justified by their deterrent impact.[4] The question here is whether they are right.

Second, I will prescind from questions of when, if ever, certain officials ought to assess the empirical credentials of deterrence arguments. For familiar reasons, judges may not be reliable at assessing the empirical validity of deterrence arguments. Let's assume that we have knowledge of the deterrent impact of private law norms.

Third, let's define "deterrence." Deterrence is a specific mode of influencing conduct. Here is how I'll normally understand it—some complexities will be introduced later:

---

[*] With thanks to Ruth Chang, Cecile Fabre, Chris Essert, John Goldberg, and Adam Perry for especially helpful written comments and suggestions, and to Ben Cartwright for superb research assistance. Errors, mine.

[1] There are many labels that can be used to refer to versions of such an outlook—"corrective justice," "Kantian theory," etc, but I think it will more distracting than beneficial to use any particular one of them.

[2] See, for example, A Beever, *Rediscovering the Law of Negligence* (Hart 2007).

[3] See especially J Gardner, *Torts and Other Wrongs* (OUP 2019) 51 ("*TAOW*") and ch 4. For a view which is similar to the one developed here in its emphasis upon deterrence (and similar considerations) being limited by a need to respect the duty-bearer's rights, and establish their responsibility to the right-holder, see A Robertson, "Constraints on Policy-Based Reasoning in Private Law" in A Robertson and T H Wu (eds), *The Goals of Private Law* (Hart 2009).

[4] For a wealth of evidence, see virtually any chapter in E Bant and others (eds), *Punishment and Private Law* (Hart 2021).

Sandy Steel, *Deterrence in Private Law* In: *Private Law and Practical Reason*. Edited by: Haris Psarras and Sandy Steel, Oxford University Press. © Sandy Steel 2023. DOI: 10.1093/oso/9780192857330.003.0008

Table 8.1 Influencing conduct through reasons

Influencing conduct through reasons (some examples)	
By adverting to pre-existing reasons	Guidance
By creating a prudential reason against conduct	Deterrence
By otherwise directly affecting the prudential reasons for or against conduct	Incentivizing etc

Deterrence (D): A deters B from φ-ing if and only if A causes B not to φ by creating a prudential reason for B against φ-ing.

Note, then, that deterrence is not merely influencing conduct, but doing so in a particular way: by creating a prudential reason. There is a resultant contrast between deterring a person from an act and guiding them away from it. Guidance away from an act involves adverting a person to the reasons against the act, rather than adding a prudential reason against it.[5] If I was about to take a left turn in order to get to Glasgow and a road sign adverts me to the fact that the left turn does not lead to Glasgow, it would be odd to describe the sign as having *deterred* me from taking the left. It guided me. There's also a contrast between *deterring* and *incentivizing*. Incentives typically provide prudential reasons *in favor* of an act or remove or attenuate the prudential reasons against it. Finally, the law might also seek to influence conduct by removing a reason in favor of the conduct. Table 8.1 captures the foregoing.

If A deters in this sense, I will say that A has a "deterrent impact." The chapter's concern is with how the deterrent impact of private law norms or their enforcement bears on their justification. To be clear, this deterrent impact could be asserted to be a reason *for* or a reason *against* the creation, maintenance, or enforcement of a particular norm.[6] If the negligence liability of medical professionals causes doctors not to accept people as patients or to incur wasteful expenditure, for fear of liability, this negative deterrent impact could be a consideration against such liability. I will refer to positive and negative deterrence arguments as "D considerations."

Fourth, what is private law? I will leave this undefined, but my examples will be from uncontroversially private law areas: tort, contract, property, trusts, and fiduciary law.

Here is the plan. Section 1 establishes that D-considerations are not necessary for there to be reasons to create private law norms. Section 2 argues that they are not sufficient, but defeasibly sufficient. Sections 3 and 4 argue that D-considerations are reasons for certain kinds of private law rules, sometimes decisive reasons for particular rules, and sometimes decisive reasons against particular rules. Section 5 considers general objections to the justificatory relevance of D-considerations: (i) that such considerations are inconsistent with the "bipolarity" of private law; (ii) that acting upon such considerations violates deontological constraints. It is shown that neither

---

[5] cf J Pike, "How the Law Guides" (2021) 41 Oxford Journal of Legal Studies 169.
[6] See also Gardner's discussion of this in *TAOW* (n 3) ch 2.

DETERRENCE IN PRIVATE LAW   125

objection precludes the decisive relevance of D-considerations in some private law contexts.

1. The Necessity of Deterrence

We can begin by assessing:

N1: The deterrent impact of a private law primary duty not to φ is necessary for that duty to be morally justified.

A duty is a primary duty (a P-duty) if and only if it does not arise from the breach of another duty. A primary *legal* duty is a P-duty that is established by legal institutions. N1 means that such a duty will only be justified if (i) it reduces the number of instances of φ-ing compared to the non-existence of the duty, (ii) by creating a prudential reason against φ-ing.

The fact that deterrence operates by creating prudential reasons—hence (ii)—reveals N1 as false.[7] It supposes that whenever the law imposes a primary duty, this could only be justified if the primary duty directs people's attention to some negative consequence that will ensue to their interests if they fail to behave in accordance with it. This is false since a P-duty's *guidance* seems defeasibly sufficient to justify it. Suppose that the existence of a legal P-duty of disclosure of medical risks owed to patients will induce doctors better to comply with their moral duties because (i) the law actually arrives at the correct moral position in relation to duties of disclosure and (ii) doctors believe that the law is more likely than they are to get the moral position right, and are motivated to comply with their moral duties. If the institution of a legal P-duty will *guide* people to greater compliance with their moral duties—at least if those moral duties are of a certain kind—(perhaps) correlated with rights, not duties whose legal regulation will undermine the value that grounds the duty, etc—then there is a *pro tanto* justification for the P-duty. The idea that D-considerations are necessary to justify a P-duty may involve a confusion between D-considerations and *guidance*. It is plausible that a P-duty must reduce the incidence of P-duty-breaching conduct *by guidance* to be justified.[8] But that is not the same as saying that it must have a deterrent impact.

---

[7] This is even more starkly shown by a variant on N1 concerned with private law *powers*. The idea that a power to change normative relations could only be justified if it had a deterrent impact is difficult to understand.

[8] It seems false, though. Even if it is known that the P-duty will not change behavior, there may be an expressive value in having such a duty. Suppose that instead of duty-imposing norms against sexual assault, there were mere liability-norms, which exposed a person to a penalty if they commit an assault, but with no primary duty against committing the assault. Suppose this were an equally effective system in terms of reducing the number of assaults—perhaps the penalties are extraordinarily high. Yet there seems to be something morally objectionable about the legal system in failing to recognize a *prohibition* upon sexual assault. It might be objected that this prohibition need not amount to a relational, private law P-duty against sexual assault. The expressive value of *prohibition* would be equally achieved by a criminal law prohibition on sexual assault. In some cases, that may be right, but the difficulty in construing criminal punishment in many cases as the enforcement of a duty *to the victim* risks victims feeling that *their* interests are not being taken seriously. If the law does nothing to reflect the moral duties *owed to the victim* arising from the wrong,

Now consider:

N2: The deterrent impact of a private law secondary duty to φ is necessary for that duty to φ to be morally justified.

A secondary duty (S-duty) is a duty that arises from the breach of another duty. The standard example in private law is a duty to compensate arising from the breach of a contractual, tortious or equitable duty.[9] Much the same can be said against N2 as against N1. If an S-duty *guides* duty-bearers to better conform to their moral S-duties, then that seems to be a defeasibly sufficient reason for creating the duty; all sorts of considerations may defeat that reason, but it seems, on its own, to be a reason for the creation of the P-duty.

In chapter 2 of *Torts and Other Wrongs*, Gardner considers what might be adduced as a defense of N2.[10] The defense is along these lines:

(1) For a legal S-duty to be justified, it must replicate or (part-)constitute a moral S-duty
(2) Moral S-duties exist only if the existence of the S-duty deters agents from breaching a moral P-duty
(3) Therefore, a necessary part of the justification of legal S-duty is an underlying moral duty that has a deterrent impact

The central idea behind this argument, expressed by (2), is that the moral norm of corrective justice—the norm requiring wrongdoers to correct their wrongs—is itself justified by "deterrence" of primary wrongs. Gardner's response is to reject (2). His argument is that, for (2) to be true, it would have to be the case that the moral norm of corrective justice is itself a social norm—that is, one widely accepted and used. As he argues, however, this seems false. If secondary duties are grounded, at least in part, in the reason which grounded the primary duty, and the possibility of some measure of conformity to that reason, there is no basis for thinking that corrective justice is an inherently social phenomenon. If the reasons that grounded the primary duty are not necessarily "social" in character, then the S-duties arising from non-conformity to that reason need not be "social" either.

---

there will be a serious risk—in some cases—of victims' feelings of self-respect being undermined. If the law has a choice between framing its response to the breach of primary moral duty as a conditional legal liability rule or a primary legal duty rule, the expressive value of a legal P-duty may decisively support its adopting a primary legal *duty* rule. For an argument in favor of the expressive justification of *remedies*, rather than private law primary duties, see S Hershovitz, "Treating Wrongs as Wrongs: An Expressive Argument for Tort Law" (2017) 10 Journal of Tort Law 405.

[9] A debate has arisen as to whether such secondary duties exist as a matter of positive law. See SA Smith, *Rights, Wrongs, and Injustices: The Structure of Remedial Law* (OUP 2019) (Smith, *Rights, Wrongs and Injustices*); J Gardner, "Damages without Duty" (2019) 69 University of Toronto Law Journal 412; S Steel and R Stevens, "The Secondary Legal Duty to Pay Damages" (2020) 136 Law Quarterly Review 283. This descriptive debate is largely irrelevant to the normative issue in the text.
[10] *TAOW* (n 3) 51.

It might be thought that the deterrent impact of *some* private law norms, or private law acts, is necessary to the justification of those norms or acts—namely, *remedial* norms, which confer on courts powers to make orders of various kinds. Consider:

N3: A private law power to make duty-imposing orders to φ is justified only if the power, or the making of the order, could reasonably be considered to be likely have a deterrent impact on the addressee(s).

Orders are generally exercises of the court's normative powers to change people's legal situation. They may be duty-imposing, power-conferring, immunity-creating, and so on. Duty-imposing orders may do at least one or more of three things. First, they might replicate a pre-existing legal duty. For instance, an order to perform a contractual obligation may replicate the content of the contractual duty. Second, they might crystallize a pre-existing legal duty. For instance, a secondary duty to pay compensatory damages is a duty to pay an unliquidated sum. An order may crystallize this duty by specifying its precise content. Third, a duty-imposing order may create a new legal duty. For instance, an order to pay punitive damages creates a duty to pay them. But it seems doubtful that there was such a duty prior to the order.[11]

According to N3, a power to make an order should only exist if there is a reasonable ground to consider that the power will have a deterrent impact. But N3 seems false for the same reason as N1. There is an intelligible case for duty-crystallizing and duty-imposing orders simply on the basis that they will guide the defendant as to what they ought to do.

2. The Sufficiency of Deterrence

Suppose there is some harm or right violation ("a bad") which it would be good to prevent. The fact that an enforceable private law norm or set of such norms would deter people in such a way as to prevent the bad seems, on the face of it, to be a reason for creating the norm: creating the norm(s) would cause good consequences to ensue, and the good consequences of an action constitute reasons for it.

Clearly, however, this reason is not *sufficient* to justify the creation of the norm. First, the beneficial deterrent impact of a norm is only one positive reason in favor of it. The norm may have other negative consequences even if it has a beneficial deterrent impact.

Second, if deterrence of (say) right violations is the end, there will often be more effective means to that end than private law (secondary, or remedial) norms.[12] If one's

---

[11] See also section 3.4.

[12] An important proviso here, however, is that D-considerations may be undefeated reasons for private law norms, even when a more effective means of deterrence is available, if the use of that other means is disproportionately harmful or costly. Perhaps criminal punishment would be more causally efficacious at deterring right violations than liability to enforcement of private law secondary duties. Nonetheless, in relation to certain right violations, punishment may be disproportionately harmful. More pragmatically, there may be non-ideal situations in which an alternative scheme of deterrent regulation is unlikely to be implemented, and the only practically available means of deterrence is through private law.

goal is to crack nuts, and one has a nutcracker and a can opener for use, even if there is *a* reason to use the can opener to crack nuts, one ought not to do so. If one's concern is to deter certain conduct, one could sometimes, for instance, impose (i) non-relational duties not to engage in the conduct (ii) actionable at the suit of those who are best able to enforce those duties, and this would plausibly sometimes be more effective than private law-established deterrence of right-violations (not to mention criminal law punitive responses to right violations).

Third, even if the norm only has a beneficial deterrent impact, is the most effective means to deterrence, and has no negative consequences, it may still be unjustified: the norm may impose duties or liabilities which it is not justifiable to impose upon a particular individual, even if it is overall beneficial. Although there might, for instance, be a weighty reason to punish an innocent to prevent further wrongs (or impose a secondary private law remedial norm upon them), the reason is, at least up to some threshold of negative consequences, defeated. By contrast, if the defendant has a moral S-duty to the victim, these exclusionary norms against interfering with the defendant in certain ways appear to be canceled, or weakened.[13]

Are D-considerations *defeasibly* sufficient to justify the creation of the private law norms? A reason is defeasibly sufficient to justify an act if no further positive reason is necessary to render the act justifiable. This is true. There could be cases in which the deterrent impact of a norm is so significant that it defeats the individual objection a person made liable has to bearing the costs it imposes, even if that person is not morally liable to bear that cost.[14] Setting aside cases when the imposition of legal liability amounts to a justified wrong, it is arguable that the considerations that contribute toward a person's moral liability to bear the costs of a norm justified on deterrent grounds operate by canceling or weakening reasons *against* imposing the cost on the person. If so, the deterrent impact is defeasibly sufficient even in such cases.

3. Deterrence Considerations as Reasons which Make a Difference

In the previous section, I suggested that D-considerations can be reasons for private law norms. But reasons are cheap. It is easy for something to bear upon the justification of something else by providing a reason for it. The fact that rescuing a drowning person will give me good exercise is a reason to do it but the rational case for doing so is overdetermined. Similarly, the fact that blowing up cars that park in my space will deter people from doing so in the future is a reason to do it, but one that is always excluded, or outweighed by other considerations.

So we can ask a more interesting question about D-considerations: do they, or are they ever likely, to make a difference to which private law rules we have decisive reason to adopt—or are they like the reason that rescue provides good exercise or the reason

---

[13] I return to this below, under section 5.2.1.

[14] For an explanation of the concept of moral liability, see J Quong, *The Morality of Defensive Force* (OUP 2020) 18.

to blow up people's cars when they park in your spot, a reason, but not one that ever, or almost ever, makes a decisive difference to what we ought to do?

This section focuses on the role of positive D-considerations, that is the beneficial deterrent impact of particular norms and their enforcement. The next section examines negative D-considerations. I will argue that positive and negative deterrence considerations can make a decisive difference.

3.1 Scarcity

In a world of very limited resources, legal systems might need to choose whether to devote resources to private law adjudication and enforcement or to other goods. In making this choice, the amount of good that will be achieved by private law duties, compared to, for instance, funding healthcare, is a relevant, and potentially determinative, consideration. The amount of good achieved by private law will include its beneficial deterrent impact. Suppose that the legal system must choose, given scarce resources, to enforce one of two equally important moral duties owed between individuals. Call them Duty 1 and Duty 2. Suppose further that the private law enforcement of Duty 1 will have significant deterrent impact, while the private law enforcement Duty 2 will have almost none. This fact about Duty 2 is surely significant to whether the legal system ought to direct its limited resources to Duty 2. Consider:

> *Rescue choice.* A is under a moral duty of easy rescue to X who is drowning and will otherwise die. B is under a moral duty of easy rescue to each of Y, Z, R, S, T who are drowning in the same pool of water and will otherwise die. C is a bystander who can choose to enforce A's duty or B's duty by forcing A or B to effect the rescue, but C can only choose one.

It seems clear that, absent any special relationships between A, B, and C, C ought to enforce B's duty here, given the fact that doing so will save a significantly greater number of lives.[15] In doing this, C violates no deontological constraint. C does not, for instance, use X as a means of saving Y, Z, R, S, T.

It might be objected that states are not like the bystander in *Rescue choice* because states have a duty to prioritize the rectification of injustice over contribution to other goods. If this duty is particularly stringent, then devoting resources to rectification of private law injustices over other goods may be justified independently of private law's deterrent impact. Even if we accept that there is a duty to prioritize justice in this way, it hardly follows, however, that D-considerations are irrelevant to the justification of private law rules. One of the effects of the deterrent impact of private law rules may be the *avoidance* of wrongdoing (perhaps, sometimes, of the injustice kind). Other things being equal, there is no reason for a third party, such as the state, to privilege rectification of injustice over avoidance of injustice or wrongdoing.

---

[15] See further FM Kamm, *Morality, Mortality Volume I: Death and Whom to Save From It* (OUP 1996), ch 6.

The upshot of this section is that normative decisions about which moral duties should receive private law enforcement, in circumstances of scarcity, is justifiably impacted upon by D-considerations. The scarcity argument impacts, then, upon decisions about the *enforcement* of primary and secondary moral duties in law. It does not itself give a reason for the primary and secondary duties not to be *recognized* in law. In that sense, the scarcity argument again underlines the fact that D-considerations are only a "part" of the normative story in private law. On this argument, D-considerations do not determine the content of the primary rights and duties, powers, and so on, but only decisions about which ones ought to be enforced.

3.2 Moral indeterminacy

Interpersonal moral rights and duties are sometimes indeterminate.[16] It may be that the postal rule of acceptance in contract law, according to which a contractual offer is accepted by post when the acceptance is posted, is required by morality. Or it may be that it is one permissible way of determining the legal enforceability of agreements or promises in circumstances where it is morally required to have *a* rule. It seems likely that many aspects of contract and property law are partly conventional—for example the *details* of rules of acquisition. We may be morally required to have *a rule* in these cases, but several rules would be consistent with the underlying interpersonal moral considerations.

Consider, for example, a Kantian justification of private property. We are required to have private property rights in order for us to relate as equals. But there are several property regimes that would fit the bill. We are morally required to adopt one of them, otherwise the enforcement of property rights will be morally impermissible: if there is no public determination of the applicable property rules, then each of us will exercise our unilateral judgment as to the content of each other's rights. This will involve interacting in ways inconsistent with our innate equality. But in selecting, for instance, which set of rules of acquisition to go for, among the sets that are each consistent with our innate equality, it seems justifiable, other things being equal, to choose the one which leads, by deterrence, to fewer wrongs or other beneficial effects, for instance. If there are two specifications of the property system, P1, and P2, both involving equal constraints on innate freedom, but P1 having greater deterrent impact, then P1 should be adopted.[17] It seems likely that there are many questions of institutional detail in private law in which foundational interpersonal moral considerations do not mandate a particular solution, and so deterrence—and other—considerations can then determine which solution ought to be institutionalized.

Consider the design of duties incurred upon becoming a trustee. Suppose that set A and set B would both give effect to the values that justify creating the power to

---

[16] For a similar argument to the one in this section, see H Dagan, "The Limited Autonomy of Private Law" (2008) 56 American Journal of Comparative Law 809, 825–26. Yitzhak Benbaji also makes an argument of this kind in his "Welfare and Freedom: Towards a Semi-Kantian Theory of Private Law" (2020) 39 Law and Philosophy 473.

[17] See again Benbaji, "Welfare and Freedom" (n 16).

declare a trust and third parties would have no reasonable objections to either A or B, but set B contains duties which are simpler to understand, and thus more likely to be complied with. Other things being equal, set B should be chosen. This is not yet a D-consideration, since the fact that a duty's content is easier to understand says nothing about what motivates duty-bearers to act in accordance with its standard. But the example illustrates the point that the choice between multiple realizations of justifiable private law relations could be informed by considerations that are unnecessary to the grounding justification of those relations.

3.3 Opting in to deterrence

This section describes two arguable examples of D-considerations justifiably determining the content of private law rules when the persons subject to the rules have voluntarily created rights with a deterrent aim or voluntarily occupied a particular position. The basic unifying thread here is that a voluntary choice may be part of what justifies the appeal to D-considerations.

3.3.1 Voluntary creation of rights aimed at a deterrent impact

In relation to certain interests, compensation *ex post* will be highly inadequate: compensation will not serve to restore the value of the interest, or will only do so highly imperfectly. In relation to these non-compensable interests, in circumstances in which there is a significant prospect of the interest being invaded as a result of others' self-interested decisions, a person has an interest in others being subject to deterrent measures. In these circumstances, a person may enter into a bargain with another which requires the other to pay a supra-compensatory sum in the event that the interest is invaded by the other.

In English law, such contractual arrangements are sometimes enforceable: a liquidated damages clause will not be unenforceable as a penalty simply because it has a deterrent aim, and could only conceivably be justified as a deterrent.[18] Such clauses are enforceable so long as the sum is not "disproportionate" to the right-holder's interest in performance of the primary contractual duties. Specifically, the clause will not be enforceable when "the sum or remedy stipulated as a consequence of a breach of contract is exorbitant or unconscionable when regard is had to the innocent party's interest in the performance of the contract."[19] One situation in which this will be so is likely to be when the interests in question are straightforwardly compensable by an ordinary award of compensation. Effectively, then, English law gives limited effect to contractual arrangements that are designed to have a deterrent impact.

Now it might be said that the justification of the legal enforcement of these arrangements is simply the parties' agreement: the fact of the parties' agreement, not the intended deterrent impact of the agreement, is what justifies the law's enforcement. In short, agreements give rise to content-independent reasons for legal enforcement of those agreements. If so, the deterrent impact of the contractual right

---

[18] *Cavendish Square Holding BV v El Makdessi* [2015] UKSC 67; [2016] AC 1172 (*Cavendish v Makdessi*).
[19] ibid [255] (Lord Hodge).

132 SANDY STEEL

to supra-compensation is not what justifies the existence of that right, nor its being enforced.

Given that not all agreements are morally enforceable at law, we can reasonably ask, however, why it is justifiable for courts to enforce agreements of this particular kind— agreements about the normative consequences of right violations. Part of the answer might be that enforcement will contribute to the continued existence of a beneficial practice of private deterrence arrangements. If it were somehow hypothetically known that agreed remedies clauses never had any deterrent impact upon anyone's behavior, intuitively it seems that a major plank of the justificatory case for enforcing them is removed.

3.3.2 Fiduciary liabilities to account for profits

Fiduciaries are legally liable in English law to account for the profits made from their fiduciary position without the consent of their principal.[20] In some cases, this can be justified as a means of enforcing, either specifically, or in a next best way, a promise made by the fiduciary to acquire a right for the benefit of the principal.[21] It might be contended that this promissory strategy generalizes to justify all profit-stripping against fiduciaries: a fiduciary, it might be said, undertakes to the principal not to make a gain from its position. In ordering the fiduciary to account when this occurs, the remedy merely enforces this promissory duty, either specifically, or by enforcing a next best secondary legal duty that arises once the gain has been made.

This promise-based explanation seems, at least sometimes, to put the cart before the horse in the order of justification. Suppose A has extensive legal powers over B's assets and B is especially vulnerable to those powers being misused to B's detriment. From these facts alone, it may be appropriate that the law expose B to certain liabilities, such as a liability to have gains stripped. The positive justification of these liabilities is not sourced in A's having promised them. Compare the duties of government ministers. If we are designing the office that government ministers should hold, we would include liabilities to account for profits from those positions. Any promise that the incumbent of such an office makes upon assuming the office adds to the stringency of their duty not to profit, perhaps, but the moral duty or liability is already there in virtue of facts about their position. Of course, once these positions or offices become legally recognized, it will generally be true that people *will* objectively be undertaking the duties attached to the positions or offices. But this adds to the justificatory basis of the duties rather than providing their sole source. Even if we wish to say that the fiduciary undertakes to give up gains by assuming the fiduciary role, it is still an open question why the law attaches to the fiduciary role *this particular liability*.

Consider, then, a possible explanation: this liability is in place in order to enhance conformity to other duties or rules. Perhaps, as Matthew Conaglen argues, the liability enhances conformity to the fiduciary's non-fiduciary duties by removing the

---

[20] See generally L Smith, "Fiduciary Relationships: Ensuring the Loyal Exercise of Judgement on Behalf of Another" (2014) 130 Law Quarterly Review 608, 628–31.

[21] For an undertaking-based justification, see J Edelman, J Varuhas, and S Colton (eds), *McGregor on Damages* (21st edn, Sweet & Maxwell 2020) para 15-005.

temptation to act out of brazen self-interest.[22] Perhaps, as Irit Samet argues, the liability immunizes the fiduciary's decision-making from the insidious effect of self-deception or bias.[23] Both of these plausible arguments involve something close to deterrence, namely, incentivizing: both arguments appeal to the fact the liability rule will remove a reason in favor of acting to make a profit in these circumstances; the removal of this reason is expected to improve the fiduciary's decision-making.[24] If the account of profits rule can reasonably be expected to have these effects, then this seems to be defeasibly sufficient basis for adopting it. This is not to say that the fiduciary's voluntarily assuming their position—to the extent this is the case—has no justificatory role. The choice to assume the position might be considered to diminish the fiduciary's objection to serving the incentivization goal. The liability to account comes with the job, so to speak. This suggests a more general point: in designing the rules of "optional" private law duties and liabilities—those which one has a reasonable choice as to whether to assume the burdens of the position—one's objection to being subject to rules which have a deterrent impact or incentivizing purpose seems weakened. I explore the point further below.

3.4 Specific deterrence orders and liability

An injunction is an order to do or not to do something other than the payment of money. As noted above, an order (in relation to duties) can be duty-creating, duty-crystallizing, or duty-replicating.[25] Guidance is a sufficient *pro tanto* justification for duty-creating and duty-crystallizing orders. In these circumstances, the morally motivated subject may genuinely be uncertain as to what to do, given the indeterminacy of the moral position, and need guidance from the law.

It is harder to see how duty-replicating orders can be justified simply by guidance. If the intention were simply to guide, the court could simply remind (by declaration) the duty-bearer of their existing duty. Part of the justification of duty-replicating orders, when backed by a liability to sanctions, is plausibly to add a new prudential reason against non-compliance, that is, deterrence.[26] At any rate, the justification of a legal liability to the imposition of a setback to one's interests for the breach of a private law duty-replicating order is surely, in part, the likely deterrent impact of such liability. The fact that the imposition of these costs are not simply retributive in character is

---

[22] M Conaglen, *Fiduciary Loyalty: Protecting the Due Performance of Non-Fiduciary Duties* (Hart Publishing 2010).

[23] I Samet, "Guarding the Fiduciary's Conscience—A Justification of a Stringent Profit-stripping Rule" (2008) 28 Oxford Journal of Legal Studies 763.

[24] Lionel Smith is reluctant to describe a justification of the no profit rule which appeals to the good consequences of fiduciary decision-making as a deterrence rule, because it is not a sanction; my notion of deterrence is broader, but still would exclude the liability to account. See his "Deterrence, Prophylaxis, and Punishment in Fiduciary Obligations" (2013) 7 Journal of Equity 87, 4.3–4.4.

[25] Text at n 11 above.

[26] It is true that the law *could* do this—add a prudential reason—without *ordering* the defendant to comply with their duty; it could simply make the defendant liable to a sanction: Smith, *Rights, Wrongs and Injustices* (n 9) 136, 147. The *ordering* aspect seems justifiable, however, as a means of *demanding* compliance; a demand in these circumstances is more appropriate than a mere reminder.

shown by the fact that the sanctions will often not be applied, or discontinued, if the replicated duty is eventually conformed to.[27] This shows that the aim of the sanctions was to induce behavior, not simply to mark wrongdoing against the court's authority.[28] Liability to such sanctions can be understood as a form of specific deterrence: the provision of prudential reasons to avoid some conduct to a particular person in light of their prior conduct. Here deterrence seems justified simply by a legitimate concern that the duty-bearer will not comply with their duty. Establishing liabilities with the aim of specific deterrence can be justified as a means of securing conformity with interpersonally justified duties.

4. Overdeterrence

Suppose that the enforcement of legal duties to compensate for negligently caused medical injuries leads medical professionals to take excessive care. Let's say that care is excessive when its costs are greater than its expected benefits. Suppose further that there is a moral requirement to treat patients in accordance with this cost–benefit standard, and this moral requirement is legally recognized by a primary legal duty. Of what justificatory relevance is the fact that the enforcement of the secondary duty reduces conformity to the primary duty?

It is a reason against the enforcement, though not necessarily the imposition, of the secondary duty. If the negative deterrence impact is caused by the threat of *enforcement*, this is not a reason itself for doing away with the secondary *duty* of compensation, only legal liability in relation to that duty.[29] This reason against enforcement will often, however, not be a decisive reason. It depends. If the enforcement of the package of primary and secondary duties increases conformity to the cost–benefit norm compared to the conformity that would exist if there were no enforcement, then there might still be reason to enforce the primary and secondary duties.

Suppose, however, that the existence of enforcement of the secondary legal duty *reduces* conformity to the cost–benefit norm below the level that would exist if the secondary duty did not exist, with the result that there is more wrongful harming in the world than would otherwise be the case. Could there still be a case for the secondary duty? One reason for having the secondary duty would be to give effect to the defendant's duty of justice to compensate the claimant after breach of the cost–benefit norm (if such a duty exists). One countervailing reason is the fact that the existence of secondary legal duty contributes to the occurrence of wrongful harm, namely, the occurrence of more breaches of the cost–benefit norm.

So the legal system, in this example, has a choice: (i) enforce secondary moral duties and do more (corrective) justice, at the cost of more wrongful harm in the future, or

---

[27] For examples, see ibid 152–53.

[28] For complexities here surrounding the nature of civil and criminal contempt, see D Rolph, "The Ultimate Sanction: The Purpose and Role of Contempt in Private Law Litigation" in Bant and others, *Punishment and Private Law* (n 4) 137–38.

[29] It is clearly conceptually possible for the law to impose secondary duties of compensation without providing enforcement thereof. Indeed, this is the most plausible view, I think, of various "immunities" that exist in relation to, say, torts in combat in war.

DETERRENCE IN PRIVATE LAW   135

(ii) refuse to enforce secondary moral duties, with fewer wrongful harms in the future, but less (corrective) justice. An argument for (ii) is that, by failing to enforce secondary moral duties, the legal system will *fail to assist* subjects in enforcing their moral rights of corrective justice, with the result that harm that ought to be compensated goes uncompensated. By contrast, with (i), the legal system will *positively contribute* to the occurrence of wrongful harm, by creating the secondary legal duty. In short, under (ii), the legal system will *allow* wrongful harm to occur, while under (i), the legal system will *do* wrongful harm. Other things being equal, we might think, it is worse positively to contribute to the occurrence of wrongful harm compared to failing to assist in the prevention of wrongful harm.
Consider:

> *Hospital Bridge.* A negligently harmed B. A must take B to hospital in A's car in order to prevent this harm killing B. A knows that if A drives across the only bridge to the hospital, it will collapse due to the negligent construction of the bridge. Five people will die as a result.

In this example, intuitively, A ought not to drive B across the bridge to save B's life. It seems clearly impermissible to contribute to the deaths of five innocent people in order to conform to one's duty to prevent one's wrongful acts killing one person. Suppose in the standard trolley case that the single person tied to one track is there due to the trolley driver's wrongful act and the trolley is heading toward that single person. Still, the trolley driver ought not to turn the trolley from the single person to the five. This would be true even if the stakes were lower for each person and the driver paid compensation to the five.

If A ought not to conform to A's (*pro tanto*) duty to prevent A's wrongful negligent conduct killing B, if this would contribute to the wrongful negligent deaths of five others, then it seems that the legal system ought to choose option 2, other things being equal. Unlike A, the legal system, even if it is failing in a moral duty in failing to assist a person to enforce that person's rights, it is not a moral duty that arises from the legal system's own wrongful conduct. In the medical professionals example, the wrongful conduct of the medical professionals is not caused by the law's intervention. When the law does not provide enforcement of medical professionals' secondary moral obligations, it is not, on the face of it, failing to counteract the effects of any earlier action undertaken by the legal system. Even if we think that the legal system owes private law enforcement to its citizens in virtue of prohibiting the exercise of moral enforcement rights that would exist in the state of nature,[30] *Hospital Bridge* shows that complying with one's own duties of preventive or corrective justice is not always sufficient to justify contributing by one's action to the infliction of wrongful harm on others. In short, the fact that the legal system may have a *pro tanto* duty to assist in enforcing duties of corrective justice does not always provide a justification for breaching its own *pro tanto* duty not to contribute to the occurrence of wrongful harm.

---

[30] I assess this Lockean argument in detail in S Steel, "On the Moral Necessity of Tort Law: The Fairness Argument" (2021) 41 Oxford Journal of Legal Studies 192.

5. General Objections to Deterrence

5.1 Bipolarity

Perhaps the most general objection that might be made to the justificatory relevance of D-considerations in private law stems from considerations about the bilateral structure of private law. Here is Weinrib's elegant explanation of the justificatory relevance of bilaterality:[31]

> the corrective justice argument highlighted the incompatibility of economic analysis with the bilateral structure of the plaintiff–defendant relationship. This structure requires that reasons for liability should be such as to link a particular defendant to a particular plaintiff ... The reasons, in other words, have to embrace both parties in their interrelationship rather than deal with either of the parties independently. Economic analysis failed to do this, because the incentives that it postulated were necessarily directed to the parties separately.

Notice immediately that Weinrib is here referring to the *reasons for liability*. The bilateral "constraint," as we might call it, applies to those reasons. Suppose we grant that the reasons for liability have to be bilateral in character in some sense. It does not follow (and Weinrib does not claim so)[32] that D-considerations have no justificatory relevance to private law. At most, it only follows that D-considerations cannot be *reasons for liability*. Not all private law questions concern the reasons for liability. D-considerations, as we have seen, can be offered as *reasons against liability*.

There is, however, a conflict with Weinribian bilaterality if it implies that *all* of the reasons for a liability must be bilateral. In *Scarcity*, the issue is which moral remedial relations should be legally enforced. D-considerations are relied upon, positively, then, to generate a case for a particular liability. In *Indeterminacy*, there is already a positive justification for holding the defendant to be under *a* legal liability of some kind, but no justification, absent deterrence, for their liability to be concretized in that particular way rather than others. The deterrent impact, again, is relied upon positively as a reason for a particular concretization. Finally, in relation to *Specific deterrence orders*, the particular kind of liability is at least partly justified, positively, by its possible deterrent impact. None of these conflicts with Weinribian bilaterality should, I think, be considered problematic, however. In each case, there is an interpersonal justification for a liability—the liability-bearer does not have an in principle moral objection to bearing the costs of the liability—and deterrence is merely operating at a secondary stage to fill in the detailed content of that liability.

The more difficult category, from the perspective of the bilaterality constraint, is what I termed "opting in to deterrence," in particular, the fiduciary's liability to account

---

[31] EJ Weinrib, *The Idea of Private Law* (rev edn, OUP 2012) x.
[32] EJ Weinrib, "Deterrence and Corrective Justice" (2002) 50 UCLA Law Review 621.

for profits. The problem arises as follows. Suppose Samet and Conaglen are right that the justification of the liability to give up gains made from the fiduciary position is to enhance fiduciary decision-making, by removing a reason for taking decisions that are clouded by self-interest.[33] But suppose that a fiduciary nonetheless acts in their self-interest and makes a gain, without causing any loss to their principal. The goal of ensuring that the fiduciary makes decisions in the best interests of the principal has failed in this case. If the fiduciary has no further decisions to make on behalf of the principal, then removing the gain will not increase the probability of compliance with any future duty of the fiduciary *to this principal*. If that had been true, then removal of the gain could arguably be consistent with the bilaterality constraint: one would be removing an incentive in order to ensure future conformity to a relational duty.[34] Instead, however, the removal of the gain can only be justified as a means of making more likely, in the future, that fiduciaries act in a disinterested manner, even though that goal failed in this particular case. That is a reason for liability which is not bilateral in character. In principle, then, it seems likely that there is no reason to give the gain exclusively to the principal unless this is generally necessary to achieve the deterrent impact. At most, it seems justifiable as one effective means of giving effect to the fiduciary's duty (which I explain in the next section) to contribute to the protection of the fiduciary relationship in general.[35]

This incentives-based justification, on the face of it, seems to saddle the liability to account with the same objection often made to deterrence-based justifications of punitive damages: the objection that the beneficiary of the award gains a "windfall."[36] Here are two tentative points in response. First, this objection seems less pressing in the context of voluntarily assumed relationships, especially in the context of a commercial relationship: the liability to account can be understood as part of a freely chosen set of arrangements between the parties. Second, the windfall objection is only a *pro tanto* objection: if the benefits of the liability are reasonably expected to be significant, perhaps some windfalls can be tolerated. Suppose that the existence of punitive liability saves x lives each year, but distributes financial windfalls to claimants. It is not obvious that doling out some undeserved financial gains in order to save lives is all things considered unjustifiable.

---

[33] I Samet, "Guarding the Fiduciary's Conscience—A Justification of a Stringent Profit-stripping Rule" (2008) 28 Oxford Journal of Legal Studies 763; M Conaglen, *Fiduciary Loyalty: Protecting the Due Performance of Non-Fiduciary Duties* (Hart Publishing 2010).

[34] Though, I still doubt it: the incentive to comply with the duty to the principal could be achieved by the gain evaporating into thin air, or in the absence of gain-evaporating devices, it being given to a third party.

[35] James Penner intriguingly suggests that the fiduciary's liability to give up the gain to the principal can be justified because the liability is in the form of a "penalty" rather than a "punishment," the latter being, for him, a conceptually "public" act in some sense. Penalties have no necessary relationality however (think of speeding fines) and so some further considerations are needed to justify giving the "penalty" to the principal. See Penner, "Punishments and Penalties in Private Law, with Particular Reference to the Law Governing Fiduciaries" in Bant and others, *Punishment and Private Law* (n 4) 127.

[36] On such justifications, see eg C Sharkey, "Punitive Damages Transformed into Societal Damages" in Bant and others, *Punishment and Private Law* (n 4). There are several other justificatory issues surrounding punitive damages that are not raised by the liability to account.

5.2 Deontological constraints

Suppose that the effect of the liability and order to account is indeed to improve fiduciary decision-making. Another family of moral objections is that the order treats the fiduciary as a mere resource to be exploited to achieve good effects in the future. Normally, we might think, it is especially difficult to justify harming a person non-consensually simply in order to confer some good on other people. This exploits the person, or opportunistically uses them, or treats them as a mere means. These, or related ideas, are often raised as the central moral problem with deterrence arguments.[37]

To get a handle on the moral problem at stake, consider a few examples. Compare: it is permissible to withhold life-saving medication to one stranger in order to provide the medication to five other strangers who need it, but it is not permissible to withhold such medicine from a stranger to observe the fatal progression of that person's disease to gain medical knowledge to save five other strangers.[38] Similarly, while it seems permissible to protect five strangers from a runaway trolley by turning the trolley in a direction such that one stranger will be killed as a side effect, it seems impermissible to push a large person in front of the trolley to stop it, killing that person in doing so.

It is controversial what explains these judgments, if anything does, but here is one reasonably plausible possibility:[39]

> *Utility.* It is especially difficult to justify infringing a person's rights on the basis of her usefulness to others.[40]

Let's assume that this or a similar principle is valid. Two questions then arise for the inquiry in this section. First, does this principle have any application to the contexts in which I have argued deterrence considerations make a rational difference? Second, even if the principles apply to such contexts, can the objection raised by those principles be met?

5.2.1 Applicability of constraints to private law questions

In *Scarcity*, *Indeterminacy*, and *Overdeterrence*, these principles do not seem to apply.

Consider *Scarcity*. Suppose, again, that the legal system can only enforce duty 1, and not also duty 2, and chooses to enforce duty 2 because of its significantly greater deterrent impact. Those who lose out on protection of their moral rights by this choice cannot justifiably complain by reference to *Utility*. If failing to enforce the rights of the beneficiaries of duty 1 is itself an infringement of their rights by the legal system,

---

[37] See Smith, "Fiduciary Relationships" (n 20) on using people as a means in the fiduciary context.

[38] This example is taken from KH Ramakrishnan, "Treating People as Tools" (2016) 44 Philosophy & Public Affairs 133.

[39] These and others are catalogued and criticized by Ramakrishnan (ibid). *Utility* is Ramakrishnan's favored principle.

[40] For a similar principle, framed in terms of what contributes to a person's flourishing, see NJ McBride, *The Humanity of Private Law: Part I: Explanation* (Hart Publishing 2018) ch 3.

the justification for this infringement is not the utility of those persons' rights being infringed for the benefit of others. The deterrence benefit will not be caused by the infringement of their rights itself. Contrast the scarce medication example. In failing to provide the medication to one stranger (assume this infringes their rights), one does not use them for the benefit of another, albeit that the benefit to the other five would not have occurred had the medication been provided to the stranger. The overdeterrence situation is closely connected. In *not* legally enforcing a person's secondary moral right to compensation, by reference to the detrimental deterrent impact of acting otherwise, the law is not infringing a person's moral rights simply on the basis of her usefulness to others. The law is infringing their right in order to avoid breaching its own duty not to violate other people's rights not to suffer harm. This harm will be partly caused by the legal system's actions in enforcing the secondary moral rights of compensation.

In *Indeterminacy* situations, it is also difficult to argue that this principle applies. The justification for the private law norm is already complete by reference to some ground other than deterrence. So in holding a person to the demands of that norm, one may be infringing their rights—that is, doing something that they would normally have an entitlement to be free from—but one is not necessarily doing so simply on the ground of their usefulness to others. Or, if this is a situation in *Utility* applies, in so far as one's resources are being used to benefit a specific other person, it is defeated to the extent that one has an (enforceable) moral duty to that other person. Similarly, in relation to *Deterrent orders*, the legal system may be infringing the duty-bearer's right by applying a sanction to them, and this imposition may trigger *Utility* in so far as the aim of the sanction is to induce the duty-bearer to benefit another person. But the duty-bearer's objection under *Utility* seems defeated or substantially weakened by their duty to make those resources available to the right-holder. Conversely, deterrent orders can often be justified as a means of giving effect to a right-holder's moral remedial right to enforce their rights by necessary and proportionate means.

Utility does seem to bite in relation to cases in which the reasons for a liability are purely D-based, such as, on one view at least, a fiduciary liability to account for profits or, on some views, punitive–deterrent orders not geared at specific deterrence of the duty-bearer. In these cases a defendant's resources will be taken or used purely to benefit others. It might be doubted that deontological constraints apply to cases other than bodily use or bodily harm. If they do not, then these principles may not have much bearing on the award of remedies, and enforcement of remedial duties, which ultimately will have an effect on the duty-bearer's *property*. At least in so far as the removal of a person's property negatively impacts upon their life, however, it is plausible to think that the same or similar constraints apply. Indeed, the apparent wrongfulness of harmless trespasses against property gives some support for the application of constraints to cases of harmless use of property, too.

5.2.2 Defeating constraint-based objections

Sometimes it is permissible to impose a burden upon a person even if *Utility* applies. It is permissible to harm a person deliberately in justified self-defense, and sometimes even if this involves the use of that person's body. For instance, if the only way of B's protecting himself from a missile thrown by A with an intention to kill B without

140 SANDY STEEL

justification, then B may use A as a means to protect B from the missile (eg by pulling A in front of the missile).

Tadros has offered an explanation of this. He describes two bases on which the objections given by these principles can be defeated or diminished in force, rendering the use or harm potentially permissible:[41] (i) A's having an enforceable moral duty to bear the burden imposed by B; (ii) A's having had a reasonable opportunity to avoid bearing the burden imposed by B.[42] I cannot fully assess (i) and (ii) here, but here are some observations, with an eye to private law.

5.2.2.1 Duties to bear deterrent burdens

The idea behind (i) is that a person's objection to being used to pursue some good is defeated if they are under an enforceable moral duty to pursue that good. Normally, we are each free to set our own ends; that is partly what grounds the deontological constraints. But, when we are under a moral duty to bear a burden, and the duty is one of sufficient importance that it may be enforced, it is not open to us to say that we are free not to bear the burden, or that we are treated as a mere tool for the pursuit of the good when we are made to do as the duty requires. Tadros provides a complex general argument as to why and when wrongdoers come under duties to *protect* their victims from future harm by bearing burdens that are aimed to deter others from inflicting harm.[43]

Here is an argument why the fiduciary could be said to be under a moral duty to give up the gain. The fiduciary's duty to account for the gain made from the fiduciary position to the principal could be justified by the risk such gain-making poses to the value of the fiduciary relationship generally. A fiduciary who keeps a gain in such circumstances creates such a significant risk to the institution in virtue of the possible temptation given to other fiduciaries, who may then make morally sub-optimal decisions in breach of their assumed moral duties. The duty to give up the gain arises in virtue of its contribution toward reducing the risk posed to the valuable social institution. This duty is not necessarily owed *to* the principal. The justification of the duty is general value of the social institution, not the particular interests of the principal. To the extent that the fiduciary comes under such a moral duty, it is plausible to think their objection to being required to serve as a deterrent is reduced or eliminated. Another situation in which such duties to bear a deterrent burden arises in private law may include duties to fulfil contractual deterrence duties. More generally, a person may become morally liable to bear a burden that is intended to induce them to comply with a private law duty when that burden seems to be a necessary and proportionate

---

[41] The relationship between these bases is not entirely clear in V Tadros, *The Ends of Harm: The Moral Foundations of Criminal Law* (OUP 2011). In *To Do, To Die, To Reason Why: Individual Ethics in War* (OUP 2020), Tadros now rejects the role of opportunities to avoid harm as generating liability.

[42] Tadros, *The Ends of Harm* (n 3) ch 8 for (ii), drawing on Scanlon, particularly *What We Owe to Each Other* (Harvard University Press 1998). Sometimes Tadros writes (eg at 175) that the force of the objection is "diminished" or "eroded" in relation to (ii), in proportion to the degree to which the harm was avoidable by the person suffering it.

[43] For an important part of the argument, see Tadros, *The Ends of Harm* (n 41) 277. The basic idea is that sometimes compensation is not sufficient next best conformity to a duty not wrongfully to harm. Sometimes protection from future harm is required, and sometimes this protection must be provided by bearing a deterrent burden.

DETERRENCE IN PRIVATE LAW 141

means of enforcing their duty. This explains the justifiability of specific deterrence orders.

5.2.2.2 The significance of opportunities to avoid harm

Consider this account of the permissibility of harming a culpable attacker in self-defense.[44] If a person is not permitted to harm a culpable attacker in self-defense, that person's opportunity to avoid harm is significantly diminished: the person may be required to die due to another person's serious wrongdoing rather than act. Such a person therefore has a serious moral objection to a principle prohibiting self-defense against culpable attackers. By contrast, a culpable attacker has no objection to a principle permitting self-defense against them. Such a person can simply avoid choosing to breach their serious moral obligations. The fact that the attacker had ample opportunity to avoid causing harm, and the fact that the victim would have substantially diminished opportunity to avoid harm were acting in self-defense impermissible, seems to support the permissibility of harm imposed on culpable attackers. One's moral complaint against suffering harm is sometimes diminished by the fact that one could have chosen to avoid the harm at minimal or no cost.[45]

In the private law context, we can readily think of situations in which a person may be said to be provided with adequate opportunity to avoid the imposition of a burden imposed for the purposes of deterrence. An agreed secondary contractual obligation is one example. It seems plausible that the promisor does not have much complaint to such enforcement when the sum is not "disproportionate" to the interest in protecting the interest in performance. Assuming the promisor is a sophisticated commercial party, and absent any vitiating factor, they had adequate opportunity to avoid entering into such an agreement. More generally, we find the law attaching positive duties— roughly, duties to confer benefits—more readily in circumstances in which such duties can be avoided without significant cost.[46] Similarly, a person who takes on a role in which the law clearly attaches fiduciary obligations may often be said to have adequate opportunity to avoid being liable to account for profits made from that position. This may be the only way in which the social value of the institution is maintained through deterrence, and the fiduciary could normally easily avoid incurring the obligation to account by seeking the principal's consent, or by not assuming the fiduciary position at all.

6. Conclusion

Deterrent impact is not necessary for an enforceable private law norm to be justified. Nor is it sufficient. It can, however, sometimes be a reason for having such a norm. The reasons provided by D-considerations can decisively support (i) the adoption of

---

[44] This is drawn from Scanlon and Tadros, both (n 42) above.

[45] "Cost" is a moralized notion here: a person's being unable to satisfy a desire to harm is not a "cost" for these purposes. See furtherN Kolodny, "Political Rule and its Discontents" in D Sobel, P Vallentyne, and S Wall (eds), *Oxford Studies in Political Philosophy*, vol 2 (OUP 2016) 4.3.

[46] I discuss this in much greater detail in S Steel, *Omissions Liability in Tort* (forthcoming, OUP 2023).

particular private law rules in circumstances of scarcity; (ii) the adoption of particular rules in circumstances in which the law has a choice between different modes of crystallizing pre-legal moral relations; (iii) the availability of specific deterrent orders; (iv) the content of particular liabilities in circumstances in which the provision of remedial rights to private litigants is a particularly effective deterrent, and the defendant has a moral duty to bear the deterrent burden or otherwise cannot reasonably object to its being imposed; (v) considerations of overdeterrence may require legal institutions not to enforce certain private law duties, instead establishing limited immunities from suit.[47] In general, what enables deterrent impact to have justificatory force is either (i) the fact the burden imposed by the law is one which there is already an independent individualist justification for the person burdened to bear, or (ii) the fact that the law would itself be an agent of greater harm if deterrent impact were not acted upon.

---

[47] Since the deterrent impact of the private law is achieved mainly through making persons liable to court orders and enforcement, the deterrent impact of liability will typically be relevant precisely to that: the creation of *liability to enforcement* or proceedings, rather than to the content of primary and secondary norms.

PART II
RESPONDING TO WRONGS

9
Finishing the Reparative Job
Victims' Duties to Wrongdoers

Cécile Fabre[*]

1. Introduction

The literature on reparative justice focuses for the most part on the grounds and content of wrongdoers' duties to their victims. An interesting but neglected question, which John Gardner raises in *From Personal Life to Private Law*, is whether a victim is under a duty to her wrongdoer to (as Gardner puts it) help him "finish the reparative job" by accepting his amends and, when the amend takes the form of financial reparations, by using it so as to repair the wrong.[1]

Gardner answers in the affirmative with respect to financial reparations. It is fair to say, I think, that he raises the question without fully answering it. In this chapter, I use his remarks as a springboard for an account of victims' duties of that kind. I argue that victims have much greater latitude than he grants them. Section 2 sketches in broad terms two standard approaches to reparative justice, namely the restorative approach and the backward-looking approach of which Gardner's own account is an example. Section 3 rejects a duty to accept financial reparations, while section 4 rejects the duty to use reparative payments in conformity with reparative ends.

---

[*] Earlier drafts of this chapter were presented at the Nuffield Political Theory, the KCL Juris Workshops, and a workshop on Gardner's philosophy of private law held in April 2021. I thank audiences for illuminating discussions. For written comments on earlier drafts, thanks are owed to Gideon Elford, Helen Frowe, Alexander Georgiou, David Miller, Haris Psarras, Gopal Sreenivasan, Sandy Steel, and Frederick Wilmot-Smith.

[1] J Gardner, *From Personal Life to Private Law* (OUP 2018) 107 (*"FPLPL"*). Some way into the drafting of this chapter, I became aware of John CP Goldberg's (then) forthcoming review of the book, in which he takes up the question of victims' duties. He is critical of Gardner's view, as I am, but places greater emphasis than I do here on the question of how to construe those duties in the first instance, and less emphasis than I do on normative grounds for resisting them. (JCP Goldberg, "Taking Responsibility Personally: On John Gardner's *From Personal Life to Private Law*" (2021) 14 Journal of Tort Law 3.) The question of victims' duties to wrongdoers in a reparative context arises in the literature on forgiveness. Outside the issue of forgiveness and aside Goldberg, Linda Radzik is to my knowledge the only other philosopher who gives serious attention to victims' reparative duties to wrongdoers. However, her heavily qualified argument in favor of victims' duties "lumps" reparations together with apologies. (L Radzik, *Making Amends* (OUP 2009) 126–36; L Radzik, "Tort Processes and Relational Repair" in J Oberdiek (ed), *Philosophical Foundations of the Law of Torts* (OUP 2014) 243–244.) RA Duff and V Tadros cursorily claim that victims are not under duties to accept compensation but do not mount a sustained argument to that effect. (RA Duff, "Repairing Harms and Answering for Wrongs" in J Oberdiek (ed), *Philosophical Foundations of the Law of Torts* (OUP 2014) 216; V Tadros, "Secondary Duties" in PB Miller and J Oberdiek (eds), *Civil Wrongs and Justice in Private Law* (OUP 2020) 200.)

Cécile Fabre, *Finishing the Reparative Job* In: *Private Law and Practical Reason*. Edited by: Haris Psarras and Sandy Steel, Oxford University Press. © Cécile Fabre 2023. DOI: 10.1093/oso/9780192857330.003.0009

In those two sections, I rely on the following simplifying assumptions: the wrong-doing is relatively minor; the wrongdoer and the victim are not tied by bonds of friendship or family; there is only one wrongdoer and one victim. I relax those assumptions in section 5 and show that those additional features sometimes impose on victims duties of acceptance and use which they would not have otherwise.

Some preliminary remarks. First, I focus on cases in which an agent violates some right(s) of another person's. Within the category of rights-violations, I focus on private wrongs. I do not address reparations in the aftermath of large-scale political conflicts; nor do I consider cases in which the state is deemed to owe reparations for its (officials') wrongdoings (save for a brief comment at the close of section 5). I also set aside cases in which the breach is a violation of a contractual right. My concern is with violations of rights to property and physical integrity in interpersonal, non-contractual contexts.[2]

Second, I am mostly interested in victims' duties to wrongdoers. Whether victims are under moral duties to parties other than wrongdoers to accept the latter's payment or to use those payments in conformity with reparative ends is a separate question which I postpone until the final section. Accordingly, unless otherwise specified, when I speak of victims' duties, rights, or prerogatives, I mean *vis-à-vis* wrongdoers.

Third, individuals owe it to one another not to humiliate one another, not to seek to exercise domination over one another, and so on. Victims' latitude to refuse reparations is constrained by those moral considerations. Turning down a payment in order to make the wrongdoer feel worse or in one's debt is morally wrong. I take that point as fixed throughout and assume that the victim's attitude towards the wrongdoer is of the right kind.

Finally, my concern is solely with victims' *moral* duties. If my defense of victims' entitlements has relevance to or interesting implications for the law, all the better for it. But I leave it to those more competent than I am to say so.

2. Reparative Justice: A Primer

Suppose that Walter crashes into Violet's car in a bout of careless driving. He is under a *pro tanto* duty to her to remedy the wrong he has inflicted on her, for example to have her car fixed at his expense and to compensate her for the inconvenience she has suffered as a result of the crash. Correlatively, she has a right against him that he take the appropriate measure.[3] This intuitively appealing claim raises serious

---

[2] Thanks to Sandy Steel for inviting me to consider contractual breaches—even though I regretfully decline the invitation for lack of space. I consider postwar reparations in C Fabre, *Cosmopolitan Peace* (OUP 2016), ch 6. Furthermore, nothing I say in this chapter should be taken to imply that remedial measures are necessarily responses to rights violations: I take no stand on this particular point. Stephen Smith offers a useful typology of damages some of which, he claims, are not properly construed as compensation for losses or harms while others are not responses to a wrong. See SA Smith, "The Significance of a Civil Wrong" in PB Miller and J Oberdiek (eds), *Civil Wrongs and Justice in Private Law* (OUP 2020). For a typology of remedies which are not responses to rights violations, see N Cornell, "What Do We Remedy?" in PB Miller and J Oberdiek (eds), *Civil Wrongs and Justice in Private Law* (OUP 2020).

[3] I adapt Gardner's own example, which he borrows from an episode of the series *Curb Your Enthusiasm*. *FPLPL* (n 1) ch 3.

complications, notably with respect to how much one may reasonably ask wrongdoers to do to repair their wrong, whether monetary compensation is an appropriate remedy for non-financial harms, and whether Walters owes it to Violet all things considered to repair the wrong. I prescind from addressing those complications. Instead, I take it as a given that Walter owes financial reparations to Violet—say, for the sake of expository simplicity and as a placeholder, £500—and thus, correlatively, that she has a right to it.

Before considering whether Violet is under a duty to accept the payment and, if so, to use it to the ends for which it is meant, it is worth saying a few words about the grounds of Walter's duty. On the restorative or reconciliatory approach to reparative justice, by acting as he did, Walter caused damage to his relationship to Violet. He owes it to her to repair their relationship. In order to do that, he must atone for his wrongdoing. When atonement must take the form of, *inter alia*, financial reparations—he owes it to her to do just that.[4]

On such a view, to the extent that victims are under duties to wrongdoers to repair and promote a good relationship and that accepting and using payments serves such ends, it seems intuitively plausible to say that victims are under *pro tanto* duties to wrongdoers to help the latter finish the reparative job. However, there are at least two familiar problems with the restorative view. First, it does not adequately account for reparative duties when there is no relationship to begin with. Second, it presses the wrong kind of reasons in support of those duties in general. For it seems that, by its lights, one (or even the) reason why Walter is under a duty to Violet to drive carefully in the first place is that, should he fail to do so and crash into her, he would damage his relationship with Violet. But this does not seem right: Walter is under a duty to her to drive carefully by dint of his general duty to road users and pedestrians to give due consideration to their fundamental interests in physical safety. This is so whether or not there is a relationship to salvage.[5]

On so-called corrective approaches to reparations, Walter's reparative duty is not grounded in the damage he did to his relationship with Violet (even if, we may readily suppose, he *did* cause such damage). Rather, it is connected to his primary duty to others to take reasonable care while driving. The task of an account of reparative duties is to explain the nature of this connection. On Gardner's influential view, which he dubs the continuity thesis, the reasons which ground Walter's primary duty to drive carefully are not extinguished by his dereliction: they continue to apply to him.[6] On another view, it is the right and its correlative primary duty which survive, not the reasons which grounds the primary duty: the reparative duty is the next best thing to

---

[4] See eg J Thompson, *Taking Responsibility for the Past: Reparation and Historical Justice* (Polity 2002); L Wenar, "Reparations for the Future" (2006) 37(3) Journal of Social Philosophy 396; Radzik, *Making Amends* (n 1); Radzik, "Tort Processes and Relational Repair" (n 1).

[5] In response to first objection, Linda Radzik argues that even in those cases, there is a relationship to salvage, albeit a purely moral one (Radzik, "Tort Processes and Relational Repair" (n 1) 238. See also M Walker, *Moral Repair—Reconstructing Moral Relations after Wrongdoing* (CUP 2006) ch 1). My concern with this move is that it relies on such a broad understanding of what constitutes a relationship as to empty it of explanatory content. For the wrong-kind-of reason objection, see eg R Kumar, "Why Reparations?" in J Oberdiek (ed), *Philosophical Foundations of the Law of Torts* (OUP 2014). Gardner himself is skeptical of the reconciliatory approach; FPLPL (n 1) 91–98.

[6] See, in particular, J Gardner, "What is Tort Law For? Part 1. The Place of Corrective Justice" (2011) 30(1) Law and Philosophy 1.

148 CÉCILE FABRE

respecting the right.[7] On yet another view, Walter's duty is grounded in his breach of his primary duty to Violet to take reasonable care while driving.[8]

On whichever backward-looking account one endorses, the wrongful harm which Violet suffered at Walter's hands is repaired only if she is brought back as close as possible to where she was before the crash. For this to happen, it is not enough that Walter should offer to do that which will put her back in that position—say, for the sake of argument, compensate her for the inconvenience and pay to have the car fixed: Violet must accept Walter's payment and use it to put herself back, as close as possible, to where she was before the crash.[9] Hence our two questions:

1. On what grounds, if any, is Violet under a duty to Walter to accept the payment?
2. On what grounds, if any, is Violet under a duty to Walter to use it conformably?

3. Acceptance

When discussing the question of acceptance, Gardner makes two points. First, turning down a reparative payment is tantamount to thwarting the wrongdoer's attempt to fulfil his duty to repair. Victims are under a duty not to do so—or, as he puts it, a duty to help wrongdoers "finish the reparative job". However, second, a victim may refuse a reparative payment as a way to put the past firmly behind her and to make a fresh start, and if to do so is the next best thing. There is no duty of acceptance if one's refusal is grounded in reparative considerations. But there is a (*pro tanto*) duty not to refuse the payment for non-reparative reasons.[10]

---

[7] A Ripstein, *Private Wrongs* (Harvard University Press 2016), ch 8; EJ Weinrib, *Corrective Justice* (OUP 2012), ch 3.

[8] Tadros (n 1). Restorative and corrective approaches are not the only games in town. In the philosophy of tort law, they have formidable rivals in the economics approach and the civil recourse approach. Very roughly put, on the economics approach as defended by Richard Posner and Guido Calabresi, the aim of tort law is to assign liabilities following a legal breach in such a way as to maximize economic efficiency. On this view, the fact that Walter *wronged* Violet plays no role in ascertaining what he owes her. On the civil recourse approach as defended by, in particular, John CP Goldberg and Benjamin C Zipursky, that fact is crucial. But whereas the corrective approach grounds Walter's reparative duty in his breach of his primary duty, the civil recourse approach grounds it in Violet's right *to seek recourse* against Walter (JCP Goldberg and BC Zipursky, *Recognizing Wrongs* (Harvard University Press 2020)). Unlike the economics approach, the corrective and the civil recourse approaches conceive of the legal rights and duties of torts, and, by implication, the moral rights and duties of reparative justice, in relational terms; and they thus both open the door to an account of what, if anything, victims (or plaintiffs) owe to wrongdoers (or defendants). I do not examine in detail what the civil recourse approach may have to say about this issue, partly in deference to the fact that this chapter is a contribution to a volume on Gardner's works, partly because I have a (not fully formed) reservation* about its central claim in so far as it applies to reparative justice as distinct from tort law. (*To wit, that Walter's reparative obligation to Violet is not grounded in Violet's right to seek redress but, rather, in the mere fact that he wronged her. Whether she has the right to enforce or waive the performance of his duty (which is what the right to seek remedies amounts to) is a separate question.)

[9] I say "for the sake of argument", for it is possible in principle that some remedial measure other than a payment might sometimes do the job. But in this chapter, I assume that nothing other than payment to fix the car and compensate her for the inconvenience will do.

[10] *FPLPL* (n 1) 217–18 and 228–29. This paragraph reconstructs what I take Gardner's position to be, in the light of the pages just mentioned and in the light of his endorsement of the duty to use conformably in ch 3. More on the latter in section 4.

I disagree with Gardner, on two grounds. For a start, his way of framing the question threatens to render the latter moot. He sometimes describes Violet's refusal in terms of not thwarting Walter's *attempt* to fulfil his duty to repair, sometimes in terms of not thwarting his *performance* of the duty. This is unfortunate, for these are not the same. Walter attempts to fulfil his duty if (for example) he writes a check without realizing that his bank account does not have enough funds: Violet thwarts his attempt if she, for example, surreptitiously steals all of his pens, as a result of which he cannot write the check. Contrastingly, Walter performs his duty if he writes the check with enough funds to cover it and sends the check to Violet. Now, as Gardner has it, she thwarts the performance of his duty by not cashing the check. But it is wholly unclear why that is the case. Walter's duty to pay is simply a duty to write a check with sufficient funds to cover it. So long as he does this precisely, he *has* performed his duty and Violet's refusal to cash the check cannot be aptly described as thwarting his performance.[11] If this is correct, the question of whether Violet is under a duty not to thwart Walter's performance of his reparative duty does not get off the ground. That said, let us take Gardner at his word and assume, with him, that however one construes Walter's duty to pay and Violet's acceptance, the question of whether she is under a duty to accept remains on the table. Even so, as I now argue, Violet is not under the stated duty to Walter. More expansively put, (i) Violet is not under a duty not to pre-empt his offer by indicating that she will not accept it; (ii) she is not under a duty to do what she needs to do in order to have Walter's rights in respect of the requisite amount of money transferred to her; (iii) she is not under a duty not to return the payment to Walter once she receives it.

As far as I can see, Gardner does not provide a defense of the view that Violet is under the relevant duty.[12] Here is one. Generally, we are under duties not to thwart—and, indeed, perhaps even to help—one another in the performance of our duties. Suppose that, at time t_1, I am under a duty to you to rescue you from the pond in which you are drowning. As I am about to wade in at t_2, your life-long murderous enemy stands in my way and refuses to budge, thereby making it impossible for me to save you, whereupon you die. Assume that the land on which we both stand is publicly owned, so that prior to your getting into difficulties in the water, I and your enemy are equally entitled to stand where we are. That he wrongs you, grievously so, by refusing to let me go through is beyond dispute. I also think that he wrongs me.

I suspect that not everyone will agree. Some might say that by making it impossible for me to save you, your enemy has extinguished any duty I had to you to rescue you and that I am in exactly the same situation at t_2 as the bystander who is too far away to

---

[11] See, respectively, ibid 106 and 217. For an incisive discussion of this point, see Goldberg (n 1). I am indebted to Adam Slavny and Gopal Sreenivasan for helping me clarifying my thoughts on the ambiguity in and consequent exegetical difficulty with the term "duty not to thwart the performance of/attempts to perform the duty to repair."

[12] It might be thought that the answer, for Gardner, lies in his general account of duties, including reparative duties, as delegable. On this view, Walter delegates to Violet the task of seeing to it that the reparative job is finished. (*FPLPL* (n 1) 107.) However, even if it makes sense so to construe Violet's action, we still need to know on what grounds she is under a duty to Walter to agree to fulfill his delegable duty. (On delegable duties, the continuity thesis, and cases such as Walter and Violet, see AS Gold, "Delegation and the Continuity Thesis" (2021) 40 Law and Philosophy 645.)

do anything and watches in impotent despair as you drown.[13] But this does not ring true. For the fact is that, unlike the bystander, I *was* in a position to rescue you. It is not merely understandable but appropriate that I should round on your enemy and ask on *my* behalf as well as on yours what on earth he is doing. I now have a grievance against your enemy, on my own behalf and which the bystander does not have to the same extent, for preventing me from rescuing you.

The point applies, *mutatis mutandis*, to reparative duties. Suppose that I thoughtlessly knocked you over into the pond. Of all the possible rescuers, it behooves me other things being equal to get you out. In this case too, I am owed a duty not to be thwarted in my reparative endeavor. Or—going back to Walter and Violet—suppose that unbeknownst to Violet, Violet's daughter intercepts Walter's check before it gets to her mother, and cashes it for herself. That she wrongs Violet is beyond doubt. I believe that she also wrongs Walter.[14]

Here are two considerations in favor of the view that one is under duties to duty-bearers not to thwart them. First, on plausible conceptions of well-being, a life that goes well is one that is lived in compliance with the demands of morality. This, in fact, is a recurrent theme in Gardner's works, particularly in *From Personal Life to Private Law*. In so far as we owe it to one another not to impair our opportunities for a good life (at least not without warrant), we owe it to one another not to thwart our fulfilment of our duties, reparative or otherwise (at least not without warrant.) Second, irrespective of the impact of one's failure to comply with the demands of morality on one's well-being, to respect another person as a moral agent is to recognize in them the ability to do the right thing in the light of their own judgments, and to support them in their successful exercise of that ability. This partly explains why manipulating, exploiting, or coercing someone into committing a wrongdoing is a wrong done to them, and not merely to the victims of that wrongdoing. The rationale for the duty not to act in such a way as to get someone to do wrong is also a rationale for the duty not to act in such a way as to make her fail to do right. To put the general point in Gardnerian parlance, we do not merely have reasons to try to live by the demands of morality, we have reasons—grounded in well-being and moral agency—to succeed in doing so. Likewise, we (sometimes) are under *duties*, and do not simply have reasons,

---

[13] Another skeptical point: suppose that your enemy pushes you under the water and kills you before I manage to get to you. In this case too he has made it impossible for me to fulfill my duty of rescue. The intuition I harness here seemingly implies that he wrongs me, which seems wholly implausible. I agree with the judgment of implausibility. But I am not committed to it. There is a salient difference between depriving someone of the means she needs in order to fulfill her duty, and acting in such a way as to change the facts which gave rise to that duty in the first instance. Thanks to Adam Slavny and Sandy Steel for pushing me on this.

[14] One may wonder whether Violet and Walter have a moral claim against Violet's daughter and, if so, whether they both ought to have a legal claim to remedy against her. To the first question: I am inclined to say "yes," though it is not always clear what the nature of the daughter's wrong is. Is it an act of theft against both Walter and Violet? Against Walter only, if she intercepts the check before it reaches Violet? An act of theft against Violet but an exercise in thwarting Walter's performance of his reparative duty if she seizes the check after it reaches her mother? To the second question: this depends on when, legally speaking, Walter is deemed no longer to have a title to the money, and when the money is deemed to belong to Violet. Thanks to Zoë Sinel for drawing my attention to this fascinating and hugely complex issue and to Alexander Georgiou for a helpful discussion.

VICTIMS' DUTIES TO WRONGDOERS   151

not merely to try but to succeed, and others owe it to us not to thwart our performance of those duties.[15]

Those considerations strike me as compelling. Indeed, as we shall see later on, they support a duty of acceptance in some more complex cases. However, they do not support the claim that *Violet* is under a duty of acceptance to Walter in the simple case. As I noted at the outset, Violet has a right against Walter that he repair the wrong he did her. On the interest theory of rights (which Gardner and I both endorse), to say that someone has (i) a right, (ii) a permission, and (iii) a power in respect of ϕ is to say that some interest of hers is important enough to, respectively: (a*) impose on third parties a duty to respect or promote ϕ, (b*) deny third parties a claim that she not ϕ, (c*) render third parties liable to her changing her and their jural relationships over ϕ.[16] Generally, agents have two broad categories of interests: first-order interests in the goods necessary to lead a flourishing life on the one hand, and second-order interests in exercising some degree of control over what third parties do to or for them in respect of those first-order interests. Walter wrongfully sets back Violet's first-order interest in the goods of physical security and use of her car, which grounds his reparative duty to her. Violet also has a second-order interest in deciding whether or not she will accept the payment. The question is whether her second-order interest is important enough to be protected by a permission (or no-duty) *vis-à-vis* Walter not to accept the payment.

I believe that it is. To see this, consider non-reparative duties to rescue. In the pond case, you do not owe it to me not to relieve me of my duty to rescue you. Your interest in deciding whether or not to remain alive surely outweighs my interest in seeing to it that you do remain alive; and it is important enough not merely to be protected by a power, *vis-à-vis* me, to waive my duty, but also by a permission, *vis-à-vis* me, to do so. To be sure, your need for rescue will go unmet if you refuse my help, but such is your prerogative.

I see no reason to treat differently reparative duties to pay. Violet's interest in deciding whether or not to accept Walter's payment outweighs his interest in it being the case that she actually gets the payment. The wrongful harm which Violet incurred at Walter's hands will go unrepaired if she turns down the payment, but that too is her prerogative.

The claim that Violet does not owe it to Walter to accept his payment finds support in restitutive justice. Here are some examples, drawn from two nineteenth-century literary masterpieces. First, in George Eliot's *Middlemarch*, Nicholas Bulstrode, the town's banker and one of the main characters, is seen, and wants to be seen, as a devout Christian in words and deeds. Yet he has made his fortune by illicitly depriving his first wife's daughter and grandson of their rightful inheritance, a fact of which Middlemarchers are clearly not aware. Decades later, he offers the impoverished

---

[15] On the wrong of getting someone to act wrongly, see also JW Howard, "Moral Subversion and Structural Entrapment" (2016) 24(1) Journal of Political Philosophy 24. If the second consideration in favor of the duty not to thwart duty-bearers is apt, then it is *pro tanto* worse to stymie someone in the fulfillment of her duty than it is to thwart her in the commission of a supererogatory act.

[16] WN Hohfeld, *Fundamental Conceptions as Applied in Judicial Reasoning* (Yale University Press 1919). The *locus classicus* for the interest theory of rights is J Raz, *The Morality of Freedom* (Clarendon Press 1986) ch 7.

grandson, Will Ladislaw, to return to him the equivalent of what he took from him. Ladislaw refuses the offer, essentially because Bulstrode's original business, on which his current fortune is built, was a pawnshop doubling up as a fence shop. Ladislaw is impetuous and particularly sensitive about his difficult family circumstances. But it is the manner of his refusal, which betokens (paraphrasing Eliot) merciless arrogance towards the older man, that gives us pause—not the refusal itself. By hypothesis, the money is *his* and, precisely for that reason, it is for him to decide whether or not to accept it.

Second, Victor Hugo's *Les Misérables*. The hero, Jean Valjean, steals silverware from the bishop who gave him hospitality. He is caught by police officers who drag him back to the bishop's house to return the goods. The bishop's mendacious assertion to the police that he gave the silverware to Valjean sets the latter on his long and difficult road to redemption—as hoped for by the bishop. Even if Valjean had not understood the bishop's message, it would be odd to say that he would have been wronged by his benefactor's refusal to accept the goods. We do not owe it to thieves to take back the property they have stolen from us.[17]

One final point. My rejection of Violet's duty of acceptance is compatible with the view that victims are under some circumstances under duties of acceptance to wrongdoers in respect of the latter's reparative duties to pay. Suppose that bystander Brenda offers to pay up *in lieu* of Walter. However, Walter is willing to pay, as is his duty. Indeed, he insists—for no reason other than the fact that it matters to him that the wrongs he has occasioned not go unrepaired. I am inclined to think that, *if* she is minded to take a payment, she is under a *pro tanto* duty to him to accept his payment rather than Brenda's in this case.[18]

4. Use

I have argued that Violet does not owe it to Walter to accept his payment. Suppose that she does accept the money. The question is whether she owes it to Walter to use it in conformity with the reparative ends which mandated it in the first instance. Those two

---

[17] G Eliot, *Middlemarch* (OUP (Oxford World's Classics) 1999) (first published in 1871–1872) VI.lxi; V Hugo, *Les Misérables* (Gallimard—Bibliothèque de la Pléiade 2018) (first published in 1862) I.xii. My point about the bishop applies irrespective of the fact that Valjean did not willingly return the silverware.

[18] Suppose that Walter is destitute and that paying reparations to Violet would cause him severe hardship. It might be thought that, given that Brenda is willing to pay in his place, Violet ought to accept her payment rather than his: far from being under a duty to him to accept, she is under a duty to him to refuse. Whether this is correct depends on, *inter alia*, whether reparative obligations, in the same vein as distributive obligations, are subject to a no undue cost proviso (something like "ought" implies "can"). If they are, and if Walter thus is not under a duty to pay yet insists on doing so, then we may worry that Violet's refusal, in so far as it is grounded in concern for his well-being, is unduly paternalistic. If Walter is under a duty to pay, either because reparative duties are not subject to the no undue cost proviso or because, though they are, his duty does not run afoul of the proviso, then Violet is not under a duty *to him* to take Brenda's payment rather than his, though she may, perhaps, be under an undirected duty of charity to do so. These twists on the initial case raise the difficult question of the relationship between the principle that "ought" implies "can" and the moral foundations of civil law (on which question see eg A Slavny, "Should Tort Law Demand the Impossible?" in PB Miller and J Oberdiek (eds), *Civil Wrongs and Justice in Private Law* (OUP 2020); Frederick Wilmot-Smith, "Law, 'Ought' and 'Can'" (2021, unpublished), on file with author.

questions, of acceptance and use, must be kept separate. Even if Violet is under a duty to Walter to accept his payment, it does not follow that she is under a duty to use that payment conformably. Conversely, even if she is not under a duty to accept the payment, it does not follow that if she does accept it, she has full latitude as to how to use it.

Assume, following Gardner's expository lead, that Violet gives the money to her daughter instead of fixing her car. Assume further that helping her daughter not only does not help Violet fix her car but, moreover, does not make good on the inconvenience Violet incurred as a result of the crash. For example, Violet's daughter decides (with her mother's foreknowledge) to treat herself to a holiday. Walter complains: "you shouldn't have done that! I gave it to you to fix your car." According to Gardner, he has a legitimate grievance.

Gardner's initial example—from *Curb Your Enthusiasm*—is more complex than appears at first. The victim, Heineman, does not inform Larry, who rear-ended his car, that he has given Larry's reparative payment to his daughter; Larry finds out when he notices that Heineman has clearly not fixed his car and confronts him. Larry's sense of grievance is colored by the fact that Heineman acted surreptitiously and against their shared understanding that Heineman would fix the car.[19]

I am not sure that Larry has a grievance under those circumstances. I am tempted to say that short of having promised Larry to use the money conformably, Heineman is allowed to change his mind without informing him. In any event, Gardner's core analysis of the example clearly indicates that there is more to Larry's grievance than his having been deceived: "That Heineman did not spend the money on replacing the smashed taillight means ... that Larry's attempt to do the right thing by the light of the continuity thesis has been frustrated. Hence Larry's indignation."[20] That being said, Gardner does not tell us *why*, setting aside Heineman's deceit, Larry's indignation is justified and why, more generally, victims owe it to wrongdoers to use the latter's payments conformably. As far as I can tell, the closest he comes to offering an argument is when he claims that a victim who says that her use of the payment is none of the wrongdoer's business "is ... dropping [him] prematurely from the justification equation."[21] I confess that I am not sure how to parse that statement. One can of course readily concede that Walter would have a grievance if Violet's daughter intercepted the check and, instead of having the car fixed as asked by her mother, spent it on herself. For as I suggested above, third parties are under duties to duty-bearers not to thwart them in the performance of their duties. But we do need an argument in support of *Violet*'s duty of conformable use.

It is quite possible that, had Gardner been pressed on this point, he would have said that the duty of conformable use is grounded in the same considerations as ground the duty of acceptance.[22] If so, my rejection of the latter applies to the former. In the

---

[19] See, especially *FPLPL* (n 1) 226. I am grateful to Andrew Gold for prompting me to disentangle those various dimensions of the case.

[20] ibid 103.

[21] ibid 106. As an aside, Gardner notes that the claim that a victim owes it to her wrongdoer to use his reparative payment conformably raises the question of whether his claim against her ought to be enforced by the courts, ie by means of supervising how she spends the money. His reasons for rejecting courts' involvement are persuasive (ibid 227–28).

[22] Thanks to Alexander Georgiou for the suggestion.

remainder of this section, I scrutinize another argument one might be tempted to deploy in support of that duty. To wit, if Violet spends the money to non-reparative ends without Walter's consent, she is appropriating from him something which he was not under a duty to give her—to wit, £500 *to help her daughter go on holiday.*[23]

I agree that Walter is not under *that* duty. Even so, it does not follow that she wrongs him if she chooses to spend the reparative payment in this particular way. At t_1, before the crash, Violet has a car. Here are some of her options:

1. Keep the car.
2. Sell the car and give the proceeds of the sale to her daughter.

As she has no spare cash, she cannot give any to her daughter without selling her car. Let us suppose for now that her car is no longer roadworthy as a result of the crash. (I shall relax this assumption presently.) At t_2, after the crash and before Walter's intervention, she is minus her car and still with no spare cash for her daughter. Walter owes it to her to get her as close as possible to where she was at t_1. The next best thing is to get the car fixed for her. However, as Gardner rightly argues, she may have good reasons for asking that he give her money instead—not least the fact that she may not want to have any further interaction with him, that she would incur greater inconvenience still if he took charge, etc.[24] Let us stipulate, then, that he owes it to her to give her £500, period, bearing in mind (to repeat) that he does not owe it to her to help her fund her daughter's holiday. At t_3, having received the payment, here are some of her options:

1*. Pay for the car to be fixed with Walter's money and keep the car.
2*. Pay for the car to be fixed with Walter's money, sell it, and give the proceeds to her daughter.
3*. Let the car go unfixed and give Walter's money to her daughter.

At t_1, Violet had the option of foregoing fixing her car and helping her daughter. At t_3, Walter's payment gives her two different ways of reaching this state of affairs: options 2* and 3*. I take it that Walter would have no grounds for objecting to her opting (as per 2*) to have the car fixed, sell it, and help her daughter with the proceeds: she would be left without a car, but she would be able to help her daughter without being £500 out of pocket. If so, it is hard to see on what grounds he could object to her bypassing the sale altogether and using his payment directly to help her daughter (as per 3*).

My claim turns on the fact that Walter gives her money. If he reimbursed her for the car repairs *ex post*, or gave her a repair voucher to be spent at her garage of choice, she would not have option 3*. He does not owe it to her to give her that option. Rather, given that she has independent reasons for asking for money *ex ante*, she now has that third option, which is merely another route for her to do what she was able to do before the crash, to wit, foregoing her car and helping her daughter.

I have stipulated so far that Walter's carelessness results in Violet losing a roadworthy car. Suppose now that the car, although damaged, is still roadworthy (as in

---

[23] Thanks to the audience at the KJuris workshop, where I presented this paper in March 2021, for a good discussion of this point.

[24] *FPLPL* (n 1) 106.

fact is the case in Gardner's original story).[25] In that scenario, at t_3, she now has the following options:

1**. Pay for the car to be fixed with Walter's money and keep the car.
2**. Pay for the car to be fixed with Walter's money, sell it, and give the proceeds to her daughter.
3**. Drive around with a damaged car and give Walter's money to her daughter.

In this case, her situation at t_3 is better in one respect than it was at t_1, for she now has an option which she did not have then, namely the use of her car *and* spare cash to help her daughter. Could Walter object to her choosing option 3** on the ground that he did not owe it to her to give her cash to help her daughter and that by using the payment in this way, she is appropriating something that did not belong to her? I doubt it. If it is the case that (as I argued above) Violet does not wrong Walter by fixing and selling the car for her daughter's benefit, it is hard to see why she wrongs him by opting to help her daughter directly. To say that she does implies that she owes it to him *not* to take advantage of the fact that he wronged her in the first instance and did what he was under a moral duty to do anyway, namely offering payment. That seems unduly demanding of her.

I suspect that in this and the previous (kinds of) case, the thought that Violet owes it to Walter to use the payment conformably draws intuitive force from the fact that she gives the money to her daughter. Suppose however that she decides to keep it for herself, not with a view to spending it here and now but in case she might want to spend it on something completely unrelated to the harms she incurred at Walter's ends. For all she knows, she might revise her conception of a good life in ways that may well necessitate spare cash. For example, she might want to leave some money in her will, which she currently does not have, to the Cats' Protection League, or she might rediscover her love for playing an instrument and then decide to buy a new one, and so on. It seems extraordinarily counterintuitive to insist that she owes it to Walter *not* to do that. There is no principled reason for treating differently Violet's decision to delay spending the reparative money until such time as she has a better sense of how to spend it, and her decision to spend it now for the sake of her daughter. Consequently, she does not wrong Walter by helping her daughter.[26]

So far, I have assumed that Violet has preferences in respect of how to spend the payment, which include fixing the car and giving money to her daughter and which she may justifiably weigh as she wishes. Suppose that she is utterly indifferent as between fixing the car and treating her daughter to a nice trip.[27] She can (i) let her daughter decide, (ii) fix the car in conformity with the reparative ends for which the money is meant, or (iii) toss a coin. Must she opt for (ii) in this case? I doubt it. If the rationale for holding Violet under a duty of conformable use is the same as the rationale for holding her under a duty to accept the payment in the first place, then, given that she does not owe Walter a duty of acceptance (as per my argument in section 3), it is hard

---

[25] I am grateful to Massimo Renzo for pressing me to distinguish more carefully between those two variants.

[26] For similar points, see Goldberg (n 1).

[27] Thanks to Adam Slavny for the suggestion.

156   CÉCILE FABRE

to see why she would be under a duty to him to opt for (ii). Pending argument to the contrary, what she does with the money is none of Walter's business.

5. Complications

I have argued that, in the kind of case under consideration so far, a victim is not under a duty to her wrongdoer to accept his remedial payment and to use that payment conformably: she may let the reparative job go unfinished. I have relied on three simplifying assumptions: Violet and Walter do not or barely know each other; the crash is relatively minor; they are the only parties involved in the crash. In this section, I relax each assumption in turn.

5.1 Special relationships

Suppose that Walter and Violet stand in a special relationship: they are colleagues, parent and child, siblings, partners, or neighbors.

Some wrongdoings are such that, when committed by and against individuals who do stand in a special relationship, payments are not in order: only apologies will do. In many cases, however, payment will be owed. Does the fact of Walter's and Violet's social, familial, professional relationship make a difference to their normative relationship as wrongdoer and victim?

There are two ways in which the presence of a special relationship might be morally salient. First, we might think that other things equal, individuals are under more stringent duties to their associates—be these duties not to harm or duties to help—than to strangers, and, thus, are under more stringent reparative duties to the former than to the latter. On this view, other things equal, it is worse unwarrantedly to harm or fail to help a friend than to impose the same harm on or withhold the same help from on a stranger.[28]

Even if and when that is true, however, such that the fact of their relationship has a bearing on the stringency of Walter's reparative duty to Violet, it is not clear that she is now under a duty to accept his payment and/or use it conformably which she would not have absent that relationship. Granted, it is possible that if she turns down Walter's payment or uses it to help her daughter, she will thereby damage their relationship. It is also possible that she is under a duty to try and maintain that relationship (suppose that they are siblings, for example, or close friends). But this would not ground a duty to help Walter finish the reparative job? For a start, such a relationship seems beyond repair if what it takes to maintain it is the acceptance and/or conformable use of a reparative payment *qua* payment. While Violet might value that relationship enough to have a reason to accept Walter's payment and use it to fix her car, I doubt that she is under a *duty* to him to do so—as distinct from a duty to try and repair the relationship

---

[28] Note: this does not imply that, contrary to what I said in section 2, reparative duties, in such cases, are best justified by appeal to reconciliatory ends—any more than my duty not to, eg, lie to or assault my friend is grounded in the importance of preserving that friendship.

by some other means. Moreover, the wrong kind of reason objection to restorative defenses of wrongdoers' reparative duties also applies here. If victims are under duties to wrongdoers to accept their reparations, this is so by dint of a general obligation to help wrongdoers fulfil their duties *tout court*, and it is unclear why the fact of a special relationship should change that.

The second way in which the fact of a relationship might and in fact does make a difference is this. Parties in a special relationship can be under duties to do things for one another which they are not under a duty to do for outsiders. Suppose that Walter—a rugby fanatic impatient with the modern game's concern for player safety—previously failed to take seriously the possibility that his teenage son, a reluctant rugby player keen to please his oppressive father, might have suffered a concussion in a particularly rough game, despite the boy complaining of headaches over the following few days. Had Walter taken him to Accident & Emergency, in fulfilment of his parental reparative duty of care, his son would not now suffer from cognitive impairment. Violet, who is a close friend of Walter's, knows all of this; she knows too that Walter is racked with guilt. A few weeks later, he crashes into her, totaling the car but mercifully not injuring her. Yet she knows that if she refuses his payment towards a new car, he will be utterly crushed by what he will see, yet again, as a failure to do right. Now, we might think that he needs professional help. Yet under those circumstances, it seems that she owes it to him, her friend, to take the payment (which, I maintain, she would not do were they strangers to each other). However, I doubt that she owes it to him to use it to get a new car. To say otherwise is to confer on him claims to govern how she leads a life which, surely, he does not have.[29]

5.2 The nature of the wrongdoing

It might be thought that the claim that Violet is not under a duty to Walter to accept his payment or to use it conformably unduly trades on the fact that, in the examples under discussion, Walter's wrong is relatively minor: the car is damaged, but it is nothing that a straightforward repair cannot fix, and Violet emerges unscathed from the crash. Suppose instead that she sustains fairly serious injuries. Walter owes her considerably more by way of reparative payment, such as something towards the cost of her rehabilitation, and perhaps even retraining if she has to change career as a result. Might there be something to the thought that, although it seemed an exaggeration to say that, in the minor crash case, she *wronged him* by declining the payment or by using it to help her daughter, it does not seem an exaggeration to say so in the serious crash case?

Perhaps. I conceded in section 3 that Walter might feel very bad at the prospect that his wrong might be left unrepaired. Let me put the concession more strongly: the more serious a wrongdoing, the more appropriate it is for wrongdoers to experience guilt, remorse, shame, and so on. Sometimes, those feelings can blight a life. Now, agents generally are not under a duty never to act in such a way as to adversely affect someone's life. But past the threshold at which the adverse effect constitutes a harm,

---

[29] Thanks to Sandy Steel for pushing me on this point and furnishing the example in broad form. The rugby twist is mine.

158 CÉCILE FABRE

they can be under such a duty. The thought, then, is this. Even if Violet is not under a duty to Walter to accept his payment or to use it conformably, she is under duties of acceptance and conformable use in cases in which Walter's feelings of guilt reach the harmfulness threshold.[30]

I am not entirely sure what to think of this putative move. If Walter's feelings are appropriate, in the sense that they are not shaped by an irrational interpretation of the facts of the case and that they are commensurate to the wrong he has committed, it is not clear that Violet owes it to him to help alleviate them. If his feelings are not inappropriate, whether she owes him anything depends on the magnitude of his wrongdoing and the costs to her of helping him. It seems that for wrongdoings of a certain magnitude, Violet owes him precisely nothing by way of acceptance or use, however debilitating his feelings might be. Suppose, then, that he has not wronged her to such an extent as to extinguish any duty she might have in respect of his offer of payment. Admittedly, it seems implausible for her to aver that it would be costly to her merely to accept a payment (on the assumption that she does not have reparative reasons to refuse it).[31] If so, then she may well be under a duty of acceptance. However, it is hard to believe that she also owes it to him to spend the money conformably. Acceptance should suffice.

5.3 Multiple victims

Many (most?) wrongs have multiple victims. Consider the following variants of our initial scenario. In the first variant, suppose that Walter rear-ends both Violet and Vivien in one fell swoop. He is under a duty to each of them to make financial reparations. Let us further suppose, first, that the damage he does to Violet's car is much more serious than the damage he causes to Vivien's, and second, that he does not have the financial resources to make payments to both of them. Violet, let us thus suppose, has a stronger claim than Vivien on his reparative resources.

If Violet decides not to accept the payment, she will make it possible for Walter to fulfil his reparative duty to Vivien. Suppose that she does accept the payment (as is her right) but, instead of fixing her car, gives it to her daughter (who does not have any claim, distributive or otherwise, to it). As a result, not only does the wrong which she suffered goes unrepaired (as is her prerogative), so does Vivien's.

In the one-victim case, I argued that Violet did not owe it to Walter not to give the money to her daughter. The question here is whether the fact that he has a *pro tanto* duty to another party makes a difference to what she owes him. I do not (I confess) have a very firm intuition about this kind of case. But I am inclined to think that it does

---

[30] These rough and ready points raise a number of difficulties which I cannot address here, such as what the threshold is and whether it is determined solely by the magnitude of the harm (the answer is "no"), and whether and when agents can forfeit their claim not to be adversely affected (the answer is "yes").

[31] The assumption is necessary, otherwise the question under consideration is moot. For if Violet has reparative reasons to refuse the payment altogether, then she is—by Gardner's lights and indeed my own—clearly entitled, at least *vis-à-vis* Walter, to do so. The question is not moot if we assume that she lacks such reasons. For with that assumption in hand, the question then arises as to whether the seriousness of the wrongdoing *alone* makes a difference to her duty to him.

not. If, absent Vivien, Violet does not wrong Walter by not using the money conformably, it is hard to see why Vivien's predicament makes a difference and thus implies that Violet *wrongs Walter*.[32]

In the second variant, Walter causes serious damage to Violet's car which, in turn, occasions serious harm to Violet's young son Victor. For example, Violet can no longer drive Victor to the hospital for a thrice-weekly dialysis. She also cannot afford to pay for taxis. In the parlance of reparative justice, Walter's wrong has a primary victim, Violet, and a secondary victim, Victor. He owes reparation to Violet for the damage he caused to her car and the adverse impact of his recklessness on her ability to discharge her parental duty to Victor. He also owes it to Victor to make it possible for Violet to help Victor overcome the harm which he caused him.

If Violet turns down the payment or uses it to (for example) save up for a holiday, she remains unable to discharge her own duty to Victor and wrongs him. But she also wrongs Walter. For in effect, she is intercepting the reparative payment which Walter owes Victor. While she does not owe it to him to accept or use conformably whatever he owes that does not relate to her parental duties, she does owe it to him, and not just to her son, not to thwart his performance of his reparative duty to Victor. The well-being and moral agency arguments which I sketched out in section 3 in support of the view that your mortal enemy owes it to me not to make it impossible for me to rescue you do apply to this particular case.

Of course, the issue arises because Walter needs Violet's cooperation to repair the wrong he did to Victor. Were Victor old or well enough to take himself to the hospital, matters would different. I do not think that this stipulation renders the case under scrutiny overly rarefied. On the contrary: the point which it drives home applies to any case in which a wrongdoer depends on another party, with whom he does not have a fiduciary relationship, for the fulfilment of his reparative duties to his victims.[33] There may not be many cases of this kind in interpersonal relationships other than family relationships. But there are many such cases in the political realm. For example, think of reparations owed to victims of colonial oppression or of unjust wars, and which must be paid by wrongdoing states to those victims via the latter's governments. When those governments' officials steal those payments to fill their own private coffers, they wrong their citizens primarily, but also (if less obviously and less damningly) the citizens of wrongdoing states.

6. Conclusion

John Gardner has a demanding view of what victims owe to wrongdoers in respect of the latter's reparative payments. I have argued that victims have greater latitude, in that regard, than he gives them. It is not simply that it is up to victims to decide

---

[32] This is compatible with the view that Violet owes it *to Vivien*, if she accepts the payment, to use it conformably. I find that view somewhat implausible, though.

[33] Suppose that a wrongdoer W entrusts X with the task of fulfilling his (W's) reparative duty to Y. W acquires a right against X that the latter fulfill his duty. If X does not comply, his dereliction is a breach of this particular duty. In the case I have in mind here, Violet wrongs Walter notwithstanding the fact that, by my stipulation, he has not asked her to discharge his reparative duties to Victor on his behalf.

what conformity with reparative ends requires (though I believe that it is, as indeed does Gardner, who says that respect for the autonomy of victims require that they be given some latitude, within reasonable bounds, to make such judgements).[34] Rather, my point is that it is largely up to them, *vis-à-vis* wrongdoers, to decide whether or not to pursue those ends in the first instance.

I do not claim to have provided a full answer to the question at hand. In particular, I am unsure whether and to what extent my arguments in favor of victims' latitude apply to cases in which a service, rather than financial reparations, is owed. I am also unsure about their purchase on victims' duties, or lack thereof, to accept and use conformably financial reparations for breaches of contractual rights. John Gardner is one of very few philosophers to invite us to reflect on what if anything victims owe to wrongdoers in response to the latter's fulfilment of their reparative duties. That there is so much still to ponder, in the light of his work, is a measure of his enormous influence, and of our loss.

[34] *FPLPL* (n 1) ch 6.

10
Wrongs, Remedies, and the Persistence of Reasons
Re-Examining the Continuity Thesis

John Oberdiek[*]

1. Introduction

The continuity thesis, in John Gardner's rendition, holds that the reasons grounding one's primary duties are the very reasons grounding one's secondary duties.[1] In the context of tort law, the continuity thesis entails that the defendant must remedy the injury he has tortiously inflicted on the plaintiff for the selfsame reason that the defendant was duty bound to avoid tortiously harming the plaintiff in the first place. In this way, secondary duties are continuous with primary duties. This proposition has been enormously influential and is one of Gardner's signal contributions to tort theory. But like all influential philosophical claims, it has not only attracted proponents. What is striking is not that the continuity thesis has drawn critics, though, but that its critics have converged on a single criticism. Stephen Smith, Victor Tadros, John Goldberg and Benjamin Zipursky, and Charlie Webb all offer versions of the same charge: the continuity thesis accords wrongdoing no distinctive significance.[2] It is my aim here to explore and assess this criticism in its various iterations, and it is my conclusion that the continuity thesis has the resources to deflect it.

---

[*] My thanks to Sandy Steel and Haris Psarras for including me in this volume, and to the other contributors for their feedback at the workshop. In addition, I am grateful to Peter Chau, Andrew Gold, John Goldberg, Robert Mullins, Matthew Shapiro, Adam Slavny, and especially Rahul Kumar and Sandy Steel for their written comments, and to Timothy Macklem for discussion. Lastly, I am grateful to John Gardner for leaving such a rich legacy.

[1] J Gardner, "What is Tort Law For? Part 1: The Place of Corrective Justice" (2011) 30 Law and Philosophy 1, reprinted in *Torts and Other Wrongs* (OUP 2019) ("*TAOW*"). All page references are to the reprinted version. All references to the "continuity thesis" are to Gardner's version of it. Ernest Weinrib in *Corrective Justice* (OUP 2012) and Arthur Ripstein in *Private Wrongs* (Harvard University Press 2016) offer versions as well. For discussion, see S Steel, "Compensation and Continuity" (2020) 26 Legal Theory 250.

[2] See SA Smith, "Duties, Liabilities, and Damages" (2012) 125 Harvard Law Review 1727 and SA Smith, "The Significance of a Civil Wrong" in PB Miller and J Oberdiek (eds), *Civil Wrongs and Justice in Private Law* (OUP 2020); V Tadros, "Secondary Duties" in Miller and Oberdiek (eds), *Civil Wrongs and Justice in Private Law*; JCP Goldberg and BC Zipursky, *Recognizing Wrongs* (Harvard University Press 2020); and C Webb, "Duties and Damages" in PB Miller and J Oberdiek (eds), *Oxford Studies in Private Law Theory*, Vol I (OUP 2020).

John Oberdiek, Wrongs, Remedies, and the Persistence of Reasons In: *Private Law and Practical Reason*. Edited by: Haris Psarras and Sandy Steel, Oxford University Press. © John Oberdiek 2023. DOI: 10.1093/oso/9780192857330.003.0010

2. The Continuity Thesis and Its Presuppositions

The continuity thesis is an account of secondary duties, those that obtain by virtue of violating a primary duty. Gardner defines it as "the thesis that the secondary obligation is a rational echo of the primary obligation, for it exists to serve, so far as may still be done, the reasons for the primary obligation that was not performed when its performance was due."[3] Elaborating, he maintains, "the reasons why one must pay for the losses that one occasions are the very same reasons why one must not occasion those losses in the first place, when it is true that one must not occasion them."[4] So, on Gardner's view, a defendant is liable to pay compensatory damages to the plaintiff whom he has tortiously injured for the very reasons he first had a primary duty not to wrong the plaintiff. Once the defendant has wronged the plaintiff and the harm has been done, it is no longer possible for the defendant to abide by the primary duty enjoining him to avoid wrongfully injuring the plaintiff, yet the reasons that justified that initial (breached) duty persist and now justify compensating the plaintiff.

The continuity thesis comes into yet clearer view by taking up an *ex ante* perspective, as doing so draws attention to the way the reasons constituting one's primary duties persist even after one has violated those duties. Before any remedies are called for, before anyone has wronged anyone else, tort law first imposes primary duties on persons to treat others in certain ways. These duties are themselves compositions of normative reasons which bear on anyone and which guide (or in the case of a duty, direct) our conduct in light of what non-normative facts obtain. On this picture, what anyone should do or must do is a product of the standing reasons bearing on one's conduct at all times and the state of the world at the time one acts. What reasons there are do not change with the circumstances, but what one has reason to do, what those reasons counsel in favor of or command, can indeed change depending on the circumstances. These reasons, moreover, need not have anything at all to do with the treatment of others, for they are far broader in scope than that. Even where they do relate to the treatment of people, though, the reasons may not *require* that one treat another in a particular way—not every other-regarding reason is a duty, after all. But in the case of a duty, where the multifarious reasons bearing on one's conduct neither depend on one's will nor merely count in favor of treating another a certain way but mandate it, these normative reasons coalesce around a particular course of action or rule out a particular course of action.[5] One who violates one's duty is guilty of wrongdoing.[6] Whereas in the case of conduct that accords with one's duty the underlying reasons have been satisfied, in the case of wrongdoing, the reasons that constituted the now-breached duty persist. In Gardner's words, "If one does not fully conform to a reason—if one does not do exactly what it is a reason to do—the reason does not evaporate ... Instead, it now counts as a reason for doing the next best thing, and failing

---

[3] *TAOW* (n 1) 33. Gardner uses "duty" and "obligation" interchangeably and I follow him in that usage.

[4] ibid 34.

[5] Duties are both "categorical" and "mandatory," according to Gardner. J Gardner, "Wrongs and Faults" (2005) 59 The Review of Metaphysics 95, 103.

[6] ibid 100.

that, the next best thing again, and so on."[7] In this respect, according to Gardner, "[r]easons await full conformity."[8] And it is because of this fact that "there is no need to seek an independent rationale for the law's secondary duty ... [For] when a primary duty is breached, a next best performance of the same duty is automatically called for without further ado. Often—often enough to dictate the common law's standard remedies for wrongdoing—the payment of reparative damages counts as such a next best performance."[9]

The continuity thesis follows from an entirely general claim about normative reasons, the "conformity principle," to which Gardner evidently subscribes and which was first advanced by Joseph Raz: "One should conform to reason completely, insofar as one can. If one cannot, one should come as close to complete conformity as possible."[10] The conformity principle is general in two senses, both in its application as well as in its operation. It is general, first, in applying outside the context of law and indeed outside the context of remedies; the conformity principle is a claim about reasons as such, regardless of provenance or application. In this respect, the continuity thesis simply specifies how the conformity principle applies to a particular class of reasons, namely, private law's primary and secondary obligations and their relationship. More importantly for present purposes, the conformity principle is also general insofar as it holds regardless of why one fails to conform to the reasons bearing on one's conduct. On Raz's view, these "very common" causes include "mistakes, irrational motivations, weakness, incompetence, bad luck, or other factors."[11] There are a host of explanations for why one might fail to conform one's conduct to the normative reasons that bear on it, but the normativity of the reasons—what makes them have force as reasons, counting in favor of this or that conduct—is indifferent to them. Regardless of why there is non-conformity, in other words, a dishonored reason will still demand conformity.[12] The explanation of why one has to "come as close to complete conformity as possible" with a reason that one has not already conformed to completely is, in this way, a fact about reasons and not a fact about the substance of the conduct triggering a standing reason's call for next best, imperfect conformity. It is this

---

[7] ibid 103.

[8] ibid 103.

[9] ibid 106. Gardner elaborates on the empirical point in "What is Tort Law For?" (n 1) 72.

[10] J Raz, "Personal Practical Conflicts" in P Baumann and M Betzler (eds), *Practical Conflicts* (CUP 2004) 189, reprinted as "Reasons in Conflict" in J Raz, *From Normativity to Responsibility* (OUP 2011). All page references are to the original.

[11] Raz, *From Normativity to Responsibility* (n 10).

[12] There is nothing in the Razian conception that forbids certain kinds of explanation for non-conformity from negating the normativity of the reason that would have otherwise counseled against the non-conformity. For example, while there is a raft of reasons that count against killing another person, killing permissibly in self-defense may not in fact constitute non-conformity with all of those reasons; some may not apply or might be negated in such cases. Gardner himself may dispute this. He writes: "That a norm-violation was justified is indeed irrelevant to the application of the continuity thesis, and at the deepest level it is equally irrelevant to the law of torts. Torts are wrongs—breaches of obligation—and one owes damages for their commission even if one's wrong was justified, never mind excused." Gardner, "What is Tort Law For?" (n 1) 70. Gardner here has in mind the fact that trespassers are legally liable to pay damages even for justified trespasses. But of course battery is not battery if it is committed in justified self-defense. Perhaps in such cases there is thus no wrong. But if so, it is difficult to understand why without reference to the fact that the force used in self-defense, which would normally be battery, is justified.

164 JOHN OBERDIEK

feature of the conformity principle, embedded within the continuity thesis, that makes the continuity thesis open to the criticism that it cannot accord wrongdoing its proper significance.

3. The Criticism

As indicated at the outset, the continuity thesis has attracted a great deal of attention, and among it, its fair share of criticism. While different critics of course press different points,[13] it is notable that many have also converged on a criticism, and so I will refer to it as *the* criticism of the continuity thesis. What is the criticism?

Stephen Smith was the first to formulate it, and in his words, the problem is that the continuity thesis embodies a "model in which wrongs qua wrongs have no signif-icance."[14] "The wrongness of the defendant's action," Smith contends, "is irrelevant in the continuity thesis' explanation of substantive duty to pay damages."[15] Similarly, Victor Tadros alleges that, "[a]s breach of a primary duty is not one of its grounds, breach does not explain secondary duties in an important way" according to the con-tinuity thesis.[16] John Goldberg and Benjamin Zipursky agree with Smith and Tadros. Recounting a professional negligence case where a physician was held liable to his pa-tient for botching her surgery, they ask whether the continuity thesis provides a plau-sible account of that liability:

> Are the reasons requiring McCurdy to pay Ditto the same as the reasons for him to exercise care in performing surgery on her? In fact, the preservation of Ditto's phys-ical well-being, the avoidance of infection, and the recovery of her self-image and emotional well-being are not the principal reasons for McCurdy's being required to pay damages. To the contrary, the liability of McCurdy constitutes *accountability* for

---

[13] Two notable and related ones stand out. Goldberg and Zipursky, for example, do not think that the con-tinuity thesis can explain why damages should be privileged as the next-best conformity to the disregarded reasons constituted by breach. See Goldberg and Zipursky, *Recognizing Wrongs* (n 2) 154–58. Charlie Webb contends that the continuity thesis cannot explain why, when there is breach, we know that damages are demanded as a matter of course and without further consideration of the reasons that explained the pri-mary duty. See Webb, "Duties and Damages" (n 2) 22. I think in both cases the answer lies in Gardner's comment, quoted above "What is Tort Law For?" (n 1) 72: "when a primary duty is breached, a next best performance of the same duty is automatically called for without further ado. Often—often enough to dic-tate the common law's standard remedies for wrongdoing—the payment of reparative damages counts as such a next best performance." Much too briefly, the payment of damages is the law's settled and efficient way of operationalizing next best conformity to reason. In this respect, next best conformity is really "next best conformity," meaning that it is administrably feasible and close-enough next-best conformity. That the remedy for breach is foreordained in this way, obviating the need to inquire into the reasons for the (breached) primary duty, is itself a manifestation of this efficient operationalization. In this respect, it is interesting that Ripstein believes that Gardner's version of the continuity thesis leaves the "content of the duties enforced by tort law" more "open" than Ripstein's version does. Ripstein, *Private Wrongs* (n 1) 250. If this is correct, it underscores the fact that Gardner's commitment to damages as the next best remedy is not especially deep, which, it seems to me, is as it should be. Obviously, this requires a more thorough discussion.

[14] Smith, "Duties, Liabilities, and Damages" (n 2) 1753.

[15] Smith, "The Significance of a Civil Wrong" (n 2) 162.

[16] Tadros, "Secondary Duties" (n 2) 185.

having carelessly interfered with her physical and emotional well-being. That is why McCurdy ultimately incurred a duty to compensate her.[17]

Although Goldberg and Zipursky's complaint is not couched in the same terms as Smith's and Tadros', it is nevertheless, I think, at bottom the same complaint: secondary duties are predicated on accountability for wrongdoing, and not, as the continuity thesis maintains, on honoring the reasons that underwrite an agent's primary duties. Charlie Webb, too, is unpersuaded by the continuity thesis' account of secondary duties, and he gets to the heart of the criticism in the course of elaborating on what is by now a familiar refrain:

> the continuity thesis leaves my wrongdoing with no role to play in the justification of my duty to make good your losses. While, on this view, my duty to compensate you is indeed triggered by my wrong, the reasons I owe you compensation are not found in or connected to that wrong. I owe you compensation for the same reasons I owed you the primary duty I breached, a duty which was not triggered by or grounded in any prior wrongdoing. Instead, my breach is significant only for the change it makes to our factual circumstances and, in turn, to what these reasons now require of me, no different in kind to the way my reasons for delaying my trip out when I see it is raining become reasons to put up my umbrella if I am now out and the rain starts to fall.[18]

Smith, Tadros, Goldberg and Zipursky, and Webb thus all agree that the continuity thesis fails because it accords an inapposite role to wrongdoing in the explanation of secondary duties.

Note that the criticism is *not* that the continuity thesis does not assign *any* role to wrongdoing in its account of secondary duties, Webb's own words notwithstanding. As Webb himself explains, the duty to compensate is indeed "triggered" by the commission of a wrong on Gardner's view. The problem is rather that this is the wrong way for wrongdoing to figure in the explanation of a wrongdoer's remedial obligations. As Tadros puts the point, "[t]he only role for breach is that is causes, or gives rise to, facts that are sufficient on their own to ground the secondary duty, however they arose."[19] In this way, the continuity thesis allows the violation of a duty to play "a merely causal or counterfactual role in explaining the grounds of secondary duties," and in Tadros' judgment, that is "unsatisfactory."[20]

One way to put the criticism is that, according to the continuity thesis, wrongdoing plays no *distinctive* role in the explanation of secondary duties. The breach of a primary duty is just a change in the non-normative factual background affecting what the reasons that had demanded conformity with the now-breached primary duty presently demand. Paraphrasing Webb, breaches of duty are like rainy days: now that it's raining, the reason that I had to stay inside to avoid getting wet counsels in favor of opening an umbrella so that I stay as dry as I can. According to the continuity thesis,

---

[17] Goldberg and Zipursky, *Recognizing Wrongs* (n 2) 160–61. Italics in the original.
[18] Webb, "Duties and Damages" (n 2) 23–24.
[19] Tadros, "Secondary Duties" (n 2) 188.
[20] ibid 188 and 189.

the criticism alleges, the breach of a primary duty is nothing more than a factual trigger of one's secondary remedial duty. But wrongdoing, the criticism continues, is more distinctive than the continuity thesis allows.

What is interesting is that the continuity thesis is exposed to this criticism because of the conformity principle that is baked into its bricks. More specifically, what the criticism targets in the continuity thesis is what I have referred to as the conformity principle's second form of generality, its generality of operation. Recall that the conformity principle holds that reasons call for conformity, but where complete conformity is not possible, then the principle calls for incomplete conformity. According to Raz, any number of causes might thwart complete conformity, some of which have a moral valence but many of which do not. A breach of duty, in other words, may well activate a secondary duty, but only in so far as *anything* that prevents conformity with a reason invites next best conformity with that reason. Wrongs thus have no special standing among these utterly prosaic impediments to conformity with reason according to the criticism; they elicit secondary duties no differently than rain elicits umbrellas. But that cannot be right. Surely there is something that is distinctive about wrongdoing, such that "wrongs *qua* wrongs" have "significance."

While much of the criticism of the continuity thesis rests at this conceptual and intuitive stage, in effect laying bare the continuity thesis' mechanics and declaring that there must be more to wrongdoing than it recognizes, some have pressed the criticism beyond that point. In my view, these elaborations reveal that at the source of the criticism is a skepticism that the continuity thesis can make sense of the relational character of duties in tort law. In the remainder of this section, I introduce this more specific concern and then in the next, I begin to develop a defense of the continuity thesis.

After articulating their version of the criticism of the continuity thesis, Goldberg and Zipursky attempt to anticipate the kind of counter-argument that Gardner might mount. They imagine that one might defend the continuity thesis by characterizing the reasons underlying one's primary duty to another at a higher level of generality so as to link up seamlessly with the reasons underlying the secondary duty. Thus, in discussing the medical malpractice lawsuit, they posit a general concern with the patient's self-esteem or well-being as the potential reason underlying both the primary duty the doctor had to operate on the patient with care and the secondary duty the physician acquired to remedy the wrong he committed when he failed to do so. Goldberg and Zipursky go on to identify three interconnected problems with this move. First, considerations like well-being are "far too generic" to do the work they must in explaining the basis for anyone's primary duties in tort law.[21] Second, the reason that a liable defendant owes damages to the plaintiff they have wronged is based on an "interest in being compensated" for the wrong, a reason that obviously cannot figure in the explanation of the primary duty and is in any case not identical to one's interest in well-being.[22] Third and finally, any interest-based explanation cannot be all there is to the explanation of secondary duties because no purely interest-based account can make sense of "the relational nature of tort law."[23]

---

[21] Goldberg and Zipursky, *Recognizing Wrongs* (n 2) 161.
[22] ibid.
[23] ibid.

Tadros develops his version of the criticism by charging that the continuity thesis cannot make sense of the special responsibility wrongdoers have for righting their wrongs. He presents two hypothetical cases, *Fix 1* and *Fix 2*, which are constructed to reveal this supposed failure of the continuity thesis. Tadros recasts the relevant duties as wholly positive, rather than as a negative primary duty paired with a positive secondary duty, so as to eliminate any obfuscating effect of mixing positive and negative duties. His hypothetical tandem of cases are as follows:

> *Fix 1*: Alice can rescue Cath from serious harm at t at some minimal cost to herself and fails to do this. Later, at t_2, only Alice can fix the harm that resulted at t that she failed to prevent.
>
> *Fix 2*: Beth can rescue Cath from serious harm at t at some minimal cost to herself and fails to do this. Later, at t_2, only Alice can fix the harm that resulted at t that Beth failed to prevent.[24]

Tadros notes that Alice may have a duty to help Cath at t_2 in both cases, but that that duty will be more stringent in *Fix 1* because Alice breached a primary duty to Cath in that case alone. The continuity thesis, Tadros concedes, correctly implies that Alice only has an authentic secondary duty in *Fix 1* for this reason, for there is nothing secondary about Alice's duty in *Fix 2*—she played no role in harming Cath after all. Yet, he continues, the continuity thesis cannot explain why the duty Alice owes to Cath at t_2 is more stringent in *Fix 1* than in *Fix 2*, precisely because "breach is not a ground of Alice's primary duty in *Fix 1*."[25] The stringency of the duty that Alice owes to Cath at t_2, in other words, is entirely unaffected by whether Cath needs Alice's aid at t_2 on account of Alice's breach at t. By Tadros' lights, Alice has more reason to aid Cath in *Fix 1* than in *Fix 2* because of what Alice has done to Cath in *Fix 1* but not in *Fix 2*. The continuity thesis, though, merely registers the formal fact that only in the former case is that duty appropriately construed as secondary in nature. Tadros protests that there is more to wrongdoing than that.

The foregoing reveals a further convergence in criticism of the continuity thesis. In developing the criticism, Goldberg and Zipursky along with Tadros allege more specifically that the failure of the continuity thesis to ascribe any distinctiveness to wrongdoing lies in the thesis' inability to account for the special connection that a wrongdoer has to the wrong they are now required to remedy. According to Goldberg and Zipursky, Gardner's problem is ultimately that the continuity thesis is indifferent to the relationality of duty as such. As Tadros sees it, Gardner cannot account for the special stringency of secondary duties, which owes to the special responsibility one has to right one's wrongs. These more specific criticisms are closely related and can be combined in the following way. According to this combined specification of the criticism, wronging another is distinctive because it marks the disregard of a relational duty, an obligation that one owes to another and not just generally, and because they are relational such duties exert a particularly strong demand on those obligated by them, a fact that the continuity thesis cannot explain because it cannot make sense

---

[24] Tadros, "Secondary Duties" (n 2) 189.
[25] ibid.

of the relationality of duty grounding that fact. My strategy in defending the continuity thesis on this front will be to argue that relational duties are unique in generating claims, which are transmitted from relational primary duties to relational secondary duties upon breach of the former; that violating a claim-based primary duty necessarily wrongs the one whose claim was violated; that such violations are unlike other kinds of non-conformity to reason, making them in that sense distinctive; that the relational duties so understood are underwritten by values unique to them, in turn giving rise to reasons unique to them; that the continuity thesis is wholly compatible with relational duties so understood; and that accordingly, the continuity thesis can in fact accord wrongs the distinctive role in grounding secondary duties that the criticism alleges it cannot.

4. Reasons, Relationality, and Claims

In this section, I hope to make the case that Gardner's continuity thesis has the resources to fend off the criticism that Smith, Tadros, Goldberg and Zipursky, and Webb all make of it. The source of that criticism, I have argued, lies in the continuity thesis' assimilation of Raz's conformity principle, holding that reasons call for conformity to the extent possible, even if imperfectly. The conformity principle appears not to differentiate between the causes of non-conformity, and as a result, it appears not to give wrongdoing its due. It appears, in other words, to treat breaches of duty like any other kind of non-conformity to reason.

Let me begin by acknowledging that the breach of a duty owed to another is not just like other forms of non-conformity with reason. In breaching such a duty, one wrongs another, victimizing them. And as a result of wronging them, the victim has a claim that one right the wrong one has inflicted.[26] This dynamic is unique. No other form of non-conformity with reason involves wronging another person. That makes breaching a duty owed to another a distinctive form of non-conformity. What makes this particular context different? It is not that the duties one owes to others are necessarily categorical, for one can have categorical reasons—those that do not depend upon one's will—that have no other-regarding aspect. I may not care about medieval art, for example, but I nevertheless have a categorical reason to respect it in so far as such art has value quite apart from what I happen to care about.[27] It is also not that the duties that one owes to others are necessarily mandatory, for one can also have mandatory reasons that are not other-regarding. My commitment to getting into shape, for example, is not simply another reason bearing on my conduct to be weighed against all of the other *pro tanto* reasons, instead that commitment rules out certain unhealthy activities like eating ice cream and binge-watching shows all day. If it is not the categoricity or mandatoriness of the duties we owe to others that makes their violation in some sense special, though, then what is it? It is, I believe, their relationality.

---

[26] I discuss this in J Oberdiek, "Method and Morality in the New Private Law of Torts" (2012) 125(189) Harvard Law Review Forum 201.

[27] See J Raz, *Engaging Reason* (OUP 1999) 321.

The relationality of duty is one of tort law's most well-settled and defining features.[28] It is the relationality of duty, for example, that makes torts wrongs. Were the duties recognized by tort law non-relational, it would still be wrong to violate them of course—all duties are categorical and mandatory, after all—but doing so would not wrong anyone. Only the breach of a duty that is owed to another, only the breach of a relational duty, wrongs the one to whom that duty is owed. This is an implication of Cardozo's famous point in *Palsgraf*.[29] And it seems to me that this observation is the first step in defending the continuity thesis against the criticism that it cannot make sense of the distinctiveness of breach as the ground of secondary duties.

If the duties that tort law recognizes are not simply categorical and mandatory but also relational, it will begin to explain what is special both about the breach of a relational primary duty and the relational secondary duty that is triggered by that breach. Secondary duties are not like free-standing duties to aid, they are instead conditioned upon the violation of some primary duty. Their character is therefore a reflection of the character of the primary duty that conditions them. This is why secondary duties are duties at all[30] but also why they are relational. As R Jay Wallace puts the point, "the relational structure of the secondary obligation derives from the relational structure of the primary wrong that gives rise to it."[31] Now, if one must treat another in accordance with a relational primary duty, then the person owed that treatment has a *claim* to it, and that claim will in turn be transmitted to the secondary duty that one owes to the individual in case one breaches that primary duty. The secondary duty, again, is imbued with all of the same features of the antecedent primary duty, including that it generates a claim. In my view, it is this fact, the fact that someone has a claim to next best conformity, that distinguishes secondary duties from other cases where next best conformity with reason is called for. This in turn shows that the continuity thesis can do precisely what the criticism denies it has the resources to do: "secondary duties are explained by the moral significance of breach itself."[32]

Non-conformity with a relational primary duty is not like other forms of non-conformity to reason. No other kind of non-conformity amounts to a wrong, because no other kind of non-conformity flouts a claim. Violating a duty that one owes to another, then, is not akin to being caught in the rain by mistake. While the conformity principle may well call for next best conformity in both cases, this does not show that the two instances of non-conformity are on all fours with one another. For

---

[28] I explore the relationality of duty in tort law in J Oberdiek, "It's Something Personal: On the Relationality of Duty and Civil Wrongs" in Miller and Oberdiek, *Civil Wrongs and Justice in Private Law* (n 2). I have in mind (a species of) what Gardner refers to as "loosely relational duties" as opposed to "strictly relational duties." See J Gardner, *From Personal Life to Private Law* (OUP 2018) ch 1.

[29] Judge Cardozo in *Palsgraf* famously holds, "What a plaintiff must show is 'a wrong' to herself; i.e. a violation of her own right, and not merely a wrong to someone else, nor conduct 'wrongful' because unsocial, but not 'a wrong' to anyone." *Palsgraf v Long Island Railroad Co.*, 162 N.E. 99, 100 (N.Y. 1928).

[30] Gardner writes, "When things are not so easy is when we are left with old unconformed-to reasons that are both categorical and mandatory, that is, when we had duties that we failed to perform and hence acted wrongfully. In such cases the reason left over and clamoring for conformity does not surrender to a change in our personal goals. It continues to exert mandatory force such that at least some conflicting reasons (some of the otherwise powerful reasons that we have to get on with our lives) are excluded from consideration and cannot suffice to defeat it." Gardner, "Wrongs and Faults" (n 5) 105.

[31] RJ Wallace, *The Moral Nexus* (Princeton University Press 2019) 94.

[32] Tadros, "Secondary Duties" (n 2) 189.

only one gives rise to a claim. One can go yet further: even when comparing the non-conformity of two primary duties, if only one of those duties is relational, then only the secondary duty that the relational primary duty gives rise to will be founded upon a claim, and so in this respect, that secondary duty will have a different character than the secondary duty generated by the non-relational duty. It is not clear to me whether this entails that one necessarily has *greater reason* to fulfil a relational secondary duty than a non-relational secondary duty. It may be that there is no difference in the stringency between relational and non-relational duties, much as moral reasons are not inherently stronger than non-moral reasons.[33] But that is also not the point, for I am not attempting to establish that one necessarily has greater reason to abide by one's relational duties than one's non-relational duties. The argument addresses most directly the *character* of relational duties, and concerns the *way* they bind, not *how much* they do. There are any number of dimensions along which different kinds of reasons and even different kinds of duties may be compared, and to conclude that there is a difference between two classes of reasons or duties along one dimension does not entail that there is an inherent difference between the two classes in terms of their stringency. Put another way, conceding *arguendo* that there is no difference between kinds of duties along the dimension of stringency does not entail that there is no difference in the way that the two classes of reasons come to bind (to the same degree, *ceteris paribus*). To say that a relational duty is grounded by a claim that some person or class of persons has, then, does not imply that relational duties as such are more stringent than non-relational duties as such. My argument is simply that relational duties have a distinctive character or cast, for only relational duties give rise to claims, and therefore breaching a relational duty alone constitutes a wrong. Raz is right that non-conformity to reason calls for next best conformity regardless of the kind of reason it is, but the character of that "call" can vary depending on the kind of reason that it is and, thus, upon the kind of duty that it is.

This might seem to concede Tadros' point. His claim, again, is that Alice owes Cath a more stringent duty in *Fix 1* to assist her at t_2 than in *Fix 2*, because Alice only put Cath in the position of needing assistance at t_2 in *Fix 1*, but that the continuity thesis cannot explain that fact. Tadros is too quick to diagnose a defect in the continuity thesis. In the first instance, it is not obvious that it *is* a fact that Alice's duty to Cath is more stringent in *Fix 1* than in *Fix 2*. Perhaps we think about *Fix 1* and *Fix 2* differently. Alice's duty to Cath in *Fix 1* may not in fact be more stringent, it may just have a different character. And that difference in character may be enough to differentiate the cases appropriately. That is, it may be that Alice's respective duties are equally stringent in *Fix 1* and *Fix 2*, but it would not follow from that that the continuity thesis is thereby shown to be mistaken. The continuity thesis is not undermined by showing that there is no difference in the *stringency* of the two duties at t_2. The way to undermine the continuity thesis is to show that it cannot allow for *any* significant difference between the

---

[33] Raz, *Engaging Reason* (n 27) 268–72, 313, 314. Raz argues that when a moral reason is overriding, and so is what one should act on at the end of the day—though it is "implausible" that this will always be so—it will not be "because it is a moral reason," or "an instance of a class of moral reasons," but because of its "nature." The same could be said of relational and non-relational duties.

two duties at t_2.[34] Yet if it is the case that Alice owed Cath certain treatment in *Fix 1* at *t* by virtue of a relational duty, then Cath had a claim against Alice at *t* that she so assist her, and when Alice failed to do so, Cath's claim was transmitted to Alice's secondary duty, providing Alice with a substantively different duty to aid at t_2 in *Fix 1* than in *Fix 2*, where Cath had no antecedent claim to transmit. And that is true even if the two duties bear the same stringency. Tadros maintains that his hypothetical pair of cases shows that the continuity thesis fails because it cannot attach the right kind of importance to wrongdoing, but he assumes without warrant that the way to establish that distinctiveness is to show that the duty in *Fix 1* is more stringent than the one in *Fix 2*.

Perhaps Tadros could reply that Cath's need for aid in *Fix 2* generated a new claim binding on Alice, such that Alice would wrong Cath in *Fix 1* as well as in *Fix 2* were she not to aid her at t_2. This would seem to show that the continuity thesis cannot differentiate between the duties in the two cases after all, as both would be based on claims. But if Cath's predicament is sufficiently bad to generate a claim *de novo* at t_2 against whomever is in a position to help her, then while it is true that Alice would accordingly be subject to a claim in *Fix 2*, she would be subject to two independent claims in *Fix 1*—one due to the violation of the relational primary duty and the other the *de novo* claim—so once again it would be possible to ascribe significance to the fact that she wronged Cath in *Fix 1*. This in turn suggests a further reply to Tadros about stringency. Imagine *Fix 3*, where Alice can either aid Cath, whom she has left in the predicament of needing aid as in *Fix 1*, or Doris, where Beth failed to aid Doris initially and now only Alice can help, but not both. It seems to me clear that Alice must assist Cath. Alice owes it to Cath to aid her because, even if both Cath and Doris have a claim on Alice that she help them, Cath's claim is either more stringent or fortified by a second claim or in some other way dominant by virtue of the initial primary duty-based claim Cath had that Alice help her. And that is to say that Alice's initial wrong of treading on Cath's claim, generated by the relational primary duty that Alice owed to Cath, determines Alice's conduct following the breach. This seems to be the result that Tadros is seeking, and it seems clear that the continuity thesis can provide it.[35]

This claim-centric account of secondary duties holds the key to responding to Goldberg and Zipursky as well. Their complaint, again, is that the continuity thesis errs in ascribing the basis of secondary duties to a defied primary duty, instead arguing that secondary duties are based on "accountability." Yet Goldberg and Zipursky's account of secondary duties is not in fact at odds with the one developed here. Relational primary duties are based on claims. It is by virtue of a claim that a claimant is owed the treatment that any primary duty defines. In this sense, a relational primary duty

---

[34] Tadros may elide the distinction between the stringency and character of duties. After arguing that the continuity thesis fails, Tadros writes, "the question why breaching primary duties grounds secondary duties and affects their stringency and character is hard to answer." Tadros, "Secondary Duties" (n 2) 191. One way to put my point is that while stringency is an aspect of the character of a duty, it is not its only one, and to vindicate the continuity thesis it is necessary only to show a difference in character even if not in stringency. Still, I think it may yet be possible to show that the continuity thesis can account for the greater stringency of secondary duties in at least some cases, as I explain below.

[35] On this score, Sandy Steel may be too quick to concede Tadros' stringency point. He imagines one line of response to the criticism as follows: the continuity thesis is "an account of when and why a compensatory duty arises, not its stringency. This would reduce the theoretical ambition of" Gardner's version of the continuity thesis. Steel, "Compensation and Continuity" (n 1) 277.

172 JOHN OBERDIEK

makes the one subject to that duty *accountable* to the one to whom the duty is owed. If one violates a relational primary duty, then the claim as well as the accountability that it entails is transmitted to the relational secondary duty—one is accountable *ex post* because one was accountable *ex ante*. For again the relational structure of secondary duties is a reflection of the relational structure of the primary duty that conditions it, and it is that relational structure that gives rise to a claim. It follows that that secondary duty is also based on accountability.

Central to this defense of the continuity thesis is the idea that claims can be grounded in values. This is because the continuity thesis reflects Gardner's commitment to the Razian picture of reasons, as is evident in the continuity thesis's incorporation of Raz's conformity principle. On this picture, which I find compelling, any normative reason that applies to anyone applies in virtue of some value that would be realized, advanced, protected, or otherwise respected by it so applying.[36] In short, one has the reasons one has because there is value in it. When talking about one's claims, we focus on that subset of value that implicates interests—underlying our claims are interests, and specifically well-being interests.[37] This is why, in trying to rehabilitate the continuity thesis only to find it ultimately beyond repair, Goldberg and Zipursky are exactly right to seek out some interest, like a concern with well-being, that might persist through breach to justify liability. But of course it is their verdict that this is an impossible task, as on their view an "interest-based analysis of reparative obligations utterly fails to capture the relational nature of tort law."[38] Abstracting from the continuity thesis, they are arguing more broadly that the interest- or value-based Razian conception of reasons cannot support relational duties.

It is worth pausing to observe that Goldberg and Zipursky themselves rely on just such an interest-based conception to explain secondary duties. For as they see it, the liability of the physician in their medical malpractice example is based on accountability for interfering with the plaintiff patient's "physical and emotional well-being." Interfering with another's well-being is a quite straightforward interest-based ground for a secondary duty.[39] They also state that it is the patient's "interest in being compensated" for having been wronged that "grounds her claim to damages."[40] This is once again a clear statement that interests ground claims. Finally, Goldberg and Zipursky subscribe to the interest theory of rights—although they resist that characterization[41]—and thus accept that (inherently relational) rights are based on

---

[36] Raz writes, "I will further proceed on the basis of a common though not unchallenged assumption about the dependence of reasons for action on values: Only if an action realizes or protects, or is likely to realize or protect, some good, or if it contributes to the realization or protection, or is likely to contribute to the realization or protection, of some good, can there be a reason for its performance, and the fact that it is so related to the good will be (part of) that reason ... The assumption is of a one-way dependence. Reasons, it assumes, are rooted in values." Raz, *Engaging Reason* (n 27) 252.

[37] See T Macklem and J Gardner, "Value, Interest, and Well-Being" (2006) 18 Utilitas 362, 373.

[38] Goldberg and Zipursky, *Recognizing Wrongs* (n 2) 161.

[39] For ease of exposition, I gloss over the distinction that is otherwise important in Goldberg and Zipursky's theory between duty and liability, as it is not important in this context.

[40] Goldberg and Zipursky, *Recognizing Wrongs* (n 2) 161.

[41] Torts, they hold, "cluster around interferences with certain distinctive but widely recognized aspects of individual well-being." ibid 236. Though this is a seemingly clear endorsement of the interest theory, Goldberg and Zipursky do not embrace it: "It is natural but mistaken to read this language to suggest that we subscribe to an 'interest theory' of rights such as Raz's." ibid 236, fn 3. Their resistance here is, I think, based on a misunderstanding. They reject the interest theory because they do not believe that "the rights that are

interests. *Tu quoque* arguments of course leave unanswered the underlying charge, but the fact that some of the most ardent defenders of tort law's relationality nevertheless trace secondary duties to interests suggests that an interest-based approach can make sense of secondary duties.

Relational duties and thus claims can be founded on interests. An "interest-based analysis of reparative obligations," in other words, can capture "the relational nature of tort law." Yet even if Goldberg and Zipursky themselves are not best positioned to dispute that claim, it is widely and roundly disputed. The crux of the case against an interest-based account of relational duties, secondary or otherwise, turns on the supposed nature of well-being. Arthur Ripstein, for example, maintains that no such account is possible because individual well-being is "non-relational" and a relational duty cannot be derived from a nonrelational source.[42] The idea that well-being is non-relational, though, seems clearly wrong. One has an interest in how one is treated by others; anyone's life is affected by how others relate to them. This quite simple observation has expansive implications: a particular structure or pattern of interpersonal relations can be valuable to those subject to it, and further, can be valuable enough to warrant the protection of a right, thus grounding a claim. In this way, a claim to a certain form of treatment by others is something that can be founded, ultimately, upon an interest.

Ripstein anticipates this kind of counterargument but he does not have a convincing answer to it. Focusing on the torts of battery and trespass, he concedes, "People certainly do have an interest in being free of unauthorized touchings and unauthorized use of their property," but Ripstein does not think this supports an interest-based approach because, as he goes on to note, "as the word 'unauthorized' indicates ... the interest itself cannot be characterized except by reference to the concept of a right."[43] It seems to me, though, that no reference to an antecedent right need be made. Thus one could simply say that anyone has an interest in having bodily autonomy or in having the exclusive use of and discretion over certain things, and that those interests are sufficiently important to make interferences with either interest unauthorized. Ripstein himself nearly telegraphs this rejoinder when he observes that any autonomy-based interest "is an interest in standing in a certain type of relation," though he immediately continues, "that is, in having a certain type of right."[44] But his two characterizations of the interest are not equivalent. The "interest in standing in a certain type of relation" is

correlative to these duties are not identical with the interests that warrant the imposition of the duties." ibid. They illustrate their point by reference to patent rights: "The legal duty not to interfere with another's invention has a legal right correlative to it, and it is the right of the patent owner, but it is far from clear that the core normative reasons generating this right pertain to an interest of the owner's. To the contrary, it is plausible that the interests that provide the principal grounds for having patent protection are the benefit to members of society that will inure to a system that incentivizes scientific and engineering breakthroughs by granting something akin to property rights in certain inventions." ibid. There is nothing in the preceding that Raz need disagree with—far from it. Raz is forthright that interests beyond those of the right-holder, and more specifically, interests that derive from the common good, can justify an individually held right. See J Raz, "Rights and Individual Well-Being" in J Raz (ed), *Ethics in the Public Domain* (OUP 1994).

[42] Ripstein, *Private Wrongs* (n 1) 68.
[43] ibid 71.
[44] ibid 72.

precisely the interest that I maintain is sufficient to ground claims and therefore relational duties, including secondary duties. It is that interest that *justifies* "having a certain type of right," it is not an interest that is *synonymous* with "having a certain type of right." There is a great deal more that needs to be established in order fully to substantiate the conclusion that relational secondary duties and the claims that correspond to them can be founded on interests, but I hope that I have at least begun to make the case, and in any event, have made enough of that case for present purposes.

So, secondary duties are based on claims, claims are relational, and they are ultimately founded upon interests, specifically, those aspects of well-being that are themselves relational. It is in anyone's interest to be treated by others in certain ways, and that relational value grounds the claims that people have against one another that they do so. It is those interests, in other words, that underwrite the claims corresponding to relational primary duties, and according to the continuity thesis, just as those interests persist through breach, so too do the claims they justify. These, then, are the bases of secondary duties. But which interests are these? The continuity thesis will only be vindicated if the interests that underwrite the claims corresponding to secondary duties are the same interests that correspond to the claims corresponding to the relational primary duties whose violation triggers the secondary duties.

There are some non-starters. The interest that Goldberg and Zipursky contend grounds a claim of damages, an "interest in being compensated,"[45] is quite clearly incompatible with the continuity thesis. It is only intelligible once the primary duty has already been breached, after all, and therefore cannot be the interest that first justifies the primary duty. But have they identified the correct interest? In their botched surgery example, the reason that the patient has an interest in being compensated is that, as Goldberg and Zipursky put it, the surgeon "carelessly interfered with her physical and emotional well-being."[46] The patient's claim of redress represents "accountability"[47] for having so interfered. Now, given that Goldberg and Zipursky characterize the accountability as accountability for interference with well-being, it is surprising that they also state that well-being is "too generic"[48] an interest to ground tort law's specific duties. What I wish to focus on, though, is the role of accountability in the justification of a secondary duty. For the value in *that* seems to me to be something that the continuity thesis can accommodate and that can also make sense of the distinctiveness of wronging another, thereby according wrongdoing its rightful place in the explanation of secondary duties.

If one accepts both that reasons are rooted in values and that duties give one reasons of a particular kind, then duties are ultimately predicated on certain values. Relational duties, I have further argued, have a distinctive character, manifested in the way that they bind—they give rise to claims. And one perspicacious and not-uncommon way to explicate claims and their corresponding relational duties is in just the terms that Goldberg and Zipursky appeal to: accountability. As Stephen Darwall puts it while addressing Goldberg and Zipursky's position, "injured victims of violated bipolar

---

[45] Goldberg and Zipursky, *Recognizing Wrongs* (n 2) 161.
[46] ibid.
[47] ibid.
[48] ibid.

obligations owed *to them* have a distinctive standing to hold their injurers respon-sible."[49] This is consonant with Wallace's point noted above that the relational aspect of secondary duties is derived from the relational aspect of the primary duties whose vio-lation triggers them. Accountability is just another way of characterizing relationality and the claims that it generates. The question now is whether this can be understood as a value, which in turn underwrites both primary and secondary duties.

It seems to me that it can be. It seems to me that one can say something like the following. Everyone is accountable to everyone else to respect their well-being. Well-being has different aspects and so can be specified in a variety of ways, reflecting the narrower interests that correspond to individual torts. Thus, everyone is accountable to everyone else to respect the specified aspects of well-being reflected in the torts that safeguard those interests. Take the tort of battery. It protects the value of bodily au-tonomy or integrity. More than that, though, it does so through the recognition that there is value in a structure of interpersonal relations whose boundaries are marked by claims held by individuals against one another not to interfere with their bodies in certain ways. The pattern of claim-based relations that is constituted by this net-work of specific claims is something that is valuable to everyone with such a claim.[50] It is not merely that having bodily autonomy is a good. It is that having the standing to hold others accountable for how they treat one's body is a good. And this is a value that ultimately underwrites a relational duty both *ex ante* and *ex post*: the value in having the standing to demand respect for one's bodily integrity persists from primary to secondary duty. So, if some individual interferes with another's bodily integrity in violation of a relational primary duty, the tortfeasor owes it to the victim of the battery to redress the wrong and so incurs a secondary duty, and the tortfeasor incurs this secondary duty to redress the wrong precisely because there is value in equipping the victim with the standing to demand respect for bodily integrity. That accountability-based reason was binding from the beginning, and it persists.

In one of his final papers, Gardner offers a puzzled response to Smith's version of the criticism. Gardner writes, "But the duty going unperformed *is* the wrong. So, on my view, it is exactly what effects the change of duty—that is, the replacement of the pri-mary duty with the remedial duty. What larger change than that were we expecting?"[51] Gardner continues:

> Smith may reply: that is the very change we were expecting, but the wrong did not ground it. It was only a necessary and sufficient condition for it. A ground is more; it has to be a reason too. And, on the "continuity thesis" view, the wrong is not the reason for the remedial duty to come into existence. The only reasons for the remedial duty to come into existence are the reasons that went unconformed when the duty went unperformed. I am not sure that there is a real difference here… The reason for the new duty is the reason given by the continuity thesis itself—namely, that the

---

[49] S Darwall, "Civil Recourse as Mutual Accountability" in *Morality, Authority, & Law* (OUP 2013) 180. Italics in the original.

[50] It can be valuable even to people without one. See Raz, "Rights and Individual Well-Being" (n 41).

[51] J Gardner, "Damages without Duty" (2019) 69 University of Toronto Law Journal 419. Italics added, but existed in the original draft.

original duty went unperformed. The wrong was indeed the ground of the remedial duty.[52]

There is no getting around the fact that the continuity thesis is a deflationary account of secondary duties. For Gardner that is a feature and not a bug. It does not over-populate the conceptual scheme we rely on in making sense of our duties to one another with reified conceptions of wronging. The question is whether such an account, though spare, delivers everything it must. The criticism of the continuity thesis is that it cannot account for the distinctiveness of wrongdoing and its role as the ground of a secondary duty. I hope to have shown that the continuity thesis can accommodate the distinctiveness of wrongdoing without friction while offering a plausible account of how the reasons that explain one's relational primary duties, secured by claims, persist through breach.

[52] ibid.

11

The Next Best Thing to a Promise

Dori Kimel

Promises are not unique in being voluntarily assumed obligations,[1] but they are unique, at least among obligations owed to others, in being self-authored: the promisor can, and paradigmatically does, make up the promise's content.[2] That does not mean that promisors have complete control over the content or normative implications of their promises or of the obligations they place themselves under through promising. Notably, promisors do not control the scope of things that can be promised, and are limited, perhaps among other things, to the realm of the intelligible, the possible, and the morally acceptable: for a promise to beget a moral obligation its subject must be something that can conceivably be the subject of a moral obligation. Similarly, would-be promisors are limited to promises for which willing promisees can be found. Since a promise is given to a promisee, in whom a rights corresponding to the promisor's obligations are vested along with the responsibilities associated with the role of promisee, it seems odd to think of a promise as something that can be foisted upon an unwilling recipient; and the willingness or consent of the would-be promisee again falls outside the promisor's control.

Notwithstanding such restrictions on the scope of what can be promised (or to whom), the promisor's creative license *qua* promisor is immense, and her control over the content and shape of the moral obligations by which she can be bound through promising appears to be unique among other moral obligation. It is this quality of promise that has made its very possibility such an enduring mystery for prominent philosophers through the ages, and has made the power to make promises, for others, such a definitive manifestation of the idea (or ideal) of an autonomous agent—one that is able to exercise control over her own destiny to the extent of authoring her own moral obligations.

Some, however, believe that limits on what promisors can author or control stretch much further than restrictions on the sheer scope of things that can be promised. John Gardner appeared to think that authoring the core content of the obligation undertaken through promising—specifying, that is, what it is that you undertake an obligation to *do*—is all the promisor authors. Thus the promisor cannot control the

---

[1] For an account of what is special about promises as voluntary obligations see J Raz, "Promises in Morality and Law" (1982) 95 Harvard Law Review 916. Raz's point is that promises are an "extreme case" of voluntary obligation, in the sense that their voluntariness is part of the justification of the obligation, as opposed to merely a condition with which to meet objections.

[2] I say "paradigmatically" because the promisor may, for example, be invited by the promisee (or by third parties) to make a specific promise with a fixed content.

Dori Kimel, *The Next Best Thing to a Promise* In: *Private Law and Practical Reason.* Edited by: Haris Psarras and Sandy Steel, Oxford University Press. © Dori Kimel 2023. DOI: 10.1093/oso/9780192857330.003.0011

deontic component of the obligation: it is always strict;[3] and the promisor cannot control the reparative dimension of the promise—that is, the normative aftermath of a breach, or what she owes the promisee (and possibly others) post breach. No matter what the relationship between promisor and promisee is like, what kind of promise has been broken or what the circumstances of the breach have been, what is owed to the promisee post breach, where possible and at least by default, is "the next best"— coming as close as possible to the promised performance.

In a limited subset of promises, identifying the "next best" may be straightforward enough: you breached a promise to do something today that can still be done tomorrow, do it tomorrow; you breached a promise to do something that can be straightforwardly monetized, hand over the money. In other cases, the identity of the "next best" performance may be a more speculative affair. Whether it can be identified straightforwardly or not, the remedial obligation of "next best" performance would rarely be less onerous than the primary promissory obligation; usually it would be just as onerous, sometimes more. Be that as it may, by default, at least, the next best is owed.

In introducing this view on the remedial dimension of promises, Gardner shared a starting point with and borrowed an example from Neil MacCormick: a university lecturer "has promised to take his children to the beach one afternoon, but before setting off he is visited by a student in a condition of apparently suicidal depression." The lecturer attends to the student and thus fails to keep his promise to his children; and the judgment offered by MacCormick (and endorsed by Gardner) is that although the lecturer did the right thing in breaking the promise in such circumstances and bears no blame or fault, "he now owes it to his children as soon as possible to make good their disappointment by taking them to the seaside" or "giving some similar or better treat."[4]

Neither MacCormick nor Gardner has developed this position much further in the context of promissory obligations specifically, or, for that matter, in the broader yet still distinct context of content-independent obligations, because while drawing on examples from the promissory domain, both were ultimately not interested in promises (nor in contract) but in obligations in tort. Both viewed this position as intuitive, and hence used it as a way of giving initial intuitive appeal to shared observations and diverging explanations concerning reparative obligations and their rationale in tort law, and in morality in general. Beyond the shared observation that reparative obligations arise post wrong independently of fault, MacCormick has argued that they are grounded in respect for the wronged party, whereas for Gardner the very same reasons that "added up to make the action obligatory" in the first place, having "not been satisfied by performance of the primary obligation", post breach "call for next-best satisfaction, the closest to full satisfaction that is still available."[5]

---

[3] I have expressed doubt in this thesis elsewhere; see "Personal Autonomy and Change of Mind in Contract and in Promise" in G Klass, G Letsas, and P Saprai (eds) *Philosophical Foundations of Contract Law* (OUP 2014) 96, 103–08.

[4] N MacCormick, "The Obligation of Reparation" in his *Legal Right and Social Democracy: Essays in Legal and Political Philosophy* (OUP 1992) 212–13.

[5] "What Is Tort Law for? Part 1. The Place of Corrective Justice" (2011) 30 Law and Philosophy 1, 33.

The promissory example may look like a surprising choice with which to attempt to lend such theses (regarding damages in tort) intuitive appeal. Promises are typically embedded within robust frameworks of already existing relationships between promisor and promisee, and the norms of those relationships sometimes govern the post-breach scenario more prominently and conspicuously than would any distinctly promissory norms. Moreover, the self-authored nature of promises raises the possibility, perhaps in conjunction with the previous point, that the promisor and promisee in the first place jointly have a different understanding about what the former would owe the latter in the event of a (faultless) breach, in which case respect for the promisee would not necessarily entail what it does for MacCormick. The content-independent nature of promissory obligations, meanwhile, makes this a particularly difficult terrain on which to introduce what has become known as the "continuity thesis" for Gardner. Being content independent, a promissory obligation makes the promised action obligatory without any further reasons "added up." As Chaim Gans elegantly put it, "actions are duties under the duty to keep promises by virtue of having been promised, and not due to any other of their qualities."[6] If there is any context in which the notion that the same reasons ground an obligation pre- and post-breach would seem particularly implausible, this is it.

There may, however, be a simple explanation for the appeal of promissory examples for MacCormick and Gardner. The position for which they argued (and for which they went on to offer different explanations) may seem intuitive *for lawyers* with respect to promises, because it is a lot like this in the common law of contract: remedial duties following breach of contract typically arise irrespective of fault, and are typically of the "next best" variety—aimed at placing the plaintiff in as good a position as that in which it would have been had the contract been performed. Not only is it like this in the law of contract but contract theorists have frequently argued that it is like this in the law of contract precisely because contracts are promises, and it is like this with promises.[7]

But perhaps it is like this in contract law not because contracts are like any other promises, but because they are not? Or not like all promises but only a particular subset of promises? In other words, inasmuch as contracts are promises (or consist of promises), "next best" remedial obligations arising irrespective of fault in breach may be the correct approach because of the particular kind of promises we find here or the particular context in which we find them, and not because of something which is true of promises *qua* promises.

The focus of this essay is not contract but promise, and my main aim will be to cast doubt on the notion that breached promissory obligations always beget "next best" reparative obligations, either by necessity or even by default. For the most part I will do so symptomatically, that is by attempting to weaken and ultimately dislodge the intuitive appeal of this position. To that effect, I will highlight, first, the scope for confusing performance that is owed to the promisee as the primary obligation under the

---

[6] C Gans, *Philosophical Anarchism and Political Disobedience* (CUP 1992) 74.

[7] See eg C Fried, *Contract as Promise: A Theory of Contractual Obligation* (Harvard University Press 1981) ch 2. I have argued to the contrary in "Fault and Harm in Breach of Contract" in O Ben-Shahar and A Porat (eds), *Fault in American Contract Law* (CUP 2010) 271–88.

180   DORI KIMEL

promise, and performance that is owed as a reparative obligation post breach. I will then discuss the major variables which can and routinely do inform what the promisor owes the promisee when a promise is broken. Their cumulative effect is to suggest that whereas "next best" reparative obligations sometimes emerge post breach, their emergence is often grounded in contingent or contextual features of the promises broken, the manner in which they were broken, and the relationship between the parties, and is thus not indicative of the character of promissory obligation or reparative obligation in promise in general.

1. Has the Promise Been Broken?

The distinction between cases where the promise has been broken, so that if anything is owed to the promisee it genuinely belongs in the realm of reparative obligations, and cases where, perhaps despite appearances, the promise can still be performed may seem trivial. However, several factors can make the distinction somewhat harder to draw in certain types of case, and make it easier to mistake one scenario for another—particularly, I suspect, the latter for the former.[8] Even MacCormick's original example seems to me to be open to interpretation by reference to this distinction. Where the promise in fact has not been broken and can still be performed, the "next best" intuition is of course correct but lacks special meaning: it is tautological with the sentiment that a promise has to be kept (in which case the "next" is superfluous), or, at most, it captures the common-sense implication thereof that where it may be too difficult or impossible to perform fully or optimally, performance as near as possible to optimal is still required and is still, simply, a matter of keeping the promise rather than giving what is owed post breach.

Examples of broken promises in analytical literature, where quite typically the promise is encapsulated in a few words and the required performance consists in one highly specified act set within an exacting timeframe, can give the impression that keeping and breaking promises are binary affairs. But it need not be so. In much the same way that performance, particularly of an obligation that is imperfectly specified, or stretches over time, or has multiple components (etc) can be complete or incomplete, optimal or sub-optimal, so can a breach thereof be full or partial, final or temporary, and so on. That alone can make it easier to confuse situations whereby if the promisor still owes anything to the promisee a reparative obligation must be at work, with situations in which performance is still possible, or can still be improved or can still be resumed.

Certain additional factors, generally belonging in the realm of promise interpretation, can make the distinction between broken and unbroken (or not yet broken, or not fully broken) promises particularly illusive, sometimes even where the promise is

---

[8] Another distinction that can occasionally breed confusion is between cases where a promise has been broken and cases where it has been extinguished without being broken, eg because it was conditional and the condition has not been met, or because the failure to perform was not accompanied by the required fault requirement. I will return to former at the end of this section, and to the latter in section 4.

THE NEXT BEST THING TO A PROMISE   181

to be found toward the highly specified, one-act end of the spectrum. All such factors can of course overlap, making matters fuzzier still. I will mention two.

1.1 Essence and periphery

One complete promise, or one complete speech act which brings a promise into existence, can be made in a few words, or at any greater length. Which components of the speech act set the precise parameters of the promised action can be a matter of interpretation. The distinction between clauses which define performance and clauses which fulfil a range of subordinate or peripheral functions in an agreement is highly familiar to those tasked with drafting or interpreting commercial contracts, but it can feature in simple, non-conditional promises, too.[9] Certain words can merely give the performative core of the promise color or context, or account for hoped for yet not guaranteed aspirations associated with it, and so on.[10]

Interpreting a component of a promise-as-communicated as belonging in the essence of the promised performance or as merely forming part of its periphery can sometimes be straightforward, sometimes genuinely contentious. I may promise a friend who is weary of using public transport during a pandemic that I will pick her up from the airport, and do so by saying "don't worry, I promise I'll be there tomorrow in my blue car." "Tomorrow" clearly is in the essence of the promised performance in this case—that is when her flight arrives. A subsequent breakdown of the blue car, resulting in my turning up promptly at the airport in my other, differently colored vehicle would hardly justify treating this scenario as anything other than one in which I keep my promise. If I turn up in a car-sharing scheme vehicle, the change (relative to the terms of the promise) in ownership status may not merit different conclusions, but as an interpretive matter it could be less straightforward: since the promise was made in response to concerns about COVID safety in public transport, it would depend on whether car-sharing schemes are understood as public transport, or as significantly more COVID-secure than other public transport means.

Even time clauses can sometimes plausibly be interpreted as merely peripheral, so that their subsequent violation need not amount to a breach of the promise. That is more likely to be the case, for example, where the core commitment is to a continuing or long-term state of affairs, and the time clause is meant to signify the strength or the finality of the commitment, or express the enthusiasm or urgency associated with it rather than to set a rigid schedule for commencement. Imagine a long-standing conflict between parents and children over whether or not to adopt a dog. It is a war of attrition, in which the children resourcefully manage to rebuff every argument against and come up with increasingly irresistible arguments in favor, until finally the parents give in, and promise: "Next week we're getting a dog!"

---

[9] In conditional promises, the condition is usually (albeit not necessarily) clearly distinguishable from the performance to be delivered upon its fulfilment.

[10] An alternative analysis of such cases may be that only a part of the speech act which included the promise is *the promise*—namely only those words which define performance—whereas the rest is not part of the promise itself. Since nothing turns on the choice between the two analyses for present purposes, I will not develop the distinction further.

182 DORI KIMEL

It then turns out that it simply takes longer to find a dog, and a suitable candidate is only found three weeks later. That the parents are duty-bound to adopt this dog *now* is surely correct, but why? Is it because, having broken the promise, they come under a reparative obligation to do the next best thing? I do not think so. The performative core of the promise is getting a dog (or starting to work on getting a dog more or less immediately); "next week" is peripheral. They can still perform, in which case performance is still their (primary) promissory obligation and their children's primary promissory right.

1.2 The literal and the contextual, explicit, and implicit

Another factor that can contribute to a tendency to confuse yet to be performed promises with broken promises concerns not the role assigned to certain words or clauses in promissory undertakings, but their meaning. Particularly in the context of an established personal relationship between promisor and promisee, it is not unusual for words to acquire non-literal meanings, for things that otherwise need saying to go without saying, and for a host of similar linguistic phenomena typifying informal communication under conditions of significant familiarity to manifest themselves. The necessity and appropriate scope for contextual interpretation has long been a staple debate for contract lawyers and theorists, with distinct camps forming along well-established battle lines (discrete versus relational contracts, formalism versus contextualism, etc). In the promissory context, however, the case for limiting interpretation as much as possible to the literal or ordinary meaning of words over the contextual, or for categorically privileging the explicit over the implicit (etc) would always ring hollow—the more so the more informal or familiar the setting of the promise being interpreted.

Time clauses again provide an example. In the previous example, I demonstrated how time clauses are sometimes not meant to set a schedule at all, or that in as much as they do, adherence to the schedule is not part of the core promissory obligation. A more familiar possibility is that the time clause *is* part of the performance promised, but the words by which it is created do not necessarily carry their literal meaning. In much the same way that among building-material traders a "four-by-two" piece of structural timber is not expected to carry precisely those dimensions, in certain settings or among close familiars "tomorrow" may connote "the next opportunity" rather than the 24 hours the other side of midnight. Perhaps the conclusion that no promise was broken in the dog adoption example could be made out more easily by reference to the possibility that "next week" was meant to be part of the promised performance, but that the words stood for "soon" or "as soon as a suitable candidate is found." The intuitive quality of the assertion "he now owes it to his children as soon as possible to make good their disappointment by taking them to the seaside" in MacCormick's example may similarly owe to that: it is natural to take "this afternoon" in a context such as this to stand for "when I'm back from work" or "as soon as I'm free to do so." In which case, no special obligation of reparation kicks in: the original promise is still there, capable of being kept; of course the father has to keep it, and take the children to the seaside as soon as he is free do so.

Or perhaps not. Perhaps time clauses are always literal when small children are involved; let us modify the example sufficiently to ensure that whatever the intuition, it indeed relates to a post-breach scenario. Suppose the date is significant: it is some anniversary that the children like to commemorate annually on the beach, on that precise afternoon; "this afternoon" was intended and taken in its literal meaning, and as an integral part of the promise; the promise is well and truly broken. I think that, in such a case, MacCormick's analysis regarding the father's reparative obligation would be no longer intuitively compelling. Sure, he would still owe the children *something*— they have been waiting, excited to go to the beach, and he didn't come; undoubtedly he must explain to them what happened. But once he has done that, must he follow that up by "giving some similar or better treat"? It may still sound like the nice thing to do, perhaps in some ways the right thing to do—the children experienced disappointment, after all, and alleviating it by providing them with an equally stimulating treat seems like a healthy parental instinct. But suppose the father resists this instinct and decides instead to use the event as an educational experience: the children have an opportunity to learn that sometimes, even legitimate expectations can be (legitimately) frustrated, disappointments have to be got over; that's life. We may find this a harsh or unpleasant approach to parenting but would we be right to accuse the father of conceptual confusion relating to the normative aftermath of the promise? I do not think so. To make sure, nor do I think that that the lesson he would unwittingly be teaching them is that adults cannot be trusted: provided that he adequately explains the circumstances and established that the breach has been the right thing to do, as an educational experience it would be the intended one.

Incidentally, it looks as if the same conclusions could emerge in similar scenarios whereby the original promise can no longer be performed, even absent a breach. Suppose that, again, the precise date is an integral part of the promise, but this time the promise is conditional: "I'll take you to the beach tomorrow if no emergency comes up at work." The emergency at work has left the children disappointed, although the promise has not been broken—it has been extinguished with no wrong having been committed. I think it would look just as harsh for the father in this scenario to leave it at that and not offer an alternative treat, or use it as an educational experience relating to living with disappointment. But if the same intuitions hold whether or not the wrong of a breach has been committed, that is another indication that these are not rooted in the nature of reparative obligations in promise but something else.

2. Is the Promised Action Otherwise Required?

We now look at cases where a promise has indeed been broken, and a factor that can often prop up the "next best" intuition (or inform it as an overall judgment) is, simply, that the promised performance (or its close approximation) is strongly supported by reason or is even obligatory on its own. "On its own" requires some elaboration because there are two distinct possibilities here: it may be independently desirable (or required, or obligatory) entirely irrespective of having been promised, or it may become desirable (or required or obligatory) only once it has been promised or breached but by virtue of some other reason or principle, with the promise (or its breach) merely having brought it under that other reason's or principle's ambit. Neither scenario, however, captures a conceptual truth about promises.

2.1 Independent desirability

Patrick Atiyah saw the typical promise as a sort of formal acknowledgement (or "admission," as he called it) that the promisor is already, irrespective of the promise, duty-bound to perform the promised action.[11] Some promises may indeed be like this—I may promise my neighbor to return an item which belongs to her and is long due back—in which case their breach is unlikely to affect what the promisor owes the promisee anyway, namely performance or its closest approximation.[12] Of course, not all promises are like that, and not all promised actions need be independently desirable or supported by reason in any way, let alone obligatory.

Typical examples in analytical literature on promissory obligation do not tend to concern promises to do that which is obligatory regardless, but they do tend to involve promises to do things which are reasonably desirable and supported by reason on their own: they tend to involve promises to quit smoking, not to take it up; or, as in the examples given by MacCormick and Gardner in the present context, they involve pleasing prospects such as visiting the seaside, or attending a lecture delivered by John Gardner.[13]

The independent desirability (even short of obligatory status) of the promised performance may, in certain cases, affect our intuitive response and possibly our overall judgment as to what the promisor owes the promisee post breach, or even our judgment as to whether or not there has been a breach. We may think that, upon a simple change of mind, someone who promised her friend to take up smoking owes nothing more than an account of the change of mind, whereas if the promise has been to quit smoking, she may not be so easily let off. It is possible that the explanation for that is that the more supported by (independent) reason the promised action, the more justified and probably more relatable the promisee's disappointment upon breach, and hence this disappointment presents itself more strongly as meriting a more robust form or redress. Or it may simply be that the more supported by reason the promised

---

[11] See P Atiyah, *Promises, Morals, and Law* (OUP 1983) ch 7.

[12] A possible complication may arise in a case where the promise does not merely replicate an existing moral obligation that is owed to the promisee, but adds a new promisee. Suppose I promise my mother that, from now on, I will keep all my promises; my next breach of promise, involving a third party, would be a breach of my obligation to that third party as well as of my obligation to my mother. My (non-promissory) obligation to keep all my promises from that moment on would of course remain intact, but would I still owe it to my mother as well? Would I wrong *her* the next time I break a promise to a third party? I think I would, but that it is more plausible to argue for that conclusion on the basis of an interpretation of the original promise as accounting for such scenarios, such that the breach is not complete and performance can simply resume, in which case I owe it to my mother as a primary promissory obligation rather than as a reparative "next best."

[13] This is an example Gardner provides in *From Personal Life to Private Law* (OUP 2018) 98–99. It will be discussed later.

action is independently of the promise, the more plausible it is to interpret the promise as leaving sufficient scope in the first place for alternative (or later, or sub-optimal, or non-continuous, etc) performance, so that it is not taken to have been broken by conduct which would have more clearly constituted an irrevocable breach otherwise. The independent desirability of quitting smoking would make it more plausible to interpret the utterance "I promise that this is my last cigarette," notwithstanding the literal meaning of the words used, as transferrable onto the cigarette after that—the promisor has undertaken to bring about an appealing state of affairs, the point and purpose of the promise clearly survive the first slip in performance or its delayed start, in which case promissory performance can and should simply resume. Where the promised action does not have such an obvious and independent point and purpose, such an interpretation may look less compelling.

Be that as it may, that the promised action is independently desirable or strongly supported by reason is a contingent matter, and not something that is true of promises in general. It may be impossible to promise the morally impermissible, but as a threshold of desirability this limit is vanishingly low; and it may be impossible to make a promise to an unwilling promisee, but the desirability (for the promisee, or in general) of the promised act is not the only reason for which a promisee may accept a promise, and is hence far from guaranteed.

2.2 Triggered desirability

In the second scenario where the promised action is desirable or required "on its own," the desirability is not entirely independent of the fact that the action has been promised, but is a sort of a side effect of that fact. The promise, that is, besides serving in itself as a reason to perform the action also brings the action (or the failure to perform it) under the ambit of some other reason to perform it (or to make amends for a failure to do so), or even under the ambit of some other moral principle which can render it obligatory. Taking the children to the beach may be independently desirable, but absent the promise it is not the father's obligation to do so. Once a promise to that effect has been made, the children expect and look forward to be taken to the beach. So now, besides creating a moral obligation to take the children to the beach, the promise also brings the action under the ambit of the (let's suppose) moral obligation not to disappoint the reasonable expectations one creates in small children. If the promise is then broken, that non-promissory obligation kicks in; taking the children to the seaside at the next opportunity may indeed be the only way forward, and for that reason.

That a promise such as this happens to trigger a different moral principle, and that it is this principle (if anything) that grounds MacCormick's conclusion as to what the father ought to do next, is corroborated by the fact that such an account can explain how the same conclusion seems appropriate even absent the wrong of the breach and the opportunity for any reparative obligations to arise. This may indeed be the answer to the question that was left open at the end of section 1. The conditional promise "I'll take you to the beach if no emergency comes up at work" would have

186   DORI KIMEL

generated the same expectations in the children; their father is an academic, after all, and emergencies are not generally foreseen. This promise has not been broken, but the result in both cases is the same because the normative aftermath of both is primarily governed not by reparative obligations but by a separate moral principle which is triggered equally by the justified breach of the original example, and by the unfulfilled condition in the other.[14]

Not all promises, however, are like that. Promises the breach of which triggers some separate, non-promissory moral obligation to give the promisee the promised performance or its closest approximation may not be too rare, but such eventualities are far from a constant in promissory breach. The principles triggered most commonly belong in three groups: principles related to special vulnerability or need in the promisee, or the special responsibilities of the promisor toward the promisee; principles of reciprocity; and principles of harm prevention. Thus the triggering of any such principles would depends on a host of variables, primarily related to the identity of the promisee or the nature of the relationship between promisor and promisee, the circumstances leading to or surrounding the breach, and to reciprocal dimensions of the promise or the circumstances surrounding its making or its breach.

The beach example demonstrates the possibility of "triggered" principled belonging in the special vulnerability or special responsibility group, and reciprocity principles will receive separate attention in the next section. By "harm prevention" I mean circumstances in which the breach, absent some special reparative measure, would cause the promisee some ascertainable harm other than the disappointment or loss associated with not receiving the promised performance. The most common examples of that are cases where, in anticipation of performance, the promisee has incurred some expenses, forgone some opportunities, and the like. It is worth noting that in such cases, the reparative obligation mandated by the triggered harm-prevention principles would only rarely (and at any rate as a contingent matter) amount to "next best" performance. The loss or expenditure incurred in reliance would often be easier or cheaper to redress compared to the performance of the promised action or its closest approximation, and at any rate the orientation of the mandated response is placing the promisee in as good a position as that in which she would have been absent the promise, and not absent the breach.

3. Bilaterality

There is a theoretical tendency to think of promises as unilateral. This tendency is habitually evidenced in objections to the analogy between contract and promise which are based on the notion that the former are bilateral whereas the latter are unilateral.[15] Promises are seen as very close to (or as barely distinguishable from) vows or oaths, so

[14] Depending on how exactly the triggered principle is formulated, it may be triggered absent a promise altogether, or absent any action intended to generate expectations in children or even involving the conscious risk that such expectations would be generated.

[15] See eg A de Moore, "Are Contracts Promises" in J Eekelaar and J Bell (eds), *Oxford Essays in Jurisprudence* (3rd series, OUP 1987).

that the distance between them and bilateral agreements is great—great enough, for some, as to render any promissory account of contract misleading.

Whatever "unilateral" is taken to mean exactly—be it one party, or one-sided or non-reciprocal—I think this tendency is mistaken, or at least grossly exaggerated; promises are hardly ever as unilateral as it is common to think. I have alluded already to my belief that the role of promisee cannot be foisted upon candidates without their consent. The promisee is not mere audience to the promisor's undertaking, and the promise is not always pure reward for its recipient. The unique right to the promisor's performance comes with a bundle of associated powers or prerogatives, and with those come responsibilities. It is the promisee to whom the promisor is accountable in the matter of the promise, it is the promisee alone who possesses the power to release the promisor or to agree on modifications, and it is for the promisee to consider and balance reasons for or against exercising all such powers, and to listen to excuses or accept or reject justifications, and so on. It can all amount to very little in one case, but prove quite onerous in another. And even when very little is in fact required of the promisee in practice, the promise itself ties her in a certain bond with the promisor, and that, even as an abstract matter, can be undesirable. I may be happy for every smoker to quit smoking if they can and wish, but reasonably reject promises to that effect offered to me by strangers on the street: "good luck with the quitting, but I will have nothing to do with this project" would be a sound response.

The upshot is that the promisee must agree to act as promisee—and for that reason alone I think it more accurate to think of promises as, in fact, a particular kind of bilateral agreement. It is a private case of agreements—one where one party undertakes an obligation to perform, and the other agrees to act, in the relevant sense, as the recipient of the obligation and (where needed) its gatekeeper, with the bundle of potential responsibilities that go with that. It is a bilateral agreement even in as much as it is the case that some or all of the promisee's responsibilities *qua* promisee are not obligatory, or not quite as obligatory as those of the promisor *qua* promisor. The mere acceptance of the promise need not amount to *a promise* to discharge the role of the promisee *well*; but even if it is not enshrined in obligations, promissory or other, the role of the promisee is governed by norms, and its acceptance implies at least some commitment to pay them due attention and be reasonably governed by them.

Having said that, a distinction can still be made between the paradigmatic promise, where this is *all* the promisee gives, and cases where, say, promises are exchanged one in return for another, or other agreements are struck whereby both parties play the roles of promisor and promisee *vis-à-vis* each other, or something else is given in return for the promise. Think of it as a distinction between weak bilaterality and strong bilaterality, or imperfect and perfect bilaterality, the latter describing a spectrum whereby the closer the agreement to the "perfect" end, the more proportionate the responsibilities each party assumes—be it in deontic status or onerousness or degree of self-sacrifice, or as the case may be.

Examining our intuitions regarding what the promisor owes the promisee when a promise is broken by reference to this variable in isolation—let us concentrate on cases where the promise is broken with no fault, no loss in reliance has been suffered by the promisee, the promised action is not otherwise required, etc—it is clear, I think, that where there is strong bilaterality, or the closer we are to perfect bilaterality, the more we would veer toward "next best performance" as the appropriate response to a breach, and vice versa: the more one-sided or altruistic the promise, the less obvious it would seem that anything beyond an explanation as to the reasons for its breach are owed.

Suppose a colleague and fellow road cyclist is about to visit Oxford for a week. I know she will miss cycling in this period, and so I promise her that during her stay she will be able to use my bike. I then break the promise, with no fault on my part: the bike is stolen on the morning of her arrival, or I lend it to someone for whom it is the only way to get to hospital for life-saving treatment, and it will be a week before I can get it back. I certainly owe my colleague an explanation in such a case, but do I owe more? If she rents a bike instead, must I pay for it? It is far from clear that I must, and I do not think that this intuition is grounded in the fact that the "next best" obligation would be more onerous or more expensive than the promissory obligation which has been breached. This, after all, is often the case, and I do not think that the conclusion would change if I happen to be in a position to source a similar bike myself with relatively little effort or expense. It would certainly be nice for me to do so, perhaps ungenerous not to; I would do it, but I do not think that it would be my obligation.

What would, by contrast, at least weaken the intuition that I owe no more than an explanation is movement along the bilaterality spectrum toward a more reciprocal arrangement. Suppose the promise I have made was less altruistic and one-sided: the colleague in question has made the equivalent promise to me; or perhaps she has already lent me her bike when I visited her city last month, and my own promise was offered in return. I suspect that in such a case, notwithstanding the greater effort or expense involved in providing next best performance, treating it as something that I *owe* my colleague would be far more plausible.

One possible explanation for this difference may be that in the more reciprocal case, but not in the altruistic one, a breach which is not followed by next best performance would bring my conduct into conflict with some other moral principle, making it a private case of the scenario discussed in the previous section. The "other" principle in question may be a principle against ingratitude, or perhaps advantage-taking, or suchlike. Under some such principle, the fact that the "next best" performance is somewhat costlier or more onerous than the gesture I had already received (or what I originally owed under the promise) would likely make no difference: even if under the reparative obligation I now have to do more for my colleague than she has done (or has undertaken to do) for me, the disparity would be smaller than the disparity between receiving her bike last month and doing nothing for her now. Where the disparity in the latter equation case would in fact be the great one, the conclusion may well change.

The paradigmatic contract involves strong bilaterality, and contract law as a whole can be viewed as far more focused on facilitating an arena for truly reciprocal agreements than it is interested in altruistic undertakings. While neither is true of promise, this may well be an important part of the explanation for the claimant-centric nature of remedies for breach of contract, as well as for their general orientation toward securing the benefits of the bargain rather than merely protecting parties against incidental harms.

4. Variations in Fault

The notion that fault in breach of promise can affect what the promisor owes the promisee may elicit starkly contrasting instincts in layers and other thinkers. I suspect that, to non-lawyers, the converse—the thought that the promisor generally is in just the same position *vis-à-vis* the promisee post breach whether it was possible or impossible to keep the promise, whether the breach was accidental or careless or intentional, whether it was justified, whatever its motives, etc—would be anything but intuitive. Lawyers, meanwhile, may again have the law of contract in mind. This, after all, is a branch of the law where fault plays a conspicuously limited role, and where its role in the selection of remedies for breach in particular is minimal. At common law, at least, remedies for breach are (with very few exceptions) claimant-centric, not defendant centric; as such, they aim to place the claimant in a certain position post breach largely regardless of the circumstances that brought the breach about, the motive for it or the state of mind accompanying it, and regardless of questions such as whether it was avoidable or not, excusable or justified.

But this is the law of contract, and there is a host of reasons—logistical, functional, and ideological—why the law of contract should be like this.[16] For instance, that it is primarily meant to facilitate (strongly bilateral) commercial activity, that it has (related) special reasons to prioritize certainty and predictability of outcome or to encourage expenditure in reliance, that it is bound by constraints of procedural efficacy, and that in awarding remedies it is strictly concerned with furthering its own facilitative objectives and with protecting parties to contract from harm rather than with subjecting parties to moral scrutiny. Indeed, by largely ignoring fault the law of contract can be said to be shielding parties from moral scrutiny which would go beyond the law's legitimate remit and to which they would not necessarily wish voluntarily to subject themselves through contracting, while also shielding courts from having to conduct such scrutiny in adjudicating private disputes.

No such considerations apply to promise, and here it may seem odd to think that failure to keep a promise in circumstances where keeping it turns out to be impossible or where breaking it turns out to be *the right thing to do* should generally result in the emergence of the very same reparative obligation that would typically emerge in the wake of a breach that is unjustified or inexcusable. All the more so in as much as the thought is that in either type of case, the reparative obligation in question is the most demanding one.

Perhaps the most straightforward way to explain why it seems odd would be that in cases of the former type (impossibility, justification), at the point of breach the promisor treats the promise—and hence also the promisee—appropriately, whereas in cases of the latter type she does not. In the former, the promise—and hence also the promisee—figures correctly in her practical reasoning; in the latter it does not. It looks like a significant difference. So the promisor may indeed owe the promisee *something* in either type of case, but performance or its closest approximation, in the absence

---

[16] See Kimel, "Fault and Harm in Breach of Contract" (n 7).

of independent reasons to give it, would appear to follow much more naturally from failure to act appropriately on the promise and to treat the promisee appropriately in the first place. Indeed, the fact that the promise has not figured appropriately in the promisor's practical reasoning in the first place can lend Gardner's sentiment that the reasons grounding the obligation are "still with us awaiting satisfaction" particular intuitive force: a promissory obligation has been created, but then has not been treated as such by its creator; it still awaits. But where it *has* figured appropriately—the promisor turns up for the subsequently canceled flight he needs to take so as to keep his promise, or correctly identifies an emergency as *justifying* a breach—that sentiment loses much of its intuitive appeal. Does the "satisfaction" of the reasons grounding a promissory obligation not consist primarily in treating it not as an absolute obligation, not as something that cannot be defeated or frustrated by any conceivable eventuality, but in treating it appropriately as the obligation that it is?

In setting out their positions on the character of reparative obligations, both MacCormick and Gardner have used primary examples which are emphatically of the no-fault variety: a life-or-death emergency makes breaking the promise to take the children to the seaside patently the right thing to do—the breach is fully justified; or in Gardner's other example, keeping a promise to deliver a lecture at a particular time and place becomes impossible when flights are canceled due to a hurricane.[17] Do the arguments in which they each ground the thesis that the same reparative obligation—and the most demanding one, at that—arises just the same in cases such these and in cases of blameworthy breach make this conclusion seem less odd? I do not think so; on the contrary, it seems to me that their narratives provide reasons to doubt this very conclusion, and suggest particular grounds for thinking that fault in breach can indeed have an effect on the reparative obligations arising in its wake.

4.1 Reasons awaiting satisfaction

Suppose promissory obligations, as Gardner appeared to view them, were always strict liability. If that were true, still it would not be a reason for thinking that the same reparative obligations arise whether the promise-breaker acts with fault or not. A strict liability obligation can be broken (so that the wrong of breaking it is committed) without fault; but a strict liability obligation can also be broken *with* fault, and the obligation's "strict liability" status simply does not mean that the normative aftermath of both scenarios must be identical. Strict liability offences in criminal law tend to be of the less egregious, "regulatory" variety, part of the rationale for making them strict liability is minimizing the complication and cost associated with prosecution and trial, and the punishments they attract tend to be moderate—hence, in practice, where such an offence is committed it is rarely explored whether it has been committed with fault, and convictions usually result in identical sentences whatever their circumstances. It is not hard to imagine, however, a legal practice whereby the sentence handed down

---

[17] *FPLPL* (n 13).

THE NEXT BEST THING TO A PROMISE   191

following a conviction of some such offences is allowed or even required to be sensitive to fault.

Returning to promissory obligations, I have already suggested that Gardner's specific argument in support of next best reparative obligations does not provide an explanation for why the normative aftermath of fault and no-fault promise-breaking need be identical, but merely begs the question. As he put it:

> Once the time for performance of a primary obligation is past, so that it can no longer be performed, one can often nevertheless still contribute to satisfaction of some or all of the reasons that added up to make the action obligatory. Those reasons, not having been satisfied by performance of the primary obligation, are still with us awaiting satisfaction and since they cannot now be satisfied by performance of that obligation, they call for satisfaction in some other way. They call for next-best satisfaction, the closest to full satisfaction that is still available.[18]

The promisor in the lecture example has placed himself under an obligation to give a lecture at a particular date. Since this is a promissory obligation, the reasons that "added up to make the action obligatory" have nothing to do with the desirability of the lecture; rather, they are that the action has been promised, in conjunction with whatever reasons there are for thinking it obligatory to keep promises. If the promisor had simply forgotten to turn up, or chosen not to turn up because the weather on the day was suitable for a trip to the seaside instead, he can be said to have failed to respond appropriately to the reasons that have made the action obligatory, and *in this sense* those can be said to have not been "satisfied." That is, what has left them unsatisfied is not the failure to perform as such, but the failure to respond to them appropriately as reasons which ground an obligation; the eventual failure to perform is merely a symptom thereof.

By contrast, no equivalent disregard to the reasons that have "added up to make the action obligatory" is demonstrated where the lecturer does turn up for the flight, and the flight is canceled because of a hurricane. Here, as in the children to the beach example, the failure to perform is not symptomatic of reasons awaiting satisfaction. It is plausible to think of reasons as "satisfied" when they figure correctly in reasoning, not necessarily when the actions they are reasons for are performed—certainly not when these actions are performed in the presence of stronger or higher-order reasons not to perform them. Indeed, it is tempting to suggest that in an alternative scenario in which the father keeps his promise and takes the children to the beach on the specified afternoon notwithstanding the need to give attention to a suicidal student, no reasons whatsoever are satisfied, and that includes the reasons that have made the promised action obligatory.

In his first-person account of the lecture example, Gardner relates that he "owed" his hosts and audience "profuse apologies for not having lectured on schedule," followed by an extraordinary effort, similarly owed, to find an alternative flight the following day. The apologies certainly, and the alternative arrangements probably, would have

---

[18] Gardner, "What Is Tort Law for? Part 1" (n 5) 33.

been the obligatory response had he been at fault for the breach, and it may be that one explanation for the need for "next best" alternative arrangements in certain fault cases is that the failure to treat the promise as the obligation that it is in the first place is best redressed by treating it as such in the second place. (Even so, it would probably be more accurate to think that what still awaits satisfaction is not the reasons that added up to make the promised action obligatory, but the higher-order requirement to respond to reason.) In the circumstances of the example, however, even the profuse apologies strike me as misplaced: there is scope for expressing regret or simply disappointment at the frustration of an anticipated event due to forces of nature, but what is there to apologize for? Meanwhile, in these no-fault circumstances there may still be good reasons to try to reschedule and deliver the lecture as soon as possible thereafter, and these may indeed be, for the most part, the same reasons to make the promise in the first place. They are not, however, reparatory obligations, and, for all we know, they are not obligations at all but merely reasons: it is a reasonable request, it would be a valuable and pleasant thing to do, and so on. The efficient way of making it happen in the first place involved making a promise; the promise did not get us there, but we still have those reasons to try and get there.

4.2 Respect for the promisee

MacCormick's argument, to my mind, suffers the same fate. His argument is clearer, and, as an account of the moral foundation of obligations of reparations in general, perhaps more persuasive; but rather than establish that fault can have no effect on the scope or shape of reparative obligations for breach of promise, it gives specific grounds for thinking otherwise. For him, obligations of reparation are "claimant-centric": their "primary moral foundation," as he put it, is "found in respect for the person hurt or harmed in a given case."[19] Respect demands that the hurt or harm caused through the commission of a wrong is redressed, and since the measure of respect is redressing the harm done, fault in causing it is not a necessary condition for the emergence of a reparative obligation.

Whereas MacCormick's emphasis has been on establishing that fault is not a necessary condition for the *existence* of reparative obligations, his account ultimately embraces the further conclusion that fault need not affect their *content* either: the content is determined by the harm or hurt to be redressed, and (hence) is not sensitive to the circumstances under which it has been caused, fault or no fault included. If you have broken someone's fence, it would be disrespectful to leave her with a broken fence even in as much as you bear no fault or blame for the breaking. Respect for the fence-owner not only grounds your obligation to do *something* about it, but also determines what it is that you ought to do: mend her fence or pay for mending the fence. Demonstrating this with promissory obligations, MacCormick takes the "hurt" or "harm" in question *ex hypothesi* to consist in failing to receive the promised performance. So whether the promise has been broken with fault or without matters

---

[19] MacCormick, "The Obligation of Reparation" (n 4) 213.

THE NEXT BEST THING TO A PROMISE   193

not: respect for the promisee demands next best performance in any event. The father did the right thing in breaking the promise to take the children to the beach, but the children had a right under the promise to be taken, and the justification for the breach did not affect it in any way; respect for them requires "equal or better treat" as soon as possible.

I do not wish to contest the notion that fault is not a necessary condition for the *existence* of obligations of reparation in promise. Indeed, I do think that the promisor always owes the promisee *something* when a promise is broken, including in instances where breaking it has been the right thing to do. At minimum, that something is an account: the father did the right thing in breaking the promise, but he certainly owed the children an explanation why they were not taken to the beach; the lecturer in Gardner's example was similarly not at fault for failing to turn up, but he certainly owed his hosts an account of the circumstances which prevented him from doing so. This can indeed be couched as a matter of respect for the promisee. I will return to this later.

Focusing on the *content* of the reparative obligation, I do not wish to contest the notion either that an obligation of "next best" performance can sometimes arise in the absence of fault in breach: fault, after all, is only one of several variables that determine what it is exactly that the promisor owes the promisee post breach, and various combinations of such variables may yield "next best performance" even absent any fault. Fault can, however, have an effect on what is owed, and in several different ways. Sometimes it can also be the one consideration that determines whether next best performance is called for or not.

A fairly trivial illustration of the effect that fault can have on the content of reparative obligation—in fact, an effect it would always have—has already emerged in the discussion of Gardner's canceled flight example. Where there is fault in the breach, an apology is called for; where there is not, it is not. We can apologize for being forgetful or clumsy, or for failing to respond appropriately to reasons that apply to us in any other way; however, bearing in mind the difference between apologies and mere expressions of regret about the circumstances or sheer empathy for the promisee, there is no apologizing for a hurricane, nor (usually) for doing what is unmistakably the right thing to do in the circumstances. And the distinction between an apology and an expression of regret or empathy must indeed be borne in mind, because where fault attends the breach an apology would be an important component (at least) of what the promisor strictly owes the promisee, and indeed as a matter of respect.

This fairly trivial point may be a gateway to something further reaching. To put it as a direct riposte to MacCormick's *ex hypothesi* step, fault may have a bearing on the content of the promisee's primary right under the promise, and hence also on what is taken to be the harm done through the breach such that redressing it is now a requirement of respect. The point I have in mind can be offered as a matter of promise interpretation, or, perhaps more ambitiously, as a conceptual matter—that is, as an interpretation of the norms governing promissory liability in general rather than as an interpretation of an individual promise.

As a conceptual matter, it may be suggested that since the obligation to perform is (typically, at least) not absolute, nor should the corresponding right to performance which is vested in the promisee be understood as absolute. I may have plenty of good reasons to pick someone up from the airport—it would be nice for her, I would enjoy

194   DORI KIMEL

it too, etc—but, as things stand, they are plain reasons, in competition with any reason to do otherwise that I may have. Once I make a promise to that effect, things change. Some conflicting reasons have been removed from the competition; now, picking her up is something that, relative to certain reasons for doing otherwise, I *must* do. But it is a relative must, not an absolute: something I must do even in the presence of certain reasons for not doing it, but not all reasons.[20] It may even be thought that this sort of relativity is but another example of the general limits on the scope of what can be promised, namely that which, in terms of intelligibility, possibility, and moral permissibility can conceivably be the subject of a moral obligation. So in much the same way that it is impossible to create a promissory obligation to commit murder, it is impossible to create a promissory obligation to go to the beach when a life can be saved by not doing so.

If that is true of the obligation, so the argument continues, the corresponding right of the promisee ought to be understood in the first place as similarly relative: the promisee is entitled to the promised action even in the presence of certain reasons to do otherwise, but not in the presence of all such reasons. And the distinction between the two groups of "reasons to do otherwise" would normally correspond neatly to fault: I am at fault precisely in those cases where (and for the reason that) I fail to deliver the promised act in the absence of reasons relative to which it is not the case that I must deliver it, whereas one thing that can render me not at fault is the presence of such reasons. If the failure to perform was no-fault, in other words, it may mean that a reason (to not perform) in the presence of which the promisee had *no right to the promised action in the first place* was indeed present. In such cases, the promisee may well still have a right to something under the promise—probably not an apology, certainly an explanation, perhaps more. She may even be entitled to next best performance, but under this analysis the reason for that cannot be that this is what she was owed (or had a right to) as a primary right under the promise *simpliciter*, such that denying it to her is tantamount *ex hypothesi* to harm or hurt that must be fully redressed as a matter of respect. The broken fence and the broken promise are just not the same.

As a matter of promise interpretation (or promise formation, for that matter), fault can in fact play a double role—it can be part of the primary obligation and its corresponding right, thus informing the question whether the wrong of a breach has been committed in the first place, or it can be a condition for the breach to trigger any or all reparative obligations. Even in the absence of an express provision to that effect, it cannot always be taken for granted that a promise is meant to set (or that it ought to be taken as setting) a strict liability obligation. In as much as the obligation includes a fault element, non-performance absent fault (or absent sufficient fault) would not amount to a breach. Similarly, and again even in the absence of an express provision to that effect, it cannot always be taken for granted that the promise does not condition

---

[20] Here I am relaying on Gans' account of generic obligations as "practical musts of limited absoluteness" (*Philosophical Anarchism and Political Disobedience* (n 6) 21). This account is close to Joseph Raz's more familiar account of obligations as exclusionary reasons, by reference to which the point would be that the promissory obligation is excludes certain types of conflicting reason, but not all.

the emergence of reparative obligations, or some such obligations at least, on fault in breach.

In certain cases, it may be the promisor's intention (or the joint intention of the promisor and promisee) to vest in the promisee an absolute or near absolute right to the promised act, or to set next best performance as the reparative obligation no matter the circumstances of the breach. Such cases need not be rare, and in certain contexts—that of commercial transactions, for example—it may be the norm. Yet in other contexts, interpreting a promise along either of these lines would seem unnatural and strained. An altruistic promise to a friend to pick her up from the airport, for example, would be unlikely to be expressed as cumbersomely as this: "I promise to pick you up unless circumstances arise in which it is either impossible for me to do so, or in which not picking you up would be the right thing to do"; yet this, or something like it, would be the natural interpretation of the words "I'll pick you up" in this context. Similarly, the promisor in such a case would be unlikely to spell out a provision regarding reparative obligations, such as "Should I fail to pick you up on the day in such circumstances, I will owe you an explanation and no more"; yet it probably would be entirely natural to interpret the promise in this manner as well.

Considerations relating to fault are, of course, but one element that may inform the interpretation of a promise in the context in which it has been made. In certain contexts, something like the exclusion of next best performance as the reparative obligation may be a reasonable interpretation irrespective of fault in breach. Indeed, in this latest example, it is unlikely that the promisee would expect next best performance (pay for a taxi!) if she receives a text message from her friend upon landing, saying "I'm sorry, I completely forgot." The norms of the background relationship (friendship), in conjunction with the altruistic nature of the promise, would make this an implausible interpretation of what the promise entails regarding post-breach obligations even in as much as the promisor has been at fault. Nevertheless, of all the many elements that can generally inform the interpretation of promises, either in terms of setting up the primary obligation or in terms of agreeing on reparative obligations, fault is bound to be rather prevalent and rather dominant, and would often account for the difference in terms of whether or not "next best performance" is taken to be a reasonable interpretation of what has been agreed. If it is, granting it to the promisee can be couched as a matter of respect by the logic of MacCormick's argument; but not otherwise.

There is another way in which fault can make the difference in terms of whether or not "next best performance" is owed, and which can also be put in terms of respect. Where a promise is broken with fault—but usually not otherwise—the breach itself, and not just a subsequent failure to offer appropriate reparation, is disrespectful toward the promisee. This initial disrespect can often recommend "next best performance" as a particularly natural and appropriate response. It is, after all, disrespect in terms of failing to treat the promisee appropriately *qua* promisee; next best performance, where it is still possible, is the obvious way for the promisor to redeem herself by treating the promisee now (as near as possible to) how she should have treated him in the first place, and hence also the obvious way with which to rectify the particular form of disrespect shown to him. A faultless breach—that is, breaking a promise in circumstances where it is the right or the unavoidable thing to do—usually manifests no disrespect for the promisee at all.

5. Relationship Norms

There is no one typical kind of background relationship between promisor and promisee in the context of which promises are made or exchanged. Promises can be given to complete strangers, but this is hardly the standard scenario; it is more common for promises to feature in contexts where the background relationship has distinct, sometimes dense normative underpinnings. The potential effect of such norms on the incidence and content of reparative obligations is more than just another variable: it is, if you like, a super variable, one which tends to interact with and strongly inform all the other variables I have listed thus far. The background relationship can incorporate its own norms of communication and interpretation; its own norms can be "triggered" by a promise or by its breach such as to make performance (or particular reparative responses post breach) "otherwise required"; the relationship can involve distinct patterns of bilaterality or mutual reliance; and the norms of the relationship can provide particular standards by which to evaluate fault in breach (or evaluate what constitutes a valid justification or excuse) as well as by which to determine the effect of fault on the appropriateness of any or all reparative measures.

There is more: relationship norms can inform what promises it would be appropriate, desirable, necessary, or even possible to make in the first place. (Certain acts which are merely supported by reason in other contexts, for example, may be obligatory in the context of a friendship, obviating the need for a promise in order to elevate them to "obligatory" status, or changing the role of the promise to something akin to Atiyah's "mere admission").[21] Relationship norms can affect the meaning and the value of the promised performance, *inter alia* by endowing it with particular symbolic significance which may far transcend its material value, and similarly affect the sense in which or the extent to which a breach is harmful or hurtful.[22] And, in much the same way that relationship norms can inform all dimensions of the role of the promisor, so can they comprehensively inform the role of the promisee: which promises to accept and which to decline in the first place, how wide the discretion associated with this role, how to exercise it.

I find it hard to imagine an argument to the effect that, as far as reparative obligations go, none of this matters. How can it not? Practically everything on this list attests to the fact that the background relationship between promisor and promisee can and usually does have an effect—direct or indirect, potentially transformative—on the question of what the promisor owes the promisee in the aftermath of a breach and what reparative measures, if any, are called for. A reparative obligation which may be obvious in the context of one type of relationship may be less obvious in another, or in direct competition with alternative responses, or merely desirable or just permissible, or so inappropriate as to make it the case that seeking it or even offering it would be distasteful. And of course, the stricter or more demanding the reparative obligation, the more the

---

[21] Atiyah, *Promises, Morals, and Law* (n 11).

[22] For my own thoughts, see *From Contract to Promise: Towards a Liberal Theory of Contract* (Hart 2003) 66–78, 97–99.

case for or against it is liable to be affected by relationship norms, and the broader the spectrum of possibilities describing its ultimate appropriateness.

"Next best performance" is, in fact, probably the most obvious example of a reparative measure that can look entirely natural in one setting, and utterly alien in another. In the context of commercial, detached, strictly goal-oriented relationships a reparative obligation such as this would often be natural (indeed, as we have seen, possibly irrespective of fault); and it can be equally natural, for entirely different reasons, in relationships involving small children. In other contexts, meanwhile, it may be appropriate or even obligatory to offer it, but at the same time appropriate or even obligatory for the promisee to decline. And in other contexts still, as much as contemplating it would be an affront to the other party, likely to be taken as a repudiation of the relationship between promisor and promisee rather than signaling the willingness to be governed by its norms. This, incidentally, can affect either party equally; the norms of the relationship, after all, can play a part in governing the role of the promisee as much as they govern the role of the promisor. If my car breaks down as I am about to keep the promise to a friend to pick her up from the airport, a demand by the promisee that I pay for a taxi to pick her up instead, thus adding to the costs I am already poised to incur having my car repaired, would seem like nothing short of a violation of the norms of friendship. It may be a case wherein, as promisor, I still ought to offer it, whereas as a promisee who is also a friend, she must decline. But it may be thought, more plausibly I think, that the mere offer of next best performance in circumstances where declining it is so patently what the promisee-friend ought to do, would in fact be an affront, akin to questioning the friendship or testing the promisee's understanding of it. The reasonable thing to do in such circumstances would probably be to the skip this sort of dance, report the breakdown, and leave it at that.

Against such a wide spectrum of possibilities, can anything more definitive be asserted in general? Not much, I believe; there is no precise formula in operation in this matter, nor necessarily a clear trend. The richer or more complex the background relationship and the denser the network of norms it comprises, the more such norms are likely to militate either against or in favor of particular reparative measures depending on the particular promise and the circumstances of its breach. I do not think it correct to assume, for example, that the closer or more personal or less formal the relationship, "next best" obligations are necessarily *less likely* to arise. In a close personal relationship such obligations may sometimes arise even in situations where they would not arise absent the relationship, but sometimes the other way around.

One argument that may be made in last ditch defense of the uniform "next best" approach is that in cases where background relationship norms militate against that particular reparative measure, these norms do not alter (primary or reparative) promissory norms but merely come into conflict with them. Promissory norms, so this argument goes, may sometimes be defeated in such conflicts, but that does not change the fact that they uniformly ground "next best performance" as the default reparative obligation. It is, after all, merely a *prima facie* obligation—that it is sometimes defeated, or that it is sometimes justified to break it or wave the right to it is no argument against its existence.

This sort of analysis, to my mind, would sometimes make sense before a promise is broken, that is when primary promissory obligations are still at stake. Say the promisor's circumstances change—not so as to make performance impossible or a breach justified, but enough to make performance considerably more onerous than first envisaged. In this scenario, the demarcation between the parties' roles as promisor and promisee on the one hand and as friends on the other, as well as the demarcation between the distinct clusters of norms by which these roles are governed, would be clear and conspicuous enough as to validate the distinction between what they owe each other *qua* promisor and promisee and what they owe each other *qua* friends. Thus it would not seem fictitious or terribly artificial in this scenario to suggest that the promisee has a (promissory) right to performance, but also an obligation—a friendship obligation—to release the promisor, or that it is the promisor's obligation (*qua* promisor) to perform, but also right (*qua* friend) to be released.

Post breach, by contrast, when considering reparative obligations, such distinctions would usually seem highly artificial and dubious. As we have seen, promissory norms on their own do not ground reparative obligations the same way they ground *the* primary obligation. Not only is the range of possible reparative obligations far wider (compared to the one primary obligation: performance), but it is considerably more context-sensitive to begin with. Remember all the other variables: the case for treating "next best performance" (or anything else, for that matter) as *the* default reparative obligation in isolation from all relationship norms is non-existent to begin with. There is no one default relationship between promisor and promisee either, and, to complicate matters further, the norms of the relationship can be implicated in the kind of bearing that each one of those variables has on grounding the appropriate reparative obligation in a given place. Whatever that obligation is, tracing its origins to separate, potentially competing sets of "promissory" and "relationship" norms would usually be futile.

6. Conclusions

I will end with three observations for which the discussion thus far has provided tentative, not conclusive foundations.

6.1 Is *anything* always owed?

First, on the question of *the* reparative obligation arising from a breach of promise: is there anything that the promisor always owes the promisee when a promise a broken, irrespective of all the variables discussed? Is there one thing that is owed even where the promise is entirely altruistic, the promised act is not obligatory on its own, the promisor was not at fault for the breach, the norms of the background relationship offer no special case for any particular measure?

It may seem that all the discussion thus far has done, beyond casting doubt on the notion that "next best performance" is the uniform reparative obligation, is set the stage for saying "no"; for saying, that is, that the only way to answer the question as to which reparative obligations arise when a promise is broken is "it depends." We have seen that the total of what the promisor owes the promisee post breach indeed depends on several different variables. Those variables, moreover, can interact with one another in numerous different combinations and to numerous different effects. The inescapable conclusion is that the aftermath of a breach of promise often requires some serious moral footwork, taking in the circumstances and characteristics of the case in hand. Contrary to MacCormick's and Gardner's theses, there is no one formula or one abstract principle that produces the one overall correct result in all cases; instead, it is always necessary to embrace and give appropriate weight to a plethora of potentially pertinent considerations, and those considerations belong in distinct categories and can originate from or be grounded in multiple normative spheres. It means that the overall answer is, indeed, *it depends*, but (as this chapter has sought to show) there is no mystery as to what it usually depends on. This is why, complex as it may sound, the moral footwork in question is precisely what parties to promises do, and usually quite seamlessly, when a promise is broken. That the overall answer is *it depends* does not make promise, as a moral institution, any less useful, appealing, or valuable. On the contrary, it is precisely this variability, and this ability to interact with and be shaped by the multitude of normative spheres applying to the promisor, the promisee, and the relationship between them, that makes promise the infinitely adaptable, multi-purpose, potentially freedom-enhancing and relationship-strengthening institution that it is.

Having said that, the answer I would give the narrower question as to whether there is anything that is *always* owed to the promisee post breach is, in fact, in the positive. Even where a promise is entirely altruistic, and it is broken in circumstances where keeping it is impossible or breaking it is the right thing to do, and no other consideration points in favor of any additional reparative obligation, the promisor has an obligation to give the promisee *an account*, where the circumstances of the breach have not made it plain, of why the promise has not been kept. Note that this detail emerged in the analysis of all the examples we have encountered along the way, however disparate they were otherwise. The obligation to give and the corresponding right to receive such an account strike me as a conceptual entailment of the promise's status as a bilateral, individually owed obligation, with all three of those terms doing equal work in grounding the conclusion.

Being bilateral, and involving the promisee as the holder of unique prerogatives (eg to accept or reject the promise, to release the promisor) and unique rights (eg to receive the promised act), the promise *concerns* the promisee as much and as personally as it concerns the promisor. As an obligation, the promise renders the promised action something the promisor must give relative to certain conflicting reasons, albeit not all; and correspondingly, something the promisee must receive relative to certain, but not all, conflicting reasons. It means that the promisee has special grounds to expect or demand the promised act, subject from the start to the possibility that circumstances may arise in which such an expectation would be frustrated or such a demand would have to be withheld, perhaps replaced with different demands, possibly requiring the exercise of discretion on her part, and so on. All this is, if you like, part the story of the promise, and the story of the promise is the promisee's story in much the same way that it is the promisor's.

200 DORI KIMEL

Where reasons have arisen relative to which the promised action is no longer something the promisor must do, this is a crucial development in the story of the promise, and it clearly concerns both parties. *That* such reasons have arisen may be all of which the promisee must be informed; what those reasons are may be optional. As a conceptual matter—unlike, say, as a matter of what would be courteous or generous or required by norms originating elsewhere—the issue is one of bare accountability toward the promisee, the accountability necessary in order for the promisee to understand her situation and to be able to play her role as promisee; it may not require much. But leaving the promisee ignorant of that development altogether, thus behaving toward her as if the story of the promise is not *her* story at all, amounts to a repudiation of her very status as promisee.

As a unilateral repudiation of the promisee's role under the promise, the failure to give an account of the breach also amounts to a particularly emphatic form of disrespect. The obligation to give an account can therefore be viewed as grounded in respect for the promisee, and as the one respect-based obligation that depends for its existence on nothing other than the fact that a promise has been made, and subsequently broken.

6.2 Reparative obligations and self-authorship

Next, the question of the promisor's control over the reparative obligation. I started the essay by raising the question as to what dimensions of the promise are within the promisor's control, suggesting that theses such as MacCormick's and Gardner's, to the effect that the reparative obligation is a constant, seemingly remove the choice of reparative obligation from the realm of that which is self-authored in promise. This query has subsequently been abandoned, but with the case for seeing the reparative obligation as a constant having been questioned, we can give it another glance.

The question as to what the promisor controls is logically different from the main question that MacCormick and Gardner, as well as I thus far, have addressed directly. Even if it is thought that "next best performance" is always owed, it is still possible to argue that it ought to be seen as merely the default position, and one from which the promisor (perhaps with the agreement of the promisee) may explicitly depart. And even if, as I have argued, next best performance is not always owed, some independent case may still be made in support of seeing the promisor's control over the reparative obligation as limited.

As for the first option, I have argued for the view that no single reparative obligation is *the* default position; that whereas an account is always called for, the appropriate overall reparative response inevitably depends on the combined effect of several variables on a given case. Still, in each case *some* reparative obligation, perhaps next best performance, may emerge as appropriate, and hence it may be seen as the default in the particular case. But with no default reparative obligation that is conceptually linked to the very idea of a promise nor to the very idea of an obligation, the case for denying the power of the promisor (perhaps with the agreement of the promisee) to depart from what would have been the default in the individual promise strikes me as implausible. If next best performance (or something else) in the event of a breach really were part of the very concept of a promise or an inevitable normative implication of its status as an obligation, there would perhaps be scope to argue that the self-authorship power of the promisor cannot extend to altering it; that attempts to alter it would be tinged by conceptual confusion as to the meaning of the obligation that the promisor purports to take. By contrast, if next best performance is merely the appropriate response in light of contingent dimensions of individual promises, no such accusation can be made. By specifying, at the time of making the promise, a reparative obligation that is different, perhaps lesser than the reparative obligation that could have been expected otherwise in the circumstances, the promisor perhaps makes the promise less meaningful, or a lesser source of reassurance for the promisee. But she does not, or not necessarily, make it less of a promise.

This will have to remain a tentative conclusion in the present context, but I cannot think of a good argument to the general effect of seeing the control of the promisor over the reparative obligations as limited on any other grounds. An argument to such an effect can only take the shape of an interpretation of promise as a moral practice, showing it to be, simply, *better*—more useful, fairer, more valuable, less dangerous— with such limitations in place. Such an interpretation strikes me as unlikely, particularly when it is remembered that the promisee has the power to either accept or reject the promise, and hence the promisee can also negotiate, at the time the promise is offered, the reparative dimension of things. So control over the reparative obligations post breach is not entirely part of the self-authorship power of the promisor, but really part of the joint authorship power of the promisor and the promisee. It seems like a good idea.

This is not quite the end of the story. In the previous section, I argued that there is one thing that a promisor does always owe the promisee post breach, namely an account. If I was right about that, then there may be at least one limit in principle on the promisor's control over the reparative obligation. A promise which specifies a limited reparative obligation—more limited than the obligation that would have arisen otherwise—is still a promise, and can still be binding on its terms. "I promise to pick you up from the airport, but if I fail to turn up I don't owe you as much as an explanation," by contrast, sounds to me like an oxymoron. Those who believe that vows can be binding may think that an utterance such as this may have the binding force of a vow; a promise, however, it is not. Sometimes promises are broken without the breach being disclosed to the promisee, let alone without the promisor offering the promisee an account of the circumstances of the breach or (for that matter) an apology where the breach is with fault. In such instances the promisor commits more than one wrong, and that does not, of course, make the promise any less of a promise. Specifying in advance, however, that the promisee will not be entitled to have her rights under the promise respected is different: in such a case, no intelligible promise is offered up for the promisee's consideration to begin with. The proposed removal of bare accountability to the promisee in the event of a breach would be a case in point. I do not see it as a default reparative obligation from which the promisor or even the promisor and promisee jointly can depart, because the absence of bare accountability for a breach entirely dissociates the promisee from the promise, and a promise with no promisee is no promise.

6.3 Reparative obligations in promise and elsewhere

At the start, I noted the possibility that remedies for breach of contract may be what they are—almost entirely claimant-centric, orientated toward securing the full benefits of the contract, independent of fault, and so on—not because contracts are like promises but because (at least in some ways) they are not; or because they are, at most, a very particular subset of promises, and as such hardly representative of the general case. The discussion that followed gave this thought some substance and credence, revealing the limited extent to which reparative obligations in contract law can be seen as a true reflection of reparative obligations in promise—be it in light of possible characteristics of promise (or promissory relations, or breach of promise) falling outside the spectrum of phenomena represented in contract law, or in light of distinct characteristics of contract law which do not feature in and do not inform extra-legal reality.

MacCormick and Gardner, in drawing on promissory examples, have attempted something more ambitious still—that is, using those as indicative of the logic and content of reparative obligations not in contract but in a more distant branch of the law, or in morality in general. Their common intuition appears to have been that once a promise is made, the promissory obligation simply joins the existing constellation of obligations binding the promisor, and for all intents and purposes behaves like the rest of them. This, perhaps, is also their common error. Promises are special in being self-authored, content-independent obligations that bind their parties, however minimally or expansively, in a joint venture of sorts—one in which their roles are constituted by norms of conduct and accountability capable of sometime seamless interaction with any number of the norms governing their relationship more broadly. The error is the failure to appreciate the extent to which the unique qualities of promissory obligations are capable of uniquely shaping their reparative dimensions.

12

The Place of Regret in the Law of Torts

Zoë Sinel[*]

The puzzle of private law's remedial obligations and the relevance of human emotions in law were significant themes in John Gardner's scholarship. In part because of his influence, much of my own scholarship is motivated by questions of how reparative acts can count as rational responses to tort law's primary wrongs, and whether our feelings matter at all from the law's perspective. One of Gardner's most influential contributions to private law theory is his solution to the problem of reparation for wrongs. This is the problem of explaining how it is that a remedial action rationally responds to one's initial failure to do as one ought. Gardner's solution to this problem relies in part on the moral emotion of regret. This chapter offers a new way to understand Gardner's solution to the problem of reparation for wrongs; it also argues for a revised conception of regret's place in private law and private life. Although ultimately I arrive at positions somewhat orthogonal to Gardner's, I am deeply indebted to his work on these subjects.

Regret is a retrospective emotion.[1] In regret, an agent looks back from a present standpoint on decisions she made, actions she took, or even the life she has led, and wishes she had decided, acted, lived differently. Regret can thus take as its object that which has yet to be repaired and that which cannot be repaired.[2] Regret is directed toward what one leaves behind, toward the moral residue of one's missteps. We might say that regret's "constitutive thought" of "how much better if it had been otherwise"[3] seems particularly salient in the law of torts. Tort law consists almost entirely of situations in which someone has failed to do what he or she ought to have done *vis-à-vis* another.[4] Indeed, a gloomy way to view tort law is *as* the law of interpersonal failure. More specifically, regret seems an apt response to three features of

---

[*] Thank you to Andrew Botterell, Erika Chamberlain, Hanoch Dagan, Chris Essert, Cécile Fabre, Andrew Gold, Randal Graham, Ori Herstein, Dori Kimel, Joanna Langille, Ryan Liss, Jason Neyers, James Penner, Stephen Pitel, Anne Schuurman, Adam Slavny, Sandy Steel, Fred Wilmot-Smith, and Ben Zipursky for their helpful feedback on earlier drafts.

[1] For similar definitions, see M Zeelenberg, "Regret" in D Sander and KR Scherer (eds), *The Oxford Companion to Emotion and the Affective Sciences* (OUP 2009) 336; RJ Wallace, "Justification, Regret, and Moral Complaint: Looking Forward and Looking Backward on (and in) Human Life" in U Heuer and G Lang (eds), *Luck, Value and Commitment: Themes from the Ethics of Bernard Williams* (OUP 2012) 176. For a more capacious definition, see: J Landman, "Regret: A Theoretical and Conceptual Analysis" (1987) 17 Journal for the Theory of Social Behaviour 135, 153.

[2] See AO Rorty, "Agent Regret" in AO Rorty (ed), *Explaining Emotions* (University of California Press 1980) 491. But see C Bagnoli, "Value in the Guise of Regret" (2000) 3 Philosophical Explorations 169, 178.

[3] B Williams, "Moral Luck" (1976) in B Williams (ed), *Moral Luck: Philosophical Papers 1973–1980* (CUP 1981) 27.

[4] I say "almost entirely" so as not to at this early stage exclude those who understand remedies as responsive not just to wrongs but to rights as well.

Zoë Sinel, *The Place of Regret in the Law of Torts* In: *Private Law and Practical Reason.* Edited by: Haris Psarras and Sandy Steel, Oxford University Press. © Zoë Sinel 2023. DOI: 10.1093/oso/9780192857330.003.0012

tortious wrongdoing: (i) the deleterious but reparable wrongful consequences of a wrong that have yet to be repaired, "the reparable"; (ii) the deleterious and irreparable consequences of a wrong, "the irreparable"; and (iii) the fact of the wrong itself, "the wrong."

In private law theory circles, no-one took more seriously the connection between regret and tort law's remedial obligations than John Gardner. His scholarship provides a picture of tort law in which regret plays an important role with respect to the reparable, the irreparable, and the wrong. According to Gardner, for the reparable, regret provides an extra reason to motivate an agent to undertake actions of repair; for the irreparable, regret signals an agent's appropriate disposition to the legal duty violated; and, as to the wrong, regret stresses that the wrong itself is a normatively salient feature of our legal world. It is partly due to his reliance on regret and its role in our personal narratives that Gardner is able to offer an intuitively appealing picture of tort law's rights, wrongs, and remedies. Intuitive appeal notwithstanding, the picture is misconceived. Moreover, as I will show here, it is an analysis of regret—the very emotion that lends Gardner's account much of its appeal—that illuminates many of these misconceptions.

This chapter makes two complementary claims. First, I contend that regret has no role to play in private law's remedial responses to wrongs because the wrongs in private law are normatively inert; there is no legal *remainder* or residue that regret can take as its object.[5] Establishing this feature of tort law's wrongs and remedies is the chapter's primary aim. Second, I conclude with the suggestion that it is by virtue of its very exclusion from tort law that the emotion of regret is possible. Regret's irrelevance in tort law allows regret space to operate in our personal lives.[6]

1. Reparation for Wrongs: Puzzles and Gardner's Solutions

1.1 The puzzle of reparation for wrongs

Without exaggeration, we might say that the problem or puzzle of reparation for wrongs lies at the heart of tort law's justification. The puzzle puts pressure on a core feature of tort law's remedies, namely, that those who breach duties owed to another must take steps to remedy these breaches. The question is, why does the wrongdoer's breach put the wrongdoer under a duty to make it as if the breach did not happen? If, for example, we think that what is normatively significant is the damage itself—the fact of the injured party's unfortunate situation, her harm—then the exclusive goal should be to ameliorate this negative state of affairs. Tort law's obsessive focus on the past

---

[5] I echo Ori Herstein's claim that there is perhaps no "legal remainder" in private law. Herstein challenges the "private wrong" conception of private law. I leave engagement with this provocative thesis for another day, but I acknowledge that this challenge is perhaps one upshot of the suggestion I advance here. (O Herstein, "The Remainder: Deserting Private Wrongs?" in P Miller and J Oberdiek (eds), *Civil Wrongs and Justice in Private Law* (OUP 2020).)

[6] For present purposes, I only gesture at what this role might look like. Further exploration of this idea as well as sustained analysis of the role of emotion more generally in the law of torts is undertaken in Z Sinel, *Just Feelings: A Tort Law Theory of Emotion* (manuscript in progress).

might seem irrational. Responses to wrongs, so the thought goes, should be oriented toward the fixable future, not the immutable past. "[W]hat is bad cannot be undone,"[7] wrongs cannot be erased, they and their unfortunate consequences are blots on our personal narratives, stains we can only try in vain to expunge.[8] The only rational response to wrongs and their consequences is to make things better from here on out; to dwell on past wrongs is nothing more than irrational crying over spilled milk.[9] For those of us who think the fact of his wrong *does* mean that the wrongdoer stands in a special obligatory relation of repair toward the person wronged, the challenge is to explain the connection between his initial obligation not to commit the wrong in the first place and his subsequent remedial obligations with respect to this wrong and its consequences.

The puzzle contains two related but distinct aspects. The first concerns the nature of the connection between the initial or primary obligation and the remedial or secondary obligation. I label this aspect the *puzzle of continuity*. It is, at its core, a question about the formal relationship between obligations, their breach, and subsequent obligations of repair. The second concerns the *content* of the obligation of repair, specifically, how the actions that the obligation mandates respond rationally—in that they seem to satisfy the actions made mandatory by the initial obligation—to the initial obligation that has been breached. How, we might ask, can performance of a reparative obligation really make it as if the wrong never happened?[10] I call this second aspect the *puzzle of repair*.

The puzzle of continuity concerns the connection between a secondary duty of repair and the breach of a primary duty. To explain how remedies are rational responses to rights violations, we must posit a connection between the remedy and the infringed right. Sometimes this connection seems obvious: if I owe you $100 to be paid on Monday, but fail to do so on that day, then it seems intuitive that I ought to pay you that same $100 (perhaps along with an explanation, an apology, or an interest) at the next available opportunity. This late payment seems not so much a remedy as it is a continuation of the original duty. Note, however, the added parenthetical requirements attached to the late payment; these belie the notion that late payment is equivalent to prompt payment. If late payment were just the same as punctual payment, why would an explanation, apology, or interest payment be rational and even perhaps necessary? All else being equal, we prefer the punctual over late payment of debts.[11]

The connection between rights and remedies in the late payment scenario seems intuitive, but when we look at tort law's most common remedy, monetary damages, matters take a mysterious turn: how is the payment of monetary damages a rational response to a non-pecuniary injury (eg bodily injury, pain and suffering, psychological

---

[7] R Bittner, "Is It Reasonable to Regret Things One Did?" (1992) 89 The Journal of Philosophy 262, 268.

[8] In Gardner's recent description, such wrongs leave an "indelible residue." J Gardner, *From Personal Life to Private Law* (OUP 2018) 123 ("*FPLPL*").

[9] For support for the idea that the primary aim of private law is forward looking, see V Tadros, "Secondary Duties" in P Miller and J Oberdiek (eds), *Civil Wrongs and Justice in Private Law* (OUP 2020) 186.

[10] See A Ripstein, "As If It Had Never Happened" (2007) 8 William & Mary Law Review 1957.

[11] We can imagine a situation in which I would prefer late over punctual payment: Imagine that I know I am going to be shaken down by the faculty bully for my coffee money at 12 p.m. every Wednesday. I would much prefer in this situation, if you owe me a debt due at 11 a.m. on Wednesday, that you pay me after noon.

distress)? What is the connection between the primary obligation not to cause bodily injury and the secondary obligation to pay damages for the bodily injury caused? It seems counterintuitive to think that the payment of a monetary award is continuous with an obligation not to maim or injure another's person. From the continuity aspect of the problem of reparations for wrongs, the question is, how does one's normative requirement at *t* continue or transform into an equally obligatory requirement, often one with a completely different content, at *t + 1*?

The puzzle of continuity concerns how the normative force of a breached obligation is transmitted to the equivalent normative force of a remedial obligation. It asks, why is it not the unfortunate situation of the plaintiff that generates the duty rather than the fact of the defendant's breach? The puzzle of repair, by contrast, concerns not formal continuity but substantive effect. It asks, how can an obligation to Y somehow respond to one's failure to perform one's antecedent obligation to X? If I negligently damage your physical person, causing loss of limb, how does a conventional sum for non-pecuniary loss satisfy my original obligation? The contents of the two duties—do not maim, for the primary, and pay a conventional sum, for the secondary—seem too different for satisfaction of the latter to count as satisfaction of the former.

If you think that part of the reason for the tort defendant's obligation of reparation involves in a non-arbitrary way the fact of his prior breach, then solutions to the puzzles of continuity and repair are required. Gardner aims to provide these.

1.2 Gardner's solutions: The continuity thesis, its derivative role, and the placebo effect

Gardner's lodestar is Joseph Raz's "conformity principle": "One should conform to reason [that is, what the balance of reasons counts in favor of] completely, insofar as one can. If one cannot, one should come as close to complete conformity as possible."[12] Raz considers this a truism about reasons. It simply describes what it means when we say we have reasons that apply to us. Even if outweighed or overruled, reasons do not by virtue of these cease to be reasons for the action that they recommend.

Gardner takes this feature of how reasons operate—their persistent call for conformity—and applies it to a certain type of reason, a categorical and mandatory reason, that is, an obligation. In Gardner's view, the primary and remedial obligations are not the same. This is because although they are a type of reason, obligations are importantly different from ordinary reasons in that they do not allow for imperfect conformity.[13] Unlike reasons, it is not possible to satisfy an obligation *more or less*; either you perform it or you do not; once an obligation is breached, it can no longer be fulfilled. Second, and relatedly, "obligations ... are individuated according to the action that they make obligatory."[14] By contrast, reasons can count in favor of a number of different actions that serve the reason that grounds them.

---

[12] J Raz, "Personal Practical Conflicts" in P Baumann and M Betzler (eds), *Practical Conflicts: New Philosophical Essays* (CUP 2004) 189. Gardner explicitly acknowledges his debt to Raz in J Gardner, "What is Tort Law For? Part 1. The Place of Corrective Justice" (2011) 30 Law & Philosophy 1, 33, fn 56.

[13] Gardner, "What is Tort Law For?" (n 12) 33.

[14] ibid 29.

THE PLACE OF REGRET IN THE LAW OF TORTS   207

In claiming that an obligation ceases to exist when we fail to perform it, Gardner sets himself the task of explaining why it is that performing the remedial obligation does seem somehow rationally related to the initial obligation. In other words, how do we account for the fact that when we do the next-best thing to perfect performance, we seem to be responding rationally to the original obligation? Given that obligations cannot be imperfectly conformed to, how can it be that this "imperfect" performance counts as any degree of conformity with our original obligation that we breached? Gardner's answer is that this apparent "imperfect" conformity is actually perfect conformity with a *new* obligation, an obligation that is grounded in and called for by the same reasons that grounded the first obligation and which failed to be satisfied, but, because of the nature of reasons, their tenacity, did not disappear as a result.

Continuity is a problem for Gardner because on his theory the primary obligation is "discharged" by its breach.[15] To understand Gardner's solution to this problem, we need to know what it means for obligations to be discharged by their breach. Obligations, for Gardner, are special kinds of reasons,[16] and he takes reasons to be *facts*, considerations existing in the world by virtue of which certain propositional statements are true, counting either for or against a certain action, belief, or emotion. Thus, the fact that I have a duty is a special type of reason—a mandatory and categorical reason—for or against the action or omission that is its object. A reason is a fact that counts in favor of φ because φ-ing would be an appropriate response to some value—it would promote, protect, respect it, etc. When Gardner states that the duty comes to an end following its breach, what he is saying is that the fact of the duty (the fact that I have the duty) no longer exists. I can no longer do what it tells me to do; it can no longer perform its key normative role of guiding my actions directly. Considering Neil MacCormick's example of a (justified) breach of a promise to take one's children to the beach today,[17] Gardner notes, "the obligation to go to the beach on the next suitable occasion is a different obligation, because it calls for a different action, from the original obligation to go to the beach today."[18] By "discharged" Gardner does not mean "put to an end," but something more like "removed from active service." If the primary obligation no longer exists and cannot be conformed to, the source of the secondary obligation's normative force is mysterious. Gardner needs to bridge the primary and secondary obligations.

The bridge is purportedly provided by Gardner's well-known continuity thesis, according to which "the secondary obligation is a rational echo of the primary obligation, for it exists to serve, so far as may still be done, the reasons for the primary obligation that was not performed when its performance was due."[19] The idea is that the secondary obligation directs conformity with the unconformed-to reasons left behind

---

[15] "[Following its breach] [m]y original obligation is, we should now be able to agree discharged (put to an end) by its breach." (ibid 32.)

[16] For Gardner, like Raz, an obligation is not a reason because an obligation is not a fact by virtue of which some proposition's truth may be assessed. Only facts can be reasons; however, the fact that one has an obligation is a reason. (ibid 31; J Raz, *Practical Reason and Norms* (2nd edn, OUP 1990) 51.) Throughout, I will say, "has an obligation" and mean by this "the fact that one has an obligation."

[17] N MacCormick, *Legal Right and Social Democracy: Essays in Legal and Political Philosophy* (Clarendon Press 1982) 212.

[18] Gardner, "What is Tort Law For?" (n 12) 30.

[19] ibid, 33.

when one did not conform to the primary obligation. While one can no longer satisfy perfectly one's primary obligation, this does not mean that one should not do something, specifically, something that responds to the reasons that counted in favor of performing the primary obligation. In other words, in so far as what one does consequent the wrong serves in some way the reasons one had to perform the primary obligation which one failed to perform, then one's perfect satisfaction of this secondary obligation *counts* as reparative of one's initial failure.

What gives the secondary remedial action the normative force of an obligation? Gardner gestures toward this answer in his 2018 explanation of how the continuity thesis works:

> the reasons that I did not conform to still call for conformity even once the time for perfect conformity with them is over. Now they call for the nearest-to-perfect conformity that is still available. *And when they were reasons that originally put me under a duty, a duty that I breached, they are not simply to be returned to the mêlée of other reasons that now apply to me. They now place me under a duty of repair.*[20]

But *why* do these reasons not simply return to the melee? And, moreover, how is it that the *reasons* left over provide *normative* (in the sense of obligation-grounding) force for the secondary obligation if the primary obligation is discharged and all that is left are some of the reasons that counted in favor of performing the action that the obligation made mandatory (that is, not the obligation itself)? How do these reasons provide obligatory force to the secondary obligation? As Sandy Steel has perceptively asked: "What does it mean for a reason to ground a duty?"[21] Solutions to these problems are necessary to understand how the obligation of reparation is normatively connected in a non-arbitrary way to the primary obligation. I will return to address this important question in section 2.3, but for now it is sufficient to grasp the main contours of the puzzle of continuity, why it is a problem for Gardner, and how he tries to solve it.

Let us turn our attention to the puzzle of repair. Our guiding question for the reparative puzzle is simple: how can damages count as repair for an irreparable wrong? In *From Personal Life to Private Law*, Gardner placed solving this problem as the central task of the book:

> I am trying to get to the bottom of a puzzle about so-called "general damages" for torts and breaches of contract. The puzzle concerns the longing to repair the irreparable ... I have come to grasp over the years that the remedial apparatus of private law is itself extremely hard to explain and defend.[22]

In Gardner's view, general damages are acknowledgements of the rational remainder left behind by irreparable wrongs.[23] They foster the illusion that the irreparable is

---

[20] *FPLPL* (n 8) 126 (my emphasis).
[21] S Steel, "Compensation and Continuity" (2020) 26 Legal Theory 250, 259.
[22] *FPLPL* (n 8) 4.
[23] ibid 155.

reparable. They can repair in the sense of the continuity thesis, but only in a derivative fashion.[24] The continuity thesis applies derivatively to such damages if what the wrongdoer did was wrong in part because it *disappointed* the plaintiff and in so far as payment of general damages is understood as assuaging this disappointment. Only in this way do general damages serve as a mechanism of repair.[25] They are awarded alongside damages that do seem reparative in the sense of compensating the wronged party by restoring to her means she happened to already have but of which she was wrongfully deprived. Thus, by calling general damage awards "damages" and by having them also come from the defendant to the plaintiff, we are drawn into the illusion that they are reparative. On Gardner's account, we come to think of these damage awards as reparative, and, working like a placebo, they become so.[26]

To conclude, for Gardner, tort law's obligations of reparation pose two puzzles, the *puzzle of continuity* and the *puzzle of repair*. His continuity thesis addresses the first directly and the second only derivatively. An important hallmark of his solution is the separateness of primary and secondary (reparative) duties. Another crucial feature is the role he assigns to reparative obligations in our personal narratives and specifically the important place he gives to regret. In this next section, I explore this second key feature of Gardner's account.

2. The Place of Regret

Recall that the constitutive thought of regret is wishing that things had been otherwise and that in this picture we can see three places for regret in the law of torts: (i) with respect to the reparable, (ii) with respect to the irreparable, and (iii) with respect to the wrong itself. Gardner endorses this picture and offers an account of tort law's remedial obligations that relies on our intuitions regarding regret's role in dealing with wrongs and their consequences. The secondary obligation is an attenuated version of the primary obligation that precedes it. Secondary obligations are only "second best." For Gardner, between the first-best solution of performing one's primary obligation and the second-best solution of performing (or being ordered by a court to perform) an obligation of reparation, a gap exists, a space occupied by the actor's feelings of regret, of feeling that things would have been better had she performed the primary obligation in the first place. In his account, regret responds to a rational remainder, an "indelible residue."[27] This residue or remainder, I argue, does not exist in tort law. If my argument succeeds, then we have good reason to doubt regret's relevance in explaining tort law's remedies—at the very least, we have good reason to doubt its relevance in accounts like Gardner's that rely on our intuitions about such remainders and their moral significance.

[24] ibid 154.
[25] ibid.
[26] ibid.
[27] ibid 123.

2.1 The reparable

When I spill your milk, my reparative actions—the mopping, the wiping, the purchase of replacement milk—are all acts that effectuate repair. These actions make it as close as possible to the case that certain material effects of my wrong—the mess, your milk-thirst—never happened (or, at the very least, cease to persist). These are the reparable effects of wrongdoing. Regret, in Gardner's account, has a role to play here. Regret motivates the repair of what has as of yet gone unrepaired. If repair is still possible, then regret serves as extra motivation toward repair.[28] Regret is a painful emotion; "[r]egret is characteristically felt as a particular sort of painful feeling, a pang, a stab, waves of stabs."[29] By repairing the consequences of my wrong, I assuage my painful experience of regret. Regret furnishes an extra reason to repair: a reason to assuage what Bernard Williams famously called agent-regret.[30] Amelie Rorty echoes this moral significance of regret, but also points to its prophylactic benefits, explaining, "[b]ecause it is a painful feeling that agents are motivated to avoid, properly focused regret can conduce to agent responsibility, sensitizing a person to preventative and remedial measures."[31]

Perhaps regret works like this, but for at least one obvious reason,[32] it does not strike me as apt in tort law, namely, that by the time a defendant is under a tort-imposed obligation of reparation, the time for instantaneous emotional responses to wrongs and whatever actions these responses might recommend is long gone. If I truly felt regret when I committed a wrong and felt it painfully enough that it motivated me to reparative action, perhaps we would not need the law of torts at all.[33]

Furthermore, even if we allow that regret has this motivational force, it is not the case that any action must flow from the experience of it.[34] We might suppose, following Rorty, that by acting reparatively we drown out the feeling of regret. As she explains,

> regret is not itself strongly tied to remedial or retributive action… A person who becomes absorbed in trying to remedy the negative consequences of his action rarely *feels* regret, because his thoughts and attention are not on what he did, but on what he is trying to do.[35]

---

[28] ibid 140.

[29] Rorty, "Agent Regret" (n 2) 496.

[30] Williams, "Moral Luck" (n 3). In Gardner's terminology, repair serves a "pain-relief" reason; *FPLPL* (n 8) 141.

[31] Rorty, "Agent Regret" (n 2) 501.

[32] Indeed, this is a reason acknowledged by Gardner in his recognition that repair via the continuity thesis is at best a second-best response to wrongdoing and usually is a third- or even a fourth-best solution.

[33] I tend to disagree with this conclusion regarding the non-necessity of a tort law in a world of morally pure agents. For elaboration on this idea, see Z Sinel, "De-Ciphering Self-Help" (2017) 67 University of Toronto Law Journal 31.

[34] Rorty, "Agent Regret" (n 2) 496.

[35] ibid 502.

THE PLACE OF REGRET IN THE LAW OF TORTS   211

A final reason to doubt regret's relevance with respect to the reparable is that, unlike the law of public wrongs (criminal law), in the sphere of private law, an agent's internal motivation is irrelevant. As Raz correctly points out, regret (agent-regret) is essentially self-referential:[36] "agent-regret relates to one's sense of who one is. When I agent-regret an action of mine I feel bad or sorry about being or having become the kind of person who acted in that way."[37] Tort law is notably indifferent to this kind of soul-searching. The law of torts does not care why the defendant has fulfilled any of his primary legal obligations, or even why he has not.[38] It is even less interested in his reasons for paying a court-ordered remedy. Indeed, the reason the defendant pays compensation to the plaintiff is *not* because the defendant wants to, but because the court orders him to. The very fact that a plaintiff must take a defendant to court in the first place is evidence of the defendant's lack of internal motivation to pay. Tort law cares only about conformity, not compliance.[39] Conformity only requires that one do what the reason recommends, whereas compliance requires that one do what the reason recommends by acting on or for that reason. If it is a part of tort law that regret motivates an agent toward repair, then tort law's doctrines would support the relevance of compliance as opposed to conformity with its obligations. Notably, this is not the tort law we happen to have.

2.2 The irreparable

Although by fulfilling a secondary obligation of paying damages we respond rationally to some of the same reasons we had to perform the primary obligation, Gardner is quick to note that by the lights of the continuity thesis, the amends we make can only ever be incomplete.

> By hypothesis, when the continuity thesis applies, the time for perfect conformity is over. One did not do one's duty. All one can do now is perform another duty, a secondary or fallback duty, fulfillment of which serves the same reasons but allows for only imperfect conformity with them... There is always ... what we might call a "rational remainder," a residue of unconformed-to reason, a remnant of the past that remains stubbornly inaccessible to reparative resolution by the lights of the continuity thesis.[40]

Gardner's response to this rational remainder is the reasonable emotion of regret. Regret (agent-regret) is the apt response to what goes unrepaired.[41]

The irreparable consequences of wrongdoing pose one of the more difficult problems in any justificatory story about tort law and its usual remedy of monetary

---

[36] J Raz, "Agency and Luck" in U Heuer and G Lang (eds), *Luck, Value, and Commitment: Themes from the Ethics of Bernard Williams* (OUP 2012) 140–41.
[37] Raz, "Agency and Luck" (n 36) 140.
[38] *Bradford v Pickles* [1895] AC 587 (HL).
[39] Raz, *Practical Reason and Norms* (n 16) 178–82.
[40] *FPLPL* (n 8) 127. See also, Raz, *Practical* (n 16) 142.
[41] *FPLPL* (n 8) 140.

212   ZOË SINEL

damages. And here we have the "purest case" for regret,[42] the purest because the traditional object of regret is that which is unrepaired. As Williams writes, in some situations, "there is no room for any appropriate action at all. Then only the desire to make reparation remains, with the painful consciousness that nothing can be done about it."[43] Given its lack of practical effect, is regret rational when it is directed toward the irreparable?

Gardner answers, "Yes." Indeed, one still even has a reason to repair, understood as a reason to succeed but with no derivative reason to try: the agent will continue to have a reason that counts in favor of repair but, because repair is impossible, he will have no reason to try to bring this state of affairs about.[44] The regret one feels with respect to the irreparable nonetheless calls out for expression. And this expression involves the practice of apology as well as the institution of general damages.[45] When a defendant pays general damages they express the idea of reparation—the intention of wanting to repair—which, placebo-like, can effectuate a feeling of reparation in the plaintiff. As Gardner explains, in these situations, "[t]he most that is available now ... is sensitivity to a reason that one did not conform to. We can still *respect* the reason ... by holding ourselves to it and feeling the right way about it."[46]

Thus, with respect to the irreparable consequences of his wrongs, the agent's emotional responses, specifically his reaction of regret, perform a significant role in Gardner's theory and his explanation of the logic of general damages. With respect to the irreparable there is nothing that can be *done*; however, this fact itself gives us reason to feel regret—to wish things had been different. The experience of regret does not on its own give a wrongdoer a reason to express it, but, when he does—for example, by apologizing or paying general damages—these expressions signal something crucial about the wrongdoer, namely, that he has the appropriate disposition toward his wrongdoing and its effects. Furthermore, through this expression a certain magic can happen whereby the victim of the wrongdoing might come to *feel as if* the impossible has occurred and the irreparable wrong has been made right.

2.3 The wrong itself

The third potential object for regret is the fact of the wrong itself.[47] This is the regret an agent feels "towards his own past actions," not just toward states of affairs that may be the product of his own or another's or no-one's actions.[48]

---

[42] ibid.

[43] Williams, "Moral Luck" (n 3) 27.

[44] ibid 144–45.

[45] ibid 150.

[46] ibid 151.

[47] It is perhaps controversial to suggest that one can regret a wrong apart from its deleterious consequences. I am not sure what I think about this. It would not make sense, for instance, to regret saving the life of a suicide even though one has committed the wrong of battery. Nonetheless, it does not seem far-fetched to think that, in the composite of a wrong which has deleterious consequences, part of what one regrets is the commission of the wrong itself.

[48] Williams, "Moral Luck" (n 3) 27. Here Williams is drawing a distinction between general regret of the "aw, that's a shame" variety and the more specific form of agent-regret.

Recall that, on Gardner's account, compliance with the secondary obligation can only count as imperfect compliance with the primary obligation.[49] For Gardner, the fact of the unperformed duty—of the wrong itself—is a stubborn remainder, something to be regretted. Contrary to Gardner, I contend that the past wrong casts no shadow—that it is normatively inert. This thesis regarding the normative inertness of wrongs requires some unpacking. Although neither explicitly endorse this thesis, it is implicit in both Arthur Ripstein's and Ernest Weinrib's work. How, Ripstein asks, do "damages really ... make it as if a wrong never happened"?[50] Simple, Weinrib replies, "once the defendant destroys the plaintiff's object, the specific action that the duty requires is different, but it is not a different duty."[51] Normative continuity between wrongdoing and repair is maintained through recognition that the original duty is the same as the remedial duty. The normative relations of right and duty stay the same, although their respective contents are transformed by the breach.[52]

I call this broadly Kantian argument the "unity thesis." Here, the rights and duties of private law are best understood through analysis of a single Kantian tenet—the Universal Principle of Right (UPR)—according to which "[a]ny action is *right* if it can coexist with everyone's freedom in accordance with a universal law, or if on its maxim the freedom of choice of each can coexist with everyone's freedom in accordance with a universal law."[53] Under the UPR, persons are understood as essentially independent—that is, agents whose choices are their own, not those of another. The freedom is negative: freedom *from* the choices of another. When I have a right, that is because my status as a human agent gives me certain claims to be independent of and from your choice and your actions. My right is fundamentally a protection of my own choice, and so, unless *I choose* to waive or abandon it, the right remains intact. So, it just does not make sense to say that when a defendant wrongs a plaintiff, the plaintiff's right goes away.[54] There is no normative change brought about by the violation of a right. It cannot be that by virtue of his wrongdoing a wrongdoer deprives a fellow autonomous agent of her right to independence from his choice.[55] The right remains, although the means to its full realization might be set back. The duty of repair is thus simply the duty to restore these means since it "simply gives [one] back what [one] had all along."[56]

Notably, the original obligation–right relation does all the normative work at both the initial and remedial stages. It is because I continue to have a right to my vase and to my intact arm that I can justly demand compensation from you, the person who has

[49] *FPLPL* (n 8) 127 and 142.

[50] Ripstein, "As If" (n 10) 1958.

[51] EJ Weinrib, "Two Conceptions of Remedies" in CEF Rickett (ed), *Justifying Private Law Remedies* (Hart Publishing 2008) 13.

[52] ibid 12. Also see EJ Weinrib, *The Idea of Private Law* (Harvard University Press 1995) 135.

[53] I Kant, *The Metaphysics of Morals* (1785) (M Gregor tr, CUP 1996) 6:231.

[54] See B Herman, *The Practice of Moral Judgment* (Harvard University Press 1993) 163; J Timmermann, "Kantian Dilemmas? Moral Conflict in Kant's Ethical Theory" (2013) 95(1) Archiv für Geschichte der Philosophie 36, 40–41.

[55] Ripstein, "As If" (n 10) 1978–79. See also A Ripstein, "Civil Recourse and Separation of Wrongs and Remedies" (2011) 39 Florida State University Law Review 163, 177. See also EJ Weinrib, "Civil Recourse and Corrective Justice" (2011) 39 Florida State University Law Review 273, 279.

[56] A Ripstein, *Force and Freedom: Kant's Legal and Political Philosophy* (Harvard University Press 2009) 304.

broken them.[57] In this way, the unity theorists provide us with a straightforward explanation for the connection between rights and remedies: remedies just are different manifestations of the same relation of equal freedom that the right originally was understood to manifest.

One potentially troubling aspect of this account of remedies for wrongs is its annihilation of the relevance of the wrong itself.[58] It appears that, juridically speaking, the unity account is indifferent as between the position of a wrong never having been committed in the first place and a wrong having been committed but subsequently remedied via a court order. Unlike Gardner's view, in which there is a gap between the commission of a wrong and its subsequent repair, a gap that must be bridged through the continuity thesis and responded to with feelings of regret, on the unity account, there is no need to offer any bridge and there is no room for regret because, strictly speaking, there is no gap that could call for either.

Those sympathetic to Gardner's way of looking at things might think that if performing the initial obligation and subsequently performing the reparative obligation were indeed identical—two sides of the same coin—then our moral reactions to them would be equally identical. Yet, plainly, they are not. Someone who performs her obligations immediately is more praiseworthy than someone who breaches and subsequently undertakes reparative action.[59] According to our moral reactions at least, there is a rational remainder between the acts of doing and repairing. And this rational remainder between doing the best and doing the next-best thing is aptly captured by Raz and Gardner as a gap that we *rationally* respond to through the emotion of regret: "Not being able to conform with reason completely is a matter of regret."[60]

The story Gardner tells about reasons and regrets seems sensible. Indeed, as I have just suggested, it almost seems absurd to think, as unity accounts would insist, that wrongs cannot be objects of regret. Gardner arrives at his conclusion about the persistence of wrongs and relevance of regret through his insistence on the separateness of primary and secondary obligations. I will now suggest that this understanding is flawed and, further, that the problems with Gardner's picture of reparation for wrongs begins and ends with his principle for individuating duties. *Pace* Gardner, I argue that the primary obligation does not disappear following its breach. Rather, the primary and secondary duties are just two expressions of the same overarching obligation. If this is right, then there is no wrong left over for regret to take as its object.

In Gardner's view, duties should be individuated according to the *action* that they make mandatory.[61] The reason the primary obligation goes away is that it is now

---

[57] How is it that a money payment can be a replacement for a broken window or a dented car or a ruined sweater? If we think of these sorts of things as entitlements to a certain realm of freedom: I am free from your wrongful breaking of my window, denting of my car, ruining of my sweater, then we can think of money as a replacement for this deprivation of freedom. You cannot have a right to a certain state of affairs continuing, but you do have a right to get back to the state of equal freedom. As the universal means, money allows one to be put in the same position as one was in before the wrong.

[58] I find it intriguing that one of the most common criticisms of Gardner's continuity account is that it fails to give wrongdoing distinctive significance. See SA Smith, "Duties, Liabilities, and Damages" (2011) 125 Harvard Law Review 1727; Tadros, "Secondary Duties" (n 9); JCP Goldberg and BC Zipursky, *Recognizing Wrongs* (Harvard University Press 2020). For the reasons above, I think this criticism misses the mark.

[59] See PF Strawson, "Freedom and Resentment" (1962) 48 Proceedings of the British Academy 1.

[60] Raz "Personal" (n 12) 189. See also Raz *Practical* (n 19) 203.

[61] Gardner, "What is Tort Law For?" (n 12) 29.

THE PLACE OF REGRET IN THE LAW OF TORTS   215

impossible to perform the action that it mandated. This principle of individuation according to actions, without perhaps the assistance of lessons from action theory,[62] produces some odd results.

First, it is uncontroversial that many (if not most) of our duties are duties to perform more than one action. Take, for example, the duty of a bailee. It is his duty to maintain the bailed property in such a way as a reasonable owner would. This duty makes mandatory several different actions to take positive care of the property: not to leave the shed where the property is stored unlocked, not to leave its window open, not to fail to provide it with water and light if the bailed property is a plant, etc. It does not make sense to refer to each of these as a different obligation. They are all grounded in the obligation of being a bailee. Second, we can see that more than one obligation can be the source of an action. Let's say that the provincial government legislated a minimum speed of 40 kilometers per hour (kph) and a maximum of 50 kph. Anyone driving over 50 kph or below 40 kph will run afoul of this new law. Suppose that I also promise my mother that I will not drive over 50 kph. This limit means something to her, apart from the fact that it is the law. My promise to my mother is separate from my obligation to obey the law. Yet Gardner would have to say that the obligations were the same, as they make mandatory the same action, and this cannot be right. We can see that they are distinct if we imagine that the government legislated a new maximum limit of 60 kph while retaining its 40 kph minimum. Although I am no longer bound legally to drive at 50 kph, I am still bound to perform this action by virtue of my promise to my mother. Likewise, if my mother changed her mind and released me from my initial promise and made me make a new promise never to exceed 70 kph, no one would say I am now at liberty to speed.

A further difficulty with Gardner's individuation thesis for obligations lies in how he justifies a different individuation thesis for reasons from that for obligations.[63] In his view, obligations pick out a particular action that must be performed, while reasons indicate a more general action that can be conformed to in several different ways. Is this right? Yes and no. What Gardner means is that obligations serve two roles in providing reasons for action. First, as obligations, they make the act obligatory. If I have an obligation to φ and X-ing contributes to φ-ing, then I ought to X. Second, as operative reasons, obligations generate other reasons to perform actions that contribute to my ultimately φ-ing. These actions on their own are not severally obligatory; however, they derive their justifications from an obligatory reason for action, the obligation.

The double role of obligations in practical reasoning, however, fails to save his individuation thesis for obligations. It is unclear, in other words, why a secondary (remedial) obligation is not just one of the further instrumental or constitutive actions called for by the primary obligation. Given my primary obligation to take my children to the beach today, it is not clear why it is not the case that taking my children to the beach tomorrow given the additional fact that today has passed is not just an auxiliary reason

---

[62] Perhaps a distinction between act-tokens and act-types could help. Act-types can be understood as more general descriptions of actions, while act-tokens are the particular acts. Take the example of "A repaying her debt to B" as an act-type. A may repay this debt in a number of different ways—that is, by performing a number of different act-tokens, such as: "repaying B immediately," "repaying the debt in cash," etc.

[63] Gardner, "What is Tort Law For?" (n 12) 31.

helping me identify how I can best (in light of the changed circumstances) satisfy my operative reason (my promise). Saying that each makes a different action mandatory is unhelpful insofar as any obligation makes various actions mandatory, although all can be described under the single action of "perform your obligation."

A further, perhaps more telling, problem with Gardner's account concerns how the force of the reasons for the original obligation—those which make it obligatory— transmit this normative pressure to the remedial obligation, making it obligatory, for the same reasons, but yet as a different obligation. What makes the original duty obligatory is relatively clear—for example, it could be the fact that you made a promise— but it is unclear what grounds the remedial duty for Gardner. We cannot say that the non-normative fact of one's breach generates a (normative) reason like a remedial obligation. A plausible answer to this puzzle of continuity emerges from Gardner's coauthored work with Timothy Macklem. According to Gardner and Macklem, when a mandatory reason is not complied with, what sticks around is the exclusionary force of the reason. It is now no longer a reason to exclude reasons that count against performance of the action it mandates, but a reason to exclude reasons simply to forget about its breach:

> Where one fails to do as a mandatory reason would have one do, however, the enduring force of the reason is different. It continues to be a mandatory reason even after one's failure. Just as some reasons not to perform the required action were excluded by virtue of the fact that the action was required, so some reasons to forget all about one's non-performance of the action afterwards are excluded.[64]

For Gardner, an obligation consists of two parts. The first is a straightforward reason to perform the action that the obligation mandates. I have an obligation not to steal your bicycle. The first part of the obligation is a reason telling me not to steal your bicycle. It could in turn give rise to various other reasons that would assist or enable conformity with this first-order reason, for example if I were tempted daily to liberate your bicycle from your unlocked garage on my way to work, this temptation would provide me with a reason to choose a different route, perhaps to buy you a lock, etc. In addition to this reason not to steal your bicycle, an obligation consists of a second part, a second-order reason, a reason not to act for certain reasons that might counsel against acting on the first-order reason. That I do not have my own bicycle and that I enjoy the feeling of wind in my hair as I merrily bike around, strictly speaking, are reasons for me to "borrow" your bicycle. The reason not to steal your bicycle is *obligatory* precisely because it pre-empts these reasons. I cannot act on these reasons and consider my action rational. Such reasons, in other words, are excluded. They do not enter the balancing scales when I am figuring out what to do about my bikeless state.

If I breach my obligation and abscond with your bicycle, it is clearly now impossible for me to conform to the first-order reason. Having stolen it, I can no longer *not* have stolen it. But what about the second part of the obligation? What about its exclusionary force? On Gardner's analysis, we might say that it is precisely the exclusionary

---

[64] J Gardner and T Macklem, "Reasons" in J Coleman and S Shapiro (eds), *The Oxford Handbook of Jurisprudence and Philosophy of Law* (OUP 2002) 467.

force of the obligation that sticks around, excluding reasons to treat the obligation's violation as just crying over spilled milk. The first-order reason to perform the action is discharged by the breach. One can no longer do what the obligation mandated; however, the exclusionary reason (the second prong of the protected reason—reasons not to act on reasons contrary to the performance of the first-order reason) sticks around. It is not discharged. What persists then is the deontic structure, or form, of the obligation. That an obligation consists of two types of reason, a first-order reason to X and a second-order reason *not* to act on reasons *not* to X, accounts for the continuity between primary and secondary obligations. The first-order part of the obligation is sometimes discharged, but its exclusionary force sticks around. The rationale for the primary obligation does come into play, but only at the stage of determining the appropriate content of the secondary obligation. Thus, the structure provides the normative force, while the rationale gives evidence for the appropriate content.

This gloss on Gardner's continuity thesis is inspired by Gardner's scholarship, but it is not clear that he would have endorsed it.[65] In Gardner's view, it is not the second-order reason—the reason to exclude other reasons from consideration, including the reason to ignore the reason as obligatory—that sticks around, but rather it is the rationale for the original obligation that remains. Whatever considerations in the world that served as reasons for my initial obligation are what continue and serve to ground my reparative obligation following my failure to satisfy my original obligation.

To see the problem with Gardner's solution to the continuity puzzle more clearly, let's return to the promise example. If I am explaining to another why I am taking my children to the beach tomorrow, I might say because I failed to do as I originally promised. If, however, I am pushed to explain why failing to do as I promised is normatively significant, all I am left with is the explanation that *I made a promise*—that is, the original obligation. Hence, if we trace the normative force back to the original obligation, then Gardner's view appears to collapse into an endorsement of the unity thesis, where the only relevant normative feature is and remains that of the original obligation.

One could respond on Gardner's behalf that because, for him, rights are based on protected interests, this collapse is overstated. The obligation is based on underlying reasons and, given the change in circumstances, these reasons can give rise to new obligations. I have certain reasons not to take your tuque: it is winter, and you need it to keep you warm or it possesses a certain resale value, and so on. Once I take it, these reasons cannot demand that I not take it, *because I have already taken it*. In other words, they no longer serve the role of guiding my actions. Instead, these same reasons tell me to give the tuque back. There is, as such, a difference compared to the unity view, according to which I must give the tuque back and I must not take it in the first place *because it is yours*. Nonetheless, Gardner might say that the reasons stay the same, even though he identifies different reasons as relevant than would a proponent of the unity thesis. As such, his continuity still relies on a type of identity. The reason I must give the tuque back, for Gardner, is based on the same rationale for not taking it

---

[65] Note Steel's rejection of something like this view as amenable to Gardner's in Steel, "Compensation and Continuity" (n 21) 259. Although he appears to be open to this solution in J Gardner, "Damages Without Duty" (2019) 69 University of Toronto Law Journal 412.

218 ZOË SINEL

in the first place, although he will call it a different obligation because it is impossible to be guided by the actions mandated by the initial obligation (not to take the tuque).

But, in fact, the reasons are not the same. Gardner, though acknowledging the "extra reason" provided by the fact of the obligation's breach, ignores that this fact in his account changes the set of reasons that potentially grounds the new remedial obligation.[66] If he were to say that the breach is the fact that provides the justification for the obligation, he risks endorsing an independent principle of compensation—a principle that is engaged whenever there is a breach of an obligation that requires repair—and, thereby, abandoning his solution to the puzzle of continuity.

To save Gardner's account from the discontinuity inherent in accounts that rely on an independent principle of repair, perhaps it is worthwhile to explore again whether the continuity thesis can be absorbed into the unity account. At first glance, unity theorists like Weinrib and continuity theorists like Gardner appear to hold starkly contrasting positions. To illustrate:

> *Weinrib*: The defendant's breach of the duty not to interfere with the embodiment of the plaintiff's right does not, of course, bring the duty to an end, for if it did, the duty would—absurdly—be discharged by its breach.[67]

> *Gardner*: [Following its breach] [m]y original obligation is, we should now be able to agree, discharged (put to an end) by its breach.[68]

Closer analysis of the terms "obligation" and "duty," however, reveals that this contrast might be overstated. Weinrib relies on a Kantian understanding of duty and obligation, according to which duty is the "matter of obligation" while obligation is "the necessity of a free action under a categorical imperative of reason."[69] This means that the duty is a *specific action* required in order not to violate the obligation. There can be many ways to discharge (and to violate) one's obligations, but the fulfilment of different duties (understood now as different specific actions) does not entail that there are a corresponding number of different obligations. Obligations are not individuated according to the action that they make mandatory, *pace* Gardner, for they can make multiple actions mandatory (ie create multiple duties) but remain the same obligation. Gardner, notably, refuses to draw any real distinction between duties and obligations, but it is clear that what he terms "obligation" is what Kant and Weinrib would refer to as a "duty." This might mean that there actually is no dispute here. The difference lies only in the definition of the terms "obligation" and "duty." Perhaps, Weinrib and Gardner agree. Both Weinrib and Gardner think that different acts are required before and after the breach. But they use the word "obligation" differently and so Weinrib thinks that the same obligation covers both actions—although they are different duties—and Gardner thinks they are different obligations. While this is an appealing

---

[66] In Gardner's words, "the extra reason for action that consists in the very fact that it was obligatory not to have done what one did." Gardner, "What is Tort Law For?" (n 12) 35.
[67] Weinrib, *The Idea of Private Law* (n 52) 135.
[68] Gardner, "What is Tort Law For?" (n 12) 32.
[69] Kant, *The Metaphysics of Morals* (n 53) 6:222.

compromise, as I will argue in section 3, the difference between Weinrib and Gardner is more than terminological.

To summarize, the first puzzle of reparations for wrongs, the puzzle of continuity, is only a puzzle if you think, as Gardner does, that the primary obligation exits the normative playing field after its breach. On this account, you must explain how a *new* obligation responds to a discharged obligation. I have suggested that this is an inaccurate picture of private law's remedial obligations. The so-called secondary obligation does not arise phoenix-like out of the ashes of the primary obligation's breach, but normatively speaking is the same obligation. Now, the problem here is that we seem to be departing from some of our commonsense intuitions regarding the significance of wrongs. On this view, it is almost as if they have none. Wrongs cast no shadow, they leave no remainder and thus, I suggest, leave no space for regret. I think this is the correct conclusion, but we must acknowledge that this runs against certain fundamental human psychological intuitions regarding the nature of wrongdoing and our moral emotional reactions to it.

3. No Regrets (in the Law of Torts)

Thus far we have seen that regret is irrelevant with respect to the reparable, the irreparable, and the wrong itself—the three putative objects of regret in Gardner's response to the puzzle of reparation for wrongs. It is irrelevant with respect to the reparable because the defendant's motivations are equally irrelevant. It is irrelevant with respect to the irreparable (both the irreparable consequences of the wrong as well as the wrong itself) because, contrary to our intuitions, legal wrongs leave nothing behind for regret to take as its object. In this final section, I want to explain, on the one hand, why, nonetheless, we might still find the picture Gardner offers so appealing, and, on the other, to persuade you that, despite this appeal, there is no room for regret in the law of torts. One way to illustrate this point is by looking at a place where regret does have a role: in situations when one cannot do what one has a non-legal obligation to do because one has another conflicting (non-legal) obligation. This is the situation of conflicting imperfect obligations. There is no better place to analyze such a situation than the moral philosophy of Kant.

Kant famously or, as many would see it, infamously, stands as the moral philosopher for whom conflicts of obligations are impossible.[70] If obligations are by definition that which are necessary, then it cannot be that an agent can have an obligation to X and an obligation not to X.[71] When imperfect obligations conflict, according to Kant, it is not the case that "the stronger obligation takes precedence ... but that the stronger *ground of obligation* prevails."[72] When imperfect duties conflict, the ground for the unfulfilled obligation does not disappear.[73] To borrow an example from Jens Timmermann, if

---

[70] Indeed, Bernard Williams' pivotal work on agent-regret takes this as his point of criticism of Kantian moral theory: the fact that we feel regret undermines a theory like Kant's in which, allegedly, regret has no role to play. See S Wolf, "The Moral of Moral Luck" in C Calhoun (ed), *Setting the Moral Compass: Essays by Women Philosophers* (OUP 2003).

[71] Kant, *The Metaphysics of Morals* (n 53) 6:224.

[72] ibid.

[73] Timmermann, "Kantian Dilemmas?" (n 54) at 56, fn 59.

I have an imperfect obligation of gratitude toward my benefactor, but I am unable to repay him because of the desperate poverty of my parents, the ground of the imperfect obligation to my benefactor remains despite the obligation's unrealizability. After deliberation, I come to the determination that the only obligation that applies to me is my filial duty, but this does not mean that I am free to ignore my yet-to-be-realizable and yet-to-be-realized obligation to my benefactor. If we take a closer look at how regret arises here, we can see what a close fit Gardner's theory has with the situation of conflicting ethical duties.

According to Barbara Herman, the ground of the obligation that Kant refers to are facts of a certain sort. What grounds the obligation of beneficence, on Herman's account, is the "fact that we are dependent beings, a fact that is salient in an agent's circumstances of action through the claim of need."[74] Because the grounds are facts and because facts cannot conflict, grounds also cannot conflict. Rather the conflict occurs "in the agent" when there are two grounds, and she cannot act for both. Situations in which grounds conflict call for deliberation and the product of deliberation is an obligation.[75] When conflict happens in the agent in this way, the question is what happens to the ground that the agent could not act in favor of? According to O'Neill, "[u]nmet *rationes obligandi* are not simply wiped off the map, as (on some readings) unmeetable prima facie duties are wiped away: they maintain their claims on us."[76] And this claim is meted out in "the price of unmet demands in residues and remainders such as regret, agent regret, and remorse."[77] Thus, regret's role is to show the agent's commitment is genuine in that she was appropriately committed to the moral ground.

What is interesting and important for my purposes is that Gardner seems to think of the duties and rights of tort law as following this pattern. Just like in situations of putative conflicting obligations, the wrongdoer in Gardner's theory is left full of regret and the primary significance of this emotion is that it reveals the agent's appropriate disposition toward the obligation to which he failed to conform. Recall Gardner's analysis of the practical consequences of irreparable wrongdoing: "The most that is available now ... is sensitivity to a reason that one did not conform to. We can still *respect* the reason ... even in our nonconformity with it, by holding ourselves to it and feeling the right way about it."[78] As well, on both the Kantian account of ethical dilemmas and Gardner's account of tort's breached primary obligations, it is the obligating reason, not the obligation, that sticks around demanding conformity. In the Kantian picture, the reason has yet to become a full-fledged obligation through the process of deliberation and as such has not yet been satisfied. In Gardner's picture, the obligation disappears because it is no longer realizable.[79] It is a mistake, however,

---

[74] Herman, *The Practice of Moral Judgment* (n 54) 167.

[75] ibid 168.

[76] O O'Neill, "Instituting Principles Between Duty and Action" (1997) 36 Supp Southern Journal of Philosophy 79, 92.

[77] ibid. See also Timmermann, "Kantian Dilemmas?" (n 54) 58: "Because the weaker ground continues to make its force felt I will regret that I *had to do* as I was morally bound to do."

[78] *FPLPL* (n 8) 150.

[79] For a similar story, see Timmermann, "Kantian Dilemmas?" (n 54) 56–57.

for Gardner to use as his model for tort law's remedial obligations the Kantian picture of conflicting ethical obligations. In so doing, Gardner affixes his analysis to duties of virtue, not duties of right—to duties that are defeasible, that require judgment to apply, and that are capable of conflict. Conflict of this sort is not possible for duties of right.[80]

Gardner is right about regret as a moral feeling that responds to our inability to do as the general moral rule requires but is wrong about its place in law and its relevance. Regret, as Katherine Gasdaglis recently and persuasively argues, reveals that we manifest the appropriate respect for the (moral) law, that we are appropriately morally constituted.[81] It is a feeling, however, that is irrelevant with respect to our performance of and conformity with the legal obligations of tort law.

4. Conclusion

I would like to close this chapter with what might seem to some like a counterintuitive notion, namely that it is the very irrelevance of regret in the law of torts that creates the possibility of regret. I call this the shadow theory of emotion in tort law.

We can see how the shadow theory works if we imagine a world in which regret did matter for tort law's remedies. Imagine that the government passed the *Regret Act*. Pursuant to this statute, if defendants revealed sufficient and appropriate regret for their wrongs, their damages could be reduced. Likewise, if they failed to show regret, damages could be increased, and perhaps even punitive damages would be made available. What kind of world is this? It is a world in which law mandates a particular emotional response. It is a world, moreover, that flows from the logic of a theory like that of Gardner, according to which there is no hard and fast line between private law and personal life. If regret is relevant for private law in the way that Gardner suggests, then it might be unobjectionable to have the presence or absence of regret entail legal consequences. I suggest that we might be loath and should be loath to endorse this kind of world.

Moreover, legislation of this sort would be self-defeating. If we want to encourage true expressions of regret, these cannot be externally enforced. By definition, authentic regret comes from within the agent (albeit an agent shaped by external social and legal forces), not from without. Mandating regret is therefore impossible; an emotional response cannot be coerced or legislated.[82] Tort law's exclusion of regret, in sum, gives regret a place to operate in our non-legal interpersonal interactions.

---

[80] ibid 44–45. O'Neill, "Instituting Principles Between Duty and Action" (n 76) 86–87.

[81] K Gasdaglis, "Moral Regret and Moral Feeling(s)" (2021) 64 Inquiry: An Interdisciplinary Journal of Philosophy 424.

[82] I leave to one side the issue of whether regret might be appropriate and legally salient in other legal contexts, that is, contexts outside of private law. For instance, it is common to take a criminal's regret over her crime into account at the sentencing stage of a criminal trial. If criminal punishment is justified on the basis of an individual's willed (that is, subjectively intended) violation of the state's law, then it is perhaps unproblematic that the criminal's mental state is brought back into play in sentencing determinations. Further analysis of this issue, however, lies outside this chapter's scope.

In this chapter, my aim was to shed light on Gardner's contributions to private law theory with respect to his solution to the problem of reparations for wrongs and the role of the emotion of regret within this problem. At this stage, I am content merely to signal that the exclusion of emotions in tort law might be part of a larger picture of our moral and social interpersonal lives.

13

Primary Duty = Secondary Duty?

Claudio Michelon[*]

One of John Gardner's most salient contributions to private law theory is his proposal and defense of the continuity thesis.[1] The continuity thesis addresses one of the enduring questions in the field: what is the relationship between the primary duty and the secondary (or remedial) duty in the law of torts?[2] The continuity thesis is not, of course, the only "live" attempt to tackle this problem, and, in fact, Gardner's claim stands in a complex relation with its closest rival, the identity thesis.[3] That complex relationship is not yet fully understood and, as a result, the arguments for and against each thesis are muddled to the point that it is difficult to see which advantages either of them might have over its rival.[4] My primary objective here is to clarify each thesis, defend each against objections that have been leveled against them, and, at the end, present reasons why the continuity thesis offers a better framework within which to understand the relationship between primary and remedial duty. I start by discussing the deceptively credible arguments for and against the identity thesis. Once these arguments are laid to rest, we can have a better sense of what the dispute is really about, and of the (limited, but significant) role that each thesis plays in addressing what I will call below the "normative question." That, in turn, should help us see the *type* of argument that is capable of settling the matter, as well as the *type* of argument

---

[*] I would like to thank comments on earlier drafts at the conference that gave origin to this volume, and at the Edinburgh Centre for Legal Theory, in particular, Amalia Amaya, Antony Duff, Cécile Fabre, Euan MacDonald, George Dick, Hanoch Dagan, James Wolffe, John Oberdiek, Martin Kelly, Haris Psarras, Sandy Steel, and Zoë Sinel.

[1] J Gardner, "What is Tort Law For? The Place of Corrective Justice" (2011) 30 Law and Philosophy 1. Page numbers are for the republication of this article in J Gardner, *Torts and Other Wrongs* (OUP 2019) ("*TAOW*") ch 2. Gardner adds detail to his conception of the continuity thesis in his *From Personal Life to Private Law* (OUP 2018) ("*FPLPL*") 125–28. This addition shows that there are more than one continuity theses and that what can be said in favor of one version might not apply to other versions of it. I will return to this point in the last section of this chapter.

[2] Stephen R Perry was not the first to formulate this question, but he has presented it particularly clearly in his "The Moral Foundations of Tort Law" (1992) 77 Iowa Law Review 449, 479.

[3] Whose best-known contemporary defense is put forward by Ernest Weinrib. The claim goes back to Weinrib, *The Idea of Private Law* (Harvard University Press 1995) 135, but is more thoroughly developed in E Weinrib, *Corrective Justice* (OUP 2012) 81ff. See also A Ripstein, *Private Wrongs* (Harvard University Press 2016) ch 8. Further afield, there are other intriguing attempts address this problem, such as Goldberg and Zipursky's attempt to relate primary and secondary duties via a Hohfeldian power that arises from the violation of the first and allows the victim (and court) to create the second; see, for instance, JCP Goldberg and BC Zipursky, *Recognizing Wrongs* (Harvard University Press 2020) 163.

[4] Sandy Steel, in his enlightening discussion of the matter, sees no advantage in what he calls "reasons continuity" *vis-à-vis* "duty continuity." (S Steel, "Compensation and Continuity" (2020) 26 Legal Theory 256). While I accept that neither thesis can provide a complete answer to the normative question and that both theses provide credible ways to frame substantive arguments that can bear on that question, I also believe reasons continuity to be superior to duty continuity, for reasons presented below.

Claudio Michelon, *Primary Duty = Secondary Duty?* In: *Private Law and Practical Reason.* Edited by: Haris Psarras and Sandy Steel, Oxford University Press. © Claudio Michelon 2023. DOI: 10.1093/oso/9780192857330.003.0013

that can complement the general framing provided by either thesis in offering a complete solution for the normative question. With that in place I argue that, against the background of the distinction between, on the one hand, reasons for action *simpliciter* and, on the other hand, duties, the continuity thesis is superior to the identity thesis, as it can deliver all the benefits the latter, while avoiding its handicaps.

1. Primary Duties, Secondary Duties, and Their Identity

Much of tort law is structured around the fact that the breach of a primary duty (such as the duty I have not to drive over the speed limit or the doctor's duty to provide certain information to her patient) gives rise to a secondary duty (typically, but not exclusively, the duty to pay a certain amount of money to someone as compensation). In fact, for some, all tort law is structured around this fact. The norms that constitute the positive law of torts take the breach of duty (perhaps combined with other conditions, such as the occurrence of damage) to be a sufficient condition for the existence of the secondary duty.

Consequently, purely as a matter of the positive law, the relation between breach of primary duty and the rise of a corresponding secondary (or remedial) duty is one in which the former is a sufficient condition (or part of a conjunction of facts that are, taken together, a sufficient condition) for the latter. But that is not, of course, what either the continuity thesis or the identity thesis is trying to shed light on to. The question they are trying to address (or, perhaps more accurately, to frame) is why the breach of the primary duty *should* be at all relevant for the existence of a secondary duty. Call it the "normative question."

A satisfactory answer to that question would mean progress in two related ways. First, and more obviously, it would shed light on the reasons that justify the existence of secondary duties, and clarity about those reasons would, in turn, allow for a better understanding of how they relate to other reasons bearing on the existence of such duties and on the legal regime that regulates them.

The identity thesis offers an elegant and deceptively simple frame within which to address the normative question. According to the identity thesis, a primary duty d is identical to the secondary duty that results from the violation of d. In other words, the primary duty and the remedial duty that ensues from the breach of the primary duty *are one and the same duty*. Weinrib ascribes this thesis to Blackstone and, in fact, uses the latter's words to offer a formulation of the identity thesis: "the plaintiff's injured right and the right restored by the defendant are the same right or its equivalent."[5] Weinrib clearly does not take the connector "or" as marking a disjunction but, instead, as expressing a conjunction.[6] Leaving aside the complications that would result from taking "its equivalent" to be a disjunct, the identity thesis can be more simply

---

[5] Weinrib, *Corrective Justice* (n 3) 91–92, citing 4 Bl Comm 9.

[6] Taking the "or" as a disjunction would dramatically weaken the identity thesis, as it would imply that the secondary duty does not need to be the same as the primary duty, but only, in some way, its equivalent. The latter, formulated in this rather generic manner, would not be particularly controversial and, in fact, it would be compatible with the continuity thesis (a compatibility that both Weinrib and Gardner reject).

stated as the claim that "having a duty to φ is *the same* as having a duty to remedy the failure to φ."

An answer to the problem of how to frame the normative question follows. If the differences between primary duty and secondary duty are only apparent and, thus, underneath appearances, they are *the same* duty, having a primary duty to, say, drive carefully, is *the same* as having a secondary duty to pay damages for not having driven carefully. Fulfilling the remedial duty would be just another way to fulfil the primary duty.[7] The answer to the normative question of why the breach of the primary duty should be relevant to the existence of the secondary duty appears to be simple: if my duty can be fulfilled by performing either of two actions (the one specified by the primary duty and the one specified by the remedial duty), the impossibility of fulfilling the duty by performing the action specified in what legal doctrine calls the primary duty leaves as the only possibility of fulfilling that duty the performance of the action specified in what the doctrine refers to as the remedial or secondary duty. If one had a duty to do either φ or φ*, and it is no longer possible to do φ, then the only way to fulfil the duty is to do φ*.

In spite of the crispness and elegance of its solution to the normative problem, the identity thesis goes against an intuitively appealing conception of how to individuate obligations. According to this conception, duties should be individuated by the actions they make obligatory (call it "action-individuation").[8] The action of driving carefully and the actions by which I might make amends for not having driven carefully (say, paying some money into your bank account) are different actions. That is true for all actions specified by primary duties *vis-à-vis* all actions specified by the corresponding secondary duties. So, if action-individuation is true, no primary duty is identical to the corresponding secondary duty: they are necessarily different. Having initially appeared to subscribe to the identity thesis,[9] John Gardner later raised precisely this objection against it.[10]

If the identity of two obligatory actions were indeed a necessary condition for duties to be identical and if, as a consequence, the identity thesis turned out to be false, the issue of the relationship between primary and secondary duties would remain open. So, it is not surprising that Gardner thought it important to object to the identity thesis before putting forward his own attempt to tackle the framing of the normative question (his version of the continuity thesis).

---

[7] Complications arise to the identity thesis if one wishes (as its proponents appear to do) to sustain both that (i) they are *identical*, and that the (ii) fulfillment of the primary duty is preferable to the fulfilment of the secondary duty. If they are identical, why would it be preferable not to wrong someone rather than wronging them and then paying compensation? I take this to be the point that Zipursky was trying to make in BC Zipursky, "Rights, Wrongs, and Recourse in the Law of Torts" (1998) 51 Vanderbilt Law Review 1, 73–4. I cannot address this question here, but Weinrib's answer to this challenge, in Weinrib, *Corrective Justice* (n 3) 93, needs further motivation, for it is not clear how a Kantian framework could explain the relevance of the presumably accidental (or at least, not substantial) differences between primary and remedial duty.

[8] Action-individuation is not only intuitively appealing. It has been assumed as true in contemporary works on the metaphysics of duty (in particular, P Vranas, "The Individuation of Obligations" (unpublished manuscript with the author)).

[9] J Gardner "Wrongs and Faults" (2005) 59 The Review of Metaphysics 95, 106.

[10] Gardner, *TAOW* (n 1) 55–56.

226   CLAUDIO MICHELON

For all its appeal, however, it is not clear that action-individuation is the right way to individuate duties. Weinrib objects that this way to individuate obligations is both under-inclusive and over-inclusive.[11] In spite of the fact that these two objections are not ultimately convincing, understanding why they fail will help us see that the meta-physics of duty individuation cannot provide the silver bullet with which to defeat the identity thesis. If the identity thesis is to be objected to, we need a more robust conception of duty individuation.

The under-inclusiveness charge departs from the claim that one can have multiple duties to perform the same action. For instance, one could have a contractual duty toward a certain person not to reveal confidential information to third parties while simultaneously having a statutory duty toward the same person not to reveal the same confidential information to the same third parties. But if duties are individuated by the action each makes obligatory, there could be no *two* such duties. The contractual and the statutory duties would be one and the same and the apparent existence of two duties would not correspond to normative reality. This might strike one (and it certainly struck Weinrib)[12] as implausible. In fact, there are good (albeit not conclusive) reasons to think that there are two different duties here. For starters, there would be two separate regimes of consequences resulting, respectively, from contractual rules and statutory/common law rules. Furthermore, these duties (or at least the diverse regime of legal consequences that results from their breach) seem to be subject to different vicissitudes. One might disappear (say, by a time bar) while the other remains.

However, while that might be the case, the existence of two separate duties in such situations does not deliver a killer blow to action-individuation. Peter Vranas has distinguished between what he called "coarse-grained" conceptions of duty individuation, which take the distinctiveness of the obligatory action as both necessary and sufficient to individuate a duty, and "fine-grained" conceptions of duty individuation, according to which the distinctiveness of the action is sufficient, but not necessary, to individuate duties.[13] In fine-grained conceptions of duty individuation the duty's distinctiveness can *also* be a function of some other property not shared by the duties such as, for instance, their respective normative grounds, or the beneficiary of the duty. In such fine-grained conceptions of duty individuation, the same "modular" action (in our example, not revealing confidential information) could be required by different duties, if each of those duties were to possess a different ground (in our example, the contract and the statute).[14] This more modest variety of action-individuation, which

---

[11] Weinrib, *Corrective Justice* (n 3) 89–91. The labels "under-inclusive" and "over-inclusive" are not Weinrib's, and are adopted simply for ease of reference.

[12] ibid 91.

[13] Vranas, "The Individuation of Obligations" (n 8), who, having made the distinction, goes on to defend a coarse-grained version of duty individuation. The distinction is not formulated by Vranas in exactly the way I presented it above.

[14] There is widespread consensus among private law theorists that primary duties in tort law must be fine-grained. For instance, most agree that they should be specified also by the identity of the person benefiting from the duty. See, for instance, Ripstein, *Private Wrongs* (n 3) 3–4; Weinrib, *The Idea of Private Law* (n 3) 114–26. But there is no reason to believe that a conception of duty individuation that allows for a richer array of criteria of individuation (in addition to action-individuation) couldn't be shared by someone who, like Gardner, endorses action-individuation.

takes the distinctiveness of the obligatory action as sufficient (but not necessary) to differentiate duties, is not vulnerable to the over-inclusiveness objection, and if it turns out to be true, it would be sufficient to disprove the identity thesis. So, we are back where we started. But perhaps action-individuation, even in its modest variety, should be dismissed for the diametrically opposed reason.

The over-inclusiveness charge against action-individuation of duties is grounded on the claim that there are at least some duties that can be fully discharged by the performance of different actions.[15] So, for instance, if I have an obligation to pay a certain amount of money to you (say £100), I might do so by handing you a check, by handing you cash, by making a deposit into your bank account, *inter alia*. Some of those actions can be even further specified (I can fulfil the duty in cash by giving you ten £10 notes, or by five £20 notes). If that is correct, there are multiple actions that can correspond to the fulfilment of the *same* duty. Thus, defining the identity of a duty by reference to one particular action (as action-individuation proposes) would leave an important remainder: it would leave unexplained the fact that the performance of multiple actions could count as a fulfilment of the same duty. If each duty is individuated by a single action, how is that possible? Would there be multiple, perhaps alternative, duties? But that would be a very cumbersome way to conceive of legal duties. Even the action of paying £100 in five £20 notes can be further broken down into an incalculable number of ways.

This objection is more demanding than it would appear at first sight. To see why, notice that action-individuation is not vulnerable to the over-inclusiveness objection if each of the different actions that counts as the fulfilment of the duty could also count as the action that individuates the duty. So, handing you five £20 notes (under a set of specified circumstances) can also *count as* "paying you £100." What individuates the duty would indeed be an action, but there are many types of actions (under certain descriptions) that, in a specified set of circumstances, also *count as* the action that specify the duty: describing an action as "handing you five £20 notes" *is* not incompatible with describing it as "paying you £100" (in the right specific context).

So, for the objection to work it must be the case that the disjunctive set of actions that count as fulfilling a certain duty cannot be each also described as different ways in which to perform the action that individuates the duty. So, it cannot be the case that the action of "giving you five £20 notes" and "giving you ten £10 notes" could both be described as "paying you £100" (in the right specific context). But that seems implausible. I might show love to my wife by buying her flowers and by buying taking on by myself all the housework we used to share. Both actions can be appropriately described as showing love to my wife. So, again, action-individuation remains a plausible conception of how to individuate duties.

The discussion above allows us to see, at least in outline, how a conception of duty individuation that is neither reliant on actions nor incompatible with the identity thesis might look. A duty might be individuated purely on its grounds (call it "ground-individuation") and indeed, a ground-centered conception of duty individuation appears to be what Weinrib, Ripstein, and others have in mind. The ground that

---

[15] Weinrib, *Corrective Justice* (n 3) 91.

228   CLAUDIO MICHELON

identifies the duty is, presumably, what is required by corrective justice in an instant case. As Weinrib puts it:

> the right and its correlative duty continue to exist with different specific content before and after the injustice. Underlying the succession of specific characteristics of the right and its correlative duty is the relationship that the parties have through the plaintiff's connection with the object of the right. That relationship remains identical throughout the metamorphosis that the defendant's injustice has wrought in the object of the right. To put it in familiar philosophical terms, the diachronic identity of the right is merely a juridical exemplification of the category of substance as that which persists through change: during the legal relationship the existence of the right remains constant, but the way in which the right exists changes.[16]

This common ground implies something along the lines of the following disjunction: "either comply with primary duty to ϕ in situation S *or* comply with remedial duty to ϕ^* in situation S*." Hence, if the obligation's normative "ground" is the touchstone of duty individuation, the duty to ϕ and the duty to ϕ^* would in fact be one and the same duty, as they possess the same ground. The appearance of there being different duties would then be an illusion engendered by an intuitively appealing, but ultimately misguided, conception of duty individuation (ie action-individuation).

Thus, it would appear that ground-individuation can be formulated without any obvious obscurity or contradiction. Of course, this does not give us a reason to prefer it to fine-grained action-individuation. Weinrib's argument for favoring it contains a number of moving parts and, in the next section, I will try to render it as clearly as I can. With that in place we would be in a better position to evaluate the identity thesis (that relies on ground-individuation) and its relative advantages and disadvantages in relation to a version of the continuity thesis (that does not).

Before moving on to discuss Weinrib's argument for why ground-individuation should be favored as an explanatory template for the relation between primary duty and secondary duty, it is important to ask which type of problem the individuation of obligation is. The intuition on which the plausibility of action-individuation lies could be reasonably conceived as a metaphysical intuition. One might think that, at the metaphysical ground floor, duties are individuated purely on the basis of the actions they mandate, and all other properties they might possess (their ground, their addressee, etc) are simply add-ons to a more primitive structure that is identified purely on the basis of the actions commanded.

There are *prima facie* good reasons to support such a metaphysical conception of duty individuation. For starters, irrespective of any other property a duty might be thought to possess, a duty is always going to be a duty to act in a particular sort of way. It is true that the attachment between a duty and the action (or actions) mandated could be a mere necessary accident, not the distinctive mark that individuates the duty. However, a theory that individuated duties solely on the basis of the action they mandate would be conceptually simpler than one that had relied on additional basic

---

[16] Weinrib, *Corrective Justice* (n 3) 92.

features (like fine-grained duty individuation) and more consilient than one that left the connection between duty and action unexplained (like ground-individuation).[17] This would be a reason to prefer a coarse action centered theory of duty individuation to both fine-grained action-centered and ground-centered conceptions of duty individuation: it is simpler, as it requires less conceptual scaffolding.

But let us assume for a moment that (i) one such metaphysical conception of duty individuation is indeed simpler; and that (ii) simplicity and consilience are, in the absence of countervailing considerations, good reasons to favor one theory over its rivals;[18] and/or that (iii) one of the other interesting contemporary attempts to justify coarse-grained metaphysical conceptions of duty individuation (that are not solely predicated on consilience and/or simplicity) is correct.[19]

It would still be worth asking whether a conjectural victory by coarse action-individuation at the metaphysical ground floor would appease Weinrib, Ripstein, or, for that matter, Gardner. Should their beliefs about duty individuation in connection to the particular context of the normative question concerning the relation between primary and secondary duties in tort law yield to an eventual metaphysical triumph by coarse-grained individuation? Should they abandon their beliefs on, respectively, ground-based individuation and fine-grained action-centered individuation, so as to fall in line with coarse-grained individuation?

I believe not, for in spite of the metaphysical flavor of the intuitions that favor action-individuation and in spite of the fact that the rival theses are sometimes expressed in metaphysical vocabulary and tone,[20] the relevant disagreement between those who defend action-centered individuation and those who defend fine-grained individuation of duties, within the context of explaining the connection between primary and secondary duties, is not best understood as a disagreement about the metaphysics of duty (at least not *primarily* about it). In order to see why, let me now turn to Weinrib's argument for the identity thesis and the ground-based individuation of duties.

2. Grounds, and the Identity of Primary and Remedial Duty

Weinrib's argument in favor of what I called ground-based duty individuation is an instance of a particular justificatory strategy. Recall that what needs justification is the claim that having a duty to ϕ is *the same* as having a duty to remedy the failure to ϕ. One of the ways in which the claim can be vindicated is to show that both duties are

---

[17] Although, of course, the diametrically opposite argument could be made in favor of ground-individuation if it is assumed that all duties must possess a ground of some sort.

[18] On simplicity as a way to adjudicate between explanations, see the discussion in PR Thagard, "The Best Explanation: Criteria for Theory Choice" (1978) 75 Journal of Philosophy 76, 91

[19] Vranas, "The Individuation of Obligations" (n 8).

[20] Gardner is categorical that "obligations (and more generally norms) are individuated according to the action that they make obligatory (or, in the case of other norms, empower or permit)"; Gardner, *TAOW* (n 1) 57. Weinrib's attack on action-individuation, in turn, is couched in distinctive metaphysical language: "As a juridical instantiation of the category of substance, the right and its correlative duty persist *through* change; they do not remain *un*changed"; Weinrib, *Corrective Justice* (n 3) 93.

grounded on the same higher-level duty.[21] Grounding primary and secondary duties on a higher-level duty explains some of the central claims that Weinrib makes about the relationship between them, in particular the claim that the causative event (the violation of the primary duty) should be seen (primarily) as "the reason" and not simply as "a condition" for the remedy.[22] I will come back to this claim later, as it will prove important to unpack it in order to evaluate the relative merits of the continuity thesis *vis-à-vis* the identity thesis, but before that I need to provide more detail on what this justificatory strategy looks like, some of its implications, and on plausible attempts to formulate the type of higher-level duty that is needed for this strategy to be successful.

A popular version of this strategy relies on the existence of a relation between each duty (primary and remedial) and the victim's right not to be negatively affected by others (in a way that is incompatible with their freedom).[23] What primary and remedial duties share in this account is that a failure to discharge either of them can be described as a violation of that same right.[24] The same point can be made from the point of view of the Hohfeldian correlative to this right: primary and remedial duties are specifications of a higher-level duty not to negatively affect others (in a way that is incompatible with their freedom). Notice that this strategy does not imply that the higher-level right (or correlative duty) needs to be as abstract as I phrased it above. In fact, there might be a number of higher-level rights/duties covering different types of primary/remedial duty pairings. Sandy Steel discusses this strategy with reference to a higher-level duty "to respect the victim's right to their body."[25]

Now, if primary and remedial duties are the only two specifications of a higher-level duty in a particular set of circumstances, and if they cannot be both fulfilled, it would follow that, in order to fulfil the higher-level duty, I would need to perform either the action required by the primary duty (ϕ) or the action required by the remedial duty (ϕ^*); and if it is no longer possible to ϕ, then the only way to fulfil the duty is to ϕ^*. And thus, the ground-based identity of primary and remedial duties (whose common ground is the higher-level duty) would explain why the violation of the primary duty (ie the causative event) is the reason for the remedial duty.

One charge that has been leveled against this version of the higher-level duty strategy is that the duty is defined so abstractly that it becomes unilluminating regarding the problem that it intends to shed light onto (the relationship between the remedial and the primary duty). Sandy Steel believes, rightly, that some of the most interesting aspects of the normative relationship between them are left unexplained by this particular answer to the normative question.[26] Accordingly, he puts forward an

---

[21] Although there might be different ways to conceive of "grounding," what I take this relationship to be for the purposes of this chapter is simply a relationship between, on the one hand primary and remedial duty and, on the other hand, a more abstract duty, so that the former are specifications of the latter for a particular set of circumstances.

[22] Weinrib, *Corrective Justice* (n 3) 82 and *passim* in ch 3

[23] Although this phrasing of the higher-level right is inspired by Weinrib's account, I am not here making an interpretative point on Weinrib's thought, but instead simply presenting what I take to be a plausible Kantian-inspired version of the higher-level duty.

[24] This is, roughly, what I take to be Weinrib's main contention; Weinrib, *Corrective Justice* (n 3) 91. A similar point is made in Ripstein, *Private Wrongs* (n 3) 241ff.

[25] Steel, "Compensation and Continuity" (n 4) 256.

[26] ibid.

alternative way in which to vindicate the identity thesis (roughly, what he calls "duty continuity") which is also an instance of the higher-level duty strategy, but relies on a different conception of the higher-level duty's general form.

Steel's higher-level duty is a duty not to act in such a way as to "be a causal source of damage," of a certain type, suffered by the victim.[27] So, differently from the first version discussed in the previous paragraphs, the higher-order duty here is a duty that selects a set of actions on the basis of their ability to place the agent in a certain state: the state of having caused the relevant damage. One advantage of Steel's account, if compared to the alternative attempt discussed above, is the fact that it puts more meat on the bones of the higher-order duty. The violation of the primary duty places the wrongdoer in a new continuous state (the state of being a source of the relevant damage suffered by the victim). That state persists until a new event occurs. Providing compensation is one of the events that has the effect of effacing that stain caused by that state in the moral patrimony of the wrongdoer. If there no longer is a damage, the wrongdoer cannot be in a state of being its cause.

I cannot afford to dwell here on which version of the higher-order duty strategy is best and, as I mentioned above, I will also refrain from discussing some of the difficulties that arise for this strategy from the apparent normative asymmetry of primary and remedial duty.[28] Rather, I will flesh out one of its implications that helps understand a normatively relevant difference between the identity thesis and Gardner's continuity thesis.

Consider again Weinrib's claim that the causative event is the reason for, rather than a condition to, the remedial duty.[29] As a condition, the "causative event has to be understood ... as the occasion that triggers the operation of a normatively independent remedial policy."[30] As a reason, it has to be understood "as the reason that grounds the remedy as a matter of justice."[31] The problem with considering the causative event as a condition, rather than the reason, is that it might cause a "disjunction between the injustice of the causative event and the remedial response"[32] for "the injustice occasions the remedy, without grounding it."[33] As he puts it:

> On the one hand, the causative event is seen as some sort of injustice that requires a remedy; yet on the other, the remedy's operation is independent of the reason for thinking that the causative event was an injustice to begin with. Thus, so far as the remedy is concerned, the injustice of the causative event is both *indispensable* and *superfluous*.[34]

---

[27] ibid 256–58.

[28] See n 7.

[29] Weinrib accepts that the causative event is both a condition and the reason for the remedy. The real alternative is to consider whether it is a condition *because* it is the reason or whether it is the reason *because* it is a condition; Weinrib *Corrective Justice* (n 3) 98.

[30] Weinrib, *Corrective Justice* (n 5) 98.

[31] ibid.

[32] ibid 85.

[33] ibid 86.

[34] ibid 86.

But this overstates the point. Could not the causative event be both indispensable and non-superfluous? Perhaps the causative event could be both indispensable and be *a* relevant reason, without being *the only* reason that justifies the secondary duty. It would appear the causative event could in principle (i) be a necessary condition for the remedial duty, without being a sufficient condition for it, while also being (ii) a reason in favor of the remedial duty, without being a conclusive reason in favor of the remedial duty.

The disjunction between, on the one hand, the causative event being *a* condition or, on the other hand, it being *the* reason is presented as exhaustive and exclusive (thus excluding from consideration the possibility that the causative event could be *a reason* and *a condition*) because primary and remedial duties, as we have seen, are just specifications of a higher-order duty. They derive all their normative force from this higher-level duty. Duties, as is well-known, behave in a binary fulfil/breach manner. We can either fulfil the higher-level duty or we can breach it. We might even be justified in breaching the duty. But the only normative relevance of the causative event, in this view, is that it makes it the case that the only way to fulfil the higher-level duty is to act as required by the remedial duty. That is why the causative event could not be *a* reason in favor of the existence of a remedial duty, but only *the* reason for it. Both primary and remedial duties are normatively grounded exclusively in a higher-level duty. No other normative consideration appears to be able to penetrate this hermetic pairing. But that is precisely one of the apparent differences between the continuity thesis and the identity thesis. In the next section I consider whether the continuity thesis does indeed allow for more reasons to come into play in an explanation of the normative relation between the primary and secondary duty and, if so, whether that is an advantage in relation to the identity thesis.

3. Duties, Reasons, and Continuity

As we clear away the metaphysical intuitions and claims about duty individuation and gain more clarity about how the identity thesis relies on a vindication of primary and secondary duties by a higher-level duty, the proximity between the identity thesis and the continuity thesis becomes more manifest. The continuity thesis, as formulated by Gardner amounts to the claim that:

> the secondary obligation ... exists to serve, so far as may still be done, the reasons for the primary obligation that was not performed when its performance was due.[35]

But duties *are* reasons for action.[36] Thus, on the face of it, there appears to be no contradiction between, on the one hand, the identity thesis (as vindicated by a higher-level duty type of justification) and, on the other hand, the continuity thesis. But perhaps the continuity thesis should be interpreted in a more stringent way. Maybe the

[35] Gardner, *TAOW* (n 1) 61.
[36] J Gardner and T Macklem "Reasons" in JL Coleman, KE Himma and SJ Shapiro (eds), *The Oxford Handbook of Jurisprudence and Philosophy of Law* (OUP 2004) 466.

claim is really that the reasons for the primary obligation (the ones that the secondary obligation exists to serve) are not, or at least do not need to be, duties. On that interpretation, a gap remains between the identity thesis and the continuity thesis. And it is a significant gap.

In order to see why, notice that defending a higher-level duty account of the relation between primary and remedial duty does not imply a commitment to denying that reasons other than the violation of the primary duty might bear on the existence of a secondary duty (or, which is a separate point, on the judicial availability of the remedy). In fact, one would not even be committed to believing that *the* reason for the remedy is a conclusive reason in favor of remedying the situation (or a reason in favor of granting legal standing to the victim to demand a judicial remedy). Although the duty is individuated by its ground (the higher-level duty), it is still the case that the secondary duty is a duty to perform a particular action (or, perhaps, one among a limited set of possible actions) and there might be perfectly respectable reasons not to perform that particular action that are not derived from the higher-level duty. Unless one subscribes to a very rosy picture of our normative landscape, duties might sometimes conflict and, at times, breaching one of them will be a lesser evil.[37] If a defender of a higher-level duty account of the identity thesis accepts that sometimes duties conflict and that, in such cases, one might need to breach a duty in order to fulfil a more important one, she would not be bound to claim that the higher-level duty that connects primary and remedial obligation should always prevail over all other duties.

One can without difficulty imagine a host of other reasons that (i) are not duties and that (ii) bear on the action that would be demanded by the secondary duty that specifies the higher-level duty. Take the action of "paying £100,000.00 to the victim" for instance. If in doing so, the wrongdoer will be pushed below a wealth threshold that would inevitably cause the wrongdoer and his family immense suffering, the wrongdoer would have a reason not to pay the money to the victim. Moreover, this fact is also a reason against having the remedial duty (under certain circumstances). Neither is it difficult to think of instances of reasons that count against bestowing upon the victim legal standing to pursue judicial remedies. Think of a case in which granting the victim legal standing would cause a level of disarray in the judicial system (presumably one of MacCormick's juridical consequences),[38] so that the decision would not leave positive private law (which is a public good) in a worse state than it would have been had the remedy not have been made judicially available.[39] In what follows, I will not address facts that might count as a reason against the availability of judicial remedies but instead focus on reasons against the performance of the action required by the secondary duty and reasons against the existence of the remedial duty. Reasons like that push in the opposite direction to the duty. Call them "potentially countervailing reasons." How could a defender of the higher-level duty vindication of the identity thesis respond to the existence of those reasons?

---

[37] ibid 467–68.

[38] N MacCormick, *Rhetoric and the Rule of Law* (OUP 2005), 104ff. John Gardner makes the point that judges deciding cases are not only bound by reasons stemming from corrective justice, but must also take into account the impact of their decision on the legal system in J Gardner "Public Interest and Public Policy in Private Law" in *TAOW* 310–11.

[39] *TAOW* 315.

234 CLAUDIO MICHELON

Leaving aside the claim that none such reason is a real reason, there appears to be a number of possible responses. The first, less interesting, response is to accept that at least some such reasons might conceivably countervail the high-level duty that grounds primary and remedial duties, but claim in addition that this would make the decision alien to private law (or corrective justice, or private law adjudication). These would have no place in a pure or rational system of private law. But such response invites the question, "so what?" Perhaps the answer to that further question is simply that there is an epistemic advantage in seeing the normative and conceptual structures of corrective justice in lab conditions.[40] This might indeed be good grounds on which to ignore the "impure" reasons that bear on the remedial action and/or on the existence of the remedial duty, but we must be clear about how far that epistemic advantage can carry us. From that epistemic advantage nothing follows about the strength of those impure reasons and how they relate to the strength of the higher-level duty identified under lab conditions. We might be justified in bracketing out certain reasons to obtain greater clarity about the shape and dynamics of a subset of reasons, but that says nothing about how the higher-level duty relates to the other reasons that bear on the case. This response, regardless of its epistemic merits, leaves the normative question untouched.

A second response might be to accept that at least some of those reasons could affect the existence of the remedial duty, provided they could be cashed out in terms of a "system of rights."[41] Within this system of rights, reasons against the remedial duty are placed at a level above the higher-level duty that makes primary and remedial duties identical: they are reasons to conclude that the higher-level duty that *appears* to ground both the primary and the remedial duties is just a mirage. The justification for that is that the existence of a higher-level right/duty is given by general considerations about the whole system of rights and, on that basis, it might turn out that a *prima facie* right/duty is not a real duty. Thus, it turns out that a reason pushing against the action required by the secondary duty is not simply a reason against that secondary duty being inferred from the violation of a primary duty but a reason for there not having been a primary duty in the first place. Clearly, some potentially countervailing reasons could be in fact captured by one such system of rights. But many might not be tamable in that way. In relation to the latter, the question remains as to how their strength relates to the strength of the higher-level duty.

Regardless of whether one accepts the "system of rights" account of some potentially countervailing reasons, a third alternative open to the defender of the identity thesis is to claim that the higher-level duty simply cannot be countervailed by the reasons pushing in the opposite direction, because the former would be indexically prior to the latter.[42] Duties, after all, are reasons of a special kind, they are *mandatory reasons*, that is to say, they have a special type of force. They are not simply (i) reasons to do something but also (ii) reasons not to act on a given set of countervailing reasons

---

[40] I take it that this was the investigative project Weinrib outlined in his "Aristotle's Forms of Justice" (1989) 2 Ratio Juris 211.

[41] See Weinrib's system of rights in Weinrib, *Corrective Justice* (n 3) 86 and 110–15.

[42] Or, if we are focusing on the availability of judicial remedies, it might be claimed that positive law should prevent judges from considering reasons that pull in the direction opposite to the higher-level duty.

(regardless of how strong the latter might be).[43] Feature (ii) means that certain types of reason are excluded from bearing on the action for not being *the type of reason* that could countervail the reason provided by the duty. The duty is insulated from them and, as a result, the matter of how strong they are (either individually or jointly) is not a relevant factor in determining the right thing to do. In current philosophical jargon, they are excluded by kind, not by weight.[44] That is a distinctive feature of the identity thesis and the ground-based justification for the identity that is predicated on the existence of a higher-level duty.

Thus, claiming that the identity of primary and remedial duties is a result of them both being grounded on a higher-level duty is tantamount to claiming that they are grounded in (i) a reason for action that is also (ii) a reason to exclude a certain set of reasons from the reasons that would be able to defeat that reason for action. Accordingly, a defender of the identity thesis does not need to deny that the potentially countervailing reasons (like pushing the wrongdoer below the poverty line) are real reasons. They can simply claim that they are not the kind of reason that could countervail the reason provided by the higher-level duty.

Notice that the exclusion promoted by a duty does not need to be (and, in fact, seldom is) absolute. For something to count as a duty, it is sufficient that it excludes by kind a non-empty set of reasons. The identity thesis could be vindicated by the (necessary) existence of a higher-level duty even if the set of reasons "excluded" is not particularly extensive.

Contrast all that with the continuity thesis. The continuity thesis does not require that the fact that grounds either the primary or the secondary duty be another higher-level duty. This fact might give you a reason for action, while not implying that other reasons bearing on the action required by the remedial duty should be excluded by kind from the set of potentially justificatory reasons. The continuity thesis is not incompatible with the reason that grounds the primary duty being, sometimes, a duty (ie that certain primary duties are indeed grounded on reasons that are mandatory), but it does not assume that to be the case. Moreover, it does not assume that the violation of the primary duty, and the consequent frustration of the reason that grounds that primary duty, should necessarily generate a duty. Perhaps all that is left from the violation of the primary duty (its "echoes," to use Gardner's image) are non-mandatory reasons for action. In other words, the truth of the continuity thesis does not imply that the remedial duty should be itself grounded on a duty.[45]

---

[43] J Raz, *Practical Reasons and Norms* (2nd edn, OUP 1999) 58–59; Gardner and T Macklem "Reasons" (n 36) 466.

[44] Raz famously introduces the distinction, which is now commonplace, in his discussion of exclusionary reasons in Raz (n 43) 35ff.

[45] In this chapter's first footnote I raised the possibility that the conception of the continuity thesis defended here is not what Gardner had in mind. In *FPLPL* 126 he appears to claim that the primary duty's grasp on the existence of the secondary duty is in part due to its ability to exclude some countervailing reasons. It is certainly true that the remedial duty has exclusionary force, but Gardner might be suggesting also that the primary duty's exclusionary power carries over to the reasons that justify the *existence* of a secondary duty. If that is how Gardner sees the continuity thesis, we should perhaps start talking about continuity *theses*, as this would be a very different claim to the one I believe to be superior to the identity thesis. To be sure, the passage allows for an interpretation that is compatible with my favored conception of the continuity thesis.

We are now in a position to see more clearly crucial differences between the identity thesis and the version of the continuity thesis I am defending here as superior to the identity thesis. First, the identity thesis makes an important additional commitment, *vis-à-vis*, the continuity thesis. Both see in the reasons that ground the primary duty the key to answer the normative question, but the identity thesis is also committed to the claim that this reason, whatever it might be (and there might be many such reasons), would always also be a reason to exclude a certain set of reasons *by type* from the justification of both the primary and the remedial duties. The continuity thesis has no such implication. It might indeed be that, in relation to a particular primary duty, the reason that grounds it is indeed another, higher-level duty, but this is not assumed to be the case. The continuity thesis is compatible with the reason that grounds the primary duty implying no exclusion by kind of any other reasons.

Second, and as a consequence, if the identity thesis were true, the existence of a primary duty would need to meet a heavier justificatory burden than it would need to meet were the continuity thesis true. For a primary duty could only exist, according to the identity thesis, if there were a higher-order reason (i) of which it was a specification *and* (ii) which excluded by type a non-empty set of potential reasons. For every particular primary duty there would need to be a fact that both is a higher-level reason for action *and* possesses exclusionary force which would have to be justified in the higher-level duty. The continuity thesis is not committed to the same burden as, at least in principle, there would be no need to justify the exclusionary nature of the grounding reason for there to be a justification for the primary duty. Notice that in both the identity and the continuity thesis, the question of exclusion might arise, but only in the former will it arise *necessarily*. In relation to these first two contrasting features, we can already see some reasons to favor the continuity thesis over the identity thesis. The former can give you all the latter can, while not being committed, like the latter, to the straitjacket of vindicating the exclusionary force of higher-level reasons.

Third, the continuity thesis is not committed to there being any reasons excluded by kind from the justification of the remedial duty. In fact, even if the reason that justifies the primary duty is a higher-level duty (something that, as we saw, is not incompatible with the continuity thesis), the continuity thesis does not commit to any duties "carrying over" to the justification of the remedial duty. The identity thesis, in contrast, is committed to there being at least one non-empty set of reasons excluded from the justification of the remedial duty, those that it inherits from the exclusion put in place by the higher-order duty. Thus, the continuity thesis allows for the possibility that the justification of the remedial duty is exclusively a result of the weight of the reasons bearing on the remedial action (although, of course, the continuity thesis is not incompatible with there being duties bearing on that action that stem from the violation of the primary duty). Here again, the continuity thesis is more capacious than the identity thesis.

Those are important differences between attempts to provide an answer to the normative question and each offers a rival framework within which to investigate the availability of reasons to justify the remedial duty. Moreover, each framework has different substantive implications, as the identity thesis is committed to there being at least one potentially countervailing reason whose weight would be irrelevant to the final balance of reasons that vindicates the availability of a remedial duty. But neither should be taken to provide a complete answer to the normative question. That answer would be necessarily predicated on *substantive* considerations.

To illustrate that, let me consider briefly how each framework would deal with the fact (and potentially countervailing reason) that, paying the victim £100,000 would drive the wrongdoer below a certain level of wealth, with drastic negative consequences for her family. If the continuity thesis is true, reaching a conclusion about the existence of a remedial duty grounded on the violation of a primary duty would still depend on answers to a number of questions. What reason or reasons ground the existence of the violated primary duty? Is there another way to conform to those reasons, now that the primary duty has been violated? If so, which action or actions by the wrongdoer would allow her to conform to those reasons (eg paying the victim £100,000)? Are there any other reasons that might bear on performing this action or these actions (eg the fact that, by paying the victim £100,000, the wrongdoer would fall below the poverty line, with drastic negative consequences for her family)? How does that reason's strength interact with the reasons that grounded the primary duty? In order to answer the latter question, it would be necessary to ask if any of the reasons that grounded the primary duty was itself a mandatory reason and, if so, whether the other potentially countervailing reasons is part of the set of reasons the mandatory reason excludes by kind? If they are not excluded, finally, one needs to consider the question of how much weight needs to be assigned to each reason so as to determine which one should guide the action to be performed by the wrongdoer. It might turn out that, at the end of this road, the fact that paying compensation would throw someone below the poverty line would outweigh the reasons that grounded the primary duty in the first place, and no secondary duty would be justified.

Similarly, if the identity thesis (as vindicated by a higher-order duty) is true, reaching a conclusion about the existence of a remedial duty grounded on the violation of a primary duty would still depend on answers to a number of questions. It is still necessary to know about which higher-level duty grounds the primary duty and, as duties are mandatory reasons, which types of reasons are to be excluded from the set of reasons that bear on the existence of both the primary and the secondary duties. If the potentially countervailing reason is part of the set of excluded reasons, then the higher-level duty cannot be defeated by it and, as the primary duty can no longer be discharged, the only action that could count as discharging the higher-level duty is the one required by the remedial duty. On the other hand, if the potentially countervailing reason is not part of the set of excluded reasons it is necessary to check its weight against the weight of the higher-level reason. Whichever is stronger would then control the action.

Notice that, although the reasons excluded by the higher-order duty are the same in relation to the primary duty and the remedial duty, the set of reasons that bear on the existence of the primary duty and the set of reasons that bear on the existence of the secondary duty might not identical. Take again the fact that having a duty to pay the victim £100,000 would (under some conditions) push the wrongdoer below the poverty line. This reason pushes against the existence of such remedial duty. But it is not a reason against having a duty, toward the victim, to drive carefully so as not to cause her bodily harm, even though having no such primary duty would also have the same beneficial effect of not pushing the wrongdoer and his family beyond the poverty line.

Thus, each rival theory frames the normative reasons that can ultimately answer the normative question differently and, in doing so, each has different implications regarding those substantive normative reasons. Clarity about this conceptual framing also helps avoid certain temptations, among which is the temptation of thinking that, if primary and secondary duties were identical, all that needs to be grounded in reasons is the primary duty (say, the duty of driving carefully so as not to endanger someone else's health) and not the duty to perform the particular remedial action that might undo the harm. As we have seen above, the possibility of having to pay someone an amount of money that would push the wrongdoer below the poverty line might be a reason for the wrongdoer to drive carefully, but it is not a reason for her not to have *a duty*, toward the victim, to drive carefully. But it might well be a reason against the wrongdoer having a duty, toward the victim, of paying her compensation.

If the analysis above is sound, there is indeed a relevant difference between the identity thesis and the continuity thesis, but that difference does not stem from a deeper disagreement on the metaphysics of duty, as one might surmise from reading the central voices in this debate. More importantly, the disagreement is not best understood as a disagreement between substantive normative attempts to answer the normative question, but rather as two rival ways of framing the investigation of the reasons that bear on the normative question. As such they are not best seen as one size fits all complete answers to the normative question, but as ways to organize our thoughts as we address the normative question that is raised piecemeal by particular primary duties and particular remedial duties. I also hope to have shown that there are reasons to prefer the framing provided by the continuity thesis to the one provided by identity thesis, not least because the former appears to be able to deliver all the advantages that the latter can claim to deliver, while keeping itself freed from some of the methodological and substantive commitments that the first implies.

Such conceptual framing is, therefore, an important part of the answer to the normative question. But it is not the end of the story. Not by a long shot.

14
The Role of Plaintiffs in Private Law Institutions

Larissa Katz and Matthew A Shapiro

1. The Power to Sue—Three Models

In common law systems, when someone's private law rights have been violated, the wronged individual initially determines whether the wrongdoer will be held accountable, by deciding whether to sue the wrongdoer in court and press her claims through the various stages of civil litigation. The victim of the wrong alone—not some government official or other third party—enjoys the *power to sue*. Why? According to what we'll refer to as "the conventional view," the victim should be the one who decides whether to call the wrongdoer to account precisely because she's the one who suffered the wrong; it's the very fact that *her* rights were violated that gives her the power to sue.

John Gardner emphatically rejected the conventional view. By portraying the power to sue as either a component or a necessary entailment of every private law right, he argued, the conventional view commits a "legalistic fallacy"[1] and begs the question as to why victims of rights violations should have the *further* right to haul the wrongdoers into court and subject them to the court's authority. Gardner insisted that the power to sue is a distinct right from the substantive rights recognized by private law that requires its own, distinct justification. And when he turned to providing that justification, he grounded the power to sue not in considerations personal to the victim but rather in institutional considerations regarding the structure of the legal system as a whole. The role of plaintiff, for Gardner, is an institutional one that must be explained in institutional terms. But a close examination of his writings on private law reveals that Gardner equivocated about the precise nature of that role, with implications for both the doctrinal compatibility and the normative appeal of his account of the power to sue.

Gardner criticized the conventional view of the power to sue for eliding what he saw as a justificatory gap between the substantive rights recognized by private law and the procedural powers afforded victims of rights violations. According to Gardner, the conventional view falsely depicts the former as "entail[ing]" the latter.[2] Too many private law scholars, Gardner lamented, have been misled by the lawyer's maxim *ubi ius, ibi remedium* into supposing that a right doesn't truly exist unless there's a remedy for its violation, a notion Gardner dismissed as a "legalistic fallacy."[3] "It does not follow,"

---

[1] J Gardner, *From Personal Life to Private Law* (OUP 2018) 204 ("*FPLPL*").
[2] ibid 216.
[3] ibid 204. For a purported attempt to invoke the *ubi ius* principle without committing the legalistic fallacy, see J Goldberg and B Zipursky, *Recognizing Wrongs* (Harvard University Press 2020) ch 3. For a similar

---

Larissa Katz and Matthew A Shapiro, *The Role of Plaintiffs in Private Law Institutions* In: *Private Law and Practical Reason*. Edited by: Haris Psarras and Sandy Steel, Oxford University Press. © Larissa Katz and Matthew A Shapiro 2023. DOI: 10.1093/oso/9780192857330.003.0014

he insisted, "from the fact that I owe you a duty of repair that you enjoy any kind of permission to make me perform it, or for that matter a power to conscript others into making me perform it."[4] Rather than a component of every private law right, the power to sue in common law systems is one of the "normative incidents" of the breach of those rights, an additional feature that requires some "explanation."[5] Put another way, the conventional view for Gardner tends to flatten private law's normative landscape. Whereas the conventional view builds the power to sue into the substantive rights recognized by private law, Gardner sought to disaggregate the bundle of normative relations that goes under the heading "private law right" into three distinct elements: (i) a "primary right" not to be treated in a certain way, (ii) a "secondary" right of repair when the primary right has been violated, and (iii) a "tertiary right" to decide whether to enforce the secondary right in cases of breach of the primary right.[6] As a distinct right, this last, tertiary right—the power to sue—requires some "additional argument" beyond the considerations justifying the existence of the primary and secondary rights.[7]

Gardner thought that this need for an independent justification for the power to sue was especially pressing because he regarded that power as an extraordinary feature of the legal system. As Gardner explained, the power to sue is actually a bundle of distinct powers—namely, "the extensive legal powers of the person who claims to have been wronged (the plaintiff) to initiate, maintain, and terminate court proceedings against the person whom she claims to have wronged her (the defendant)"—as well as a right to non-interference by third parties in the exercise of those powers.[8] The power to sue thus confers on plaintiffs significant power over both the defendant and the courts: with regard to the defendant, the plaintiff enjoys "a largely undirected legal power ... to determine whether [the defendant's duty of repair] is concretized and enforced through the courts," and as to the courts, the power to sue imposes a corresponding "duty ... to assist" the plaintiff in the exercise of her power "when ... validly exercised by the issue of proceedings."[9] All these powers, moreover, are "radically discretionary," in that "the conditions for the[ir] valid exercise ... are few and proforma, and that there are scant legal duties regulating their exercise."[10] Such vast discretionary powers, Gardner thought, demand a compelling justification, one that the mere existence of the underlying substantive rights a plaintiff is seeking to enforce can't supply.

When Gardner canvassed various candidates for such a justification, he found considerations personal to the plaintiff to be insufficient and instead settled on a

---

kind of normative argument for giving victims of rights violations the power to sue, see AS Gold, *The Right of Redress* (OUP 2020).

[4] *FPLPL* (n 1) 204–05.

[5] ibid 55–56.

[6] ibid 213–14.

[7] ibid 205. See also J Gardner, *Torts and Other Wrongs* (OUP 2020), 93 ("*TAOW*").

[8] *FPLPL* (n 1) 199. See also *TAOW* (n 7) 3 (defining "civil recourse" as the "legal power for someone who holds herself to have been on the receiving end of a tort (a 'plaintiff') to summon the alleged tortfeasor (a 'defendant') before the courts, and to do so unilaterally (without the leave of any official), with a view to obtaining a court-imposed or court-approved remedy against the defendant").

[9] *TAOW* (n 7) 85–86.

[10] *FPLPL* (n 1) 201.

distinctively institutional account of the power to sue. He didn't, of course, dismiss the plaintiff's personal interests altogether, acknowledging that the plaintiff's "tertiary right ... exists to protect her against unremedied violations, by the defendant, of her primary and secondary rights," such that "[s]he is the right's principal beneficiary."[11] But there are many possible institutional arrangements for safeguarding and enforcing the substantive rights recognized by private law, and in Gardner's view, the plaintiff's own interests—particularly her autonomy—fail to justify the extraordinary, discretionary power plaintiffs enjoy over both defendants and the courts.[12] The power to sue, Gardner contended, is an institutional power that far exceeds any kind of analogous power we enjoy in private life and, as such, "rests for its defence on the contribution that its existence makes to one or more public goods" realized through the public institutions of the legal system.[13] Gardner didn't purport to identify all the public goods the power to sue might serve, but among the possibilities he mentioned were promoting more efficient dispute resolution by giving plaintiffs leverage to obtain settlements, avoiding some of the drawbacks of public prosecution, forestalling "counterproductive" intermeddling by ill-placed third parties, and dispersing power so as to prevent the formation of an "oligarchy of officials."[14]

Gardner thus conceived of the power to sue as casting plaintiffs in an institutional role whose purpose is to promote various public goods, but the precise nature of that role remains somewhat ambiguous in his writings. More specifically, at various points, Gardner seemed to suggest three different models of the power to sue: (i) as a power to *conscript* public authority for private purposes, (ii) as a *power-sharing* arrangement between plaintiffs and the courts, and (iii) as a quasi-public *office*. While these are obviously overlapping conceptions, they emphasize different features of the power to sue and thus raise slightly different normative concerns.

1. *Conscripting Public Authority.* Gardner most often presented the power to sue as involving a kind of private control over public authority. With the power to sue, Gardner argued, "public authority (the authority of the court) is put at the disposal of the wronged person.... The wronged person, in short, is given a right not only against the wrongdoer but also against the court, a right to conscript the court (and its officers) in his or her quest for corrective justice against the wrongdoer."[15] The authority over which plaintiffs are granted control—that they are allowed to "conscript"—is public because it's the authority that public institutions (ie courts) exercise over other private individuals. And because that public authority is coercive, the power to sue enables plaintiffs to control the exercise of coercion over others, whether to compel the defendant to discharge his reparative duty of corrective justice or to "coercively obtain" a settlement from the defendant and thereby "secure the performance of [the defendant's] reparative duty by less wasteful means [than litigation]."[16]

---

[11] ibid 211.

[12] ibid 212–13. On this point, John took himself to be primarily arguing against A Ripstein, *Private Wrongs* (Harvard University Press 2016); E Weinrib, *The Idea of Private Law* (2nd edn, OUP 2012).

[13] *FPLPL* (n 1) 210.

[14] ibid 209–10.

[15] *TAOW* (n 7). See also *FPLPL* (n 1) 205.

[16] *FPLPL* (n 1) 208–09. One of us has explored the various ways in which the procedures of civil litigation delegate coercive power to the parties. See MA Shapiro, "Delegating Procedure" (2018) 118 Columbia Law Review 983–1065.

And yet, even as Gardner emphasized the public, coercive nature of the authority "put at the disposal" of plaintiffs, he considered it a feature of the power to sue that plaintiffs may exercise that authority for reasons that are fundamentally personal or private. In recognizing a particular wrong as a tort, he argued, "[t]he law is selecting some people for a measure of official support in their personal affairs that most other clients of the welfare state can only dream of."[17] A plaintiff's quest for corrective justice, for Gardner, is therefore a "personal affair," and "[t]he support of the law in dealing with personal injustices that one faces is a kind of social assistance—a public sponsorship of one's cause."[18] What's more, Gardner took it for granted that plaintiffs would often exercise their power to sue for the most self-interested of reasons, in as much as the plaintiff is

> a non-official who stands to profit personally, whether financially or otherwise, from the outcome of the proceedings. Indeed, she is *meant* to profit personally if her claim succeeds. A large and obvious conflict of interest is no barrier, then, to having the draconian legal authority to bring the court's authority to bear on the dispute, and to wield it against the defendant.[19]

Nor did Gardner see any significant legal constraints on plaintiffs' ability to deploy coercive public authority for such private purposes. The power to sue is, for one thing, unilateral, in that a plaintiff need not get approval from any government official before filing a lawsuit.[20] For another, Gardner believed that "the plaintiff has no legal duty to exercise her legal powers at all, or to exercise them in any particular way if she does exercise them, including to exercise them reasonably."[21] She may thus exercise her powers for any reason or no reason at all. This means that the power to sue affords plaintiffs "[t]he latitude ... to err in exercises of authority over others—over the court and, through the court, over the defendant."[22] Indeed, "[i]t is not as if the plaintiff's errors are merely tolerated by the law," but rather "her errors are positively supported and sponsored by the law."[23]

What emerges from Gardner's private law theory, then, is a model of the power to sue that puts public authority in the hands of private parties, while imposing virtually no accountability for the misuse of that authority—what Gardner himself described as "a typical *illiberal* arrangement."[24] And yet, Gardner seemed to think that such an arrangement is justified by virtue of its contribution to various public goods. Although he criticized the privatization of government power in many other contexts,[25] he seems to have been less concerned when it came to the power to sue.

---

[17] *TAOW* (n 7) 86.
[18] ibid 305.
[19] *FPLPL* (n 1) 200.
[20] ibid.
[21] ibid.
[22] ibid 202.
[23] ibid.
[24] ibid.
[25] See eg J Gardner, "Criminals in Uniform" in RA Duff and others (eds), *The Constitution of the Criminal Law* (OUP 2013) 102.

2. *Power-Sharing.* While we think this first, conscription model best captures Gardner's thinking about the power to sue, some of his statements point to other possible models. One alternative model views plaintiffs not as controlling or conscripting public authority for private purposes but rather as *sharing* the power to enforce private law rights (and the costs of enforcement) with the courts. Gardner thus noted private law's "generous terms for power-sharing and cost-sharing as between the aggrieved party and the legal system."[26] But whereas Gardner's statements in support of the conscription model depicted plaintiffs as pursuing a "personal" quest with the aid of the court, some of his other statements portrayed them as participating in the court's basic task of doing justice. The power to sue, as Gardner sometimes described it, is a power to "launch" legal proceedings[27] or to seek to "enforce" the defendant's duties of repair "by applying to the court for an award of damages against the tortfeasor."[28] That's the relatively limited sense in which "[t]he authority of the court to tackle and resolve the dispute, in private law cases, is subject to the authority of the plaintiff,"[29] and the plaintiff has the power "to determine the powers of the court."[30]

On this view, power is shared between the plaintiff and the court because the process for enforcing the plaintiff's private law rights may be initiated only by the plaintiff herself, but that process, once initiated, is fundamentally under the court's control. The power to sue involves rights-holders in a joint enterprise with the court whereby rights-holders interpret their rights and, when they feel aggrieved, decide whether to seek redress, while courts stand ready to take up the invitation to do justice.

This power-sharing model avoids, or at least mitigates, the most "illiberal" implications of the conscription model. It also seems to accord with Gardner's more general account of adjudication, particularly in private law cases. For Gardner, private law adjudication is always an allocative task, in two respects. First, the stakes in every case are necessarily "zero sum," in that one party's gain is the other party's loss, so the court can't avoid distributive questions in deciding how to resolve a dispute.[31] Second, the rule of law requires courts to do justice according to the law, which means deciding cases according to general rules, and that, in turn, requires courts to decide how to distribute various goods between the more general classes of potential litigants to which the parties before them belong.[32] Courts never have occasion to engage in either of these allocative tasks, however, until a dispute is brought before them by a plaintiff.[33] The allocative tasks in which doing justice according to the law consists are always performed at the behest of private parties. Plaintiffs, in this way, "play ... a role in the administration of justice and the maintenance of the rule of law."[34]

The power-sharing model thus suggests a different institutional role for plaintiffs from the one they play under the conscription model. Under the conscription model,

---

[26] *TAOW* (n 7) 86.
[27] *FPLPL* (n 1) 201–02.
[28] *TAOW* (n 7) 103.
[29] *FPLPL* (n 1) 199.
[30] ibid 200.
[31] *TAOW* (n 7) 94–99.
[32] ibid 88–91.
[33] J Gardner, *Law as a Leap of Faith* (OUP 2012) 256–59.
[34] *FPLPL* (n 1) 214–15.

plaintiffs are expected to exercise the power to sue in pursuit of their personal projects and, in doing so, to incidentally promote various public goods. Plaintiffs' institutional role under the power-sharing model, by contrast, more closely approaches a genuine partnership, as plaintiffs engage the court's function of doing justice according to the law in the particular case, rather than just unwittingly contributing to more systemic objectives.

3. *Plaintiffs as Quasi-Officials.* The power-sharing model of the power to sue can be understood as a more public version of the conscription model: rather than underwriting a purely "personal" quest, the power to sue involves plaintiffs in the courts' public task of doing justice according to the law. A third model casts plaintiffs in an even more public role. To be clear, we don't think Gardner actually meant to endorse this model; still, some of his statements do suggest it, so it's worth mentioning, if only as a contrast to the first two. The third model doubles down on the institutional nature of the plaintiff's role and conceives of the plaintiff as a quasi-official exercising public authority. In one passage, Gardner thus referred to plaintiffs as "acting officials" and included them among the "officials of the legal system."[35] Although he appears not to have repeated that formulation elsewhere, he did suggest that plaintiffs perform essentially the same functions as public prosecutors.[36] And in explaining how the power to sue might "avoid ... unhealthy concentrations of power in public officials and agencies" and thereby "ensur[e] that the law and its institutions do not become a tool only of an oligarchy of officials," Gardner likened the role of the plaintiff to that of the juror, another kind of acting official who makes "important decisions about the use of public authority."[37]

The quasi-official model can't be reconciled with Gardner's numerous statements, quoted above, in support of the conscription model. On Gardner's view, plaintiffs may exercise the public power put at their disposal for any reason or no reason at all, and thus may abuse that power with near impunity. But that is not how the official exercise of power is structured in a liberal state that adheres to the rule of law. While officials often have discretion to choose among several reasonable courses of action, they are typically held accountable for unreasonable, let alone ill-motivated, exercises of their power. So we simply don't see how plaintiffs can be considered officials—even "acting" ones—if, as Gardner repeatedly insisted, there are few meaningful constraints on their power to sue.

2. Three Queries

We find much that is compelling in Gardner's account of the power to sue. In particular, Gardner, in our view, rightly conceptualized that power in institutional terms,

---

[35] *TAOW* (n 7) 106.

[36] *FPLPL* (n 1) 209.

[37] ibid 210. Elsewhere, he gives this point a more private spin, suggesting that "the legal system is more likely to be justly maintained, and in particular justly maintained as a public good, if all sorts of people somewhat randomly draw the courts' attention to all sorts of injustices. The randomness is one way of mitigating the problem of 'regulatory capture', in which those who are supposed to be held answerable to the rules effectively dominate the administration of them." *TAOW* (n 7) 311.

attending to the institutional purposes it serves, rather than treating it as an obvious moral entitlement of victims of rights violations.[38]

At the same time, Gardner's account of the power to sue—and particularly the first model, which he seemed to favor—leaves us with three, related queries. The first concerns how the plaintiff's status as an institutional actor relates to the reasons justifying her power to sue. The second query asks what the detachment of the plaintiff from the reasons that justify that power says about the plaintiff as a moral agent. The third query concerns how private and public power are combined in institutional roles and the nature of the distinction, if any, between them. As we will see, the resources within each model to resolve these questions vary, exposing some quite serious weaknesses in the first model and some underappreciated reasons for favoring a version of the second (which we begin to sketch in section 3).

2.1 Query 1: Power and reasons

On any version of Gardner's account, a plaintiff has an extraordinary legal power, not merely a Hohfeldian claim-right, enabling her to enlist (or even "conscript") courts and public resources in determining whether and when to subject a defendant to the use of public authority.[39] As with any power that is constitutive of an institutional role, one would expect the plaintiff's reasons to have some bearing on what counts as a proper exercise of the power to sue. Unlike rights (which just *are*), powers involve the exercise of discretion—they require decision-making.[40] The decisional aspect of powers means that reasons matter in the justified exercise of a legal power. The power to decide a matter of concern to others for any reason or no reason at all amounts to arbitrary discretion—the very nightmare that, for liberals generally, law and legal institutions are meant to dispel.[41] This relationship between powers and reasons— and, more to the point, the idea that powers must be exercised for the purposes for which they are conferred, or at the very least for reasons not inconsistent with those purposes—is expressed across a broad legal terrain from public law[42] to private law.[43]

---

[38] For that reason, we follow Gardner in understanding the power to sue at least partly in teleological, rather than purely deontological, terms.

[39] For further explication of private law "rights of action" in terms of the traditional Hohfeldian categories, see K Barker, *Enforcement in Public and Private Law: Paradigms, Exceptions, and Hybrids* (OUP forthcoming) ch 2.

[40] The decision she is thereby making marks an action of the powerholder as an exercise of that power: for example, when possession of property is transferred from A to B, it is a function of A's decision that B, in taking possession, is her bailee, trustee, or buyer, and so the new owner.

[41] L Katz, "Ownership and Offices: The Basic Building Blocks of the Legal Order" (2020) 70 University of Toronto Law Journal 267–86.

[42] See L Smith, *The Law of Loyalty* (OUP forthcoming) ch 9; L Katz, "The Regulative Function of Property Rights" (2011) 8 ECON Journal Watch 236–46 (connecting abuse of power in the public law context and the abuse of "right" in private law). See also HLA Hart, "Discretion" (2013) 127 Harvard Law Review 652–65.

[43] The principle holds for trustees, donees of a power of appointment, and even property owners. See L Katz, "Spite and Extortion: A Jurisdictional Principle of Abuse of Right" (2013) 122 Yale Law Journal 1444–82. It also governs the exercise of contractual powers. See eg *Wastech v Greater Vancouver Sewage and Drainage District* [2021] 2021 SCC 7.

Institutional actors, from trustees to police officers,[44] are justified in their claims to extra powers and privileges only to the extent that they exercise them for appropriate institutional purposes.[45]

In other contexts, Gardner recognized that acting for appropriate reasons is a requirement for the legitimate exercise of institutional power and justified action more generally. For example, he insisted that officials exercising extraordinary powers fall short when they fail to act *for* the reasons that justify the power (even if their action ends up being in conformity with those reasons).[46] Justifying extraordinary power over matters that concern others is not a once and for all thing, complete at the time of allocation of the office or role to which it attaches. Put another way, holding an office or occupying an institutional role is not in itself a sufficient justification for a decision or action taken by the institutional actor or officeholder. Indeed, Gardner always resisted such magical thinking about offices, rejecting the idea that once you have an office—and so a warrant to make a decision that is not otherwise morally yours to make—you are somehow in a different moral sphere altogether. A person wielding extraordinary powers cannot simply point to the existence of the office or role to justify the powers. It is only in acting in a particular case for the very reasons for which those powers are justifiably conferred that the decision or conduct in that case is justified. Correspondingly, one who does not exercise her powers *for* the reasons they are conferred is acting without warrant and so without justification.[47]

Against this backdrop, it's all the more striking how reluctant Gardner was to allow that reasons or purposes constrain a plaintiff's power to sue—even as he insisted that the plaintiff has these extraordinary powers over others as an institutional actor, and not in her personal life. Recall that, for Gardner, the plaintiff's exercise of her extraordinary power over officials, and through officials over defendants, is almost entirely undirected and unregulated; a plaintiff "has no legal duty to exercise her legal powers at all, or to exercise them in any particular way if she does exercise them, including to

---

[44] See L Smith, "The Motive, Not the Deed" in J Getzler (ed), *Rationalizing Property, Equity and Trusts: Essays in Honour of Edward Burn* (Butterworths 2003); M Thoburn, "Policing and Public Office" (2020) 70 University of Toronto Law Journal 248–66.

[45] To be sure, the purposes underlying institutional powers aren't always "public"; sometimes, one private party is empowered to act to advance the private interest of another. For examples of such "private administration" see Smith, *The Law of Loyalty* (n 42) ch 8. Nor do we mean to deny that various ulterior goods can legitimately be realized through a kind of "invisible hand" mechanism, in which institutional actors exercise their powers for reasons that do not include all the good consequences their actions produce. What we find concerning—and what Gardner's account of the power to sue seems to countenance—is a situation in which an institutional actor is under no rational constraint at all, but rather remains free to exercise her powers for any reasons. It's that kind of arbitrary discretion that gives rise to the various problems we go on to canvass in the main text.

[46] *R v Dadson* [1850] 4 Cox CC 358. In that case, a guard shot a fleeing thief whom, it turned out, he was legally permitted to shoot. But since the guard was not aware of the circumstances that would otherwise have justified the shooting (that the victim was a felon), the guard's conviction was upheld. See J Gardner, "Why Blame?" in I Solanke (ed), *On Crime, Society, and Responsibility in the Work of Nicola Lacey* (OUP 2020) 85–86.

[47] Gardner might have been even more inclined to view the plaintiff as a kind of official—he was already somewhat inclined—had he noticed that the plaintiff, like other officials, enjoys *extra* privileges that ordinary people would not have, to do what would be a wrong, but for her role. Take, for example, legal permissions to make statements that might otherwise be defamatory in the course of a judicial proceeding: *Kimball v Ryan* [1936] 283 Ill App 456. All the more reason to expect some closer relationship between plaintiffs as institutional actors and reasons.

exercise them reasonably."[48] Elsewhere, he insists that the plaintiff still acts within her authority when she is making baseless, even stupid, decisions, enjoying a "latitude...to err" in ways that "are [not] merely tolerated by the law" but "positively supported and sponsored by the law."[49] In civil litigation, there is no requirement for the plaintiff to be reasonable at all, and she does not lose her authority to another simply because she makes unreasonable choices about whether and how to enforce her rights.

For Gardner, this apparent detachment of the plaintiff from the purposes of her role seems to be a feature of the role itself, not merely a function of other institutional choices we have made. We can imagine an account along these latter lines. It would deny any institutional expression of moral constraints on the exercise of a plaintiff's power without denying that plaintiffs as institutional actors are (morally) obligated to exercise their powers for the reasons for which they are conferred. This would explain the latitude plaintiffs have in terms of the absence of institutional checks on their decision-making, itself a contingent policy choice. Within this set of institutional arrangements, a plaintiff would be free to exercise her power to sue without external review of her reasons and certainly without the say so of any other official. This view would align with some of the very reasons of public good that Gardner sees as justifying private litigants' having the power to sue in the first place: to subject a plaintiff to external review by officials might well undermine the institutional goal of, say, diffusing power.

Is this what Gardner was getting at when he described the radically discretionary nature of plaintiffs' power to initiate legal proceedings? Does his account compel plaintiffs to attend to reasons as a moral matter (a morality adapted, of course, to the institutional circumstances in which the plaintiff operates), albeit without a further institutional apparatus for enforcing those moral limits in the form of reviewing officials? This is not the move we see Gardner making here. On Gardner's account, the plaintiff's power to sue is free of any *internal* constraint on its exercise in the form of a principle of abuse of right or power. Gardner's account does not require that the plaintiff act for (or refrain from acting for) any reasons in particular. There are two categories of reasons that might have informed a principle of abuse of power in this context, and Gardner rejected both. The first are the reasons of public good that Gardner thinks justify that power to sue. On such a view, a plaintiff abuses her right when she does not act in order to promote the good outcomes that justify her having that power. But on Gardner's account, the plaintiff isn't bound to attend to those reasons. Nor does it seem she could intelligibly attend to them and still advance the systemic objectives Gardner believed she is supposed to serve. Gardner offered these public goods (such as the better results of a plaintiff-led model over a prosecutorial model; the reduction of information costs due to a plaintiff's familiarity with the conflict; and the effect of dispersing an oligarchy of officials) as reasons for an overall institutional arrangement rather than reasons aimed at the level of particular acts or decisions. And as we'll see in the next section, Gardner suggested that plaintiffs would realize these public goods through their individual decisions to sue only if they

---

[48] *FPLPL* (n 1) 200.
[49] ibid 202.

pursued what they took to be their own interests, not if they directly considered the public goods in their decision-making.

The other category of reasons that might constrain plaintiffs' exercise of the power to sue are the reasons of corrective justice that pick out the plaintiff as the principal beneficiary of the standing to sue. On such a view, a plaintiff abuses her power when she is not exercising it to see (corrective) justice done. But while reasons of corrective justice explain the substantive rights a plaintiff has and also why she is the principal beneficiary of the initiation of a suit, Gardner did not treat the plaintiff as compelled, legally or morally, to exercise her power as an institutional actor *for* those reasons. One could readily imagine incorporating such a rational limitation into the second and third models of the power to sue outlined in the previous section. If plaintiffs share power with the courts to administer justice in their individual cases, then one might suppose that they should be under the same obligation as courts to exercise their power for (or at least consistent with) that purpose. And if plaintiffs temporarily hold a public office, then one might think that they should have to attend to the reasons that constitute their office, just like all other public officeholders, including judges and even jurors. But as the first section showed, Gardner repeatedly insisted that plaintiffs may exercise the power to sue and thereby "conscript" public authority for virtually any reason, even if, in doing so, they subvert the very reasons of corrective justice that private law adjudication is supposed to serve. Indeed (and as the next section elaborates), Gardner made clear that the contribution of the power to sue to various public goods *depends on* plaintiffs' being free from significant limits on the exercise of that power. Gardner thus appeared to foreclose the kinds of restrictions on plaintiffs' reasons that the power-sharing and quasi-official models of the power to sue, with their focus on the plaintiff's institutional role in the administration of justice, seem to implicitly invite, confirming his commitment to the conscription model. For Gardner, corrective justice supplies the form and (much of) the substance of private law adjudication, but doesn't similarly inform plaintiffs' exercise of the power to sue.

In this respect, there is an asymmetry on Gardner's account between the plaintiff and the defendant in civil proceedings. The reasons of corrective justice and the continuity thesis that account for the defendant's duty to repair also account for the defendant's position institutionally: his liability to enforcement proceedings subject to his right to defend himself. For Gardner, the defendant's moral position as wrongdoer is more or less unified with his institutional position as defendant. In contrast, the plaintiff's moral position as victim and institutional position as plaintiff are decoupled.

What Gardner's account leaves us with is a view of the plaintiff as detached from the reasons or purposes that justify assigning her extraordinary institutional powers.[50] The purposes or reasons for assigning those powers to her are no concern of the plaintiff in her institutional role; nor is the plaintiff compelled to attend to reasons of corrective justice in exercising her powers. It is indeed precisely on the basis that the plaintiff's power to sue is radically discretionary that Gardner distinguished the legal power to sue from any analogue in personal life.[51] The position of the plaintiff

---

[50] Those powers include the power to force others to answer or be stuck with making amends whether they committed the wrong or not and the privilege of making false statements that would otherwise be defamatory.

[51] See eg his discussion of *The Treasure Seekers* in *FPLPL* (n 1) 145–52.

in law differs from that of the victim in personal life in that the former is not subject to a reasonableness limit in bringing suit.[52] In personal life, the questions of who has the authority to enforce another's duty and of how enforcement should proceed are resolved on the basis of what, all things considered, would be reasonable for a person to do in the circumstances.[53] Plaintiffs in civil suits, by contrast, have a power to sue that is subject to no such principle of abuse of power, notwithstanding the far greater powers attached to that institutional role. On Gardner's account, it is the institutional power that is radically discretionary and "illiberal," unconstrained by reasons even as its closest analogue in private life is inherently constrained by the moral criterion of reasonableness.

Gardner's insistence on the radically discretionary character of the plaintiff's power to sue goes beyond what fidelity to legal doctrine requires.[54] While he acknowledged rules against "malicious" or "bad faith" litigation conduct, he downplayed other doctrinal evidence that might have led him to revise his account of the undirected nature of the power to sue in ways that we think would be more in keeping with his view that the plaintiff is an institutional actor, even an officeholder. At least in the United States, the jurisdiction with which we are most familiar, it is true that plaintiffs have no general obligation to be reasonable in their litigation conduct. Plaintiffs need not exercise litigation powers *for* particular reasons, nor do they necessarily violate any rules by exercising those powers for reasons other than those for which the powers are conferred. But there are myriad restrictions on litigation conduct that is ill-motivated or particularly unreasonable. For example, plaintiffs are subject to sanctions not only for filing lawsuits motivated by an "improper purpose," but also for pressing claims that are so legally or factually unsupported as to be frivolous.[55] They must also avoid unduly burdensome litigation conduct, such as discovery requests that aren't "proportional to the needs of the case."[56] Even taken together, these kinds of restrictions don't amount to a comprehensive reasonableness requirement. But they nevertheless belie Gardner's portrayal of the power to sue as almost completely undirected, and they provide a doctrinal basis for reconsidering the first model of that power, which Gardner so clearly embraced, in favor of the second or third.[57]

In the end, it seems that Gardner regarded the radically discretionary nature of the power to sue as a feature of that power by institutional design, not a defect that should be explained away or repaired. That position has the somewhat curious implication that the myriad, though modest, doctrinal limits on plaintiffs' discretion to exercise the power to sue diminish the institutional position of the plaintiff.

---

[52] ibid 207.

[53] ibid 206.

[54] For other ways in which an account of the power to sue such as Gardner's—and particularly his conscription model—might be inconsistent with tort and civil procedure doctrine, see O Herstein, "How Tort Law Empowers" (2015) 65 University of Toronto Law Journal 99–132.

[55] Fed R Civ P 11.

[56] Fed R Civ P 26(b).

[57] These and other doctrinal limits on the power to sue are in addition to the *moral* limits that constrain plaintiffs' exercise of that power, which we discuss in the next section.

2.2 Query 2: The passive role of plaintiffs and moral agency

How we think Gardner would come out on the first query leaves us with a second query, about the relationship between people and the institutions they serve in their capacity as institutional actors. As seen in response to the first query, on Gardner's account, plaintiffs are detached from the purposes of their institutional role—plaintiffs need not attend to the reasons of public good that justify their powers, nor even any of the reasons of corrective justice that account for why they are the power's principal beneficiaries. At the same time, the plaintiff, on Gardner's view, is only contingently connected to the underlying conflict, in virtue of the institutional criteria that justify assigning her the power to initiate proceedings to resolve it.

One implication of this view is that the plaintiffs are neither full participants in the institution they serve nor full owners of their own conflicts. Various institutional goals are achieved through them, but not by them. Plaintiffs are put in a position of radical freedom just because things work better that way overall. In having and exercising the broad latitude they enjoy to initiate and manage legal proceedings, they are the means of bringing about other things that we really care about: the good outcomes (including the diffusion of public power) that Gardner thought justify the existence of such an extraordinary power.[58]

As it turns out, and as Gardner readily acknowledged, people tend to take a very different view of their role as litigants. Many assume that their (deeply felt) personal connection to their conflicts is sufficient to justify their having the power to sue.[59] On this view, the state takes something that belongs to plaintiffs when it takes over the prosecution of their private law claims.[60] Gardner dismissed this as a "legalistic fallacy," an erroneous import from law (ie how we do things in law) into morality (ie a right to have it be done that way). He insisted that the power to sue is not a moral entitlement, and certainly does not deserve to be the right that it is (with massively discretionary powers over the use of public authority) independent of the institutional criteria that justify it. But the legalistic fallacy should have given Gardner more pause than it did: for is it not the case that the institutional aims he described as justifying the power to sue are advanced by the legalistic fallacy and perhaps even depend on it? To put it crudely, private litigants are set up with a private power that invites a kind of false morality, leading to the legalistic fallacy. If we accept Gardner's account, the very nature

---

[58] Gardner draws an analogy between the private power to sue and freedom of expression, which he also thinks is justified instrumentally. See *FPLPL* (n 1) 212. We don't resist his claim that some of our freedoms can be instrumentally justified for reasons of public good. (Indeed, one of us has argued previously that many of our rights—property, for instance—depend on reasons of public good for their existence.) The problem is not the reasons of public good that justify having those powers; it is the detachment of the actor from those reasons in her institutional role.

[59] It is of course not just laypeople who "feel" this; this is the view of a great many philosophers of tort law. See eg Goldberg and Zipursky, *Recognizing Wrongs* (n 3); J Oberdiek, "It's Something Personal: On the Relationality of Duty and Civil Wrongs" in P Miller and J Oberdiek (eds), *Civil Wrongs and Justice in Private Law* (OUP 2020) 301–21; Ripstein, *Private Wrongs* (n 12).

[60] cf N Christie, "Conflicts as Property" (1977) 17 British Journal of Criminology 1–15 ("State, lawyers, convert conflict to non-conflict, make it disappear ... [define] the interpersonal conflict away, by making crime about larger social forces; or take over the conflict.").

of the power to sue (its radically discretionary nature, the freedom to err, to be selfish, to act for *any* reason in the role) leads to a moral mistake upon which the institutional role is in fact premised. The institutional role of the plaintiff—to wield a radically private power over the use of public authority and thereby to bring about the institutional goods Gardner described—can be seen to rest on a kind of "noble lie": we are in a position that is *designed* to be exercised freely and without regard to the institutions it serves. We are useful idiots: from the standpoint of the reasons that we may (falsely) think are necessary and sufficient to justify our decisions in civil litigation—reasons of corrective justice—even our errors are just part of the strategy, yielding the outcomes the institution is meant to generate through us.

This picture of how the plaintiff is supposed to relate to her institutional role accords with the first model of the power to sue, whereas the second and third models suggest grounds for resisting it. On the first model, remember, the plaintiff is invited to "conscript" public authority for her own private purposes without regard for the usual limits on such authority, a radical form of discretion that is justified by its supposed contribution to various public goods. The "legalistic fallacy" is, on this view, a useful fiction, lulling victims of private law wrongs into (falsely) regarding their lawsuits as a way of personally vindicating their rights so that they will play their necessary, but incidental, part in the broader institutional scheme. By contrast, such false consciousness seems to sit much less comfortably with the second and third models of the power to sue, suggesting an alternative, more authentic relationship between plaintiffs and their institutional role. An arrangement in which plaintiffs and courts share power to administer justice in individual cases seems to assume that plaintiffs have an accurate understanding of the enterprise in which they're participating; otherwise, it's hard to see how they're genuinely *sharing* power to do justice, as opposed to merely *serving* the authority of the court. Likewise, official action is typically deliberate—not only in the sense described in the previous section (ie officeholders are supposed to exercise their powers *for* specific reasons), but also in the sense that officeholders understand the basic nature and contours of their office, as well as its place in the broader institutional structure. In embracing the utility of the "legalistic fallacy," Gardner appears to have foreclosed alternative conceptions of the power to sue that would allow the plaintiff to understand her institutional role on its own terms.

The detachment that Gardner proposed between the plaintiff and her role—the very detachment that the legalistic fallacy resists—not only makes of people something other than what they as moral actors take themselves to be, but also requires that they take themselves to be something other than what the institutional role actually consists in. All of this leaves us rather cold. Moral agents, living what they are led to think of as their own personal lives, are being made players in the lives of the rest of us.

2.3 Query 3: The function of private power in public institutions

Gardner's account of the power to sue raises a third question for us: what is private about the power to sue and how does conceiving of the power as private fit with Gardner's view of the plaintiff as institutional actor? Gardner insisted (on all three versions of his account) that the power to sue is a private power that a person holds *qua* institutional actor. One sense of private is the *deeply* private—the personal. We speak of private interests as ones in which others don't have a share (the personal), and we speak of private actors as those acting in a personal capacity, in their own name and on their own behalf. Private powers can be ours in this sense when they exist for reasons personal to us and when private actors exercise them in their own name and on their own behalf. But this is clearly not the sense of "private" that Gardner invoked in this context. Of course, he had a more robust idea of the personal than most. He thought there were many areas of moral life that do not depend on law and about which it might even be better if the law (and officials) remained quiet. Morality, direct and unmediated, guides our actions in these spheres. But Gardner also recognized that some matters lack determinate answers in morality and thus stand to be resolved on contingent empirical grounds through institutions—matters, in short, of *policy*. Law and institutions are needed to provide (artificial) determinacy in matters of policy like this. Without law and the institutions it authorizes to make policy decisions, we have no authoritative answers for these sorts of questions, for morality provides none. For Gardner, the matter of enforcement—whether to enforce, how to do so, and by whom—is a policy matter in criminal law and private law alike. Of course, the powers to make policy decisions are usually held by public actors who operate under special duties and whose decisions are subject to review.[61] But there are, on Gardner's view, sometimes contingent practical reasons for assigning such powers to institutional actors outside officialdom.[62] The assignment of the power to sue to private parties— individuals who operate outside the network of officials who make up government and act subject to special duties—is one example of this. In so far as the power to sue is private on Gardner's account, it is not private in the sense of being a personal power: it is not ours for reasons personal to us, nor is it a power we exercise on our own behalf even if we do exercise it primarily for our own benefit. It is rather, a private *institutional* power.[63]

The public–private distinction Gardner was drawing is not, then, the more familiar distinction between the personal and the public or institutional: the question of enforcement *is* an institutional matter beyond personal life. So, in virtue of what is the power to sue private? It seems that what makes the power private for Gardner is just

---

[61] For an overview of the various review mechanisms in public law administration, see Smith, *The Law of Loyalty* (n 42) ch 10.

[62] Hart and Sacks made a similar point about the role of private discretion in institutional decision-making: "Private powers are one of the great instruments for postponing to the future decisions which do not have to be or cannot be made today. That is, it is difficult to define the scope of the power, the manner of its exercise and what happens if it used for unauthorized purposes or defectively. But it is easier than telling people the substance of what they must or must not do." HM Hart and AM Sacks, *The Legal Process: Basic Problems in the Making and Application of Law*, W Eskridge Jr and PP Frickey (eds) (Foundation Press 1994) 133–34. This was also HLA Hart's view about discretion as a form of decision-making: "society's ability to regulate the future is inherently limited by imperfect information and an imperfect understanding of aims"; hence the need for discretion. See Hart, "Discretion" (n 42).

[63] We should also bear in mind how Gardner conceived of the private domain (which he preferred to call personal life): a domain in which we actually do not enjoy anything like the arbitrary discretion he thinks characterizes the plaintiff's power to sue, but rather a domain governed by reasons and requirements of reasonableness. We have seen this already in his discussion of the personal standing a person has to enforce her or someone else's rights, which does not allow the victim anything like the latitude he thinks institutions allow the plaintiff. Purposiveness—acting for reasons—is built into the very nature of the rights and powers we have in personal life.

its radically discretionary quality. It is a form of institutional power not bounded by the usual duties that attach to officials—duties to consider its exercise, to make the selection, to make that selection for the very reasons the power is conferred. It is private power in that it is pure discretion. Thinking of private power in this way—as a tool for policy-making about morally indeterminate matters—resolves one problem: how the power to sue is an institutional power, not a personal one, and yet still distinct from public power in the hands of officials. But it leaves on the table another: the question of how this radical discretion in the hands of institutional actors can be reconciled with a commitment to legality in the law and its institutions. That quandary is perhaps most acute if we conceive of plaintiffs as occupying an office or as sharing public authority with the courts. But the worry persists even if plaintiffs are instead "conscripting" public authority for private purposes, in as much as the rule of law precludes granting control over the state's coercive apparatus to those who are free to wield it arbitrarily.

Gardner's insistence on the detachment of the plaintiff from her institutional role and on the disconnect between the plaintiff and the reasons that justify that practice leaves us at an impasse. In the next section, we sketch a way to resolve it.

3. Power-Sharing Revised

Gardner's core insight was that questions of enforcement of private law rights, and the powers to enforce those rights, are policy matters in private (non-official) hands. Plaintiffs, on any version of Gardner's account, have the power to make important decisions about the use of public authority for institutional reasons and as such are themselves institutional actors. We agree that there are good normative and doctrinal reasons for conceiving of plaintiffs as institutional actors who share power with judges in a decentralized form of administration of justice. Gardner's own account of the plaintiff's role as institutional actor, however, leaves us with some significant concerns. In light of our three queries, the most appealing model of the plaintiff's role that emerges from Gardner's private law theory is, in our view, the second, according to which plaintiffs and courts share the power to administer justice. But if plaintiffs are truly partners with judges, should we not expect them to attend to the reasons that constitute that practice—the reasons of corrective justice (along with the continuity thesis) that, on Gardner's own telling, guide both how courts develop substantive private law and how courts resolve the particular dispute before them? Recall from our discussion of the first query that on Gardner's account, plaintiffs have radical discretion; they are unconstrained by reasons and free from review by officials. But we can maintain that public–private distinction, allowing that administrative law does not regulate the sphere in which the plaintiff operates, without landing where Gardner does: with the plaintiff holding a fundamentally illiberal power. Discretion is a basic and ineliminable aspect of any system of law, but it can and ought to be contained within the law and grounded in reasons, just as rules are.

In a genuine power-sharing model, there is a common normative foundation grounding the power of each institutional actor. For the institution of private law adjudication, that normative foundation is the enterprise of determining the rights and obligations of the parties and doing corrective justice between them. Each of the participants—plaintiff, defendant, and court—plays a distinct role in that enterprise and accordingly enjoys distinct powers to advance it. Most relevant here, plaintiffs enjoy the powers to initiate and drive the proceedings, while courts enjoy the power to conclusively determine the validity of the plaintiff's claims. But the key point for our purposes is that all the participants' powers are grounded in the same institutional practice. Plaintiffs, just like their judicial co-participants, have a power rooted within that practice and so are constrained by the reasons that justify it. Plaintiffs abuse their power and act outside their institutional role when they exercise their power for reasons radically inconsistent with those upon which the practice is grounded.[64] Even if a plaintiff is not required to act *for* reasons of corrective justice, she abuses her tertiary enforcement right when she sues out of spite or for arbitrary and capricious reasons or wields her other various litigation powers disproportionately. And as we noted in our discussion of the first query, that is more or less the view found in civil procedure doctrine, which (at least in the United States) cabins plaintiffs' discretion much more significantly than Gardner acknowledged.

Gardner's power-sharing model, when juxtaposed with his statements emphasizing the institutional imperatives served by the power to sue, also leaves us with a second worry. Recall that not only does Gardner want to view the plaintiff's role as a private role, rather than a public office bound by duties to act for particular reasons; he also wants to deny that plaintiffs *own* their conflicts as they own their cars and houses. For Gardner, the plaintiff's power lies somewhere between an office (ie power subject to special duties) and property (ie power that we have for reasons personal to us). Gardner seemed to assume that to conceive of the plaintiff's role as an institutional one, resting on institutional criteria, is to rule out the possibility that a plaintiff might have a moral claim to the power to sue. That, in our view, is mistaken. In developing his institutional account of the power to sue, Gardner took as his foil private law scholars who purport to ground that power in plaintiffs' individual "independence" or "autonomy."[65] But such values aren't the only personal considerations that potentially justify allocating the power to sue to the plaintiff. There are other moral reasons, also personal to the plaintiff, that we think have some role. The violation of one's rights not only gives one rights to corrective justice (what Gardner referred to as secondary rights); it also generates a further interest, personal to the rights-bearer, in determining whether and how those secondary rights are enforced. More than just a "beneficiary" of the civil process (as Gardner put it), a plaintiff whose rights have been violated has a personal stake in decisions about whether and how that violation is addressed. These personal reasons include, first, the dignity interest (or rightful honor) of the rights-holder, the interest in not abasing oneself by letting rights violations go unanswered;[66] and second, an interest in not being a stickler—that is in not always insisting on standing on one's rights, especially when doing so would be harmful,

---

[64] For a jurisdictional account of abuse of right, see Katz, "Spite and Extortion" (n 43).

[65] See n 12.

[66] One of us has argued that various procedural features of civil litigation can be understood as responding to this interest. See MA Shapiro, "The Indignities of Civil Litigation" (2020) 100 Boston University Law Review 501–79.

unjust, or oppressive. Both of these are moral reasons, personal to us and bearing on the kind of persons we are, and they make enforcement a matter of personal concern that goes beyond the vindication of one's primary and secondary rights that Gardner thought made plaintiffs "principal beneficiaries" of the process. In a regime in which private law rights can be enforced, morality counsels against both being a stickler and standing down gratuitously. More than just a beneficiary of an institutionally justified power, a rights-holder is morally implicated in how enforcement decisions within that institution are made: it reflects badly on her personally when the decisions fail to track these moral reasons—when her rights are enforced inequitably or when her rights violations go unanswered in circumstances where her self-honor and dignity demand a response. That is so even when some other actor, such as an official, makes decisions about enforcement in her stead, for it is ultimately *her* rights being over-enforced or neglected, and thus *her* status as a rights-bearer being impugned as either overbearing or illusory. The enforcement or non-enforcement of a personal right says something about the rights-bearer whose right is being enforced. So, when individuals are granted primary rights of the kind recognized by private law, they acquire an interest in seeing that those rights are enforced in an appropriate manner. That interest is a reason to afford them some measure of control over decisions about whether and how to enforce—something like the power to sue.

We agree with Gardner that these kinds of personal considerations are insufficient to justify always giving plaintiffs the power to sue. But in our view, they support a *presumption* that rights-holders themselves should hold that power by default. That is because rights-holders are generally better placed than government officials to strike the right balance between vindicating their rightful honor and avoiding sticklerism. We think there are contingent but fairly predictable worries that public prosecutors would not serve plaintiffs' moral interests in the manner of enforcement well enough to categorically displace the presumption in favor of plaintiffs in that role. Public prosecutors might give certain categories of rights violations (or certain categories of victims of rights violations) short shrift and let even serious rights violations go unremedied. This seems to be one concern with the relative dearth of criminal prosecutions in cases of police brutality, with many worrying that prosecutors are insufficiently motivated to prosecute abusive police officers, whether because of ideological affinities or because of other shared institutional interests. In other contexts, we can imagine that public prosecutors might insist on prosecuting rights violations just to make a point, even a socially valuable one, when the right-holder herself might be inclined to stand down. Consider, for example, the recent case in which a white woman walking her dog in New York City's Central Park made a false report to the police accusing a black birdwatcher of having threatened her. The woman was criminally charged with making the false report even though the birdwatcher had expressed strong misgivings about her suffering any serious consequences for her wrongdoing.[67] While the birdwatcher would hardly have been a stickler had he decided to stand on his rights, he seemed to

---

[67] T Closson, "Amy Cooper, Who Falsely Accused Black Bird-Watcher, Has Charge Dismissed" *New York Times* (New York, February 17, 2021). The charges were ultimately dropped after she completed a diversion program.

worry that such a response would still have been disproportionate. The birdwatcher, as a rights-holder, had an interest in exercising a kind of equitable discretion to avoid not just extreme forms of sticklerism, but also what he regarded as a less egregious but still disproportionate kind of enforcement—an interest that a regime of public prosecution for private rights violations fails to recognize. Any institutional arrangement in which public prosecutors enforce private rights without regard to a plaintiff's interest in holding on to what she has or her interest in letting go to avoid being a stickler, would violate her continuing moral interest in the manner of enforcement. These worries, combined with the institutional factors Gardner himself noted, account for the strength of the presumption that enforcement is a matter for the plaintiff in the common law tradition.[68] On the other hand, the presumption is rebuttable, in that it can be overcome in particular contexts by institutional or policy considerations that counsel in favor of lodging the power to enforce private law rights with some actor other than the right-holder. Our account does not rule out other institutional arrangements that are a better fit with the moral and institutional criteria that we think bear on the plaintiff's role. Another institutional actor could ensure that these moral reasons are given the appropriate weight in the decision-making process. There are conceivable situations where these moral reasons are better served by a public prosecutor, and there are situations where it seems quite certain that they would not be. For example, it may be that victims of sexual assault in a particular time and place may feel social pressure to decline to stand on their rights in a way that does not track a duty of self-honor. Or perhaps commercial owners, confronting harmless trespass, may be inclined for business reasons to be sticklers for their rights, insisting on exclusion just in order to gain leverage over their competitor. So, it is possible, we concede, that the presumption that rights-bearers have the power to sue will be displaced in favor of a prosecutor who could better track these moral reasons—albeit without undermining the reasons of public good that also militate in favor of the plaintiff's having the power.

There is considerable doctrinal support for the idea that the plaintiff's power to sue is at least partly grounded in these kinds of personal considerations, subject to overriding institutional imperatives. Lawsuits generally *must* be prosecuted by the "real party in interest," the person whose rights are fundamentally at stake in the action.[69] Members of damages class actions have a right to opt out and either go it alone or sit on their rights.[70] Various equitable doctrines allow courts to deny sticklers the relief they may be entitled to at law.[71] Such rules reflect the idea that plaintiffs have a personal,

---

[68] The kinds of personal moral interests that we identify resonate with some of the considerations that John Goldberg and Ben Zipursky adduce in support of their principle of "civil recourse." See Goldberg and Zipursky, *Recognizing Wrongs* (n 3). But we think our account of the power to sue departs from theirs in treating the enforcement of private rights as only *presumptively* a matter for the rights-holder, with the possibility that the presumption might be rebutted in certain categories of cases by countervailing policy concerns.

[69] Fed R Civ P 17(a).

[70] Fed R Civ P 23(b)(3).

[71] *Brownstone v Geller* [1980] 91 Ill App.3d 823. See also *Pickering v Rudd* [1815] 4 Camp 219 (KB) (UK) (refusing to treat the permanent encroachment of a nail and board into the airspace above the plaintiff's garden as trespass, in the absence of any interference with the plaintiff's ordinary use). See also *Messina v Arena Developments Ltd* [1985] BCJ No 751 (Can); *Kingsbridge Development Inc. v Hanson Needler Corp* [1990] 72 OR2d 159 (Can Ont H Ct J). For an insightful discussion of how Gardner's version of the

moral stake in the question whether, and how, their rights are enforced. Meanwhile, other doctrines curb plaintiffs' discretion in certain contexts for the sake of counter-vailing policy considerations. The class action and other representative devices exist in the first place to facilitate the vindication of rights in circumstances in which we worry that individual rights-holders may be loath to seek a remedy—because, say, their individual claims are too small to be worth the trouble. Members of class actions for solely injunctive or declaratory relief have no opt-out rights, since such relief is indivisible among the individual class members and benefits them all equally.[72] And administrative agencies can sometimes intervene in, or even take over, individual plaintiffs' lawsuits when necessary to vindicate more systemic policy objectives fully.[73] In the doctrine, then, we see repeated attempts to recognize the moral significance for individual rights-holders of decisions about whether and how to vindicate their rights, even as that solicitude sometimes yields for the sake of the kinds of institutional objectives Gardner rightly emphasized.

4. Conclusion

Our own proposed power-sharing account of the power to sue has more of the features of both office and property than Gardner's model allows. Plaintiffs as private insti-tutional actors join public officials (judges) in the administration of the system of rights.[74] We agree with Gardner that the power to sue depends on reasons of public good: when those reasons are gone, "it no longer deserves to be [the right] it once was."[75] But on our account, the institutional role of the plaintiff is not a detached one, a passive vehicle for decentralizing power otherwise left to public officials. Rather, we conceive of litigants as active participants in an institutional practice, constrained to act for reasons consistent with (or at least not completely antithetical to) the purposes of that practice. At the same time, on our view, the allocation of the power to sue is not independent of moral reasons personal to the plaintiff. Moral reasons of correc-tive justice (*pace* Gardner) are relevant to the plaintiff's tertiary enforcement right, for the fact that one's rights were violated gives one a personal stake in decisions about

---

continuity thesis might itself ground such equitable limits on plaintiffs' pursuit of corrective justice, see AS Gold, "Delegation and the Continuity Thesis" (2021) 40 Law and Philosophy 656–60.

[72] Fed R Civ P 23(b)(2).

[73] For example, under Title VII of the Civil Rights Act of 1964, the Equal Employment Opportunity Commission or the Department of Justice may intervene in an employment-discrimination suit when "the case is of general public importance." 42 USC § 2000e-5(f) (2018).

[74] And indeed the authority to do so is not limited to their power to sue, but is also found in the position they take about how things stand between them and others even outside of courts. As one of us has argued, plaintiffs' institutional role is continuous with the role that rights-bearers have outside court in *interpreting* their substantive private rights. Rights-bearers have a power to make a determination of how things stand *vis-à-vis* others that, on uptake by another, is appropriately accepted by courts—as their co-participants in the administration of justice—as final. See L Katz, "Blowing Hot and Cold: The Role of Estoppel" in Oberdiek and Miller (eds), *Civil Wrongs and Justice in Private Law* (n 59) 131–53.

[75] *FPLPL* (n 1) 212.

whether and how the violation is remedied. The role of enforcer thus belongs, defeasibly, to the right-holder for reasons personal to her. But as Gardner rightly stressed, institutional considerations still matter, for corrective justice consistent with dignity and equity is done through institutions—courts—and rights-holders can be at most only co-participants in that process.

15
Private Law Rights and Powers of Waiver

Haris Psarras[*]

1. Introduction

An established view in legal philosophy has it that private law rights are waivable—that is, that right-holders are free to give them up. In this chapter, I challenge this view and argue that not all private law rights are waivable. I also argue that waivability operates differently in different types of private law rights. My argument uses as a springboard John Gardner's tripartite classification of private law rights. The classification has first been launched to support an analysis of the place of corrective justice in private law and to explicate the extensive discretion of the plaintiff in civil litigation.[1] But, as I argue, it can also serve as a basis for a theory on the waivability of private law rights or, at least, for the version of such a theory that I propose in this chapter.

The argument proceeds as follows: section 2 explains why and how the orthodox view that private law rights are waivable should be re-examined if we want to tackle the question of waivability comprehensively, viz, tackle it with regard to different types of private law rights. Section 2 also introduces Gardner's tripartite classification of private law rights into (i) primary rights (rights that preclude others from unlawfully interfering with the right-holder), (ii) secondary rights (rights to remedy breaches of primary rights), and (ii) tertiary rights (rights to effectuate secondary rights in court), and argues that using this classification as the basis of an analysis of the waivability of private law rights will enable us to take such an analysis in a more promising direction.

Section 3 argues that a primary right is a claim-right over what another person ought or ought not to do, normally matched with a power to waive the correlative duty toward the right-holder and a power to withdraw the waiver. Section 4 concentrates on secondary and tertiary rights. It considers a secondary right as the residue of a primary right that has been breached and explains why secondary rights are unwaivable. Furthermore, section 4 contends that a tertiary right also invests the right-holder with two powers that apply in relation to two different agents: first, in relation to the wrongdoer, a waivable power to sue her; second, in relation to a civil court, an unwaivable power to lead the process of judicial ascertainment of the relevant primary and secondary rights through starting, continuing, and discontinuing proceedings against the wrongdoer.

---

[*] Some points discussed in this chapter were first presented at a webinar on John Gardner's philosophy of private law on April 9, 2021. I am grateful to webinar participants for enlightening comments. Special thanks to Hanoch Dagan, Christopher Essert, Cécile Fabre, Dori Kimel, Matt Shapiro, Zoë Sinel, Sandy Steel, Robert Stevens, and Frederick Wilmot-Smith. Errors are my own.

[1] J Gardner, *From Personal Life to Private Law* (OUP 2018) 207–11 ("*FPLPL*").

Haris Psarras, *Private Law Rights and Powers of Waiver* In: *Private Law and Practical Reason*. Edited by: Haris Psarras and Sandy Steel, Oxford University Press. © Haris Psarras 2023. DOI: 10.1093/oso/9780192857330.003.0015

2. Waivability and Types of Private Law Rights

The idea that private law rights are waivable has been an orthodoxy in private law theory since Hart defended it in the course of his critical engagement with an account of rights and duties advocated by Bentham.[2] After rejecting a distinction between duties in private law and duties in criminal law drawn on the basis of the mistaken belief that private law secures the separate interests of different individuals while criminal law secures the general interests of society,[3] Hart draws a distinction between private law and criminal law on the basis of the control over the duty of another that the law gives to a right-holder. He argues that in private law a right-holder is being given "the fullest measure of control" over a duty that another person owes to her— that is, a level of "exclusive control" that amounts to the power to "waive or extinguish" such a duty.[4] Also, he contrasts that with the fact that in criminal law a person "has no power to release anyone from its duties" or "to determine whether the duties ... should be enforced or not."[5]

In the same vein, other scholars who have celebrated waivability as a characteristic feature of private law rights have also done so while contrasting private law duties to criminal law duties.[6] Such formulations of the idea that private law rights are waivable are as good as they can get, given the scope of the argument that they are intended to serve. If the question that an argument grapples with is what differentiates private law duties from duties in criminal law, then the assertion that private law duties correlate to waivable rights, while criminal law duties do not, may be a satisfactory answer. Yet, clearly, this does not mean that all private law rights are waivable, let alone that all private law rights are waivable because they are private law rights. For one thing, for a private law right (or, indeed, for any right) to be waivable, in the sense discussed by Hart in the extracts I highlighted above, it has to be correlative to a duty.[7] And the fact that private law duties can, in principle, be juxtaposed to criminal law duties on the basis of

---

[2] See HLA Hart, "Legal Rights" in *Essays on Bentham: Jurisprudence and Political Philosophy* (Clarendon Press 1982) 162, 181–88; originally published as "Bentham on Legal Rights" in AWB Simpson (ed), *Oxford Essays in Jurisprudence: Second Series* (Clarendon Press 1973) 171.

[3] Hart, "Legal Rights" (n 2) 183.

[4] ibid 183–84.

[5] ibid 184.

[6] See R Stevens, "Private Rights and Public Wrongs" in M Dyson (ed), *Unravelling Tort and Crime* (CUP 2014) 111, 117–18; NE Simmonds, "Rights at the Cutting Edge" in MH Kramer, NE Simmonds, and H Steiner (eds), *A Debate over Rights: Philosophical Enquiries* (OUP 1998) 113, 141–42. Note, also, that by "private law duties" and "private law rights," in this context, we normally refer to duties and rights in the law of obligations, not in property law. For an in-depth normative account of property rights, see JE Penner, *Property Rights: A Re-Examination* (OUP 2020), which also covers questions on waivability (see ch 4).

[7] Note that, in technical terms, the normative entity that is waivable in situations involving rights known as "waivable rights" is not the right itself, but the duty that the right correlates to (see Hart, "Legal Rights" (n 2) 184). In this sense, the accurate way to express the normative phenomenon of waiving is to say that a right-holder gives up a right through waiving another person's duty that is correlative to that right. Terms and formulations such as "waivable rights" and "waiving a right" are used for the sake of simplicity. In private law theory and in general jurisprudence their usage is widespread; see, among others, NJ McBride, *The Humanity of Private Law. Part I: Explanation* (Hart Publishing 2018) 73, 171; R Stevens, *Torts and Rights* (OUP 2007) 105; DN MacCormick, "Rights in Legislation" in PMS Hacker and J Raz (eds), *Law, Morality, and Society: Essays in Honour of H.L.A. Hart* (Clarendon Press 1977) 189, 196.

the view that the former are correlative to rights (arguably, to rights that are therefore considered to be waivable), while the latter are not, does not exclude the possibility that there may be types of private law rights that are not correlative to duties and may therefore be unwaivable.[8]

At this point we have established that some prominent arguments or declarations in favor of the waivability of private law rights have not been formed in a manner that would rule out justified skepticism toward the idea that private law rights are inherently and invariably waivable. In his criticism of this idea, Gardner took a more decisive step. He spotlighted as a reason why waivability should not be considered as built into the nature of private law rights, not only the idea that not all private law rights are "duty-based" (as he terms rights that are correlative to duties), but also the bolder idea that not even duty-based rights (in private law, in other areas of law, and beyond law) are necessarily waivable.[9] Moreover, Gardner's argument on this point enables us to deduce an explanation for some people's attraction to the view he rejects.[10] The erroneous treatment of all rights in private law, and beyond, as invariably subject to an alleged power of the right-holder to waive them can be traced back to the mistaken consideration of all different entitlements that are roughly classified into the "rights" category as rights correlative to duties and, hence, as waivable rights. This consideration may be doubly mistaken. First, because the underlying assumption that rights correlative to duties are, by definition, waivable may, as noted earlier, have to be rejected; second, and most importantly, because even if the assumption holds, it does not follow that other entitlements (such as legal powers, authority claims, or other claims in law)[11] that are occasionally described as "rights" in an approximate sense are also waivable.[12]

Gardner may have been right in attributing the appeal of the idea of waivability of private law rights to widespread ambiguity between rights, in the broad sense of the term, and rights correlative to duties. But this does not explain Hart's endorsement of the idea. Hart (unlike other theorists who may have been trapped in ambiguity over "right" as a term and "right" as a concept) is well aware that a number of legal entitlements loosely called "rights" (ie powers, liberties, immunities) are not correlative to duties.[13]

The problem with what appears to be Hart's endorsement of the idea of waivability is of a different nature. Hart is committed to the view that to have a right in private law is not merely a matter of being owed a duty correlative to your right but a matter of having a "special form of control" over such a duty—that is, to have the legal power to waive or extinguish the duty.[14] It must be his commitment to this view that makes Hart

---

[8] Of course, Hart, following Bentham, acknowledges that rights correlative to duties (in his words, "rights correlative to obligations") are only one type of rights, and that there are also rights resulting from permissive laws or legal silence, which he calls "liberty rights"; see Hart, "Legal Rights" (n 2) 165–66.

[9] *FPLPL* (n 1) 203–04.

[10] But for Hart's cautious stance on the matter see ibid 203, fn 10.

[11] For these and other legal concepts casually denoted by the term "right" see WN Hohfeld, "Some Fundamental Legal Conceptions as Applied in Judicial Reasoning" (1913–1914) 23(1) Yale Law Journal 16, 30–31.

[12] *FPLPL* (n 1) 204.

[13] Hart, "Legal Rights" (n 2) 164–65. See also note 8, above.

[14] ibid 184–85.

262 HARIS PSARRAS

leave no room for entitlements loosely called "rights" on his list of private law rights. In fact, Hart keeps his version of such a list all too short, allowing only for the two following types of private law rights that are correlative to respective duties and can be waived: (i) rights not to be harmed, and (ii) rights to receive compensation for harm following litigation.[15]

Yet familiarity with ordinary legal practice suggests that a full list of the types of rights that are secured by private law institutions would be longer. Moreover, some types of private law rights that are known through practice, but had not been explicitly acknowledged by Hart, have more recently received increasing attention from philosophers of private law. Some such further types of private law rights that have been theorized in recent scholarship are: (i) an entitlement to reparation,[16] which can also be conceived of as a right to a remedy[17] (note that rights of this type are more general than—and antecedent to—the rights that Hart considers as rights to compensation);[18] (ii) a right of action or a right of redress,[19] which can also be framed in terms of a right to assert and vindicate a right to a remedy through the courts;[20] (iii) less heavily institutionalized normative claims, that are yet detectable in the rationale of ordinary practices in private law, such as entitlements reflecting private law's commitment to what has been described as relational justice.[21]

Looking through these additional types of rights, one may be unsure as to how they should best be classified but would note that at least some resist their classification as rights correlative to duties and count as rights in a broad sense of the term—essentially being powers or liberties or even broader claims in conformity with moral reasons that have been incorporated into the law. Now, a sceptic may argue that a number of these types of rights are products of theorization of private law more than they are reflections of day-to-day practices in civil litigation. But even if there is some truth in the sceptic's concern, still the vindication and specification of remedial entitlements in court as well as the enforcement of remedies through the execution of court decisions are normative practices integral to private law and yet not fully analyzable in terms of correlations between rights and duties.

These remarks on some types of private law rights that Hart did not explicitly acknowledge, suffice to explain why and how the established view on the waivability of

---

[15] ibid 184. Here, Hart also acknowledges that a right-holder, following a breach of a duty owed to her, is entitled to bring a lawsuit to remedy the harm caused or—in case of a continued breach—to put an end to the breach. However, Hart does not consider this entitlement as a separate right in private law nor discusses its possible waivability. In light of this, it is fair to say that, on Hart's list of private law rights, rights to sue are not classified as a separate type of rights.

[16] On the notion of an entitlement to reparation, see EJ Weinrib, *The Idea of Private Law* (OUP 2012) 143–44.

[17] On a right to a remedy, see *FPLPL* (n 1) 212.

[18] One way to explain the difference between a right to compensation and an entitlement to reparation is to note that the former is a court-ordered right to a particular and judicially determined remedy, while the latter is the reason why a court is under a duty to order that remedy following successful litigation over breach of duty. On court-ordered rights see SA Smith, *Rights, Wrongs, and Injustices: The Structure of Remedial Law* (OUP 2019) 75, 82–84.

[19] On rights of action or rights of redress as expressions of "the principle of civil recourse," see JCP Goldberg and BC Zipursky, *Recognizing Wrongs* (Belknap Press 2020) 113, 122–24.

[20] See *FPLPL* (n 1) 209.

[21] On relational justice, see H Dagan, "Autonomy and Pluralism in Private Law" in AS Gold and others (eds), *The Oxford Handbook of the New Private Law* (OUP 2020) 177, 178–79, 190–93.

private law rights should be reviewed. Waivability has been seen as inherent in private law rights in view of the belief that private law duties—in contrast to criminal law duties—are correlative to rights; a belief associated with the idea that rights correlative to duties are waivable. Now, regardless of the plausibility of a contrast between private law and criminal law in these terms and regardless of the credibility of a direct link between the correlativity of rights and duties and the waivability of rights, the fact that a number of entitlements in private law, like those mentioned earlier, may not be correlative to duties calls for the orthodox view on waivability to be re-examined. Its re-examination should be performed on the basis of a typology of private law rights that, first, acknowledges both the private law rights in the strict sense of the term (ie those that preoccupied Hart) and any private law entitlements that resist classification in Hart's categories; and, second, enables us to appreciate interconnections between different types of rights—interconnections that become more noticeable through a comprehensive portrayal of private law rather than through representations that concentrate on either substantive or remedial private law.

Gardner's tripartite classification of various entitlements in private law as primary rights, secondary rights, and tertiary rights is a good candidate for this task. In the remaining sections of the chapter, it will serve as the basis for my re-examination of the orthodox view. I will also use it as the basis for an alternative analysis of waivability in private law rights; an analysis that lies beyond the intended explanatory scope of Gardner's taxonomy, but is compatible with it and serves its spirit. A good way to introduce Gardner's classification to readers who are not familiar with it, is to recall an example that he draws from a fictional representation of commonplace tensions in interpersonal relationships: Alice, a girl in Nesbit's *The Story of the Treasure Seekers*, has been treated disagreeably by her brother Horace Octavius (H.O.); their older brother, Dicky, intervenes and requires H.O. to apologize to Alice for his misbehavior. Gardner tells us that Alice has three rights that are of interest to us when we look at the incident from a normative perspective.

First, Alice has a primary right not to have been treated disagreeably by H.O. Second, she has a secondary right to an apology from H.O. Third, she has a tertiary right to assert and enforce her right to an apology from H.O. herself and—within reason—in the way she sees fit; that is, regardless (and, indeed, to the exclusion of) others' leaping to her defense.[22] If we turn from interpersonal relationships that unfold in a private circle (such as the relationship between Alice and H.O.) to relations regulated by private law, the normative landscape, Gardner argues, remains unaltered. In the eyes of the law, a person has a primary right not to be wronged by another; that is, a right that another (i) does not do certain things that set her back in the life she already has or (ii) protects her from having her life set back.[23] Such a right can also be described as an "initial entitlement,"[24] in the sense that it covers what a person is owed to by another, in the first place.

---

[22] See *FPLPL* (n 1) 207–09.

[23] ibid 182.

[24] ibid 192, fn 42 citing G Calabresi and D Melamed, "Property Rules, Liability Rules, and Inalienability: One View of the Cathedral" (1972) 85(6) Harvard Law Review 1089.

Now, in the event of a breach of her primary right, the right-holder has a secondary right, that is, an entitlement to a remedy (eg reparative damages) available as of right for the breach.[25] She also has a tertiary right to initiate litigation and take the lead in the unfolding of court proceedings, in order to have her secondary right authoritatively established in court and receive a remedy in the form of a court order. The continuity between a primary and a secondary right is the flipside of the continuity between a primary and a secondary duty and, as such, it also lies at the core of the so-called continuity thesis, which has marked the culmination of Gardner's endeavor "to make a case for moral norms of corrective justice."[26]

That being said, it should be noted that the continuity thesis is not part and parcel of the tripartite classification of private law rights. It may well be that in Gardner's work the continuity thesis and the tripartite classification act as mutually supportive components of an account of private law that stresses the key role of corrective justice among a number of values served by private law. But the continuity thesis and the tripartite classification can also be seen as two conceptually separable theorizations of the intersection between substantive and remedial private law. One way to highlight their separability is to acknowledge that they are intended to address different questions. The continuity thesis purports to explain corrective justice in private law as a matter of practical reasons that underlie obligations that have been institutionalized as private law duties;[27] the tripartite classification aims to explain what claims correspond to such private law duties and what additional entitlements render such claims justiciable and remediable.

In light of the fact that the tripartite classification is a self-standing theoretical tool, its credibility is not undermined by an ongoing controversy over the continuity thesis.[28] In any case, my account of the tripartite classification in the rest of the chapter makes only occasional reference to the continuity thesis and is not premised upon its endorsement; this is also one of the reasons why my argument does not address objections against the continuity thesis.

Let us now turn to the second stage of the argument to explore how the consideration of private law rights on the basis of their tripartite classification enables us to gain a more nuanced understanding of their waivability. The remaining two sections of the chapter discuss different types of rights as follows. Section 3 covers primary rights; section 4 covers secondary and tertiary rights. First, each section discusses puzzling aspects of the freedom (or lack thereof) to waive private law rights that the orthodox view (ie the view that private law rights are waivable because right-holders in private

---

[25] ibid 192.

[26] J Gardner, *Torts and Other Wrongs* (OUP 2019) 61 (*"TAOW"*).

[27] In Gardner's words, the continuity thesis is "the thesis that the secondary obligation is a rational echo of the primary obligation, for it exists to serve, so far as may still be done, the reasons for the primary obligation that was not performed when its performance was due" (ibid).

[28] For criticisms of the continuity thesis, see eg Goldberg and Zipursky, *Recognizing Wrongs* (n 19) 159–63; S Smith, "Duties, Liabilities, and Damages" (2011) 125(7) Harvard Law Review 1727, 1737–38, 1754; Z Sinel, "Through Thick and Thin: The Place of Corrective Justice in Unjust Enrichment" (2011) 31(3) Oxford Journal of Legal Studies 551, 559–63. For moderate renderings or restatements of the continuity thesis that respond to or acknowledge objections that it has attracted, see, respectively, S Steel, "Compensation and Continuity" (2020) 26(3) Legal Theory 250, 266–71 and L Radzik, "Tort Processes and Relational Repair" in J Oberdiek (ed), *Philosophical Foundations of the Law of Torts* (OUP 2014) 231, 239–42.

law may freely waive the correlative duties) is not in a position to make sense of; second, it proposes a way to grasp such aspects with reference to legal practice through arguing that different types of private law rights are different clusters of entitlements and that some of these entitlements are waivable, while others are not.

3. The Waivability of Primary Rights

Primary rights are the natural place to start an inquiry into the waivability of private law rights. One reason for that is that they are prior to secondary and tertiary rights in the sense that the latter two are remedial rights, whereas primary rights are substantive rights: a secondary and a tertiary right arise after and because of an infringement of a primary right.[29] But there is also another reason why it is natural to start with primary rights, a reason that has to do with how we normally understand the practice of waiving rights. To elucidate this, let us recall that primary rights are intended to protect the right-holder against others' unlawful interference with various valuable states of affairs that she enjoys under the law.

As it has been acknowledged by advocates of the rights-based theory of private law, regardless of whether a primary right has emerged through a person's voluntary undertaking of a duty toward another, who therefore then becomes a right-holder (as it happens with contractual rights), or has arisen for other reasons (as is the case with rights in tort or equity), it is a right that correlates to a duty; that is, a claim-right that another person acts in accordance with a duty she has toward the right-holder to do or not to do something.[30] Of course, a primary right, so understood, is a claim-right in the Hohfeldian sense of the term.[31] In other words, it is what Hart describes as a "right correlative to [an] obligation."[32] Considering that normally to waive a right is to waive the correlative duty, primary rights are the paradigmatic type of waivable rights in private law. Moreover, primary rights should make the strongest case for the orthodox view. If there are different types of waivable rights in private law, then it should be more straightforward to establish waivability in the case of primary rights.

Yet closer consideration of constraints that apply to waiving primary rights shows that the orthodox view is not watertight even in its strongest case. In principle, primary rights in private law are waivable, but not for the reason given by the orthodox view. Also, their waivability is subject to exceptions and qualifications. The weaknesses of the orthodox view become apparent if one considers some highlights of private law practice. Such highlights also indicate that a tripartite-classification approach to private law rights is better in tune with the practice of waiving primary rights in private law.

The reason that the orthodox view would appeal to, to justify its unconditional commitment to the waivability of primary rights can be found in Hart's description of the

---

[29] See *FPLPL* (n 1) 207–08.
[30] See eg Stevens, *Torts and Rights* (n 7) 4–5, 11; see also S Steel, "On the Moral Necessity of Tort Law: The Fairness Argument" (2021) 41(1) Oxford Journal of Legal Studies 192, 194.
[31] Hohfeld, "Some Fundamental Legal Conceptions" (n 11) 32.
[32] Hart, "Legal Rights" (n 2) 166, 168.

right-holder as "a small-scale sovereign" who enjoys "the fullest measure of control" over the correlative duty.[33] But the espousal of such a justification of waivability, which also indicates a close association between the orthodox view and the will theories of rights[34] (note that Hart constructed his advocacy of what has by now become the orthodox view through a rejection of Bentham's version of the benefit theory of rights),[35] leads an argument in support of the orthodox view to mistakes.

One such mistake is the claim that primary rights are correlative to duties that are not only waivable, but also extinguishable;[36] a claim that is deduced from the orthodox view's consideration of the right-holder as a person who enjoys full control over the duties owed to her. Though the idea of waivability of duties largely corresponds to some long-standing practices in private law,[37] the idea that all private law duties are extinguishable is erroneous. The error persists, even if we take private law duties to be extinguished only at the request of the holders of the correlative rights, as the orthodox view proposes.[38] To illustrate, consider the textbook examples of a contract of slavery[39] or of a TV game show in which players would agree to remain locked up in the TV producer's premises indefinitely even if they were to change their mind later.[40]

What renders such contracts void or unenforceable is that some primary rights in private law (at least, the type or rights that such contracts are intended to extinguish or compromise) and the correlative duties are inextinguishable. It may well be that different schools of thought would provide different justifications for the inextinguishability of the smaller or larger group of private law duties that each of them considers as inextinguishable. And it may also be that not all such justifications are equally remote from the orthodox view's consideration of the right-holder's autonomy as the top value served by private law rights.[41] Even so, it remains the case that if in private law not all duties correlative to primary rights are extinguishable then the orthodox view's attempt to justify what it claims to be the invariable waivability of

---

[33] ibid 183.

[34] ibid 162.

[35] ibid 174, 183.

[36] ibid 184.

[37] Largely, but not wholly, as the law sometimes rules out waiving some duties; see eg the issue of waivers of liability in tort as discussed in Edward L. Rubin, "Toward a General Theory of Waiver" (1981) 28(3) UCLA Law Review 478, 532, 558.

[38] Some scholars use the term "inalienable right" to describe a right correlative to a duty that is not extinguishable (see eg NJ McBride and R Bagshaw, *Tort Law* (6th edn, Pearson 2018) 20; MacCormick, "Rights in Legislation" (n 7) 198–99), though the term is typically used to describe a right that cannot be transferred from the right-holder to another person (see eg R Stevens, "Not Waiving but Drowning" in A Dyson, J Goudkamp, and F Wilmot-Smith (eds), *Defences in Contract* (Hart Publishing 2017) 125; Stevens, "Private Rights and Public Wrongs" (n 6) 115–16).

[39] Stevens, "Private Rights and Public Wrongs" (n 6) 116; A Ripstein, *Force and Freedom: Kant's Legal and Political Philosophy* (Harvard University Press 2009) 38.

[40] For a different version of this example, in which players are locked up for a specific yet too lengthy period of time, see McBride and Bagshaw, *Tort Law* (n 38) 20.

[41] For instance, a justification of the inextinguishability of some rights on the basis of the idea that a right-holder is her own master throughout her life (for this idea see eg Ripstein, *Force and Freedom* (n 39) 36) directly opposes the orthodox view's take on extinguishability, but does so through appealing to a value that the orthodox view holds in high esteem (ie individual autonomy). For an endorsement of inextinguishability through an appeal to the benefit theory of rights, whose take on the values that underlie rights protection is diametrically opposed to the orthodox view's take on this matter, see eg McBride, *Humanity of Private Law* (n 7) 40.

PRIVATE LAW RIGHTS AND POWERS OF WAIVER 267

primary rights on the basis of a portrayal of the right-holder as a "small-scale sovereign" fails.

The failure of the orthodox view's justificatory enterprise is due to its attempt to offer a defense of primary rights' waivability across the board; that is, a defense that allows for no exceptions or qualification. Inevitably, even a single exception to the allegedly unvarying extinguishability of correlative duties suffices to subvert the orthodox view's justification of the waivability of primary rights. In a nutshell: (i) if the hypothesis that primary rights are waivable is premised on the idea that a right-holder has "the fullest measure of control" over the correlative duties (as the orthodox view proposes through considering the right-holder as a "small-scale sovereign");[42] and (ii) if it is subsequently established that at least some private law duties are inextinguishable; (iii) then, the justification of the waivability of primary rights on the basis of the "full-control" idea fails. This is because the very fact that some private law duties are inextinguishable indicates that right-holders do not have full control over them; if they did, then there would be no inextinguishable duties in private law.

Now, if the issue with the orthodox view were only a matter of a failed argument proposed in its favor, and if the point that primary rights are invariably waivable were accurate, though not inferable from the "full-control" idea, then that would arguably leave the key claim of the orthodox view unscathed. After all, the orthodox view—one could argue—is a view on the waivability of private law rights, not a view on why such rights are waivable. Though this may be true, a closer inspection of the relationship between the orthodox view and ordinary aspects of private law practice indicates that the weaknesses of the orthodox view are not primarily a matter of failed justification. In fact, even the key claim of the orthodox view appears to be at odds with routine practices in waiving primary rights.

Consider that the orthodox view is not in a position to account for waivers barred under statute or even for waiver withdrawal. How could the statutory bar to the application of *volenti* in road traffic accidents[43] be explained by the orthodox view without it appearing inconsistent with its commitment to the idea of invariably waivable primary rights? Also in tort, is withdrawal of consent (which amounts to withdrawal of waiver), not in tension with the idea of a right as solely a matter of control over an applicable correlative duty?

One could argue that the reason why the orthodox view has no satisfactory answers to these questions is that it does not allow for exceptions. Is it, then, that by treating the statutory bar to *volenti* as an exception to a generally applicable rule of free waivers or by acknowledging that waivers are withdrawable, the orthodox view would insulate itself from criticism? That would be an option for the orthodox view if there were room for it to reconcile such an exception or qualification with its claim that the exercise of the free will of the right-holder is the ultimate normative consideration that a primary right is intended to protect and the critical link between a right-holder and her right.[44]

---

[42] See notes 4 and 33 above.

[43] Road Traffic Act 1988 ("*RTA*"), section 149(3).

[44] For an effective argument in favor of the addition of such qualifications to the orthodox view, see G Sreenivasan, "A Hybrid Theory of Claim-Rights" (2005) 25(2) Oxford Journal of Legal Studies 257, 267. The argument also demonstrates how such an addition marks a departure from the orthodox view toward a hybrid theory incorporating elements from both the will theory and the interest theory tradition.

Yet it is hard to think of a justification for statutorily barring a waiver without appealing to normative considerations beyond those that are associated with the portrayal of a right-holder as a small-scale sovereign. And it is equally hard to contemplate a reason why a right-holder would retain a normative link with a right after waiving it if the key link between a right-holder and her right is seen to be her freedom to exercise it until she possibly decides to waive it, thus alienating herself from it for good. But, clearly, the retention of a link between a right-holder and her right is a conceptual pre-requisite for the orthodox view to account for withdrawals of waivers. This is because for the orthodox view to remain consistent with its line, waiver withdrawal should be normatively grounded on the very reasons that the orthodox view would appeal to, to justify its claim that a right-holder is in full control of the correlative duty, in the first place.

It appears that the orthodox view reaches an impasse when it attempts to make sense of practices in private law that do not sit well with its commitment to the treatment of the right-holder as a small-scale sovereign. Let us now turn to the tripartite classification to see how it can contribute toward an alternative theorization of waiving primary rights. Now, given that the tripartite classification is not a theory on the waivability of rights, it is unsurprising that its endorsement does not necessarily lead to a specific conclusion on the matter. However, its insights into the nature of primary rights and other types of rights in private law enable us to advance our understanding of their waivability.

First, the tripartite classification rejects the idea that the power to waive a primary right is built into the nature of a primary right.[45] Second, it also rejects the idea that having a primary right entails having some form of power over the duty-bearer.[46] This point concerns any form of power, not just a power to waive the correlative duty; notably, it also concerns a power to seek reparation for a breach of duty.[47] More specifically, according to the tripartite classification, the powers related to the assertion and enforcement of a primary right constitute a separate right in private law: a tertiary right; a set of "radically discretionary procedural powers"[48] that are not normally recognized to right-holders of substantive rights in other areas of law (eg in criminal law), let alone in other normative systems and in morality.

The dissociation between a primary right and a right-holder's powers over the duty-bearer, along with the consideration of the right-holder's discretionary procedural powers as constitutive of a separate right are two key features of the tripartite classification. They enable it to accommodate the idea that the will of a right-holder has high normative significance in the practice of rights in private law without yet treating such a will as the normative core of a primary right, as the orthodox view does. This explains why, according to the tripartite classification, a power to waive a primary right is not

---

[45] *FPLPL* (n 1) 204.

[46] The point, as Gardner puts it, is that a right-holder of a duty-based right is not necessarily a "holder of normative power" over the duty-bearer, which means that it is a mistake "to read a normative power back into the relationship between a (strict sense) right-holder and the person who owes her a duty" (ibid).

[47] Note the argument on why the doctrine *ubi ius, ibi remedium* is not a conceptual truth; note, also, the rejection of the idea that rights are "equipped automatically with remedies for their breach" in or outside the law (ibid).

[48] ibid 201; see also 209.

seen as built into the nature of a primary right. Clearly, this does not mean that, from the perspective of the tripartite classification, primary rights cannot be matched with powers of waiver. Of course, they can, as the ordinary practice of primary rights in private law indicates.

The third key insight of the tripartite classification into the nature of primary rights is their consideration as duty-based rights (ie as rights correlative to duties) in a theoretical framework in which a duty is not the flipside of the institutionally protected will of the right-holder, but a mandatory categorical reason not to wrong the right-holder.[49] This conception of a duty does not mean that interfering with protected aspects of the right-holder's life without her consent does not count as a form of wrongdoing. It means that non-interfering unless consent is given is not the sole form of complying with a primary duty in private law.[50] It also means that interfering without consent may not count as wrongdoing in some cases.[51]

In light of these insights, we can offer a picture of the waivability of primary rights in private law that is more complex and realistic than the one advocated by the orthodox view. Thus, a primary right can be seen as a claim-right over what a duty-bearer ought or ought not to do in order not to wrong the right-holder. As such, a primary right in private law is neither inherently waivable nor inherently unwaivable. But in many legal systems primary rights have been institutionalized as clusters of rights and powers. This form of institutionalization consists in matching primary rights with powers of waiver and powers to withdraw a waiver. It is a widespread practice across different legal traditions, and therefore cannot be left out of the picture when we theorize the operation of primary rights in private law. But acknowledging the practice of waivers does not entail endorsing the orthodox view. Though waiving a right is a manner for the right-holder to exercise control autonomously over duties owed to her, the right-holder's will is not the only relevant consideration to the practice of waivers. Policy considerations, including considerations of public good, may also be relevant,[52] as is the case with statutory bars to waivers. And such restrictions on waivers cannot be left out of the picture either.

An argument can be made for such restrictions to be accounted for without yet considering them as curtailing the autonomy of the right-holder. This would go as follows. The exercise of a power of waiver of a duty to φ can be considered as a conferral to the duty-bearer of a liberty to φ or not to φ until the waiver is withdrawn.[53] But given that for the period of time covered by the waiver the right-holder cannot successfully exercise her power of assertion and enforcement of her primary right,[54] the exercise of

---

[49] ibid 118, 207.

[50] In what appears to be a light-touch version of the interest theory of rights, Gardner has conceptualized the typical form of a primary right in private law as corresponding to a duty which exists because the right-holder is especially vulnerable to or dependent on the duty-bearer's actions, regardless of how small the right-holder's aspect of life that is at stake may be; see ibid 120. In this sense, respecting the will of the right-holder on a matter may in some cases be all that is required of a duty-bearer even if acting against the right-holder's will entails no loss for her.

[51] For an example see D Parfit, *On What Matters* (OUP 2011) 178.

[52] See eg *FPLPL* (n 1) 210–11.

[53] For conceptualizations of a power of waiver along these lines see Penner, *Property Rights* (n 6) 82 fn 26; Stevens, "Private Rights and Public Wrongs" (n 6) 115.

[54] More broadly, on different types of relationship between powers of waiver and powers of enforcement when they are held by the same person see MH Kramer, "Some Doubts about Alternatives to the Interest

a power of waiver in private law can equally well be considered as a conferral to the defendant of an immunity from liability in the course of civil proceedings for not φ-ing.[55] Thus, a statutory bar to a waiver can be conceptualized not only as an exclusion of the power of a right-holder to grant a liberty to the duty-bearer to φ or not to φ, but, alternatively, as an exclusion of the defendant's immunity from liability for not φ-ing. This latter form of conceptualizing a statutory bar to a waiver acknowledges the role of the court in the assessment and assertion of the statutory bar.

It is telling, in this respect, that the bar to the application of *volenti* in the Road Traffic Act[56] has been formulated in terms of excluding not the negation of the defendant's primary duty not to risk negligent harm to the plaintiff, but the negation of the defendant's liability in case the risk of negligent harm that has been willingly accepted by the plaintiff, eventuates.[57] This formulation suggests that what is excluded here is not a power of waiver of a primary right, but the consideration of such a waiver in court also as a waiver of a power of enforcement. So understood, a statutory bar to a power of waiver does not necessarily curtail the autonomy of the right-holder; rather, it eliminates the normative implications that a waiver of a primary right would otherwise have for the powers of enforcement that primary rights in private law are normally paired with.

Finally, the consideration of the power to withdraw a waiver as a separate power that stays with the right-holder after she exercises her power to waive a primary right accounts for the fact that the right-holder retains a link with reasons underlying the legal recognition of a primary right even after she waives it. If the recognition of a primary right reflected only law's respect for the will of the right-holder as it is manifested through actions covered by the right, and if the power of waiver were part and parcel of the primary right itself (as the orthodox view argues), then the issuance of a waiver by the right-holder would leave us looking for separate reasons to justify a subsequent waiver withdrawal.

By way of contrast, the tripartite classification's consideration of a primary right as underlain by reasons requiring that the right-holder is not wronged as well as by public good considerations, and its treatment of a primary right in private law as a triple normative package (a package comprising a claim-right, a power to waive the claim-right, and a power to withdraw the waiver) enable us to explain why the link between the right-holder and the power to withdraw a waiver remains intact even after the "claim-right" part of the package is waived. Moreover, the reasons that underlie the institutionalization of this triple normative package also furnish all three constitutive parts of the package with a unified justificatory basis.

Theories of Rights" (2013) 123 (2) Ethics 245, 250–53. Gardner classifies powers of enforcement, along with other procedural powers, under tertiary rights.

[55] The situation would be somewhat different if the power of enforcement were vested not in the right-holder but in enforcement officials; see ibid 252 (point iii).

[56] *RTA* (n 43).

[57] Section 149(3): "The fact that a person so carried has willingly accepted, as his, the risk of negligence on the part of the user shall not be treated as negativing any such liability of the user" (ibid). See also McBride and Bagshaw, *Tort Law* (n 38) 705–06.

4. Limitations on the Waivability of Rights to Remedies

The orthodox view on the waivability of remedial rights in private law can be found, in a nutshell, in Hart's remarks on a breach of right that empowers the right-holder to initiate court proceedings. Hart indicates that the right-holder (i) "may leave [her right] 'unenforced' or may 'enforce' it by suing for compensation" or for another remedy and, at a later stage, (ii) "waive ... the obligation to pay compensation to which the breach gives rise."[58] Though the orthodox view models its conception of waivability of remedial rights after its approach to primary rights' waivablity, its recognition of two different types of remedial rights (ie (i) rights to assert an infringed primary right in court through asking for a remedy and (ii) rights to enforce a remedial right that has been established by court order) demonstrates its awareness that, unlike primary rights, remedial rights operate through the agency of not one, but two normative actors: the plaintiff and the court. Furthermore, the treatment of the waivability of each of these two types of rights in different terms indicates that the orthodox view also acknowledges that the different institutional roles of the plaintiff and the court in the remedial process have an impact on whether and how different types of remedial rights may be waivable.

Despite acknowledging such complexities, the orthodox view's picture of waivable remedial rights is partly misconceived and incomplete, while it also fails to address key issues related to institutional and normative limitations on giving up rights or other entitlements following a breach of a primary right. First, it is partly misconceived because it considers in terms of waivability of rights the choice of a right-holder to start or not start a lawsuit against the infringer of her primary right as well as her choice to ask or not ask for the enforcement of a court order against the infringer if she wins the lawsuit. Of course, the right-holder is presented with these choices following a breach of right.[59] But choosing not to sue, or—if she decides to sue and the lawsuit is successful—not to enforce a court order against the defendant does not amount to a waiver of a right. Such choices, if made, are simply choices not to exercise the respective powers (ie the power to sue and the power to enforce a court order). If anything, the point of having a power is to choose whether and when you exercise it. Choosing not to exercise a power, while you are still entitled to exercise it at any point you change your mind, is a key manifestation of the normative fact that you have a power; it is not an act of waiving it.

Second, the orthodox view's approach to remedial rights is incomplete. This is because it discusses two types of remedial rights and neglects others. The remedial rights that have been highlighted by the orthodox view correspond to the two categories that in Smith's recent elaborate account of remedial rights have been classified as (i) action rights, and (ii) enforcement rights.[60] But there is also an additional type of remedial rights: court-ordered rights. Those are "rights established by judicial orders," such as a

---

[58] Hart, "Legal Rights" (n 2) 184.
[59] The right-holder also has further choices as the case progresses in court; it is she, in her capacity as a plaintiff, who controls litigation.
[60] Smith, *Rights, Wrongs, and Injustices* (n 18) 80–82, 84–85.

plaintiff's right to receive £100 compensation from the defendant because a final court order places the defendant under a duty to pay £100 compensation to her.[61] Evidently, court-ordered rights are rights correlative to duties. Considering that the paradigmatic type of a waivable right is a right correlative to a duty, it is striking that the class of court-ordered rights is absent from the orthodox view's list of remedial rights. This is striking because according to the orthodox view, remedial rights, as any other private law rights, are waivable; and, even more so, because the two other types of rights on the list are not rights correlative to duties but powers whose waivability can hardly be defended with reference to the orthodox view's portrayal of the right-holder as a small-scale sovereign.

But perhaps the absence of court-ordered rights from the orthodox view's list of waivable remedial rights is not that surprising. When we look at the everyday practice of court-ordered rights we realize that we do not think of them as waivable rights. A successful plaintiff who does not wish to benefit from her court-ordered right would choose not to exercise the enforcement right that empowers her to employ the state's coercive power in order to enforce the court decision. The idea of waiving a court-ordered right sounds odd, not only because the plaintiff may choose not to proceed to enforcement but also because the idea of her waiving at will a duty that has been generated and imposed upon the defendant by a court order appears to undermine or interfere with the exercise of the court's authority. Once a court decides a case through issuing an order that terminates litigation, the violated right and the infringed duty that triggered the lawsuit, eventually re-emerge, but this time they come in a new form. Now they are not substantive rights and duties that may be waived if the right-holder decides so; they are highly specific remedial rights and duties ascribed to the right-holder and the duty-bearer through the binding decision of a court, which is also enforceable by state coercive mechanisms.

The courts' and the state's role in the conferral and exercise of rights and duties at the remedial stage of a relationship in private law makes a full endorsement of waivability regarding court-ordered and other remedial rights less appealing. In addition to that, there is also another consideration that challenges the idea of invariable waivability when it comes to remedial rights. A remedy, in civil law and beyond, is sought as a manner to address a past breach of law. Of course, a remedy changes the normative position of the litigants or other parties to a dispute. But the change produced by the issuance of a remedy does not come out of nothing. Rather, it is carried out against the background of prior substantive rights and duties;[62] more specifically, prior substantive rights and duties that have been infringed.[63] And it is intended as an authoritative resolution of such infringements through a court order that produces new—or, according to some, re-emerging[64]—rights and duties (ie court-ordered rights and

---

[61] ibid 82.

[62] But see ibid 100, where it is argued that although a wrong-responding court order is "issued in response to the defendant's wrongdoing, (t)he label 'wrongdoing' does not tell us anything about (its) content."

[63] On remedies as alterations of normative situations that arise in virtue of past incidents of non-compliance to the law, see also S Steel, "Remedies, Analysed" (2020) 41 (2) Oxford Journal of Legal Studies 539, 543–44.

[64] On the idea that private law rights survive their violation, see eg A Ripstein, *Private Wrongs* (Harvard University Press 2016) 250–51.

duties) to make up for earlier rights and duties (ie substantive rights and duties) which, regardless of whether we consider them as gone for good or as revivable, are no longer normatively operative.

To sum up, the problem with the application of the orthodox view to the domain of civil litigation is not only its consideration of remedial powers as waivable rights correlative to duties, but also its neglect of institutional limitations on the waivability of court-ordered rights (these are limitations related to the conferral of such rights to the plaintiff through the exercise of a court's authority) and of normative limitations related to the fact that a remedial right does not have a life of its own but emerges as a result of the breach of a substantive right. Let us now turn to the tripartite classification to explore its potential to account for constraints on the waivability of remedial rights. Though, as noted previously, the tripartite classification does not directly concern questions of waivability, here the argument is that the conceptualization of private law rights that has been advocated by the tripartite classification enables us to gain a better understanding of the limited waivability of remedial rights, always in reference to how waivability works in ordinary legal practice.

The tripartite classification covers two types of rights that can be classified as remedial: secondary rights and tertiary rights.[65] A secondary right is defined as a right to a remedy for a breach of a primary right,[66] while tertiary rights are a set of different types of rights through which a plaintiff asserts in court her infringed primary right and her right to a remedy and later, if needed, moves on with the enforcement of a court order made in her favor. Note that both types of remedial rights acknowledged by the orthodox view (ie (i) powers to bring, continue, or discontinue civil proceedings and (ii) enforcement rights) are classified by the tripartite classification as tertiary rights.

Yet secondary rights are not acknowledged by the orthodox view. Other accounts of remedial rights, such as Smith's account,[67] may cover types of rights not considered by the orthodox view (see eg court-ordered rights) but also disregard secondary rights. In fact, Smith's account comes together with an argument that rejects the very idea of secondary rights and denies their status as a separate type of rights or, at least, as a separate type of legal rights.[68] Arguments that deny the existence of secondary rights claim that a right-holder whose primary right has been infringed, has no legal right to a remedy prior to (i) the authoritative assertion of the infringement of her right in court and (ii) the conferral of a specific remedy issued through a court order. In other words, according to these arguments, a remedial right in law emerges when a court-ordered right to compensation, injunction, or another judicially crystallized remedy is bestowed on a plaintiff.

---

[65] Beyond his tripartite classification, Gardner has adopted, in passing, a narrower sense of remedial rights that covers only some types of remedial rights; see J Gardner, "Damages Without Duty" (2019) 69(4) University of Toronto Law Journal 412, 413.

[66] *FPLPL* (n 1) 242.

[67] Smith, *Rights, Wrongs, and Injustices* (n 18) 80–86.

[68] See eg ibid 191–99. For a different argument against secondary rights see JCP Goldberg and BC Zipursky, "Tort Law and Responsibility" in Oberdiek (ed), *Philosophical Foundations of the Law of Torts* (n 28) 17, 29–32.

274 HARIS PSARRAS

A number of doctrinal and philosophical arguments have been developed in defense of the legal status and the normative significance of secondary rights.[69] More specifically, regarding the question of waivers that concerns us here, additional arguments can be made to defend secondary rights as a self-standing category of legal rights in light of its role in a persuasive normative account of waiving rights in remedial law, but also with reference to specific practices of waiving rights that attest to the recognition of secondary rights by the law.

In terms of the significance of the very idea of secondary rights for an account of waivability in private law, it should be noted that secondary rights, as understood in the course of the tripartite classification, enable us to account for what I earlier described as normative limitations to the waivability of a remedial right. Note that a remedial right, even when it comes in the judicially crystallized form of a court order, is related to a substantive right whose breach is intended to address. It is revealing that accounts of remedial rights that do not recognize secondary rights are not committed to the idea of a necessary normative link between an infringed substantive right and the remedial right that addresses the infringement; in fact, such accounts allow for remedial rights to be seen in some cases as altogether new rights.[70] However, this view is not compatible with the hypothesis underlying a project for a comprehensive account of waivability of rights in private law. If there is no necessary link between substantive and remedial rights, then there is no need to believe that considerations of waivability that apply to substantive rights may still be relevant to waiving (or not having the power to waive) rights at the remedial stage.

By way of contrast, the tripartite classification acknowledges the normative connection between secondary rights and infringed primary rights. It considers a secondary right as the residue of an infringed primary right that emerges straight after the infringement. Thus, secondary rights are seen to emerge for moral reasons (more specifically, reasons of corrective justice) that have found institutional expression in private law.[71] The institutionalization of these reasons leads to the recognition of secondary rights as legal rights. This approach to the status of secondary rights also has implications for the question of waivability.

If secondary rights are residues of infringed primary rights they must be unwaivable. This is because secondary rights are (in virtue of their nature as residues of infringed primary rights) correlative to duties, just as much as primary rights are correlative to duties. The duties that secondary rights are correlative to are residues of the infringed primary duties. In essence, following infringement, primary duties either have their correlative primary rights replicated in the form of secondary rights (as it happens with infringements that terminate the correlative right; for example in the case of destruction of property) or retain their correlation with remains of their correlative primary rights that are still conducive to compliance, and, at the same time, obtain an additional correlative relationship with a secondary right (as happens with

---

[69] See Gardner, "Damages Without Duty" (n 65); S Steel and R Stevens, "The Secondary Legal Duty to Pay Damages" (2020) 136(2) Law Quarterly Review 283.

[70] See eg Smith, *Rights, Wrongs, and Injustices* (n 18) 74.

[71] See *FPLPL* (n 1) 212–13.

PRIVATE LAW RIGHTS AND POWERS OF WAIVER   275

infringements of primary rights with a time-sensitive element; for instance in a case of false imprisonment).[72]

Following this line of argument, it can be maintained that there are no waivers of secondary rights in private law. The correlativity of secondary rights to residues of primary duties indicates that waiving a secondary right would require waiving a primary duty which has already been severely compromised, if not terminated, due to an act of wrongdoing. Giving up a secondary right in a personal relationship which unfolds outside the legal domain may be normatively meaningful; wrongdoing in such a relationship can be addressed through an appeal to moral values that complement or transcend corrective justice or through emotions with motivational potential for action-guidance.[73] But in law things are different as private law systems normally adhere to remedy-based reparative operations.[74]

Apart from these normative considerations, there are also aspects of legal practice that reflect the recognition of the unwaivability of secondary rights by legislators and courts. Consider, for instance, the "reasonableness" test that applies to exclusion or limitation of liability clauses.[75] When the validity of such clauses, which are normally considered as waivers of tertiary rights (eg waivers of rights to sue for damages),[76] is assessed in court, the use of the "reasonableness" test (as provided for in the relevant statutory provisions) also requires consideration of the circumstances under which liability arose or would have arisen.[77]

These circumstances occur upon breach of a primary right regardless of the initiation of a lawsuit, yet they are considered as circumstances that give rise to liability. Given that the term "liability" here does not refer to a remedial duty asserted in a court order (note that the litigation process is still in progress when the validity of a liability clause is assessed), it must refer to the duty to provide a remedy; a duty that occurs independently of the exercise of an action right and, of course, prior to the conferral of a court-ordered right to the plaintiff. In other words, we are here presented with a secondary right—a right which is not only untouched by the waiver of a power to sue, but also encapsulates the normative considerations that will then be used in court to set a benchmark for the assessment of the validity of the waiver.

The unwaivability of secondary rights and its exploration against the background of clauses intended to act as waivers of tertiary rights takes us to the issue of tertiary rights' waivability and calls for devising an account that could tackle the issue in light of the tripartite classification. Remember that the orthodox view's failure to address

---

[72] Such an automatic normative transition from primary rights to secondary rights upon infringement of a primary right has been theorized in terms of a principle termed as the "right in, right out" principle in *TAOW* (n 26) 73–74.

[73] Consider forgiveness as a way of giving up a secondary right in a non-regulated personal relationship to which considerations of corrective justice may also apply.

[74] Though this argument in favor of the unwaivability of secondary rights reflects considerations associated with the continuity thesis, such as the treatment of a secondary obligation as a "rational echo of the primary obligation" (see *TAOW* (n 26) 61–63), it is also compatible with theorizations of private law on the basis of corrective justice that reject the continuity thesis and conceptualize rights to reparations not as secondary rights but as surviving primary rights (see eg Ripstein, *Private Wrongs* (n 64) 245–52).

[75] Unfair Contract Terms Act 1977 ("*UCTA*"), section 11 and section 24.

[76] See eg McBride and Bagshaw, *Tort Law* (n 38) 356.

[77] *UCTA* (n 75), section 11(3).

the question of waivability of tertiary rights is primarily a matter of a mistaken "elevation" of the plaintiff's powers in litigation to the status of claim-rights that correlate to duties. But it is also a matter of the orthodox view's inability to accommodate the institutional limitations that courts' dominant role in civil litigation imposes on the scope and operation of the waivability of tertiary rights.

The tripartite classification is not vulnerable to such criticism. This is because it conceives of a tertiary right as a cluster of entitlements that includes not only rights correlative to duties but also powers toward different actors in civil litigation. Let us take a closer look to the most representative tertiary right: a right-holder's right to initiate a lawsuit for infringement of a primary right. From the perspective of the tripartite classification, this right involves (i) a right against third parties not to usurp the right-holder in her asserting or enforcing her infringed right in court through starting civil proceedings against the wrongdoer;[78] (ii) a power against the wrongdoer to initiate a lawsuit;[79] (iii) a right and a power to put the court under a duty to evaluate her lawsuit and, upon assertion of the alleged act of wrongdoing, provide her with a remedy.[80]

This approach to the multiple facets of a tertiary right enables us to account for the complex picture of the practice of waivability of action-rights and other tertiary rights in civil litigation. Arguably, when it comes to tertiary rights we are presented with a situation of limited waivability, a situation in which waivability applies only to some entitlements among those that constitute a tertiary right. Let us set aside, for now, the right against others not to replace the right-holder in her potential role as the initiator of a lawsuit.[81] And let us consider, through the prism of practices on exclusion or limitation clauses, the right-holder's power to sue the wrongdoer as a twofold power, its one horn is exercised against the wrongdoer, while the other authorizes the court to activate its adjudicative powers with regard to the civil proceedings issued to it by the right-holder in her institutional capacity as a plaintiff.

Each of these two powers appears to have its own status when it comes to waivers. The power against the wrongdoer can be waived on the basis of an exclusion of liability clause. But the same cannot be said of the power toward the court. Its consideration as a waivable power would be at odds with the fact that the validity of an exclusion of liability clause is assessed by the court in the course of civil proceedings. Furthermore, waiving the power against the wrongdoer to sue her amounts to the disability of the right-holder to have her primary and secondary rights asserted in court (ie not a disability to sue but a disability to have the court hold the defendant liable); it therefore also amounts to an immunity for the wrongdoer. But the powers of the court to adjudicate a claim after proceedings are launched are public powers toward the litigants and, most importantly, duties toward the plaintiff from which the court cannot release itself.[82]

---

[78] See *FPLPL* (n 1) 207–08, 210.

[79] ibid 199; Gardner, "Damages Without Duty" (n 65) 413.

[80] See Gardner, "Damages Without Duty" (n 65) 413; cf Steel, "On the Moral Necessity of Tort Law" (n 30) 194.

[81] This question pertains to the transferability of tertiary rights, which should be treated separately from their waivability, also in light of equitable subrogation.

[82] See *FPLPL* (n 1) 201.

Even the plaintiff's possible choice to discontinue litigation is not a waiver. Consider, for instance, that a second claim can be made after discontinuation of a first claim (though the court's permission is normally also required). This suggests that a court remains duty-bound to exercise judicial authority on the plaintiff's request until the cause of action is extinguished. Not all tertiary rights are amenable to such analysis, but, overall, it can be contended that normative and institutional considerations related to a well-functioning civil litigation system limit their waivability.

5. Conclusion

This chapter argued that Gardner's classification of private law rights into primary, secondary, and tertiary rights can also serve as a starting point for a new approach to the waivability of rights in the law of obligations and in civil litigation. Acknowledging that different types of rights perform different normative functions enables us to challenge the orthodox view, which endorses invariable waivability of rights throughout the domain of private law. Closer consideration of the legal theory and practice on powers of waiver indicates that waivability operates differently in different types of substantive and remedial rights. More specifically, the conceptualization of different types of private law rights as clusters of claim-rights and powers or other entitlements supports an argument in favor of the waivability of primary rights, the unwaivability of secondary rights, and the limited waivability of tertiary rights.

PART III
THEORIZING PARTICULAR AREAS OF PRIVATE LAW

16

How is Tort Law Political?

Jenny Steele[*]

"Law is in and of society, adapting to its contours, giving direction to change. Therefore, blurred boundaries—between law and morality, law and politics, law and economics, law and custom—are signs of good order."[1]

1. Introduction

In much contemporary private law theory, the search is on for boundaries. Public policy and political considerations especially have been cast as external to the law's own reasoning. This may be a protective move, inspired either by a wish to avoid intervention (if private law is openly political, will it inevitably be laid open to critical political scrutiny or meddling?) or perhaps by the threat of disciplinary annexation, particularly by the policy sciences.[2] A different perspective suggests that judges are engaged in understanding the context of decisions just as they are in reasoning from a select range of principles.[3] Reasons, as John Gardner reminded us, are multiple and varied in private law just as in any other domain, but for practical reasons must be "played up or played down" according to the context of a decision.[4] To some extent, this speaks to institutional specialization. But it is very different from the categorical exclusion of all but a few reasons.

How is it decided which reasons to "play up or play down"? It has been argued that common law judges are expected "to know how social relations emerge and what happens to them as circumstances change,"[5] and that law will be neither

---

[*] I would like to thank TT Arvind for his comments on a draft of this chapter.

[1] P Selznick, *A Humanist Science: Values and Ideals in Social Inquiry* (Stanford University Press 2008) 112.

[2] This fear is identified by Gardner in relation to law and economics in particular. Importantly, he argues that economic analysis goes wrong not in denying the autonomy of private law from policy, but in asserting "the autonomy of public policy from everything else": J Gardner, *From Personal Life to Private Law* (OUP 2018) 8–9 ("*FPLPL*").

[3] "Context" is a complex idea in its own right, and is explored by TT Arvind and J Steele, "History, Context and the Problem of Juristic Method: The Chancery Amendment Act 1858 and the Law of Contract" in TT Arvind and J Steele (eds), *Contract Law and the Legislature* (Hart Publishing 2020) ch 3.

[4] J Gardner, "The Negligence Standard: Political Not Metaphysical" (2017) 80 Modern Law Review 1–21, 2.

[5] Selznick, *A Humanist Science* (n 1) 111.

Jenny Steele, How is Tort Law Political? In: *Private Law and Practical Reason.* Edited by: Haris Psarras and Sandy Steel, Oxford University Press. © Jenny Steele 2023. DOI: 10.1093/oso/9780192857330.003.0016

effective nor just without some "empirical" element to its reasoning, which takes account of what has been tried and what has worked (or not). On this view, law is not so much condemned to slip into politics (or economics or morality) when it considers a wide range of issues and the practical effect of decisions. Rather, as Selznick argues in the passage that appears as the epigraph to this chapter, just and effective law is law whose boundaries are blurred and which realizes its ideals or principles with the assistance of varied reasons. Ideals and principles adapt to what will and will not work. This is in sympathy with Gardner's approach to tort law's "political" elements.

John Gardner's theoretical contributions to "private law"—by which he essentially meant the law of contract and tort[6]—are against current trends in private law theory in their accommodation and promotion of a sense of openness and contextualism. They are also able to accommodate the sense that "law and morality" is a boundary as blurred as "law and politics," or any others.[7] Reasons, Gardner urged, were not to be confined to categories, and could be used across a wide range of different contexts, including law, personal life, and political decision-making:

> Public or private, individual or collective, personal or institutional, in law or in love, in parliament or in the supermarket, all valid reasons for action count.[8]

The solution in one context may for good reasons be different—broader or narrower—from the solution in another. This reflects the fact that the realization of reasons in different contexts will call for different solutions. But if decision-making is sound and institutions are working effectively, reasons in different domains will be comprehensible. Gardner's approach, too, suggests that boundaries are blurred when the law is in good order. While *From Personal Life to Private Law* presents a sustained argument that our reasons for action in our personal lives are also immediately relevant to reasons for action in private law, "The Negligence Standard" makes the same point about the availability of similar reasons across both private law, and decisions by "governmental agents" (which may be called, "political" decisions).[9]

In this chapter, I address Gardner's take on the particular relationship between tort and the political. Flagging of a link between tort and the political is most evident in his discussion of the negligence standard, which he urged should be seen

---

[6] Gardner offered the explanation that property was, for his purposes, essentially a footnote to the law of tort and contract, providing "some of the detailed rules" by which there is liability for torts such as conversion (*FPLPL* (n 2) 14). I explain below why some reasons why this appears unrealistic, particularly given Gardner's focus on security in private law. He did not question the existence of a category of unjust enrichment or restitution, but was less interested in this than in contract and tort. See J Gardner, *Torts and Other Wrongs* (OUP 2019) chs 1, 8, and 9, and Chapter 19 in this volume.

[7] Despite the availability of reasons across all domains, there are still distinct areas of specialization. On some questions of law, there "is no point at all in asking a philosopher," and this reflects the inevitable plurality of values and reasons applicable to private law: *FPLPL* (n 2) 13–14. The list of examples includes the choice of negligence or strict liability for defective products.

[8] Gardner, "The Negligence Standard" (n 4) 2.

[9] Notes 4 and 2.

as "political not metaphysical" (a point that was not confined to the negligence standard alone but was applicable to the choice of liability standard in general).[10] This was a knowingly provocative statement, since the negligence standard in particular has often been perceived as expressing a legal principle about the appropriate extent of responsibility, having at least some relationship with morality.[11] Equally, Gardner set out the reasons why distributive questions (which are typically associated with the political) are inescapably a part of the law of tort, and not merely external to it.[12] The law must decide how to operationalize its principles, in this case corrective justice, in a manner that is appropriate. This too was knowingly against the current of orthodoxy, which has sought to avoid distributive questions in private law on the basis that they are the proper subject of political (generally majoritarian) decision. In both of these two senses in which tort could be called political, Gardner's position is, essentially, one of reassurance. Tort is unavoidably political, but is none the weaker for that.

Finally, Gardner argued that tort could, through its distribution of security rights, be seen as promoting a "mode of social power" which is in some sense distinctive and potentially (if the appropriate rights are distributed)[13] deserving of political support. This mode of social power is not socially conservative, and is even capable of "rivaling wealth."[14] This is the most unguarded and ambitious of the suggested connections between private law and the political. It is briefly made, in keeping with the style of *From Personal Life to Private Law*. Here, tort is offering something to politics. It is not completely clear how we should read the reference to a "mode of social power," but it is not a narrowly legal reference: it is about the protections that citizens can expect or achieve via law, and their broader significance. Progressive politics would on this view need to work "with" security, not against it, and the aspect of wealth that most needs to be rivaled (perhaps combated) is the aspect that enhances insecurity, through capital mobility. Tort begins with the protection of value, through security rights, and not of "autonomy": at core it is a preserver of value in the form of the continuity of a life.[15] This is the claim that interests me most. Can tort be seen as advancing protection of security rights in a progressive fashion, and can it be urged that this is of distinctive political significance, despite all the blurring of boundaries and transferability of reasons already mentioned?

---

[10] Gardner, "The Negligence Standard" (n 4).

[11] Having said that, any relationship with moral culpability has long been recognized as problematic. The non-exact fit between morality and law was noted by Lord Atkin in *Donoghue v Stevenson* [1932] AC 562. For problems faced by various "moralist" positions regarding negligence see J Goudkamp, "The Spurious Relationship Between Moral Responsibility and Liability for Negligence" (2004) 28 Melbourne University Law Review 343.

[12] J Gardner, "What Is Tort Law For? Part 2. The Role of Distributive Justice" in J Oberdiek (ed), *Philosophical Foundations of Tort Law* (OUP 2014).

[13] This too appears to be a political and distributive question: it matters to Gardner whether the rights are distributed to the "security rich" or the less security rich.

[14] *FPLPL* (n 2) 194.

[15] ibid 231. One issue raised, which is not pursued here, is how this is consistent across human and non-human claimants, such as corporations and other organizations. It may be that it is not intended to be consistent, and indeed much of the discussion focuses on "general" damages. But this would restrict the breadth of the claims being made quite radically. We could however accept the points being made about security, without associating this with "continuity of lives."

In section 2, I briefly explore the three elements of Gardner's account of tort already noted. In that section, these are described in terms of *choice* (rather than discovery) of responsibilities for a wide range of appropriate reasons (the choice of standard); with *distribution* (rather than only correction) on the basis of multiple considerations (the choice of when to "operationalize"[16] corrective justice); and with a potential political significance for tort's protection of security, in the sense that it embodies a form of *social power*. In relation to the first and third, Gardner himself refers to the political. Although he does not use the term in relation to the second, his position here dismantles a division between the role of private law (correction), and of political or "policy" decisions, which it is sometimes argued are not the preserve of private law but should be left for collective processes (associated with distribution). It is important to point to all three distinctive features because it is when we consider what it is that tort is distributing that we are pointed to the value of security that is the third element above—and to Gardner's ambitions for tort.

In sections 3 and 4, I turn specifically to this last appeal to the political, namely the suggestion that understanding tort as distributing security rights can lead us to identify a powerful form of security that can compete with other forms of power—particularly, with wealth. Gardner points (briefly) to other areas of political life and debate where notions of security have been, and are, significant, but does not engage with aspects of security that exist in other areas of private law (except to say that contract and tort are essentially alike in this respect—and to some extent, they are). Some of these aspects of security are introduced in section 3. The problem is illustrated by the contention already mentioned, that security, as contained in the law of tort, may be capable of "rivaling wealth." It could be argued that "security" is, in fact, the very essence of wealth, and this is linked to both property, and contract: security through use of private law structures (not necessarily chiefly adjudication) is what makes wealth "enduring," and reflects efforts to achieve "priority"—both of which have been identified as important in distinguishing wealth from mere assets (while at the same time, it might be added, tending to evade scrutiny as political), and as underpinning the creation of huge and pervasive inequalities of security that Gardner is keen to avoid.[17] However, this is a problem well worth thinking about, and we should grasp the opportunity. In section 4, I return to consider what, if anything, is distinctive about the protection of security through tort, whether this assists our understanding of tort, and whether this is any sense a counterpoint to other implicit understandings of security in private law.

---

[16] This is not the expression used by Gardner, but is chosen to summarize his account of the selection of possible claims of corrective justice which will be given effect by law.

[17] K Pistor, *The Code of Capital: How the Law Creates Wealth and Inequality* (Princeton University Press 2019). Throughout her book, Pistor discusses how private law makes wealth enduring (durability); achieves priority against other interests (priority); creates enforceability across jurisdictions ("universality"); and ensures "convertibility" into state money (at 3). These features between them can be described in terms of a powerful form of security.

2. Three "Political" Connections: Choice, Distribution, and Power

2.1 Choice: The political nature of the negligence standard

Probably the most obvious, because the most clearly flagged, way in which Gardner suggested that tort is "political" lies in his identification of the "negligence" standard with the political (rather than, he added, the metaphysical).[18] The basis for the negligence standard is not to be *found* (in metaphysics), and must be chosen for other reasons, which may be truly varied. This is a reflection of the fact that the realm of metaphysical responsibility is, on Gardner's account, very broad.[19] Basic responsibility he argues, is fundamentally strict. In fact, there are few metaphysical limits to "basic responsibility." To adopt a negligence standard, far from marking the boundary of what is morally required or legitimate, is a deregulatory choice.[20]

Gardner's theory of tort is decidedly "non-toxic" (a phrase he uses to explain the motivation for his shift to private law, from criminal law theory).[21] It is deliberately short on blame.[22] This is partly because of the breadth of "basic responsibility" already noted. The law only gives effect to a few of the available duties, and if it recognizes that some of them may be breached without individual fault, this cannot make responsibility in law more stringent than "basic" responsibility. The *political* nature of the negligence standard, and of any standard adopted by the law of tort, is partly a description of this relative freedom to decide (or necessity of deciding) which responsibilities should be reflected in the law. That will be done in what was described, in section 1, as an "empirical" fashion, including understanding of social relations, and observation of what has worked before.[23] The connection between legal decisions in relation to negligence and its responsibilities (plural), and metaphysical responsibility (singular), can be expected to be quite remote.

The meaning of "political" in this instance, despite the banner headline, is dilute. The primary purpose of the label is to draw attention to the existence of a plurality of available reasons. Tort's conclusions are neither compelled, nor provided, by morality or metaphysical responsibility, and the reasons available to reach those conclusions are as plural as in any other context. In a sense, we are told more about what the negligence standard is not, than about the reasons why it should particularly be called

---

[18] Gardner, "The Negligence Standard" (n 4).

[19] Some have thought too broad: see the exchange of views in A Duff, "Cliff-top Predicaments and Morally Blemished Lives" (2019) 19 Jerusalem Review of Legal Studies 125–40; M Dempsey, What We Have Reason to Do: Another View from the Cliff-Top" (2019) 19 Jerusalem Review of Legal Studies 141–54; J Gardner, "As Inconclusive as Ever" (2019) 19 Jerusalem Review of Legal Studies 204–24, 215–17.

[20] Gardner, "The Negligence Standard" (n 4) at n 42.

[21] *FPLPL* (n 2) 4: "I saw more prospect of making both moral peace and philosophical progress with private law's ... less toxic remedial apparatus."

[22] Arguing that blame, condemnation, and so on ("all that blaming jazz") are not the right place to start when thinking about responsibility, see Gardner, "The Negligence Standard" (n 4) at 18. More pertinent are complex questions of "blameless but responsible agency": ibid, citing B Williams and T Nagel, "Moral Luck" (1976) 50 Proceedings of the Aristotelian Society 115, 123–27.

[23] Gardner refers to "the fairness, the efficiency, or more generally the reasonableness" of responsibilities being assigned in a particular way: Gardner, "The Negligence Standard" (n 4) 21.

"political." If reasons are transferable across the legal, personal, and political domains, why emphasize this particular description? It may simply direct our attention back to the existence of multiple valid reasons in all decision-making contexts, and to the impossibility of deriving an answer from philosophy.

I would argue that there are elements of Gardner's examination of the negligence standard which can draw us closer to understanding the institutional context of tort. These factors help us to understand which reasons to play up, and which to play down, and in this sense perhaps *how* (in what distinctive way) tort law is "political." Gardner's account directs us to the significance of the fact that tort reasoning typically carves out some *roles* and some *relationships* in which responsibilities—according to potentially different standards—are assigned.[24] It is this "assignment" of responsibilities (plural), which occurs in a distinctly role-based way,[25] that Gardner identifies as associated with "pliable politics." In private law, we do not have one general "responsibility" to others: our responsibilities vary with our roles and with the relationships we have with others. Assignment is "pliable" because it is determined according to a wide range of reasons and considerations; and because there is a considerable range of possible answers that a decision-maker could rationally give.

Gardner argues that responsibilities are typically allocated according to particular tasks that are performed,[26] therefore, we owe duties *qua* drivers or teachers or employers which raise different contextual questions and thus, different political choices may be made about the applicable standard. But he also, importantly, links these choices with the nature of different relationships, rather than according to tasks alone, discussing the responsibilities between two drivers in terms of "symmetry", and the responsibility of a boiler installer for a domestic client in terms of "asymmetry."[27] These different circumstances, and different relationships, bring with them different available reasons for determining liability and choosing an appropriate standard. These questions are "in the broadest sense" political.

The choice of standard is therefore not a function of the boundaries of "moral" responsibility, nor (to recall our starting point) of a specialist range of reasons that is exclusive to private law. This move is especially important when courts are tempted to give the impression of applying a narrow range of reasons.[28] On the other hand, the reasons will reflect the structure and purpose of the law of tort. The reasons will need to be institutionally appropriate.

---

[24] On the central importance of relationships to tort, see also J Steele, "Regulating Relationships: The Regulatory Potential of Tort Law Revisited" in J Goudkamp, M Lunney, and L Macdonald (eds), *Taking Law Seriously: Essays for Peter Cane* (Hart Publishing 2022) ch 10.

[25] This includes instances where responsibility is "assumed": such assumptions relate to specific roles or activities of the assumer.

[26] Gardner, "The Negligence Standard" (n 4) 4–5.

[27] Gardner, "The Negligence Standard" (n 4) 20–21. There is room to quibble or problematize: driver-pedestrian cases are asymmetric; what of boilers installed for commercial clients and/or as part of a larger construction scheme? The point is that these features of tort relationships add complexity to the choice of standard and to the reasons which may be brought to bear. Compare the analysis of varied perception of market relationships, including the importance of symmetry and asymmetry, in TT Arvind and J Steele, "Remapping Contract Law: Four Perceptions of Markets" in *Contract Law and the Legislature* (n 3) ch 19.

[28] This is occurring at present in the tort of negligence, where cases decided for a plurality of reasons are being brought under the umbrella of "causing harm or failing to confer a benefit" (acts omissions).

Whether or not the language of the "political" is fully required,[29] Gardner takes an important step in separating his account of tort reasons from identification of the boundaries of moral responsibility, and part of this involves a sensitivity to the institutional context in which tort is required to use reasons. Those reasons, however, are not to be artificially confined.

2.2 Distribution: The unavoidable distributive element of tort

Second, tort is inherently and unavoidably distributive. It is not the domain exclusively of corrective justice.[30] While Gardner did not expressly relate this to the notion of the "political," it is an essential step toward his proposal that tort may offer something to politics. If anything, the distributive element deserves to be labeled more clearly as "political" than the choice of standard. Gardner argued that the distributive in tort is not to be connected with the most obvious element of the political in relation to distribution: distribution of assets. To argue that tort is distributive does not necessarily mean it can only be justified if the existing distribution, which it aims to restore, is just. Importantly, Gardner's account of the distributive aspect of tort is—like the account of choice of standard—tied to its internal operation.

Tort does not merely have distributive *effects* (observed from an external vantage point). There has to be a way to decide which claims of corrective justice are to be satisfied; this is, by its nature, distributive reasoning, but it is not focused on distribution of assets. It is focused on the distribution of security (in a particular sense).[31] Drawing on MacCormick,[32] corrective justice claims are treated as familiar in personal life; the institutional role of private law (in this instance, tort) is positioned in terms of deciding which of these claims will be supported by legal liability. This choice is in itself distributive and (as ever) will draw upon a wide variety of reasons. Thus private law achieves a distribution and its reasons for doing so are not restricted by the conditions of corrective justice thinking, because this will not provide the boundaries that are needed. Once again, law is not in danger of carving out wide responsibilities that go beyond some moral minimum. Rather, law must determine which of the many possible claims of corrective justice are appropriately selected to ground legal liability.

Even accepting that reasons for corrective justice are also found in non-legal settings, it might be that the availability of a tort process has additional distinctive roles in that it will stimulate (by making available), and crystallize (by offering the sources of argument), as well as distribute corrective justice. In other words, the link

---

[29] Gardner rejects Rawls' argument that the political domain is one of distinctive reasons, Gardner, "The Negligence Standard" (n 4) 1–2.

[30] Gardner, "What Is Tort Law For? Part 2" (n 12).

[31] In *FPLPL* (n 2) ch 5, Gardner expressly linked tort with the distribution of security. Earlier, in the concluding section of "What Is Tort Law For? Part 2" (n 12) he spoke rather in terms of distribution of risk, and drew on Tony Honoré, "The Morality of Tort Law: Questions and Answers" in T Honoré, *Responsibility and Fault* (OUP 1999) 67. While the two may appear to be simply different sides of the same coin, the focus on security shifts attention from the consequences of an actor's actions, to the good that is being protected and distributed through tort. Some of the implications are explored in section 3.

[32] N MacCormick, "The Obligation of Reparation" Proceedings of the Aristotelian Society, 1977–1978, New Series, Vol 78 (1977–1978) 175–93.

with "personal life" may be overstretched, and the link with law quite particular. But whatever the questions of detail, Gardner has identified an essential distributive element in tort which helps to explain its reasoning processes. It is unavoidable that legal decision-makers will have to decide why it is right to attach liability—and thus operationalize corrective justice—in one instance of harm done by proposed wrongdoing but not another. Distributive questions are intrinsic and unavoidable. This function is closely connected to the institutional nature of tort, as a means of responding to claims that must nevertheless be framed in terms of corrective justice. But this gives considerable scope for choice and for what, in section 1, was described as "empirical" reasoning (we might also call this, less threateningly, trial and error, or more threateningly to some,[33] "experience"), because of the broad scope of responsibility. And reasons for resisting claims may come in many varieties, certainly including consideration of the relational setting and roles of claimant and defendant in that relationship. Relational questions—including the kind of consideration of "asymmetry" referred to above—will be relevant to the distribution of corrective justice effected by tort.

2.3 Power: Tort's security is a political force

The final point brings together the elements that have been observed to date. What is it that tort is distributing? We noted above that the response must be framed consistently with corrective justice.[34] But in a further move, again inspired by MacCormick, Gardner argues that what is being distributed is security, or security rights. Gardner links this with "holding on," a tendency which can be observed in our personal lives, and he searches for the source of the puzzle that holding on is sufficiently valued to be the model for legal remedies. He finds this in the integrity of a life, rather than in choice or autonomy.[35]

This move is significant partly because it completes a shift from focus on *wrongdoing*, to the good that is supplied (and distributed) by the law of tort. Taking the step from what conduct and harm is being sanctioned to what, distinctively, is being distributed when tort liability is imposed sheds important light on the nature and operation of the law of tort. Equally, this plays to the *prospective* (as well as retrospective) nature of tort's allocations of responsibilities, associated with recognition of tort relationships in which responsibilities are allocated.[36] Security is, Gardner argues, a "mode of social power" which is independent of wealth—even though, of course, the wealthy are more able to access protection through law. The value of security is even, on Gardner's account, capable of *rivaling* wealth—by which he seems to mean, at least, that the right to preserve what we have against some people some of the time

---

[33] Because of its realist connotations, and link to OW Holmes (*The Common Law* (Little, Brown, and Company 1881) 1).

[34] J Gardner, "What is Tort Law For? Part 1: The Place of Corrective Justice" (2011) 30 Law and Philosophy 1.

[35] *FPLPF* (n 2) ch 5.

[36] Gardner explains the retrospective and prospective nature of responsibilities in terms of the continuity thesis. Responsibilities face both ways, but give rise to separate duties to avoid harm, or to compensate: Gardner, "The Negligence Standard" (n 4) 3–5.

is independent of whether we have the resources to purchase our own security (which would of course favor the wealthy).[37] There are signs, however, that the point is more ambitious than this. In particular, he places security as a counterpoint to capital mobility, which is identified as the source of deep insecurity (destabilization).[38] This points to a deeper ambition, that security could more *directly* rival wealth, by holding back aspects of wealth, or correcting some of its impact, through advancing security in the form of holding on. Tort law, on either view, is "for the people," not for the few.

This time the link with the political is different. It is not based on analysis of tort reasoning alone but is to some extent normative, since Gardner urges that the protection of security interests could and should be seen as politically important. While securing what we have could be seen as distributively regressive, Gardner nevertheless thinks it could potentially be a powerful corrective to the priority of wealth. Emphasizing other areas where security is recognized as important, he argues that while security is plainly by definition "conservative," it is not socially conservative but can be identified with the advancement or protection of social justice. It is certainly true that insecurity is a powerful social problem.[39] But to achieve a link between tort's distribution of security rights, and the avoidance of insecurity in this broader political sense, is a task of considerable difficulty.

On the one hand, politics is already suffused with security, as Gardner begins to recognize. His discussion refers to *social* security, but he treats this as a separate phenomenon, and not of the same set of ambitions as tort. There is room to question whether the two are really so distinct.[40] On the other hand, security can already be seen as a prevalent issue in private and commercial law, and this in itself means that the claim that security through tort can be a mode of social power to rival wealth must be met with some healthy skepticism. How does security through tort differ from security through property or contract, which are so important to wealth?[41] Implicated here is Gardner's perception of private law as essentially modeled on obligations, rather than property (and obligations modeled on tort).[42]

Despite this, I suggest that our understanding of tort will be enhanced by following Gardner's lead and perceiving it in terms of distributing security rights, and in terms of role-based (or relational) responsibilities. This will need to be an understanding that is institutionally framed, and the "mode of social power" involved may turn out to be limited. It might be argued that we are simply falling into a trap here, of treating different ideas together simply because they are, or can be similarly labeled. Perhaps Gardner's idea of security is narrower even than I consider it to be in the discussion that follows, and that it needs to be tied much more specifically to the idea of "continuity of a life" that he sketches. That, however, would make his approach much more

---

[37] *FPLPL* (n 2) 194.

[38] ibid 193.

[39] Insecurity of housing, employment, food, and other resources are undeniably important political and legal issues.

[40] Risk has long been identified as operating in both domains (for discussion see J Steele, "Risk Revolutions and Private Law" in S Worthington, A Robertson, and G Virgo (eds), *Revolution and Evolution in Private Law* (Hart Publishing 2018); with reference to "security" see the discussion that follows in section 3.

[41] The most important legal sources underpinning wealth and inequality are identified by Pistor, *The Code of Capital* (n 17) 3, as contract law, property rights, collateral law, trust, corporate, and bankruptcy law.

[42] *FPLPL* (n 2) 14.

290   JENNY STEELE

narrowly applicable than it appears. The approach would have much weaker application to actions by non-human claimants, and to understanding the continuity between tort and contract. This interpretation, I think, is ruled out by the centrality given to security in the conclusion to *From Personal Life to Private Law*, where it is argued that security is the central preoccupation, always, of private law: "The big questions for private law are always: Whose security is to be protected? Against Whom? In what way?"[43]

3. Reflecting on Security and Private Law

Security is a pervasive theme of private law as well as politics, though perhaps due to its very pervasiveness it has not had the focus it might merit. It is related to the notion of risk, which has begun to have somewhat more attention among tort lawyers,[44] and which was previously identified by Gardner as distributed by the law of tort.[45] Security, however, tends to focus attention on the response to risk (not simply by the law but also by parties), rather than on its creation. The notion of security is arguably more central than risk to private law, reflecting not just what people formally have responsibility for but what parties are seeking to achieve through their (prospective) arrangements and through their claims, as well as the contested issues at stake. Security is multifaceted and deeply engrained in private law, but its presence has tended to be implicit, or to go without saying. Perhaps we should follow Gardner's lead and give some close consideration to the notion of security. Because it is so pervasive, that would be a large undertaking. This section identifies a few features of security which are pertinent to the present discussion.

3.1 Security and confidence

Security can be perceived narrowly in terms of keeping something intact ("holding on") or as near to this as possible, as Gardner does. But it can alternatively be associated with confidence: a *sense* of security. This need not be a sense of total security. Security commonly lies in arrangements that will make a risk manageable, both in terms of apprehension and reality, should it be realized: enough can be secured to be relatively at ease with the risk. In other words, security can be and typically is a matter of degree, and it may be associated with confidence or peace of mind (a sense of security; or acceptable degree of security). On the other side of the coin, formal security rights without confidence might be considered to be no security at all. Equally, security arrangements can be complex, with multiple sources of security addressing different elements of varied risks to a greater or larger extent. The choice of how much

---

[43] ibid 231.

[44] M Dyson (ed), *Regulating Risk Through Private Law* (Intersentia 2018); Steele, "Risk Revolutions in Private Law" (n 40).

[45] Gardner, "What Is Tort Law For? Part 2" (n 12). See the discussion in n 31.

security to pursue is sometimes one of balance, or negotiation, since security of different degrees typically comes at different costs.

3.2 Security versus wealth?

A difficulty facing the suggestion that tort's security rights represent a social force "capable of rivaling wealth" is that "security" could also be said to be the very essence of property and to underpin wealth. These however may embody different forms of security. The kind of security provided by tort is considerably more limited, even if Gardner might argue that it is richer.[46]

Tort reflects a relational form of security. As Gardner neatly encapsulates it, "we are to enjoy security against others to whose actions we are vulnerable, or with whom we have special relationships."[47] This is—happily—a long way from an understanding that tort deals in duties to behave in certain ways that are owed to the world in general. It starts with the claimant as much as the defendant, and identifies the relationship in which this form of security is created. It is a more illuminating understanding of tort than the defendant-centered view.

The form of security that underpins wealth is more extensive than this. It seeks priority and it seeks to be enduring and as universal as possible.[48] This is the basis of security of assets in a dynamic sense—the sense that builds wealth. Holding on and wealth are not opposed. It is more that the tort notion of holding on is, if Gardner is on the right track, different, and at the same time much more limited in what it can achieve. Tort's security rights are only rights against certain duty-holders, while universality and priority are the basis of wealth.

Further, tort's security rights are more or less only as accessible as the legal remedy. That is to say, rarely are the structures associated with tort sufficiently focused on prevention to achieve security in the form of *confidence*—unless repeated sufficiently often (routinely), or perhaps with enough force to bring about predictable changes in behavior. Wealth works differently: the confidence that assets are secure is the basis of the ways that wealth can be created, maintained, and used to create more wealth.[49] Security, and particularly universality, is also the very basis of capital mobility, with which Gardner was seeking to make a contrast (and which he was perhaps hoping tort could help to resist).

The security associated with the possibility of a tort claim looks puny in comparison. This makes more problematic Gardner's tendency to attribute analytical priority to tort over other elements of private law. It may be true that the big questions of private law always address security, as Gardner argues.[50] But if so then tort's preoccupation with the distribution of security in the form of corrective justice does not look dominant in private law as a whole. For example, if Pistor is correct, then private law in

---

[46] Because of its connection with value in the continuity of a life.

[47] *FPLPL* (n 2) 231.

[48] See n 17.

[49] Pistor, *The Code of Capital* (n 17), argues that the securing of wealth through private law is the basis of capital growth and inequality.

[50] *FPLPL* (n 2) 231; see also n 45.

the form of contract, property, trust, corporate and bankruptcy law, are the very basis of inequality.

The enlightening effects of a focus on security are more diverse than this. For example, the pervasive notion of security and its association with property is also illustrated, though quite differently, by the historic argument that lack of security is a reason to introduce new forms of "property," to level up in security terms. Famously, Charles Reich argued, in effect, that clients of the state did not have the security associated with property.[51] To create a "new property" to meet this problem meant building security of a new type, through new procedural rights such as due process.[52]

While few would argue that this project was realized, we could learn from this that substance and process—and associated rights—are linked in significant ways in private law. If we want tort to provide security in the confidence sense identified above, and not just in a formal sense associated with the substantive legal position, then the possibility of securing remedies needs to be real and predictable. Tort has, in practice, needed the assistance of other structures in order to progress toward this in any context. This includes the presence of insurers and in some areas the introduction of compulsory insurance, the availability of new duties through statutory intervention, the role of public authorities as repeat defendants in certain areas, and the availability of funding structures capable of easing some sorts of claims. In addressing tort's political role and contribution in terms of security, we should not neglect the influence of structures which assist and promote security. The addition of such structures introduces fresh dynamics and values, whether by bureaucratizing tort claims, perhaps even reducing its formal rules to something close to a checklist for lower-level decision-makers,[53] or through introducing new forms of moralism.[54] In other words, the attempt to make tort's security rights meaningful—an essential aspect of being "powerful"—introduces new dynamics of security.

Security is such a widespread idea we do not always think about it. Tort would have to incorporate a truly compelling idea of security, to muscle in on wealth or to indicate that property really could be just a footnote to obligations, and not vice versa. Identifying the basis of tort in security—and in value—is not enough. Tort's security is inclined to be insecure, creating a serious shortfall in its ability to amount to a form of "social power." In seeking to make up this shortfall in at least some circumstances, the essential supporting structures introduce important new dynamics to its political contribution.

---

[51] CA Reich, "The New Property" (1964) 73 Yale Law Journal 733

[52] Note also the argument by D Super, "A New New Property" (2013) 113 Columbia Law Review 1773, couched expressly in terms of security: reforms of due process had failed, and new reforms should aim at securing what is essential to vast swathes of society—rather than the most wealthy. This makes the point about inequality of security, but once again relates it to private law (specifically property).

[53] S Halliday, J Ilan, and C Scott, "Street Level Tort Law: The Bureaucratic Justice of Liability Decision-Making" (2012) 75(3) Modern Law Review 347–67. The emphasis here is on small claims relating to road defects, and the search for "bureaucratic justice" which is transferable in principle to all contexts.

[54] The link between insurance and moralism is of long-standing. See for example C Heimer, "Insurers as Moral Actors" in R Ericson and A Doyle (eds), *Risk and Morality* (University of Toronto Press 2003).

3.3 Who can secure? Who should secure?

Associated with recognition of security and its significance is a perception that we should generally anticipate risks and secure our own interests. There are exceptions and qualifications. There are some relationships and arrangements in which the location of the responsibility to insure is clear, such that tort would risk undermining this set of arrangements if it does not recognize the responsibility to insure when assigning responsibilities.[55] Tort, otherwise, would be creating insecurity (in arrangements, and in the sources of repair). Beyond this, it is often recognized that different roles are associated with a greater or lesser ability—or even tendency—to anticipate and secure than others. As with the location of duties, so with location of responsibility to secure, tort has developed in respect of particular roles. Having few assets or less knowledge or expertise in relation to a particular risk means being unable to afford or anticipate the need for security. This is recognized in some "asymmetric" tort cases (to continue Gardner's term), and influences the identification of those for whom a defendant may have responsibility (including cases where there is an "assumption" of responsibility through assuming a role).[56]

In tort, we seek remedies in our guise as particular classes of people, in particular relationships with others. As claimants we may be visitors, trespassers, employees, neighbors, consumers, pedestrians, drivers, clients, school children, children in care, parishioners, commercial rivals, family members, ex-employees, patients, prisoners, citizens subject to state power, and so on—and all of these imply a specific role on the part of the defendant. These roles make a difference to the analysis of our security claims. Tort is occupied with the security relationships associated with these roles; here, I think Gardner's theory is enlightening and fitting.

4. Tort, Politics, and Security Rights

Do any of the features of security visited in section 3 help us to think about the essential argument, that tort is distributing security rights through the particular medium of corrective justice, and that it is thereby contributing distinctively, potentially, to politics, through its value of security independent of wealth (and possibly, though we have doubted this, rivaling it)?

Shifting from wrongdoing *per se* to role-based responsibilities and the distribution of security rights can indeed illuminate the political role of tort—and the institutional concerns that underpin it. This interpretation helps explain why duties are (as Gardner

---

[55] R Merkin and J Steele, "Allocation of Risk and Tort Law" in *Insurance and the Law of Obligations* (OUP 2013) ch 8. As is pointed out in that chapter, this is a comfortable fit with Gardner's analysis of prospective responsibilities and tort duties (referring to J Gardner, "Backwards and Forwards with Tort Law" in J Keim-Campbell, M O'Rourke, and D Shier (eds), *Law and Social Justice* (MIT Press 2005)).

[56] It was the basis for creating some responsibilities under the Employers' Liability Act of 1880 (and some degree of security without breach of duty in the Workmen's Compensation Acts). These enactments were aimed at providing security for some of those who could not afford to do so themselves, at a time when the background was an absence of duties in the workplace.

suggests) role-driven (including the roles of both claimant and defendant and their interaction). When is it—and when was it—D's duty to secure the interests of C, either by avoiding the harm or failing that, by ensuring some protection? It is *because* there is such widespread use of security ideas that the question of how to distribute security rights makes sense to the courts—not because it is something entirely distinctive encountered primarily in relation to tort. Recalling the points made in section 1, security duties and the implications of their location within social relationships fall within the broad field of experience of the courts.

As such, there is an internal comprehension of security within relationships. Externally, these points about security are also directly relevant to the political standing of tort law. Here, tort has proved to be politically vulnerable. For example, political concerns encapsulated as "compensation culture" proceed on the basis that the accusation that "every harm gives rise to a claim" is correct—as if tort really was concerned with universal standards of behavior, giving rise to liability irrespective of the context. That is a view that Gardner's approach quite rightly rejects. The reality is that tort law sifts much more carefully than this, and balances interests and considerations in determining how to distribute security rights. This sort of misunderstanding—a denial of the specific political role of tort—has sometimes led to legislation which in the end either reiterates what tort does anyway,[57] or introduces more moralism (often reflecting "autonomy" arguments) than was there before, in order to restrain remedies.[58] The first of these is a frustrating illustration that although the boundaries of law and politics tend to be blurred when all is working well, political capital sometimes means taking action against false targets. The second is more serious, and illustrates that "moralism" can be a political choice.

The link between tort, security, and politics is also illustrated by the observation that much of tort law, and much of the political debate about tort reform, is driven by the organizations charged with putting security into effect. The political debate that has been summarized in terms of "tort reform" has been about the limits of responsibility for security, and the location of some such responsibility with claimants. Closely linked are arguments—promoted by insurers—for the "division" and thus limitation of responsibility, according to causal share.[59] This is an agenda based in the price of security.

When addressed in terms of security, tort can indeed be seen as politically distinctive. It allocates certain security roles in a relational context, and in this way it also distributes security. It does this while attending to a range of reasons. In a sense, this is in principle a form of security that "ordinary people" can access. Sometimes, the relationships are even understood in terms of asymmetry, or perhaps vulnerability.

---

[57] Examples in the United Kingdom are section 1 Compensation Act 2006; and the Social Action, Responsibility and Heroism Act 2015. It is not being suggested that these will necessarily *make no difference*—statutes can certainly have unintended consequences. Rather, the point is that the effort was essentially wasted. These are "political" in the sense of being based in party politics, and interest group politics.

[58] See eg P Cane, "Reforming Tort Law in Australia: A Personal Perspective" (2003) 27 Melbourne University Law Review 649.

[59] K Barker and J Steele, "Drifting Towards Proportionate Liability: Ethics and Pragmatics" (2015) 74 Cambridge Law Journal 49–77.

There are areas of tort law that have been shaped by a sense of "fairness" or social need which are not purely legal ideas, and which permeate both case law and legislative activity. Like much else in tort law, despite its necessary use of general principles this too is achieved in a context-by-context fashion.

For tort to embody a mode of social power that could rival wealth, however, faces considerable challenges, to the point of being unlikely. Tort's relational sense of security is not as powerful as the more extensive and effective security devices created in the protection of wealth. It is constrained by the relational form, and in the absence of structures that make its remedies predictable and reliable, it offers only an insecure form of security. Its distributive decisions are moreover highly visible, inviting political scrutiny.[60] This scrutiny owes its existence partly to the fact that the kind of security advanced by tort consists of remedies, which tend to highlight the "cost" of security. In addition, there are repeat players on the receiving end of tort judgments, to the extent that its remedies and even its funding regimes—not to mention standards and principles—will always be capable of being politicized and challenged. For these reasons, tort as a whole is unlikely to achieve the sense of autonomy that would be required—if it was possible at all—to provide a counter to existing sets of values. That is partly why tort's successes have been sectoral not general. They occupy areas where it can be said to be socially useful or at least acceptable for the distributive effects of tort to operate.

5. Conclusion

Gardner's argument is that tort is chiefly not a question of rights that cannot be transgressed, nor of behavior that deserves sanctions, but of security. That security is distributed through choosing when to respond to claims of corrective justice. That is a relational view, which I have suggested is a more promising fit with the frame of tort than the alternatives he rejects. The choices involved in responding to some claims of corrective justice are "political" in the broad sense (they attend to broad reasons). For these reasons, only in a certain sense does tort offer security. It does this through relational allocations of security duties (responsibilities) and connected duties.

However, I have also proposed that there is a danger in moving from the discovery that tort distributes security, to a claim that it encapsulates a form of security that is of wide political significance. Gardner associates tort's security with the integrity of lives. I have suggested that the potential of tort's notion of security to "rival wealth," as Gardner hoped, is truly limited, and that it compares poorly with the forms of security already used to underpin creation of wealth. Lives are not secured with confidence through tort, but some responsibilities to secure are indeed recognized. If we lower our sights, tort's potential to influence the cost and location of security duties is both

---

[60] Contrast the role of private lawyers in advancing wealth through creations that are effectively only occasionally tested in the courts, thus reaping benefits where there is a time lag. The indeterminacy of private law protection is in this instance—unlike the instance where security depends on a remedy (in tort)—an advantage to those asserting rights, again increasing inequality: Pistor, *Code of Capital* (n 7) 215.

real and significant. The broader political implications of tort—whose visibility tends to keep its power in check—flow precisely from this.

Tort's areas of greater effectiveness will tend to be areas of consensus, rather than challenge—but the institutional capacity to produce remedies and thus to invite consensus is still significant. This is evidenced over time by statutory support not only for the principles of tort law but—in some areas—for the security of its remedies, whether through revision of funding regimes, or through areas of compulsory liability insurance. Only with this additional assistance can tort provide security with any degree of generality, and thus confidence. In this way, we can see that the institutional ability of courts to decide appropriately between claims of corrective justice and thus distribute security rights does offer something of political significance. There could be an appearance of circularity, in the sense that tort's decisions take into account reasons which are also transferable to a non-legal context: what will be the impact, the cost, the consequences for law and for future parties, of recognizing a claim? But these reasons are indeed played up or down as is appropriate for the decision-making context.

Amidst the very pluralism of values and of reasons that Gardner notes, tort's political contribution is unlikely to be found in a unique "power," particularly one (security) which is already pervasive and exists in stronger forms. If we ask *how* tort law is political, however, the answer is likely to relate to its institutional structure and goals, and this is indeed where Gardner helps us to focus our attention. Looked at more modestly, its political contribution perhaps lies in its development of just and appropriate allocation of responsibilities of security, made possible by its institutional form, and inviting facilitation and support.

17
The Value of the Neighbour Relation

*Christopher Essert**

1. Introduction

In this chapter, I want to defend the claim that the duty of care in negligence law, the duty that is in commonwealth legal systems most commonly associated with Lord Atkin's statement of the so-called neighbour principle in his speech in *Donoghue v Stevenson*, can be understood as relationally structured. Where I come from— Toronto—this is pretty close to a truism. So one of the most interesting and remarkable parts of John Gardner's writing on tort law is, to me, the few pages in *From Personal Life to Private Law* where he denies what I take to be truistic. Gardner argues that the neighbour principle brought on a revolution in tort law precisely because it created a kind of non-relational duty. My plan, though, is not simply to repeat the standard Toronto-plan talking points, points of which Gardner was a perceptive reader and pointed critic, but instead to show how the duty can be understood as relational even on Gardner's own view of what a relational duty needs to be. As we'll see, Gardner's rejection of the claim I'll defend turns out to depend on some deeper claims about the nature of value.

2. Gardner on Relational Duties

I want to begin by setting out what I understand to be Gardner's idea of a relational duty and his treatment of the neighbour principle, which are contained in a few pages in *From Personal Life to Private Law*.[1] Gardner tells us that a "strictly relational duty"

> is a duty that one has for the reason that one stands in some special relationship with the person to whom the duty is owed. By a "special relationship" I mean, in turn, a relationship other than the relationship that we are all said to have with each other simply as persons or human beings or God's creatures, etc. A special relationship, we might say, is not just a relationship with someone but a relationship with someone *in particular*, from which others must inevitably be left out.

---

* For comments on an earlier draft, I'm grateful to the attendees at this volume's workshop session, and in particular to Andrew Gold, John Goldberg, Ori Herstein, John Oberdiek, David Owens, Prince Saprai, Sandy Steel, and Nicos Stavropolous.

[1] J Gardner, *From Private Life to Public Law* (OUP 2018) 23–24 ("*FPLPL*"). In the quoted passages, italics will be Gardner's and underlining will be mine.

Christopher Essert, *The Value of the Neighbour Relation* In: *Private Law and Practical Reason*. Edited by: Haris Psarras and Sandy Steel, Oxford University Press. © Christopher Essert 2023. DOI: 10.1093/oso/9780192857330.003.0017

298   CHRISTOPHER ESSERT

Gardner is quite clear in what he's saying here: I owe you a strictly relational duty not to *v*, say, if I owe you that duty because you are my R, where "R" could be filled out in any number of ways, including "spouse" or "patient" or "employee" or "student" or "child" or "guest" or whatever.

The important idea in Gardner's view is that the value of the relation that obtains between you and me—as spouses, as student and teacher, as guest and host—is the explanation for the existence of the duty. That is, it is a good thing that there is such a thing as marriage—"a world in which marriage exists is better than ... a world in which it does not"[2]—and the duties that spouses owe to each other in virtue of their marriage are partly constitutive of the marriage itself. That is, what it is to be married is to owe certain duties to one's spouse, so marriage cannot exist without such duties. So the duty exists because the marriage itself exists and the marriage is the reason for the duty. So the duty is (strictly) relational.

And notice also another (as it will turn out) crucial feature of this account: part of Gardner's idea of a relational duty is that it arises in the context of a relation, as he puts it, "from which others must inevitably be left out." Part of what it is to be married is to owe duties to one's spouse that one does *not* owe to others. I think this leaving-out is also part of the value of the relation (and I think Gardner thinks so, too). Marriage is what it is in part because of the fact that one does not owe duties of marriage to those to whom one is not married. I take it that this is implicit in what I said before this paragraph began, but it will be important to us later to have this rendered explicit. When I have to choose between helping my wife and helping you, my explanation, "I helped her because we are married," also implicitly communicates the idea that I did *not* help you because we are *not* married. The relational duties of marriage draw a line, as I'll come to say, between those to whom they are owed and those to whom they are not. And one of the important and valuable things about marriage is precisely the fact that it draws these lines. When two people who have cohabited for a long time get married, it is possible that the only thing about their lives that changes upon marriage is the creation of these duties and the drawing of these lines. So (I want to say) a world in which marriage exists is better than a world in which it does not precisely because the former rather than the latter is a world in which these lines can be drawn, and the drawing of these lines is itself valuable. Our lives are enriched by the existence of the relation of marriage so conceived.

Now let's begin to move toward tort law. It's obvious—to Gardner, to me, to everyone who looks at the law without an urge to distort it to fit it into some preconceived theoretical shape—that there are strictly relational duties of the relevant sort in private law. What it is to be a trustee is to owe certain duties to the beneficiary of the trust that one does not owe to others, and the value of trusteeship lies (at least) in part in the existence of these duties; what it is to be a party to a contract is to owe duties that arise out of the contract that are owed to the counterparty and not to others; and so on. Our question is about if or how this idea applies to the tort of negligence in English and Canadian law after the House of Lords' landmark judgment in *Donoghue v Stevenson*.[3]

---

[2] ibid 29.
[3] [1932] AC 562 (HL).

The big idea that emerges from that judgment is the so-called neighbour principle. Here is the famous passage from Lord Atkin's speech:

> The rule that you are to love your neighbour becomes in law, you must not injure your neighbour; and the lawyer's question, Who is my neighbour? receives a restricted reply. You must take reasonable care to avoid acts or omissions which you can reasonably foresee would be likely to injure your neighbour. Who, then, in law is my neighbour? The answer seems to be—persons who are so closely and directly affected by my act that I ought reasonably to have them in contemplation as being so affected when I am directing my mind to the acts or omissions which are called in question.[4]

An important thought, which Gardner captures, is that there is a sense in which the neighbour principle *vastly* expands the scope of the duties that tort law imposes on us. Before *Donoghue*, it was necessary for a plaintiff to show how they and the defendant were already—that is, before and independently of the events giving rise to the injury—related, through what we can call an *independently comprehensible relation*, something like spouse–spouse, or doctor–patient, or employer–employee, or student–teacher, or parent–child, or guest–host, or whatever. (These relations echo, intentionally, the examples I used above to illustrate Gardner's idea of a strictly relational duty.) The neighbour principle says that such an independently comprehensible relation is not required for negligence liability, that we can owe duties in negligence to those with whom we seem to have no relation other than (something like) risker–riskee.[5]

Now the question, as I said, is about the possibility of understanding this duty to be strictly relational. Gardner thinks it cannot be so understood. He begins by giving what turns out to be a bad interpretation of the principle. According to that interpretation, the category of "my neighbour" in law

> includes all and sundry, people with whom one has no relationship apart from the very action that would constitute the breach of duty. The fact that one has a special relationship, then, can no longer be the reason why one has the duty.[6]

As Gardner notes, and as I said, this is a bad interpretation of the principle. Because Lord Atkin is very clear that I don't owe the duty of care to "all and sundry." Rather I owe it only to those "who are so closely and directly affected," that I ought to take care.

We can see the idea this way: when I am contemplating acting, we can suppose that there are some class of people who, as the principle says, are so closely and directly affected by my act that I ought to think about them and adjust my action accordingly. These people are my neighbours. The law says that when I injure them, I wrong them by breaching the duty of care. Gardner says that there is no special value associated with this duty. It is worth quoting him at length:

---

[4] ibid 580.
[5] For a similar treatment of the relation between relational duties of care and pre-existing relationships, see JCP Goldberg and BC Zipursky, "The Myths of *Macpherson*" (2016) 9 Journal of Tort Law 91, 101–04.
[6] *FPLPL* (n 1) 47.

300 CHRISTOPHER ESSERT

The relationship that holds between Atkin neighbours does not meet this condition. That is not to say, of course, that there is no value in your having or performing your duty of care towards me, when I am your Atkin neighbour. Of course there is: that someone is kept out of harm's way is analytically valuable; and inasmuch as your having a duty to keep me out of harm's way contributes (instrumentally or consti-tutively) to keeping me out of harm's way, the duty too is valuable. But that is not the issue. The issue is whether there is any value in my being positioned relative to you such that your action threatens to put me in harm's way, and such that I need the protection of a duty of care owed by you. Should I want to be in such a vulnerable po-sition, cherish or sustain it when I am in it, etc.? Apart from the fact that it lands you with a duty of care towards me, in other words, is there anything to be said in favour of my being your Atkin neighbour? If not, then we are not in a special relationship in the relevant sense, and the duty of care is not, after all, strictly relational.

And that is indeed the correct verdict, the one that explains the paradigm shift that *Donoghue v Stevenson* represents in the history of the modern law of torts. The duty of care owed to one person by another in the law of negligence today is not based on the value of the relationship of Atkin neighbour that holds between them. It is based, rather, on the value in the life of the one to which breach of the duty of care by the other poses a threat.[7]

I think Gardner's conception of the value of the duty of care as lying in the value of the life of the person to whom it is owed is pretty seriously incomplete as an explanation of the breadth of the duty. But we'll come back to that.

The point to unpack now is this: in this passage, where Gardner denies that the neighbour relation has any distinctive value—where he denies that there is anything good about your and my being neighbours in this sense—he neglects, it seems to me, his own point, which I raised earlier, to the effect that part of the idea of a valuable rela-tion that gives rise to strictly relational duties is the idea that some people are excluded from that relation. When we remember that point and apply it to the present context, we see that part of the idea of the neighbour principle is precisely that not everyone is my neighbour. Put it this way. Gardner asks:

> Apart from the fact that it lands you with a duty of care towards me, in other words, is there anything to be said in favor of my being your Atkin neighbour?

If we reframe the question, we can see that the answer is yes. How should we reframe it? To ask this:

> Apart from the fact that it lands you with a duty of care towards me, *a duty which you do not owe to others*, is there anything to be said in favor of my being your Atkin neighbour?

---

[7] *FPLPL* (n 1) 48–49.

In other words, the duty of care in negligence gets its value in the same way that other relational duties do: from the way that it draws lines between those to whom it is owed and those to whom it is not owed, between those with whom one is in the relevant relation (in this case the neighbour relation) and those who are, as Gardner says, "left out." This is, in fact, something that Lord Atkin says, right before he introduces the principle: "acts or omissions which any moral code would censure cannot in a practical world be treated so as to give a right to every person injured by them to demand relief. In this way rules of law arise which limit the range of complainants and the extent of their remedy." Right from the start, Lord Atkin is telling us that part of the point of the neighbour principle is not merely to extend liability—as it in fact does on the facts of the case, where a duty is found that could not have been found under the old categories of pre-existing duty—but also at the same time to limit it. But this idea—the idea that a neighbour-principle version of the duty of care not only explains why there is liability to one's neighbours but *also* explains why there is not liability to those who are not one's neighbours—is much more closely associated with another famous torts case.[8]

3. The Duty of Care as a Liability-Limiting Principle

The other case is *Palsgraf v Long Island Railroad Co.*[9] I doubt that anyone reading this chapter needs these next six sentences but, just in case, the outline of case is as follows. As a train was departing from a railway station, the defendant's servant, a guard, saw a passenger rushing to get onto a train while carrying a package. The guard gave the passenger a push to assist him in boarding. The push caused the passenger to drop his package. The package contained some fireworks or explosives, which exploded upon being dropped. The explosion resulted in some scales, some distance away, to fall onto the plaintiff, Mrs Palsgraf, causing her injuries. The central holding of the majority judgment, written by Judge Cardozo, is that while the guard may have been negligent to the passenger whose package it was—since, having been pushed, he might have fallen and been hurt—he could not have been negligent to Mrs Palsgraf, because the explosion and thus the injuries that Mrs Palsgraf suffered were totally unforeseeable to the reasonable person in the guard's position.

The defendant did not act in the way that a reasonable person in its position would have acted: it was careless or, arguably, even negligent. But the reason that the defendant's actions were careless was that they imposed unreasonable risks of injuries to the passenger with the package or perhaps to his property and *not* that they imposed unreasonable risks of injuries to Mrs Palsgraf. Nobody could have foreseen what happened to Mrs Palsgraf, it was a kind of one in a million event, the possibility of which would have been regarded, in the words of a different case, as "fantastic and far-fetched."[10] Cardozo's famous judgment centers on the idea that Mrs Palsgraf—or any plaintiff in a tort case—needs to sue on the basis of the defendant's breach of a duty

---

[8] This idea has lately returned as an explicit theme in some decisions of the Supreme Court of Canada. See, for instance, *Deloitte & Touche v Livent Inc* (Receiver of), 2017 SCC 63 [31].

[9] 248 NY 339 (CA).

[10] *Overseas Tankship (UK) Ltd v The Miller Steamship Co* [1967] AC 617 (PC) 641.

302   CHRISTOPHER ESSERT

owed to the plaintiff and not merely on the basis of the defendant's having breached some other duty, one owed to a third party or perhaps to nobody in particular. He says, that is, that she must sue "for a wrong personal to her, and not as the vicarious beneficiary of a breach of duty to another."[11] Cardozo in this judgment is very clearly articulating some kind of relational conception of the duty of care. For instance, he says that "[t]he conduct of the defendant's guard, if a wrong in its relation to the holder of the package, was not a wrong in its relation to the plaintiff, standing far away."[12]

The whole point of *Palsgraf*, as far as I am concerned, is that the defendant's actions, while perhaps careless or perhaps negligent in respect of package man, were not wrongful to Mrs Palsgraf. In other words, the whole point of *Palsgraf* is that you can act carelessly and injure someone and *not wrong them*. I want to say that it is this very fact that is the clearest way to see the value of the neighbour relation. Do I mean that it's good that sometimes you can injure someone while not wronging them? I do, but I don't mean just that. I mean that the lesson of *Palsgraf* is about the line between those whom you wrong when you injure them through your carelessness and those whom you do not wrong when you injure them through your carelessness. The value of the neighbour principle is in the fact that it allows us to draw that line between these two kinds of people. Without that line, Cardozo tells us, "Life will have to be made over, and human nature transformed."[13] How so?

Think again about the facts of *Palsgraf*: there, the defendant acts in a way that (we can assume) was careless, that was not the way that a reasonable person would act. And the plaintiff is injured. But Cardozo's point is that the plaintiff's injury is not a part of a wrong done by the defendant to the plaintiff. Again, as I said, the official explanation for that is in direct contradiction to Gardner's claim about the duty of care: Cardozo tells us that negligence and risk are both "terms of relation," which suggests that the duty of care here is relational at least in some sense.[14] The thought is that the defendant did not owe the duty of care to the plaintiff, so when the plaintiff was injured as a result of the defendant's carelessness, there was no duty to be breached and so no wrong. But let's try to explain the case using just the neighbour principle that is Gardner's central issue of concern. In those terms, the idea has got to be that the plaintiff loses this case because the plaintiff is not the defendant's neighbour, which is to say that Mrs Palsgraf was not "so closely and directly affected" by the defendant's act that the defendant "ought to have her in mind as being so affected." In other words, the likelihood of what happened to her was "so small that in the circumstances a reasonable man would have been justified in disregarding it and taking no steps to eliminate it."[15] So we have now two kinds of potential plaintiffs: those on whom we impose risks that are unreasonable, risks that ought to be taken into account, and those on whom we impose risks

[11] *Palsgraf* (n 9) 342.

[12] ibid 341.

[13] ibid 343.

[14] Gardner discusses not only "strictly relational duties" but also "loosely relational duties" (at eg *FPLPL* (n 1) 50), which are duties owed by one person to another justified not by the value of the relation between the parties but by something else, and indicates that it might be OK by his lights to talk about the duty of care as loosely relational in that sense, and that doing so might help to understand some other important parts of private law. But that's beside the present point, which is that I think (and will argue) that the duty of care is strictly relational, where Gardner does not.

[15] *Overseas Tankship* (n 10) 642.

that are merely "fantastic and far-fetched"[16] and so can be disregarded. The neighbour principle, I am saying, is the principle that allows us to draw a line between these two different kinds of plaintiffs. And this is a line we want to draw. Why?

Here, once again, is Gardner's criticism of the idea that the duty of care is relational:

> The issue is whether there is any value in my being positioned relative to you such that your action threatens to *put* me in harm's way, and such that I *need* the protection of a duty of care owed by you. Should I want to be in such a vulnerable position, cherish or sustain it when I am in it, etc.? Apart from the fact that it lands you with a duty of care towards me, in other words, is there anything to be said in favour of my being your Atkin neighbour?

I take it that the answer to this question lies just in understanding the idea of the neighbour principle. When you are my neighbour, you are someone to whom I owe a special kind of concern—I guess we should call it "care"—such that, if I injure you, I wrong you. So the relation between us as neighbours is the realization of the idea that I should—that I am obligated to—adjust my conduct so as to try to avoid injuring you. You have a kind of claim on my conduct. By contrast, when you are not my neighbour, Lord Atkin's principle tells us, I do not have this duty, I do not have any obligation to adjust my conduct to avoid injuring you. (Again: the risk is so small that a reasonable person would feel comfortable disregarding it.) And if I do in fact injure you, I don't wrong you. Rather, your being injured was just something bad that happened to you. It's true that I played a kind of causal role in your being injured, but there is a clear sense in which *I didn't do anything to you*, a sense in which (if you want to talk this way) your injury wasn't my fault.[17]

Now it is obviously true that it is bad that I injured you in this second kind of case where you are, by hypothesis, not my neighbour. Maybe there are some moral or legal consequences that might follow from that. But in thinking that I didn't wrong you, we are committed to thinking that, before I acted, I owed you no duty not to act the way that I did, and that you could not demand of me that I not act that way. Why? Well, were you to be able to demand that of me, you'd have, in some sense, too much control over me. You'd be able to demand that I not act in a way that imposed a risk on you that (again, by hypothesis) is so small that I would be "justified in disregarding it and taking no steps to eliminate it." You can see, I hope, that there'd be a kind of contradiction in imposing a duty in that case: the reason we impose duties in negligence is so that we do not impose unreasonable risks on one another. But, of course, "in the crowded conditions of modern life even the most careful person cannot avoid creating some risks and accepting others."[18] What we need to avoid is swinging the pendulum too far in the other direction, and creating duties that proscribe the creation of any risks of injury on others. Duties like that would, given the inevitability of risk-creation, effectively make it impossible for us to live our lives, to do anything at all. So an essential

---

[16] ibid 641.

[17] In full-on Toronto-plan style, we could say that you and I were not doer and sufferer of the same injustice, although I don't know that that formulation illuminates what we are currently thinking about.

[18] *Bolton v Stone*, [1951] AC 850 (HL) 867.

304 CHRISTOPHER ESSERT

component of human lives and our social world as we understand those things is that sometimes we are permitted to impose risks on one another, so long as those risks are small. The central idea of the duty of care, as I am trying to understand it here, is that it is constitutive of the difference between these two kinds of cases. In other words, you are my Atkin neighbour, as Gardner puts it, precisely when my actions impose a risk of injury on you that is sufficiently large that we think that, were you injured in that way, I would have done something wrong to you. And you are not my Atkin neighbour when I don't impose a risk of that magnitude on you, so that even if I injure you carelessly, I have not wronged you.

4. The Value of Line-Drawing

Let me say all that in a different way. The neighbour principle allows us to draw a line between those who are our neighbours and those who are not. The specific value of that relation—that line-drawing—is that it allows us to recognize that, in acting, there are those whose safety we must take account of and those who we can feel free to disregard.[19] The importance of this is that the possibility of disregarding some is essential to our being able to act at all. That is the upshot of Cardozo's idea that "prevision so extravagant" would remake our social world: without the neighbour principle's entailment that not everyone is my neighbour, I'd be in a way normatively paralyzed by the possibility of wrongful injury to others. Without it, we'd essentially be in a world of strict liability, with all the familiar problems such a world would bring.[20] By contrast, of course, without the neighbour principle's official content—the idea that some people *are* my neighbours and are owed duties as such—I'd be unrestrainedly free to impose whatever risks on others and those others would be, in a mirror-image sort of way, normatively paralyzed by that possibility. So, as I'll explain, the neighbour principle recognizes and realizes an important kind of relational idea.

What relational idea is this? I guess I am inclined to say that the duty of care and the neighbour principle can be understood as arising out of our *relation as equals*. What I have in mind when I use that expression is, I think, a relatively common idea to the effect that we should arrange our political and legal institutions to realize and vindicate the idea that none of us is the natural inferior nor superior of any other. I won't say anything in defense of that idea because, as Samuel Scheffler puts it, it is one that appeals to many, either because they accept it as a part of a broader understanding of society as a "fair system of cooperation among free and equal people" that is "implicit in the public political culture of a modern democratic society" and thus "represents a point of normative convergence" among those with diverse values and outlooks or because they think that "living in a society of equals is good both intrinsically and instrumentally."[21]

---

[19] To something like the same effect see JCP Goldberg and BC Zipursky, "The Moral of *Macpherson*" (1998) 146 Pennsylvania Law Review 1733, 1825ff.

[20] SR Perry, "The Impossibility of General Strict Liability" (1988) 1 Canadian Journal of Law & Jurisprudence 147.

[21] S Scheffler, *Equality and Tradition: Questions of Value in Moral and Political Theory* (OUP 2010) 227.

THE VALUE OF THE NEIGHBOUR RELATION   305

What I'll do instead is say something about how the neighbour principle can be tied to this idea of relating to one another as equals. The essential thought is one that is associated with Ernest Weinrib's pathbreaking work on private law.[22] Contrast the world we live in—the world of the neighbour principle—to two nearby possible worlds. One is the world in which we are liable for all the consequences of our actions, no matter how much care we take. This would be a world in which, to take an example we've discussed already, the defendant in *Palsgraf* would be liable for the plaintiff's injuries. In such a world, people in the position of that defendant would be in a very real sense subordinated to people in the position of the plaintiff: the justification of such a rule would need to be tied to the importance of protecting plaintiffs from being injured, but that protection would be so extensive as to efface the possibility of the defendants' acting at all, since any actions, no matter how carefully undertaken, impose at least some risks on others. But how could one person's safety be indisputably more important than another person's ability to act at all? That would seem to amount to thinking that the one person is in some basic sense more important than the other. Such a liability regime would be inconsistent with the parties relating as equals.[23] A second neighbouring possible world is some version of the converse of the first, a world of subjective fault (a world in which the defendant in *Vaughan v Menlove*[24] is not liable for the plaintiff's injury) or perhaps a world where we let losses lie where they fall. In either of these worlds, the parties to a negligence case would be unable to relate as equals in precisely the converse way of the parties in the first case. Here we would be endorsing a rule that says that defendants' interests in being able to act are indisputably more important than plaintiffs' interests in being able to live safely, a result which, properly understood, could only be justified by according a kind of superiority to defendants and a kind of inferiority to plaintiffs.[25]

The world of the neighbour principle is different than either of these. The neighbour principle tells us that sometimes defendants wrong plaintiffs when they injure them accidentally and at the same time it tells us that sometimes defendants do not wrong plaintiffs when they injure them accidentally. And the explanation of the differences between those two kinds of cases is to be traced (through a series of steps involving explicating the idea of reasonable foreseeability and so on) to the idea that plaintiffs and defendants can relate as equals precisely through the neighbour relation so understood. Now in trying to explain things this way, I chose the language of comparing

---

[22] The argument below closely tracks one in EJ Weinrib, *The Idea of Private Law* (OUP 2012).

[23] It was suggested to me that *Vincent v Lake Erie Transp Co*, 109 Minn 456 (1910), is an exception to this rule, in that, there, fairness or equality seems to require the defendant to compensate the plaintiff for its losses even though the defendant took reasonable care, which is to say for losses that the defendant had no duty not to impose. But I think that's not the right reading of the case. *Vincent* is a straightforward trespass case—as argued in, for instance, A Ripstein, *Private Wrongs* (Harvard University Press 2016)—so the defendant was clearly under a duty not to use the plaintiff's dock. Now, you might—indeed, you should!—ask how the kind of strict liability associated with trespass could be consistent with the idea of equality I'm working with. But that is a different topic than this one.

[24] (1837) 132 ER 490 (CP).

[25] Although I use the words "plaintiffs" and "defendants" throughout this paragraph, it's important to avoid thinking that this is a matter of competing classes of persons. The point is that, *in each interaction*, the terms of that interaction need to be consistent with the two parties' relating as equals, and each of the alternatives fails that requirement.

possible worlds quite intentionally, because I want to connect these thoughts to Gardner's desideratum for the existence of a relational duty. Recall that Gardner argues that a relational duty arises out of the value of the relationship to which it belongs, a value understood in terms of the way that a world in which such a relationship exists is better than a world in which it does not. And so we can see that the value of the neighbour relation as I've tried to elucidate fits this model: it is that it is constitutive of a kind of equal relations between neighbours in respect of the subject matter of negligence law, which is to say (roughly) accidental injuries. In the crowded conditions of modern life, none of us can avoid imposing risks on others: sometimes that is OK, because the risks are small enough to justifiably disregard, given that avoiding them would make action too difficult; other times it is not OK, because the risk is large enough that it should not be imposed on others.

Tying this to Gardner's desideratum, then, the idea becomes that the neighbour relation is valuable because it is a relation of equals, and a world in which our legal relations are relations of equals in this way is better than a world in which some are permitted to subordinate others.[26] That seems something close to analytic to me. But you might want to deny it, as Gardner himself seems to do when he says: "Personally I do not share the taste for constituting people as juridical equals that lies at the heart of this view."[27] Fine. We are not going to settle *that* question here. My point is just that the form of the account that I am providing is entirely consistent with the idea of a strictly relational duty as Gardner understands it.

[26] Two points here are worth making, one simpler than the other. The simple one can come first: even if you deny that relating as equals is as important as I think it is, it is very hard to deny that it is a good thing, that it is valuable in Gardner's sense of valuable, namely having "potential to contribute to human lives and their quality." (That quotation is from J Gardner and T Macklem, Value, "Interest, and Well-Being" (2006) 18 Utilitas 362.) Second: there is a lot of interesting stuff to say about exactly how we should think about the argument of the last few paragraphs. In the text above, I've followed Gardner in articulating the argument in what we might call value-first terms: his idea is that we should compare how good the world with the relationship is to how good the world without it is. This form of thought echoes, I think not coincidentally, the Razian account of certain normative ideas like the normative power to make promises: on Raz's view, really simplified, we have the power to promise because a world in which we have the power is better than a world in which we lack it. There's another way of proceeding here, though, which you might call "transcendental," if you were into using words like that, which claims that there is some sense in which it is impossible for us to envision a morally acceptable world without the power to promise, and so we have the power to promise. (This is essentially Seana Shiffrin's account of promising.) That other way closely parallels what Cardozo seems to be saying in *Palsgraf*. The claim is not that the world with the duty of care is better than a world without it, but rather that "[l]ife will have to be made over, and human nature transformed," before we could eliminate the duty. For what it's worth, I think it's helpful to keep both of these ideas in mind at the same time, because (as the text above indicates) I think that the precise way in which a world with the duty of care (and, incidentally, a world with the power to promise) is better than a world without it is that the former is a world in which we can relate to one another as equals where the latter is not, and so the former is a world that is morally acceptable where the latter is not. So the argument is not strictly speaking transcendental in the way that some arguments in metaphysics are, but rather it is what we could perhaps call morally transcendental, in that it claims that a certain normative phenomenon is a necessary constituent of a morally (or, if you prefer, normatively) acceptable world.

[27] J Gardner, "Tort Law and Its Theory" in J Tasioulas (ed), *The Cambridge Companion to the Philosophy of Law* (CUP 2020) 352 at 364.

5. Relating as Equals, Relating as Neighbours

Here's another angle onto Gardner's view. It seems that the only candidate for a relation that could make the duty of care relational, after *Donoghue*, is the relation, roughly, of risker–riskee. But the idea that we are in a valuable relation when I impose a risk on you seems ... odd? What could be valuable about being exposed to a risk, is what Gardner seems to be worrying: "should I want to be in such a vulnerable position, cherish or sustain it when I am in it, etc.? ... is there anything to be said in favour of my being your Atkin neighbour?"[28]

Here's one way to respond. I think that Lord Atkin is saying, actually, is that the physical relation of risker and "riskee" that Gardner is talking is not the same as, the legal (juridical, moral) relation that is our target of concern. Indeed, the legal relation—our being Atkin neighbours—can actually obtain in the absence of the physical relation of being at risk. This can be true in a variety of ways. First, think about the official statement of the principle itself, which says that whether or not you are my neighbour is a question that is to be answered "when I am directing my mind to the acts or omissions which are called in question." But I can be "directing my mind" to something before I actually do it. Actually, that's the point here, isn't it? I should be thinking about what I am about to do before I do it, precisely so that I can see if it might risk injury to anyone else. So when I direct my mind in this way I create a relation between myself and my neighbours, a relation that (as I've argued) is valuable because of the way that it draws a line between neighbours and others. And when things are going the way that they ought to go, I will adjust my conduct in the light of the risks created to my neighbours. But I will be under no duty to adjust my conduct in the light of the fantastic and far-fetched risks I might impose on others, since I know (and they know) that even the most careful of us cannot avoid imposing risks like that.

I think what Gardner is pointing to here does expose a kind of ambiguity in the way that we think and talk about the duty of care. Because the neighbour relation is a kind of valuable relation, but there is also another valuable relation—the one that is probably properly called "relating as equals"—that does pre-exist the conduct or even the contemplation of the conduct. This relation does obtain between each and every one of us—it applies, I guess, to my relations with "all and sundry"—and what it demands of us is, first, that we impose on ourselves duties of care owed to our neighbours and, second, that we not impose on ourselves duties of care to others. But those duties of care that we do impose constitute, I'm arguing, a distinct relation from the pre-existing one that, in the sense I'm articulating in this paragraph, grounds them.[29]

---

[28] *FPLPL* (n 1) 49.

[29] A different way to ask the question of Gardner's that I quoted at the end of the paragraph two before the one to which this note is appended is to ask the question from the defendant's point of view. Why would I want to owe you duties of care? Wouldn't my life be better were I not to owe any duties to anyone, since there I could act freely without regard to their safety? I say no. I think part of the egalitarian idea that I am trying to articulate here is that it is good for each of us to relate to others as equals. In particular, it is good for *me* to live in a social world in which I must govern my conduct in a way that is responsive to your presence in the world as someone to whom I relate as an equal.

308   CHRISTOPHER ESSERT

A second way to see that the neighbour relation can obtain independently of the actual risky conduct is by noting that, as Lord Atkin says, the neighbour principle is meant to be a "general conception" of relations. And so, I think, it is meant to include cases not only like those we have been describing so far—cases where the duty of care arises because of the risk that defendant's conduct imposes on plaintiff—but also other cases. Officially, in the actual judgment in *Donoghue*, it is meant to cover the cases of duties arising out of pre-existing relations. And we can make sense of that: in those cases, the nature of the relation is such that when you and I are in such a relation, you are on the inside of the line that we drew above. Saying more than that would require more space than we have here to investigate the details of those cases. But there's another case we can look at, briefly, the case of the tort of negligent misrepresentation.

Gardner uses this tort, at one point, to illustrate the idea that tort law can contain strictly relational duties. He writes:

> Maybe some torts are (or include) breaches of strictly relational duties. Think of the tort of misrepresentation, for example, which can be committed only in the course of precontractual dealings.[30]

Now, I know that there is a significant amount of academic controversy over how misrepresentation torts operate. But let me make a series of suggestions that might help us to further develop the thoughts above. While there is, in England, a specific statutory wrong of "misrepresentation," there is, both in England and elsewhere, a distinct tort of negligent misrepresentation. This is the tort that applies whenever a defendant is in a special relation with a plaintiff, such that the defendant ought to know that the plaintiff would reasonably rely on the defendant's statements. And in Canada we understand that tort as a branch of negligence law, in the sense that we can talk about it using concepts like duty and thus, I want to say, in the sense that the duty owed in cases of negligent misrepresentation can be understood as an instance of Lord Atkin's general conception of duties.

But set that aside for a moment. Ask, even on Gardner's terms, what is the nature of the relation that grounds this strictly relational duty? The answer is that the parties need to be in "precontractual dealings." But it isn't hard to see that such an idea is obviously going to be overbroad and that we'll need to construct a category of pre-contractual dealings of a sufficiently developed state such that the tort applies. Because remember that on Gardner's view, a duty counts as strictly relational only if it arises out of a relationship that is itself independently valuable. But how does that requirement apply here? Is there such a thing as a relationship of "dealing precontractually" such that we can say that the world is a better place because such a relationship exists? It's hard to see why, except to the extent that precontractual dealings seem at least empirically necessary for us to have contracts, and (we can assume) contracts are valuable. But that seems not to get right at the heart of things: we want to be able to say that the relationship, understood in part as constituted by some sets of rights and duties that the parties owe to each other, is independently valuable.

---

[30] *FPLPL* (n 1) 46.

And how would we say that about the precontractual duties case? I take it that the only plausible answer is that it is the very existence of the duties that is of value: that is, there is something good about its being the case that, sometimes, when we are negotiating the terms of a contract, we become bound to each other in a way that obligates us to be truthful to one another. When? Well, I want to say that it depends, but that the most obvious way to think about the answer is through the neighbour principle.

Think about it this way: the core idea of negligent misrepresentation is the idea of a "special relation" that needs to obtain between plaintiff and defendant. What is required to create such a relation is a subtle matter and it differs from case to case. But in at least one class of cases, the idea is helpfully understood just by thinking that the defendant undertakes responsibility to the plaintiff through making certain representations. Whether or not a duty is created depends on the nature of those representations and the purpose for which they are made. If they are relied on for the purpose that they are meant to be relied on, then losses suffered on the basis of that reliance are recoverable. But if they are relied on for other purposes, they are not. So when, as an auditor, I make representations about a firm's finances to you for the purpose of your determining whether or not to loan that firm money, and then others rely on those representations for other purposes, I am not liable for those others' losses. Now ask: what is the nature of the valuable relation that you and I have, in virtue of the value of which we can say (as Gardner himself says) that the duty I owe you is strictly relational? It's hard to characterize the value of that relation in any other terms than that it is a relation whose point is to enable precisely this sort of reliance. In other words, the relation and the duty are sort of mutually constitutive, the point of the duty is just to draw the line around those to whom I'm liable and those to whom I'm not. So there is a really close continuity with regular negligence here: the only difference is that in that case I make you my neighbour by imposing a risk on you whereas in this case I make you my neighbour in the way that Mr Rogers used to do, by asking, won't you be my neighbour. So the idea that there is a continuity in these cases is grounded on the idea that the duty in both cases precisely serves to delineate the scope of a relation, and the relation is a valuable one because it allows for a distinction between those to whom a duty is owed and those to whom it isn't. The reasons why the scope of the duty is different in this case than in the normal case have to do with the differences between, roughly, words and representations, but we won't have room to explore that, either. But in both cases the value of the neighbour relation lies in its line-drawing, in its recognition that sometimes we are responsible for the injuries we cause others and sometimes we are not.

6. Doing Things as Equals

Here's a way to put the question that now presents itself: what, exactly, is the substance of my and Gardner's disagreement? I don't think this is all merely a kind of disagreement about legal forms. That's because Gardner actually says explicitly why he rejects the sort of view that I'm trying to defend when he says that the duty of care, rather than being based on the value of any relationship between plaintiff and defendant is "based, rather, on the value in the life of the one to which breach of the duty of care by the other poses a threat."[31] He goes on:

> I am not thinking primarily of actions that risk another's death. I am thinking primarily of actions that imperil some valuable *aspect* or *aspects* of a person's life: her relationships and roles, her plans and projects, the pursuit and accomplishment of her personal goals, and so on. She may be put in danger of no longer being able to support her family, pay her rent, pursue her career, bear children or look after them, live in her own home, save her marriage, cultivate her garden, develop her skills as a pianist or goalkeeper, take pleasure in travel or films or cooking, take pride in herself as a parent or lover, etc.

But *lots* of things imperil these aspects of our lives. Mrs Palsgraf's accident, we can assume, probably set back her ability to pursue these plans and projects significantly more than Mrs Donoghue's episode of what amounted to food poisoning. And yet Mrs Donoghue is the poster child for a successful plaintiff where Mrs Palsgraf is the poster child for an unsuccessful plaintiff. So the appeal on its face to what I'll follow Gardner in calling the value in the lives of negligence plaintiffs is going to be insufficient to explain the difference between Mrs Palsgraf and Mrs Donoghue, the difference between unsuccessful and successful plaintiffs. That is not to say that Gardner is unable to explain the difference. Those familiar with his work will be able, I think, to guess at how he'd want to do it. It is going to be a story about the balance of reasons.

But that strikes me as not quite on target. Here's a closing thought: Gardner's view as set out above is that tort law (like many other parts of our lives) is about the value or values of or in our lives, about our doing things in the world. On my view, though, it's not about the things we do but about the way we do them, in the precise sense that it's about insisting that we need to do them *as equals*. We need tort law—we need *all law*—not to get stuff done, but to get stuff done together, in a way that is consistent with our equal standing, in a way that does not just amount to some of us deciding how things will be for others because we take ourselves to be somehow superior to them. The neighbour relation is a specific and important realization of that idea, and the duties it imposes protect it rather than merely protecting the actions and lives of us considered as separate.

---

[31] *FPLPL* (n 1) 49.

18
The Liberal Promise of Contract

Hanoch Dagan[*]

1. Introduction

"The big themes of private law," as John Gardner wrote, "are also among the big themes of life."[1] And because these themes are so timeless, he added, they are not necessarily connected to liberal values: liberal civilization, after all, "has its beginning, middle, and—one hopes not too soon—its end."[2] The three themes of personal life that underlie private law, per Gardner, are thus wrong, loss, and remedy: the "trinity of torts," as he called them.[3] The absence of contract from this picture of the core of private law is not coincidental for him: tort *should* come before contract as a matter of both logical and justificatory priority.[4] Moreover, while acknowledging "Maine's pride in the shift "from Status to Contract." which put an end to feudal forms of bonded labor, Gardner was "horrified at how contract has become an all-consuming tyranny in the intervening 150 years."[5]

The main mission of this chapter is to study Gardner's rather grim account of contract. Analyzing both the insights and the pitfalls of this account is important both for its own sake and in order to evaluate Gardner's view that private law is not *essentially* about freedom.[6]

To preview briefly what lies ahead, let me begin with this last proposition regarding the role that "our characteristically modern concern to live our lives autonomously"[7] plays in private law. If Gardner's dissent relates to the questions private law must address or to the possible answers it can give—and has given—to these questions, then Gardner must be correct. But if the issue at hand relates to the role autonomy plays "in the defence of private law," as he sometimes suggests,[8] then—as I hope to show in these pages—I believe that the case of contract implies otherwise.

Gardner's picture of contract, summarized in section 2, is (as one might expect) not autonomy based. Contractualization, in his view, stands for "the *This for That* way,"[9]

---

[*] Thanks to Andrew Gold, John Goldberg, Dori Kimel, James Penner, Prince Saprai, Stéphane Sérafin, Sandy Steel, and Ben Zipursky for their helpful comments.

[1] J Gardner, *From Personal Life to Private Law* (OUP 2018) 9–10 ("*FPLPL*").

[2] ibid 6.

[3] ibid 1.

[4] J Gardner, "Breach of Contract as a Special Case of Tort" in J Gardner, *Torts and Other Wrongs* (OUP 2019) 333, 343 ("BCT").

[5] J Gardner, "The Contractualisation of Labour Law" in H Collins and others (eds), *Philosophical Foundations of Labour Law* (OUP 2018) 33, 47 ("CLL").

[6] *FPLPL* (n 1) 199.

[7] ibid 193.

[8] ibid 18.

[9] CLL (n 5) 43.

Hanoch Dagan, *The Liberal Promise of Contract* In: *Private Law and Practical Reason*. Edited by: Haris Psarras and Sandy Steel, Oxford University Press. © Hanoch Dagan 2023. DOI: 10.1093/oso/9780192857330.003.0018

which explains why breach of contract is "a special case of tort."[10] Thus conceived, contract is *necessarily* a source of alienation. Resort to contract beyond the sphere of commerce (as in the famous widget case) is intrinsically troubling: the contractualization of employment, for example, "is a process that lovers of freedom, as well as lovers of self-realisation, should resist."[11]

If the essence of contract is indeed captured by the *This for That* model, Gardner's conclusions are convincing. Fortunately, it is not. This model, which echoes, as I claim in section 3, the Kantian (and Hegelian) transfer theory of contract, is, to be sure, not incoherent; the transfer theory of contract offers a specific conception of contract, which is, as Gardner insists, both subordinate to tort and is normatively troublesome in the ways he powerfully highlights. But there are other possible conceptions of contract, and indeed there is at least one possible conception that *is* autonomy-based. The autonomy-based conception I discuss in this chapter is both more defensible interpretively and analytically than Gardner's *This for That* model and less vulnerable normatively to Gardner's devastating critique. Or at least so I argue in sections 4 and 5.

Indeed, circling back to Gardner's broader point about private law and liberalism, while the questions of private law are timeless, not all answers are equally acceptable. It is not easy to defend, let alone celebrate, a contract law modeled after transfer theory: in some contexts, such a system is positively unjust; in many others it is normatively disappointing. An autonomy-based contract law, by contrast, is neither, and it is also not subordinate to tort. Our characteristically modern concern for autonomy may not be a necessary feature of contract law. But it *is* indispensable for its defense. Similar conclusions, I surmise in section 6, may apply to private law as a whole.

2. Gardner on Contract

Gardner did not write much about contract, but his astute observations are illuminating, both in what they establish and in the significance of their presuppositions. In what follows I outline the two important propositions that explain his reservations from the central role contract plays in contemporary private law and in current society: that breach of contract is a tort, and that modern-day rampant contractualization is alarming. I then turn to the premises that ground these propositions: theses regarding the nature of contract and contractual rights that imply that contract is subordinate to tort and that contractualization risks alienation and subordination. My task in this section is to show the coherence of Gardner's view of contract, a view that makes Gardner, as I argue in section 3, a transfer theorist of contract.

[10] BCT (n 4) 333.
[11] CLL (n 5) 47.

2.1 Breach of contract as a tort

Breach of contract, Gardner insists, is simply "a special case of tort," since, just like other torts, it invokes plaintiffs' civil recourse for a wrong "in which primarily corrective justice is attempted," "in a primarily reparative mode," and "in response to claims for unliquidated sums."[12] The only distinctive feature of contractual obligations is that—unlike the other obligations vindicated by tort law—they are voluntary, but this feature only implies that "[t]ort-law obligations form the general class and contract-law obligations are a special class carved out of it."[13]

Gardner is aware of the familiar distinction between breach of contract and your garden variety tort action: that while tort damages focus "on restoring the *status quo ante*, the way things used to be before the tort was committed," with breach of contract a plaintiff is made whole by recovering on her expectation, which is supposed to bring her "as close as possible to the situation that she bargained for," namely to the way things would have been had the contract been performed.[14] But he is not impressed. "Superficial differences in measurement should not distract us," he claims, from the fact that in both cases "the aim of damages awards is to put P, so far as money can do it, in the same position as she would have been in had D's primary obligation been performed."[15]

2.2 Degrading contractualizations

Treating contract as more than just one source of obligation is one prevalent mistake, Gardner argues; another, and much more troubling mistake regarding contract given its disturbing real-life effects, is the rampant contractualization that typifies contemporary law and society.

"In modern private law, as indeed in modern culture at large, there has been a long-standing tendency towards what might be called contractual reductivism where special relationships are concerned, especially but not only in respect of special relationships that can be *initiated* by the making of a contract." Gardner agonized over this development. It is all too easy, he claimed, to perceive it "as augmenting our freedom, allowing us to craft all our special relationships to suit our particular personal goals." But we must not forget the way contractualization also *reduces* our freedom: once special relationships—such as employer–employee, landlord–tenant, bailor–bailee and so forth—are rendered "comprehensively plastic, because contractual, in law," their "relatively fixed deontic content" is eroded. This is a real loss since "the law's recognition of and support for special relationships sometimes contributes to their availability and sustainability."[16]

---

[12] BCT (n 4) 333.
[13] ibid 341, 343.
[14] *FPLPL* (n 1) 164.
[15] BCT (n 4) 340.
[16] *FPLPL* (n 1) 44–46.

314 HANOCH DAGAN

The employment relationship is Gardner's prime example, and he was deeply concerned about its treatment as "*merely* a contractual one."[17] A contractual rationale of employment "yields the wrong limits" to "the employer's authority over the employee," since once the authority has been assigned to the employer, it is "as if one's working life is not part of one's life" and "the law of contract does not imply a legal duty, on the part of the employer, to use his authority reasonably while the contract of employment subsists."[18] The resulting predicament is indefensible.

Indeed, the excesses of the "real-life labour markets of capitalist economies" in which employers "enjoy legitimate authority over such an extensive swathe" of their employees' lives "irrespective of the wisdom of the authority's exercise" is Gardner's Exhibit A in his critique of contractualization. "Freedom of contract on its own," he claims, is "a freedom-destroying monster with a freedom-friendly face." It "gives its blessing to authoritarian work regimes and lends social acceptability to the depressing idea that work is there to pay for the life of the worker without being part of that life."[19] It also invites "the exploitation of the plasticity of contractual relationships to create hybrid arrangements, some of them designed to subvert or evade the law's residual uses of the employee/non-employee distinction."[20]

2.3 Contract as *this for that*

Gardner's critique of the contractualization of employment and similar special relationships is deeply embedded in, and indeed heavily relies upon, his understanding of the nature of contract. He recurrently refers to the picture of *This for That* as capturing the essence of contract. "Contracts assign authority," he similarly writes, which only requires "that one accepts an offer from another and gives, or promises, something in return."[21]

And thus, "[o]n the *This for That* model, going to work is a cost to the employee, a sacrifice of time and effort that calls for compensation, a burden to be borne in return for wages." Work is fully alienated and "is not *supposed* to have a place within [the employee's] wider life." As long as the employer complies with his obligation to compensate the employee for her work, he has no further duties. This is why contracts "can be used to assign vast authority in the employment context, potentially subjecting people for a significant proportion of their waking hours to a regime of petty rules and capricious directions which, if it were replicated outside the workplace, would be classified as the apparatus of a totalitarian regime."[22]

Gardner borrowed the *This for That* model from Ian Macneil. But unlike Macneil, he insists that this model is not a pathology of the idea of contract. Macneil criticized "the abstract world of the law of contract" he encountered, in which the "*This for That* of atomistic, unrelated humans, non-existent in the real world" is the lens through

---

[17] ibid 45.
[18] CLL (n 5) 35, 43–44.
[19] ibid 35, 44, 46.
[20] *FPLPL* (n 1) 45.
[21] CLL (n 5) 36, 46.
[22] ibid 41, 44, 46.

which many contract doctrines are "founded or pretended to be founded."[23] His target, more precisely, was *neoclassical* contract law, which fails to do justice to both "particular types of contractual relations," and the "contractual relations" as such.[24] Gardner's point is different, and—on its face—more radical. He claims that "the problem is not that the law of contract fails to do justice to contractual relations"; in other words, it "is not a contingent limitation borne of the extant law of contract." Rather, the problem in his view is inherent to contract. Contract necessarily "regards us as *merely contractually related* humans." The *This for That* model, which defines contract, sets "a limit on the suitability of contract law" to govern special relationships such as employment.[25]

It is this last move that is crucial to Gardner's harsh verdict of the contractualization of work as the "common enemy against which liberal lovers of personal autonomy and Marxian lovers of self-realisation should equally have raged and rallied ... while they still had the chance." If contract implies the *This for That* picture, then subordination and alienation are indeed inevitable concomitants of contractualization. Contract (on this picture) is simply not fit to govern this—and many other—special relationships, and neither protection for weak bargainers nor statutory rights or implied terms aimed at augmenting employees' contractual rights "can be expected to do much to ameliorate."[26]

2.4 Contractual rights as security rights

The same idea that underlies Gardner's claim regarding the inevitability of contract's damaging effects on employment—his *This for That* view of contract—also explains his first proposition: that breach of contract is a special case of a tort. To see why, we need to consider his understanding of contractual rights, and then appreciate its reliance on the *This for That* model.

A good starting point here is Gardner's explanation why the differences in measurement between contract and torts damages are superficial. Both tort law and contract law, he writes, "use money payments ('reparative damages') as their proxy device, and use *restitutio in integrum* as the regulative ideal for their assessment." It is thus misleading to present them as "parting company on the question of which is the relevant *status quo*" in this inquiry, because both "invite us to imagine the relevant *status quo aliter* on the footing that the plaintiff's life would in other respects have carried on much as before."[27]

The reason for law's vindication—in both branches—of people's interest in the narrative of their lives to continue "on the same arc as before" lies, for Gardner, in the significance of keeping one's life "on its existing track." This interest is not necessarily related to autonomy; it merely follows from our being capable of having goals and

---

[23] I Macneil, *The Relational Theory of Contract* (Sweet & Maxwell 2001) 300–01.
[24] ibid 292.
[25] CLL (n 5) 41.
[26] ibid 41, 45–46.
[27] *FPLPL* (n 1) 163–65.

from the simple fact that the terms of our engagement with value "are set by value that is already instantiated, and by the people and things that already instantiate it."[28]

Gardner calls these rights security rights, and argues that this term aptly captures "the tort case and the contract case alike." In both cases, he maintains, "we care about the way things were before ... because we care about the way things were already *heading* for the plaintiff when the wrong came along." Thus, tort law and contract law "share the same built-in conservative feature." They both "aim to put the plaintiff's life back on its previous track, or at any rate to enable the plaintiff to put her life back on the previous track (*aliter*), even though not necessarily at its previous (*ante*) position on that track."[29]

3. Gardner as a Transfer Theorist

Gardner sees no important distinction between torts and breaches of contract, as just noted, because in both cases law vindicates the plaintiff's right to security against the defendant's intervention in "the way things were already *heading* for" her. This proposition, I now want to claim, makes Gardner a transfer theorist of contract. To see why, we first need to make it a bit more precise.

Gardner's discussion of torts is helpful here. The law of torts, he writes, "gives the potential plaintiff rights which, if they go unviolated, will help to keep her life on its existing track."[30] The key word here is *existing*, which in the context of torts is clearly correct. By contrast, the conventional reference of contract law to the plaintiff's *expectation* interest suggests that with contract this is not the case. It implies that contract brings a promisor's performance into the promisee's track in a subtly, but importantly, different way than an assignment.[31] It is thus no coincidence that Gardner marginalizes this familiar feature of contract law. Indeed, to fully establish his claim that breach of contract is a tort he should embrace transfer theorists' repudiation of this way of referring to contract's default measure of recovery, and substitute any reference to "expectation interest" with "performance interest."[32]

The idea of transfer theory, just like the *This for That* picture, implies that expectation is a misnomer. Similarly, when Gardner writes that contracts *assign* authority, he echoes Peter Benson's recent discussion of contract as an extension of a spot exchange. Transfer theory, Benson writes, follows the footsteps of contract's legacy at common law, where the "crucial conceptual move" from immediate exchange to executory contract became possible with the recognition that *all* the normative work takes place upon formation.[33]

---

[28] ibid 168, 179, 183–84.

[29] ibid 165, 183.

[30] ibid 183.

[31] cf S Sérafin, "Transfer Theory and the Assignment of Contractual Rights" (unpublished manuscript), on file with author.

[32] P Benson, *Justice in Transactions: A Theory of Contract Law* (Harvard University Press 2019) 41, 264, 353, 355, 357–58.

[33] ibid 247, 251–52.

It is not only Gardner's understanding of the essence of contract and the nature of contractual rights that shows him to be a transfer theorist. His dissenting propositions regarding the status and the stature of contract similarly demonstrate his alliance with that view of contract.

Thus, Gardner's classification of breach of contract as a tort again mirrors Benson's analysis, in which there is a "striking parallel" between breach of contract and conversion. Benson's reason for this proposition is unsurprisingly reminiscent of the *This for That* picture. A breaching promisor, Benson claims, "deprives" the promisee of the "promised performance that [he] has vested with her, as a matter of rights, at contract formation." In other words, once formation is viewed as "a form of transactional acquisition"—an extended spot exchange, in Benson's account, or an assignment, in Gardner's—any withholding of the promised performance is a failure to deliver what already belongs to another. Breach is "a per se wrongful deprivation and injury"—a violation of the promisee's security right, in Gardner's terms—because after formation the promisor is a mere possessor of the promised entitlement, the rightful owner of which is the promisee.[34] What contract lawyers refer to as a promisee's expectation interest is treated, by both Benson and Gardner, as if it is already part of her *existing* track.[35]

Similarly, Gardner's complaints that contract has no internal resources to face the possibility of transfers of authority that entail clearly objectionable alienation and subordination also presuppose other characteristic features of transfer theory.

Thus, contract per transfer theory indeed only requires, as Gardner claims, offer and acceptance and is indifferent to the nature of the pertinent performance. The parties' substantive ends have no room in the *This for That* picture in line with transfer theory's account of contract in which their respective needs, purposes, circumstances, interests, and well-being are legally irrelevant.[36] Transfer is set entirely by will and is thus blind, exactly in the way that triggers Gardner's alienation critique, to the distinction between a right to the delivery of a widget, which requires a promisor to produce and then depart from an external object, and a right to an employee's labor that is both more comprehensive and much closer to the promisor's own self.

By the same token, transfer theory is famously indifferent to concerns of substantive inequality that trigger Gardner's verdict of employment contracts' potential to bring about unacceptable subordination. Transfer theory is based on a strong commitment to *formal* equality and a clear injunction against any interpersonal obligation beyond the duty of reciprocal respect for independence. Contracting parties must not actively coerce or deceive one another; but there is no prescription against advantage-taking as such, let alone any affirmative duties, unless they can be grounded in the intentions of the actual contracting parties. Contract law, on this view, has no business in protecting particular categories of disadvantaged, inexperienced, or vulnerable individuals, and

---

[34] ibid 334, 338–39.

[35] As the text implies, transfer theory takes various shapes and not all of them require a literal transfer. Thus, Arthur Ripstein recently described his version of transfer theory in terms of "bilateral modification." See A Ripstein, "The Contracting Theory of Choices" (2021) 40 Law and Philosophy 185.

[36] Benson, *Justice in Transactions* (n 32) 24, 27, 367–69, 371–72, 377–78, 469.

318 HANOCH DAGAN

it must not "aim to redress differences in bargaining power per se or unfair and une-qual starting points."[37]

Indeed, as Arthur Ripstein explains, transfer theory—the picture of contract as the *This for That* way—sharply delimits "the contract part" of the law governing, for example, employment, so as to exclude any further "powers the state may exercise" in "restricting or shaping the arrangements that people can make," "'supplying' a va-riety of contract types so as to make life more convenient or protect people from var-ious forms of domination and exploitation," "imposing mandatory terms on some contracting situations," or "empowering associations such as labour unions to bargain collectively."[38] Ripstein, like Gardner, refers to all these rules as a regulatory apparatus, which has nothing to do with contract.

Thus conceived, Gardner seems correct in referring to contractualization as con-tractual *reductivism*—under transfer theory, as he claims, "if an employment relation-ship exists in law, it must reside in the terms of the contract between employer and employee."[39] Ripstein is untroubled by the reference to all the legal rules that restrict and shape the arrangements people can make with contract as a regulatory overlay, rather than as components of the "the contract part." At this point, however, Gardner part ways with his fellow transfer theorists.

As noted, Gardner agonizes over treating people in a special relationship like em-ployment as *merely contractually related* humans. Unlike Ripstein, he doesn't find solace in the fact that after law contractualizes employment, it "reasserts some non-negotiable aspects of the employment relationship by adding various implied terms to employment contracts, and attaching various statutory rights and obligations to them." This move, he claims, "comes too late," because "by the time the policy is being implemented, the ideological game is already up." Contract, Gardner reminds us, "has become a concept in ordinary, everyday use." And according to this concept, he adds—following the *This for That* picture of transfer theory—"contractual norms are norms created by the parties to the contract." This means that the contractualization of employment recasts the employment relationship in purely "voluntaristic terms," de-void of the features that should be regarded as constitutive to it.[40]

On this front Gardner seems to be correct. If the *This for That* picture of transfer theory captures the way law shapes[41] and ordinary people understand contract, then contractualization cannot be fully remedied by a regulatory overlay, whatever its con-tent may be. This means that the conceptual debate over transfer theory, to which I turn next, is not merely academic. The stakes, as Gardner explains, are high.

Contract can be designed around transfer theory's model of extended barter. But, as I argue in section 4, it need not and should not. Therefore, as I hope to establish in

---

[37] ibid 188, 373, 388.

[38] Ripstein, "The Contracting Theory of Choices" (n 35) 206–11.

[39] CLL (n 5) 42.

[40] ibid 36, 41–42.

[41] I use the verb "shapes" following Gardner's reference to contractual obligations as "legally shaped" (BCT (n 4) 345). Elsewhere, I've claimed that Gardner downgrades law's significance in the constitution of power-conferring institutions like contract. See H Dagan and A Dorfman, "Postscript to Just Relationships: Reply to Gardner, West, and Zipursky" (2017) Columbia Law Review Online 261, 265–66. But as long as the fact that law shapes contract is acknowledged, this debate can be bracketed.

section 5, breach of contract is not yet another wrong, and contractualization does not necessarily stand for "the *This for That* way" with its devastating effects of subordination and alienation.

4. From Transfer to a Joint Plan

4.1 Transfer theory's escape route?

Friends of transfer theory may try to push back against Gardner's conclusions regarding the implications of this view on the status and stature of contract in private law and in a decent society. One strategy may be to argue that their claim is thinner; that transfer theory need not stand for the proposition that the *This for That* way *exhausts* the idea of contract, and therefore it does not imply that contractualization necessarily entails the potential of alienation and subordination. Ripstein, for example, argues that transfer theory only stands for "the simple idea that contract is the means through which people vary the normative relations between them."[42]

This proposition indeed seems a truism. The problem is that while it is immune from Gardner's critique,[43] it fails to provide any account of how and under what conditions two people can change their respective legal relations in the typical ways afforded by contract. Once transfer theorists want to say a bit more about contract law and contractualization they necessarily "thicken" their theories. Ripstein himself does so by adding that contracts "are enforceable because they create new rights as between the parties in a way that is consistent with the freedom of both,"[44] which for him surely means independence (and not autonomy), and Benson's extended elaboration of transfer theory invokes a conception of "juridical autonomy," which similarly "presupposes particular notions of freedom and equality specified in terms of the innate mutual independence of all persons in relation to others."[45]

The convergence between these propositions and between their implications as to the division of the "contract part" and the "regulatory part," along the lines shared by Gardner and Ripstein, does not seem coincidental. It suggests that the *This for That* picture can function as a model of contract if it implies, as it does for Gardner, that as long as there is a *This* and a *That* which are exchanged—as in a barter, which contract in this view extends—we have a contract, period. This means that for the current purposes I can bracket the differences between the various accounts of transfer theory,[46] and focus on the question whether contract can stand for something other

---

[42] Ripstein, "The Contracting Theory of Choices" (n 35) 210.

[43] Recall that the conception of contract Gardner criticizes is more robust than the sheer application of a normative power.

[44] Ripstein, "The Contracting Theory of Choices" (n 35) 210.

[45] Benson, *Justice in Transactions* (n 32) 373, 468–69.

[46] I have criticized transfer theory on its own terms elsewhere, both in general and with regard to Ripstein's and Benson's accounts of it. See respectively H Dagan and M Heller, *The Choice Theory of Contracts* (CUP 2017) 33–40; H Dagan and M Heller, "Autonomy for Contract, Refined" (2021) 40 Law and Philosophy 213, 215–38; H Dagan, "Two Visions of Contract" (2021) 119 Michigan Law Review 1247.

320 HANOCH DAGAN

than an assignment of authority or a similar conception that falls under the *This for That* model.

4.2 Contract's intertemporal dimension

Let's return then to Ripstein's "simple idea that contract is the means through which people vary the normative relations between them." Gardner seems to agree that this is the function of contract, and to appreciate its value. As he puts it, "there is something to be said for our having the ability to add to our obligations, shaping our normative arrangements with others, forging commitments, [and] developing relationships."[47]

Instantiating this idea in the *This for That* way works well with respect to a certain type of commitments, such as a future delivery of a widget for an agreed-upon price, which indeed looks like a spot exchange projected to the future. The conceptual bridge between spot exchange and contract can be crossed, as Benson argues, by fast-forwarding the legally significant point of normative reassignment from the time of delivery to the moment of formation, thereby "legally effacing" the temporal gap between agreement and performance. Because all the normative action takes place in formation, the function of contractual rights is indeed to secure the ability of the promisee to hold on to her *existing* track. This move works nicely because on this picture, as Benson puts it, "a transaction is not a cooperative venture"—at all relevant times "there is no 'ours' ... only a 'mine' and a 'thine' "[48]—so the only thing that is at stake is securing the reassignment of the *This* and the *That*.

In this type of case, in order for the contractual parties to be able to reshape their normative arrangements as assignors and assignees, all they need from the law is enforcement services and no more. This entails Gardner's picture of contract in *strict* voluntaristic terms, under which *all* contractual norms are norms created by the parties. To be sure, contract law need not limit itself only to the agreement's express terms; defaults are not out of place. But these defaults must be premised on the parties' presumed intent. Law's ambition, on this view, must be strictly limited to supplement the parties' express terms with implied-in-fact terms that are likewise grounded in the parties' joint will (or the content of their consent).[49]

So far, so good. But things look very different once we move from this simple widget contract to your garden-variety wholly executory contracts whose performance are arranged in a temporal sequence. Where performance is sequential, as it so often is, the parties' script cannot be easily translated into as a set of disconnected exchanges of *This for That*. In fact, often—where the object of their agreement is the pursuit of a project (say, the promisor will build the promisee's home)—their script would have an irreducible inter-temporal dimension. In this type of cases, thinking about the contract in terms of *These for Those* seriously misrepresents what the parties are all about.

---

[47] BCT (n 4) 344.

[48] P Benson, "The Idea of a Public Basis of Justification for Contract" (1995) 33 Osgoode Hall Law Journal 273, 316–17.

[49] See Benson, *Justice in Transactions* (n 32) 23, 123–24, 131–34; B Langille and A Ripstein, "Strictly Speaking: It Went without Saying" (1996) 2 Legal Theory 63.

Here, formation does not stand for a set of reassignments of the parties' entitlements. Rather, it is the moment in which they embark on a *new* path, in which they are *interdependent*.

Unlike the transfer view of contract, which nicely fits what economists call "the complete contingent contract," in these arrangements parties contemplate interactive engagements that require complex adaptations. To be sure, most agreements fall neither at the perfectly contingent nor the clearly incomplete, relational pole of the spectrum but rather at some point along this continuum.[50] But even in this middle-of-the-road types of cases, transfer theory's picture of *This for That*, which effaces the normative significance of contract's inter-temporal dimension by re-presenting the promisor as an assignor and the promisee as the possessor of a promised entitlement, fails to capture the idea of contract.

In all these other cases, contract law cannot and does not merely offer enforcement services for the parties' fully scripted agreement, but rather *proactively* facilitates their *cooperative* endeavor. Indeed, proactive facilitation is the name of the game of modern contract law. This is why its capacious fabric of default rules goes far beyond what can be reasonably accounted for as implied in fact terms.[51] It is no coincidence that this robust body of law is conventionally understood as an apparatus for filling gaps in incomplete contracts in order to *expand* the scope of the possible cooperative engagements that may be conducive to the parties' plans.[52]

The difference between these two views of contract law's defaults—as either implied-in-fact terms or gap-filling devices—demonstrates the practical takeaway of the choice between the rival pictures of contract: transfer vs a joint plan. (Further implications will be discussed in section 5.) It also suggests that while transfer theory safeguards, as advertised, the parties' independence, it *limits* contract's ability to function as a planning device and therefore curtails its empowering potential. Which of these paradigms should serve as the core case—the basic class—of contract?

Even if historically contract has indeed emerged from spot exchange,[53] its vocation need not be dependent on this path. There are two reasons for replacing transfer theory with one that understands contract as a plan. First, as we've just seen (and as Macneil intimated), as a *legal* theory transfer theory fails to account for a significant subset of the legal phenomenon it seeks to elucidate; while the planning picture of contract can easily accommodate the simple reassignment cases, the *This for That* picture is incapable of accounting for the cooperative ones. Moreover, transfer theory is not very attractive normatively; adopting it as law's compass would dramatically curtail the way contract currently empowers people to shape their normative landscape. Whereas transfer theory extends the range of exchanges people can make *vis-à-vis* the

---

[50] See CJ Goetz and RE Scott, "Principles of Relational Contracts" (1981) 67 Vanderbilt Law Review 1089, 1089–91.

[51] See Dagan, "Two Visions of Contract" (n 46) 1255–59; H Dagan and O Somech, "When Contract's Basic Assumptions Fail" (2021) 34 Canadian Journal of Law & Jurisprudence 297.

[52] See eg CJ Goetz and RE Scott, "The Limits of Expanded Choice: An Analysis of the Interactions between Express and Implied Contract Terms" (1985) 73 California Law Review 261, 261.

[53] But see R Kreitner, "Toward a Political Economy of Money" in U Mattei and JE Haskell (eds), *Research Handbook on Political Economy and Law* (Elgar 2017) 7, 10 n 9.

322 HANOCH DAGAN

world of barters, modern contract law provides them the indispensable infrastructure that also enables them to join forces in their respective plans into the future.

4.3 Empowering plans and self-determination

Once we replace the *This for That* picture with one of a joint plan, we can see why conceptualizing contractual rights as security rights misses on contract's distinctive role in private law. Unlike torts, contract is *not* duty-based. Rather, it is first and foremost a power-conferring institution. Contract is, as Charles Fried argued, "a kind of moral invention"[54] precisely because the normative powers it confers *expand* people's ability to legitimately recruit others to advance their own goals, purposes, and projects—both material and social. Duties are, of course, relevant to contract law. But contract law's duty-imposing rules (as in the doctrines governing the bargaining process) would be meaningless in the absence of (power-conferring) contracts; their role is to protect our ability to apply the powers enabled by contract.[55] Similarly, while contract indeed allows us to create duties, the point of these duties is not the protection of people's pre-existing rights, but rather their empowerment. Accordingly, the duties contract law imposes rely on, and should thus be shaped by reference to, the normative commitments that explain and justify the legal powers that constitute contract in the first place.[56]

By expanding the available repertoire of secure interpersonal planning engagements, contract law, as noted, dramatically augments people's ability to plan. In that it makes a crucial contribution to their autonomy because self-determination involves planning. People, to be sure, may change their plans, and autonomous persons must be entitled to do so. But having a set of plans arranged in a temporal sequence is typically key to the ability to carry out higher-order projects, namely, to self-determine.[57]

This autonomy-enhancing function of contract depends, of course, on the reliability of contractual promises, which explains why a contractual right is the right to expect, namely, why contract law does not merely protect promisees' actual reliance. To perform its mission of ensuring the reliability of wholly executory contracts, contract needs to recruit law's authority and coercive power against promisors even before promisees have actually been harmed.[58] Moreover, because contract's empowerment potential depends on people's ability to count on the representations of others, an autonomy-enhancing view of contract implies that individuals may be required to

---

[54] C Fried, "The Ambitions of Contract as Promise Thirty Years On" in G Klass (ed), *Philosophical Foundations of Contract* (OUP 2014) 17, 20.

[55] The same point, in fact, justifies the tort rules applicable to contractual relationships. cf A Dorfman, "Conflict between Equals: A Vindication of Tort Law" (unpublished manuscript), on file with author.

[56] See H Dagan, "The Value of Choice and the Justice of Contract" (2019) 10 Jurisprudence 422, 426–29. Some transfer theorists view contract law's power-conferring core as "non-contentious," while others seem to dissent. Compare Ripstein, "The Contracting Theory of Choices" (n 35) 200 with Benson, *Justice in Transactions* (n 32) 67, 438. Gardner discusses at some length (*FPLPL* (n 1) 199–216) the "powers of the parties," but by that he refers to their powers of civil recourse, rather than the normative powers that undergird contract as such.

[57] cf CR Beitz, "Property and Time" (2018) 26 Journal of Political Philosophy 419, 427.

[58] See Dagan, "Two Visions of Contract" (n 46) 428.

satisfy promisees' expectations even if they only inadvertently invoked the convention of contract with no subjective intention to be legally obligated.[59]

These last observations pose a serious challenge to anyone who, like Benson and Ripstein, insists that our private law obligations must only be negative. If the only interpersonal duties private law can legitimately impose are duties of non-interference—if affirmative duties to assist are beyond its legitimate scope—then these expansions of contractual liability are illegitimate. On this view, only transfer theory can rehabilitate contract's legitimacy, since only if a contract is understood and shaped as an assignment can liability in contract fit private law's organizing idea of liability for misfeasance only.[60]

If indeed private law's legitimacy were properly restricted to vindicating people's independence, this conclusion would have been inevitable, notwithstanding its disappointing implications to people's self-determination. Fortunately, as I argue in some detail elsewhere, it is not.[61] Private law can be legitimate even if law does not strictly adhere to the vision of interpersonal independence as long as it takes seriously the more fundamental requirement of interpersonal justification. While private law cannot justify its power merely by reference to its public benefits, it can be legitimate if its injunctions are premised on people's right that others respect their self-determination, and not only their independence (or security).

This means that while there are good reasons to resist excessive interference with people's autonomy that many affirmative interpersonal duties to aid others entail, a blanket rejection of affirmative duties is unwarranted. As HLA Hart explained, since some, but not all, infringements of our independence ignore "the moral importance of the division of humanity into separate individuals and threaten ... the proper inviolability of persons," we must always distinguish "between the gravity of the different restrictions on different specific liberties and their importance for the conduct of a meaningful life."[62] The duties of private law need not track the misfeasance–nonfeasance distinction; they need not—and are not—only duties of abstention.

Because people are justifiably expected to pay some modest price to benefit others with whom they interact, there is no reason to bypass the modest interpersonal burden that law imposes on promisors who voluntarily invoke the contract convention while engaging with promisees. Promisees *are* justified in expecting promisors to submit themselves to the jurisdiction of contract law notwithstanding the cautionary burden this may impose on them, because this is the modest price each pays so the other can benefit from contract law's potential to advance their self-determination. Because transfer theory is not needed to save contract's legitimacy, there is no good reason to incur its autonomy-reducing implications.

---

[59] See JS Kraus, "The Correspondence of Contract and Promise" (2009) 109 Columbia Law Review 1603, 1620–25.

[60] Benson, *Justice in Transactions* (n 32) 8, 12, 16–17, 19, 24, 27, 66, 364, 367–69, 371–72, 377–78, 385, 393–94, 469.

[61] See H Dagan and A Dorfman, "Just Relationships" (2016) 116 Columbia Law Review 1395; H Dagan and A Dorfman, "Justice in Private: Beyond the Rawlsian Framework" (2018) 37 Law and Philosophy 171.

[62] HLA Hart, "Between Utility and Rights" (1979) 79 Columbia Law Review 828, 834–35.

5. Liberal Contract Meets Gardner

A contract law premised on the *This for That* model is, as Gardner claims, subordinate to tort and its social ascendancy may well be unfortunate, as he also maintained. Replacing the model of transfer with that of a joint plan reinstates, as I've just argued, contract's distinctiveness. But what does it do to Gardner's two propositions with which I've started? To address this question, we need to consider some of the implications of an autonomy-based—not to be confused, of course, with independence-based—account of contract.

Just as transfer theory comes in different forms, there are also different autonomy-based contract theories.[63] In what follows, I focus on one specific theory, which I have developed with Michael Heller in recent years, that is, I think, particularly receptive to face Gardner's challenges. Contract, on this view, which Heller and I dub choice theory, is a joint plan co-authored by the parties in the service of their respective goals. Because law's justification for enforcing contracts is premised, as noted, on the liberal commitment to reciprocal respect for self-determination, contract law on our account is guided by contract's autonomy-enhancing *telos*.[64]

5.1 Contract remedies and the plan

Shifting from transfer to a joint plan challenges Gardner's proposition that breach of contract is a tort by pointing out to an important difference between tort damages and damages for the breach of contract.[65] Tort damages are, as Gardner claims, characteristically unliquidated,[66] and the compensation owed by tortfeasors is a matter for the law to determine. Under the *This for That* picture, similar analysis applies to contract. Cases of liquidated damages are thus, for Gardner, of little theoretical purchase as they simply pre-empt the basic action for unliquidated damages at the point of contracting in order "to save trouble and expense later."[67]

This analysis does not survive the shift from transfer to a joint plan. There is no reason to exclude categorically the question of contract remedies from the parties' script. Quite the contrary: their plans can, as they sometimes do, cover the eventuality of breach as well; and if they can *ex ante* device together a mutually satisfying formula for this contingency, a facilitative law should not hesitate to follow suit. *Ex post*

---

[63] See H Dagan, "Autonomy and Contracts" in M Chen-Wishart and P Saprai (eds), *Research Handbook on The Philosophy of Contract Law* (forthcoming).

[64] See generally H Dagan and M Heller, "Choice Theory: A Restatement" in H Dagan and B Zipursky (eds), *Research Handbook on Private Law Theory* (Elgar 2020) 112.

[65] Another remedial context in which choice theory challenges transfer theory relates to specific performance. The latter tends to explain (or explain away) specific performance's very limited scope by reference to exogenous reasons; the former, by contrast, sees this feature as a necessary entailment of liberal contract's inherent concern for the autonomy of the future self. Compare *FPLP* (n 1) 227 and BCT (n 4) 340 with H Dagan and M Heller, "Specific Performance: On Freedom and Commitment in Contract Law" 98 Notre Dame Law Review (forthcoming).

[66] BCT (n 4) 333.

[67] ibid 341.

fairness review may well be appropriate where promisors are vulnerable to making sub-optimal choices (more on that soon). But where sophisticated parties to complex commercial contracts use a liquidated damages clause in anticipation of possibly unverifiable harms of breach—or for any other reason that fits their cooperative engagement (say, as a signaling device)—an autonomy-enhancing contract law must respect their script and thus validate its full effect.[68]

5.2 Indigenous limit and floor

I turn now to Gardner's most significant challenge to contract: his claim that alienation and subordination are the inevitable concomitants of contractualization. As we've seen, Gardner powerfully explains how transfer theory's *This for That* model entails this troublesome implication,[69] and because he subscribes to that theory, he sharply criticizes the contractualization of special relationships such as employment. But his critique, as I presently show, is inapplicable to an autonomy-based theory of contract. In fact, once contract is understood and designed in line with its autonomy-enhancing *telos*, the alarming consequences Gardner highlights become pathologies, *abuses* of the idea of contract, which a properly designed contract law places beyond the scope of enforceable agreements.

An autonomy-enhancing contract law—liberal contract—necessarily makes qualitative distinctions among the various choices contract enables based on how they implicate the parties' self-determination. Specifically, it conceptualizes contract's utility surplus as a means to the superior end of autonomy, and thus distinguishes between the use of contracts for strictly instrumental purposes and its use in the pursuit of one or both parties' "ground projects"—the projects that make people who they are and give meaning to their lives.

The former category, epitomized in the case of commercial contracts, lends itself to the familiar cost-benefit analysis that renders commensurate all contract rules and terms. By contrast—since facilitating preference satisfaction is important to liberal contract only because *and to the extent that* it is conducive to people's self-determination—the latter category cannot be easily analyzed in these terms. Preferences that undermine self-determination should be generally overridden. A liberal contract law cannot legitimately facilitate transactions in which the parties' welfare enhancement threatens to efface their self-determination.[70]

In other words, liberal law should delineate the scope of enforceable contracts so that it does not end up facilitating co-authored scripts that might render one party into the sheer instrument of the other's plans or purposes. Many contract types—even certain service contracts—are largely free from this risk. But contracts that implicate people's ground projects are typically vulnerable on exactly this front.

---

[68] See Dagan and Heller, *The Choice Theory of Contracts* (n 46) 94.

[69] See similarly H Collins, "Is the Contract of Employment Illiberal?" in H Collins and others (eds), *Philosophical Foundations of Labour Law* (n 5) 48.

[70] cf H Dagan and R Kreitner, "Economic Analysis in Law" (2021) 38 Yale Journal on Regulation 566, 572–74, 585.

An overly intensive or overly extensive promisee's dominion in contracts that affect a constitutive feature of the promisor might endanger the latter's self-determination. Thus, in so far as these contract types are concerned, an unlimited promisee's dominion is autonomy-*defying*. These and others contractual scripts purporting to give a promisee an excessive dominion over the promisor's activities are therefore beyond the limits of (liberal) contract. Specifying this prescription requires attention to the characteristics of the specific contract type at hand: it translates variously in, for example, spousal contracts, contracts for membership in certain meaningful communities, and—my focus here—employment contracts.

The workplace's hierarchical structure, which was imported from "the former legal tradition of status obligations," is currently instantiated through an implied duty of obedience.[71] Conceptualizing a failure to perform as an insubordination along these lines may fit transfer theory, in which the employee is a mere possessor of the employer's entitlement to contract's performance. But the obvious autonomy-*reducing* implications of an implied duty of obedience suggest that it is wholly out of place in a genuinely liberal view of contract. Guided by liberal contract's autonomy-enhancing *telos*, and substituting the view of contract as a transfer of authority with its understanding as the parties' joint plan, liberal law must push in the *opposite* direction. A genuinely liberal contract theory prescribes that employment contracts can give a promisee-employer only a *limited* dominion over the promisor's activities.

In this account of the employment contract, managerial control, if it is to be a part of the parties' relationship, must be, as Sabine Tsuruda claims, merely instrumental. Thus, the requirement that workers "carry out orders to do particular things, such as following prescribed procedures or complying with grooming policies" is acceptable. But employers must not be legally authorized "to act as a moral authority over the lives and choices" of their workers, and their managerial control must not extend to workers' "agentical activity." Tsuruda acknowledges that the "interpersonal and interdependent character of work" can justify *some* employer control over "what employees do and say while they are at work." But she correctly insists that employers must not have a legal right "to quiet obedience and moral deference."[72] A truly liberal employment contract *cannot* authorize employers' arbitrary and unaccountable authority.

Liberal contract's prescription of limited promisee authority is not the only normative resource for addressing Gardner's charge that contractualization necessarily involves alienation and subordination. Another resource *internal* to contract in its conception as a joint plan is its commitment to relational justice; that is to reciprocal respect for self-determination. This obligation arises from people's right of self-determination, the same right that, as noted, justifies the enforcement of contract in the first instance. Therefore, when someone resorts to contract law's empowering potential, her uses should be limited to interactions that respect the other party's self-determination. This obligation cannot be too onerous, but neither is it limited to a negative duty of non-interference.

This principle has significant consequences for the structure of contract law, and its manifestation in employment are thus continuous with the larger universe of

---

[71] See H Collins, *Employment Law* (2nd edn, OUP 2010) 10, 34.
[72] See S Tsuruda, "Working as Equal Moral Agents" (2020) 26 Legal Theory 305, 307, 313, 337.

contract law. Relational justice undergirds a long list of rules—prescribed by courts, legislatures, and regulatory agencies—that govern both the pre-contractual stage and the life of an ongoing contract.[73]

Consider contract law's careful, but important, deviations from the *laissez-faire* mode of regulating the parties' *bargaining process*. For example, note the expansion of the law of fraud beyond the categories of misrepresentation and concealment to include affirmative duties of disclosure, or the modern rules dealing with unilateral mistake, duress, anti-price gouging, and unconscionability. Concern for relational justice also best explains key rules *during the life* of a contract, as epitomized by the duty of good faith and fair dealing. This duty, now read (in many jurisdictions) into *every* contract, protects the parties against the heightened interpersonal vulnerability that contract performance engenders and solidifies a conception of contract as a cooperative venture.

Indeed, viewed from this autonomy-based understanding of contract, many employment and labor law rules, which some see as necessary impositions on its logic and others as politically controversial interventions, are actually ingrained in contract's liberal DNA. The institutional pedigree of work law's floor of minimum terms and immutable rights on topics like safety in the workplace, non-discrimination, minimum wages, working hours, and labor organization, is admittedly not within the common law of contract. But so is the case of many other contract rules in modern-day societies. What is crucial for our purposes is that once relational justice is recognized as an endogenous, indeed indispensable, component of the liberal idea of contract, proudly premised on contract's own justificatory foundation, this floor of acceptable employment arrangement can find a happy home within, and not only without, contract. This is a lesson with some practical timely significance: it implies that (liberal) contract cannot be the refuge from work law's floor of minimum terms and immutable rights.[74]

5.3 Contract types and special relationships

Finally, recall that part of Gardner's contractual-reductivism critique relates to the way contract necessarily deprives special relationships of their distinctiveness. Because "the professional obligations of police officers, social workers, architects, and solicitors" cannot be grounded in contract, for example, the contractualization of these roles implies, he claims, a total assimilation, which in effect erases their distinctive meaning.[75]

This inference may well follow transfer theory. But it does not follow the way contract is viewed if it is designed in line with its liberal, autonomy-enhancing *telos*. Contract law in this view (and in contemporary law) is very different from the

---

[73] For a detailed defense, both normative and positive, of the role of relational justice in contract law, on which the following paragraph draws, see H Dagan and A Dorfman, "Precontractual Justice" (2022) 28 Legal Theory 89; H Dagan and A Dorfman, "Justice in Contracts" (2022) 67 American Journal of Jurisprudence 1.

[74] See H Dagan and M Heller, "Can Contract Emancipate? Contract Theory and the Law of Work" (2023) 23 Theoretical Inquiries in Law 49.

[75] CLL (n 5) 37–38.

open-ended *This for That* framework imagined by transfer theory as "the contract part." Indeed, contract law takes seriously its *proactive* facilitative role in many types of interactions and thus its responsibility to secure the availability and viability of multiple contract types in the various contracting spheres. A genuinely liberal contract law develops an inventory of contract types for each sphere of human interaction, which offers people different modes of cooperation in the pursuit of joint plans.[76] This menu, as Fried recently observed, is crucial for "party autonomy and self-fulfillment ... because human interactions and legal interventions are hardly imaginable without them." Just like "language that enables thought[,] without types, our minds would be blank."[77]

Once we replace the open-ended ideal of transfer theory with this robust repertoire of contract types—the "nominate contracts" as they are called in European civil law systems[78]—we can see that liberal contract need not deprive special relationships of their distinctive meanings; that it, moreover, actually participates in the creation and maintenance of these meanings.[79]

Gardner may have still been worried that "the contract part" cannot possibly include mandatory rules that are at times crucial in order to sustain the deontic content and thus solidify the meaning of, say, serving as an architect. This assumption, again, befits transfer theory.[80] But it is (again) inapplicable to its rival, liberal view of contract. Mandatory terms that stabilize and channel cultural expectations regarding types are often needed in order to maintain the rich inventory of types liberal contract requires. And as long as these terms are salient and there exists a sufficient range among types in the relevant sphere of human activity, they are also unobjectionable from contract's own perspective since parties who resent the "specification" of one such type would simply opt for another.[81] Therefore, these mandatory terms need not be summarily excluded from "the contract part." Once transfer theory is properly set aside, the specter of total assimilation, in which contract-makers can fully "customize the deontic content" of their engagement, is no longer an inevitable feature of contractualization.[82]

---

[76] See generally Dagan and Heller, *The Choice Theory of Contracts* (n 46) 93–109, 116–16. To clarify: liberal contract's prescription of robust pluralism implies that while all contract types are ultimately answerable to contract's autonomy-based *telos*, different contract types also follow more "local" values—notably utility and community (or some balance thereof). These values are either constitutive of or instrumental to people's autonomy, and therefore have their proper place in an autonomy-based theory of contract. ibid 43–45, 51–64, 79–80, 84–85.

[77] C Fried, "Contract as Promise: Lessons Learned" (2019) 20 Theoretical Inquiries in Law 367, 377–78.

[78] See eg B Markesinis and others, *The German Law of Contract: A Comparative Treatise* (Hart 2006) 162–63.

[79] cf RW Gordon, "Unfreezing Legal Reality: Critical Approaches to Law" (1987) 15 Florida State University Law Review 195, 212–14.

[80] Ripstein, "The Contracting Theory of Choices" (n 35) 209.

[81] Dagan and Heller, *The Choice Theory of Contracts* (n 46) 4, 111–12.

[82] This does not mean or imply that all special relationships can or should find their home as contract types; some are better understood as what I call "offices." See H Dagan and ES Scott, "Reinterpreting the Status-Contract Divide: The Case of Fiduciaries" in PB Miller and AS Gold (eds), *Contract, Status, and Fiduciary* (OUP 2016) 51, 56–60, 62–66.

6. Private Law and Liberalism

I want to believe that if Gardner was able to devote more of his scholarly attention to contracts he would have discarded transfer theory, notwithstanding its proud legacy and the distinction of its contemporary carriers. But my critique of his implicit reliance on that theory, which obscures—as I hope to have established—the promise of contract, should not marginalize Gardner's contribution to our understanding of contract. Maybe because of his outsider outlook, Gardner, who took transfer theory as a given, importantly clarified why shaping and thinking about contract along its lines entails the disappointing conclusions to which he powerfully objected. Fortunately, this is a path we can avoid. Transfer theory should be discarded. An autonomy-enhancing theory obviates Gardner's sad account of contract and contractualization, and offers a rather happy legal trajectory.

But isn't it too parochial? Before closing, it is apt to return to Gardner's warnings with which I've started. Because "the main concerns that drive and structure private law are ordinary human concerns," he argued, "the most durable features of private law are . . . more ecumenical than various more ephemeral features." Gardner acknowledged that many aspects of contemporary private law are—and should be—"coloured by distinctively liberal preoccupations." But he claimed that they need to be restored to "their proper parochial place." The heightened importance of autonomy that typifies modernity bears on "how to tailor to our contemporary needs a set of doctrines that have a more ecumenical and hence less ephemeral set of rationales and resonances." But it is nonetheless "anachronistic to read this [commitment] back into the whole history of private law, and in particular to think that an emphasis on personal autonomy is necessary to justify or make intelligible private law's most durable features." This is why Gardner insisted that an autonomy-based account of private law "misses deeper and less sectarian concerns," and that rather than autonomy, private law, at bottom, is about security—"our timeless human concern to preserve the lives we already have."[83]

This chapter shows that the shift from autonomy to security is not cost free. A security-based contract law is possible. But it entails the disturbing consequences that Gardner himself highlighted. Elsewhere, I seek to establish that similarly troubling consequences follow parallel security-based conceptions of other branches of private law, which entrench understandings of property as "sole and despotic dominion" and oust the obligation to respect others' self-determination from the core of tort law.[84] Comparative law and legal history may (or may not) support Gardner's thesis insofar as it relates to "private law's most durable features." But because this exercise cannot *justify* these features—since, more specifically, excluding autonomy from private law makes it less justifiable—we should be careful not to *mis*represent them as more ecumenical and less controversial. Liberalism may well be historically contingent, but liberal values are indispensable for a just private law.

---

[83] *FPLPL* (n 1) 8, 183–84, 195–96, 199.

[84] See respectively H Dagan, *A Liberal Theory of Property* (CUP 2021); H Dagan and A Dorfman, "Against Private Law Escapism: Comment on Arthur Ripstein, Private Wrongs" (2017) 14 Jerusalem Review of Legal Studies 37.

19
The Reasonably Loyal Person

Andrew S Gold[*]

John Gardner's contributions to fiduciary theory arise in his discussions of neighboring fields. Perhaps for this reason, some of his major contributions take the form of puzzles left to be solved. This chapter explores a leading example of such a puzzle: the apparent absence of the "reasonably loyal" person from fiduciary law. Tantalizingly, Gardner only hints at his views on why there is no reasonably loyal person in fiduciary law. Still, his initial exploration of this question offers profound insights. I will consider Gardner's puzzle—why is there no reasonably loyal person standard?—together with his proposed answers. The inquiry sheds light on fiduciary loyalty, on loyalty in our personal lives, and on how the two interrelate.

The central concern is whether the law can look to extra-legal standards to fill in legal loyalty obligations—that is whether the law can engage in "buck passing," as Gardner refers to it. There is cause for doubt, if fiduciary law's relationships lack law-independent counterparts. This chapter will suggest that these relationships do have law-independent counterparts, and that the law can readily pass the buck to extra-legal loyalty norms. Indeed, it may do so in multiple ways. That leaves open whether such buck passing is desirable. I will suggest three reasons why it might be: (i) buck passing to extra-legal loyalty practices is a useful anti-opportunism device; (ii) buck passing allows fiduciary loyalty to better accommodate the lived experience of extra-legal loyalties; and (iii) buck passing provides an interface between legal and extra-legal conceptions of loyalty that can facilitate legal evolution.

1. Buck Passing and the "Reasonably Loyal" Trustee

To begin, we will need an understanding of what buck passing means. On Gardner's account, the law sometimes delegates resolution of a problem to non-legal standards: the law "helps itself to standards of justification that are not themselves set by the law."[1] Thus, when the reasonable person standard is used, courts are not asking a legal question as to how someone should act. The basic idea is expressed "by saying that the question of what a reasonable person would have thought or done or said or decided

---

[*] I am grateful to participants at an Oxford conference on John Gardner's contributions to private law theory, at fiduciary law workshops, and at a summer faculty workshop at Brooklyn Law School. I am also thankful for comments from Anita Bernstein, Hanoch Dagan, Cécile Fabre, Joshua Getzler, Ethan Leib, Paul Miller, Haris Psarras, Lionel Smith, and Fred Wilmot-Smith. Any errors are my own.

[1] J Gardner, "The Many Faces of the Reasonable Person" in *Torts and Other Wrongs* (OUP 2020) (hereinafter, "Reasonable Person") at 279.

Andrew S Gold, *The Reasonably Loyal Person* In: *Private Law and Practical Reason*. Edited by: Haris Psarras and Sandy Steel, Oxford University Press. © Andrew S Gold 2023. DOI: 10.1093/oso/9780192857330.003.0019

THE REASONABLY LOYAL PERSON   331

(etc) is a question of fact, not a question of law."[2] In such cases, the law is allowed to "help itself *pro tempore* to standards of justification that are not themselves set by the law."[3] As a consequence, "[a] ruling which is arrived at "on the facts" is to that extent not subject to legal generalization."[4]

Let us adopt this starting point as a given. I will assume for discussion that tort law's reasonable person is best seen in buck passing terms. I take it that buck passing is a conceptual possibility (irrespective of whether it is the best interpretation of tort law's reasonable person), and I wish to consider the insights we can glean from seeing the legal landscape in this way.

Why engage in buck passing? There are multiple reasons why the law might do so, but Gardner locates a moral reason in Aristotle's reflections on law and equity. As Aristotle indicated, legal rules are inevitably overinclusive.[5] Equity, however, provides a means to resolve cases in a less rule-based fashion, permitting "discretionary departures, within limits, from mandatory legal rules."[6] Aristotle's account does not end there—he was famously also concerned with those who are sticklers for justice "in a bad sense."[7] But for present purposes, our focus will be on equitable reasoning as an alternative to rule-based reasoning.

Rule following can provide justice according to law, but it is not the only way to provide justice—and in some settings, it may not be the best way. In Gardner's view, the courts' resort to equity can be justice's "rebellion against law."[8] As he argues:

Not every manifestation of justice is an act of following a sound rule. For some, just rulings are not governed by nor capable of being elevated to any sound rule of justice. They are based on a weighing of allocative considerations in their raw, unruly form. Solomon's justice was justice ad hoc.[9]

Suppose that law's use of equity does provide justice in this *ad hoc* way. Even so, the challenge posed by legal rules is not fully evaded in Gardner's view, for he sees the law of equity itself as "a body of legal rules which license discretionary departures, within limits, from mandatory legal rules."[10] And this means that the law's equitable measures

---

[2] ibid.

[3] ibid.

[4] ibid. at 280.

[5] See ibid at 282 (citing Aristotle, NE 1137b10ff).

[6] See ibid at 284. There is another way that equity may intersect with Gardner's thought. I have argued elsewhere that equity allows for a special application of Gardner's continuity thesis. See AS Gold, "Delegation and the Continuity Thesis" (2021) 40 Law & Philosophy 645. While Gardner discusses legal norms of corrective justice as a means to assist wrongdoers in conforming to their reasons for action, he often has in mind defendants. Equity can assist *plaintiffs* in conforming to their reasons for action when those plaintiffs are themselves wrongdoers.

[7] See Aristotle, Nicomachean Ethics in J Barnes (ed), *The Complete Works of Aristotle*, Vol 2 bk V (Princeton University Press 1984) 1796 ("It is also evident from this who the equitable man is; the man who chooses and does such acts, and is no stickler for justice in a bad sense but tends to take less than his share though he has the law on his side ....."). For recent analyses of equity as a response to such sticklers, see AS Gold, *The Right of Redress* (OUP 2020) 195–202; D Klimchuk, 'Equity and the Rule of Law" in LM Austin and D Klimchuk (eds), *Private Law and the Rule of Law* (OUP 2014) 247.

[8] See J Gardner, "The Virtue of Justice and the Character of Law" in *Law as a Leap of Faith* (OUP 2012) 254.

[9] See ibid.

[10] See Gardner, "Reasonable Person" (n 1) 284.

"wed the judge to further rules," with the end result that both over-inclusiveness and under-inclusiveness remain a part of the picture.[11] This seems right, and the more so when we recognize that equity's interventions can crystallize into a rule-like form.[12]

Gardner suggests a potential answer is to engage in buck passing, for it means that the rule-like features of law can be evaded. Indeed, when buck passing decides a legal question, it is by definition resolved through something other than the law:

> One more radical solution is to build into a legal rule ... a legally deregulated zone in which the many and varied underlying reasons are to be confronted by the decision-maker in their ordinary form, and applied direct, unmediated by law. Now there is, if you like, a non-rule embedded in the rule.[13]

In this sense, buck passing is a step beyond equity.

The reasonable person is a prime example of this approach, as a measure which can "take the edge off the rule."[14] Importantly, it is not the only such measure. The reasonable person also has "neighbors"—persons who share features in common with the basic, plain vanilla reasonable person but with added qualities, heightened standards, or special constraints. Examples include the "reasonably competent carpenter" or the "ordinary prudent man of business."[15] These neighbors, moreover, allow for a kind of middle path between pure buck passing and legally delineated standards of conduct. As Gardner indicates, "[the reasonable person] exists to create legally deregulated zones in the law. Yet, with a bit of tweaking, he can also help, as needed, to put a little bit of law back in."[16]

There are various ways of putting a little bit of law back in. In some cases, the reasonable person is reined in by customary standards. Examples include cases where the law borrows the customary standards of a trade or profession, as happens with medical doctors. One might think that figuring out what the reasonable person would do in such cases is sufficiently reined in to become a question of law. But Gardner suggests that, properly understood, this is "an example of the law passing the buck to customary standards"; we are still confronted in these settings with a question of fact.[17] In other cases, the reasonable person is subject to specialized standards. Thus, the reasonable person might become the "reasonable civil engineer or the reasonable neurosurgeon or the reasonable hairdresser."[18]

---

[11] ibid.

[12] For further discussion of the ways that equity can supplement law, see PB Miller, "Equity as Supplemental Law" in D Klimchuk, I Samet, and HE Smith (eds), *Philosophical Foundations of the Law of Equity* (OUP 2020) 92.

[13] See Gardner, "Reasonable Person" (n 1) 284.

[14] ibid at 285.

[15] Note that Gardner's use of the male gender (eg the "reasonable man") in contexts where the courts use that wording is not accidental; he wishes to draw attention to the problematic features of that conception of the reasonable person. See ibid at 278–79. While I will generally use gender-neutral language in describing the reasonable person, I quote his language directly as it is a component of his argument.

[16] ibid at 289.

[17] ibid at 290. Gardner clarifies that in this setting, such customary standards are not examples of customary law. ibid.

[18] ibid at 291. Note that in some cases, the reasonable person might be modified in light of what is customary within a given community. cf A Bernstein, "The Communities that Make Standards of Care Possible" (2002) 77 Chicago-Kent Law Review 735.

In yet other cases, the reasonable person is subject to distinctive rational priorities. As Gardner emphasizes, "there are many ways of being reasonable, and some are associated with one trait of character, some with another."[19] Different virtues can predominate in the reasonable person's thoughts, with different consequences for his or her conduct. This last category of reasonable person—involving distinctive rational priorities—is of particular importance. Various traits, such as prudence, can be tacked onto the "reasonable person," and in some settings the law does so. A quick survey of the reasonable person's neighbors, however, shows that they are a rather incomplete bunch; the village of reasonable people is missing some inhabitants.

And here we arrive at the concern that motivates this chapter. Conceptually, it is not a large step from the reasonably prudent person to the reasonably loyal person. Why not take that step? On Gardner's view, there is an intriguing absence in the law's characterization of fiduciary loyalty:

> Is the person of "undivided loyalty" supposed also to be the person of reasonable loyalty? Clearly the law thinks him justified (hence reasonable) in what he does. He is held up as setting the proper standard of behaviour for the role of trustee. But interestingly he is not described as a "reasonably loyal trustee" or the like.[20]

Are obligations that rely on buck-passing, like the "reasonable person" in tort law, different in this respect from fiduciary loyalty obligations? Not everyone may agree that the "reasonably loyal" person is absent from fiduciary law, and jurisdictions vary. Still, the "reasonably loyal" formulation is not typical in fiduciary settings, and I will take it as a given that there is such an absence. With that assumption in place, I will suggest that it is still possible to develop a useful buck-passing account of fiduciary loyalty (whether or not the "reasonably loyal" person is currently a component of fiduciary law). The remainder of this chapter will discuss reasons why.

2. Assessing Arguments Against a "Reasonably Loyal" Trustee Standard

2.1 The excusatory latitude concern

As Gardner suggests, there are some settings in which a "reasonable person" standard is designed to provide someone with an excusatory latitude. Criminal law is a classic setting. Someone acting under duress when confronted with grave threats may act based on a justified fear, without it being the case that what she does in response to that fear is a justified action. On this view, one can perform unjustified actions in response to a justified emotion. The justified emotion provides an excuse. Significantly, then, the reasonable person "may be free of vice, but he is decidedly not free of shortcomings."[21]

---

[19] See Gardner, "Reasonable Person" (n 1) 296.
[20] ibid at 298.
[21] ibid at 275.

334   ANDREW S GOLD

The reasonable person is justified in what he or she does, but the reasonable person is not "justified in every which way at once."[22]

Something similar might be said for fiduciaries. As Gardner notes:

> [W]hen applied to virtue-names like "loyalty" the qualification "reasonable" allows a measure of excusatory latitude. That is what we get with "reasonable fortitude" and "reasonable self-restraint" in the criminal law.[23]

That is not necessarily a bad thing in the right context, but perhaps fiduciary law is not the right context. There could be good policy reasons—or perhaps moral reasons—for treating trustees differently. Gardner does not indicate these reasons, but given the risks of fiduciary abuses of power, it is not overly difficult to imagine them. As he concludes:

> To be reasonably virtuous, we might think, it is sufficient but not necessary to perform justified actions, so long as one performs unjustified actions only on the strength of justified beliefs and justified emotions and the like. We may want to deny any such excusatory latitude to trustees.[24]

Someone who is reasonably loyal could, perhaps, engage in unjustified actions on the justified belief that their conduct passed muster. Yet, opportunistic fiduciaries, like corporate directors, can also manufacture arguments for the reasonableness of behavior that involves half-hearted loyalty, self-serving behavior. Good faith fiduciaries may also rationalize sub-loyal conduct as reasonable without realizing that it is not loyal, and this could pose the greater risk. In turn, such cases could erode valuable relationships between fiduciary and beneficiary (whether intrinsically valuable or valuable for their systemic consequences). Fiduciary law regularly engages in over-inclusive legal rules and stringent remedies to discourage opportunism and limit the effects of cognitive biases; it may have good cause to act similarly in adopting standards of loyalty that deny an excusatory latitude.[25]

2.2 The absence of a "law-independent" trust relationship

Alternatively, Gardner suggests that the "reasonably loyal trustee" is not used because the trust law relationship does not have a counterpart legal relationship to pass the buck to:

---

[22] ibid.

[23] ibid at 298.

[24] ibid at 298–99.

[25] Limited exceptions, however, may exist. Both inside and outside the law, loyalty obligations have internal constraints that limit certain types of otherwise loyal behaviors. For discussion of legal settings, see AS Gold, "The Internal Limits on Fiduciary Loyalty" (2020) 65 The American Journal of Jurisprudence 65. On such constraints in friendship settings, see TM Scanlon, *What We Owe to Each Other* (Harvard University Press 1998) 164–65. On the import of cabining such constraints in fiduciary law, see AS Gold "Pernicious Loyalty" (2021) 62 William & Mary Law Review 1187, 1224.

A second explanation is that the role of trustee (unlike that of parent, businessperson, observer, physician, etc.) has no law-independent existence. There is no measure of a "reasonably loyal trustee" until the law says just how much loyalty is expected of a trustee. So here, we might conclude, there is little or no scope for the law setting trustee standards to pass the buck to "those considerations which ordinarily [ie apart from this very law] regulate the conduct of human affairs."[26]

Courts could still provide guidance as to what must be done by such a fiduciary, but, as Gardner further adds:

> That being so, we now know, the reasonable person and his familiars would not be the right choice to do the standard setting. They would be reined in to the point of having little or no work left to do.[27]

In sum, there may be nowhere to pass the buck to, and to the extent law fills the gap to address this challenge, we are back in the world of legal rules with their attendant weaknesses.[28]

3. Fiduciary Loyalty as a Different Kind of Loyalty

3.1 Is fiduciary loyalty not genuine loyalty?

The above possibilities suggest that if we are to address Gardner's puzzle, we will need to think through fiduciary loyalty's relationship to extra-legal loyalty. Before proceeding further, it will be important first to address a related concern raised by Stephen Smith's work. Smith is also troubled by the relationship between legal and extra-legal loyalty obligations, but his worry is more radical than Gardner's worry. Smith contends that there is a mismatch between fiduciary loyalty and extra-legal counterparts, for he believes fiduciary loyalty is not loyalty at all.[29] If we hold that view, there is little need to figure out whether buck passing is possible in fiduciary settings, since fiduciary "loyalty" is a conceptual mismatch for real-world loyalty, full stop. Gardner's puzzle is not much of a challenge if it turns out that fiduciary loyalty is not loyalty in the first place.

---

[26] See Gardner, "Reasonable Person" (n 1) 299 (brackets in original).

[27] ibid.

[28] Note that it is possible to think of other reasons why fiduciary law does not use a "reasonably loyal trustee" standard. One is the possibility of harm to the value of special relationships, if the "reasonably loyal trustee" approach produces too many qualifications of a fiduciary's loyalty obligations. Alternatively, some might think that a "reasonable" loyalty standard is problematic because it implies that loyalty can be a matter of degree. I have doubts about this latter perspective. For one thing, the differences between loyalty to friends and loyalty to best friends imply that loyalty practices can include matters of degree. For another, courts seem to recognize degrees of loyalty. Cf *Donahue v Rodd Electrotype Co. of New England*, 367 Mass 578, 593–94 (1975) (suggesting the "utmost good faith and loyalty" owed by partners calls for something more stringent than the loyalty owed by ordinary corporate directors).

[29] See SA Smith, "The Deed, Not the Motive: Fiduciary Law Without Loyalty" in PB Miller and AS Gold (eds), *Contract, Status, and Fiduciary Law* (OUP 2016) 213.

336   ANDREW S GOLD

Smith's concern is grounded in a feature of loyalty obligations that is easily recognizable in our non-legal lives (what Gardner would term our "personal life"). He denies that we can have "instant loyalty."[30] Loyalty is something that requires people to have a history together, a meaningful prior relationship. Thus, he contends: "Helping someone whom you have just met—for example helping a stranger to cross the street—is commendable, but it is not an instance of loyalty."[31]

As Smith further argues:

> [T]he impossibility of acting loyally or disloyally towards others—unless you are already in a meaningful relationship with them—is a problem for loyalty-based accounts of fiduciary law regardless of how "meaningful" is defined.[32]

The difficulty stems from a central feature of fiduciary law: "fiduciary relationships may arise—and do arise in full force—between parties who have no prior relationship."[33] The examples are legion, and they are especially prominent in commercial settings, as with money managers or corporate directors.

Notably, Smith's goal is to understand loyalty as that word is commonly used in ordinary language. He recognizes that courts sometimes use terms of art, and that fiduciary loyalty might mean "loyalty" in some specialized sense.[34] Yet, with that cautionary note, he contends that "the way that courts and commentators employ the concept of loyalty suggests that the concept is meant to carry its ordinary meaning."[35] He does not think that fiduciary loyalty is presented as having a special sense, and thus it is problematic if fiduciary loyalty does not match loyalty's ordinary meaning. There is another implication, however. If Smith's claims are right, buck passing to the loyal person should be a non-starter for fiduciary law. We need not worry about the "reasonably loyal trustee" on this view because fiduciary law isn't genuinely concerned with loyalty as usually understood.[36]

3.2 The problem with emphasizing meaningful relationships

Yet Smith's account does not fully track ordinary usages of loyalty, or at least not all such usages. It is a mistake to think that fiduciary loyalty always needs to be built on a meaningful relationship if it is to count as genuine loyalty, as ordinarily understood.

---

[30] ibid 214 ("[A]scriptions of loyal behaviour always have a temporal element: there is no such thing as instant loyalty.").

[31] ibid.

[32] ibid.

[33] ibid at 215.

[34] ibid at 220.

[35] ibid. Smith also suggests a motivational requirement; when acting loyally, he contends, one must be motivated by a meaningful relationship. See ibid at 215. This argument loses much of its force if one can have derived loyalty outside of a meaningful relationship. That said, the relevance of loyal motives for fiduciary law raises complexities that cannot be fully addressed here.

[36] Another option is to find that fiduciary loyalty is a kind of loyalty but also that it is *sui generis*. See eg PB Miller, "Dimensions of Fiduciary Loyalty" in DG Smith and AS Gold (eds), *Research Handbook on Fiduciary Law* (Elgar Publishing 2017).

True, the loyalty we owe to friends and others within meaningful relationships is a paradigmatic instance of loyalty, and one of the most salient in our daily lives. This is also a loyalty that must be built up over time. Still, insisting that loyalty requires prior meaningful relationships may be an example of relying too much on the most common cases (or the most idealized cases).

Smith is concerned with ordinary usages of loyalty, and I share his methodology. Ordinary usages of loyalty, however, are incredibly broad—they range from loyalty to friends, to family, to country; from loyalty to a cause through loyalty to a sports team. One may also be loyal to the terms of a relationship, and not just the parties to that relationship.[37] The "loyal opposition" is a special case of loyalty in some polities.[38] Even brand loyalty has its place, such as when we buy Coke versus Pepsi.[39] Not all of these loyalties have plausible linkages to fiduciary loyalty, but we should recognize the very wide-ranging palette that fiduciary theorists can work with if ordinary usages are our starting point.

Moreover, instantaneous strong feelings of attachment to others do sometimes arise, and in some cases these attachments may incorporate feelings of loyalty. Some cases are ambiguous. Is it realistic to say that a mother can feel loyalty to her infant at the instant the mother first sees her child's face? One might say that it is love rather than loyalty in this context. Still, a case can be made that such cases involve both love *and* loyalty, and in any event other examples exist. As an alternative example, consider someone moved by a deeply motivational speech (for a literary illustration, consider a soldier who heard the St Crispin's Day speech in Shakespeare's *Henry V*).[40] If the speech strikes the right chord, it could produce immediate loyalty to the speaker, or to the cause she represents, or to the country she supports. Or, imagine someone has just saved your life. Some might feel an instantaneous loyalty—of a type—to the rescuer.[41]

Another way to discern instantaneous loyalty obligations is to consider more institutional types of relationship. If we shift to these other settings, loyalty's basis begins to look very different. In these settings, at least, loyalty obligations may have a transactional origin; we may consciously opt into loyalty.

Simon Keller notes that we can sometimes make a choice to be loyal:

Some kinds of loyalty are such that the loyal agent is able to choose the object of her loyalty. If you are loyal to a political party, for example, then your loyalty probably originated in a choice to favor this party over others, and is probably experienced as an ongoing choice; you could, at least in principle, transfer your loyalty to a different party, if you choose.[42]

---

[37] See J Raz, *The Morality of Freedom* (OUP 1986) 354–55.

[38] For discussion, see J Waldron, *Political Theory: Essays on Institutions* (Harvard University Press 2016) ch 5. I thank Paul Miller for the example.

[39] On the range of loyalty practices, including brand loyalties, see S Keller, *The Limits of Loyalty* (CUP 2007) 22.

[40] See W Shakespeare, "The Life of Henry the Fifth" in S Wells and G Taylor (eds), *William Shakespeare: The Complete Works* (OUP 1986) (Original Spelling Edition) 660.

[41] cf Keller, *The Limits of Loyalty* (n 39) 4 (suggesting loyalty to someone "who did something kind for you many years ago").

[42] See ibid at 58.

338   ANDREW S GOLD

This understanding opens up the possibility that we can adopt loyalty obligations from the moment we join an organization or begin an employment relationship, or for that matter a fiduciary-type relationship.

Nor is this phenomenon limited to commercial or corporate contexts. Speaking from experience, when I first moved to Chicago in 2004, I made a choice to be loyal to the Chicago Cubs, and I understood this to require an instantaneous loyalty to the team. When Chicago's other baseball team then won the World Series shortly afterwards, I was in no position to switch teams, as my loyalty to the Cubs was already in place. I understood it to apply from the moment I made my choice. While my choice was somewhat idiosyncratic, it is not unheard of for people to decide on a sports team loyalty on the spur of the moment.

Such choices may also be more formalized. In honor cultures, feudalistic societies, and some organizational settings it is possible to pledge loyalty, and loyalty oaths and promises to act loyally are a long-standing practice. Quite famously, loyalty oaths have been required as a prerequisite for holding various public offices.[43] While there is evidently a public law aspect in some of these cases, these oaths don't make much sense if their reference to loyalty couldn't bind someone within a commonly accepted meaning of loyalty in our personal lives. And, one can just as easily comprehend a loyalty oath as a prerequisite to membership in a club, a society, or a social clique.

A loyalty oath is hardly something required of a close and trusted friend, and it would be bizarre in most settings for a family member to pledge loyalty to another family member. As Smith notes, promises between parties in a close relationship may signal that the relationship is not so close after all.[44] Yet these oath-taking contexts are contexts where loyalty is a central preoccupation. It would be strange to think that such oaths were intended to have anything less than an instantaneous effect once made. If, for example, an individual taking a loyalty oath as a precondition to holding office says he will be loyal as soon as the relevant bonds form—hopefully!—this would surely not suffice for the participants in the practice. The oath is meant to create an obligation of loyalty from the moment it is uttered.

Role-based loyalties also implicate instantaneous loyalties, at least some of the time. It isn't difficult to think up archetypal lawyer–client relationships in which a lawyer feels an immediate loyalty obligation to her client—whom she might otherwise not have supported given her suspicions of wrongdoing—in light of how the lawyer perceives her role as an attorney. What motivates such a lawyer, moreover, is not necessarily that the law tells her to act in a certain way. We can plausibly imagine cases where what makes the difference is that this is a part of her self-conception, a part of how she understands her role in the legal system, and a part of how she understands her extra-legal relationship to her client.

Keller's work offers a helpful nomenclature that fits these lawyer–client settings. As he argues, loyalties may be "non-derived" or "derived."[45] A non-derived loyalty

---

[43] See A Kent, EJ Leib, and JH Shugerman, "Faithful Execution and Article II" (2020) 132 Harvard Law Review 2111, 2141–46 (providing history of oaths of office from the medieval era).

[44] See Smith, "The Deed, Not the Motive" (n 29) 215 n 7 (citing D Markovits, "Promise as an Arm's Length Relation" in H Sheinman (ed), *Promises and Agreements* (OUP 2011)).

[45] Keller *The Limits of Loyalty* (n 39) 58.

is a kind of loyalty that is not itself a manifestation of another, deeper commitment. In the case of a derived loyalty, however, loyalty is itself the product of another prior commitment:

> Your loyalty to a political candidate might be derived from a more fundamental commitment to certain political values, or from a more fundamental loyalty to a candidate's political party... You might maintain your loyalty to the Red Sox out of loyalty to your father, with whom you used to go to the games.[46]

A long-standing prior loyalty—one which may even have built up over time—can plausibly support an instantaneous loyalty to something else. The instantaneous loyalty is an expression of the prior background loyalty. Attorney–client settings are a rich source of examples for this kind of loyalty. A deep-seated loyalty to the justice system could readily support a lawyer's derived loyalty to her client (and it could do so instantaneously). Moreover, her prior loyalty to the justice system might be an extra-legal loyalty, and the derived loyalty to her client could be an extra-legal loyalty as well.

There is also no evident reason why the prior commitment that supports a derived loyalty obligation should be a loyalty obligation itself. We might have prior obligations of various sorts that are expressed through our subsequent, instantaneous loyalty to something else. To modify Keller's example, why couldn't one instantaneously be loyal to the Red Sox because one promised to one's father that one would be loyal to the Red Sox? Once we allow for derived loyalties that find their source in a prior loyalty-based commitment, it seems artificial to limit the category of derived loyalties to only those cases where the prior commitment is itself a loyalty obligation.

In each of the above examples, we confront long-standing practices that use the terminology of loyalty, that are adopted in non-legal settings or from an extra-legal point of view, and that are engaged in by parties who take their loyalties seriously. They involve obligations that recognizably fit patterns of loyalty in other contexts (eg they call for selfless behavior and require efforts to advance the best interests of a beneficiary). Given these features, it is possible to see these practices as loyalty practices, even if they involve kinds of loyalty that would be utterly inadequate for friendships or family relationships.[47]

There is room for fiduciary loyalty to be built upon agreements, undertakings, oaths, or other loyalty-creating transactions. Not everyone sees loyalty in this way, but enough people do to bring such instantaneous loyalty within ordinary usage. If buck passing does not work well in fiduciary law settings, the reasons why are not built into the concept of loyalty itself.

---

[46] See ibid at 58–59. As my father was a fan of the New York Yankees, I have qualms about the specifics of this hypothetical, but the argument nonetheless seems sound.

[47] In this respect, the divide between thin and thick versions of loyalty resembles the divide between thin and thick versions of trust. On the latter divide, see M Harding, "Fiduciary Relationships, Fiduciary Law, and Trust" in Smith and Gold (eds), *Research Handbook on Fiduciary Law* (n 36) 58, 60. For further discussion of the idea that loyalty can be thin or thick, see I Samet, "Fiduciary Loyalty as Kantian Virtue" in AS Gold and PB Miller (eds), *Philosophical Foundations of Fiduciary Law* (OUP 2014) 125, 126; GP Fletcher, *Loyalty: An Essay on the Morality of Relationships* (OUP 1993) 40.

340   ANDREW S GOLD

4. The Existence of a Law-Independent Counterpart

4.1 Fiduciary relationships with law-independent counterparts

The possibility that fiduciary loyalty is genuine loyalty still leaves us with the question of law-independent counterparts. Some may argue that any relationship that is built around the exercise of legal powers will lack a law-independent counterpart. If that view were adopted, then trust relationships would be on very shaky ground, given their close conceptual linkage to legal ownership of property. Indeed, even agency relationships might be in trouble. One of the most basic and important features of agency law is that it enables a principal to enter into a legally binding contract by means of the conduct of an agent—legally binding contracts, of course, only exist within systems of law.

Yet, as Gardner notes, the idea of buck passing is consistent with the idea that a reasonable person would take the law into account in deciding how to act.[48] We may also have morality-based reasons for exercising or not exercising legal powers that apply in roughly the same fashion that they apply in our private lives. For example, I argue in *The Right of Redress* that there are moral reasons not to bring a private right of action, notwithstanding its legal legitimacy.[49] Reasons to show mercy, or reasons to forgive, could militate against bringing suit. This same point applies to the fiduciary in respect to her fiduciary authority, with the added consideration that the fiduciary's reasons for exercising (or not) her legal powers may center on reasons of loyalty. While not decisive, these features suggest the potential for extra-legal loyalty-based relations in contexts where legal powers are involved.

The example of trust law is nonetheless a difficult one, given the degree to which legal concepts can be central to its structure. Perhaps some trusts do have law-independent counterparts. It is telling that some theories of the state's relation to the people it governs, such as John Locke's, make use of a trust analogy.[50] Moreover, some theories of morality suggest a trust structure could justify moral duties (as TM Scanlon suggests with respect to the moral obligations humans owe to other animals).[51] Indeed, Gardner himself describes aspects of our ethical obligations in terms of an "implied trust."[52] While these references to a trust relationship are somewhat loosely made, they signal that trust-like, law-independent relationships could be a part of political and moral theorizing.

Whatever our views on law-independent counterparts for trusts in the formal sense, it is also worth considering whether other fiduciary relationships have law-independent counterparts. Gardner's query about the reasonably loyal trustee is

---

[48] See Gardner, "Reasonable Person" (n 1) 282, 293.

[49] See Gold, *The Right of Redress* (n 7) 192–95.

[50] See J Locke, "The Second Treatise of Government" §149, in David Wootton (ed), *Political Writings of John Locke* (Signet 1993) 337 ("[T]he legislative being only a fiduciary power to act for certain ends, there remains still in the people a supreme power to remove or alter the legislative when they find the legislative act contrary to the trust reposed in them.").

[51] See Scanlon, *What We Owe to Each Other* (n 25) 183.

[52] See J Gardner, *From Personal Life to Private Law* (OUP 2018) 105 ("*FPLPL*").

apparently aimed at fiduciary relationships generally. I think such counterparts exist in non-trustee fiduciary settings, and I will turn to some examples now.

Agency relationships are a likely candidate. With or without the law, we often have people act on our behalf, in much the way that agency law empowers us to act. Some aspects of agency relationships are necessarily law-dependent—it does not make much sense to speak of someone acting as a legal substitute for another in the absence of the law. The capacity of an agent to sign a legally binding contract on behalf of another does not plausibly pre-exist a legal system. Nonetheless, in our personal lives we can still have someone make a promise on our behalf.[53] We might think that an agent's powers to contract on our behalf have law-independent analogues that are close enough to support buck passing to the loyal agent. Moreover, notions of loyalty as obedience regularly crop up in extra-legal settings,[54] suggesting that the extra-legal loyalty of agents could be a fruitful context for this approach.

Joint ventures and partnerships are another classic category. We often team up with others in pursuit of a project or series of projects, with or without the law. These relationships are probably vital for the success of pre-legal societies. They are also easily discernible parts of modern life, with their own distinctive forms of loyalty.[55] Further, the law will recognize their legal validity even in cases where the participants were entirely unaware that they had formed a legally recognized relationship, and this in itself may be indicative of a law-independent notion of partnerships.[56] The loyalty owed to team members is so deeply ingrained in loyalty practices that buck passing is almost certainly a feasible option for at least some partnerships.

Parent–child relationships are a prominent but also more complex example. Here, there is some jurisdictional variation, as parent–child relationships are not uniformly considered to be fiduciary. But, in those jurisdictions that do treat these relationships as fiduciary relationships, it is overwhelmingly evident that these relationships have law-independent existence. Indeed, the law-independent forms of this relationship are more prominent and arguably more important than the legal forms. And, here too, the relationship at issue has been used to theorize the state's loyalty obligations to its citizens.[57] Where parent–child relationships are considered to be fiduciary, it is a reasonable choice for courts to consider the factual question of what a loyal parent would do.

---

[53] For an interesting discussion of such extra-legal representative powers, see A Reinach, "The Apriori Foundations of the Civil Law" in JF Crosby (ed), *VIII Realist Phenomenology* (Transaction Books 2012) 82–83. Reinach suggests that one can also request, admonish, inform, thank, or advise in the name of another. See ibid at 83.

[54] See Keller, *The Limits of Loyalty* (n 39) vii (emphasis added).

[55] On the distinctiveness of partnership loyalty in legal settings, see EJ Criddle, "Stakeholder Fiduciaries" in PB Miller and M Harding (eds), *Fiduciaries and Trust: Ethics, Politics, Economics, and Law* (CUP 2020) 105.

[56] On the possibility of entering into fiduciary relationships without realizing it, see G Klass, "What if Fiduciary Relationships are like Contractual Ones?" in Miller and Gold (eds), *Contract, Status, and Fiduciary Law* (n 29) 93, 102; AS Gold, "Trust and Advice" in Miller and Harding (eds), *Fiduciaries and Trust: Ethics, Politics, Economics, and Law* (n 55) 35, 51–53.

[57] See eg E Fox-Decent, *Sovereignty's Promise: The State as Fiduciary* (OUP 2011). I have argued against the parent–child analogy for purposes of theorizing the state–citizen relationship, but the usage of such analogies is still indicative of the law-independent existence of parental loyalty obligations. cf AS Gold, "Reflections on the State as Fiduciary" (2013) 63 University of Toronto Law Journal 655.

Lastly, some fiduciary relationships are based on the unique circumstances of a given fact pattern. Such *ad hoc* fiduciary relationships are often built in part upon friendships, and these relationships can thus incorporate the kind of loyalty that develops gradually within meaningful relationships (they accordingly can also fit Stephen Smith's account of loyalty reasonably well).[58] If so, these relationships are premised on the existence of *involvements* which take shape incrementally without a specific act of relationship creation.[59] They bring two or more parties together in a way that is not formally announced, but which is readily apparent to the participants and to third parties in the relevant community. Such extra-legal involvements are also clear cases of law-independent relationships.

4.2 Fiduciary relationships without law-independent counterparts

Interestingly, the lack of a law-independent counterpart in a given moment need not be fatal to a buck passing account. A fiduciary relationship that lacks a law-independent counterpart *ab initio* may not always lack a law-independent counterpart in the future. The loyalties owed within a given relationship can evolve over time. For example, it may become an expression of loyalty for two friends to call each other on their birthday given their past practices of doing so, even if initially their friendship did not require birthday calls.[60] This is true even against a backdrop of rule-based obligations; relationships built on contracts can implicate evolving loyalty obligations that effectively supersede the terms of the agreement.[61] And a version of this process may hold true for fiduciary relationships that begin with a legal mandate, rather than a contractual one. Parties to such a relationship may then end up with a law-independent counterpart even if they did not begin with one.

At a larger scale, the loyalty obligations that attach to an entire category of special relationship may also evolve over time, extending beyond (or in place of) the terms set by law. There was a time in history when lawyer–client relationships did not exist. Now, there are characteristic forms of loyalty—extra-legal loyalty—that lawyers customarily show toward their clients. These are products of social norms which have taken time to form, but which are presently recognizable and suitable for factual inquiries into what a loyal party would do. Whenever it was that lawyers first appeared on the scene, there would have been no law-independent counterpart that was a perfect fit for the lawyer–client relationship; this relationship only needed to exist when law existed. That doesn't preclude the subsequent emergence of a law-independent relationship for an entire legal category like the lawyer–client relationship. While some

---

[58] See eg *Burdett v Miller*, 957 F.2d 1375 (7th Cir 1992) (Posner, J) (finding an *ad hoc* fiduciary relationship in part based on a friendship).

[59] See D Owens, *Shaping the Normative Landscape* (OUP 2012) 97 (citing E Goffman, *Interaction Ritual* (Doubleday 1967) ch 7).

[60] See ibid at 108. See also ibid at 101.

[61] D Markovits, "Sharing Ex Ante and Sharing Ex Post: The Non-Contractual Basis of Fiduciary Relations" in Gold and Miller (eds), *Philosophical Foundations of Fiduciary Law* (n 47) 220–23. See also Owens, *Shaping the Normative Landscape* (n 59) 107 (suggesting obligations of friendship can start life with a promissory obligation, but concluding that no obligation constitutive of friendship is a promissory obligation). Gardner shows apparent sympathy for Markovits' understanding. See Gardner, *FPLPL* (n 52) 44–45.

of the extra-legal loyalty at issue may simply be a direct reflection of whatever the law has mandated, other features can be products of custom within a community.[62]

These possibilities suggest law-independent counterparts can evolve for fiduciary relationships that do not initially have such counterparts. Assume, however, that we are dealing with a fiduciary relationship that does not evolve in this way. Courts may still borrow from another fiduciary sphere that does have a law-independent counterpart. Doctrinal borrowing is already well-established in fiduciary law. In *Meinhard v Salmon*, Judge Cardozo looked to trust law loyalty in thinking about joint venture loyalty.[63] Corporate law regularly builds on both trust law and agency law. The loyalty required for novel fiduciary relationships is frequently based on analogies to more established fiduciary relationships,[64] and legal transplants are commonplace.[65] Similarly, in cases where a fiduciary law relationship has no law-independent relationship that is a genuine counterpart, the law might pass the buck to the loyal participant in some other fiduciary relationship—one that does have a law-independent counterpart. If that legal relationship is close enough in its central features, this kind of buck passing could work quite well.[66]

Note also that specialized legal concepts often implicate a higher level, more abstract concept (eg employment-related concepts can be understood at the specialized level of employment relationships or, alternatively, at the more abstract level of contract relationships).[67] If trust law lacks a law-independent counterpart at the level of the trust relationship, we might move up the ladder to the more abstract idea of a fiduciary relationship. In that case, a court could buck pass to whatever it is that a loyal *fiduciary* would do, even if it cannot readily buck pass to whatever it is that a loyal trustee would do. A higher level of abstraction could mean greater indeterminacy, but for some disputes the most basic answers (eg no self-dealing) may suffice.

5. The Buck Passing Account Revisited

Let us now turn briefly to the merits. In assessing the merits of buck passing to the loyal person, it is important to recognize the flexibility involved in adopting this approach. This flexibility is built into Gardner's understanding of the buck passing idea. While he sees buck passing as a kind of legally "deregulated" zone, it is a deregulated zone that can be shaped, enhanced, and customized in various ways. With that in

---

[62] A powerful illustration is the tendency of plaintiffs' lawyers to eschew "blood money" when representing their clients. For discussion, see T Baker, "Blood Money, New Money, and the Moral Economy of Tort Law in Action" (2001) 35 Law & Society Review 275.

[63] 249 N.Y. 458 (N.Y. 1928).

[64] On the role of analogies in fiduciary law, see DA DeMott, "Beyond Metaphor: An Analysis of Fiduciary Obligation" [1988] Duke Law Journal 879.

[65] Such transplants may also be problematic. See E Rock and M Wachter, "Dangerous Liaisons: Corporate Law, Trust Law, and Interdoctrinal Transplants" (2002) 96 Northwestern University Law Review 651.

[66] Compare Gardner's discussion of buck passing to the "reasonably competent carpenter" in determining liability for an ordinary house owner. cf Gardner, "Reasonable Person" (n 1) 292.

[67] For helpful discussion, see S Deakin, "Juridical Ontology: The Evolution of Legal Form" (2015) 40 Historical Social Research 170, 173.

mind, it is quite plausible for the law to occasionally use a buck passing strategy in assessing fiduciary loyalty.

First, a buck passing account of fiduciary loyalty could be adopted without employing the excusatory latitude of the "reasonably loyal" person. One might simply ask, factually, what a loyal person would do in a given set of circumstances. Or, one might use what Gardner refers to as an enhanced standard if the circumstances call for it. Second, buck passing to the loyal person can be subjected to legal constraints. If courts are concerned that extra-legal loyalties will be *overly* stringent—that they will be harmful because unregulated loyalty can become excessive—then the law can place boundaries around this legally unregulated zone. As Gardner expresses the idea, courts may "put a little law back in." Buck passing to the loyal person is consistent with various carve outs or constraints where the law imposes legal rules.

In short, the law can pass the buck for fiduciary loyalty without the excusatory latitude of the "reasonably loyal" person, and it can opt for narrower limitations on loyalty where appropriate. What the above possibilities suggest is that fiduciary law can buck pass in a manner that is not overly excusatory nor overly inviting of loyalty's excesses. Still, that just means that buck passing is an option. Are there any arguments that actually work in its favor? As noted, I will suggest three possibilities: (i) the buck passing approach to loyalty is a useful anti-opportunism device; (ii) buck passing allows fiduciary loyalty to better match extra-legal loyalties; and (iii) buck passing provides a valuable interface between legal and extra-legal concepts of loyalty that can facilitate legal evolution.

Our first basis for buck passing is actually an extension of Gardner's Aristotelian justification. Recall that, for Gardner, there is a moral argument for buck passing that draws on Aristotle's argument for equity. On this view, buck passing is a step beyond equity as a response to the over-inclusiveness of legal rules. This view indicates one reason why buck passing to the loyal person could be valuable, for loyalty is capable of acting much like the law of equity acts in other realms. Loyalty can mold itself to the particularities of new fact patterns,[68] subtly addressing opportunism while also providing predictability and accessibility to those familiar with loyalty practices. Indeed, Henry Smith has offered a powerful theory of fiduciary law as equitable, with loyalty as an important component.[69] On this account, fiduciary loyalty, with its associated burdens of proof and strict remedies for breach, is an anti-opportunism device that tracks equity's proxies for opportunism while going beyond them.

We should be careful not to confuse acting loyally with acting equitably in the realm of our personal lives (it would be an interesting but also distinct development for the law to pass the buck to the "reasonably equitable person"). After all, it is possible for individuals to be equitable toward someone while still falling short of what loyalty requires. I might act equitably toward an acquaintance by partially forgiving her debt, given the difficulty my acquaintance will have in paying this debt; if I acted loyally toward her as a friend, however, I might forgive the debt in its entirety. Likewise, one can be loyal toward someone by giving her a very large share of a pool of assets, with the

---

[68] On fiduciary law's atomistic quality, see DeMott, "Beyond Metaphor" (n 64) 915.

[69] See HE Smith, "How Fiduciary Law Is Equitable" in Gold and Miller (eds), *Philosophical Foundations of Fiduciary Law* (n 47).

effect that one is inequitable toward someone else who thereby gets a smaller share. The equitable person is not inevitably loyal, and the loyal person is not inevitably equitable.[70]

But these considerations don't preclude the law from using loyal behavior— including the factual question of what a loyal person would do—as a mechanism for policing opportunistic behavior, in much the same way that the law of equity operates to address opportunism in other settings. Loyalty is often a very good tool for combatting opportunism by those who exercise fiduciary discretion. Loyalty is also accessible to fiduciaries, beneficiaries, and even courts in a way that other standards might not be. While we ought not view the loyal as perfectly equivalent to the equitable, what is loyal can function as a rough proxy for what is equitable.

Another reason to buck pass is that this enables the law to accommodate the extra-legal loyalties that fiduciaries actually experience. Indeed, it allows for this loyalty to match beneficiary expectations in a better way. One basic reason for such accommodation is that, where successful, it will lessen the burden on fiduciaries who take their loyalties seriously; they will not face a conflict between what the law deems loyal and what they subjectively feel is loyal.[71] Another possibility is that the loyalty at issue will be easier for regulated parties to understand, as it will be more accessible.[72] A further consequence may be to improve compliance by limiting perceived gaps between legal and extra-legal standards. Where legal obligations diverge from their perceived moral counterparts, this divergence can decrease compliance with those legal obligations.[73] The same could be true for loyalty.

Buck passing also permits something else that is implicit in the above suggestions. Buck passing may allow external, non-legal understandings of loyalty to eventually be incorporated into internal, legal understandings of loyalty. In such cases, the value of buck passing is how it affects the law's content in contexts that do not involve buck passing. This claim might appear to be in tension with some of Gardner's other legal theory commitments, but it need not be.

Gardner emphasizes that when read as a whole, his account of buck passing is an argument against incorporationism; that is, it is an argument against the view that standards like the reasonable person, once applied by courts, are by that fact alone legal standards.[74] Yet, if we accept Gardner's anti-incorporationist view (I take no position here), it would not follow that the standards which emerge from a buck passing approach can *never* be incorporated into the law. Particularly in the fiduciary

---

[70] In this respect, as in others, the virtues relevant to the law may be in tension. Gardner was of course well aware of such tensions. See J Gardner, "The Virtue of Justice and the Character of Law" in *Law as a Leap of Faith* (OUP 2012) 238, 252–53 (describing differences between rules of justice and of loyalty).

[71] See generally AS Gold, "Accommodating Loyalty" in Miller and Gold (eds), *Contract, Status, and Fiduciary Law* (n 29) 185. For a general account of the accommodationist approach, see SV Shiffrin, "The Divergence of Contract and Promise," (2007) 120 Harvard Law Review 708. Relatedly, this may also be a means to limit contractual reductivism regarding fiduciary loyalty. For Gardner's arguments against such reductivism, see Gardner, *FPLPL* (n 52) 44–46. While I believe fiduciary loyalty is sometimes contractual, there are reasons to hope that not all forms of fiduciary loyalty will be understood in that way.

[72] See Gold, "Accommodating Loyalty" (n 71) 200.

[73] See ibid 198–99. cf P Robinson and J Darley, "The Utility of Desert" (1997) 91 Northwestern University Law Review 453 (discussing a similar idea in the criminal law setting).

[74] See Gardner, "Reasonable Person" (n 1) 302–03.

context, where fact finders are typically judges and not juries, one might anticipate that understandings of loyalty that surface in a buck passing context could gradually migrate over to the law, and even become legal rules. For example, it is now a legal rule that a corporate director's loyalty doesn't require intentional violations of positive law, but this legal rule could have evolved from a factual analysis of what a certain kind of loyal person would do.

Legal concepts are at least somewhat mutable.[75] They are also "defeasible"—that is, they are partly open-ended or indeterminate.[76] These features exist to varying degrees within legal systems, and certainly within private law, but it should be evident that fiduciary law's concepts have both characteristics. Fiduciary loyalty also evolves with regularity, especially in heavily litigated fields like corporate law. Although this is ultimately an empirical question, fiduciary loyalty concepts thus appear susceptible to the influences of extra-legal conceptions of loyalty. If that hypothesis is right, the loyalty that manifests in a buck passing context could readily cross over to the law's own conceptions of fiduciary loyalty.

Granted, it may not always be obvious when courts are engaging in buck passing, especially in the fiduciary setting. As noted, juries are not the usual fact finder in fiduciary law cases, and judges do not always identify buck passing cases as such.[77] *Meinhard v Salmon* itself may provide examples of a court buck passing to the loyal person, yet that is less than clear.[78] But this very ambiguity between incorporated legal standards and potential buck passing may allow for the conduct of the extra-legally "loyal person" to influence the legally adopted rules that govern loyal fiduciaries. Particularly where courts do not always identify buck passing cases as such, there is room for judicial pronouncements on loyalty that begin as buck passing to end as legal rules.[79]

Importantly, the resulting legal standards may not precisely match whatever it is that the extra-legally "loyal person" or the "reasonably loyal person" would do as a factual question. They may, nonetheless, be influenced by that factual question, and they may approximate its answer. If so, the result could be more recognizably loyal, to the untrained eye, than what the law would otherwise have provided. That approximation is itself valuable.[80] Fiduciary loyalty is a kind of loyalty, but it is often quite distinct

---

[75] See Deakin, "Juridical Ontology" (n 67) 180.

[76] See ibid 173.

[77] As Gardner recognizes, a court may engage in buck passing where the court itself is the fact finder. See Gardner, "Reasonable Person" (n 1) 301.

[78] At times, Cardozo uses language that suggests he is applying standards of loyalty that are extra-legal in their source. For example, see *Meinhard*, at 468 ("A managing coadventurer appropriating the benefit of such a lease without warning to his partner might fairly expect to be reproached with conduct that was underhand, or lacking, to say the least, in reasonable candor, if the partner were to surprise him in the act of signing the new instrument."). That reading is not conclusive, however, and *Meinhard* is an isolated case. For a suggestion that fiduciary relationships regularly draw on "precepts of social morality and practice," see S Fitzgibbon, "Fiduciary Relationships Are Not Contracts" (1999) 82 Marquette Law Review 303, 338–40.

[79] Such a process is also consistent with fiduciary law's pattern of adopting rules and standards that work in combination. On that pattern, see Smith, "How Fiduciary Law is Equitable" (n 69) 273; RH Sitkoff, "An Economic Theory of Fiduciary Law" in Gold and Miller (eds), *Philosophical Foundations of Fiduciary Law* (n 47) 197, 202–03. The rules might be legal while the standards result from a buck passing approach.

[80] The benefits of using legal concepts of loyalty that are "recognizably loyal" may roughly track the benefits of using legal concepts that are "recognizably moral." On the latter, see AS Gold and HE Smith, "Restatements and the Common Law" (manuscript on file with author); AS Gold and HE Smith, "Sizing Up Private Law" (2020) 70 University of Toronto Law Journal 489.

from its extra-legal counterparts. The need for a gap between legal loyalty and extra-legal loyalty can be real. Still, the gap between legal and extra-legal loyalty need not be a huge gulf, and buck passing to the loyal person could be a way to maintain a close but reasonable distance between the law's understanding of loyalty and the understanding of fiduciaries themselves.

6. Conclusion

John Gardner was onto something important when he asked why there is no "reasonably loyal trustee," and pursuing his question further leads to a range of insights. This chapter suggests that buck passing is a realistic option for fiduciary law. A fiduciary's loyalty can be a question of fact just as much as it can be a question of law, and for most fiduciary relationships both perspectives are available. Under the right circumstances, both perspectives could also be desirable.

20

Corrective Justice and the Right to Hold on to What One Has

John CP Goldberg and Benjamin C Zipursky

1. Agents and Patients; Duties and Rights

John Gardner's *From Personal Life to Private Law* is an extended meditation on personal responsibility, both moral and legal.[1] Its focus is on agents more so than patients—on those who act more than those upon whom others have acted. Thus it aims to emphasize deep connections between interpersonal moral duties and duties recognized in the private law of contracts and torts, to explain why both kinds of duties require not only actions meeting a standard of conduct but the avoidance or achievement of certain results, and to capture how breaches of these duties generate secondary duties of repair. By contrast, it mentions only begrudgingly the rights of those upon whom others have acted—*patients* or, in more familiar terms, *victims*.[2]

The exception to this pattern is Chapter 5, titled "The Way Things Used to Be." Here readers are told explicitly that their attention is being turned to "the one whose life was disrupted or interrupted, the patient as opposed to the agent."[3] Whereas previous chapters explained why wrongful injurers incur duties to repair losses resulting from their wrongs, Chapter 5 considers why, within tort and contract law, victims are entitled to demand that they be restored to something like the condition they were in prior to having been wronged. Why should these bodies of law operate on the premise that victims are entitled to be so restored?[4]

As Gardner notes, questions such as these are often raised in connection with concerns about unequal distributions of wealth. (Is it just for a Rockefeller to be able to obtain a large tort judgment against an hourly-wage worker who negligently damages the Rockefeller's car?) But the problem goes deeper. Even if there is nothing unjust about the status quo, there is still a question as to the basis of the victim's claim to having it re-established. Might the very idea of restoration—an idea that Gardner takes to be a core principle of private law—rest on nothing more than "irrational sentimentality"?[5] What case can be made for law that vindicates "holding on" rather than "letting go"?[6] Note that the reference to "holding on" is not merely a reference

---

[1] J Gardner, *From Personal Life to Private Law* (OUP 2018).

[2] ibid 52–57. Gardner does not deny that agents' duties correlate with patients' rights. Instead, he de-emphasizes rights in part to dissociate himself from those who mistakenly maintain that such rights connect analytically to powers enjoyed by victims to hold to account those who have violated their rights.

[3] ibid 162.

[4] ibid 165.

[5] ibid 182.

[6] ibid 167.

John CP Goldberg and Benjamin C Zipursky, *Corrective Justice and the Right to Hold on to What One Has* In: *Private Law and Practical Reason*. Edited by: Haris Psarras and Sandy Steel, Oxford University Press.
© John CP Goldberg and Benjamin C Zipursky 2023. DOI: 10.1093/oso/9780192857330.003.0020

to possessions. In the realm of interpersonal wrongs, often what is being restored is the "arc" or "narrative" along which the victim's life had been proceeding.[7] The question is whether a victim has reason to want to be able to get his or her life back on the track on which it was proceeding before she was wronged by another. Leaving aside concerns about transaction costs associated with having to change tracks, what is it about existing goals that gives them a distinctive value, such that private law should offer victims the opportunity to pursue them once again?

Gardner's answer to these questions resonates to some degree with what might loosely be termed an "existentialist" strand in Bernard Williams' work.[8] Acting for goals, Gardner says, is what gives human life value. In addition, for certain things to be our goals they must be things to which we are committed. It follows that "an unlooked-for deflection from one's goals" must be regarded as something undesirable. (It is of course different when one decides to change one's own goals.) "Once we have this commitment, we cannot treat the life we are living on the same footing as some other possible life, as just another life for whatever it is worth independent of our commitments. This one is ours and we cannot live it without giving it a certain rational priority."[9] From an impersonal perspective, any in a vast range of goals one might pursue is equal in value to others. But, as rational beings conscious of the fact that a finite human life can involve the pursuit of only some goals, we cannot but adopt the "rationally necessary illusion" that our goals are especially valuable.[10] What makes them special need not be anything intrinsic to them but merely the fact that they are ours.

That our goals have special value for us permits us in turn to appreciate in a more impersonal manner the significance of goals. We can grasp why another person's goals matter for her, and why we often will and should support others in their pursuit of those goals even if we don't ourselves assign value to those goals. We can further appreciate the impersonal value that attends each person being committed to some goals and not others, for it is just such selective commitment that makes living a valuable human life possible. All humans are valuers, and, as such, are sensitive to a vast range of values. Yet we recognize that it would make a hash out of human life for any of us to attempt to pursue all values alike. As valuers, Gardner adds, humans give and owe respect to value not in the abstract but to value as it is actually instantiated in the world. We have, he claims, more "stringent" reasons to support and care for actual friendships than we do to make new friends. Likewise, we have more stringent reasons to respect the valuable goals that others already have than we do to help them acquire those goals to begin with. To "relate properly" to value means relating to it as instantiated value—to things that already exist.[11]

With this account of value in place, Gardner turns to the question of restoration. Thus far, he has sought to explain why one has reason to hold on to the life one has. As he acknowledges, this explanation does not entirely answer the question of what one

---

[7] ibid 168.
[8] ibid 172 n 15 (citing Williams, "A Critique of Utilitarianism" in JJC Smart and B Williams, *Utilitarianism: For and Against* (CUP 1973)).
[9] ibid 174.
[10] ibid.
[11] ibid 180.

350   JOHN CP GOLDBERG AND BENJAMIN C ZIPURSKY

has reason to do when some important aspect of one's life has been taken away. Having reason to hold on is one thing. Having reason to *go back* is another.

And yet the two are related. The rationality of holding on is crucial to the explanation of why each of us has primary moral and legal duties to avoid setting others back in certain ways, whether by causing them bodily harm or depriving them of promised performances. These primary duties protect the lives we have; they help the beneficiaries of these duties keep their lives on their existing tracks. In this sense, they correspond to what Neil MacCormick called "security rights."[12] Distancing himself from the approach to private law articulated by Arthur Ripstein, Gardner maintains that these security rights are not aspects of a liberal principle of equal freedom. They are rooted in general features of the human condition rather than a particular political or "sectarian" conception of a life well led.[13] Human engagement with value consists of engagement with the instantiations of value, whether or not those engagements are self-chosen or self-directed in the requisite sense: there is value in living a life even if it is a life one has fallen into.

Once one sees that primary duties and rights are tied to the reasons each of us has to hold on—to value—the goals we have, one can begin to grasp the connection between holding on and going back. According to the continuity thesis, breaches of primary duties (violations of primary rights) give rise to secondary duties (and secondary rights). The breaching party owes it to the right-holder to conform as much as possible to the reasons underlying the duty that was breached. And the right-holder has a right that the breaching party so conform. Thus, if an actor negligently injures another, the actor has reason to take reparative actions so as to make it as if the other's setback never happened, and thereby to restore her to her prior condition. Crucially, for Gardner, the status quo ante is composed not only of the victim's pre-setback health and holdings but also the path or paths she had already carved for herself and that she would have proceeded down in the absence of the rights violation.

Gardner concedes that the foregoing account faces a complication. Often a violation of a security right will be such that it is not possible to enable the victim to get her life back on track—often she will be required to "let go" of some significant aspect of the life she had been leading. Does it make sense, in these contexts, to think about repair as restoration? He says that it does. It may be that certain important aspects of the life one was leading are not fully restorable. But in authorizing compensation for these permanent losses, private law presumes that one is being restored to one's life in other respects. If our imagined negligence victim loses her eyesight because of the tort, and cannot continue to work as a pilot, her life cannot proceed on the same track. But compensation that allows for her to cover her expenses and train for a new job enables her to reassemble a version of the life she had been leading.[14]

Chapter 5 concludes by discussing how private law, as a law of obligations, can be understood as a scheme for allocating security rights. By defining what counts as a

---

[12] ibid 183 (citing MacCormick, "The Obligation of Reparation" (1978) 78 Proceedings of the Aristotelian Society 175 at 177).

[13] ibid.

[14] Gardner allows that there may be some cases—for example, of catastrophic injury—that test the limits of this conception of "getting one's life back." But the core concept remains. Note that he gestures at a somewhat distinct treatment of contract remedies. ibid 188–89.

wrongful injury, it allocates initial "entitlements." Moreover, as famously emphasized by Calabresi and Melamed, it protects those entitlements in the particular manner of enabling those who have suffered rights violations to obtain compensation sufficient in principle to restore the status quo ante.[15] Which entitlements the private law protects, and how it protects them, are, according to Gardner, questions of distributive justice. In this sense, the common supposition that corrective and distributive justice are distinct forms of justice is mistaken. Private law is a law of distributive justice, where the things being distributed are primary duties not to injure and rights not to be injured, as well as secondary duties and rights of restoration. In other words, it is "a specialized juridical scheme for allowing some people, often at the expense of others, to hold on more tightly, with the support of the law, to what they already have, or recently had, in their lives."[16] Tort law is in this sense "conservative": it protects people in what they have. Whether it is conservative in other senses—for example, by privileging the Rockefellers—depends on its substantive rules. Tort law that protects ordinary individuals against being injured by wealthy and powerful actors and entitles these ordinary individuals to restorative payments when injured, might actually serve progressive political ends.

> [T]he first question of distributive justice facing the law of obligations is not how to distribute wealth but how to distribute legal obligations that give the law of obligations its name. What these legal obligations are primed to offer … is not wealth but security. This security could, if the obligations are well-distributed, be relatively independent of wealth and indeed be a mode of social power capable of rivaling wealth.[17]

As Gardner points out, it is thus no accident that the powerful have in recent decades pushed aggressively for law reforms that promise to reduce their legal liabilities.

2. Value Theory and the Continuity Thesis Reconceived

Our comments in this chapter aim to be largely constructive. In particular, we are inclined to credit the arguments sketched above with bolstering the power and plausibility of corrective justice theory as applied to tort law. In keeping with prior work, we ultimately conclude that, even with these improvements, corrective justice theory provides a less compelling account of tort law than our preferred wrongs-and-recourse theory.[18] Because the differences between the two accounts have struck some readers as quite modest, we conclude by highlighting differences we regard as especially significant.

As we see it, Gardner's continuity thesis provides a way of shoring up an attractive but vulnerable aspect of Ernest Weinrib's account of corrective justice.[19] When

---

[15] ibid 192 (citing G Calabresi and D Melamed, "Property Rules, Liability Rules, and Inalienability: One View of the Cathedral" (1972) 85 Harvard Law Review 1089 at 1097.)

[16] ibid 193.

[17] ibid 194.

[18] JCP Goldberg and BC Zipursky, *Recognizing Wrongs* (Harvard University Press 2020).

[19] For a thoughtful exploration of various iterations of the continuity thesis, see S Steel, "Compensation and Continuity" (2020) 26 Legal Theory 250.

analyzing areas of private law such as tort and contract, it is common for scholars to speak of primary duties not to injure others and secondary duties of repair that wrongful injurers incur when they breach their primary duties. While Weinrib might accept this primary/secondary language as part of a loose articulation of his view, it is not, strictly speaking, in keeping with it. On his account, there is only one duty: the defendant's duty to avoid wrongfully injuring that is correlative to the plaintiff's right not to be so injured. Weinrib famously claims that it is absurd to suppose that the defendant's violation of the plaintiff's right would somehow extinguish that right.[20] But if the right remains, the correlative duty does as well. Once the injury has occurred, the defendant's compensation of the plaintiff for having injured her is the only way for him to respect her right. To say the same thing, the duty owed to the plaintiff and breached by the defendant remains intact after the breach, and compensation paid to the plaintiff by the defendant is compliance with *that duty* in so far as compliance is possible.

Weinrib's contention that the violation of a right against being wrongfully injured does not put an end to that right seems deeply counterintuitive. Intentionally killing another without justification is a violation of that person's right not to be wrongfully deprived of her life, and the termination of the victim's life would seem to terminate her right to it. Damaging someone's reputation by convincing his neighbors that he is a child molester likewise puts an end to his right not to have his reputation so damaged. Negligently running someone down and crushing his legs puts an end to his right not to have his legs crushed by another's negligent act. And so on. None of this undercuts the plausibility of a claim that victims enjoy a right to reparations based on a violation of right. It does, however, tend to undermine the plausibility of the claim that the right that was violated still exists after its violation. It likewise undermines that the thought that the payment of compensation is a performance of the duty not to injure (as much as it can be performed).

Gardner's continuity thesis offers a looser and more plausible alternative to Weinrib's explanation of the link between the duty not to injure and the duty to compensate. On his account, too, a person's legal right not to have his or her legs crushed by the negligence of another is violated when another breaches the legal duty to refrain from negligently crushing that person's legs. However, once this duty is breached, it is no longer possible to comply with it. Instead, what remains of the duty and its corresponding right are *the reasons requiring vigilance and respect for the intactness of another person's bodily integrity*. Unlike the primary duty that no longer survives, the reasons for the duty survive its breach. And these reasons entail other duties—in this case, a duty to provide funds that will enable the victim to recover so far as possible from his injuries. On this account the defendant's duty of compensation is continuous with, but not identical to, the defendant's duty not to injure the plaintiff: the same reasons warranting the duty not to injure another negligently support the duty of compensation to the person one has so injured.

While Gardner's rendition of the continuity thesis strikes us as an improvement over Weinrib's, it has problems of its own. Here we highlight one. The analysis, if it

---

[20] EJ Weinrib, *The Idea of Private Law* (Rev edn, OUP 2012) 135.

is sound, should cover central cases of injury and repair covered by private law. And one such case involves injuries that are beyond repair. If an actor's negligent conduct caused the victim to suffer permanent loss of function in his legs, the value of intact and working legs—which we posited as a principal reason for recognizing the duty to take care not to cause damage to them—cannot be a reason for a compensatory damages award in anything like the way it was a reason to take care not to cause bodily harm in the first place. The payment of compensation does not protect or secure the possession of intact and working legs. Yet tort law still awards compensatory damages for such damage.

It would perhaps be tempting for Gardner to address this puzzle by recasting the relevant reasons such that they encompass a broader or more abstractly defined interest: for example, the victim's interest in happiness or in having a normally functioning body. One might argue that the primary duty to be careful not to crush another's legs exists because of these broader interests. The duty of repair generated by the breach of the duty to avoid injuring then can be understood as answering to the same reasons, namely, the victim's interest in happiness and healthy functioning. The sameness of the reasons for the primary duty and the secondary duty thereby preserves the continuity thesis.

However, this imagined move concedes too much. For one thing, the interest in happiness and healthy functioning is so generic as to weaken severely the explanatory and interpretive force of Gardner's theory. In a related but more pointed manner, one might observe that the duties of care in negligence law are focused largely on physical harm, and—whatever else one might think of Razian interest theories of rights of the sort that Gardner employs—it is quite plausible to think of negligence law's duties of care not to cause physical harm as rooted in at least somewhat better-defined interests, like those of bodily integrity. Sticking to the continuity thesis by shifting to a generic interest in happiness or well-being and rejecting the relevance of interests in bodily integrity one worries, is throwing away the baby with the bathwater.

Chapter 5 of *From Personal Life to Private Law* suggests that Gardner was contemplating a rather different way of rescuing the connection between primary and secondary duties upon which corrective justice theory relies. Again, the strategy involves identifying a broader interest that encompasses the interest protected by the primary duty, but one not so broad or disconnected from bodily integrity as a generic interest in happiness or physical functioning. Each of us, he argues, has an interest in being able to live a life that is on a track. While this interest is broader in an important respect than the interest in intact and working legs, one might nonetheless describe the extension of the interest here as *vertical* rather than *horizontal*. On this version of the continuity thesis, the reason behind the duty not to injure another carelessly that generates the duty to compensate for negligent injury is the victim's interest in keeping his life more or less on track, and in controlling the deviation from normality moving forward.

We are unsure whether this move ultimately succeeds: at least on our initial reconstruction, it carries its own over-generality problems. Nonetheless, there does seem to be something gained by it. Consider another torts case. In this one, the defendant steals the plaintiff's car and wrecks it. If the plaintiff sues for conversion and prevails, the defendant will be ordered to provide compensation to cover the cost of a replacement car. One can describe the stability of owning a car that the compensatory payment helps to secure in terms of rights: there was a right in owning a car, not just a right in having the car at one's disposal. And, indeed, because the car is personal property, the ownership of it includes control over when the owner sells it or licenses others to use it. The interest in not have the car taken by another without permission, the interest in not having it destroyed, and the interest in being compensated in the event that it is destroyed are all plausibly unified in a single property right. Indeed, these are arguably constituents of the owner's property right in the car.

A similar account can be offered in the domain of contract. A homeowner contracts with a painter to paint the homeowner's house, providing one-third of the $9,000 fee up front. The painter paints a small part of the house but then quits, breaching the contract. The painter will be required to pay compensation in an amount sufficient to cover the cost of someone else finishing the job. The interest in having the house painted and in the interest in being paid money when the defendant breaches come together here through a single right created in the contract. A right exists to have the house painted and to have damages paid if it is not. Both the interest in having the house painted and the interest in having compensation if the house is not painted are aspects of the contractual right.

While these examples in one respect help make the case for the plausibility of Gardner's rendition of corrective justice theory, they also feed into a criticism one of us has previously made, namely that it improperly generalizes from property and con-tract law to tort law.[21] A right against wrongful invasion of one's bodily integrity, for example, seem quite different from a right to receive an agreed-upon performance. When a contractual promisor is under a duty is to complete a task, and fails in that duty, it is quite cogent to speak of the promisor as being under a duty to do the next best thing. When the "thing" in question is avoiding causing catastrophic injury to an-other, the idea of doing the next best thing is far less intuitive.

Corrective justice theorists insist that tort rights are really not so different from contract and property rights. Certainly this seems to be Weinrib's and Ripstein's view. They argue that the right not to suffer a wrongfully inflicted physical injury, like the right to contractual performance, is a right that bundles together the right not to suffer bodily harm and the right to receive compensation for such harm. We have argued against this integrated picture. The right against wrongful interference with bodily in-tegrity is basic in certain respects, as is the right against false imprisonment, and the right not to have one's reputation smeared. The duty not to crush someone's legs, im-prison them falsely, or defame them is not part of an integrated package in the way that the duty not to interfere with someone's possession of property, or the duty to perform a contract, arguably is. To put the point in a less tendentious way, the interference with these interests—for example, the wrongful crushing of someone's legs—is a significant setback prior to, and specifiable independently of, the creation of a set of conventional arrangements in institutionalized form for responding to this interference. Even if we suppose it is plausible that the interest in receiving compensation to ameliorate one's condition after such a setback is related to the interest in not having been injured in

---

[21] BC Zipursky, "Civil Recourse and the Plurality of Wrongs" (2014) 2014(1) New Zealand Law Review 145, 159–65.

CORRECTIVE JUSTICE AND THE RIGHT TO HOLD ON TO WHAT ONE HAS 355

the first place, it is not plausible that—at its most basic level—the interest in not having one's legs crushed is properly cast as an aspect of a larger right that includes a right to be compensated in the event of having been injured.

Gardner's analysis of the right to be put back on track—like Ripstein's thoughtful analysis of rights against injury in *Private Wrongs*—implicitly challenges our position.[22] By describing in detail the importance of *security* in what one has, including not only one's possessions but one's health and bodily integrity, Gardner identifies a basis for the attribution of a duty of repair to the wrongdoer. More generally, in light of the centrality to a person's life of ongoing expectations and reliance on being able to continue living roughly as one has, the interest in these expectations and reliance being "satisfied" is deep and diachronic. It is because of this interest that there is a duty of repair. And it is arguably because of this interest that the primary duty exists, too. Finally, once we acknowledge that the law protects this deeper interest and that, without it, the reliance and expectations would be misplaced, it seems to be of a piece with property and contract: it is institutional, not pre-political. Although the Razian interest theory of rights that underlies the structure of Gardner's approach is somewhat alien to the Kantian foundation of Ripstein's view, the overall picture—and the overall response to critique of Weinrib's overstatement—appears similar.

3. Qualified Liberalism in Torts

A fascinating turn at the end of Chapter 5, mentioned above, is Gardner's claim that the state's guarantee of security to each person is an aspect of distributive justice. This is interesting for several reasons. Most obviously, it is deliberately ironic in the context of the ongoing debate about whether private law as it exists in Anglo-American common law leans too heavily in a status quo direction, so as to be vulnerable to critical attack from the point of view of those favoring significant redistribution. Gardner's response—echoing points made by others including George Fletcher, Greg Keating, and, in some respects, Ripstein—suggests that private law institutions are actually part of how our system secures distributive justice.

We are interested in Gardner's suggestion for two other reasons. One is that Gardner, like Ripstein, actually seems to be endorsing a *political theoretic* foundation for corrective justice and private law, not a moral foundation, a welfarist foundation, or formalistic one. Yet whereas Ripstein's connects private law's guarantees of mutual forbearance to Kantian and Rawlsian notions of a right to craft one's life in a manner independent of the demands or values of others, Gardner's draws from a different political-philosophical tradition. In the end, it is not creativity or independent choice that private law is to be valued for protecting. Instead, it is settled expectations and security, and, more particularly, equality in expectations and security. As a historical matter, Gardner's inclinations—which are in important respects more modest than Ripstein's—are well-suited to and supported by the history of Anglo-American law. For example, when the US Constitution protects due process of law, privileges

---

[22] A Ripstein, *Private Wrongs* (Harvard University Press 2016).

and immunities, and equal protection, it is acknowledging the enormous importance of equal and individual empowerment to use the legal system to protect certain expectations.

On the political front, it is worth noting Gardner's striking treatment of the UK government's proposed "bedroom tax." As he describes it, it called for a *pro rata* reduction of public housing subsidies for accommodations deemed "too big" for their occupants. When issued, the proposal raised an objection that Gardner credits, namely that it failed to give any weight to the distinction between:

> getting people out of houses they are already living in, on the one hand, and funding houses for those who are homeless or trying to move, on the other. The *status quo* should carry some weight in the distribution. Thus, say, the subsidy changes should not be retrospective ... or should be phased in only slowly for such people. People should be given an opportunity to hold on, to continue on the same track, to keep the lives they already have.[23]

Here, Gardner appears to contend that the government would (at least prima facie) be wronging people who have lived in a particular public housing unit if it forced them to move into smaller apartment just because their family has diminished in size. Gardner recognizes that in terms of overall social welfare, such a forced move might be justifiable. But he is taken by the idea that it requires some people to suffer a large hit. Within his framework, this is plausible. Yet one wants to know what this would mean for efforts by the state to engage in broad redistribution efforts. Placing significant weight on individuals' sense that they are entitled to keep their lives on existing tracks would seem to set a substantial constraint—one itself rooted in what Gardner claims to be a form of distributive justice—on distributive justice in the sense more typically invoked in discussions of how wealth and opportunities are appropriately allocated within a society.

4. Why We Don't Sign On

The version of corrective justice theory we have teased out of Gardner's reflections on the importance of the way things used to be strikes us as appealing at many levels. Its potential capacity to make sense of private law and to unify its different parts (particularly contract and tort) is impressive. It is also in several respects appealingly modest. From a moral-metaphysical point of view, its rootedness in an interest theory of rights is down to earth. Its conception of a good life is plausibly non-committal on whether it is objectivistic, subjectivistic, or some combination thereof. It also commendably avoids linking its theory of justice to the notion of a life well-lived as a bravura performance (a prominent theme in Dworkin's later work),[24] and it seems similarly untethered to the Rawlsian effort to locate a conception of justice fit for persons with

---

[23] ibid 167.
[24] See JCP Goldberg, "Liberal Responsibility: A Comment on 'Justice for Hedgehogs'" (2010) 90 Boston University Law Review 677.

CORRECTIVE JUSTICE AND THE RIGHT TO HOLD ON TO WHAT ONE HAS   357

irreconcilable conceptions of the good. These are not advantages *per se*, but we think them quite suitable as ways to think about justice in connection with private law. Additionally, Gardner's account invites nuanced consideration of the relationship of corrective and distributive justice.

Above all, Gardner is refreshingly candid about what must be acknowledged as a deeply conservative aspect of private law. The value of being able to remain roughly on track in one's life is surely one that resonates in ordinary thinking about value. One may question whether it can or should be embraced as a matter of critical or aspirational morality. But its pervasiveness in Anglo-American political culture and its entrenchment within Anglo-American private law are undeniably important facts that legal scholars are not always keen to acknowledge. Gardner's linkage of private law and corrective justice to the importance to individuals of having their lives stay on course generates an interpretive theory that is at once powerful and challenging.

All the more pressing, then, is the question of why we continue to reject corrective justice theory, even in the version put forth with such wit, insight, and eloquence by Gardner. Having labored for many years to distinguish ourselves from corrective justice theorists, we probably could produce a laundry list of answers at legal, moral, and jurisprudential levels. For now we want to focus on two interconnected reasons, both pertaining to the sense in which tort law is about legal rights and duties.

Some of our concerns can be captured by focusing on the distinction, discussed above, between two levels at which the interests undergirding tort claims might be described: on the one hand, the interest in being free of particular interferences or setbacks—such as wrongfully inflicted bodily harm, reputational damage, loss of privacy, or the like—and, on the other hand, the more general interest in stability and continuity in one's possessions, well-being, and future path. According to our reconstruction, Gardner's corrective justice theory of torts hinges on grasping how the former, further-specified interests and the latter, broader interests can be understood as components of a single underlying right. This is what explains why the duty to refrain from tortiously injuring another and the duty to provide compensation (if one does not so refrain) are connected. Some of our resistance to corrective justice theory turns precisely on wanting to disaggregate what Gardner and other corrective justice theorists aim to bundle together within the concept of a right, and, relatedly, on our rejection of the claimed connection between duties of conduct and duties of compensation.

Consider the rights not to have one's personal medical information splashed all over the internet without consent, not to have one's legs crushed in a negligently caused car accident, not to spend time in a jail cell because of a bogus charge of criminal wrongdoing, and not to have one's face disfigured by an over-the-counter pharmaceutical product sold without an adequate warning as to the risk of such injury. Violations of each of these rights all involve what might be called "interferences with interests" or "setbacks." And perhaps that is what is meant in some sense by calling them "rights invasions." On our account, however, it is critical to understand that each of these rights invasions in and of itself—without (in the first instance) any further account of the nature of the interests or reasons underlying the right—involves a mistreatment of one person by another. Each involves the breach of a relational duty of conduct owed to the victim not to injure the victim. To say the same thing, there is something importantly *self-contained* about the content of the various torts. A claim for invasion of privacy, negligence, false imprisonment, or products liability alleges the violation of a right against being subjected to a certain kind of injury as a result of wrongful or sub-standard conduct by another: the right against having one's private information broadcast to the world, against being negligently physically injured, against being unjustifiably imprisoned, and against being injured by a defective product. What generates liability in these cases is the fact that someone (the plaintiff) suffered a legally recognized form of mistreatment at the hands of another. The rights invasion is the wrong.

We don't deny, of course, that torts, and tort compensation, bear some connection to the more abstract interests of the sort that Gardner identifies. The question is how best to characterize the nature of the connection. Tort law, by empowering individuals to hold wrongful injurers accountable and to obtain compensation for their injuries, surely does enable some victims to get their lives back on track. And the knowledge that tort law is in principle available when we are wrongfully injured provides some degree of assurance that our lives will carry on as they have been, if we so choose. Furthermore, the knowledge of would-be defendants that liability will follow upon their mistreatments of others probably diminishes the likelihood that any of us will be knocked off course. In these sense, we agree with Gardner that tort law connects to security.

Still, we think more is gained than lost by insisting on these (several) freedoms from wrongfully inflicted injuries as special kinds of rights, on their own, rather than merging them with the broader, meta-right to security. We also think more is learned from keeping separate the security provided by a legal system with rights of action, ostensibly providing more reliable expectations for all. To put the point more tendentiously, while we are open to the possibility that the kind of merger of interests Gardner posits may indeed capture certain instantiations of the language of rights as it is used in private law, we think the merger model, applied to tort, tends to render more obscure the constituent normative phenomena (and the relationships among them) rather than illuminating them.

Gardner stresses the connection between private law and personal life in part to emphasize that the duties of private law are outgrowths of what might be called "natural" duties (for Gardner, ways of acting that are obligatory in light of reasons that apply to us as moral agents). We likewise view the primary duties of tort law as, in important respects, outgrowths of (putative) natural duties and the rights to which they are correlative as outgrowths of (putative) natural rights. Unsurprisingly, judges and legislatures, faced with the demands of claimants seeking remedies for perceived wrongs have, recognized as legal wrongs the violation of familiar moral duties and rights. Typically, these are negative rights against being injured in certain ways by others. They are also typically rights correlative to duties born by other persons, not duties of the state (although individuals acting in their official capacities are often subject to some of them). And they are rights whose violation can be described as temporally located.

Where we part ways, again, is in our description of what is or is *not* contained in these rights and duties. On our account, the natural duties to avoid or refrain from injuring, and the correlative rights against being so injured, as well as their legal counterparts, are self-contained. Under the rules of tort law, a breach of duty and rights violation involves an injurer who fails to comply with a legal rule or standard that directs her to refrain from injuring another in a particular manner. In tort law, rights violations are actions performed at a time or times. If D interferes with P's right at time t then nothing D (or anyone) does at time $t + 1$ can make it the case that D did not interfere with P's right. By the same token, a court need not determine whether the victim of a tort, such as an unlawful touching, has suffered a setback to her life's path or prospects in order to determine that a tort has occurred. The legal right in question, even if grounded in reasons of an enduring kind, is defined such that its violation is complete when the relevant sort of injury (in battery, the relevant kind of touching) occurs.

As explained above, the security and stability one has (in, say, one's possessions of one's legs), in a legal system that recognizes duties of repair as described by Gardner, can also be conceived of as a right, and indeed the kind of right enforced by tort law and constitutive of a system of corrective justice. Yet this is a different idea in a number of the respects described above. It is fundamentally *not* fairly interpreted as an outgrowth of a natural right (or a right correlative to a natural duty); it is fundamentally post-political, and does not even make sense except as against the backdrop of legal system. It is not merely a negative right, on this account; it is a right to be provided with correction, rectification, and compensation. And, while Gardner regards this as a right, in corrective justice, correlative to the wrongdoer's duty of repair, we regard it as a right against the state to hold the defendant accountable to the plaintiff—a right correlative to a duty in the state and simultaneously correlative to a liability in the wrongdoer. Finally, the integrated right is not temporally located in the same sense. Indeed, its whole point is to stretch out over time. Accordingly, because the interest served by the remedy is ongoing, it is misleading to see the remedy and the invasion as unified in a concept of one right.[25] There is of course in tort law a connection between right and remedy, but it is not a conceptual connection. It is a normative, political-philosophical connection. For wrongs that amount to mistreatments of a certain sort, the state provides the tort victim with the ability to demand and, upon proof of claim, to obtain a remedy from the wrongdoer.

One of the advantages of retaining clarity on the distinctions above is that doing so fosters an open-minded attitude toward whether, from a critical and constructive point of view, different legal institutions might be better suited to dealing with set of interests or constituent rights than others. Like some economists, we are open to the possibility that insurance and state compensation funds may well be superior to the common law of torts in supporting the interests in stability and getting back into one's groove—a point obscured by the unification of the interests into a right correlative to a singular duty. Conversely, we tend to think that the judiciary is ordinarily the best-suited institution to articulate the duties of conduct and rights against mistreatment that form the core of the common law of torts.

---

[25] At this stage in the discussion, we are explaining why we do not sign on to the account we have *constructed* out of themes in Chapter 5 (and beyond)—the view criticized in this paragraph and those following it is a projection onto Gardner that he might not have accepted.

Finally, a word about distributive justice. We are inclined to agree with Gardner's astute observation that a well-designed system of private law, by protecting and vindicating rights, can provide a bulwark against certain forms of distributive injustice. Yet we think it undesirable to express this idea by characterizing private law as law that "distributes" security rights or the ability to obtain compensation for their violation. To be sure, the legal recognition of rights against wrongful injury and the imposition of liability that sometimes comes with violations of these rights do provide some reassurance and security to individuals. If tort law is properly characterized as distributing something, however, it is distributing legal powers rather than legal rights and duties. Indeed, the feature of tort law that perhaps most effectively enables it to serve, at times, as a counterweight to maldistributions of wealth and power is its conferral of private rights of action—the power enjoyed by victims to press claims without official authorization, to obtain through discovery information that defendants would prefer to have kept hidden from view, and to settle them on terms they deem satisfactory.

5. Conclusion

A justly influential tradition in British moral, political, and legal philosophy combines elegant analysis and plain-speaking candor with a focus on human well-being. Like the writings of H.L.A. Hart, whose Oxford Chair he occupied for many years, Gardner's work exemplifies these virtues. Those who study private law are fortunate that a scholar originally gripped by criminal law turned his attention in our direction before his untimely death. While not a utilitarian, Gardner shared the instinct to ask always why law really matters to people, an approach very much on display in his meditations on the place of compensation, repair, and restoration in the law of tort and contract. In the end, one of his most fundamental points is simple yet deep: we care about what has been taken from us—and private law attends to this concern—because humans have good reason to be attached to what we have. As explained above, we are inclined to think this analysis serves more as an invitation to adopt a wrongs-and-recourse conception of private law than as the defense of corrective justice theory it was meant to provide. Under either approach, however, the evident humanity of Gardner's analysis enriches our understanding of the basic principles of private law.

Name Index

For the benefit of digital users, indexed terms that span two pages (e.g., 52–53) may, on occasion, appear on only one of those pages.

Adams, T. 78n.16
Alexander, L. 23n.26
Alexy, R. 43n.4
Altham, J. E. J. 86n.56
Anscombe, E. 44n.8, 49n.27
Aristotle 47n.19, 90–91, 102, 331, 344
Arvind, T. T. 281n.3, 286n.27
Atiyah, P. 184, 196
Atkin, Lord 69–70, 283n.11, 297, 299, 301, 303, 307, 308
Austin, J. 22, 23
Austin, L. M. 26–20nn.44–5, 81n.32, 331n.7

Bagnoli, C. 203n.1
Bagshaw, R. 266n.38, 266n.40, 270n.57, 275n.76
Baker, T. 343n.62
Bant, E. 123n.4, 134n.28, 137n.35, 137n.36
Barker, K. 245n.39, 294n.59
Barnes, J. 331n.7
Barshim, M. E. 98n.61
Baumann, P. 8n.22, 28n.56, 163n.10, 206n.12
Bayles, M. E. 86n.58
Beatson, J. 102n.87
Beever, A. 87n.63
Beitz, C. R. 322n.57
Benbaji, Y. 130n.16, 130n.17
Ben-Shahar, O. 179n.7
Benson, P. 316, 317, 317n.36, 319, 319n.46, 320, 320n.49, 322n.56, 323
Bentham, J. 260, 261n.8, 265–66
Bernstein, A. 332n.18
Betzler, M. 8n.22, 28n.56, 163n.10, 206n.12
Bingham, T. 77n.6
Birks, P. 102n.87
Bishop, W. 102n.87
Bittner, R. 205n.7
Blackstone, W. 224–25
Boonzaier, L. 2–3, 13–14
Bradley, F. H. 51
Brownlee, K. 59n.1, 64
Bulstrode, N. 151–52

Caesar, J. 61, 70
Calabresi, G. 11n.34, 148n.8, 263n.24, 350–51

Calhoun, C. 219n.70
Campbell, J. K. 19n.1
Campbell, R. 22n.17
Cane, P. 24n.36, 72n.28, 76n.2, 294n.58
Cardozo, B. 169, 301–3, 304, 306n.26, 343, 346n.78
Chapman, B. 86n.58, 87n.63
Chaskalson, A. 81
Closson, T. 255n.67
Coleman, J. L. 30n.66, 81n.32, 216n.64, 232n.36
Collins, H. 1n.1, 311n.5, 325n.69, 326n.71
Colton, J. 132n.21
Conaglen, M. 132–33, 136–37
Copp, D. 80, 81
Cornell, N. 146n.2
Crisp, R. 47n.21
Crosby, J. F. 341n.53
Cutts, T. 5, 103n.91, 104n.93

Dagan, H. 14, 130n.16, 262n.21, 318n.41, 319n.46, 321n.51, 322n.56, 322n.58, 323n.61, 324–11nn.63–4, 324n.65, 325n.68, 325n.70, 327n.73, 327n.74, 328n.76, 328–11nn.81–2, 329n.84
Dan-Cohen, M. 85n.54
Darley, J. 345n.73
Darwall, J. 21n.15
Darwall, S. 21n.15, 80n.25, 174–75
Dawson, W. H. 67
Deakin, S. 343n.67, 346n.75
DeMott, D. A. 343n.64, 344n.68
Dempsey, M. 72–73, 73n.29, 74n.33, 285n.19
Denis, L. 90n.78
Dickinson, E. 63
Dorfman, A. 318n.41, 323n.61, 327n.73, 329n.84
Doyle, A. 292n.54
Duff, A. 1n.1, 285n.19
Duff, R. A. 35n.94, 36n.101, 60n.2, 145n.1, 242n.25
Dworkin, R. 43, 77n.5, 356–57
Dyson, A. 22n.23, 260n.6, 266n.38, 290n.44

Edelman, J. 132n.21
Edwards, J. 1n.1

362 NAME INDEX

Eekelaar, J. 186n.15
Eliot, G. 151–52, 152n.17
Endicott, T. 81n.32, 85n.55
Enoch, D. 61n.4
Ericson, R. 292n.54
Eskridge, W. Jr. 252n.62
Essert, C. 13–14

Fabre, C. 7–8, 146n.2
Feinberg, J. 99n.72
Finnis, J. 50n.32, 77n.7, 78, 81n.36
Fitzgibbon, S. 346n.78
Fletcher, G. P. 339n.47, 355
Fox-Decent, E. 341n.57
Frickey, P. P. 252n.62
Fried, C. 179n.7, 322, 327–28
Fuller, L. L. 77, 78–80

Galoob, S. 71n.24
Gans, C. 179, 194n.20
Gasdaglis, K. 221
Geach, P. 50
Geistfeld, M. A. 322n.55
George, R. 94n.25
Georgiou, A. 150n.14, 153n.22
Getzler, J. 71n.24, 246n.44
Goetz, C. J. 321n.50, 321n.52
Goffman, E. 342n.59
Gold, A. 15, 71n.25, 149n.12, 153n.19, 239–
40n.3, 256–57n.71, 262n.21, 328n.82,
331nn.6–7, 334n.25, 335n.29, 336n.36,
339n.47, 340n.49, 341n.56, 341n.57,
342n.61, 344n.69, 345–30nn.71–1,
346n.79, 346n.80
Goldberg, J. 13n.42, 15–16, 20nn.5–6, 22n.20,
23n.29, 28n.57, 145n.1, 148n.8, 149n.11,
155n.26, 161, 164, 164n.13, 165, 166,
167–68, 171–73, 174–75, 214n.58, 223n.3,
239–40n.3, 250n.59, 256n.68, 262n.19,
264n.28, 273n.68, 299n.5, 304n.19,
351n.18, 356n.24
Gordon, R. W. 328n.79
Gormally, M. 50
Goudkamp, J. 22n.23, 266n.38, 283n.11,
286n.24
Green, L. 99
Gregor, M. P. 90n.78

Hacker, P. M. S. 20n.11, 260n.7, 266n.38
Halliday, S. 292n.53
Hamowy, R. 87n.60
Harrison, R. 86n.56
Hart, H. L. A. 39, 44, 77n.5, 77n.7, 78n.11,
89n.73, 245n.42, 252n.62, 260–63, 265–66,
271, 323

Haskell, J. E. 321n.53
Havel, V. 48–49
Hayek, F. 86–87
Hegel, G. W. F. 312
Heimer, C. 292n.54
Heller, M. 319n.46, 324, 324n.65, 325n.68,
327n.74, 328n.76, 328n.81
Henry IV, king of France 57
Herman, B. 213n.54, 220
Hershovitz, S. 20n.6, 43n.3, 125–26n.8
Herstein, O. J. 3–4, 26n.46, 70n.23, 204n.5,
249n.54
Heuer, U. 64, 73, 203n.1, 211n.36
Himma, K. E. 232n.36
Hobbes, T. 78n.14
Hodge, Lord 131n.19
Hoffmann, Lord 40n.114
Hohfeld, W. N. 151n.16, 223n.3, 230, 245–46,
261n.11, 265
Holmes, O. W. 19–20, 22, 27,
121n.28, 288n.33
Holmes, O. W. Jr. 87n.62, 121n.28
Honoré, T. 89n.74, 287n.31
Hooker, B. 47n.21
Hornsby, J. 65–66
Howard, J. W. 151n.15
Hugo, V. 152
Hume, D. 94

Ilan, J. 292n.53
Irwin, T. 47n.22

Jaffey, P. 23n.27, 24n.33
Jordan, M. 66

Kamm, F. 128n.14
Kant, I. 21n.16, 23, 24–25, 26–27, 44–45, 53,
57, 90–91, 106–10, 112–13, 116, 117, 118,
119–20, 123n.1, 130, 213, 218–21, 225n.7,
230n.23, 312, 355–56
Katz, L. 11–12, 65n.12, 245–40nn.41–3,
254n.64, 257n.74
Keating, G. 355
Keller, S. 155–339, 337n.39, 337n.41,
341n.54
Kelly, E. I. 119n.23
Kent, A. 338n.43
Keown, J. 94n.25
Kimel, D. 9, 189n.16
Kioussopoulou, L. 93n.13
Kirste, S. 1n.1
Klass, G. 178n.3, 322n.54, 341n.56
Klimchuk, D. 26–20nn.44–5, 81n.32, 331n.7,
332n.12
Kolodny, N. 141n.45

NAME INDEX   363

Kramer, M. H. 77n.9, 78n.17, 86n.59, 87n.63,
    260n.6, 269–70n.54
Kraus, J. S. 323n.59
Kreitner, R. 321n.53, 325n.70
Kumar, R. 147n.5

Ladislaw, W. 151–52
Landman, J. 203n.1
Lang, G. 203n.1, 211n.36
Langille, B. 320n.49
Leib, E. 71n.24, 338n.43
Lemmon, E. J. 88n.67
Lennon, J. 65n.11
Letsas, G. 178n.3
Locke, J. 135n.30, 340
Lunney, M. 286n.24

MacCormick, N. 9n.23, 207, 233, 266n.38, 287,
    288, 350
MacIntyre, A. 46, 47, 52n.39
Macklem, T. 30n.66, 32n.73, 34n.81, 35n.88,
    35n.90, 35–19nn.92–3, 172n.37, 216,
    232n.36, 233n.37, 306n.26
Macneil, I. 314–15, 321–22
Maine, H. 311
Malcolm, N. 78n.14
Markesinis, B. 328n.78
Markovits, D. 338n.44, 342n.61
Marmor, A. 81n.32, 85n.55
Marshall, R. 54n.46
Marx, K. 315
Mattei, U. 321n.53
McBride, N. J. 2, 13–14, 22, 23–24, 28n.57,
    33, 34, 40n.112, 47n.20, 50n.35, 52n.39,
    90n.75, 104, 138n.40, 260n.7, 266n.38,
    266n.40, 266n.41, 270n.57, 275n.76
MacCormick, N. 178–79, 180, 182–83, 184,
    185–86, 190, 192–93, 195, 198–99, 200,
    202, 260n.7
McIlroy, D. 58n.61
McInnes, M. 102n.87
McKenna, M. 80n.26
Melamed, D. 11n.34, 263n.24, 350–51
Merkin, R. 293
Michelon, C. 10–11
Mill, J. S. 45
Miller, P. B. 27n.54, 71n.25, 87n.63, 120n.26,
    145n.1, 146n.2, 152n.18, 161n.2, 169n.28,
    204n.5, 205n.9, 250n.59, 257n.74, 328n.82,
    332n.12, 335n.29, 336n.36, 337n.38,
    339n.47, 341–31nn.55–6, 342n.61,
    344n.69, 345n.71, 346n.79
Montaigne, M. de 57
Moore, A. de 186n.15
Moore, M. 23n.26

Moore, M. S. 81n.33
Murphy, L. 27, 40–41
Murray, J. 22n.17

Nagel, T. 3n.7, 87–88, 88n.65, 285n.22
Nesbit, E. 261n.12
Neyers, J. 102n.87
Norcliffe-Brown, D. 98n.59
Nussbaum, M. 52n.38, 90–91

Oberdiek, J. 8–9, 27n.54, 87n.63, 97n.58,
    120n.26, 145n.1, 146n.2, 147n.5, 152n.18,
    161n.2, 168n.26, 169n.28, 204n.5, 205n.9,
    250n.59, 257n.74, 264n.28, 273n.68,
    283n.12
O'Neill, O. 220, 221n.80
O'Rourke, M. 19n.1, 293n.55
Owens, D. 3n.6, 342n.59, 342n.61

Parfit, D. 57n.59, 73, 269n.51
Penner, J. 90n.75, 137n.35, 260n.6, 269n.53
Perry, A. 223n.2, 304n.20
Pike, J. 124n.5
Pistor, K. 284n.17, 289n.41, 291–92, 291n.49,
    295n.60
Porat, A. 179n.7
Posner, R. 148n.8
Priel, D. 109n.9
Psarras, H. 12

Radzik, L. 145n.1, 147n.4, 147n.5, 264n.28
Ramakrishnan, K. H. 138n.38, 138n.39
Rawls, J. 78, 80, 86–87, 94n.22, 95–96,
    97, 103n.90, 119n.23, 120n.24,
    287n.29, 355–57
Raz, J. 2–3, 8n.22, 20–22, 23n.24, 23n.26,
    24–25, 26–27, 28n.56, 29n.64, 34n.87,
    38, 40n.115, 43, 49, 77n.7, 80n.25, 81,
    81n.36, 86, 101n.78, 151n.16, 163–64, 166,
    168, 168n.27, 169–70, 172, 172–73n.41,
    175n.50, 177n.1, 194n.20, 206, 207n.16,
    211, 211n.40, 214, 235–23nn.43–4, 260n.7,
    266n.38, 306n.26, 337n.37, 353, 355
Reich, C. 292
Reinach, A. 341n.53
Renzo, M. 155n.25
Rickett, C. E. F. 213n.51
Ripstein, A. 10–11, 14n.49, 15–16, 20n.6, 107,
    107–8nn.5–7, 148n.7, 161n.1, 164n.13,
    173–74, 205n.10, 213, 213–4nn.55–6,
    223n.3, 226n.14, 227–28, 229, 230n.24,
    241n.12, 250n.59, 266n.39, 266n.41,
    272n.64, 275n.74, 305n.23, 317n.35, 318,
    319–20, 320n.49, 322n.56, 323, 328n.80,
    329n.84, 350, 354–56

364 NAME INDEX

Robertson, A. 289n.40
Robinson, P. 345n.73
Rolph, D. 134n.28
Rorty, A. O. 203n.2, 210

Sacks, A. M. 252n.62
Samet, I. 132–33, 136–37, 332n.12, 339n.47
Sander, D. 203n.1
Saprai, P. 178n.3, 324n.63
Saunders, A. 65n.11
Sayre-McCord, G. 89n.69, 90n.80
Scanlon, T. M. 57n.59, 93n.13, 93n.14, 94n.17, 95n.41, 101n.79, 140n.42, 141n.44, 334n.25, 340
Scheffler, S. 304
Scherer, K. R. 203n.1
Schopenhauer, A. 44–45
Scott, C. 292n.53
Scott, E. S. 328n.82
Scott, R. E. 321n.50, 321n.52
Selznick, P. 281–82, 281n.1
Sérafin, S. 316n.31
Shakespeare, W. 337
Shapiro, M. A. 11–12, 216n.64, 232n.36, 241n.16, 254n.66
Sharkey, C. 137n.36
Sheinman, H. 338n.44
Shier, D. 19n.1, 293n.55
Shiffrin, S. V. 84n.52, 306n.26, 345n.71
Shugerman, J. H. 338n.43
Shute, S. 53–55, 65n.14
Simester, A. 24n.34, 24n.38
Simmonds, N. E. 260n.6
Simpson, A. W. B. 260n.2
Sinel, Z. 9–10, 32n.74, 37, 150n.14, 204n.6, 210n.33, 264n.28
Sitkoff, R. H. 346n.79
Skorupski, J. 43n.4
Slavny, A. 87n.63, 149n.11, 150n.13, 152n.18, 155n.27
Smith, A. T. H. 24n.38
Smith, D. G. 71n.25, 336n.36
Smith, G. 339n.47
Smith, H. E. 332n.12, 344, 346n.79, 346n.80
Smith, L. 71n.24, 132n.20, 133n.24, 245n.42, 246–40nn.44–5, 252n.61
Smith, S. A. 11n.35, 22, 23n.27, 24n.33, 26–20nn.44–5, 28n.57, 76n.3, 81n.32, 102n.87, 126n.9, 133n.26, 138n.37, 146n.2, 161, 164, 165, 168, 175–76, 214n.58, 262n.18, 264n.28, 271n.60, 273–61nn.67–8, 274n.70, 335–37, 338, 342
Soames, S. 85n.55
Sobel, D. 122n.29, 141n.45

Solanke, I. 35n.89, 246n.46
Somech, O. 321n.51
Sorensen, R. 88n.66
Sreenivasan, G. 149n.11, 267n.44
Srinivasan, A. 88n.66, 88n.68
Steel, S. 28n.59, 126n.9, 135n.30, 141n.46, 146n.2, 150n.13, 151n.15, 157n.29, 161n.1, 171n.35, 208, 217n.65, 223n.4, 230–31, 264n.28, 265n.30, 272n.63, 274n.69, 276n.80, 351n.19
Steele, J. 13, 281n.3, 286n.24, 286n.27, 289n.40, 290n.44, 293n.55, 294n.59
Steiner, J. 87n.63, 260n.6
Stern, R. 90n.76
Stevens, R. 126n.9, 260n.6, 265n.30, 266–61nn.38–9, 269n.53, 274n.69
Stone, R. 5–6, 115n.21, 116n.22, 119n.23, 120n.26, 122n.29
Strawson, P. F. 214n.59
Styron, W. 56–57
Sumner, W. 47

Tadros, V. 140, 141n.44, 145n.1, 148n.8, 161, 164–65, 167–68, 169n.32, 170–71, 205n.9, 214n.58
Tamberi, G. 98n.61
Tasioulas, J. 19n.4, 306n.27
Taylor, C. 46n.16, 52n.38, 52n.39
Taylor, G. 337n.40
Thagard, P. R. 229n.18
Thoburn, M. 246n.44
Thompson, J. 147n.4
Thomson, J. J. 31nn.69–70, 88n.67
Timmermann, J. 90n.78, 213n.54, 219–20, 220n.77, 220n.79
Toulmin, S. 57
Tsuruda, S. 326

Valjean, J. 152
Vallentyne, P. 122n.29, 141n.45
Varuhas, J. 132n.21
Virgo, G. 289n.40
Voyiakis, E. 36n.99, 93n.12, 104n.95, 105
Vranas, P. 82n.39, 225n.8, 226–27, 229n.19

Wachter, M. 343n.65
Waldron, J. 3n.6, 77n.6, 80n.21, 84n.53, 99, 337n.38
Walker, M. 147n.5
Wallace, R. J. 45–46, 169, 174–75, 203n.1
Webb, C. 161, 164n.13, 165–66, 168
Weil, S. 46–47

NAME INDEX · 365

Weinrib, E. 5, 6, 10–11, 15–16, 19n.3, 23–24, 28n.58, 107, 107n.6, 108n.8, 136, 148n.7, 161n.1, 213, 213n.55, 218–19, 223n.3, 224–25, 225n.7, 226–30, 231, 234n.40, 234n.41, 241n.12, 262n.16, 305, 351–53, 354–55

Wenar, L. 101n.79, 147n.4

Widerker, D. 80n.26

Williams, B. 15–16, 45, 48, 49, 51, 52n.39, 80n.25, 86, 88n.67, 90–91, 90n.77, 203n.3, 210, 211–12, 212n.48, 219n.70, 285n.22, 349

Wilmot-Smith, F. 4, 22n.23, 102n.86, 102n.88, 152n.18, 266n.38

Wolf, S. 219n.70

Wootton, D. 340n.50

Worthington, S. 289n.40

Zalta, E. N. 23n.26, 84n.53

Zeelenberg, M. 203n.1

Zipursky, B. C. 13n.42, 15–16, 20nn.5–6, 22n.20, 28n.57, 148n.8, 161, 164–65, 166, 167–68, 171–73, 174–75, 214n.58, 223n.3, 225n.7, 239–40n.3, 250n.59, 256n.68, 262n.19, 264n.28, 273n.68, 299n.5, 304n.19, 324n.64, 351n.18, 354n.21

Subject Index

For the benefit of digital users, indexed terms that span two pages (e.g., 52–53) may, on occasion, appear on only one of those pages.

abuse of power 245n.42, 247–49
abuse of right 247–48, 254n.64
accidents 9, 62, 121n.28, 267, 301–2, 305–6, 310, 357–58
account of profits 132–33
allocation 93–95
arithmetic models 97, 102
aspirational values 64
autonomy-based theory of contract 325, 328n.76

bargaining process 322, 327
breach of contract 11, 84n.50, 96–97, 131, 179, 188, 202, 311–12, 315, 316, 317, 318–19, 324, *see also* contract
    tort, as a 313
breach of duty 19, 22, 38n.108, 39, 40, 54, 166, 224, 262n.18, 268, 293n.56, 299, 301–2, 358–59

care, duty of 301–4
causative events 229–30, 231–32
choice 285–87, *see also* politics
civil procedure doctrine 249n.54, 253–54
civil recourse 15–16, 148n.8, 313, 322n.56
    definition 240n.8
    principle of 256n.68, 262n.19
compensation, principle of 218
competition 97–100
conscription model *see* public authority conscription model
consequentialism 7, 123
contextualism 182, 282
continuity thesis 161–76
    claims 168–76
    corrective justice 351–55
    criticism 164–68
    definition 161
    derivative role of 206–9
    presuppositions 162–64
    reasons 168–76
    regret 206–9
    relationality 168–76
    wrongs 206–9

contract *see also* breach of contract
    central principles of contract law 84
    contractual relations, model of 14
    contractual rights as security rights 315–16
    degrading contractualizations 313–14
    Gardner's approach to 312–19, 324–28
    indigenous limit and floor 325–27
    intertemporal dimension of 320–22
    liberal 324–28
    liberal promise of 311–29
    liberalism and private law 329
    remedies 324–25
    self-determination 322–23
    special relationships 327–28
    This for That model 314–15
    transfer theory 316–20
    types 327–28
contributory negligence 97
conversion 282n.6, 317, 353–54
'core' of tort cases 39–41
correction 102–4
corrective justice *see also* justice
    agents 348–51
    continuity thesis 351–55
    distributive justice and 106–22
    distributive justice compared 119–22
    duties 348–51
    Gardner's scheme 109–12
    intermediate conception 113–15
    Kantian 107–9
    Kantian and Gardnerian conceptions compared 112–13
    liberalism 355–56
    patients 348–51
    principle of 8, 357
    procedural justice 116–19
    rights and 348–60
    substantive justice 116–19
    theoretical approaches 356–60
    value theory 351–55
criminal law 25n.40, 61, 67
    criminal offences, definitions of 83
    enforcement 251–52
    philosophy of 1

368 SUBJECT INDEX

criminal law (*cont.*)
  prohibition 125–26n.8
  public wrongs 211
  punitive responses 127–28
  reasonable person standard 333–34, 345n.73
  rights and 268
  strict liability offences 190–91
  theory 24, 285
  waivability 260–61, 262–63

damages *see* reparative damages
declarations 67, 133–34, 261
defamation 246n.47, 248n.50
desirability *see also* voluntary obligations/
    promises
  independent 184–85
  triggered 185–86
deterrence 123–42
  bipolarity 136–37
  considerations as reasons which make a
    difference 128–34
  constraint-based objections, defeat
    of 139–41
  constraints, applicability to private law
    questions 138–39
  deontological constraints 138–41
  duties to bear deterrent burdens 140–41
  fiduciary liabilities to account for
    profits 132–33
  moral indeterminacy 130–31
  necessity of 125–27
  notion of 133n.24
  objections to 136–41
  opportunities to avoid harm,
    significance of 141
  opting in to 131–33
  overdeterrence 134–35
  scarcity 129–30
  specific deterrence orders and
    liability 133–34
  sufficiency of 127–28
  voluntary creation of rights 131–32
distribution 287–88, *see also* politics
distributive justice
  corrective justice and 106–22
  corrective justice compared 119–22
  principle of 108–9
duress 327, 333–34
duties *see also* obligations
  care, of 301–4
  concept of 47, 48
  continuity thesis 232–38
  corrective justice 348–51
  definitions 19–22, 218–19, 261

moral *see* moral duties
  notion of 45, 48, 76
  to oneself 48
  primary and reparative, independence
    of 37–38
  private law 1–3
  reasons and 232–38
  relational 297–301
  remedial 229–32

economics 148n.8, 281–82, 281n.2, *see also* law
    and economics movement
efficiency 67–68, 148n.8, 285n.23
emotion theory 221
entitlement to reparation 262n.16
epistemic loss and gain 52–57
equality
  equal freedom, principle of 350
  formal principle of 14
  of relations *see* neighbour principle
equity 12–13, 15, 257–58, 265, 331–32, 344, 345
exclusion of liability 276
excuses 23, 55–56, 187, 196, 333–34
exemplary/punitive damages 127, 137, 221
existentialism 349
expectation interest 316, 317

fairness
  asymmetries 87–89
  models of 95–96
  morality and unfairness 88–89
  "ought implies can" 81
  unfairness and law 89
fault
  variations in 189–95
  wrongs and 22–27
fiduciary law, theory of 344
fiduciary liability 132–33
fiduciary loyalty 335–39, *see also* "reasonably
    loyal" person
  genuine loyalty and 335–36
  law-independent counterparts 340–43
  meaningful relationships 336–39
foreseeability 13–14, 70, 299, 301–2, 305–6
formalism 182

geometric models 97, 102

harm
  avoidance of *see* deterrence
  prevention of 186

incentives 124, 136–37
incorporationism 345–46

independence, principle of 107–8
individuation according to actions, principle
    of 214–15, 228–29
injunctions 133, 273, 317–18, 323
instrumentalism 6–7
insurance 41, 104n.94, 292, 296, 359
interest theory of rights 151, 172–73, 269n.50,
    355, 356–57
"invisible hand" mechanism 246n.45

justice
    allocation 93–95
    competition 97–100
    concept of 5, 110
    correction 102–4
    corrective *see* **corrective justice**
    distributive *see* **distributive justice**
    fundamental principles of 109
    Gardner's theory of 92–94, 95, 101, 356–57
    method 100–1
    moral duties 49–50
    private law 5–6
    procedural 116–19
    questions of 92–93, 104–5
    reparative *see* **reparative justice**
    scope 95–97
    substantive 116–19
    Theory of Justice (Rawls) 95–96
justifications 1–7

law
    concept of 44–45
    mirror of morality, as the 43–44
    moral duties and 51–52
    theory of 76
    try, obligation to 60–63
law and economics
    movement 281, 281n.2
legality *see also* **"ought implies can" (OC)**
    Gardner's account of 83
liberalism 70
    contract law 311–29
    corrective justice 355–56
    private law and 329
liberty 3–4, 61, 95, 269–70
    rights 261n.8
loyalty *see also* **fiduciary loyalty; "reasonably
    loyal" persons**
    concept of 336, 339

merger model 358
metaphysics of duty 225n.8, 226, 229, 238
mirror thesis 52, 53, 58
    moral duties 43–46, 58

misfeasance 108, 323
mistake 102, 104, 313, 327
mitigation 65–66, 97
moral agency 250–51
moral duties *see also* **morality**
    concept of 45, 48, 51
    duties to oneself 48
    epistemic loss and gain 52–57
    evil 48–49
    justice 49–50
    law 51–52
    law as the mirror of
        morality 43–44
    legal duties and 44, 45
    mirror thesis 44–46, 58
    notion of 2, 45
    place for 48–52
    rape, wrongfulness of 53–55
    reliability 51
    Sophie's choice 55–56
    vice 48–49
moral indeterminacy 130–31, *see also*
    deterrence
moral liability 128
moral obligation 9–10, 45–46, 48, 51, 76–77,
    109, 135, 141, 177, 184n.12, 185, 186, 193–
    94, 340
    notion of 44n.8
moralism 36, 41, 292, 294
morality 46–47, *see also* **moral duties**
    unfairness and 88–89

negligence standard 13, 40–41, 282–83
    political nature of 285–87
    principle of negligence 69–70
neighbour principle 297–310
    doing things as equals 309–10
    duty of care as a liability-limiting
        principle 301–4
    line-drawing, value of 304–6
    relational duties 297–301
    relating as equals 307–9
    relating as neighbours 307–9

obligations *see also* **duties; primary
    obligations; secondary obligations;
    voluntary obligations/promises**
    definition of 218–20
    notion of 45
officials 11–12, 61, 64, 65–66, 123, 146, 159,
    240–41, 251–53, 255–56, 257–58
    plaintiffs as quasi-officials 244,
        246–48
opportunism 330, 334, 335n.28, 344–45

370 SUBJECT INDEX

"ought implies can" (OC) 76–83, *see also*
  legality
  agents to guide 84–86
  asymmetries 84–89
  diagnosis 90–91
  fairness 81, 87–89
  Gardner's accounts of 82–83
  group members 86–87
  guidance 80–81, 84–87
  legality compared 76–81
  morality 88–89
  orthodox account 87–88
  puzzles 83
  resolution 84–89
  unfairness and law 88–89
outcomes in law of torts 96, 247–48, 250
overdeterrence *see* deterrence

pacta sunt servanda 84
parental responsibility 157, 159, 183, 341
partnerships, law-independent notion of 341
penalties 99–100, 125–26n.8, 131, 137n.35
'penumbra' of tort cases 39–41
plaintiffs 239–58
  moral agency 250–51
  passive role of 250–51
  power and reasons 245–49
  power-sharing 253–57
  private law institutions, role in 239–41
  private power in public institutions, function
    of 251–53
  as quasi-officials, model of 12, 244, 248,
    251, 253
  queries 244–53
  sue, power to 239–44
pluralism 328n.76
policy *see* public policy
politics 281–96, *see also* security
  choice 285–87
  distribution 287–88
  negligence standard 285–87
  political activism 73–74
  power 288–90
  security rights 293–95
power *see also* plaintiffs; power-sharing model
  abuse of 245n.42, 247–49
  plaintiffs 245–49, 253–57
  political 288–90
  private power in public institutions, function
    of 251–53
  reasons and 245–49
  sue, to 239–44
power-sharing model 12, 243–44, 251, 253–55
precautions 70
prevention 107n.6, 135, 291

  harm 186
primary obligations 223–38
  continuity thesis 232–38
  grounding 229–32
  identity 224–29
  reasons 232–38
private law *see also* waivability; wrongs
  deterrence in *see* deterrence
  duties 1–3
  general issues 1–7
  instrumentalism 6–7
  justice 5–6
  justification for 1–7
  liberalism and 329
  plaintiffs, institutional role in 239–41
  practical reasons 3–4
  principles of 348–49
  rights-based theory of 265
  rights, types of 259
  security 290–93
  specific areas 12–16
probability, role of 31, 136–37
procedural justice
  substantive justice compared 116–19
proceduralism 112
promises *see* voluntary obligations/promises
property rights 100–1, 107n.4, 111, 130, 172–
  73n.41, 260n.6, 289n.41, 353–55
proportionality
  arithmetic 97
  of punishment 5
public authority conscription model 12, 241,
  242, 243, 244, 248, 249, 251
public law 5, 245–46, 252n.61, 338
public policy 281
punishment
  aptitude-based assessment 98–100
  allocative action 94–95
  criminal 5, 93–94, 99–101, 125–26n.8,
    127n.12, 190–91, 221n.82
  penalties and 137n.35

rape, wrongness of 53–55
rationality 35–36, 82, 113, 350
  principle of 35
rationes obligandi 220
reasonable person standard 121–22, 301–3,
  330–31, 332–34, 335, 340, 345–46
reasonableness test 275
"reasonably loyal" persons 330–47, *see also*
  fiduciary loyalty
  arguments against 333–35
  buck passing account 330–33, 343–47
  concept of 15
  excusatory latitude concern 333–34

SUBJECT INDEX 371

law independent counterpart, existence
of 340–43
law-independent trust relationship, absence
of 334–35
reasons
continuity thesis 28–29, 232–38
duties and 232–38
excluding 31–36
outweighing 31–36
persistence of *see* **continuity thesis**
power and 245–49
practical 3–4
primary obligations 232–38
satisfaction, awaiting 190–92
secondary obligations 232–38
to try *see* **try, obligations to**
reciprocity 107–8, 186
reductivism, contractual 313, 318, 327,
345n.71
regret 203–22, *see also* **wrongs**
definition 203n.1, 221
irreparable action 211–12
'no regrets' in tort law 219–21
place of 209–19
reparable action 210–11
wrong itself 212–19
reliability 322–23
moral duties 51
remedies *see also* **continuity thesis; injunctions;**
reparative damages
contract law 324–25
remoteness 97
repair principle 218
reparative damages 15, 102n.83, 162–63,
164n.13, 264, 265
reparative justice 145–60, *see also*
victims; wrongs
acceptance 148–52
complications 156–59
primer 146–48
special relationships 156–57
use 152–56
victims, multiple 158–59
wrongdoing, nature of 157–58
reparative obligations *see* **voluntary**
obligations/promises
responsibility *see* **parental responsibility**
restitution 102–4, 151–52, 282n.6
restitutio in integrum 315
retribution 133–34, 210
rights
benefit theory of 265–66
concept of 173–74, 357, 359
contractual 315–16

doctrine of 21n.16
function of 112–13
interest theory of 151, 172–73, 269n.50,
355, 356–57
omnilateral definition of 109, 117
primary 265–70
principle of 90, 107–8
private law theory 265
remedial 271–77
security 293–95
types of 259
voluntary creation of 131–32
risk, concept of 290
rule of law 4, 76, 78, 80–81, 83, 84n.49, 86–87,
243, 244, 252–53

scarcity 129–30, *see also* **deterrence**
secondary obligations 223–38
continuity thesis 232–38
grounding 229–32
identity 224–29
reasons 232–38
security *see also* **politics**
confidence and 290–91
contractual rights 315–16
notion of 290, 292, 295–96
politics and security rights 293–95
private law and 290–93
relationships 293
of tort 288–90
wealth *vs.* 291–92
self-authorship 200–1, *see also* **voluntary**
obligations/promises
self-determination 322–23
skepticism 44, 69, 261, 289
specific performance 83, 84, 324n.65
standard of care 82, 89n.74
sticklerism 255–56
strict liability 11, 22n.19, 26, 38, 62, 87, 190–91,
194–95, 282n.7, 304, 305n.23
substantive justice 5–6, 116–17, 118, 119,
120, 122
contestable 117*t*
procedural justice compared 116–19
transparent 117*t*
"succeeding" 64, 65–67, 72, 150–51, *see also*
try, obligations to
definitions 59–60
obligations to succeed 150–51
reasons to succeed 3–4, 26, 59–60, 62,
63, 212
succeed-by-trying 68–71

Ten Commandments model 44–45

372   SUBJECT INDEX

This for That model 312, 314–15, 319–20, 324, 325
transfer theory of contract 312, 316, 317–20, 321–22, 323, 324, 324n.65, 325, 326, 327–29
   extended barter, model of 318–19
totalitarianism 61
trusts 124, 340–41
try, obligations to *see also* "succeeding"
   expressive value of trying 72–74
   intrinsic value of trying 67–74
   law and 60–63
   means to an end, as a 63–67
   reason to fail-to-φ-by-trying-to-φ 66
   reasons to try-not-to-try 66–67
   succeed-by-trying 68–71
   terminology 59–60
   trying as an end 67–74
   trying to φ as a form of φ-ing 68
   trying-to-φ as a means of φ-ing 63–64
   trying-to-φ as a means toward ends other than φ-ing 65–66
   trying-to-φ as aspiration toward phi-ing 64
   value, trying as a constituent of 71–72
   value of trying 59, 74

ubi ius, ibi remedium doctrine 268n.47
unconscionability 327
unfairness *see* fairness
unilateralism 112
universal law, formula of 90, 213
Universal Principle of Right (UPR) 213
unjust enrichment 23–24, 40, 102, 103, 282n.6
utilitarianism 32n.72, 45, 51, 57, 68

value theory 351–55
value of trying *see* try, obligation to
vicarious liability 301–2
vice 333–34
   moral duties 48–49
victims *see also* reparative justice; wrongs
   duties to wrongdoers 7–8, 145–60
   multiple 158–59
   powers of 11–12
   wrongdoers' duties to 8–11
voluntary obligations/promises 177–202

bilaterality 186–88
broken promises 180–83
contextual interpretation 182–83
essence and periphery 181–82
explicit vs. implicit promises 182–83
fault, variations in 189–95
independent desirability 184–85
literal meaning 182–83
promised action otherwise required 183–86
reasons awaiting satisfaction 190–92
relationship norms 196–98
reparative obligations 198–202
respect for the promise 192–95
self-authorship 200–1
triggered desirability 185–86

waiver, powers of *see* waivability
waivability 259–77
   primary rights 265–70
   private law rights, types of 260–65
   remedial rights, limitations on 271–77
wealth 13, 95, 233, 237, 283, 284, 288–89, 348–49, 350–51, 359
   security *vs.* 291–92, 293, 295–96
welfare
   child 73–74
   enhancement 325
   social 6, 356
   of society 95
   state 242
winning, concept of 68
wrongs *see also* continuity thesis; private law; regret; victims
   continuity thesis 206–9
   fault and 22–27
   nature of wrongdoing 157–58
   rape, wrongfulness of 53–55
   regret and 204–9, 212–19
   reparation for 204–9
   reparative justice 157–58
   responding to 7–12
   victims duties to wrongdoers 7–8
   wrongdoers' duties to victims 8–11
   wrongdoing, notion of 22, 36
   wrongful injury, definition of 350–51